Lying up a Nation

Lying up a Nation
Race and Black Music

Ronald Radano

The University of Chicago Press Chicago and London

Ronald Radano is professor of music at the University of Wisconsin—Madison.
He is the author of *New Musical Figurations: Anthony Braxton's Cultural Critique*
and coeditor of *Music and the Racial Imagination,* both published by the
University of Chicago Press.

The University of Chicago Press, Chicago 60637
The University of Chicago Press, Ltd., London
© 2003 by The University of Chicago
All rights reserved. Published 2003
Printed in the United States of America

12 11 10 09 08 07 06 05 04 03   1 2 3 4 5

ISBN: 0-226-70197-2 (cloth)
ISBN: 0-226-70198-0 (paper)

Library of Congress Cataloging-in-Publication Data

Radano, Ronald Michael.
    Lying up a nation : race and Black music / Ronald Radano.
       p. cm.
    Includes bibliographical references and index.
    ISBN 0-226-70197-2 (cloth : alk. paper) — ISBN 0-226-70198-0 (pbk. : alk. paper)
       1. African Americans—Music—History and criticism.   2. Music—United
    States—History and criticism.   I. Title.

    ML3556 .R25 2003
    780′.89′96073—dc21

                                                              2003001142

♾ The paper used in this publication meets the minimum requirements of the
American National Standard for Information Sciences—Permanence of Paper for
Printed Library Materials, ANSI Z39.48-1992.

For Colleen

It would not be wrong to consider this book itself as a myth:
it is, as it were, the myth of mythology.
—Claude Lévi-Strauss, *The Raw and the Cooked*

It must be remembered that the oppressed and the oppressor are bound
together within the same society; they accept the same criteria, they share
the same beliefs, they both alike depend on the same reality.
—James Baldwin, *Notes of a Native Son*

Truth, indeed, was designated in negro parlance "telling lies to buckra."
—James M. Phillippo on Jamaican slavery (1843)

Error is the space in which history unfolds.
—Martin Heidegger, *Early Greek Thinking*

That which we do is what we are. That which we remember is,
more often than not, that which we would like to have been,
or that which we hope to be. Thus our memory and our identity
are ever at odds, our history ever a tall tale told by inattentive idealists.
—Ralph Ellison, "The Golden Age, Time Past"

Simultaneous with the appearance of the word in the world is the
possibility of lying: in Mandekan someone who is thought incapable of
lying is said to have *no mouth*.
—Christopher L. Miller, *Theories of Africans*

"Zora," George Thomas informed me, "you come to de
right place if lies is what you want. Ah'm gointer lie up a nation."
—Zora Neale Hurston, *Mules and Men*

Contents

List of Illustrations ix

Preface xi

1 **Telling Stories, Telling Lies** Revisionist Listening and the Writing of Music History 1

2 **Resonances of Racial Absence** Black Sounding Practices Prior to "Negro Music" 49

3 **First Truth, Second Hearing** Audible Encounters in Antebellum Black and White 105

4 **Magical Writing** The Iconic Wonders of the Slave Spiritual 164

5 **Of Bodies and Souls** Feeling the Pulse of Modern Race Music 230

Epilogue **A Nation's Gift** 278

Notes 287

Index 379

Illustrations

1 Chinese Boatmen's Song (Barrow, 1806)   158

2 South American Song (Frézier, 1717)   190

3 Chinese Airs (Du Halde, 1735)   191

4 South American Song (De Léry, 1611)   192

5 Siamese Song, with Drawing of Percussion Instrument (Loubère, 1691)   193

6 Foreign Songs (Rousseau, 1768)   194

7 Persian Music Diagrams, Instrument, and Song (Chardin, 1711)   195

8 Turkish Music (Fonton, 1751)   196

9 Bird Songs and Negro Boat Song (Stedman, 1777)   197

10 Jamaican Music (Sloane, 1707)   198

11 Chinese Hymns (Amiot, 1779)   199

12 Ashantee Airs (Bowdich, 1819)   200

13 Abyssinian Airs (as Basis for Improvisation) (Combes and Tamisier, 1839)   201–2

14 Egyptian Modes and Song (Villoteau, 1826)   203

15 Title Page of *Slave Songs of the United States* (Allen et al., 1867)   207

16 First Page of the Table of Contents of *Slave Songs of the United States*   208

17 Photograph of William Francis Allen, 1830–89   210

18 Allen's Certificate of Admission to the Educational Commission for Freedmen   212

19 "Turn, Sinner, Turn O!" (1867)   215

20 "The Day of Judgment" (1867)   216

21 "God Got Plenty o' Room" (1867)   217

22 "The Trouble of the World" (1867)   218

23 "Hunting for the Lord" (1867)   219

24 "Round the Corn, Sally" (1867)   219

25 "Belle Layotte" (1867)   220

26 "Rémon" (1867)   221

27 "Shall I Die?" (1867)   222

28 Transcription of Melodies from Shouting Ceremonies, Probably Beaufort, South Carolina   225

29 "Bell Da Ring" (1867)   226

30 First Page of "Directions for Singing" from *Slave Songs of the United States*   227

31 Frontispiece and Title Page of Allens' Privately Published Book, *Family Songs* (1899)   228

32 "Let Us Cheer the Weary Traveler"   285–86

Preface

How to explain the remarkable and wondrous experience of black music? How do we comprehend its effect on countless listeners across the history of our nation? And how do we do so equitably, profitably, in a way that gives insight into the role the music has played in shaping the character of American culture overall? These are weighty matters, no doubt, and when we try to speak to them in a substantive way, words seem to fail us. It is not surprising, then, that so many of us prefer to avoid such attempts, resorting to the familiar saying, "Let the music speak for itself."

And yet we never do because it never can. For all that we hear in black music, or indeed in any kind of music, is inevitably invested in words: in the stories we tell, in the histories we recite, in the associations we make. When we listen to a jazz performance at a club like the Village Vanguard, we hear the music through the lens of history, as the space provides a kind of accompanying sound track to the sound itself. Or, perhaps more accurately, we hear the club in the music, given that we can never really separate our stories of the music from its seemingly pure sonic form. Could we, in witnessing gospel sung in an African-American church, ever expect to hear its performance displaced from the religious context?[1] Could we, to spin this somewhat differently, listen to covers of rhythm 'n' blues tunes without noting who first performed them, and would not this matter even more if the covers were recorded by whites? It is not simply a matter of describing the performances that makes the task so difficult. We must also relate the experience to the broader domain of history that inevitably casts sound as recognizable, discernible form. These contexts, these words, these ideas shape our musical perception continually; they give to black music an architecture of meaning that directly informs the way we hear. The stories we tell do not simply surround the sound but are inextricably linked to it, as sound and text work hand in hand in casting music's spell.

Over the past half century or so, the listening public has remained re-markably committed to a particular story about black music. It is a good one, so good, in fact, that it has more or less determined the way we hear performances across a range of genres, from blues to jazz to hip-hop. The story goes something like this. Black music garners its strength and power from the integrity of a greater African-American culture forged under cir-cumstances of enduring racial oppression. The qualities so often affiliated with black music—its soulfulness, its depth of feeling or "realness," its emotional and rhythmic energy, its vocally informed instrumental inflec-tions—grow directly out of the depths of social tragedy only to rise up miraculously as the voice of racial uplift. This generative background, in turn, determines the aesthetic value of modern forms. Black music of real worth speaks with certitude and conviction of the rightness of blackness against the wrongness of white supremacy. At its best, black music ex-presses a kind of cultural exceptionalism, a racially informed distinctive-ness and moral integrity that reflects its grounding in traditions of Africa and an intimately linked slave era. While recent critics have sought to qual-ify these claims to allow greater room for the range of music's expressive capacities, they almost always affirm its viable center, or what Amiri Baraka (publishing under the name LeRoi Jones) has famously called "the changing same." This is what we might call the "blues" character of mod-ern modes of analysis, through which critics propose black music as the last bastion of authenticity in a postmodern age.[2]

There are some very good reasons why listeners, musicians, and critics have remained committed to this particular narrative of black music. It is, of course, a powerful story in itself, a kind of hero's tale, one that has be-come closely related to American images of self, most obviously in black circumstances, but also widely across the color line. Equally important, though, is the kind of sustaining role this "selective tradition," as Raymond Williams would call it, has played in refusing white racism's challenge to black cultural legitimacy.[3] It was not too long ago that commentators claimed that African-Americans as a whole were a people without a culture and that black music in particular was but a reflection of European-based practices. For many, to go against the grain of orthodoxy means reflexively assuming an assimilationist position. If we begin to argue that black music is not stable, is not culturally pure, concerns mount, for this would seem-ingly lead to the conclusion that the music is not specifically black. And if that is the case, the argument continues, we are just a small step away from an even older tale, namely, that black music is simply a version of (white) American music, a story that, at its root, presumes African-Americans are incapable of creative expression. While we may now seem far from such primitive thinking, these views still carry considerable cultural weight, particularly among African-Americans who must endure their repeated eruptions during the course of everyday life.

How, then, do we affirm distinctiveness while also allowing black music some breathing room, some possibility of taking public form according to another tale? For the main story, as good as it is, tends to prescribe meaning in a way that has been limiting for many artists as it stands at odds with the historical complexities of cultural production. In this book, I seek to outline a different kind of story about black music, one that affirms the importance of cultural distinctiveness to the making of black identities while also reconsidering the efficacy of commitments to singular notions of meaning and form. It is what might be called an interventionist tale, a chronicle that aims to cut through some of the more mystified narratives by observing the music's constitution within the ideas and social forces of American life. The portrait put forward here is intended to reinforce the role of black music as a marker of blackness. Because of its intimate historical connection to ideologies of race, however, black music has inevitably assumed multiple manifestations. Its power and significance relate not simply to racial and semiotic indicators but also to a flexibility in articulating a broad range of meaning. Seen this way, black music's dynamism and heterogeneity become not limitations but sources of potency. The music assumes cultural significance in its capacity to influence and reflect the legacy of racial relations in the United States.

Our story begins from the premise that the understanding of black music's emergence is inextricably linked to a racial logic, one in which blackness defines a distinctiveness or "difference" that has been historically negotiated within a relationship between African- and Euro-Americans. That is, the qualities that define black music grow out of a cultural ground that is more common than many may realize, and this commonality is all the more so in musical circumstances, where practices literally exist in the air and are thus accessed more easily than other forms of cultural expression. Because we have continued to believe that racial differences are real, however, we as a nation and as an interracial people have repeatedly sought to enact those differences in sound, just as African-American musicians in particular have been motivated and rewarded both socially and economically for realizing versions of black musical distinctiveness. As a result, black music, as the defining expression of race, has been shaped and reshaped within a peculiar interracial conversation whose participants simultaneously deny that the conversation has ever taken place.

One might even say that black music both reveals and obscures the lies we tell when attempting to define who and what we are. As it affirms the separation of black and white, it also calls that distinction into question. It is loyal to our false commitments and biases, as it expresses what is most true.

The phrase "lying up a nation" that gives this book its title suggests something more than literal acts of deception. As an African-American vernacular expression introduced into folklore studies by the novelist and ethnographer Zora Neale Hurston, "lying" means telling a good story, a feat of no small importance in a world where stories play such an important role in the making of social structures and relations. Good stories are good because they resonate powerfully with our sense of the complexities and contradictions of life. As such, they resemble acts of cultural criticism that attempt to explain with a certain elegance the strangeness of life's ways. Tales of this order may not always be literally true, and at their best, in fact, they tend to play the line, engaging ambiguously an assembly of possible meanings. So it is with the best of black music, which seems similarly to perform lying acts. It tells stories that convey a range of meaning, its power deriving precisely from its accessibility and capaciousness, from its forceful articulation of a broad base of social realms. In its seemingly endless capacity, black music both affirms evolving myths of blackness that cast African-Americans apart from a dominant whiteness and serves to overcome the color line, proposing in sound a broader, interracial involvement. Its power derives above all from its ambiguity, from its contradictory articulation of two key realms of symbolism. The notion of lying here, then, is meant to convey the sense that stories, whether literary or musical, are always to an extent made up, and in this way they stretch the truth. But the best of them capture something of the texture of living and in the end seem the truest of all.

The book speaks to the conceit of lying in other ways. Most emphatically, perhaps, it seeks to move beyond the more familiar tales by turning directly to the historical sources that document black music's history. In no small way, *Lying up a Nation* is a conventional historical study that works from an evidentiary body of texts that supply the record of the African-American musical past. These "primary" texts, however, which were almost always written by whites, are far from objective records. As representations, they are inevitably secondary; they themselves tell stories, they convey meanings that exist beyond, while they simultaneously embody, the literal words. Partial and by nature incomplete, these tall tales grow from the white racial imagination, providing in many cases records of slave performative action from the perspective of the enslaver. As "fictional" as they are, they are nonetheless crucial, for the stories show us how the sound of black music has acquired meaning through discursive representation. Without this evidentiary body we would be left only with stories, with no historical record, and thus without the means of analyzing black music's social constitution. The best we can do is to attempt to engage the historical texts critically, reading in between the lines toward the crafting of a story that challenges conventional racialist thinking while also paying respect to the power of music and race in the formation of American identities. More than a recovery of historical representation, *Lying up a Nation* claims for black music its role as the conscience of the American experience, as the sonic truth teller of race and its multitude contradictions.

Because *Lying up a Nation* is fashioned as a narrative, with themes and events building one upon the other, it will be read most productively in its chapter-by-chapter sequence. Such an approach allows the history and its logic to unfold, a process guided at the beginning of each chapter by the orienting insights of major black critics. Readers with particular orientations and interests, however, will inevitably prefer to consult the book more casually. The following chapter outline is intended to assist both approaches.

Chapter 1 is a broad theoretical reflection on the practices of studying black music, observed within the informing contexts of contemporary musicology and black cultural studies. The aim here is to advance a way of approaching African-American music history through a proposed conversation between these two disciplinary domains. It is here, too, that the reader will learn the basic interpretive premises and critical strategies put into practice in the ensuing pages. Chapter 2 begins the historical sequence of the story, focusing on the period through the eighteenth century, in large part before the American conception of "black music" (or, as it was known at the time, "Negro music") had taken shape. The discussion involves a close look at representations of African and North American black performances with respect to the social circumstances out of which these performances emerged, giving particular stress to the role of voice, the primary possession of a possessed people. It is in the partially autonomous voice (over the assumed importance of drumming and rhythm) that we locate the basis of black music's miraculous emergence. Chapter 3 brings the story into the first half of the nineteenth century, focusing on the role of singing and other forms of music making in the circumstances of cross-racial religious worship. In this setting, we see vocal expressions infiltrating the discourses of Christianity, to the point of challenging simple determinations of music and language, and of music as a definitive marker of racial difference. Within a few decades, however, the racial and economic motivations to assign a difference to black performances become overwhelming, inspiring practices and learning that reposition black and white apart.

The final two chapters bring to bear considerations of black music that are particularly relevant to modern interpretations. Chapter 4 explores the emergence of the slave song as "spiritual" against the background of antebellum performance settings and the broader language base of romanticism that publicly translates slave song as soulful expression. The section on musical transcription will be particularly relevant to those interested in the way songs are transformed into visual form and the effects of writing on the interpretation and influence of black music overall. Chapter 5 considers another key matter in modern black music, the issue of rhythm. The discussion charts how rhythm becomes the defining quality of black music relatively late in the story, emerging in representations of "hot" music (coon songs, ragtime, syncopated music, etc.) around the turn of the twentieth century. From this historical background, the epilogue looks toward the present, briefly considering the extent to which black music may enable the overcoming of the racial categories it helped to establish.

The making of *Lying up a Nation* has been a rather complex story in itself, largely because of the tremendous support I have received from so many institutions, colleagues, and friends. The book began as a retooling of sorts, when I had the luxury of spending a year as a Rockefeller Fellow reading black cultural studies and literary theory at the Center for the Study of Black Literature and Culture at the University of Pennsylvania. Those studies, together with important engagements with an affiliated faculty (notably, former center director Houston Baker, Roger Abrahams, Gary Tomlinson, Herman Beavers, and my "fellow Fellow," Dismas Masolo) and the opportunity to stage a center conference focusing on black music and cultural theory, were all instrumental to plotting the course of my project. A subsequent fellowship at the Smithsonian Institution's National Museum of American History enabled me to follow up these theoretical explorations with a year of preliminary historical research. I am especially grateful to Charles McGovern and Pete Daniel for their support during that stay.

At the University of Wisconsin, I have enjoyed the privilege of teaching classes and seminars in both the School of Music and the Department of Afro-American Studies that relate directly to this primary research project. As such, this book has already taken form as various classroom stagings, which have been invaluable to shaping the overall argument and exploring various historical details. Guest professorships at the University of Chicago and Harvard University provided similar opportunities, and I am grateful similarly to those institutions for granting them. I would like to thank at Chicago Rick Cohn and especially Phil Bohlman, and, at Harvard, Skip Gates, Tom Kelly, Kay Shelemay, and Cornel West (now at Princeton), who made the visits possible. Similar thanks go to the broad assembly of students at all three institutions who have had an impact on my work over the course. I could not have imagined undertaking this research project without access to extensive collections such as those housed at the University of Wisconsin. I am indebted particularly to the Mills Music Library, the Rare Book Collection at Memorial Library, and the American History and Rare Book Libraries of the Wisconsin Historical Society on the Madison campus. Among the library staff, special thanks go to Geri Laudati and Steve Sundell for their continued support. The staff of the Widener and Loeb Libraries at Harvard were also crucial in the preparation of many of the images that adorn this book.

The final stages of research and writing were aided by fellowships from Wisconsin's Institute for Research in the Humanities, where I benefited from the intellectual generosity of its former director, Paul Boyer, and other institute fellows; from the Wisconsin Graduate School (in the form of an H. I. Romnes Faculty Fellowship); and from the John Simon Guggenheim Foundation. The Institute of African-American Affairs at New York University (NYU) and the music department of the Graduate School of the City University of New York (CUNY) generously provided visiting scholar status and office space during the Guggenheim Fellowship. Manthia Diawara of NYU and Steve Blum of CUNY took the trouble to make these situations work and to make me feel welcome during my visits. Financial support from Wisconsin's graduate school provided generous funding to staff a team of highly skilled research assistants: Mark Goodale, an anthropologist, who completed the bulk of research on music in colonial travelogues; Jonathan Pollack, a social historian, who worked on sections pertaining to the revival movements; Maya Gibson, a musicologist, who read on black religious performance; and Morgan Luker, another music student, who assisted in preparations during the final phase of research and revision. Patrick Burke served as my primary assistant over an extended period, and his contributions were so wide-ranging and extensive that I can hardly do them justice in this brief acknowledgment. His discoveries and insights strengthened several aspects of the manuscript. Hatim Belyamani provided valuable translations and interpretations of nineteenth-century

French travelogues as an assistant at Harvard's Du Bois Institute, while Wayne Marshall and Dave Gilbert helped to shore up some details during the production stage.

Beyond these institutionally related sources of support, I have gained so much in a personal way from a series of engagements with scores of scholars who have had an unquestionable and profound impact on my thinking about and writing of this book. It is simply impossible to cite them all, and I say this with regret, for the various conversations have meant a great deal to me. At best, I can name those friends with whom I have had more extended exchanges together with several others who have variously supplied help, advice, and research: Regina Bendix, Florence Bernault, Phil Bohlman, Jeanne Boydston, Paul Boyer, Rich Crawford, Virginia Danielson, Suzanne Desan, Dena Epstein, Steve Feld, Linda Gordon, Herman Gray, Jim Gustafson, Brian Hyer, Steve Kantrowitz, Toma Longinovíc, Susan McClary, Kirin Narayan, Rob Nixon, Bruno Nettl, Larry Scanlon, Jim Stokes, Sterling Stuckey, John Szwed, Tim Taylor, Bill Van Deburg, Chris Waterman, Shane White, Ed Widmer, and Deborah Wong. Sam Floyd generously supplied an extensive critique of an early proposal of the project that helped me greatly in finding a voice within the contested politics of musical criticism. I am also grateful to Charlie Dill and Robin Kelley for their affirmations and various readings of portions of the text, together with Kofi Agawu and Guy Ramsey, with whom I have had ongoing exchanges, culminating in this context with their expert formal reviews for the press. At Chicago, Yvonne Zipter performed virtuoso editorial acts in bringing the manuscript into proper form; Tim McGovern helped ably in several instances and in various ways; and Doug Mitchell, the consummate editor and friend, has been unyielding in his support throughout the process. Colleen Dunlavy has been there through all stages of this work, but I am thankful to her above all for something that goes even beyond love and support. She has always kept me mindful of what this is, after all: just another story in a book. Hers is quiet wisdom. She is my truest song.

Portions of this book first appeared in considerably different, preliminary forms in several essays: "Hot Fantasies: American Modernism and the Idea of Black Rhythm," in *Music and the Racial Imagination,* edited by Ronald Radano and Philip V. Bohlman (Chicago: University of Chicago Press, 2000), 459–82; "Black Noise, White Mastery," in *Decomposition: Post-Disciplinary Performance,* edited by Philip Brett, Sue-Ellen Case, and Susan Leigh Foster (Bloomington: Indiana University Press, 2000), 39–49; "Denoting Difference: The Writing of the Slave Spirituals," *Critical Inquiry* 22, no. 1 (Spring 1996): 506–44; "Notes upon the Text," *Lenox Avenue: A Journal of*

Interdisciplinary Artistic Inquiry 1 (1995): 53–59; review essay of *We'll Understand It Better, By and By,* ed. Bernice Johnson Reagon, *Journal of the American Musicological Society* 48 (Spring 1995): 144–54; and "Soul Texts and the Blackness of Folk," *Modernism/Modernity* 2, no. 1 (January 1995): 71–95.

1 Telling Stories, Telling Lies

Revisionist Listening and the Writing of Music History

Black Resonances   I begin with the famous musical moment near the opening of Ralph Ellison's novel, *Invisible Man*. It is a familiar passage in the history of American racial thought, one so excessively labored that to dally here risks the misstep of playing to the common order. Even so, the text invites reflection once more, vividly depicting as it does the strangely conspicuous obscurity of "black music" in America.[1] At this particular point, Ellison's music-loving narrator makes a startling revelation: he locates jazz at the site of its own erasure. In the loud clamor of black music, represented here in Louis Armstrong's recording of "Black and Blue," the narrator describes the uncanny experience of hearing white society's deafness to black being. What he calls, in a strategically mixed metaphor, the "beam of lyrical sound" that shines forth from Armstrong's horn ultimately loses its radiance in the public sphere and fades into the darkness of absence. Ellison enhances this association between racial invisibility and a paradoxically sited, yet silent, black sound by relying on jazz-based figures and themes. Comparing absence to the sensibility of swing, Ellison, a former jazz trumpeter, observes this through his protagonist:

Perhaps I like Louis Armstrong because he's made poetry out of being invisible. I think it must be because he's unaware that he *is* invisible. And my own grasp of invisibility aids me to understand his music. . . . Invisibility, let me explain, gives one a slightly different sense of time, you're never quite on the beat. Sometimes you're ahead and sometimes behind. Instead of the swift and imperceptible flowing of time, you are aware of its nodes, those points where time stands still or from which it leaps ahead. And you slip into the breaks and look around. That's what you hear vaguely in Louis' music.[2]

Now what a strange notion: to trace toneful elegance from social absence! And yet Ellison does so neither to deny black musical significance nor to elevate it to some racially autonomous status. This "poetry out of being invisible" betrays special insight into the peculiarly American quality of "black experience," just as it acknowledges the dependency of that experience on the historically contingent circumstances of race.[3] To be sure, Ellison is privy to the profound ironies of racial contest and engagement that form the matrix of the American social art of black music. What sets him apart from lesser critics is the way he avoids square renderings of time and culture, knowing full well what you miss when you conform to the literal rhythms of racial assumption. Ellison plays not just with the antagonisms of race but with the dynamic ambiguities that underlie the very distinction between "black" and "white" as well. His aim is not to center blackness but, rather, to do something far more subversive. He wants to claim America by revealing a conspicuously marginal and invisible black music as the nation's voice.

What do we hear when America sings? What sounds from the disembodied voice of a nation so traumatized and confused by its own racial constitution? What might the music tell us that we fail to discern in other artifacts of culture? For Ellison, black music betrays the blurred racial realities that so many Americans, asleep in the nightmare of the color line, refuse to acknowledge.[4] In the same way, in this book, I propose strategies of listening into the body of black music, to hear and feel its breath—the very materiality of sounding the nation.[5] For if Ellison is correct, we can locate in black music the silenced narratives of the social, those "unspeakable things unspoken," as Toni Morrison calls them, which resonate as musico-discursive eruptions inextricably linking black and white. Rather than coalescing as a singular, audible totality, these eruptions have constructed the racial play of sights and sounds through which we can retrospectively map a new history of black music and reconsider the trajectory of American music at large.[6]

Such attentive listening means something more than hearing "the sound itself," a concept derived from a positivist musicology that presumes art to exceed the social meanings that inevitably contain it. We need to move beyond these modern fantasies of autonomous form that have overtaken black musical studies, not to deny artistic value but in order to situate the making of art forms within the broader dimensions of culture. Black music, like all Western musical practices, is patently intermusical as it is intermediated and, finally, interracial. To claim otherwise, whether to celebrate the "structural coherence" of a masterful improvisation or to advance an essential connection to the temporal recesses of Africa, is only to foreground one of music's many social texts. Neither pure lyric nor unadulterated racial sound, the voice of black music may best be likened to a "soundtext," to a sonic palimpsest that accumulates tales on those already written. A multivocal, multitextual offering, black music communicates in the end many "musics," which, in their variety, ironically give voice to a racial nation.

Working against the consensus positions of American musical historiography, then, I propose in no uncertain terms to challenge, in this book, those strategies of containment that uphold the racial binaries informing the interpretation of black music. It goes against the grain of a pervasive, yet remarkably underanalyzed assumption that correlates an enduring black musical presence with the myth of a consistent and stable socioracial position of "blackness." Put to challenge, in particular, is the view, still common to our time and culture, of an immutable black musical essence that survives apart from the contingencies of social and cultural change. Such a seemingly commonsense opinion must either depend on a musical universalism in black form (somehow aligned with as it extends from European idealism) or presume a vital, unrelenting force that, despite claims honoring culture over nature, betrays racialist sentiments.

In registering this challenge, my aim is not, of course, to unseat the significance and integrity of black music. The commitment to a viable essence of black music that still occupies the popular imagination remains an important ideological component of national memory that emerges historically as one of the many coherence systems binding people musically.[7] Rather than a falsity it suggests what Roland Barthes called "myth": the stories we tell in giving texture and meaning in the making of our worlds. The myth of essence represents a crucial mode of musical coherence that reflects the constituting role of sound in the formation of racial subjects. Yet continuing to uphold uncritically the myth of black music as a stable form or even as a "changing same," as Amiri Baraka calls it, forestalls consideration of the interracial background from which ideologies of black music developed in the first place. The positioning of black music as a national marker of integrationist celebration, whether in the form of "America's classical music" or what W. E. B. Du Bois called "the most beautiful expression of human experience born this side the seas," depends on a broadly social circumstance out of which the music's prominence arose.[8] The tenacity of belief in black musical essence, then, is neither a "black problem" nor a "race problem." Such beliefs stretch easily across the racial divide, from scholastics to popular literature to everyday speech, even if they are condescendingly attributed to an orthodox black racialism or Afrocentrism. Championed to reinforce claims of difference, "essence" betrays a common origin in the multiracial denials of irreversible racial mixture. For claims of black essence presume white ones, too; neither will fade until "white society" gives up its commitment to racial category. "It's up to you," James Baldwin observes. "As long as you think you're 'white,' there's no hope for you. As long as you think you're 'white,' I'm going to be forced to think I'm 'black.' "[9]

Rather than merely deconstructing musical blackness, then, this study seeks, to the contrary, to enact a critical rendering of Reconstruction: to outline black music's very constitution as part and parcel of the broader emergence of race in American public history and culture.[10] Situating black music within the texture of American life means no longer easily separating "black music" from "white music," nor, indeed, black music from the rest of the social experience. It requires us to engage critically the many myths of origin, which, in their association with legacies of race, are themselves Eurocentric, in order to move toward a more socially informed interpretive practice. This reconstruction against the fall of stable raciomusical concepts will reveal not only music's expressive capacities but also its generative, constitutive effects. In order to situate black music as a social force, we need to observe its place within historically evolving structures of relations, yet hopefully without succumbing to the implied continuities and essentialisms of traditional histories of American music.[11] At the same time, these structures of relations propose another way of telling the story of black music, which, as a story, is inherently uniform and, to that extent, essential. If narrative conceptions of history escalate the violence of language and reason, they also more practically identify what gives coherence to the constructions of self, memory, and place. To give them up is to commit another kind of violence by privileging the old stories of an absolute racial binarism or, worse, to deracinate history under the cloak of an unacknowledged whiteness. As a matter of course, we must negotiate between analyses of the structures of relations that produced multiple series of black musics and the stories arising from the necessity of American racial experience. The challenge is to propose a story without succumbing to the racial fixities and transcendental concepts that more conventional renderings suggest. At the center of this story we will find the miraculous becoming of a black music that textures the nation's voice.[12]

The comprehension of black music as a form constituted within and against racial discourses is, in the end, less the invention of "theory" than a proposal developing from historically grounded inquiry. As much as this study is informed by the insights of contemporary critical perspectives of society and culture, it speaks above all to the startling paucity of evidence sustaining the common portraits of African-American musical history. Consider, for example, the assumptions we commonly make about the consistency of black musical experience and stylistic practice. Black music, it is often claimed, is soulful, rhythmically affecting, based on collective engagements of call and response, and expressive of multiple levels of feeling and desire: pain, freedom, rebellion, and sexual ecstasy, just to name a few. The soulfulness of the singing voice, the overpowering qualities of swing are, we so often assume, formal absolutes that derive from black music's inherent character and distinctiveness. We believe these phenomenal and stylistic features to be part of the stuff of the music's expressive core. They have always been there and been perceived in the same way.[13]

The historical accuracy of such claims, however, is impossible to verify, since they develop from presentist assumptions. Even if we could set aside the hermeneutical challenges of historical recovery and measure continuities empirically, we face the fact of a sonically absent history. The first recordings of black music, after all, appeared only in the early 1890s—led off by an Edison cylinder that sounded more "Irish" than "black"—and then not in significant numbers until the late 1910s and 1920s.[14] What is more, given the historical and situational complexities of any culture's legacy, the experience and meaning of African-American musical practices had to vary enormously depending on time, place, and circumstance, but our historical record provides only the most scattered documentation of events. These variances had to affect the development and interpretation of expressive practices, yet we have no way of charting the complexities of the music's overarching formation. To assume that musical practices of the present document consistent patterns of performance and reception over the course of two hundred to three hundred years is to project one past onto another. It is to assume a kind of cultural stasis that ignores the flux of musical and sociodiscursive processes as it contradicts the broader historical record. The legacies of oppression and segregation that undoubtedly contributed to black music's distinctiveness are not enough to sustain arguments of an unyielding black essence any more than parallel claims of totalities of European heritage or frontier independence defend white ones.

It is especially difficult to draw safe conclusions about performance practices from the colonial and antebellum eras. As Dena Epstein observes, prior to the 1830s, African-American performances in North America were rarely documented and only, then, as passing asides in the texts of white observers more concerned with the primary economic and social details of Euro-American experience. "Authentic answers to these questions," she writes, "are not at all easy to find, for the published literature on the thirteen colonies says really very little about the black population and still less about its music. Those contemporary documents which have been examined barely mention them."[15] When commentaries of black music do emerge, they appear cast in a racial language that, in the best circumstances, betrayed whites' conflicted sentiments toward the persistent challenges of black national presence. More conspicuous were the racist affronts of blackface minstrelsy that, whether expressing contempt or desire, effectively masked the interpretation of black performances to the point where no authentic and true source could be provided. (Ironically, as will be seen, this particular discourse was key to the invention of the very concept of the "original.") What we really have, in effect, is a fragmented body of cultural translations that mediate the course of "black music" from sound to text within the discourses of those who, for the most part, had typically antagonistic and tentative contact with African-Americans. While the narratives of African and African-American slaves added significantly to the historical picture, these texts, scattered across a long history until their flourish in the mid-to-late 1800s, cannot in themselves flesh out the picture.[16] Even if there were substantial documentation of musical practices among slaves, we would need to read it through the same discourses observed in documents composed by whites, since it is through these latter texts that even black oppositionality is attended. To rely uncritically on either group, black or white—or even on the more sizable body of commentaries appearing after the Civil War—leads to an unproductive, unreliable history, one in which a "slave period" develops from present-day perceptions of "fact" apart from the texts and circumstances in which these facts were constituted. It is to submit to a kind of critical blindness guided by unseen ideologies of presentism and race that obscure the normalizing effects of writing as such.

Of course we need to make generalizations if we are finally to propose a story arising out of the representations and structures of relations that constitute the "absent cause" of an inaccessible past.[17] But the generalizations we tend to make grow too casually from highly problematic data and monolithic conceptions of slavery, only to serve as the basis for proposing grand, overarching claims about the unity of the black musical past. These claims pervade a popular literature in which the history of black music is still contained. Indeed, they trace across some of the best examples of historical scholarship, representing what Hortense Spillers calls the "knowledge industry" of grand reifications of its subject.[18] What we might call the tenacity of black musical racialism is what permits Lawrence Levine to build with little critical discrimination a vision of a "sacred world" among slaves that rests on a conflation of temporally and geographically discon-nected information. It is what allows Sterling Stuckey to make grand leaps of faith in connecting the ring shout to modern urban circumstances (such as Thelonious Monk's dance displays during the act of musical perfor-mance) and to claim it as an informing mode of perception across the com-plex of black America. It is what enables music scholars, finally, to embrace literally and wholeheartedly Henry Louis Gates Jr.'s highly ironic challenge to the authority of French literary deconstruction (in his theory of "sig-nifyin' "), latching onto the obvious musical parallels as if they were grounded in irrefutable empirical evidence. All these strategies sacrifice a certain critical rigor in the name of an otherwise laudable desire to high-light coherences on which stories can be based.[19]

The claims of black music's transhistorical endurance do not develop from poor intentions. On the contrary, they reflect the deep political com-mitments of progressive-minded scholars who seek to defend a tradition so commonly denied a right to speak. The problem lies in the leaps many of these writers make to build a historical narrative on a textual ground uncomplicated by a parallel inquiry into the formation of the texts them-selves. In this way, they expose the pitfalls in the challenge of representa-tion. As Winfried Siemerling observes in her succinct outline of a basic premise of contemporary cultural analysis, "while it seems safe to say that discursive representation creates, by its very occurrence, a previously nonexistent specific difference that is usually valued by the groups con-cerned, it has, however, also the treacherous potential of re-inscribing and 're-presenting,' even in the act of negation, the operational categories and oppositions of the status quo."[20] Finding the formal cultural essence link-ing early eighteenth-century South Carolina to late twentieth-century Los Angeles, or even the Mississippi Delta of the 1920s to the Bronx of the 1990s, might serve in one way to advance modern initiatives of emancipa-tion and uplift, but it also extends racial mystifications by re-presenting the past with little regard for the vagaries of history. To draw simple relations between the musical expressions of James Reese Europe, Bobby Short, Sis-ter Rosetta Tharp, Anthony Davis, Frank Johnson, Little Richard, Black Patti, Don Byron, Mariah Carey, Harry T. Burleigh, Muddy Waters, Andre Watts, Charlie Pride, Mos Def, and Simeon Gilliat (the famous slave fiddler) is to propose unities without seriously considering the enormous range of contingencies that divide them. It is to submit to the surreal fantasy in which America nonetheless engages because of its racial obsessions. Do these artists need to reveal a perceivable musical connection in order to be effectively "black"?

What drives this search for an imaginary link binding all of black music is the belief in a viable and manifest difference affirming ideological commitments to "black" and "white."[21] To deny that black musical practices frequently share qualities in common would require us to forget the realities of modern racism together with the legacies of discrimination, violence, and segregation that variously compelled African-America to develop culturally distinctive practices. Indeed, to disavow the importance of difference in the formation of "black music" would mean challenging the vision of music as a social act. Yet the production of black music in response to an uncontested and ultimately invisible white normative order is part of a social process rather than an expression of some absolute, racially based quality. And it is the failure of historians and critics aggressively and repeatedly to make this distinction that has allowed us to slide backward and to succumb to imaginations of black music's a priori essence. Rather than inquiring into the American-born social grounds of racially attributable stylistic procedures, or, even more radically, elaborating on the interracial commonalities that reveal forms of musical sharing, writers and listeners have repeatedly assumed "difference" to grow from the nature of racial-cultural backgrounds. As a result, before research is even undertaken, historical projections of black music fulfill a version of Ralph Ellison's "prefabricated Negroes ... sketched on sheets of paper and superimposed upon the Negro community."[22] The vast body of research on black music becomes an attempt to document a terrain of difference without ever questioning the assumptions on which this difference is based.

For this reason "difference" as a social construct plays a crucial role in the comprehension of black music and its history. Ironically, we find the origin of this notion by turning away from a pure and exclusive African-America and observing the historical relationship between black creative agency and Euro-American naming practices. For black music's difference grows from, as it informs a racialized double vision of, self and other, reflecting the relational circumstances of interracial experience. The double vision of race reveals why "the Negro problem" historically assigned to African-America is in fact a condition of U.S. history in general and of black music in particular. Black music reveals a "double consciousness" across the color line, complicating as it informs black identity formation and underlying among whites the "deep inner uncertainty as to who they really are."[23]

Music's place in the construction of difference traces a long history. During the Renaissance (and speaking in the most general terms), music took prominence in elite circles to distinguish European creativity from the intrusions of recently colonized others whose sounding practices challenged the bounds of comprehension. And so did it signify local dangers associated with nature and magic, naming an otherness lurking within. At this point, difference specified a multiplex of cultural significations, in which an early racial concept was but a part. In *Merchant of Venice*, Shakespeare proposes an early modern alignment of sonic power and taming: "Their savage eyes turn'd to a modest gaze, / By the sweet power of music."[24] Even once notions of race had coalesced in Europe in the late eighteenth and nineteenth centuries, moreover, the incomprehensible sounding practices of outsiders, now recognized as "music" in the theories of Jean-Jacques Rousseau and Johann Gottfried Herder, expressed a broad accumulation of foreign markers serving to depict otherness.[25] In the United States, however, what had previously been barely audible obtained an intelligibility within new, specifically racialized, discursive regimes. For a variety of complex reasons to be considered over the course of this study, the perception of musical difference had grown so thoroughly racialized that music came to epitomize racial differences generally, informing opinion across the racial divide. The linkage of race and music, in fact, occupied a crucial place within the system of relations comprising the social, a linkage that, once again, describes a coalescence rather than an overarching principal of change. It was not so much a causal center as a force within a broader structural causality, the "form" of which was determined only in relation to the complex of social forces. Seen this way, the expressive power of black music can be said to derive not from a qualitative, absolute difference but from a socially and experientially determined interracialism that contradicted white supremacist ideologies and inspired musical determinations of a realm not-white. Difference spoke above all of an in-betweenness or what I will be calling here "sameness," even as it was continually figured and refigured to establish an easy separation of the races.[26]

Perpetuating absolute notions of difference, then, can only affirm racial precepts that took form at the beginnings of a colonizing modernity. And it is for this reason that this study works to rethink the informing theory of "African retentions" as it is commonly articulated in contemporary musical scholarship. The challenge is not waged against the recognition of retentions themselves, for which scholars such as Sterling Stuckey, John Szwed, and Roger Abrahams had long had to argue until being more routinely recognized in black studies from the 1970s. Indeed, retentions are part of a process of claiming "pastness" within virtually all culture groups, and the performance of pastness carries crucial symbolic value in many if not all formations of culture.[27] More exactly challenged, therefore, are the conclusions African retentions routinely propose. For theories of retention, which underlie Afrocentric thought, commonly reduce the complexity of lived experience to a static and oversimplified phenomenology of blackness. These theories are oversimplified because they give weight to the assumption that black music grows, like a living, organic form, from fixed, predetermined origins, an assumption that, after all, betrays the legacy of the color line.

It is not that African qualities do not inform American practices but, rather, that the analytical concept of "retentions" implies a historical continuity that cannot be comprehended apart from the discourses and social processes that cast this very idea into being. "Retentions" is a distinctly modern, formal concept that provides us with a lens through which we observe the African-American musical past. But since this concept is itself a representation cast within modern racial ideology, it cannot serve to explain the phenomenal complexities of performative experience across the history of America. It cannot do so because it is an abstraction based on the extraction of a hypothesized African purity that had been recast within North American racial discourses. As Stuart Hall puts it, "The original 'Africa' is no longer there. It too has been transformed."[28] There is simply no single, purely musical dimension of sound retained that can be isolated analytically since this "sound retained" can only be understood as part of a broader musical-discursive relation. And because this relation is part and parcel of the changing conceptions of racial difference, it never maintains the essential stability that "retention" implies. "If there is a lesson in the broad shape of this circulation of cultures," Kwame Anthony Appiah writes, "it is surely that we are all already contaminated by each other, that there is no longer a fully autochthonous *echt*-African culture awaiting salvage by our artists (just as there is, of course, no American culture without African roots). And there is a clear sense in some postcolonial writing that the postulations of a unitary Africa over against a monolithic West—the binarism of Self and Other—is the last of the shibboleths of the modernizers that we must learn to live without."[29]

African-American musical history thus faces a version of what Sandra Adell names a multifaceted "double bind."[30] On one hand, racism precludes documentation of a culture, denying African-America a past. On the other, the scattering of evidence that does remain conforms to a caricatured portrait deeply invested in racialist constructs of difference. To resist the evidence is to perpetuate an idea of cultural absence—a new "Myth of the Negro Past"—that writers since Reconstruction have determinedly worked to overturn. And yet to rely on that same evidence without interrogating its discursive formation means extending the legacy of racialism that constructs "blackness" and "whiteness" as viable social categories. In the end, it complicates the efficacy of historical analysis as it condemns black musical studies to the realm of metaphysics.

What promises to be a more profitable strategy is to work critically from the textual strains and figurations themselves in order to explore the ways in which conceptions of black music emerged in the first place. This requires not only interpretation of the recorded incidences of African-American performance but also a reading of them and their absences from the discursive contexts and historical circumstances they occupy. It means, too, observing the various ways in which racial discourses of performance have repeatedly tempered the American social imagination. In this respect, musicological analysis departs from the specifically musical in order to consider the parameters of Western music's broader social power and influence. Looking beyond the "music in social context" approaches that for so long preoccupied conventional ethnomusicological analysis, the present project seeks to extend the critical challenge to music/social dualisms put forward in progressive ethnographic research. Because mediation means something more than a simple correspondence of subject and object, music and society must be seen as a relation in which one is always invested in the other. The enduring idea of a purely musical "black form"—together with the binaries of oral/written, folk/art, rural/urban, black/white that go hand in hand with it—give way to the conception of a discursively constituted black music standing between as it embodies the textual and musical, as resonance.[31]

In the figure of resonance, of an utterance without beginnings, we locate a key critical concept for imagining a different story of black music.[32] Resonance describes the sounding after an unlocatable origin; it is the "afterlife" of a negative sonic inception, the "absent cause" represented in the audible outer world. As resonance is received, moreover, so is it repeatedly recast, rearticulated, and heard within the social. Conceived as a textual figuration of sound's position within a social "unconscious" and accordingly existing between and beyond an ever-present discursive sphere, it conjures a flutter of sounds and texts that give shape to resoundingly racialized constructions of difference through the continual engagement of blacks and whites.

One hears in resonance not simply soul, sorrow, or a kickin' beat, but the racio-social discourse network from which these discernible figurations arose. What is more, the resonances of black music not only reveal the social construction of race but serve to voice and ultimately to shape and advance them. As the key cultural expression of race since the early nineteenth century, "black music," in its various articulations, has projected racial notions into the public sphere, displaying incomparable potential to travel across the social landscape. As a form easily recognized by anyone who can hear patterns in sound, black music infects white bodies with a difference that they themselves have constructed. African-Americans, moreover, have similarly contributed to these same categories of difference since many identify in them a figure of racial belonging that had been determined across the lines of color as superior to white practices. In other instances, black performers have challenged the notion of difference by claiming "white" musical practices as their own, further upsetting the stability of white supremacy's faulty racial logic.[33] Many Euro-Americans, as a matter of course, have sought to preserve the sanctity of color to fulfill racialist fantasies of difference. And so with each embrace of black sound they step back from and resist an increasingly common musical ground. This is perhaps why whites for so long seemed unable to swing in a "black" style. They did not partly because of learning and largely because to do so would upset color distinctions.

From the Civil War to the rise of hip-hop more than a century later, the resonances of black music have traced a multitude of innovations according to this peculiar dialogic. The relational nature of difference has meant that the musical categories of black and white would never remain stable. On the contrary, difference fluctuates wildly as a never-ending loop of text and sound. As a supradiscursive phenomenon interwoven with the discourses that socially constitute it, black music resonates across the sites and sounds of public culture, from black to white and back again. It gives voice to authenticities of race and origin as its artificiality betrays those authenticities as part of the social imagination. Searching for the historical essence of black music leads not to a primordial nature but to the second nature of the public sphere, as myths of presence give way to modern representations of blackness as swing, soul, funk, and groove. It is this instability of difference that grants to African-America its special, seemingly miraculous musical power. And it is this same difference that continues to baffle and confuse an American populace still convinced that the blackness and whiteness of sound is fundamentally, essentially, real. The whole, authentic truth of black music becomes but a lie, a social narrative that ascribes difference in order to repress subtexts fundamentally resonant in black and white.

What I'm gesturing to here is a kind of insurgent textual listening through which one hears the story of black music emanating from the matrix of racialist orthodoxy. This listening practice is subversive in an Ellisonian sense because it locates black music's power not in a segregated racial preserve but in the relational position of a black sound confessing the mulatto truth of a white supremacist nation.[34] If it unseats the authenticity of black presence so does it reveal for African-America something more: it places claim on the totality of the American social experience that has been persistently portrayed as centered in white.

But my ultimate aim is not simply to critique black music's pervasive essentialism but rather to provide a historical theory that defends the magical, miraculous quality of black performance. I want to show that the true miracle of black sound derives neither from a simple African origin nor from an inherently "spiritual nature" that seemingly "jes grew." It emerges instead from the alchemy of modern racial logic and the ironic differences that logic produces.[35] While taking shape within the public and social, the miraculousness of black sound owes its resonant form to the obscured materiality of black utterance, and this is what makes the challenge of re-sounding the nation ultimately an act of near magical recovery. If we are to rewrite the narrative of black music we must also reclaim some semblance of the character of its effective resonances welling up as "traces," as Antonio Gramsci called them, as the primary documents of early American racial history. "Rather than talk of what we 'know' about slavery, then," following W. J. T. Mitchell's directive, "we must talk of what we are prevented from knowing [and hearing], what we can never know, and how it is figured for us in the partial access we do have."[36]

To hear black music this way is to construct a critical practice from a radical revision of its definition and history. It is to observe how a discernibly "black music" emerges as part of a broader ideological configuration and system of relations that repeatedly reinvented the substance, indeed, the very ontology of black music as such. When we hear the body of black music "speak" we begin to recognize the instabilities of race and nation that have given rise to the tragic formations of racial difference. When we hear black music "speak" we identify an ideal conception of America within the stable ideological construct of white assimilation that is fundamentally, at its very core, simultaneously black and white. This kind of subversive listening develops neither from a purely sonic experience nor from the selective visions that so often inform interpretations of the American social past. It locates black music's power not in race per se but in the wild fluctuations from sameness to difference that racial ideologies have constructed. From this mode of hearing, we identify, finally, the origins of a kind of musical-textual double speak that claims for music the unities and incommensurabilities of blackness and whiteness, at once.

Hear Me Talking to You   Subversive listening requires a special attention to the muted and muffled sonorities existing between the lines. As

Ellison and other critics have shown us, the truth about black music is rarely rendered, rarely truly heard. Judging from a broad, social vantage, black voices seem always to inhabit positions in the quieter walks of life, relegated to racially determined exteriors, of presence-in-absence, even as their sounds help to constitute the sonic architecture of the public sphere. An African-American "ghost" vocalist might stand in for a Euro-American star, sacrificing the sound of difference to a greater public cause—a theme that Julie Dash explores in her film, *Illusions* (1983). But such transgressive capacities seldom find their way back around. When the gifted voices of Harry Belafonte and Dorothy Dandridge sing in *Carmen Jones,* they perform a related sacrifice, gaining operatic authority through the actual vocal exploits of white others. Even when conspicuously present the black voice remains mystified, obscure. "They don't care nothing about me. All they want is my voice," complains Ma Rainey in August Wilson's thoughtful characterization. Ultimately, what "they" wants is for that voice (or any other mode of African-American expression) to keep its place, to entertain while remaining effectively and fixedly black. As entertainment, African-American music maintains its lowly status. "Don't misunderstand me," André Hodeir confides in his celebration of jazz, "I don't in the least claim, like most specialized critics, that jazz is *the* music of our time. . . . The riches of jazz, however precious, cannot for a moment match the riches of European music."[37]

But the efforts to contain the sonic qualities of race, of "blackness," also signify the power African-American voices convey even when they sound beyond the cloistered circumstances of the church and club. Both the form and content of this vocal power are resonant with deep history. In colonial and antebellum slavery, voice represented the most sonically conspicuous possession of a body otherwise possessed. The vocal utterance provided slaves with an expressive tool, an audible social force that served to construct group networks and structures of meaning. Within the economy of slavery, African-American slaves identified a way of crafting cultural possessions within the vessel of their own possessed self—out of the possession itself—a force that challenged the control of the master-owner. From this knowledge, blacks before and after emancipation learned to rely on the vocal practices of singing, storytelling, and preaching (together with attendant instrumental correlates and interplays) to draw out in sound a racially prescribed local wisdom. More than any other expressive phenomenon, the "vocal" sound of black music has represented the crucial place from which African-Americans have told their stories in the art forms of modern virtuosity, from the emergence of Kansas City swing to the freedom songs of the Civil Rights era. The continuing efforts to speak against the shrillest white supremacist challenges reflect the tenacity of African-Americans who have built a culture on the ability to make bodily utterance. It is this affective vocal quality that courses through the veins of a racially determined black music and rises up from the greater social unconscious to reveal a veritable miracle of sound.[38]

"Black voice," then, can be understood in two ways: as the literal, audible utterance empowering the singing or speaking subject and as a metonym referring to the broad, social impact of a highly racialized African-American performative tradition. In post-Revolutionary United States, white public recognition of the black speaking and singing voice would be the first step toward realizing an always-controversial "Negro" presence. And as the significance of that voice grew, so would its audible immediacy. Already by the early nineteenth century, the racialized voice of blackness had exceeded not only the subject but sound as such, entering into the interstices of public discourse. And as it resonated across the land, its power and influence would grow. What we might call the authenticity or realness of black music would be revealed in its fluctuation, in its socially constructed instability, wavering between sound and text to the point of complicating distinctions between music and language.

What is so striking and potentially threatening about the black voice, broadly construed, is that which lies beyond the processes of signification. If voice, or indeed, black music generally, resonates from within a constituting linguistic matrix, it also expresses a quality of experience that seems momentarily to exceed the merely discursive, even as that experience is quickly rendered within language constructs. That is, there are qualities to black music and perhaps more generally to the modern musical experience since the eighteenth century that draw us into uncharted realms beyond the limits of language. This is the quality of nineteenth-century opera suggested in Carolyn Abbate's appropriately indirect and mystified notion of the "unsung." While Abbate reserves this strategic term for the particular moments when operatic characters perceive music beyond the staged performance (namely, the sound of the accompanying orchestra), she extends it more generally to gesture to the transgressive antinarrative potential of operatic performance, and it is from this position that it has taken on a broader significance in musicology. Abbate's reflections on the unsung mark the turn to a new critical attention to the power of sound and, particularly, to the ways in which music contradicts literary theory's presumption of textual dominance.[39] Similarly, Anthony Newcomb locates music's affective capacities in its very materiality, in the residual traces left after the semiotic attribution of meaning. "It is probably more true of music than of any other art," he writes, "that the sign (if we conceive it as such) is not transparent. That is, the sign does not disappear in favor of its function as pointing to the signified."[40] The conspicuous materiality of sound as such, of sound beyond discourse that is simultaneously saturated with vague, nebulous, yet multilayered meaning, has been commonly described not as an essence but as a vocal "grain" emanating from the unsignifiable qualities of a body singing. And if this notion, which is drawn from Roland Barthes's famous essay, "The Grain of the Voice," has been somewhat labored in discussions across cultural studies and the critically informed "new musicology" of the 1990s, it also points to an aspect of experience as well as an interpretive pathway into what is perhaps especially meaningful about music. "Grain" gestures to the hyperreal, dream-like aspect of music that so remarkably and continually draws our attention. It is what incites passion, prompts deep philosophical reflection, and inspires glorious rhapsodies of poetry and prose.[41]

Critical inquiry into the power of sound has brought about something of a "musical (re)turn" in the musicologies, a turning back not so much to "the music itself" but to a reconsideration of the history and phenomenology of listening within and against the challenges put forward by contemporary literary theory. Rather than merely observing music as one of the many textual dimensions within discourse theory, scholars in ethnomusicology and historical musicology are now exploring the exceptional nature (or natures) of the musical encounter, the physically experienced, "vocal" uniqueness—what Steven Feld calls, paralleling Abbate, and in the spirit of a post-Geertzian anthropology, "vocal knowledge"—and how that uniqueness is played out variously across cultures and within the broad stretch of Western history.[42] Critics of elite concert music, in particular, have sought to examine the circumstances through which music has played a fundamental role in the construction of Euro-Western experience, and it is this body of literature, as part of the musical history of the West, that has the greatest bearing on our understanding of black music. Writing in the wake of Abbate's forceful assertion of a musical phenomenology within contemporary theoretical discussions, these scholars have greatly contributed to reclaiming music's cultural authority by demonstrating its unique expressive capacities within the social and philosophical formation of modern Western epistemology and culture.

Gary Tomlinson, for example, has sought to present to a broad intellectual audience the special place of music in the formation of Euro-Western modernity. In *Metaphysical Song: An Essay on Opera,* he shows how vocal production has been constructed over the course of the modern as a kind of opening into uncharted realms. The creation of opera, in particular, Tomlinson explains, "has been a chief staging ground in elite Western culture for a belief of two worlds, one accessible to the senses, the other not." This "potent experience of a metaphysics as well as a physics" takes on discernible formations within the contexts of European music history, notably in the relation of the supersensible within the natural order in the late Renaissance and, then, in the separation of the immaterial and the material realms, which, Tomlinson argues, is consistent with the new formation of subjectivity in the seventeenth century.[43] It is, however, the subsequent formation in Kant of the noumenon reaching beyond normal, rational understanding (yet still determined within subjective consciousness) that sets the trajectory of musical reception into the nineteenth and twentieth centuries. While stressing that musical experience should not and cannot be conceived as a transhistorical phenomenon within an essential, transcendental realism, Tomlinson reveals convincingly how the legacy of metaphysical song extends into modernism, figured in terms of the sublime, the uncanny, and the Lacanian "cry" as a quality of experience seemingly beyond description. Music at these moments brings to bear imaginations of an originary place (in both a mythic-historical and an infantile, prelinguistic sense) inextricably linked to modern conceptions of transcendence.[44]

So can the power of voice be discerned in its very absence, recalling the jazz-based silences of Ellison's *Invisible Man.* In his fascinating study of the nineteenth-century concept of absolute music, Daniel K. L. Chua proposes the discursive formation of a sonic "absolute" as an attempt to re-create music's prior vocal purity within the contexts of modern rationalism and skepticism. No longer resonant with the heavens and angels that marked its prior, premodern unity with language, ritual, and culture, the "voice" of modern music had become disenchanted, disciplined, and virtually silenced as a mere sensual form—a "pleasure of the ear," as John Calvin named it. According to Chua, the theories of absolute music, which were first fashioned in German romantic aesthetics at the turn of the nineteenth century and came to dominate intellectual musical opinion across the nineteenth and twentieth, reflect a disenchanted and discontented world. "Absolute music" is for the modernity of European high culture an attempt to recover the lost voice of the ancients. Through such musical imagining, "a disenchanted world vocalises its hope by projecting its loss as instrumental music."[45] In the broadest sense, absolute music represents an effort to identify the vocal "grain" of transcendent, embodied sound in the quietude of rational skepticism. This recovery takes place within the civilized, progressive technologies of instrumentalism and composition, which fashion absolutes beyond language as they reflect the anxiety of modern music's separation from an imagined vocal origin.

The musical (re)turn of critical musicology as it has been put forward by Abbate, Tomlinson, Chua, and others urges a new projection of the role of musical scholarship. As a version of postmodern theory's "culture of enchantment," as Mark Schneider calls it, the new musicology confronts big questions having to do with the very nature of musical power in Euro-Western elite cultures.[46] But musicology's collective critique of language studies brings us only so far. For what is this "beyond" or "unsung" realm if not in the end another dimension of the social? If we are constituted within the various structures of social relations making up our worlds, then music, in its perceived transcendence of language—and even in its very real capacity to exceed total linguistic grasp—must similarly consist in social frames, unless we claim against the logic of contemporary social theory some realm of consciousness that is otherwise free. Without reducing musical expression to the larger sphere of discourse, we need to acknowledge the simple fact of music as a social phenomenon if we are to comprehend the true extent of its significance. To their credit, a few historically sensitive scholars of European elite music have extended a (largely unacknowledged) ethnomusicological tenet, stressing how music's extradiscursivity may be itself a discursive formation, quite possibly human in nature, as it is particular to its local constitutions in culture. Discursive conceptualizations of "music" are, they explain, played out in performance and in the phenomenology of hearing, circling back into the realm of language and textuality. Accordingly, music's place in the social and its impact on the listener develop from the way that sound actually inhabits the very tissues of the discursive, just as the saturation of ambiguous meanings that music contains (as the ultimate polysemic sign vehicle) produces a quality of experience exceeding full linguistic grasp.[47]

The trouble is, these arguments rarely develop the full implications of their own logic. Even the most historically sensitive European musicology restricts the range of analysis of music's relation to the social, limiting the "nonmusical" to the arcane arenas of elite culture and the philosopher's text. This nearly exclusive commitment to internalist matters of intellectual history precludes the alternative possibility of engaging in broad-based social and class analyses common to other historical disciplines, together with the multiplex and conflicting nature of ideological formation: ideologies in the plural.[48] As a result, studies of European music history commonly fail to consider how musical experiences, as social experiences, were constituted within the domains of the racial and the political-economic, as well as the intellectual—within what Stuart Hall calls "the material force" of ideology or, once again, within the extensive, overarching frameworks that Roland Barthes names "myth."[49] Nor, for that matter, do scholars of European music, when turning to contemporary musical circumstances, typically consider the wider social and ideological contexts from which their own listening practices derive. It would seem that one could simply examine the place of European art-music in modern culture as if it were the dominant force in our musical experience and not the minority music it really is. For only in such a position of dominance might one engage in analysis without regard to the interferences of race, power, and mass culture that interpellate the critical subject.

Musicology's commitments to a specifically intellectual history thus obscure the place of elite musical culture within European social history and—even more important to this study—its relation to musical experience within the contemporary American public sphere.[50] In this way, even its seemingly progressive new historicism perpetuates the closed systems of New Criticism in its assumption that the study of history and reception can be convincingly limited to critical exegeses of philosophical treatises and safely situated in a presumably stable and secure historical "Europe." In its cloistered intellectualism, the "new musicology," as it is typically proposed, reinforces an old conception of musical practice as something divorced from the political world as well as from the challenges of representation that face the twenty-first-century historian. This traditional aspect to the new musicology perpetuates the false binary of music and society, as musicology's object remains somehow distinguished from the modern legacy of race and colonialism that, as a weighty volume of postcolonial criticism has copiously revealed, underlies a greater Western "disenchantment."[51]

As important as the new critical musicological investigations have been, we need a broader intellectual purview, considering other strategies for exploring the dimensions of the sonic, vocal power of African-American music. We need to build from new musicological initiatives while also considering the undeniable impact of American social forces in the making of the musical experience. Such a perspective begins to come into focus through the seminal anthropological investigations of music by Judith and Alton Becker, Steven Feld, Anthony Seeger, Christopher Waterman, Jane Sugarman, Veit Erlmann, and others, particularly through the important studies in popular music and cultural theory that have emerged since the

1980s, demonstrated most recently in the work of John Shepherd and Peter Wicke. This latter scholarship explores more rigorously than perhaps any prior study the relationships between what the authors call "musical processes and the processes of subjectivity"—the ways in which music is constituted within a broader network of determinations as it follows a distinctly musical logic, one intimately linked to a bodily constrained self-in-the-making.[52] What I have in mind for the study of African-American music develops from a similar desire to situate music more conspicuously within the tradition of cultural studies. I'm calling for, however, a particular kind of inquiry that relates the connotative "grain" of the musical experience to the formation of racial ideologies and, in turn, repositions "black music" at the very center of American modernity. Whereas Shepherd and Wicke attempt to isolate a peculiarly musical phenomenology within the social, I am seeking to explore how the "musical" enters into and informs the domain of language and social experience, which in turn conceptualizes the apartness of music from language as "the sound itself." Once we acknowledge music's unique relation as a phenomenon constituted at once within and against the social (together with its corresponding systems of representation) we begin the necessary step of considering how black music similarly affirms and critiques ideological formations of racial difference. Black music, I want to propose, challenges the conception of modernity as "lost voice," as disenchanted, by claiming in its miracle of production a countermodernity that acknowledges America's interracialism at the same time it inevitably divides us according to race.[53]

As a performative icon so obviously and naturally expressing racial indicators (thus enacting what linguistically oriented ethnomusicologists call "iconicity"), black music effects a certain, primary blackness beyond all other American cultural practices. Its embodied form signifies a legacy of racial meaning accorded solely to the "Negro" heritage, as if American expressions beyond African-America somehow exceed racial category. The 1990s literature on "whiteness" has prompted a reconsideration of this still pervasive assumption. Still, however inaccurate and exclusionist the formation of black music as "race music" may be—after all, we are all a part of the same socially constituted domain—it has greatly determined modern constructions of musical meaning and experience, affording to it a unique affect already in slavery but particularly once African-American expressions entered into modern public culture after the Civil War.[54] It is in this social constitution of music as something beyond discourse where we locate a crucial dimension of black music's cultural power.

The slippage between the musical and the linguistic draws from and is amplified by the slippage arising from the incommensurate relation of black to white. Just as one locates music's "grain" in those moments when sound seems to tear from the linguistic constructs that routinely contain it, so does one recognize black music's power in the momentary "sameness" that contradicts the commonsense social reality of racial distinctions. In both musical and racial experience, one senses that prelinguistic, imaginary quality deriving from the incommensurability of music to language, of black to white, a quality evoking a sense of transcendence and perfection that harkens a mythic, premodern origin.[55] The logic of modern racial difference not only ascribes blackness but does so by drawing from the legacy of figurations linking race and authenticity, a linkage that many romantic racial theorists employed when proposing a common origin of humanity. This theory of supraracial sameness was also consistent with contemporaneous theories of music's beginnings in a premodern domain. Brought together in American conceptions of black music, first in the slaves' miracle of musical production (which forced whites to recognize a form created out of the formlessness of bondage), then in the various public articulations of black music circulating after the Civil War, racial sound spoke simultaneously of difference and sameness, of the social text that determines "blackness" and of the interrelational experience suggesting unities beyond it. The sublime, transcendent quality of music at its most powerful—the Lacanian *jouissance,* the explosion of language when language cannot contain—builds a particular signification in its intersection with American racial constructs, rendering in black music occasional flashes of recognition of a human commonality within and against the authorizations of difference. It is in this respect that Ellison names the blues the "art of ambiguity," a form signifying difference as a means of transcending it.[56]

Black music's power, then, reveals in its seeming supradiscursivity a saturation of significations suggesting a "beyondness" harkening back to prior unities of music and language and of the races. (This may be what Lévi-Strauss means when he suggests that "by listening to music, and while we are listening to it, we enter into a kind of immortality.")[57] It is not that black music, and for that matter, perhaps all music in the West, merely exceeds discourse but that it concentrates signification and nondiscursive bodily experience, bringing to bear a meshing of social forces and bodily affect together with the discursive system of relations that conceives it. (In this we should recall the density or opacity Newcomb attributes to the musical sign.) Black music's power does not derive solely from its marking of difference but also from its ability to signify a difference that depends on and grows out of a common history and experience and, in doing so, reveals the sameness of a shared interracial belief in the American racial myth. Black music accumulates contradictory racial significations to produce a certain sublime vastness of meanings that, while socially and discursively constituted, communicates both more immediately and less directly than the significations of language. "The significant feature of musical communication," Steven Feld writes in an important essay, "is not that it is untranslatable and irreducible to the verbal mode but that its generality and multiplicity of possible messages and interpretations brings out a special kind of 'feelingful' activity and engagement on the part of the listener, a form of pleasure that unites the material and mental dimensions of music experienced as fully embodied." In the instance of black music, this "feelingfulness," as a kind of overdetermination or condensation of meaning within the body, is most obviously (and inextricably) linked to the experience of race.[58]

When we witness the subversive, disruptive, "scatological" vocalizations in "Heebie Jeebies," in which Louis Armstrong plays the line between speech and song, we engage not merely the pure musicality of the grain but the compression of linguistic signification that is rich with racial meaning as well. We "hear" the Sambo stereotype, the exotic images—the savage, the ghostly apparition—of Armstrong's early filmic appearances, the virtuoso of a famous 1920s studio band, together with the sublime figurations of a black sound that in its public celebrations revealed the sameness that crosses race. And we hear countless other signs and images that no casual analytic gesture such as this one can properly indicate. These articulations, which at once inform and reflect the discursive, produce the remarkable sense of authenticity and completion we associate with a miraculous sound that seemingly "jes grew."[59]

The musical experience of completion, then, which historically sustains essentialist claims of black identity, is produced by the instability of music existing within and against linguistic signification as it simultaneously challenges and sustains concepts of race. Black music centers blackness, yet it does so in continual relation to the category and experience of whiteness in America. If black music supplies a supplementary difference to whiteness, so does it complicate (through the same logic of supplementarity) white racial fixity. Black music, then, develops racial stability and "truth"—black difference—out of the instability of music's relation to discourse, just as its truth is enhanced by the social instabilities within the racial dynamic. It does not merely reflect the social, as if we could maintain a clear distinction between the realms of "music" and "society." Rather it is inhabited by the social, just as its sonic materiality—the miracle of sound arising from the formerly material-less, possessed bodies of African-American slaves—informs the epistemological contours of modernity. Black music epitomizes a formulation of sound into text and back again as a social articulation or utterance I am calling in this study *resonance.*

Against this background we might venture to claim black music as an American version of "absolute music" or, disavowing the instrumental legacy's preeminence, of "metaphysical song." Black music certainly shares many of the features of nineteenth-century musical absolutism and metaphysics. While not limited to instrumental practices, black music's formulation as a sonic beyondness in a world of disenchanted existence reflects the influence of the intellectual legacy of romantic aesthetics as it has intersected with more common local European and African-American determinations of the sacred and the transcendent. Yet black music is also a critical negative achievement, absolute not in form but in content: it proposes a "unity" within the disunity and discontentment of the modern, and its special capacity of unity derives from the racial divisions it is purported to overcome. In its sonic "purity," however, it is of course equally disenchanted, having arisen from the incommensurability of black and white. Black music therefore projects a (in this sense, "soulful") unity momentarily and fleetingly, only to return us to a cursed modernity and its racial antagonisms. It is both a manifestation of ideals and an elusive feminized seductress, repeatedly reinscribed by a legacy of rhapsodic gestures, from the coronation of the spirituals to the jungle and tribal-house styles of contemporary electronic dance music.

That the claims of black music are cast across race and genre speaks to the power of discourse in the machinery of representation in the public sphere. The language through which African-Americans in the twentieth century claim difference grows from the same racial logic. While a large share of this project is dedicated to unearthing the discursive network from which an overarching concept of black music arose, I will also be gesturing to recoveries within these discursive spaces of some historical vestige of "black voices" welling up from within. We begin to hear the voice of a historical black music in what Homi Bhabha, calls the time lag, "the disjunctive moment of its utterance: the space which enables a post-colonial contra-modernity to emerge."[60] The miracle it projects (recalling Ellison's initial gesture) is the presence out of the loss that slavery represents, fulfilling in sound a victory against the enduring skepticism and doubt of a presumably superior whiteness. While not a fixed and stable completion (in the sense of a dialectically conceived continuity), black music's victory grows from its many resolutions out of the conflicts of which it too must be a part. If Euro-Americans "won the race" in economic terms, they also—many believe—paid the price with their souls. And it is out of this economy of loss where we begin to discern a negative utterance echoing from the countermodernity that black music "sings" and that social text can only partially contain and represent. Black music gives voice to the moral victory of an African-American experience that realizes black humanity against the logical failure of Euro-modernity as such.

In twentieth-century literatures, we find direction for exploring black music's counterresonance in the vestiges of utterance that take form in the public sphere. These traces appear, for example, in the vocal effects of the Mills Brothers or in James Reese Europe's curious reference to an ephemeral folk instrument made from a branch of the chinaberry tree that can be played only while the sap runs. And we recognize determinations of a different kind in the challenges of William Grant Still, who embraces racialist thought and vernacular romance to propose a musical counter-modernity, claiming an origin of modern form in a universal peasantry to which black folk are the most likely heirs.[61] These testimonies are not, in themselves, evidence of the "truth" about black musical difference, for difference is always figured within the symbolic violence of a white mastery, incessantly determining the contours of black speaking and sounding. The inefficiency of white representations to entirely capture an aural experience at once constituted in and outside of discourse is what also enables us to gesture to the black vocal utterances that are similarly in opposition to as they are dependent on the textual sphere of whites. In the singing of modern blackness, we locate markers to follow into the past. They are the signposts from which we can trace backward as a kind of archeological recovery the "never-said, an incorporeal discourse, a voice as silent as a breath."[62]

The historical study of black music thus becomes what Houston Baker calls "blues criticism," a critical practice "for which the intent is always the foregrounding of ancestral faces—hear an America singing that has never been heard before." In this instance, the unsung or "never said" is the secret voicing or "truth content" that America confesses, an utterance that rather than emanating from "the black (w)hole" of racial singularity proposed by Baker emerges instead as a "miracle of production" developing from the contradictions of race.[63] Musicology's musical (re)turn proceeds in this instance from the broadest conception of the musically social and the socially musical, at a nexus of sound and text that grows resonant with racial signification. That music history traditionally relegates this dynamic to the realm of black music (the musical correlate of what Paul Gilroy calls in his discussion of slavery black people's "special property") pays testimony to the extent to which the racial and social have been occluded from analyses of the musical experience.[64] If, in contrast, we situate the racial within the musical, black music becomes not simply an isolated phenomenon for study but a key factor in our understanding of Western music and its history overall. The study of "unsung voices" assumes a new dimension as a form of racial analysis.

In 1928, Louis Armstrong led a seven-piece studio ensemble, The Hot Seven, in a recording of Don Redman's arrangement of "Hear Me Talkin' to Ya."[65] At the outset of the performance, Armstrong makes an announcement. He asks us to listen, to "hear me talking to you." It is an obvious reference to the title, and at first it might seem inconsequential to the ensuing performance. But what if we were to take this playful gesture literally? Hear me talking to you? What are we supposed to hear? What's the story? And who's doing the talking? Judging from what jazz musicians have repeatedly claimed, the "story" would seem to be the music itself, in the collective ensemble work and in the solos that arise from it. As Ingrid Monson puts it, jazz is "saying something," and this notion extends back prior to modern genres.[66] To tell a good story is to play a meaningful, memorable performance. It is to construct an improvisation so powerful, so emotionally and intellectually challenging that it seems to go beyond words, to reveal a deeper, more telling secret. The conceit of storytelling represents one of the enduring rhetorical gestures among musicians, the principal trope conceptualizing the art of Lester Young, Charlie Parker, and so many others. So too does the conceit lie at the heart of black music's mystification. It serves to justify claims of musical transcendence, of a power projecting meaning beyond language. For many, it is through this beyondness that one discovers much about life generally. Black music emerges as an unspoken tale that nonetheless voices a truth about life and nation.

But what precisely is the music telling us? We've tended to assume it is a tale of racial continuity and essence, and certainly the countless references to black music's qualities of transcendence and sublime affective power propose a direct, straightforward message. But could there be another story that eludes us? If we take the musicians at their word—to hear them "talking" to us and acknowledge what they have to say, we can begin to imagine a different story from the one most commonly narrated. I want to propose that we construct a critical position from the stories contained in "the music itself," in tales perhaps exceeding the intentions of the artists, yet through which we locate the truth about racial life in America.

These stories do not speak of racial absolutism. In the very materiality of their form, we can hear them revealing a sameness that is only then cast as a form of "difference" in order to uphold the racial order.

What we hear, in fact, in Armstrong's performance of "Hear Me Talkin' to Ya" is a veritable hybrid of black and white: a thirty-two-bar song form derived from the tradition of nineteenth-century popular music, the verse/chorus design of which reaches back further to common songs of the English tradition and to the interracial religious vocal practices of the camp meetings; an arrangement by Don Redman that is consistent with harmonic practices employed in Tin Pan Alley and somewhat innovative in its use of chromaticism during the transition to his alto saxophone solo; improvisations that, while conventional, display competency and imagination, reflecting a marked departure from the New Orleans–based paraphrase style of jazz from the 1910s and 1920s; a level of instrumental virtuosity and timing that draws similarly the African-American performance traditions of New York, Chicago, and New Orleans as it is securely identified with classical pedagogy and twentieth-century Euro-Western modernism; and, finally, a strikingly new rhythmic approach named "swing" that had just emerged within the urban contexts of northern blacks as it paid tribute to rhythmically generated styles reaching back to New Orleans and more generally to the early southern centers of ragtime. While African "retentions" most certainly inform this if not all of American music, to focus on these alone falsifies the depth, power, and experience of the new jazz expression. What is most obvious here is a remarkable creative invention that speaks to the impossibly complicated racial intersections at this particular moment. In sound we can hear both the documenting and proposing of a new comprehension of blackness in whiteness, of whiteness in blackness, which characterizes this place, this time. What rises beyond words is the unspoken truth of the sameness of an America that relies on black music to voice its fantasies of race.

"Hear Me Talkin' to Ya" proposes, after all, a reflective consideration of the musical experience, one that moves us from music as isolated form and toward the blurred spaces of the musical and the social. This brief discussion suggests that we might begin to think of black music not as a fixed expression sounded from one side of the color line but as a sonically articulated comprehension of a cross-racial social dynamic. For if musical experiences exceed the linguistic, so are they necessarily constrained by the social ground in which we live. The social, in turn, is textured with the residue of musical traces that resonate in the dimension of an everyday life we conceptualize as sensual, "feelingful," poetic. Armstrong's significances, for one, derive not merely from the sound of his horn but from a far more complex dynamic of relations in which "jazz," "music," and "swing" infiltrate and give substance to the intricacies of a broad stretch of American entertainment and play. We hear Armstrong in the social precisely because of his musical significance, because of the power and influence that his jazz innovations, socially determined as they are, bring forth into the everyday. When Armstrong says "hear me talking to you" he means for all of us to listen because it is about all of us whom he speaks and plays.

Speaking Past   Exposing the fallibility of black music's metaphysics does not in itself explain why claims of authenticity and essence have remained so tenacious. Given the critical power and influence of musicology's (re)turn, it would be all too easy to dismiss such orthodoxies as sorry loyalties to a naive folk humanism inconsistent with the newfound wisdom of "post" theory. And yet these orthodoxies seem to flourish in direct proportion to the critical postmodernisms that test conventional understanding of self and agency. For when text is said to stand before one's musical experience, the security of identity and the efficacy of agency are seriously challenged. As a matter of course, black music's historical role in asserting identity among marginalized people begins to slip away. And finding stability and place in the sonic-textual wash of contemporary American musical culture poses new and striking challenges as the markers of racial authenticity blur into the broader musico-discursive fabric. To disparage the commitments to authenticity is thus to be blind to the larger ideological configurations that give meaning to all cultural forms and that provide black music in particular with its exceptional, miraculous qualities.

Accordingly, reconceptualizing black music's history does not render false the realities of musical experience but, rather, seeks to establish the narrative historiographic ground from which these realities have been written. This section will observe some of the crucial stories in the making of modern perspectives of black music both to document its unmatched role in crafting identities and to propose a critical strategy that works from a repressed history. At issue here in particular is the desire to negotiate between the strengths of contemporary critical insights into textuality and representation and to comprehend the wisdom behind the vigorous resistances to them. Only then can we begin to imagine more venturesome interpretations of the in-betweenness from which the miracle of black music speaks.

Since the emergence of black music as a concept, writers and observers have variously spoken past one another, their passions and enthusiasms heightening conflicts among so many claims and gestures. While this condition is certainly not new, the increased instability of racial determinations of music in the public sphere has amplified the level of confusion and cross-speak to the point of challenging the most valiant attempts at clarity and understanding. Music's proliferation across the hypermediated spaces of public culture has created a shimmer of style and symbol that complicates racial category as it amplifies fears of racial encounter.[67] In the late 1980s and 1990s, the imagist hyperrealism of gangsta rap exhibited a performative extravagance that forcefully challenged white supremacy while simultaneously supplying a crucial marker of authenticity and style for a broad interracial cross section of American youth culture. Ambiguities of racial crossing, moreover, have grown most conspicuous in relation to celebrated artists. The phantasmagoria of signs representing Michael Jackson, for example, helps to explain his appeal as they identify the shifting sounds of meaning for those seeking to sustain racial place.[68] This decentering of reliable and secure determinations of black racial authenticity has, in turn, provided new spaces for questioning the authority of the narratives of black innovation that privilege African-American artistry. Richard M. Sudhalter's *Lost Chords: White Musicians and Their Contribution to Jazz, 1915–1945,* is one of the more conspicuous examples of a renewed desire to claim for white Americans a portion of the achievement that is jazz. Such efforts simultaneously reinforce an anachronistic racial binarism as they reveal a degree of insensitivity to the racial injustices that motivated similar arguments among some black critics. The "crimes of writing," to borrow Susan Stewart's apt phrase, are merely recent manifestations of a grand tale of negation to which black people have been repeatedly subjected.[69]

The academy has certainly witnessed its own share of "speaking past," even if its engagements have seemed less exercised than those taking place in popular public forums. If scholarly debates have appeared muted and restrained, this has had less to do with the terms of patrician decorum than with the broad-scale displacement of black music in musicological contexts. Whereas English studies has seen a tremendous flourishing of black literary criticism (even while, as Nellie Y. McKay explains, the representation of minorities still lags), black music studies takes place by and large on the exteriors of musicology's dominant conversations, which rather remarkably still remain principally devoted to matters of European elite music.[70] The severity of this limitation has not merely forced researchers to work harder amid a tenacious Eurocentrism; it has had a stultifying effect on the development of black musical scholastics and on its level of critical engagement as well. Seeking to improve matters, moreover, progressive scholars of European music have sometimes attempted to pick up the slack, assuming the responsibility of writing about African-American contributions and with glaringly inconsistent results. When Guthrie P. Ramsey, Jr., asks "Who Hears Here?" he speaks to the strangely paternalistic environment of a musicology still dominated by European programs of study and at a loss to improve a seemingly impossible situation. If we were to characterize the state of musicological research on black music, it would be one in which achievement is, as Ramsey puts it elsewhere, "slow, demanding, and sinuous," limited by enduring commitments to traditional comprehensions of musicology's object of study. Black music research thus remains outside the circle of serious critical and scholarly inquiry, a condition having less to do with black music studies as such as with the thoroughly racialized, extramusical circumstances affecting the development of criticism and scholarship as a whole.[71]

Even the most thoughtful criticisms can lead to problematic ends, reflecting at times the white "self-referential" impulse that Michael Awkward traces across a legacy of scholarly writing on black expressive culture. The important developments in jazz scholarship during the 1960s and 1970s, for example, expressed the laudable aim of demonstrating through analytical scrutiny the aesthetic value of an emerging jazz canon. In advancing those aims, however, writers also tended to decontextualize the music from the social frames that brought it into being, celebrating the genius of form as a parallel to a similarly dehistoricized European canon. By the 1980s, moreover, some scholars sought to challenge the erection of black musical canons by involving new critical strategies associated with social construction and postmodernism. In a curious thought piece published in the British journal *Popular Music,* Philip Tagg proposed nothing less than the elimination of categories of "black" and "white" as determinants of musical style and practice. Recognizing the hybrid nature of North American and European music's constitution, he offered a new story of its history in terms that ultimately erased the racial margins as part of a grand imperial mix. Tagg's essay was an early attempt to acknowledge the fictive constructedness of musical category and the degree of stylistic blurring that characterizes all musical processes. And yet as hopeful as such an ideal may sound, it reflects a remarkable naïveté about the effects of so much difference making in the namings of black music.[72]

Of an entirely different order is Gary Tomlinson's "Dialogics and Jazz: A White Scholar Signifies." This essay, which appeared in a seminal collection devoted to black music and contemporary theory, set the stage for a new kind of critically oriented jazz studies in the 1990s. Here, Tomlinson critiques what he calls the "monological" demonstrations toward canon making advocated at the time by African-American literary scholars such as Henry Louis Gates, Jr., and by many jazz critics. In Gates, he identifies a principal target, observing a contradiction between his proposals for establishing an African-American literary canon and his famous theory of signifyin', which, in its coupling of poststructuralist and black "vernacular" rhetorical practices, foregrounds dialogical (and therefore inherently anticanonical) themes of instability, parody, and play. Proposing his own intertextual engagement to comprehend jazz practices, Tomlinson proceeds to signify on Gates's own canonical appeals, together with the standardization of interpretive frames that have historically burdened jazz writing. In doing so, however, Tomlinson not only issues a useful critique but also defers the larger problem of the near exclusion of African-American music from existing academic canons. What is more, his lengthy, energetic foregrounding of European theory prior to a discussion of Miles Davis's fusion repertory (the preparation lasts twenty pages) downplays the legacy of intellectual violence advanced against others in the name of knowledge and reason—this, despite copious references to the major theorist of disciplining acts, Michel Foucault. If Tomlinson is signifying on the contradictions inherent to canon making as put forward by Gates, he is doing so within what Gayatri Spivak calls "an effectively heliocentric discourse" and from a rather certain, dedicated commitment to theory's powers. Theory becomes the truth center or "vernacular" from which Tomlinson speaks, without thoroughly considering the challenges of positioning this emancipatory tool within the context of black music studies. While dialogism derives from Mikhail Bakhtin's democratic conception of the novel, for black people, as Christopher Miller puts it, this historical association with "freedom, dialogue, and development arrives at the end of a gun barrel."[73]

Representing black music thus involves some real risk taking, and to proceed even with a clear sense of that risk chances perpetuating the positions one seeks to counter. The applications of contemporary poststructuralist theories are particularly challenging—no matter one's prescribed racial category—since their emphasis on instability and undecidability calls to mind the forms of ridicule employed historically to denigrate the putatively imitative nature of blacks.[74] In this respect, black culture's instability implies inadequacy: the inferiority of black difference is exposed as a dynamic yet ultimately nonevolving stasis that fades into the presence and light of a certain white dominance. What we might call the narrative of black music's containment begins with slavery and linguistic domination, whereby blackness remains fixed in its perceived instability, in its failure (formal, moral, or otherwise) to evolve and progress. Such views informed white supremacist interpretations across the nineteenth and early twentieth centuries, as both scholars and the general Euro-American public assumed African-American expression to be but a mirror of a racialized "white" creativity. And so do versions of such "myth(s) of the Negro past" still show up today in the continued marginalization of music by people of color and in the resistance to challenging the centrality of European music common to most academic music programs.

Marginalized within academic studies and segregated according to a racial binary in public conversations of high culture (e.g., classical music vs. classic jazz), black music as a subject of scholarly research has traditionally been left to those performers and listeners who cherish its power and effect. One of the most impressive concentrations of resources grows out of the African-American Christian church (in its many guises), which, as an institution, has historically supported the propagation and interpretation of black music. Church-based organizations, notably the National Baptist Convention, had already begun to establish forums for performance and publication by the late nineteenth century, and their efforts eventually set the foundation for the ideologies of black musical history and perception that moved in and out of African-American contexts. Circulating within many black communities was an assumption of a religious-spiritualist background to musical practices that would inform perceptions of secular practices, reaching into popular depictions of rhythm 'n' blues, jazz, and soul and informing the prophetic character of an emerging black musical scholastics. While Christian-based ecclesiastical interpretations have been part and parcel of the broader construction of black musical meaning since the interracial conversion rituals of the early nineteenth century, the new intersection of church-based perceptions and musicology's midcentury commitments to data collection and style history served to establish a mode of study seeking a racial ground of African-American originality. These approaches, replete with canons and formal modes of analysis, have functioned less to critique than to celebrate creative achievements realized in contexts of oppression.[75]

Black emancipatory scholarship—as represented in the gospel research of Horace Boyer and Bernice Johnson Reagon, the blues and spirituals studies of James H. Cone and Jon Michael Spencer, and the African-retentions arguments of Portia Maultsby, Melonee V. Burnim, and Jacqueline Cogdell Dje Dje—may be likened to what Michael S. Harper and Robert B. Stepto call a "Chant of Saints," a celebratory mix of songful rhetoric and eschatological theory honoring the African-American musical tradition.[76] Emerging from a legacy of prophetic writing, it responds to the racial uplift themes of the Civil Rights era and, more particularly, to the Black Arts writers who commonly espoused the political and emotional significance of black music. But African-American emancipatory scholarship also speaks outwardly, implicitly critiquing the overwhelming silence in the national and academic discourses regarding the legitimacy of black music and thought. "The black experience may no longer be invisible," Cornel West writes, "but it remains unheard—not allowed to speak for itself, to be taken seriously as having something valuable to say." Prophetic modes of thought accordingly develop from "protracted and principled struggles against forms of personal despair, intellectual dogmatism, and socioeconomic oppression that foster communities of hope."[77] Disavowing elite critical strategies that seemingly function successfully only in the most privileged and secure environments, these scholars have opted for an assertive, affirmative scholastics that celebrates perceived racial unities and that strenuously constrains the dimensions of critical discourse and engagement. According to their conception, black music marks the collective "we" of blackness as such, setting aside the intraracial divisions such politics betray, together with the interracial dialogism through which, in the words of Phillip Brian Harper, Black Arts practice ultimately "achieves its maximum impact."[78]

Significantly, Afro-centered musicological scholarship routinely appears skeptical of highly developed modes of scientistic and theoretical analysis, and for this reason it is frequently looked on condescendingly as a form of "black anger" or "polemics" by those who are unequivocal in their appeals to certain modes of scholarly authority. As a response to the violence of European analytical mastery, however, this skeptical "resistance to theory" makes perfect sense.[79] Giving favor to biographical portraits honoring black gospel music's heroes, to carefully documented historical chronologies, and to didactic explanations of compositional practice, black emancipatory studies express a prophetic intent to employ black music as an act of evangelical insurgency that defends the conventional sense of heritage and bolsters racial honor. It continually celebrates the very existence of a black music that arose and persisted despite a legacy of white denial and ridicule. This ecclesiastical brand of black emancipatory scholarship, then, works to tell the stories that have brought black music into the familiar terrain of narrative, employing conventional approaches of formal description to map out its aspects of style. The political determinations that motivate these approaches tend to make little impact on more analytically oriented scholars of European music who sometimes seem bemused by the motivations behind it.

A related form of activist scholarship develops from the rhetorical traditions foregrounding theories of black music's African origins. What we now call "Afrocentric" interpretation arose directly in response to a much older legacy of white-over-black narration. In their most basic incarnations, musical Afrocentricities bear a strong likeness to the white supremacist orthodoxies they seek to challenge, merely inverting the assumptions of European superiority and disavowing the historical and cultural complexities of Africa in the name of a hegemonic black America. But the enduring legacy of black racial oppression in the United States forever puts to rest such comparisons, for even the most basic forms of Afrocentricity can never exercise the power and terror that lie behind white supremacist motivations. More accurately and more commonly, Afrocentricities advance celebratory depictions frequently informed by spiritualist prophecy while giving stress to those qualities perceived positively as African and racially black. From the 1910s, African-American intellectuals such as Alain Locke, James Weldon Johnson, J. A. Rogers, Claude McKay, Maude Cuney-Hare, and John Work crafted perspectives of black music indebted to a rhetoric of romantic "jungle" primitivism that had extended from the era of African colonization. As racialized as they were, these depictions sought to challenge assumptions of racial inferiority by exalting the qualities of distinctiveness that were thought to express the essence of the Negro race. A decade or so later, the new figurations of black music had reoriented the very notion of the "vernacular," as ethnographic portraits of rural musical life recast its character with repeated appeals to a romantic Africa. In this new aesthetic, African music, and specifically an orally constituted, improvised African rhythm, represented the incorruptible core of a racially expressive capacity, the secret means by which African-American culture would transcend the controlling forces of white supremacy, and, as such, the contingencies of time and place.[80]

More recent formations of musical Afrocentricity drew energetically from the parallel institution of American anthropology and its informing ideologies of cultural relativism. While initially culpable for displacing African-American examples in the analysis of race, modern American anthropology—greatly influenced by the theories of Franz Boas—established the academic legitimacy of the "culture areas" perspective on which African-retentions arguments would be founded.[81] In *The Myth of the Negro Past*, Melville Herskovits set the framework for modern Afrocentric interpretations. Working from the discourses of Africa circulating variously within the texts of colonial travel and cultural criticism during the late nineteenth and early twentieth centuries—and paralleling Negritude writers who were themselves working from these same influences—Herskovits crafted through elaborate documentation an image of the black diaspora as a unity of African-based difference.[82] As an affirmative discourse, Herskovits's book helped to codify an alternative hermeneutics of African-American culture growing out of the critical strategies of black advancement and celebration outlined during the Harlem Renaissance. Reversing his earlier view that African cultural practices were erased during slavery, Herskovits supplied a historical basis for the emerging "commonsense" view of black culture's African origins.[83] While music played a minor role in Herskovits's analysis, its significance would increase in the retentions theories put forward after World War II and, particularly, with the growing world prominence of American jazz. By the 1960s, African-derived black music had become a key sign of black cultural retention.[84]

The scientific examination of culture characteristic of midcentury anthropology sought not to define a racial orthodoxy as much as to explain the undeniable power and import of black expression. It refused the easy reduction of black forms to versions of European mastery, seeking to determine an autonomous line of development within the larger matrix of black/white commonality.[85] In doing so, however, its practitioners inevitably drew from discourses overladen with racialist figures, reinforcing stereotypes that many African-Americans born at the turn of the century had fought against.[86] Musical studies were particularly prone to racial images that had historically informed the perception of black performance in the United States, and these same racial figurations soon carried over into musicological analysis. The theories proposed by Herskovits's students and colleagues, notably Alan Merriam and Richard Waterman, had a remarkable impact on an emerging jazz criticism, and that influence has carried forward into the retentions theories still advocated by many ethnomusicologists in the present day.[87] Both Merriam and Waterman expressed a commendable devotion to scientific objectivity as a way of transcending racial pitfalls. Just the same, their commitment to objectivity ironically obscured the degree to which their work betrayed the various discursive markings of modern racialist opinion.

Waterman's theory of "hot rhythm," first put forward in his 1948 essay, " 'Hot' Rhythm in Negro Music," is a case in point. The "hotness" he attributes to Yoruba aesthetics also relates to an unacknowledged American racial figuration, in which rhythm signifies the putative excesses of black behavior. What may appear foreign and exotic in African hotness reinvents local associations between blackness and the licentious. In another essay, Waterman explores the commonalities between African and European musical practices in theorizing acculturation in objective, music-specific terms. His portrayal of African-American music as a melding of European and African commonalities may be derived from the familiar anthropological concept of syncretism, but it also suggests a metaphorical reading in which interracial joining-in-sound parallels the liberal appeals to integration at the onset of the Civil Rights Movement. Merriam's vigorous assertions of a scientific approach to black cultural study, in its turn, revealed similarly progressive political sentiments. Through the rigors of analysis, he believed black culture's originality could be demonstrated. Yet these admirable sentiments also stood at odds with his embrace of hyperbolic images of Africa concocted in the popular imagination. His essay, "African Music," succumbs to the primitivist myth of African ferocity, proposing Henry Stanley's narrative of *Bandussuma at Usiri* as an unparalleled depiction "of the emotional impact of African rhythm." However important and influential the work of both these scholars has been, it has also helped to perpetuate fabrications of black culture that are inconsistent with their respectful intentions. These fantastic projections represent what Kofi Agawu calls the "lies" about African music that suffuse theories of racial difference across the twentieth century.[88]

Thus we can see black musical metaphysics emerging from America's own racial imagination in response to assimilationist intentions of erasure. In political terms, the metaphysical claims of black music that became emblematic of the Black Arts Movement challenged a vulnerable white supremacy that could no longer explain away the power and appeal of black musical achievement. As enabling as these racial essentialisms may have been, however, they also constrained the comprehension of black music's more fundamental insurgencies, particularly with reference to the undermining of racial categories. Carried forward into the present, this "resistance to theory," which reflects a rightful concern on the part of some African-Americanists about the violence of the new language-centered modes of analysis, can only limit critical understanding of black music's power and place in the American experience.[89] For not only do black essentialisms inhibit the positioning of black music studies within the broader critical conversations of race and culture; they also propose the curious supposition that black music plays by a different set of rules, distinct from the traditions governing American social history. Such thinking brings us dangerously close to arguing that black music is something that lies beyond the cultural mainstream and thus necessarily outside the realm of American experience overall. "If we fail to interrogate essentialist constructions of blackness," Michael Awkward writes, "we submit to a racial irrationality that heretofore marked blacks as less than human and continues to exert its influence upon what many of us hold as the most fundamental personal areas of our lives as Americans: our formulations of subjectivity and community."[90]

The ecclesiastical background of black musical studies thus explains the tenacity of commitments to rhetorics of community and coherence in black music studies. These commitments seek to inspire a sense of hope about the future by continually reaffirming the memory of black music's miraculous endurance over the course of American history. This "miracle of production," as James Weldon Johnson called it, celebrates the remarkable fact of an expressive practice arising from the very bodies of a possessed people and carrying forth into the present day. A critical program for African-American music—and the story this book ultimately seeks to tell—begins with this tale of origin, for, as I hope to show, it is what lies at the center of its musical meaning through so many informing narratives. To end there, however, leaves black music studies in a mythology that is inconsistent with the constitution of the social and with the processes of cultural change as we now understand them. How, then, do we sustain the power of black music's metaphysics within a more rigorous analysis of race and culture? Much of the value of contemporary critical theories of language develops from their power to sort out the complex ways in which rhetorics have been enacted, and their application within the frames of black cultural studies over the past twenty years has helped to replace prior racialist commitments with interpretations that magnify race as a pernicious, unstable ideological formation. We need to come up with strategies of interpretation that bring these insights into specifically musical and musicological contexts. At issue is the comprehension of the constructedness of black music's miraculous power as it has carried forward to the present day.

A few scholars of American music have proposed ways of engaging the critical potential of black literary theory while maintaining the certainties of African-American expressive practice. As a group, they follow the trend of leading African-American literary scholars of the 1980s who mapped out a similar negotiation between the structuralisms of 1960s literary theory and midcentury American conceptions of blackness. Not surprisingly, what has drawn most attention from musicologists is the body of theory that builds critical perspectives of African-American expressive culture from musical experience. Receiving the lion's share of attention is the aforementioned work of Houston A. Baker, Jr., and particularly Henry Louis Gates, Jr., who, in their commitments to stressing the importance of black music to cultural and literary studies, enacted a kind of decentering shift consistent with poststructuralist textual practices, while each in his own way acknowledged prior Black Arts affiliations. Baker's rendering of "blues dynamism" portrayed black culture as a decentered matrix of signs that nonetheless affirm.‿⁔ ‿⁔⁺ of a "vernacular" version of negative dialectics a distinctively musical expressive center. Gates, for his part, sought similar negotiations between theory and vernacularity but only after advocating a high-theoretical structuralism that marked his departure from Black Aesthetic formulas. In the critical strategy of signifyin', Gates proposed a playful revision of literary deconstruction as the basis of an ironic advocacy of retentions arguments. By the 1990s, his criticism had gained significant appeal among a few musicologists, who identified in it a sophisticated strategy for explaining black music's power. They were certainly helped along by Gates's own alignment of signifying and black music, which reflected the ongoing significance of music in African-American studies as a whole. As Gates explained it, "What I have attempted to do with literary theory is modeled on what blues and jazz musicians do with received musical conventions." His references to the revisionist properties of improvised jazz suggested relations among signifying, improvisation, and, by implication, rhythm, linked together as forces of resistance representing the expressive core of African-American authenticity.[91]

Gates's theory offered promise for the future of black musical criticism as scholars awakened to the challenge to speak to the power and nature of African-American expressive practices. Signifying provided a neat critical device easily transposed to musical analysis as it gave credit to a cultural dimension overshadowed by the power of literary studies and European music. As interesting and creative as these applications have been, however, they do not suggest viable strategies for an overarching interpretive practice. This failure is less the fault of Gates's theoretical imagination than the presuppositions from which the borrowing takes place. Whereas Gates proposes a critical perspective developing from a playful revision of deconstruction's program—his "myth of origins"—music scholars have presented literal readings of the mechanisms of signifying that ultimately deny the multiple and complex levels of meaning that determine musical experience.[92]

In his essay "Ring Shout" and his book *The Power of Black Music,* for example, Samuel Floyd observes the source of African-American cultural identity in the resistant force of a musically determined black specificity.

Following the example of Baker and Gates, Floyd employs Hayden White's concept of tropology to acknowledge discursive instability without relinquishing structurations informing continuity and identity. In Floyd's work, however, tropology becomes an openly Afrocentric notion that ultimately reduces black music to a single, performative function. Whereas Baker and Gates give stress to tropology's discursive instability, Floyd seeks to secure both music and meaning, as the indirection of black expressive practices find their origin in the wellspring of African-American musical performance: rhythm, dance, and the ring shout. In an otherwise thoughtful discussion of Miles Davis and jazz performance practice, meanwhile, Robert Walser so overworks the signifying figure that it loses nearly all critical efficacy. By the end of the essay, Walser has positioned nearly every dimension of a Davis trumpet solo within the context of signifying, and so it is unclear what about jazz improvisation is not based on this practice. His employment of transcriptional procedures in this context serves further to contradict the elusiveness of signifying, which, as a "vernacular" anticipation of poststructuralism, would seem to resist such unqualified analytical determination.[93]

Musicology's legacy of formalism thus looms large in African-American music research. The ironic, rhythmically revisionist character of signifying, which seeks to convey the perceived doubleness of black music, is subverted; the intent of tropological revision—to radicalize normative ways of knowing in order to convey a sense of creative freedom out of bounds—is obscured. Signifying becomes, against the commitments to deconstruction as a critical practice, a formal model ready for application. The logic is unmistakably circular: What was once a musically oriented, oral rhetoric grounded in African-American traditions of performance appears now refashioned according to the theoretical premises of literary criticism to be appropriated back yet again into music in order to commit to writing the authenticity of black music. The "truth value" of signifying becomes, in the end, a tautology, a recycled facsimile.

The incommensurability of these musical/textual couplings underlines why an easy transposition of music to literary studies is equally problematic. Musicologists locate a literary device that oversimplifies both the historical trajectory and the musical experience; literary scholars, in turn, play to the mystification of black music in order to reinvigorate textual criticism. A close examination of Baker and Gates's projections of music suggests that for them music is above all a stability. They reinforce dichotomies of the oral and written in ways that stabilize and, as Diana Fuss suggests, romanticize black music.[94] In this respect the musical applications of contemporary black literary studies varies little from the criticism of Stephen Henderson, Jimmy Stewart, Don Lee, Amiri Baraka and others Black Arts writers from whom Baker and particularly Gates sought to part.[95] What Houston A. Baker, Jr., has called the "black (w)holes" so resonant beyond white writing and what Gates has referred to as the musical basis of an oral "superconsciousness" are little more than ahistorical and, ultimately, idealist devotions to a "vernacular" grounding that has been reformulated in the postmodern lexicon of elusiveness: signifyin', the blues matrix, deformation of mastery, and so on. The problem lies not so much in their gestures toward the vernacular or even in their theories of an archeological strain of creative resistance but in their perpetuation of anachronistic beliefs in music's ability to rise above the circumstances of political, cultural, and social change, to overcome, as an enduring continuity, the grand discursive web of racialist representations. What we have once again is a return to the primordial wellspring of black origins, to a romantic past that transmits into the present the pure, untainted soundings of *Volk* essence.

Establishing continuities with the past without succumbing to the racialism and essentialism on which such notions are commonly based is precisely what the British critic Paul Gilroy sought to achieve in his highly acclaimed book, *The Black Atlantic: Modernity and Double Consciousness.*[96] Working from the musical impetus informing black cultural criticism since Du Bois, Gilroy proposed an interpretive practice that affirmed music's constitutive role as it challenged the cultural absolutes and authenticities that are assumed to go hand in hand with it. What made Gilroy's position so compelling among cultural critics in the 1990s was his conception of a globally based, postcolonial hermeneutics of black experience that also acknowledged the importance of racial category in local social circumstances. His turn to the diaspora served not to reassert racialist continuities but, on the contrary, to show the ways in which these putative continuities are repeatedly complicated by the diversity of black Atlantic encounter. By directly challenging the reductionist claims of Afrocentricity, Gilroy put forward a powerful vision of the seemingly endless variety of black-based creativity. This series of variation finds sameness and wholeness, after all, in the musically articulated resistances to an overarching white racial supremacy. Working against the background of philosophical critiques of Western rationalism from the Frankfurt School to French poststructuralism, Gilroy outlined the meshing of music and race within a sonically textured countermodernity that may be read as his answer to a Habermasian Enlightenment project.

For Gilroy, authenticity emerges not from an essential African-American culture but from the distinctiveness of a musically grounded experience. This emphasis on musical experience underlies a related desire to challenge the textual dominance of cultural studies in order to bring a new sonic reference point to the interpretation of black diasporic culture. Taking to task the language- and visual-based orientations of contemporary criticism, Gilroy calls for a more musically grounded interpretive practice, a radical notion that brings with it new determinations of the politics of historical analysis. Reaching toward Walter Benjamin's notion of history as "living memory"—"as it flashes up in a moment of danger"—he conceives of the black Atlantic as the resonant remembering driven by impulses of rhythm that echo forth from racial encounter.[97] In Amiri Baraka's concept of the "changing same," moreover, Gilroy identifies a dynamic figure that expresses this ironic stability-in-instability. While paying tribute to Baraka's importance, he distinguishes his own theory from the kinds of racial absolutism more common to the era when *Blues People* was written, recasting Baraka's core features of vernacular authenticity and "blues impulse" into a mix of fluctuating practices grounded in the double consciousness of the slave experience.[98] The racial experience residing in the power of black music is not a directory of racial essence but a sounding articulation of the "slave sublime": the terror of life-threatening experience that provides an insistent moral significance to the diversity of African-diasporic practices.

Gilroy's theory of black diasporic cultures was enormously influential in black cultural studies of the 1990s, and rightly so. It represented a powerful and creative challenge to the monolithic projections of an essential black spirit that had so dominated critical interpretation since the Black Arts era. At once, Gilroy revealed the inadequacy of the claims of black authenticity as he proposed a more genuinely music-centered approach distinguished from the text-based music perspectives introduced by literary scholars. More than any other writer before him, he revealed the weaknesses of the repeated gestures to musical power by those whose concerns ultimately focused elsewhere. It is ironic, therefore, that what ultimately complicates the success of Gilroy's theory is precisely this vigorous commitment to a specifically musical determination of the social experience. For in this respect, his views are really not so different from those espoused by Baraka thirty years before him. Despite the diversity Gilroy claims for the musics of the "Black Atlantic," he remains committed to the politics of center, to a transcendent, purely musical force that "gets beyond" the instabilities of discursive contest, for which "power and significance . . . within the black Atlantic has grown in inverse proportion to the limited expressive power of language." Black music's "distinctive kinesis" offers what he calls a "direct image of the slaves' will," providing a "distinctive moral basis" for the black experience. He names this musical significance the "politics of transfiguration," which "points specifically to the formation of a community of needs and solidarity which is magically made audible in the music itself and palpable in the social relations of its cultural utility and reproduction. Created under the very noses of the overseers . . . this politics exists on a lower frequency where it is played, danced, and acted as well as sung and sung about, because words, even words stretched by melisma and supplemented or mutated by the screams that still index the conspicuous power of the slave sublime, will never be enough to communicate its unsayable claims to truth."[99]

Left unexplained in this bold assertion is the exact nature of what he names "the music itself." Gilroy does not explain it, apparently because he takes its viability for granted. In an attempt to counter the foggy mystifications of black music, he succumbs to another trap: he assumes that music, despite its informing social contexts, maintains a purely sonic essence, and this, he contends, is what informs and binds a black diasporic experience. One of the virtues of the new musicology, however, is its challenge to such absolutist notions. As the previous section demonstrated, we simply cannot isolate a stable musical phenomenon from the historical matrix, as one might extract precious metals from ore or separate wheat from chaff. We cannot assume "music" to possess a consistent ontology somehow detached from the social forces that shaped it. Musicological research reveals that the very concept of "music" is grounded in a peculiarly European history that reified sound as form and assigned it through literacy its apartness from the written world.[100] What is more, music in the West demonstrates its own peculiarities of composition and form, which are not necessarily an equivalent to the various formations of the sonic among those Africans who came to the Americas, any more than it is the same as the sound worlds conceived today among the Tiv, the Kaluli of Papua New Guinea, the Suyá of Brazil. Gilroy seems clearly to recognize this given his dedication to outlining a diversity of musical formations in a richly textured narrative. But the sameness he identifies as a distinctly musical experience presupposes a stability of sound in nature, and it is this Eurocentric presumption that undermines the comprehension of difference in specifically social ways.

Gilroy's proposal thus undercuts the possibility of forging a different kind of history, one in which many "black musics" emerge out of the particular circumstances that give rise and progression to the formation of racial subjectivities. While he otherwise seeks to complicate the stable ground of bottom-up histories by showing, as Joan Scott proposes, not that individuals have experience but how subjects emerge through experience, he runs aground when he assumes black music's power to reside in its essential blackness.[101] Like Baraka before him, Gilroy privileges rhythm as a guiding principal—the "direct image" that draws together a black diasporic memory. In this way, he fails to recognize how the very idea of "rhythm" is itself constituted in an unstable discourse rather than being something natural and attributable to all music. The various performance practices among slaves, for example, may fit the modern analytical category of "dynamic rhythm," but that is not the same as saying that all Africans in North American slave communities comprehended what they were doing as "rhythmic" or even as "music," for that matter. Slave sounding was inevitably far more heterodox and contested than the singularity of Gilroy's "slave sublime" allows. And so too is the power of black music something that emerges not from a stable difference but from the transgressive nature of its racially relational "origin."

Finding musical truths among the gossamer of tall tales will remain an impossible task until we account for the way discourse itself plays a generative role in music's making. Recognizing the textual in the musical reveals the interracial conversation that characterizes the formation of black musical difference. Rather than occluding the racial, such a perspective reveals the very seat of black music's "racial" power. For black music could never have attained the same level of significance had it not developed within an interracial matrix to specify ideologies of racial difference. As a matter of course, it has come to signify both the integrationist completion of a nation as well as a racial threat to the integrity of whiteness. The idea of difference is founded on a clear distinction between white and black, just as the desire and celebration of black music as a national expression betrays that distinction as false. It is precisely this racial irony that gives black music its power. And it is precisely this irony that has created so much difficulty for Americans who espouse racialist values, from black separatists seeking to preserve racial/cultural wholes to white liberal assimilationists, who must repress the social object of their racial desire. The sublime aspect of black music's experience, that ineffable quality revealing extremes of terror and joy, appears as traces of material sound that give voice to the incommensurability of race.

An interpretation of black music as a sonic-textual resonance aims not to overturn blackness in the name of an American mainstream. Rather it reveals black music's centrality in the mainstream itself. This subversive strategy admittedly requires once again a conception of black music as an unstable, socially contingent expression. But such a conception, at least of the nonmusical aspects of expressive culture, is hardly foreign to black studies. Indeed, while "the essentialist/antiessentialist debate" that so consumed black cultural studies in the 1990s may not have reached an essay resolution, it did manage to unravel the more simplistic determinations of culture, demonstrated in the recent scholarship of Michael Awkward, Herman Beavers, Hazel Carby, Manthia Diawara, Ann Du Cille, Brent Edwards, Shelley Fisher Fishkin, Sandra Gunning, Evelyn Brooks Higginbotham, Robin D. G. Kelley, Eric Lott, Kobena Mercer, Cornel West, and many others. That a similar degree of interrogation is virtually absent from African-American musicology reflects the intellectual paucity of the discipline.

Rereading the major texts of black cultural criticism we find that the sanctity of black music was never as clearly fixed as one might think. And it is for this reason that the many voices of the black critical tradition inform the arguments put forward in this book. Frantz Fanon, for example, has won a renewed significance in postcolonial studies because he teaches us of the powers of representation to craft authenticities and truths. For Fanon, the truth of rhythm was perhaps the fundamental authenticity, and once its falsity was revealed, it undermined what little confidence he had in overcoming the bounds of race.[102] Farther back, in *The Souls of Black Folk*, W. E. B. Du Bois introduced the musically informed idea of double consciousness to speak to the inherent instability of black identity. Significantly, Du Bois stressed instability not simply to locate the prior and purely musical "souls of black folk" but, to the contrary, to celebrate in a forward-looking way African-Americans' access to modern rights and privileges, voicing an authentic vernacular sound (the "tertium quid") that had been already occupied by text.[103] And even earlier, Frederick Douglass recognized in his first autobiography how black music's social power was revealed only through a process of profound cultural shift. If he gave voice to a slave sublime in his famous struggle with Covey, so did he recall the textual distance separating his experience in slavery from that within the public realm. Through the social and through a conversion to literacy Douglass discovered black culture's essential, second nature, a denatured artifice he celebrated as expressive in sound.

Critics such as Douglass, Du Bois, Fanon, and their critical progeny did not see in black culture a stable center, any more than they sought to deny the significance of black expressive forms in the making of American culture. Their experience taught them to see change at the center of culture, to recognize the play of differences as something on which a racialized America depends. They sought not to limit the range of black expression through claims of fixity and essence but to emancipate African-American expressive capacity, to allow black culture, and, to a significant extent, black music, a limitless possibility of invention. The tenacity of black music's mystification could at times outweigh these critical insights, and at points Douglass, Du Bois, and even Ellison spoke in the language of racial authenticity that had become so ingrained in American thought. Yet so did they articulate, as a group, a progressive alternative to the enduring fixities of blackness and black music. They gestured to ways beyond the declarations of difference, declarations that, in America, "this country devoted to the death of paradox," leave us now with either a black exclusivism or a liberal pluralism that imagines music as separate but equal.[104] To explain black music's history from either of these positions is to perpetuate versions of the color line. It is to propose difference not as an invention but as an inalterable way of life.

Lying up a Nation   So begins the rehearing of black music as a challenge to the natural histories of race. The juxtaposition of African-American cultural studies against musicology's critique of authenticities reveals the need for another turn, a strategic analytical swerve that brings us back once again to the sonic-textual concept of black resonance. In this rehearing, black music becomes inextricably related to the flows and pulsations of discourse, showing up as figures cast as difference to mark soundings that would otherwise lie beyond European-American comprehension. The conception of difference records that which is both real and unreal. It designates the places that musical Africanness can inhabit as it inevitably translates those expressions into forms of strangeness that only then become accessible to European-based determination. This logical paradox is the core of a black musical hermeneutic, for no one side of the tale can be accounted for without the other. By absolving criticism of the responsibility to document a pure and truthful presence, we can proceed with a critical engagement of black music's historical narrative. In the ambiguity of truth and falsity, we locate a miraculous musical significance that is more meaningful, experientially grounded, and patently real.

The task at hand, then, is twofold. First we need to document the material record of texts that gave shape to the swirling pattern of sounds becoming modern black music. Then we may begin to listen critically, negatively, as Theodor Adorno would have it, within and without so many inscriptions to discern the soundings revealed as absence. It is this latter task that is critical for comprehending the larger story of black music. Teased out of history's record as an accumulation of discursive phantoms, these transgressive figures—"which," in the image of Foucault's flash of lightning, "give a dense and black intensity to the night it denies"—amount to a veritable countermemory that confesses the truth of a mulatto America.[105] Emerging as spaces of silence scattered across the discursive mappings of the nation's resonance, these denials of black voicings are the means by which we hear the truth of blackness "speak." As echoes (rather than as primary generations), the voicings are disrupted representations—resonances that mediate between modern hearing and those originary sounds prior to the modern era, prior even to the conception of "black music" itself. They hint at a sound and time lost beyond record, offering, in their accumulation, a memory-text of a period before African slaves had adapted to European notions of history. What these texts lose in translation they provide, in their imperfection, that which is repressed in the standard narrative: namely, the white nightmarish memory of the sameness of black music within a larger human complex. Listening to the sounds and texts of resonance becomes a task of double hearing, of discerning music and writing, difference and sameness, which invites a new imagination, a new memory of America. In this new "dream of American form," one recognizes another tale, "a story which," as James Baldwin writes about black music, "otherwise has yet to be told and which no American is prepared to hear." It is a story of "things unsaid" that lingers only in "a dangerous and reverberating silence" of black music—the kind of history that Walter Benjamin proposes as that which "seize[s] hold of a memory as it flashes up at a moment of danger."[106]

The vernacular ground of black music, then, is not some pure, oral form resonant with African-American identities. This oral-to-written formula, which narrates the logic of black music from the first major studies of slave song in the 1860s to modern depictions of *Blues People* and *Black Talk*, requires revision in favor of a dynamic process in which orality moves through textuality and back around. For the texted history of black music as discernible "form" is what helps to forge a conception of black culture into being, just as it is this writing of sound that provides the basis for the emergence of a New World black public voice. If, as Gates argues, "black people could become speaking subjects only by inscribing their voices in the written word," they would craft that texted voice on the body of black sound—on prior inscriptions of black resonance.[107] Writing informs the recognition of blackness, which becomes heard as "Negro music," and it is from this sonic-textual posture that black authors would finally publicly "speak." The black voice of contemporary African-American literature is indeed a "musical" voice, and critics have rightly turned to those capacious expressions of sound to observe a literary tradition. In this musical wellspring, however, one locates the primacy of texts, the figures that have written black music as countless representations and that created the discursive space from which music would ironically resist inscription's violence.

Revealing the history of black music, then, becomes something akin to wresting a dream from a waking consciousness: the analytical tools of contemporary theory permit one to ponder the shimmering social body and to trace, however haphazardly and ineffectively, a pattern within the vagaries of texted sound. The ultimate goal of this tracing, however, is not to reduce history to a rubble of gibberish and noise but to propose a set of stories on which to build a new perspective of African-American musical studies. Despite the charges of conservatism launched against narrative, this book seeks to work in storied forms, albeit ones enabled by the vertiginous, unstable history of black music's soundtexts. For stories in black America served the same role as the radical skepticism of the Frankfurt School and recent persuasions of poststructuralist criticism: they sought to unsettle the dominance of regressive sociopolitical forces (e.g., fascism, colonialism, and finally, reason) in favor of, if not emancipation, then at least a more egalitarian flux and play. The intention here is to propose another take on black musical history rather than a formal history as such. For it is in stories, as Louis Armstrong and Hayden White both tell us, that the social is constructed in the aftermath of God's fall from grace. Stories keep us closer to the image of the vernacular, to the realities of an American past, however inaccessible those realities may be. Like black music, the vernacular ground remains unstable, and yet it is nonetheless from this ground that the body of black music ultimately speaks.

My field guide in this expedition into the second nature of blackness is one of the seminal texts of modern African-American literature, Zora Neale Hurston's *Mules and Men*. In this ethnography, Hurston set the groundwork for the modern conception of a black vernacular, with all of its southern-based expressions of cultural difference. As is well known, she based her study on evidence collected over the course of two and a half years of research in the field. As an anthropologist trained under the tutelage of Franz Boas, Hurston undertook a seminal project of "participant observation," returning after several years' absence to her "native village" of Eatonville, Florida, in order to document the world of African-American folkways.

While accumulating a rich body of data about spells, songs, and figures of speech, Hurston devoted the bulk of her research to recording stories—tall tales of life in a world of difference. These stories were what the people of Eatonville called "lies." They were not literally lies but, rather, creative expressions of poetic license—allegories that celebrated the ironic twists of fate giving substance and texture to the art of southern black living. The better the story, the better the lie; the better the lie, the closer one gets to the ironic pleasures and terror of America's racial sublime. In an opening sequence, Hurston, standing back uncharacteristically from the text, requests a story from her friend, George Thomas. Thomas replies matter-of-factly, "Zora, you come to de right place if lies is what you want. Ah'm gointer lie up a nation."[108]

For Hurston, the voice of vernacular authenticity that so appealed to Baker and Gates was always revealed through these ironic twists. Her proposal of truthful signs of blackness betrays a reality emerging from a figurative basis. While a literal reading of Hurston's ethnographic texts and theories tend to reinforce essentialist orthodoxy, recent critics have proposed more attentive interpretations that reveal a dynamic play of meaning rendering "truth" from so many fictive accounts. As Barbara Johnson puts it, Hurston's truths of blackness stand on "the threshold of difference." The presence of black form builds from the artifice of narrative, from the series of tales through which African-America literally casts its historical memory into being. Despite her enthusiasm about an essential black nature, Hurston was also well aware of the basis of that nature in the textual representations of the ethnographic document. Seeking the pure presence of black form, she acknowledged that this form could only be observed through what she called "the spy-glass of Anthropology," an appeal less to the powers of science than to the mediations on which all claims of black essence depend.[109]

Hurston's insights suggest that the vernacular portrayals in her ethnographic work approached a didactic rhetoric intimately connected to her literary accounts. In "Characteristics of Negro Expression," for example, Hurston maps out a "vernacular" orthodoxy that builds rather obviously from modernist visual figures: asymmetry, angularity, pastiche, speed. Here, the vernacular becomes a playful artifice, a rendering that imagines black folk culture as constructivist art work, much in the same way as her "Story of Harlem Slang" (1942), as Werner Sollors writes, "[achieves] authenticity . . . not by some purist, archival or preservationist attitude toward a fixed past but by a remarkable openness toward the ability of a specific idiom to interact with 'outside' signals."[110] To be sure, Hurston's fictional style remained integral to her work as an ethnographer. If *Mules and Men* builds strategically according to the rules of scholarly distance and objectivity, it does so above all to centralize her subjects' accounts as literary voices. According to Robert Hemenway, her model for the work drew as much from the major texts of romantic encounter, notably Thoreau's *Walden,* as from the masterworks of anthropology. Indeed, Hurston's intertextuality grew so complex that at times fiction and fact intersected. Comparing *Mules and Men* with *Jonah's Gourd Vine* suggests that Hurston may have engaged in a good bit of intertextual handiwork, borrowing in spirit if not in actuality from fiction to fact. Arna Bontemps observes, for example, that some of the stories in *Mules* had already surfaced in Hurston's urban New York imagination well prior to her fieldwork. The point is not that Hurston lacked integrity or respect for the vernacular. Rather, for her, the vernacular was a realm for which history was already unattainable, even as it remained in the end the very basis of her literary art. Its potential influence in the public sphere thus depended on her ability to tell a good lie.[111]

Accordingly, in seeking the truth of black music, we might work from this same ironic mode and trace its opposites: from the texts of outsiders who cast the notion of difference, from the stories that contain the myths of the music's uncontainability; Hurston's lies offer a way toward this realization. She knew full well how the web of writing in which art exists is no reliable gauge of expression. A lover of paradox, she verged on sacrilege when she exposed, through the concept of lying, the instability of "truth," a term that had long carried profound significance in black religious and musical life. Indeed, Hurston seemed deeply aware of the modern's challenge to a cloistered black folk epistemology. Yet she also was well aware of how truthful the lies of race can be, and how black music above other forms most profoundly expresses the racial imagination. Listening to the stories resonating in black music, we too can hear those lies. They are lies about us, about who we are. They tell the truth about ourselves, revealing those quietly uttered histories buried beneath a "united" America. Let us listen to the confessing voice of this black music, to what it has to say. For in its tales of racial glory it summons the truth of an America that is common and same.

2 Resonances of Racial Absence

Black Sounding Practices Prior to "Negro Music"

The Narrative of the Life of Frederick Douglass, an American Slave (1845) is one of the great monuments in the history of African-American slavery, a text famous for bringing to the present an authentic, vernacular past. When we read Douglass's first autobiography, we commonly imagine this representative slave world as the real thing. It is a realm full of tragedy and romantic glory, of dramatic struggle and heroic confrontation. Supplying dynamic texture to these depictions is Douglass's soundtrack of slavery through which he renders slave song as a sonorous "tale of woe." Resonant with tragedy and southern horror, the song's tale becomes the centerpiece of a harrowing expression that contradicts the happy-go-lucky portraits of blackface minstrelsy common to the mid-nineteenth century. More than any other single rhetorical aspect the slave song provides a marker of Douglass's authenticity. His words about song communicate a profound truth told, a story so powerful it has served for the past 150-odd years as the conceptual starting point for the history of modern African-American culture.[1]

But such a role no single text can play. In the end, Douglass's tale is not so much a history as one of the many stories in history. Notwithstanding the tremendous symbolic power this story contains, it is but a single representation of slavery, a reminiscence by a remarkably gifted writer, who recounts his life in the antebellum era. It is no small irony that a passage published 226 years after the first arrival of Africans to North America should be so enthusiastically and uncritically received as the truth about the slave musical past. However important Douglass's recollection may be in our hearts, it cannot adequately claim representative authority as a history, at least as we in our time conceive of it. The uniformity and consistency of vernacularity is thus revealed as a discursive construct on which the modern ideology of black music has been erected.

Significantly, Douglass himself draws attention to the partiality of his own depictions by foregrounding the generative power of writing against the presumed purity and autonomy of an orally based vernacular tradition. He does so by relating in scrupulous detail his acquisition of literacy and the gains and losses that privilege would produce. In one passage, for example, he recalls how the act of writing, which he acquired through lessons from white children, gave to him the artifice through which he created his "natural," public voice. The unmediated truth of Douglass's tale emerges from the mediating powers of the written word. In another, he awards special significance to the pen, the materiality of which dramatizes writing's life-transforming properties. "My feet," Douglass writes, "have been so cracked with the frost, that the pen with which I am writing might be laid in the gashes." As James Olney observes, the pen serves here as a marker of slavery's psychic and bodily effects, measuring the vast chasm between Douglass's literate present and a sound-filled preliterate past. For Douglass, it would seem as if public reality begins with writing itself. Yet this public entry also produces distancing effects that bring slave life into focus as it remains beyond the immediacy of true comprehension.[2]

Douglass's depictions of slavery consistently work at such cross-purposes. In *The Narrative,* writing is at once a mark of civilization and a symbol of civilization's violence. It is a birthright that mutes the resonances of the slave body. And so it is with his references to song. By harnessing the power of script, Douglass seems at first to recover this musical tale of woe, bringing back to life a rarely recorded and much misunderstood sonic world. But Douglass ultimately observes this sound as something other than a recovered history. It is an experience that has changed through its conceptualization within a transformative public culture. For Douglass, slave song stands in between past and present, private and public, making it curiously inaccessible not only to the historian but also to the slaves themselves. "I did not, when a slave, understand the deep meaning of those rude and apparently incoherent songs," Douglass writes. "I was myself within the circle; so that *I neither saw nor heard* as those without might see and hear."[3] Gaining access to script, he acquires the analytical distance from slavery's circle of culture necessary for recognizing the deep meaning within it. In the process of redrawing slave sounds, however, Douglass also grows more distant from their immediacy and effect, forcing him to mediate and ultimately to reinvent them to fit the common sense of nineteenth-century northern, literate culture. What is accomplished also leaves forgotten the experience of slavery's sonic incoherence.

Douglass's portrayals of writing and the interpretations they engender pose a serious challenge to the modern conception of black music as a transhistorical essence. According to Douglass's hermeneutics of the circle, vernacular truth develops from the ground of textual artifice. It is an unstable and unreliable origin, the constructed nature of which ironically provided the basis for his own modern self-awareness. While folklorists and historians have sought to recover an ever-greater body of evidence relating to the slave musical past, they have often mistakenly assumed that past to exist within the plain view of the present. In this way, "black music" emerges as a coherent cultural object, as a "thing" that, while marking difference, is seemingly obtained by simply learning more. Heeding Douglass, however, the crafting of black music's history might better begin from a negotiation between recovery and the tools of recovery's representation, between the "facts" of the historical past and the social networks and representations that have brought these facts into the present. Confronting the ideological formation of black music means no longer seeking Douglass's place in the circle but recognizing the value to historical inquiry the circle's rupture obtains. History becomes less an act of complete recovery than of what Martin Heidegger conceived as acts of un-concealment or unforgetting, of constructing narratives within and across the dynamic separating past and present.[4]

If, as Hortense Spillers proposes, the history of American slavery (and, by inference, of slave music) shifts from a final, recoverable reality to that of a historically contingent and "*primarily* discursive" phenomenon intersecting with slavery's own heterogeneous "spatio-temporal object," so must the terrain of that history be similarly revised. What appears in the standard texts as a serviceable record of originary African practices now reveals major structural flaws—wide stretches of lacunae that "speak" above all of absence. These absences nearly drown out the faint voices of text that well up occasionally from the more ample social history of African-America. Indeed, beyond a minor assembly of historical fragments and passing references, there is, quite simply, no documentary evidence of North American slave musical practices from the eighteenth century. Whether musical practices, like so many other African-American cultural practices prior to the 1770s, were simply unrecorded, systematically repressed, or truly absent from slave experience is an issue for historical debate.[5] Nonetheless, the fact remains that there is virtually nothing from which we might even begin to craft a standard history of slave musical performance, a condition that has inspired critics and historians to seek out creative if inadequate alternatives to fill the gap: grand conclusions based on shards of evidence; anachronistic overlays of early folkloristic presumptions; presentist interpretations that frame early black music as if it were born in the here and now. So many of the stories of black music's history develop from the imposition of an odd assortment of Civil War–era discourses and modernist assessments of the vernacular onto the absent record of the slave experience. However diverting they may be, the Procrustean bed of tales cannot address in a practicable way the social necessity of accounting for an unaccountable past.

What, then, might we learn from a more critical consideration of a highly fragmented historical record? In this reading, the positive, reified form of black music assumes figurative instability, becoming a concept that emerges in its many material guises out of a collision of African-American creativity and Euro-Western incomprehension. Determined socially and relationally over time, black music takes form variously and multiply within the musico-discursive frames that reconfigure the legacy of a diversely represented slave performativity. Rather than an autonomous expression of racial/cultural impulse, black music sounds dynamically from so many New World voices constituted within as it poses radical challenges to ideologies ascribing the difference of racial blackness as such. If black music's originary voice was forged within the circle of slave performance, it was always invested in the relational dimensions of enslavement. Eventually assuming the figure of difference, it became a dynamic centerpiece of sound and text characteristic of racial encounter during the post-Revolutionary era. In this sense, we may think of black music as a key element in the formation of ideology in an emerging United States. Rather than a falsity or fiction, this ideological formation resonated out of the very texture of the social as it served to constitute and materialize thinking about race in general.[6]

Accessing a seemingly inaccessible African-American slave music thus involves something more than an objective survey of the sources, even as those sources provide the evidentiary ground from which a historical criticism might properly begin. It requires the development of interpretive strategies that trace genealogies of discursive representation alongside the analysis of those fragments of history's repression. Black music research becomes a kind of dreamwork consistent with the psychoanalytic strategies proposed by Louis Althusser and other social theorists as a mode of ideological critique. Stretching to look beyond our most tenacious musical myths we read the fragments of evidence to bring a new hearing, a new story about a forgotten slave sound world. Like the inadvertent creations of dreams themselves, black music criticism of this kind suggests a kind of magic or alchemy. Criticism creates history out of history's own negation, drawing sound from silence; it is akin to pulling culture's rabbit out of racism's negating hat. What emerges "un-forgotten" are the strains of accumulated texts that find new form in the modern as "resonance."

Resonance is a useful concept in this instance, not simply because it is a musical term but one that specifies repetition. Its origin or "sonance" is revealed from the beginning as something essentially reiterative, changing. This originary notion of history's repetition borrows from Søren Kierkegaard by way of the gifted reinterpreter of Continental philosophy, Mark C. Taylor. As Taylor explains, "In Kierkegaardian repetition/*Repetition,* everything returns, but with a difference. The re-turning of re-petition disrupts philosophy (as if from within)."[7] In the same way, since audible sound by nature involves multiple processes of mediation (whether that transference be in the form of a sounding board, a horn's bell, or a singer's larynx), it complicates the common sense of origins. Resonance establishes authenticity not as a clarion purity but as what Walter Benjamin called in his meditation on translation "the echo of the original": the sound of that which has already sounded.[8] In crafting black music's history as resonance, I am seeking less to unearth an authoritative and truthful past as to listen for a story with no beginnings, content with the fragments of texts that sound forth inscriptively from the noisy legacy of colonial violence. Resonance as a mediated beginning marks the re-presentation from which black music originates. It identifies musically "the non-place from which all historiographical operation starts."[9]

Rethinking the Circle   Resonances consist in sound as waves, and waves project, at once, from all points, as rings or circles. In his seminal study of acoustics, *Sensations of Tone* (1862), the German physicist Hermann Helmholtz explained this phenomenon by employing the analogy of rippling water. "To illustrate this kind of motion it will be again convenient to refer to the waves formed on a calm surface of water. . . . If a point of the surface is agitated by a stone thrown upon it, the agitation is propagated in rings of waves over the surface [of] more and more distant points." While Helmholtz's analogy specifies a center, this center begins from the action of something outside the ring's circularity, whether that something be a stone or, in music, a vocal utterance or instrumental gesture. In the history of water's wave motion, these rings embody re-petition, re-production. Each portion of a particular ring "sounds" simultaneously, without linear beginning, just as the ring itself forms its circular completion from that which emanates before it. When multiple circles or resonances appear, they intersect while also remaining discrete. Helmholtz continues: "Now, throw two stones at the same time on to different points of the surface, thus producing two centres of agitation. Each will give rise to a separate ring of waves, and the two rings gradually expanding, will finally meet."[10] A succession of stones or sonic projections produces a rousing calamity of interferences and intersections, while each maintains its circular configuration. In Helmholtz's depiction, the circle coheres as it is born out of incoherence, out of the disruption of the water's surface by a stone's throw. The circle endures as it is disrupted, decentered.

These physical reflections on the circular nature of sound suggest ways of refiguring the common comprehension of black music. In the figure of resonance, we identify both a mode of conceiving of origins with respect to relationality and a means of reconceptualizing social change in terms of instability and disruption—metaphors consistent with the "absent cause" of contemporary historical criticism. The accumulation of overlapping partial projections, together with the concepts from which they derive, suggest a resonant constellation of phantom "history." Traditionally, of course, the circle has symbolized just the opposite. It has identified and remains still today the preferred signature of black completion, a trope of tremendous power and influence that locates the origins of its authority in Douglass's text. The circle is what informs the "circle of culture" that Sterling Stuckey proposes as the coherence system of an enduring Africanist black America; it is the "round house" that figures Robert Farris Thompson's diasporic poetics of architectural space; it is the "ring shout" through which Samuel Floyd, working from Stuckey's historical reading, determines the centerpiece of black musical coherence. In all of these, rhythm assumes the role of a critical impulse or driving force and the source of unity's beginning. Blackness proceeds temporally from the originary geometry of the cylindrical drum.[11]

There are many reasons for the tenacity of this historical icon, including philosophical and etymological ones that support opposing claims of circularity's African, European, or even universalist origin. Beyond the African correlates described above, we find in the historical record similar configurations in which circularity signifies tangible forms of coherence, from the circles of Hell through which Dante and Virgil proceeded to the Pawnee nest figure in Native American symbolism; from the celestial wheel of Hindu cosmography to Aristotle's "unmoved mover," who generates the circular perfection of heavenly spheres and in turn sublunar motion.[12] But such recognition does not in itself defend the perpetuation of these images (unless, again, we commit to black music studies as a kind of metaphysics), any more than the rejection of these analogies as tools for the particular kind of historical analysis practiced here should deny their significance in the way people craft musical experience. My aim is to tell the story of the circle so as to resist claims of continuity and uncomplicated racial wholeness while at the same time recognizing socially generated coherences that emerge within the logic of race. Rethinking the circle means paying close attention to what is missing of the past as that past comes into focus before us. This requires bearing witness to the waves of historical texts that give shimmering public form to an eighteenth-century "Negro sound."

In the past, writers have sought to capture the essence of black music's fragmentary past by inventing strategies that might overcome the formidable hermeneutical obstacles before them. As already noted, these procedures developed less from methodological reflexivity than from an a priori assumption of racial/musical commonalities. Black music, in these instances, projects a circular history: what is always was, what was always is. In the most important study of black music published during the second half of the twentieth century, Amiri Baraka, then writing as LeRoi Jones, proposed a musical vision of African-America that would inform experiences of black culture for the next two generations. What distinguished *Blues People* was the many ways in which it brought together anew critical themes animating intellectual and cultural thought at the time.[13] Redrawing the mode of analysis by which African retentions were observed, Baraka portrayed the evolution of African-American history in terms that assigned to music a force so powerful it moved ahead inexorably despite the formidable challenges of adversarial capitalism and white supremacy. By focusing on music, he disrupted the terrain of historical research, shifting from tangible matters of society to the vagaries and instabilities of a neglected form of expression. Baraka's musical projection brilliantly anticipated the bottom-up perspective of an emerging American social history concerned with everyday life, as he affirmed the belief on the part of many African-Americans—together with communities of white artists and intellectuals—in the unrivaled significance of black music, particularly as it had been expressed in the newly fashioned modernism of post–World War II jazz. Moreover, by restating Marxian economic analysis according to the assumptions of African musical continuity (assumptions that reenacted romanticism's trope of musical metaphysics), Baraka rectified for many the incommensurability of an unrecorded history and the belief in that history's presence. Blackness endured as a result of a musical determinism in which a racial "base" reverberated with dynamic African energies, what he named, appropriating and reinventing Ralph Ellison's terminology, the "blues impulse."[14] The sounds captured in the "blues"—a general signifier for all African-American cultural forms forged under oppression—expressed a noble force of decidedly masculine will, figured as a form antagonistic to European musical sensibilities.

Subsequently, the most important historical investigations expanded on aspects of Baraka's argument while tempering his most extravagant claims and limiting interpretations to the bounds of contemporary methods of gathering evidence. In *Black Culture and Black Consciousness,* Lawrence Levine affirmed Baraka's nationalist sentiments at the same time working within more conventional scholarly parameters to unearth the foundation of slavery's spiritual past. While Levine's project stands out for its level of subtlety and insight, as well as for its uncommon attention to matters of historical change, so did it surmount the large gaps in the record of slavery by conflating a broad stretch of antebellum and postbellum evidence. Eileen Southern, for her part, amassed an enormous body of fragmentary evidence into a formidable historical narrative that purposefully resisted interpretive judgment. In her widely read textbook, *Music of Black Americans* (now in its third edition), she consistently allowed the "facts" of history to speak for themselves. Focusing positively on the sources one could locate, Southern constructed a coherent vision without considering the normalizing effect such "coherence" brings.[15]

Dena J. Epstein's monumental study, *Sinful Tunes and Spirituals* offered an imaginative portrait of colonial slave music, and in her reconstruction of seventeenth- and eighteenth-century sources we have the most valuable assertion of an Africanist expressive tradition to date. In its sheer capacity of documentation, *Sinful Tunes and Spirituals* exceeds all prior research on African-American performance during the period before the Civil War. Reflective of her professional work at the time as a research librarian at the University of Chicago, Epstein's book supplies the rich historical documentation missing in Baraka's meditation as it seeks to defend his most basic claims about musical and rhythmic continuity. Because Epstein commits to an unswervingly Africanist posture, however, she must pursue a strategy that diminishes the effect of her highly original depiction of early slave practices. Heeding Herskovits's call for more comparative studies of Caribbean and North American traditions, Epstein turns to the somewhat more plentiful (though still highly fragmentary) documentary evidence of performances from the Caribbean islands of Barbados and Jamaica, not to engage in comparison but to extend her specifically North American focus. She justifies her strategy by arguing that the islands were, with the mainland, part of the same English colonial system, and this position has subsequently gained qualified support from social historians such as Michael

Mullin.[16] Her reasoning proved less sound, however, when she assumed that the similarities between two highly complex and historically contingent political economic systems could also explain the particulars of musical and cultural conception, praxis, experience, and change. This becomes particularly problematic when we recognize the heterogeneity of African-American cultures on the mainland across the seventeenth and eighteenth centuries.[17] While giving important attention to syncretic processes showing up in late-eighteenth-century Virginia, Epstein's aim to locate a vital essence of Old World African cultural practices leads her to reduce the history of early black music to a monolithic Africanness. For Epstein, any given New World reference seemed to offer evidence of or, at the least, tendencies toward a greater African sensibility existing across a highly disparate and varied Afro–North American sphere. As such, her determinist claims of finding in the body of Caribbean evidence a secret history of North America's musical Africanness—a history "ignored in local sources [on the mainland]"—seems far-fetched.[18]

If a comparison of North American and Caribbean slave cultures shows us anything, it is the difficulty of locating in the various accounts discernibly "African" (or even Old World or ancestral) perceptions among slaves. As Sidney W. Mintz and Richard Price argue in their groundbreaking critique of African retentions theory, the social circumstances in the Caribbean were such that no claims of linguistic or group ("tribal") identity could be easily transferred to New World environments. "The problem with the traditional model of early Afro-American culture history," they explain, "lies in its view of culture as some sort of undifferentiated whole. . . . What the slaves undeniably shared at the outset was their enslavement; all—or nearly all—else had to be *created by them.*" While recent research challenges the uniformity of Mintz and Price's overarching assertions as it proposes a more nuanced claim of retentions, Caribbean developments seem best observed in terms of an unstable plurality taking shape within a highly fluid cultural dynamic of intra-African and black/white encounter.[19] Without additional evidence or alternative reasoning, one may need to put forward the same about music, particularly in mainland North America, where contests with Euro-Americans were protracted.

What aligns the major studies of black music is their curious faith in the musical presence of an otherwise absent historical picture. In all of these cases, the authors never seemed to consider seriously the reason for the paucity of accounts of slave performances. (Even if one takes into account the Caribbean sources, the degree of representation remains rather slim.) They did not do so because they appeared to take for granted a viable slave music existing prior to the late eighteenth century even though, in North America at least, Europeans and Euro-Americans rarely acknowledged one. For Baraka and Epstein, the music's viability derived from "the natural inclinations" of African rhythm, a force that reached backward as it sounded forward into later slave practices and into the twentieth century.[20] For Levine, it was far more qualified and questionable but possibly derived from the verbal arts of protest observable in West African traditions, a view consistent with the early researches on black oral traditions by Roger Abrahams, Claudia Mitchell-Kernan, and others. For Southern, the facts, however fragmentary, were enough to project a story of consistency, progression, and stable performative coherence. What held black music together as a story was blackness as such. All projected versions of what Ranajit Guha calls "statist discourse" to the extent that they employ uncritically tropes of the colonial legacy: rhythm, soul, and especially the fixities of "black music" as a racial-musical category.[21]

The state of research on slave music might therefore recommend a certain skepticism about the common projections of the early history of African-American music. If one were to set aside the assumptions we tend to make about the formation of slave music, what kind of history might emerge? What, for example, would an emphasis on instability and change bring to our conception of black culture and to the miracle of sonic art forms its history ultimately produced? Moreover, what kind of history could we fashion if we were to take the missing record of eighteenth-century slave music literally? What might the state of black music history become if we were to argue, matter-of-factly, that the historical record reflects the state of things as they were? From this vantage, gaps of documentation would reflect gaps in experience; white observers would not have seriously commented on a New World African music because slaves did not perform one. The conscious European strategies for disrupting African continuities in the eighteenth century—the separation of language groups, the severing of ethnic and familial links, the frequent prohibition of ritual practices, including conversion to Christianity—together with the circumstances of enslavement itself (savage inhumanity, short lives, extremes of labor and hardship, the practice of selling and reselling slaves) would have been enough to disengage the viability of African musical performance.[22] According to this view, while vestiges of prior practices may have endured, an edifice of coherent African musicality prior to 1700 and quite possibly prior to 1770 did not. This would suggest that the unified circle of slavery was not merely disrupted but, instead, brutally ground out of existence.

Such an argument ultimately goes against the grain of considered speculation, but it is an important position to analyze nonetheless. For taking seriously the possibility of a missing musical history, particularly prior to the 1770s, can serve to demystify black music and to clear a space for another, less circular kind of critical reasoning. One locates an interesting precedent for this line of inquiry in an important if controversial study of American religion. In *Awash in a Sea of Faith: Christianizing the American People,* Jon Butler contends that the absence of reports of African religious practices in the eighteenth century requires no interpretive ingenuity since it documents quite reasonably an absence of African religion. "Gossipy white planters such as William Byrd II and Landon Carter chattered endlessly in their letters and diaries about nearly all aspects of their slaves' lives," Butler writes, "but said little or nothing about religion." During what he names "the African spiritual holocaust" slaves were forced to conform to a "doctrine of absolute obedience" and an increasingly violent paternalism (extending from close proximity of Europeans and Africans and the emerging influence of Euro-American religions) that undermined the viability of former African religious structures. Without reducing eighteenth-century slaves to pathetic victims of white conquest, Butler makes a provocative argument for the near impossibility of sustained ritual practices in the circumstances of sheer terror and horror that was the African holocaust.[23] Religion emerges out of a variety of fragmented ritual practices that are sustained across the eighteenth century, only to cohere in new circumstances afterward, when an infusion of new African expressions around the time of slavery's abolition (1808) transforms the initial, inchoate versions of Anglo-African Christianity introduced during the prior decades. The origins of African religious retentions thus begins only after Africa is erased.[24]

Transposed to musical circumstances, Butler's image of a horrific slave existence provides a powerful antidote to the romantic portraits of a slave sound world, to the caricatured depictions of male laborers whistling songs, of heroic women moaning blues, all existing seemingly outside the dynamic of the eighteenth-century master-slave relation. For while these engaging stories frequently derive from the best intentions, they also obscure the circumstances that may well have precluded musical practices, circumstances about which we do know something and that frequently involved incomprehensible torture, brutality, rape, starvation, death by fire, and disciplinary castration and amputation.[25] If African performances did animate mainland black cultures in the eighteenth century, they conformed to the strictures of a hostile and frequently brutal environment, particularly in the low country, where life was typically and tragically brief, and only then for those who survived the middle passage and the first year of New World enslavement. Slaves lived as "bodies in pain" under constant fear of the whip, stick, shackle, pillory, and lash. Families, when permitted to form, were, particularly in the first half of the eighteenth century, just as easily torn asunder by those who possessed them. These brutalities existed across the South in the eighteenth century, where highly organized repressive tactics eliminated nearly all opportunities of overt rebellion. In one horrific depiction, the enduring violence bred loss of hope, motivating a group of Africans to march eastward from the coastal shore, singing songs of home as they entered the water to drown.[26] The torture of slaves was so pervasive, indeed, that it could constitute sport for children. As Moreau de Saint-Méry writes, "It is thought here, however, that nowhere is so much tenderness shown toward children as in Virginia; all their whims are indulged, especially those of going barefoot a great part of the time, and beating slaves with rawhide whips."[27] It is no discredit to African-Americans to recognize the limits of human capability, musical or otherwise, within the most extreme forms of oppression. It may indeed pay tribute to the humanity of early North American slaves to acknowledge that anything but the most basic forms of human subsistence could have otherwise endured. And it is with no small measure of respect to ascertain what may have been only vestiges of Africanness as remarkable feats of expression within the most barbaric of circumstances.

Such skepticism is worthy of our consideration if only because it helps to expose the degree to which histories of African-American music have been based on assumption rather than on evidence at hand. It places in relief the inadequacy of the most facile claims, which develop from little more than conjecture. For just as we take for granted the spiritual basis of the African slave—the fodder for subsequent projections of a "naturally religious" people—so do we still accept as common sense blacks' inherent musicality. Indeed, we assume that early mainland African-America was full of sound because of the circumstantial evidence of musical practices existing in historical Africa and their correspondences with those from colonial territories in South America and the Caribbean. We assume that African-America was full of sound because of the primacy and politics of black music in modern contexts, disregarding the social circumstances well after the eighteenth century that brought the music into public view. However laudable the claims of a monumental African-American creativity may be, their imposition onto past practices must be preceded by a more deliberate consideration of the historical moment. To accept without the burden of proof Africans' musical genius is to construct history from faulty logic. Worse, it risks perpetuating racialist assumptions of "natural musicians" and a culture of "feeling" that have long and enduring histories in the West. Rather than celebrating a false god, it might be more appropriate to accept what Dipesh Chakrabarty calls a "politics of despair": an interpretive strategy that highlights an absence that one may mourn because it has been lost.[28]

But to leave African-American musical history in the nonplace and nonsound of white negation risks another kind of danger. It places trust in the merits of a critical skepticism that has not always been benign. The Afrocentric proposals and retentions literatures appearing in the wake of Melville Herskovits's seminal research came about in the first place as a response to the misguided "objectivity" of writers for whom blacks seemed incapable of creating a viable culture.[29] Without situating Butler's complex study within that legacy of skepticism (it may be aligned more appropriately with the deculturation arguments of modern liberal thought), we might begin to wonder about his emphasis on systems of religion and the false expectations they raise. Butler asserts that the African spiritual holocaust on the mainland, which stretched across an eighty-year period (1680–1760), "effectively destroyed traditional African religious *systems,* but not all particular or discrete religious practices."[30] By "system," Butler appears to mean established ritual practices that were coherent, sustained, in place. But it is unclear why the acknowledged fragments of African practices, however multiple, ephemeral, radically transformed, and continually reinvented they might have been, could not have assumed great meaning. Such commitment to system certainly does not explain away a slave music, for if African performance practices were similarly overwhelmed, the fragmentary practices that did continue could still have obtained great depths of significance. Indeed, the significance of such practices might have been amplified because they operated against a powerfully oppressive regime and nourished people in times of great suffering.[31]

Of course, to assume that "Africans" from distinct ethnic groups would join together according to some performative commonality in North American settings ignores the complex linkages between musical practices and the larger system of cultural relationships. Musical practices, like all cultural practices, are learned rather than universal. To extrapolate from these practices a grand theory of retention requires that we first divorce musical actions from the particular conceptions and discursive frames in which they were constituted. At the same time, the nonverbal properties of musical communication, together with the physical bodily nature of music's expression, provide enough reason to speculate that performances involving multiple linguistically determined African groups took place on some level, even where intergroup contact may have been otherwise limited. While dispensing with mechanistic theories of syncretism and a priori assertions of Africans' inherent musicality, we begin to identify in the qualities of music-making challenges to an easy transposition of Butler's arguments about eighteenth-century slave religion (or the lack thereof) to eighteenth-century slave performance.[32]

Put simply, there were, despite the circumstances, too many opportunities for blacks to enact creative forms of aural expression for us to conclude that early slave cultures lacked music. While religious rituals presuppose commonalities of language and cultural knowledge, musical practices, though similarly informed by those knowledges, would have more easily readjusted to such interruptions. For musical performance relies on patterns of motion and physicality that become imprinted in bodily memory. These memories can be learned and passed on, creating overarching forms of behavior that might in turn be construed analytically as "retained." It has been a common insight in ethnomusicology that musical practices represent the most enduring of all cultural practices.[33] And even if one remains skeptical of such broad generalizations, there is considerable reason to suspect that slaves came to rely on musical performance because they had few other means of making manifest their humanity and social relations. Without succumbing to romantic myths of natural black feeling or of music as a universal language, we can recognize the ability for musical practices to come together more easily than grammatically specific verbal languages would otherwise permit. We can see, too, a ground for speculating on the socially constitutive character of musical expression, the power of which may have even rivaled linguistic structures in the formation of early North American slave cultures.

Clearly, then, there is another story to be told, even if Butler teaches us to forget the grand claims and presentist assumptions of a neoromantic black musical history. We need to find another strategy for observing African-American music that neither perpetuates grand visions of circular splendor, of a totalized neo-African transplantation, nor denies the possibility of a sounding presence emerging from the facts we do have. We need to identify another way of celebrating a complex and fascinating heritage without devaluing black music's significance as a viable realm of historical analysis. "To cleanse [history] of all transcendental narcissism," Michel Foucault writes, "it had to be freed from that circle of lost origin, and rediscovered where it was imprisoned."[34] In the history of African-American music, this necessarily begins by sorting from among the fragments of resonant text some of the possibilities of mainland performance. It means working positively from the "facts" while also acknowledging their place within the artifice of cultural representation in order to craft a narrative that complicates black music's easy tale of becoming. Pursuing history both negatively and positively reveals the possibility of another kind of story, of telling what Gayatri Chakravorty Spivak calls "(an)other narrative."[35]

Reinscribing the texts of an absent slave music begins from a revised circular relation, by first considering the well-documented, positive dimensions of the past that provide a template for analysis. In turning to the contours of American history, however, I want to avoid rendering a simple "context," for this context could only arise from the same body of representations that have denied slave performance its place. Still, we need this social aspect if we hope to do something more than repeat the same monocular tale of African origins. In this respect, recent researches in American social history offer valuable insight. Particularly informing are those studies developing from social constructionist perspectives that give stress to the multiple levels of change in the formation of African-American cultures. Philip D. Morgan's *Slave Counterpoint,* for example, outlines the diversity of African-American slave cultures in the particular settings of the eighteenth-century Chesapeake and Lowcountry. Through painstaking comparative analysis, Morgan replaces abstractions of the slave world with a finely grained representation of two related, though distinct slave legacies. "Too often in history," Morgan writes, "one South has served as proxy for many Souths. . . . [But] African American culture was no more monolithic than Anglo-American culture." In *Many Thousands Gone: The First Two Centuries of Slavery in North America,* moreover, Ira Berlin seeks similarly to dispel the myth of a singular black experience. Covering the wide territory of early American history, Berlin shows how the particulars of the slaves' world were greatly dependent on matters of time, place, and culture. The formation of slave experiences, he argues, derived directly from the circumstances in which they lived and worked, and these circumstances varied from town to country, factory to plantation, North to South, southern region to southern region. The accumulation of variations, in turn, created markedly different "slave cultures" across seventeenth- and eighteenth-century colonial history. "In mainland North America," Berlin writes, "slaves (like their owners) were simply not the same people in 1819 that they had been in 1719 or 1619, although the origins and color of the slave population often had not changed. Indeed, the meaning of race itself changed as slavery was continually reconstructed over the course of two centuries."[36]

Both Morgan and Berlin's researches reflect the legacy of a new American social history that sees the dimensions of expressive culture as deriving from the materiality of experience, most notably, from the broader socioeconomic modality of the master-slave relation. These materialist presuppositions lead them to focus primarily on the most visible cultural forms, which are presented as reflections of their respective economies. The authors show, for example, that the independence of the Lowcountry's task system, which frequently provided slaves with considerable free time, lead to the development of skills in fishing, hunting, and gardening. This autonomy in production, as limited as it was, produced commodities that fed back into the southern economy. The diverse circumstances of work among Virginia slaves, moreover, produced equally diverse sites of social congregation. The kitchens, blacksmith shops, dairies, weavers' cottages, and stables of Chesapeake plantations and farms not only produced commodities but also served as the proving ground of cultural practices, from storytelling to gambling to cockfighting. So did the characteristics of the lived environment inform creative expression. For example, because slaves commonly lived in cramped quarters, they relied on outdoor cooking, out of which emerged collective meal rituals and related forms of expressive culture. Morgan offers a speculative depiction, based on irrefutable archeological evidence, of slaves "gathering around a fire, pipes in hand; singing, dancing and telling stories in communal yards; congregating in front of a cooking pot." The symbolic power of the pot, finally, took on a wider significance. In upper North Carolina, a group of slaves sang and prayed over a pot prior to building a master's house. Once the walls were raised around it, the pot, as ritual centerpiece, was removed.[37]

The iconic significance of such an artifact calls to mind the role of art and expressive practices in African traditions. As Morgan, Berlin, and others have shown, the character of black cultural practices took shape at least to some degree from the plain fact of African influence across the eighteenth century. Indeed, if the existence of black religion must be left open to question, historians are more uniformly in agreement about a significant African presence in other cultural practices, even if the extent of an untrammeled Afrocentric continuity remains the subject of debate. Both Berlin and Morgan paint a vivid picture of the depth of African practices in place. South Carolina, they show, was characterized by a far greater African presence due to the rates of importation and the modes of work that sustained cultural practices. This condition led to the creation of a greater possibility of enduring African ethnicities, a distinctive Creole language, and the likelihood of deep pockets of inter-African linguistic formation. The Chesapeake, however, also displayed African influence, though with greater fragmentation; by midcentury, it had given way to a discernibly African-American culture reflecting a depth of cross-racial experience.[38] While both authors stress the varying diversity of African retentions, Berlin is particularly careful in showing how a dynamic "African consciousness" developed as a result of slaves' confrontation with an antagonistic white supremacy. Noting variances from a Caribbean environment where black populations dominated, and observing the diverse ways in which original African cultural relations were complicated and confused ("only occasionally did members of one nation congregate on a single plantation"), Berlin draws our attention to the fascinating New World formations of Africanness. "The construction of an African identity proceeded on the western, not the eastern side of the Atlantic," he writes, "amid the maelstrom of the plantation revolution." Put another way, being African grew from the constructed assembly of experiences of being different according to an emerging modern ideology of race.[39]

Empirically driven positive histories provide a sense of the social circumstances in which slave cultural practices emerged, offering an interpretive guide for reading the fragmentary evidence of musical significance. Rather than versions of reality, these texts serve to flesh out a past by working from the same limits of historical representation. Like their counterparts in American music studies, the tales of American social history take form according to the choices of relevant fact. "Every narrative, however seemingly 'full'," writes Hayden White, "is constructed on the basis of a set of events that might have been included but were left out." What is left out is also what provides coherence to what is revealed, leading White to ask, "what kind of notion of reality authorizes construction of a narrative account of reality in which continuity rather than discontinuity governs the articulation of discourse." It is a reality built on allegory, which White aligns with the moral conviction to tell stories. As allegory, story, including the story of history, "has as its latent or manifest purpose the desire to moralize the events of which it treats." Moral meaning, in turn, derives from the sense of realism histories convey. It provides "the completeness and fullness of which we can only imagine, never experience." Completion, narrative closure, and plot "give to reality the odor of the ideal."[40]

Both the music histories of slavery and their social historical counterparts are moral tales that rely on coherence and narrative to supply a sense of realism, and this realism identifies the content of their narrative form. The social historical texts of Berlin and Morgan are particularly valuable for they build their tales about life and culture from a deep under-

standing of the broad workings of the American political economy in relation to a dynamic racial ideology that evolved according to the circumstances of American slavery. Their tales are therefore more convincing
than conventional American histories of music because they leave in more,
or better, they provide a richer, more diverse context, one more consistent
with our sense of the complexity of lived experience. As valuable as these
studies are, however, they do not in themselves furnish a workable position for the course of this study. At best, they can point in their limitation to
the direction we might proceed. For as narrative histories, they supply a
coherence that ultimately precludes the possibility of another kind of evidence emerging from what is missing. While supplying important documentation, these histories, so committed to a kind of social realism of
the past grounded in the hard facts of economy and labor, leave out the
ephemeral and unseen auditory soundscape that insight into music's
power suggests. It may be argued that among slaves the acquisition of
a musical voice took place later, in the circumstances of the antebellum
environment. But, beyond the monumental work of Lawrence Levine,
historians have tended to bypass music's significance even after its documentation was indisputable. Typically, music's ephemeral qualities, historically associated with a merely reflective superstructure, take on a
marginal significance in the reconstruction of reality, having been relegated to the ornamental status of book titles: *Roll, Jordan Roll; Down by the
Riverside; Many Thousands Gone.*

There are good indications of a musical power and prominence among
eighteenth-century slaves that slipped by white observers. Bearing witness to these indications supplies a basis for a story different from the re-
alist texts of social history, which, in their commitment to fact, preclude
the possibility of an alternative historical rendering. That is, the procedure
of social history to build narratives on existing positive evidence inevitably determines history according to its most vocal historical actors,
or at the least to those having gained access to some permanence of voice
in text. In so doing, social history denies the possibility of music's centrality developing out of the relational antinomies of black and white. In their
coverage of the range, moreover, conventional social histories stick to realism as the only mode of representation. The desire to tell a story is something more than a resistance to criticism and theory; it expresses a
devotion to providing a lesson about the past, and in the history of slavery,
this lesson is one that must not be ignored. As ethically commendable as
such a strategy may be, however, to do so in the context of black music
studies is to perpetuate "the burden of history." For a truly "bottom-up"

black music history not only reaches to the margins but also considers other ways of telling "(an)other narrative." It considers new modes of awakening the voices of others whose place in the circumstance of slave culture has been quieted by the texts of white mastery and their inadvertent servants in the historical profession.[41]

The point, then, is not foolishly to dismiss the significance of social history but to find a way to turn to the absence of a missing record in order to craft a story from a lost history. In casting this politics of despair, we need to undertake a more activist postcolonial reading, extrapolating from the evidence to listen critically, negatively, to the resonances crafted within and yet beyond the text as such. We will chart our story from the antistory of eighteenth-century writing. If music speaks rationally of an irrational aspect as in the unconscious, then a history written in the language of common sense cannot bring us to that place. In this respect I want to forward a historical version of the ethnographic evocation Steven Tyler proposes in his essay "Post-Modern Ethnography: From Document of the Occult to Occult Document." It is through this strategy that we begin to imagine a music centered in society, one expressing the repressed social unconscious—or what Eric Lott aptly describes, after Jameson, "the racial unconscious."[42] This is not, then, an effort to situate music in a common narrative of continuity and dialectical evolution but to explain a way of comprehending the formation of essence within a social constructionist project that is also sensitive to the power of representation in the shaping of evidence as such. The traces of represented evidence provide a kind of musical score or fake book from which we can improvise a slave sounding world. History emerges as a critical gesture that reveals through the analysis of a fragmentary body of evidence the countervoice of slavery's pasts.

Resonance begins with the nonsound of the performer's attack; the force of the finger prior to the sounding of an instrument's string becomes a metaphor for a historical African-American sound form emerging from the non-sense of white silence. Negative listening thus proceeds as a dreamwork—an effort to reveal the shadows of texts arising from the sober claims of white writers.

Shadow Texts of a Missing History   There is a certain uncanniness to the sense of quiet about eighteenth-century slave music, given the likelihood that its qualities and character would have been so discernible, so palpable, so loud. Indeed, the "score" from which we might read the sound of black performance is as barren as it is plain: prior to the 1770s, mainland observers had virtually little if anything to say about the character of slave performances, despite a reasonable certainty on our part that there was much to hear. The references that do survive are limited, in the main, to passing comments in diaries and legal documents that recorded acts in the control and discipline of slaves. Among the first was that of the British traveler, John Josselyn, who, during a visit to Noddles Island, off the coast of Massachusetts, witnessed in 1639 an African woman, a former "Queen," who "in her own Countrey language and tune sang very loud and shril . . . [to] express her grief" over her forced mating with another slave. An account sixty-six years later was similarly brief. While acknowledging that he and his acquaintances "spake much of Negroes" (during a dinner conversation, e.g., they speculated on whether blacks' skin color would lighten after their Resurrection), the Puritan Judge Samuel Sewall commented only once in his diary of a musical act: this, a January 1705 entry describing a Negro who played trumpet to announce the New Year.[43]

Four midcentury sources together with a later recollection describe performances in militaristic settings. A 1737 publication of laws and statutes of Virginia noted in passing the existence of black trumpeters and drummers in the militia of 1723. A second source, a state publication describing the infamous Stono Rebellion of South Carolina in 1739, observes slaves dancing, drumming, and parading. While commonly read as evidence of African retentions, according to a later writer, Alexander Hewatt, the image of slaves "marching toward the south-west, with colours flying and drums beating," resembled that of "a disciplined company," calling to mind not West African ensembles but the military conventions of Europe.[44] Antoine Bonnefoy provides another indication of a "Negro" drummer and drumming, which served in this instance not to inspire insurrection but to enlist men upon instruction by his English master. A 1744 account by Dr. Alexander Hamilton, moreover, characterizes a military performance announcing the war with France in terms disparaging whites (who were most likely the drummers) and blacks alike. The music, Hamilton writes, consisted of "8 or 10 drums that made a confounded martiall noise, but all the instrumental musick they had was a pitifull scraping negroe fiddle which followed the drums and could not be heard for the noise and clamour of the people and the rattle of the drums."[45] In *Sinful Tunes,* finally, Dena Epstein unearths a handful of legal accounts that give greater definition to the picture of African performance in early America. These details arise ironically and against the grain; they inadvertently acknowledge instances of music making in their primary attempts to launch legal action against transgressive behavior. The Somerset County (Maryland) judicial records from 1707–11, for example, document a complaint about slaves "Drunke

on the Lords Day beating their Negro drums by which they call considerable Number of Negroes together in some Certaine places." In 1712, the
South Carolina legislature established statutes instructing constables of
Charlestown to disperse slaves who congregated on Sundays and holidays. And a 1741 New York proceeding against alleged slave conspirators
spoke suspiciously of a black who "huzza'd, danced, whistled and sung"
while a house blazed.[46]

Early and midcentury British and British-American ministers represent
the first community to document slave performance practices, anticipating what would become a more dynamic religious textuality in the Revolutionary period. At this point, however, the sporadic comments resemble
the fragmentary evidence observed in the legal reports, making reference
to a range of vocal and verbal expressions but with hardly a detail about
the particulars of performance. Like the legal reports that Epstein un-
earthed, the ministerial texts introduce their insights inadvertently, negatively, as a kind of outlet of frustration arising from their attempts to
convert a recalcitrant and heterogeneous African population. As a result,
the characterizations reveal qualities in proportion with their departure
from the norms of Christian worship, even as several took pains as best
they could to understand the nature of African difference.

In what may be the earliest account of its kind, Morgan Godwyn indicated in 1680 that New World Africans routinely engaged in "*Idolatrous
Dances*" and "heathenish behavior" (emphasis in the original). Significantly, however, Godwyn's criticisms focused primarily on those aspects
of performance that contradicted proper Christian behavior, expressing
confidence that Africans, like the Britains before them, would transcend
these barbarisms upon conversion.[47] By the early 1700s, Dr. Francis Le Jau,
in his report to the Society for the Propagation of the Gospel (a British
evangelical organization), spoke frequently of slaves from his experience
as an Anglican missionary at Saint James Parish near Goose Creek, South
Carolina. Le Jau's comments were mostly confined to matters of conversion and discipline (elaborating on a recent act permitting the mutilation
and execution of runaways), with only rare mention of slave customs.
When referring directly to performance, he conflated it with libidinous behavior: "I discountenance the changing of wives as much as it lyes in my
power and I hope the Danceings [*sic*] upon Sundays are quite over in this
Neighborhood."[48] Subsequent sources reporting on the peculiarities of
slave performance ranged from incredulity to abject horror. Hugh Jones,
an English-born Anglican minister and slave owner living in Virginia questioned the wisdom of baptizing slaves "who have not the least knowledge

nor inclination to know and mind our religion, language, and customs, but will obstinately persist in their own barbarous ways." In his letters to Chesapeake and Low Country colonies (1740), in contrast, George White-field charged that the slave owners, by keeping slaves "ignorant of Christianity," had committed them to a life of paganism, for why else would they "profane the Lord's Day, by their dancing, piping, and such like?" As blacks began to participate in and then lead Christian worship, the fears grew worse. Three years later, when Charles Chauncey complained that black and white boys were preaching without training, he described a condition that would become increasingly common across the colonies. If Reverend Hutson could assert in 1758 that religious practice in South Carolina was conducted chiefly by blacks, Samuel Davies would argue around the same time that many slaves were still pagans "as when they left the wilds of *Africa.*" And as occasional as they were, the references to slaves dancing "Calinda" in Louisiana seemed to confirm claims of Old World practices remaining in place.[49]

Though never substantial, the religious texts came closest to assigning discernibly musical qualities to black singing. If Davies, for example, believed that slaves were pagans, he had also allowed a thousand blacks into his ministry and acknowledged in 1756 that they had an "ear for musick" and a love of the catechisms of Dr. Watts. Similarly, in his report to the Society for the Propagation of the Gospel, the Anglican minister William Knox admonished the "stupid obstinacy" of the African who nonetheless might be taught to say grace and short prayers. He too observed that "the Negroes in general have an ear for musick" that could serve in religious instruction: they "might without much trouble be taught to sing hymns, which would be the pleasantest method of instructing them, and bringing them speedily to offer praise to God." Moreover, Knox ascribed a particular quality to black vocal practices that betrayed a perception of consistency and order. "There is a dialect to those Negroes who have been born in our colonies, or have been long there," Knox wrote. Speculating on the value of a missionary learning this dialect, he acknowledged it as an expedient strategy but could not fathom a white person actually doing so. Still, Knox had acknowledged the emergence of a particular speech quality that encouraged the identification of African-American slaves as a generalizable cultural group with distinctive, creatively generated expressions.[50]

Offering the plainest representation of slave practices were the advertisements for runaway slaves, published from the 1730s, which have been compiled in the twentieth-century researches of Carter G. Woodson and Lathan N. Windley. The ads were routinely printed by southern publishing houses, including two in Norfolk, the productions of which were devoted exclusively to slave control and trading.[51] In contrast to other types of sources, the ads included details in the context of a single-page notice that focused specifically on the slave body. Appearing across the eighteenth century, they provided quick summaries for easy identification: "RUN away from the subscriber, 10th of June last, a Negro fellow called CAJAH, about 5 feet 9 inches high, of yellow complexion, a downcast look, well made, a very slovenly fellow." "Tom, about 25 years of age . . . thick lips, a little bow legged." While serving as a means of identification rather than as a record of musical ability, the reports are important because they further demonstrate a growing awareness among whites of the creative abilities of slaves. Instrumental skills stood out, and particularly the fiddling practices that by midcentury had become common in and around Virginia, for example, "in Albermarle, a mulatto man, named GABRIEL, about 52 or 53 years of age. . . . He plays exceedingly well on the violin." Occasionally, ads acknowledged skills in performing European classical music and musical instruments, including French horn and flute. Most intriguing, however, were the references to oral practices. "James, about 30 years of age, . . . his jaw teeth are out, is remarkable fond of singing." Tom, the runaway from Dinwiddie County, was missing "one of his lower fore teeth," which, we can surmise, explained why he was "fond of whistling, which he performs in a peculiar manner with his tongue." Cajah, though apparently not a singer, was identifiable by his distinctive way of speaking: "his voice sounds as if coming out of a hollow tree."[52]

In all of the instances of eighteenth-century black musical representation there exists an ironic textuality that exceeds the intentions of the authors. Reports of African-based practices appear as transgressions from state control and Euro-Christian behavioral norms; references to slave musicianship serve first and foremost as indications of physical qualities. When Hugh Jones comments obliquely about the "barbarous ways" of the "new Negroes," we can presume the appearance of what we now call African retentions but only as a translation of an earlier mode of representation.[53] Similarly, the depictions of Cajah, Tom, and James above suggest the common use of unusual vocal practices, even as the primary purpose of the texts was to reclaim missing property. When the fragments are considered in relation to the broader content of the sources, moreover, one realizes how far they could stray from the reality we so casually ascribe to historical evidence. For example, Josselyn's seemingly straightforward representation of an African woman's songful resistance is situated between two other depictions of New World encounters. The first describes a monster-child "without a head, but having horns like a Beast . . . and rough skin like a fish"; the other is a dramatic recollection of his encounter with a hornets' nest, during which he is stung "so extreamly [on my upper lip] that they hardly knew me but by my Garments." Together, these commentaries read like the hyperbolic stories of Medieval and early modern narration, full of dragons, witches, and cannibals. "Facts" blur into tall tales and apocryphal musings that challenge the evidentiary legitimacy of the sources overall.[54]

Historical evidence at the end of the eighteenth century effects a different kind of irony. These accounts will be given greater consideration in chapter 3, but for present purposes we can observe how they cast slave performance in new modes of representation. While perhaps more committed to depicting the subject at hand, the late-eighteenth-century sources rework earlier figurative gestures as they introduce a new dramatic language aligned with the hyperbole of an emerging romanticism. Janet Schaw's travel account of her visit to Point Pleasant, North Carolina, for example, seems at first to be employing the aviary conceit common to European depictions of human singing since the seventeenth century. "I was waked by the sweetest chorister that ever I heard in my life," Schaw writes, "and whose uncommon talents I had no warnings." Reading on, however, we realize that she is literally describing a singing bird. "It pitched on a Mulberrry tree, close to the window of the apartment where I slept and began with the note of our thrush so full . . . I got up and opened the window-shutter to take a peep at my musician, but . . . he was scared [off]." What is more, Schaw is doing so in order to obtain a contrast between her "musician" and the voices of slaves. "It was very early when this little serenader roused me," she continues. "I sat down to write while it was yet cool and pleasant, and no yelping Negroes with their discording voices to grate my ears and disturb my thoughts, which often obliges me to lay down my pen, but neither they nor the sun were yet up."[55] In William Bartram's account of his visit to the Southeast, the reader learns of the ability of slaves to sing "songs of their own composition," an assignment of creative capacity unimaginable in secular texts from the earlier part of the century. The same source, however, portrays these singers in anticipation of the rhetoric of blackface minstrelsy: "contented and joyful[,] . . . the sooty sons of Afric['] forgetting their bondage, in chorus sung the virtues and beneficence of their master." Such attributions of creativity as a service to the master become increasingly prevalent across the antebellum era.[56]

The shadow texts of early slave music give us something more than the facts themselves. Indeed, the representations are part and parcel of fact, and in the majority of instances, the depictions to which we turn are by-products of a more central authors' concern with securing the marginal place of black subjects, whose intrusions, however constituted within the racial imaginations of Europeans, complicate Euro-colonial superiority. These references grow from the repressive discipline of slaves and despite the intentions of the authors. We might accordingly think of the majority of fragmentary evidence as inadvertent admissions or interruptions that slip in between the lines of a dominant voice of denial. Read this way, the fragments, as interruptions, suggest a kind of confession that betrays the lying acts of a white supremacy seeking to repress the truth of the slaves' humanity.[57] For the historian, the shards of truth, however cast in racialist rhetoric they may be, provide a precious body of evidence that can be read in the wider context of a "black experience," in much the same way that fragments of dreams indicate repressed thoughts of the unconscious. What the colonial silence sought to deny was the socially constituting capacity of slave sounds, which ascribed a commonly recognized sonic place claimed by African-Americans. Slave sounding practices supplied a kind of musical foundation for the emergence of American commonalities repeatedly cast off as black. In the most basic way, at least, a shared multiracial humanity existed despite the inhumanity of slavery.

In order to contemplate the unwritten contours of such a musical sphere, we need to situate the textual fragments within the broader historical contexts of colonial encounter and representation. Musicological dreamwork proceeds not as a spontaneous invention or fantasy but as a studied creative reflection on the basis of existing sources, an activity we may liken to critical improvisation. As a step toward such an exercise, I want to turn first to the time prior to North American silence, to black music's "prehistory," so to speak, when sources were paradoxically more substantial. I do so not to secure a substitute text but to examine the representations themselves within the emerging constructs of race and Otherness. Exploring the genealogical formation of black music from its representational origins in Africa can provide both a sense of the discursive construction of black sound together with some indication of why the discerning voices grew silent. For, as I will argue, the silence within North American texts reflected not an actual absence of slave sound but a nervousness about the displacement of a black figurative potential, the very significance of which was recognized as it was denied. Silence about slave music represented a contradiction in terms: it identified new racial assumptions of the inhumanity of slaves as it confided an awareness of the creative dangers of that same "bestial sounding," the form of which, when observed against the background of modern European discourses of music, challenged the integrity of nation and race. This positioning of a displaced sonic difference beyond the scope of white comprehension would prove a crucial step in the formation of a sonically informed, oppositional slave creativity.

The Quest for Origins: Black Music's "Prehistory"   Over the course of the first three centuries of the modern period, portrayals of non-European musical practices grew up as part of the written legacy of colonialism. References to sound mapped the aural dimensions of what Mary Louise Pratt has called in her classic study of colonial encounter the rise of Europe's new "planetary consciousness." These musical references trace a complicated and conflicted historical terrain that shifts from contacts based in exploration and trade to the trading and transport of humans; from conceptualizations of foreigners in a newly discovered global space to a peculiar hierarchy situating blackness at the bottom end of the human family.[58] The musical references themselves reflected the widening gaze of colonial exploration. Depictions of sound in travel accounts would draw the attention of European reading audiences, and their appeal among professional musicians and critics gave rise by the early eighteenth century to a new interest in theories of musical origins, cast spatially and temporally in relation to these global contexts.[59] Somewhat before this time, moreover, Africans began to occupy a conspicuous place in colonial texts once more commonly devoted to Native American and Asian peoples. This prominence owed to no special favor, of course, but rather to the debasement of the "Negro" according to an incipient racism taking shape as part of (as it informed) the new economy of slavery.[60] The confluence of colonialism's global perspective and the increasing fascination with Africa took a peculiar turn in the commentaries of French and British observers and critics, whose commitments to slavery escalated rapidly alongside the rise of a colonial economy in the Caribbean and North America. From the outset, conceptions of foreign music, and particularly "Negro music," would develop as something part and parcel of the ideological development of colonialism and race. Considerations of music thus entered into the broader discursive formation of modern European society, proposing a textual background for later North American musical representations as well as a historical indication of music's perceived power.

A remarkable body of early and somewhat obscure travel literature was brought together in the seventeen-volume compendium *A General Collec-*

tion of Voyages and Travels (1807–14), edited by the Scottish antiquary and historian John Pinkerton.[61] Pinkerton, a controversial and eccentric figure in British literary circles, sought to produce a cultural celebration of Europe's conquering achievements, suggesting a continuation of prior British accounts published, for example, as Richard Hakluyt's *Voyages and Discoveries* (1589–90, 1598–1600).[62] The collection, largely consisting of arcane, previously published material, was highly valued in its time, "being the most voluminous that had hitherto appeared, with the exception of the French *Histoire Générale des Voyages* (Paris, 1785)." As a document, the Pinkerton collection reflected the apex of a modernist mission to impart knowledge according to new schemas of documentation and classification. It embodied the sentiments of a Linnaean natural science that also informed some of the collection's featured texts, replete with Latinate references to African ecology and musical instruments. In this way, the collection stood alongside the grand syntheses appearing across the disciplines—Hume in philosophy, Blackstone in law, Smith in economics, Gibbons in ancient history, Burke in aesthetics—presenting in textual miniature the varieties of human experience.[63]

Comparatively, however, the Pinkerton collection was an intellectually modest undertaking, reflecting above all the editor's antiquarian passion for folk expressions, particularly the ballads of Scottish bards, which he gathered (and in some cases possibly fabricated, as Ritson alleged) for publication.[64] Suggesting a global version of the Border Minstrelsy (Sir Walter Scott was reportedly a friend), Pinkerton's collection offered a compilation of British sources together with continental texts in English-language translation that celebrated the glories of the travel narrative as a modern mode of documentary evidence. In preparing the collection, Pinkerton inevitably exercised his own editorial judgments, foregrounding tales of warfare, violence, bloodshed, and punishment, perhaps in an attempt to prop up an ennobled view of European qualities of "civilization." Yet he was also impressively wide-ranging, choosing accounts from across the globe and reflecting a diversity of perspectives. Interspersed among the chronicles were several, often extended elaborations on African musical practices and instruments. While still assuming a marginal place in the broader context of the travelogues, the musical depictions provided a substantial body of textual evidence, particularly in comparison with other texts and collections representing the period. Indeed, the strength of musical representation in these volumes would draw the attention of Richard Wallaschek, who acknowledged Pinkerton's compendium in his highly influential study, *Primitive Music*. An accounting of the Pinkerton collection from the vantage of the early twenty-first century follows the textual trail of a colonial legacy as it lends insight into the nature of Euro-Western depictions of musical Others.[65]

Pinkerton's African narratives (assembled as vols. 15 and 16) record a diversity of cultures stretching across the continent and its island peripheries. Seventeen narratives contain sections on music of varying lengths. Of these, the lion's share document practices from coastal areas, having been written before the discovery of quinine's defense against malaria would enable exploration of interior regions; still, at least two of the expeditions traveled to the inner territories of central Africa. The authors of the narratives pursued travel to Africa for a variety of reasons and accordingly expressed a diversity of points of view. Among the many, Father Denis de Carli, for example, recalled his mission to Congo in the late seventeenth century from the perspective of an Italian Apostolic missioner (1666–67); William Bosman, a Dutch land agent, chronicled his time on the coast of West Africa (1705); Thomas Shaw, a vicar and professor of Greek at Oxford, detailed his research travels to Barbary (1738); and the British explorer Mungo Park (1810) compiled an engaging and highly popular tale of his fateful search for the source of the Niger River.[66] In preparing the narratives, moreover, the authors followed the conventions of travel writing since Herodotus as they anticipated procedures of twentieth-century ethnographic representation (e.g., A. R. Radcliffe-Brown, Raymond Firth).[67] Texts detailed what were considered to be the essential components of society, from religion to family structure to methods of warfare. By the eighteenth century, these depictions had become more formalized according to new conventions of analysis informed by natural science. In specifying and isolating natural forms, colonial classification sought to access and finally to normalize a foreign world. The act of identification served to assimilate difference into the imperium as that difference was simultaneously constituted.

The earliest accounts of African music in the Pinkerton collection date from the mid- to late seventeenth century, when Portuguese and British missionaries traveled to the continent to Christianize native populations. While detailing a broad expanse of African society and nature, the missionaries' main objective was the religious conversion of Africans, and their observations inevitably focused on this most basic concern. From the missionaries' perspective, the matter of conversion was an emergency requiring immediate attention. According to the racial and ideological presuppositions of seventeenth-century Europe, Africans lacked an indigenous religion beyond their "heathenish" ceremonies. In religious terms, particularly, Africans were thought to exist at a considerable moral and psychic distance from Europeans, having yet to evolve to the advanced levels of modern civilized peoples. Africans, as "primitives," literally lived in another time and place. But because Africans were still commonly seen as members of the human family, their "inferiority" was often viewed as more circumstantial than fixed. "Race" had yet to define the permanent limitation it would increasingly signify a century or so later. As a consequence (albeit in a widely fluctuating discursive field), the moral and intellectual limitations of African people could seemingly be overcome, suggesting, theoretically at least, the potential for realizing advancement into civil (European) society.[68] In the circumstances of African ritual and music, then, we find paradoxical indications of difference and sameness. As African performance expressed audibly its distance from Europe, so did it reveal an astoundingly close proximity that spoke to humanity's universalism, all of which was played out in the early Pinkerton texts.

The disparate, contradictory proximities of Africa in relation to Europe took shape according to the conflicting perspectives of Christian idealism and colonial materialism. As Christians, missionaries sometimes recognized the human potential of Africans; as European explorers, they frequently condemned behavior and a performative culture that from a practical, experiential standpoint contradicted their social codes of conduct. Portrayals of the audible landscape commonly appeared within a textual frame depicting the sordid nature of diverse groupings of Africans. Prior to observing the music of the Moorish gentry, for example, Lancelot Addison, chaplain to the English Crown (1671), reported that "they are naturally uninclined to sports, being very saturnine, and loving the extremes, either to sit still, or to be in robustious [*sic*] motions. They spend much of their time in a sort of drowsy conference, but the sum of their domestic entertainments is their women and their chess-boards." In the same spirit, Addison observed their music to be "very serious and plain, devoid of levity or flourish. . . . The Moors have very harsh and sawing voices, as they will have cause to observe who have had their ears grated with their amorous sonnets." Despite these failings, however, the Moors, unlike Africans of North America, possessed creative instincts: "most towns have their peculiar sorts of music." Indeed, Addison felt compelled to detail their musical instruments from the *rabèb* to the *ahlùd,* sometimes in comparison to European instruments. In one instance, he noted a musically related racial and class hierarchy that positioned the Moors above "negras," suggesting a cultural proximity with that of Europe.[69] If musical practices made manifest the distant, primitive condition of the people of West Barbary, they also indicated similarities with western Europe that ran counter to those demonstrations and claims.

Similar contradictions about the nature of the relationship of Europeans and Africans show up in the early modern documentation of music
in the African interior. In his discussion of an Italian Apostolic mission to
Central Africa, Father Denis de Carli preceded his musical reflections by
outlining the customary dress of the Congolese. These Africans, he reported, "had only leaves of trees, and monkeys' skins: and those who live in
the open country, and lie under the trees, whether men or women, wear
nothing at all, but go quite naked without any sense of shame." Fittingly,
their musical practices sustained their debased character. Vocal music created "such a doleful tone as caused horror"; as instrumentalists, "they beat
their drums . . . which makes a hideous noise." As did Addison, however,
Carli took pains to describe musical practices and the manner of instrumental construction, indicating at least a recognition of musical potential.
If drums produced sound antithetical to a European conception of music,
they were also deserving of detailed description. Drums, Carli explained,
were played "with open hand, and they are made after this manner: they
cut the trunk of a tree three quarters of an ell long or more; for then they
hang them about their necks, they reach down almost to the ground:
they hollow it within, and cover it top and bottom with the skin of a tyger,
or some other beast." Of particular interest to Carli was the marimba, "the
most ingenious and agreeable of them all," and for which he supplied an
elaborate explanation of its construction.[70]

Africans seemed at their lowest, most debased, in the context of indigenous ceremony—those expressions of "savagery" that missionaries
sought so vigilantly to stamp out. Musical practices discussed in these circumstances tended to amplify dissimilarities, evoking through sound a
distant, primal place. Father Jerom Merolla da Sorrento, a Capuchin and
Apostolic missioner, writes with curiosity and animation about the "hellish
practices" that, among the Giaghi, "not only make use of these drums at
feasts, but likewise at the infernal sacrifices of man's flesh to the memory of
their relations and ancestors, as also at the time when they invoke the devil
for their oracle."[71] Yet even in a text devoted to recording music's role in
the "wicked pastime" of human sacrifice, one finds considerable attention
paid to qualities of performance and expression. Early in the narrative, for
example, Merolla da Sorrento gives a detailed outline of the instruments of
the Abundi of Angola. The discussion covers three pages, during which he
compares the fingering of trumpets to European flutes and hautboys
(oboes), describes the double bell (a timekeeper in modern-day drum ensembles), and supplies carefully wrought explanations of the marimba,
drums, and other instruments.[72] Most curiously, Merolla da Sorrento elab-

orates on the very drums performed at the "infernal sacrifices": "These are made either of the fruit of the tree called *Aliconda,* or else of hollowed wood with a skin over one end only." He also draws a comparison between Negro and European military drums: the former, "being covered with a beast's skin, are sounded, not with little sticks, but with the hand, and which make a greater noise than our drums do." In this instance, Europe and Africa seem somewhat aligned, as musical differences foreground similarities.[73]

The comments suggest that for missionaries African music could convey a strange, mysterious power, ranging at once across experiential opposites. It could seemingly transport its practitioners across time and space, making Africans seem uncannily similar and different. The likenesses appeared most strikingly in the context of Christian ceremony, when the "heathenism" missionaries sought to stamp out entered into a European cultural realm, apparently with the approval of the holy fathers. Carli, for example, notes matter-of-factly a fascinating intersection of performative cultures. On hearing the "horror" of Congolese singing, "I inquired of my domestics what that meant; they answered, it was the people of some Libatte, that came with their Macolonte to discipline themselves in the church, because it was a Friday in March. This surprised [*sic*] me, and I presently sent to open the church-doors, light two candles, and ring the bell. Before they came in, they continued a quarter of an hour on their knees before the church, singing the *salve regina* in their language, with a very doleful harmony."[74] Here, Carli seems conflicted, troubled with the manner in which the Congolese perform a Marian antiphon while recognizing and admiring their religious propriety. In another instance, he speaks favorably, demonstrating a remarkable degree of cultural relativism when describing the musical practices taking place after religious instruction. "Next we catechised, dividing the people into two parts, and explaining what we said to them by the help of an interpreter. That done, they fell a playing upon several instruments, a dancing, and shouting so loud, that they might be heard half a league off." While the performance was peculiar, it was "not without surprise and satisfaction, it being a confort [*sic*] of so many curious, and *to us* strange instruments."[75]

Most striking, however, is the commentary of Merolla da Sorrento, who, directly after condemning African drumming rituals, observes how drumming could be used to praise Christ. "On all the most solemn feasts mass is sung by us and our interpreters to the glory and honour of God," he writes, "after which the count's guards [within the central African kingdom] . . . give a volley of musquet-shot, with drums beating, and other music." Similarly, when drumming was used to support Christian worship, it drew praise. "I heard a great clapping of hands, and humming . . . together with a confused noise of prating among the courtiers, and drums beating, trumpets sounding, and other noisy instruments playing; all of which were only grateful to my ears, as they proceeded from pleasure conceived at what I had said."[76]

Observed together, this sample of seventeenth-century representations suggests an instability in the meaning of African music within the European colonial imagination. The status of indigenous music could shift rapidly and unpredictably, first representing the recesses of pagan darkness, then being aligned with the decorum of Christian ceremony. Seeming at times abhorrent and accessible within the common order of the day, African musical practice conveyed a disruptive potential reaching far beyond its marginal place in the travelogues. The immediacy of musical access, enveloping as it did both natural environments and the rituals and customs of culture, introduced a challenge to the escalating European ambition to colonize and contain Africa and Africans. Rather than an imposing, palpable, and manifest threat, African music insinuated itself into colonial circumstances, complicating the certain distance between familiar and foreign as well as between the emerging racial distinctions of white and black.

If seventeenth-century representations acknowledged African music by way of tentative, conflicted observation, eighteenth-century accounts reflected the same ambiguities while seeking more strenuously to bring indigenous performances under the control of European discursive practices. Demonstrating more expansive colonizing ambitions, European powers increased the range and degree of intercultural contact. This heightened familiarity, however, tended to widen the conceptual gap between the continents, as ideologies of difference codified the nature of human distinction, conflating the distancing strategies of religion, natural history, and race. Each of these modes of difference making, of course, contradicted the claims of difference itself, for in rendering Africans within the image of the human family, they also repeatedly interceded into European experience, rendering intercontinental African-European alignments that the travelogues themselves document. With the escalation of exploration, governmental commissions, scientific study, and above all enslavement, the image of the African would take greater significance not only in Europe's understanding of the world but of itself. Indeed, the rise of eighteenth-century planetary consciousness would lie at the heart of a New World conception that dramatically revised the inner, self-centered visions of the metropole.[77] Representation of African music emerges as a part of this new global conception together with a deep-seated cosmopolitan anxiety. The formalization of musical rhetoric was consistent with the increasing efforts to stabilize the position and place of Africa, just as this very same ambition produced instabilities precluding the possibility of containment and domination.

William Bosman's "New and Accurate Description of the Coast of Guinea" (1705) is in some ways remarkable among texts from the early eighteenth century for its detailed descriptions of African music.[78] The nature of these depictions, however, suggests something closer to an antinarrative, in which the author voices unrestrained contempt for the quality and character of West African expression. Bosman's account perpetuates the moralism characteristic of seventeenth-century documents, yet in the musical discussions, at least, without the tolerance that often guided the early clerics' evangelical mission. His attacks are as caustic as they are persistent. For Bosman, Africans are a morally deficient people, who "profess to worship both gods and devils" and engage in strange practices involving "dead men's heads, and skeletons." After suggesting that "the Negroes," whom he casts as "lumpish wretches," lack any concern about comfort and civility (they disregard "the charming valleys, and beautiful rivers; which they have in great abundance," in order to create settlements in the most "disagreeable place[s] to build on"), he seeks to demonstrate this position by showing how African music represents a sonic version of the same abhorrent character. While acknowledging a broad range of expression ("their musical instruments are various, and very numerous"), he reduces the lot to a monstrous sensory display: "But all of them yield a horrid and barbarous shocking sound . . . produc[ing] a sort of extravagant noise." The combination of drums and horns, in particular, seemed most irritating to Bosman. In describing them, he adopts what was by then a familiar racial association, comparing their performance to the regressive sounds and behavior of animals and children. These instrumental combinations "afford the most charming asses' music that can be imagined . . . the noise they afford is very like that our boys make with their pots they play with on holidays."[79]

Bosman's exercise is a rather simple one in that it makes his intentions direct and clear: he wants to widen the gap between Europeans and Africans. Indeed, he seeks to create a veritable gulf separating the two worlds morally, physically, and intellectually according to contemporary notions of human evolution. Given the magnitude of Bosman's contempt, however, it seems unlikely that a literal rendering completes the story. If we are to take this account as an accurate representation of his views (and not as a rhetoric inscribed for some unknown purpose), then we might suspect that the text is speaking to another concern. That concern appears as fears of familiarity, closeness, and intimacy, magnified by the recurring acts of miscegenation. It is these "international" sexual relations that really make Bosman's blood boil:

The Tapœyers or Mulattoes, [are] a race begotten by Europeans upon the Negro or Mulatto women. This bastard strain is made up of a parcel of profligate villains, neither true to the Negroes nor us, nor indeed dare they trust one another; so that you very rarely see them agree together. They assume the name of Christians, but are as great idolaters as the Negroes themselves. Most of the women are public whores to the Europeans, and private ones to the Negroes; so that I can hardly give them a character so bad as they deserve. I can only tell you, whatever is in its own nature worst in the Europeans and Negroes, is united in them; so that they are the sink of both.[80]

Situated directly after his observations of instrumental practices, Bosman's comment draws a juxtaposition of music and licentiousness, implying that hearing the "horrid and barbarous shocking sound" of African performance produces a kind of physical contact. Encountering the wildness of Africa, he reveals an anxiety that brings Africa into intimate relation with Europe. Condemning difference to project it outward, difference resonates musically back, revealing its source within.

The incommensurability of difference would become the crucible for a series of colonial representations that hinged on what we might call the nature of nature itself. The natural as untamed—as wildness or, in its Latinate form, as "savagery"—had once been claimed within the boundaries of Europe, epitomized in the medieval image of the "Wild Man." By the early modern period, however, Europe's untamed had been largely domesticated, at least to the extent of its imagination in the metropoles of Paris, London, Rome, and Madrid. Despatialized, discourses of an uncontained nature shifted inward to identify a new, "human nature," those areas of consciousness not yet "colonized" by science—a process Hayden White has described as the "interiorization of the wilderness." As a psychic interiority, wildness represented a dimension of the character of the civilized, a conceptual category or "truth" that, however fictional, reinforced a social myth.[81] For some critical observers, such as the Neopolitan philosopher, Giambattista Vico, wildness identified a positive quality supplying civilization with its creative potency; it lay at the heart of the civilized imagination.

Just as easily, however, the savagery of self was denied as it was cast out. Perceived as something beyond the circumstances of Europe, wildness amounted to a colossal colonial repression that, according to the same logic, remained similarly uncontainable within the assimilative parameters of natural history. From this vantage, eighteenth-century formulations of difference and sameness related directly to a discernibly modern psychic self-conception that denied open expression of those untamed others lurking within. Such formulations of the wild, together with other socially constituted qualities with which it was aligned (madness, witchcraft, monstrosity, etc.), would become centrally focused in discussions of music, which had been historically linked with realms of magic and mystery.[82]

Conceived as a difference that stands at once inside and outside of Europe's conception of self, the nature of nature assumed various forms as observers devised strategies for representing an unstable relation. The more straightforward narrations amplified the foreignness of the natural as part of the even plane of humanity, as difference represented a liminal connection between the civilized and primitive, yet safely sequestered in a foreign land. Encountering a village setting in Senegal, Michael Adanson (1759), the official botanist to the French Royal Academy of Sciences, found it breathtaking: "I beheld a perfect image of pure nature." In its perfection, it was also originary—"I seemed to contemplate the world in its primeval state"—and finally sacred: "the whole revived in my mind, the idea of our first parents." And so did the performances seem to bypass the imperfections as well as the reasoning of civilized thought, embodying a seminal version of authenticity. Africans, Adanson contended, were instinctual, "they are born dancing, to see the exactness of their movements."[83] In his "History of Loango, Kakongo, and other Kingdoms of Africa" (1776), moreover, the Abbé Proyart employed a descriptive language that similarly credited instinct to dramatically different forms of expression. Proyart appears to recognize a natural spirit in nearly every dimension of African performance, regardless of its expressive sentiment. "The more remote the negroes are from sweetness and nature in their concerts," he observes, "the more sentiment and truth they throw into their dances and rustic songs. Be they provoked by grief, or excited by joy, they are always the faithful expression of nature."[84]

What underlies these depictions of the nature of nature is the intellectual artifice of scientific classification, on which, as Michael Adas writes, "many eighteenth-century writers on non-western societies claimed [to base] . . . their observations and conclusions."[85] Judging from the Pinkerton texts, eighteenth-century travelogues typically recorded a greater degree of musical diversity than prior travelogues had done. But they also sought to rationalize and assimilate practices in order to render comprehensible a complex and unstable African experiential terrain. Travel writers not only wanted to describe a foreign world but to translate that foreignness into the familiar, to cast that which was fantastic and even unimaginable into an imaginable place. What gave the unimaginable stability, what provided that even plane of humanity, was an increasingly formalized conception of difference. While representations of the foreign reached back to antiquity, the peculiar planetary consciousness of eighteenth-century Europe cast difference within a systematizing, classificatory scheme; transposed into the plain view of reason, difference was normalized and finally rendered similar. "In the second half of the eighteenth century, whether or not an expedition was primarily scientific, or the traveler a scientist," writes Mary Louise Pratt, "natural history played a part in it." And so did it play a part in the constitution of difference, which, as an organizing category, assumed a central role in the interpretation of the comparative peculiarities of African people and music.[86]

The more aggressive versions of natural history sought vigorously to contain African musical nature by committing it to the orderliness of a phenomenal, known world. In a travelogue recounting his "Journey to Mequinez" (the residence of the emperor of Fez and Morocco), John Windhus, a servant to the British Crown, depicted musical practices as natural forms appearing within a fertile landscape. For Windhus, the local performances of court and governmental musicians were among the many splendors of the pleasure dome, as sound blurred into images of beauty and the taste of edible succulence. Recalling his stay at the Emperor's residence, Windhus writes, "We dined in a garden of the basha's (about three miles out of town) that he had lately planted. . . . There were fine oranges, lemons, and small apricots of a very good flavour. The walks are separated with cane-work, and there is an arbour of the same very well contrived." Windhus proceeds to elaborate on the setting, describing the wealth and fecundity of natural growth and then turns his attention to a musical performance. At a critical moment, he conflates music and nature, aligning the one with the other: "The governor had his music with him, which consisted of four persons: two of them played upon small instruments after the manner of violins; one had a piece of parchment drawn tight over a little broad hoop, with pieces of loose tin on the sides, which he shook with one hand, and drummed on it with the other; another beat time to their music, by striking the palm of his hands together, very loud and well. This part of the country abounds with fine oranges, lemons, citrons, olives, grapes, figs, melons, pomegranates, and apricots."[87] For Windhus, musical expression suggested but one quality in a complex yet ultimately containable native environment. The unpredictability of musical practice and the mystery of an instinctual natural musician would be regularized to invent a steadier, more palatable landscape of sights and sounds.

Writing at the end of the century, C. P. Thunberg, M.D., professor of Botany at Upsal (presumably, Uppsala, Sweden), represents Hottentot musical practices according to a careful calculus that positioned Africa in a secure place physically and historically distant from Europe.[88] While Thunberg was clearly contemptuous of Africans, his prose lacks the vitriol of earlier reports. Indeed, his commentaries are powerful because they are dispassionate, reflecting the character of science's textual discipline. By reducing the phenomenological complexities of Hottentot musical performance to a singular analytical dimension, Thunberg attempts to contain a potent and transgressive quality within the order of science. For example, his reference to the "Trumpet-grass," which serves as a reed for a makeshift instrument (the reed is placed between the thumbs and the cupped hands act as a resonating chamber), appears according to its Latinate classification, "*fucus buccinalis,* in which they blew like a trumpet." Similarly, his organological classifications of the *Rabekin* ("like a guitar") and the *Korà* within a series of unrelated discussions and asides—noting tools of warfare and hunting, methods of card playing, and forms of natural life ("A curious grasshopper, of a reddish colour, of the class of *hemipterae,* was seen in great numbers")—reduce musical expression to yet another element of a "barbarous" natural world.[89]

Elsewhere we see that Thunberg observes the Hottentots as a people barely beyond that of animals. What was once perhaps even admiringly authentic now marked the most debased and destitute. "So deeply plunged in sloth, and so overwhelmed with filth," they could only gesture to the propriety of civilized musical practice. Evidence of this debasement arises from their apparent lack of a sense of time. "Of the new year," he continues, "a period which most nations and even the heathens themselves almost all over the face of the earth, observe and celebrate with more or less rejoicing and festivity, the Hottentots do not seem to have any knowledge, neither do they take the least account of the course of nature. The only thing they remark is, that every year they see the bulbous plants push out of the ground, blossom and decay, and, according to this almanac, they reckon their own ages, which nevertheless they seldom or never know with any certainty."[90] These Africans, in a word, are a people without a past, without history, and in this claim, Thunberg echoes David Hume's famous challenge in his essay "Of National Characters" (1748). "I am apt to suspect the negroes, and in general all the other species of men . . . to be naturally inferior to the whites," Hume writes. "No ingenious manufactures amongst them, no arts, no sciences." As if expanding on the same sentiment, Thunberg continues, "The country has no ancient ruins, either of subverted palaces, demolished castles, or devastated cities. The people neither know the origin nor reason of the ceremonies and customs in use amongst them, and few of them can give an account of any thing that has happened before their father's time."[91]

Thunberg's dismissive posture is a particular rendering of a late-century racial ideology that had codified "Negro" difference according to assumptions of racial inferiority famously advanced by the British scholars Edward Long and Charles White. His view reflected a broad-scale tendency to project wildness to an outlying realm as a means of securing reason at home. Many Europeans were surely capable of living with the logical contradictions of difference making, which distinguished, in the form of blackness, that which had already been constituted within a colonial order. Such contradictions give evidence that racial attitudes are never singular and stable. As Barbara Fields explains, at a given moment several conflicting ideologies are commonly in place.[92]

Musical practices, which had contributed to these same conceptualizations, accordingly both suffered and gained in European eyes. Simultaneously African music seemed to assume contradictory positions at the height and nadir of civilization. While William Lempriere (1793) recognized among the Moors a passion for music characteristic of "all barbarous nations," he reasoned that they could realize creative accomplishment only up to a degree, presumably driven by a now maligned instinct. "Want[ing] of that variety which is introduced when the science has attained a degree of perfection," their performances could only produce "a very melancholy sameness." In the same vein, while Thomas Shaw, in his "Travels in Barbary" (1738), may have devoted only two pages to musical instruments, he concluded that because the population of "Bedoweens do not write down their compositions, nor aim at any contrast or variety of parts in the music itself, we cannot consider even this branch of the mathematics as a science among them."[93] Similar views occupied French-speaking observers. Abbé Rochon may have incriminated European colonizers for their "barbarous and unjust" negligence of Africans who, he seemed to believe, still possessed a potential to realize their humanity. Yet it was the Africans who consequently suffered because Europeans had failed "to introduce industry and the arts into those countries which are destitute of them." Even

Abbé Proyart, who spoke admiringly of the natural power of African sound, withdrew its connection with the civilized. "These people have no knowledge of writing, nor any signs which may stand in its stead. They have therefore no records but tradition, which is maintained by certain usages. The arts among them are still in their infancy; they exercise those only which are necessary to life, and even those in a very imperfect manner." For much of Europe, Africans had undergone a transformation from the human category of a people to that lower category of a race, and their music made manifest this devolution.[94]

What is perhaps most fascinating about the eighteenth-century accounts is the tenacity of what we might call the Bosmanian nightmare: the way a difference seemingly conquered nonetheless returns, sounding its way back into the modern, and doing so not on the even plane of phenomenal observation but increasingly on its own terms. If classifying and assigning difference became a way for the new natural history to dominate the transgressive, it also served to amplify the inadequacy of its own acts of discipline. Because naming difference was also a practice of conceptualizing self, of determining through negation what one is according to what one is not, that conception would always be understood relationally. In the same way, the figuring of African music as difference repeatedly secured its place in the foreign as well as at the center of civilized society's origins, reflecting what Jacques Derrida has famously called "the logic of supplementarity."[95] What appeared "different" would repeatedly find its place within a dominant order, only to exceed that conceptualized fixity. The imperial strategy of stabilizing the foreign also created it, turning it back as a dynamic unstable force within the life of the metropole.

The nature of African musical nature, then, reflected the nervous relation of Europe to Africa, driving repetitions of doubleness and ambiguity across eighteenth-century texts. Richard Pococke (1743) may have observed the acts of street singing and dancing as a sign of Egyptian women's weak moral character, but it was these acts he nonetheless chose to discuss; "Mr. Browne" (1799) may have interpreted Sudanese dances and drumming as expressions of the lascivious, promiscuous behavior of "savages," yet these performances were what drew his attention and inspired comment. John Windhus's elaboration on the musical dimensions of a Moroccan wedding ritual suggested a similarly voyeuristic fascination, reflecting what Anne McClintock has called the "pornotropic" character of colonial writing. In this ritual, Windhus explains, the groom seizes the woman in the boudoir in order to "make what haste he can, . . . and if such signs appear on [her clothing] as are expected, the music plays; but if he doth not send out the drawers, the music must not play: and it behoves [*sic*] him to bestir himself about this matter; for, besides the hazard of his reputation, the company will meet every day until the drawers come." Here, music is not only aligned with licentiousness but also sonically communicates in ways apparently exceeding European practices. It reveals extraordinary powers of signification as it is simultaneously reduced to a nonaesthetic cultural "function."[96]

Such contradictions abound, often outlining extremes, reflecting in their accumulation the strength of eighteenth-century disciplining strategies. When Michael Adanson observed the musical talents of Senegalese *guiriots* ("This is the name the negroes give to the musicians and drummers of the country") he recognized a contradiction between colonialist myth and West African reality. "It convinced me, that there ought to be considerable abatements made in the accounts I had read and heard every where, of the savage character of the Africans."[97] Similarly, Rochon's previously mentioned vacillation between the fact of European barbarism and the recognition of Africans' creative potential only increases when he realizes that the claims of African savagery are unfounded, applied "merely because they are unacquainted with the manners and customs of Europe." Perhaps the most startling comment appears in the text of Abbé Proyart, who, after relegating the Congolese to the recesses of humanity, acknowledges what they share with civilized nations. "The hearer is moved with them, in spite of himself; especially when he beholds their action." Africa, it would seem, not only taps the European spirit but also reveals its instinct: "the hearer is moved . . . in spite of" civilization's containing powers. Continuing, Proyart amplifies this tension as he proceeds to tell the tale of two missionaries who came upon an African woman singing of the loss of her child to slavers. The commentary mixes the objective distancing of the natural scientist with an emotional acknowledgment of human suffering. "Struck by the novelty of the sight, the missionaries stopped a moment." As the mother expressed anguish, however, the "novelty" acquired human significance: "the song of the desolated mother, the abundance of her tears, the irregular movement which agitated her by turns," eventually overwhelmed them. "The missionaries themselves, pierced with profound grief, felt their tears flow and retired weeping." Significantly, what made this moment particularly powerful was the naturalness of the African character. The woman's indications of suffering "all expressed nature with such energy." The primal, instinctual nature that distinguished Africans from civilized Europeans was precisely what drew them in relation, just as the putative objectivity of scientific rhetoric kept them apart.[98]

Sometimes comparisons of European and African music imply a reversal of the normative cultural hierarchy, reflecting the exceptional status assigned to the primitive as originary and authentic. In these instances, the primitive become momentarily something to aspire to, even to emulate. Proyart's recitation on the healing arts of the Kakongo people attributes a power to African music that recalls European folk religions and medicine. While underscoring disparities in European and African aesthetic preferences, Proyart also acknowledges that local musical practices reveal special therapeutic potential. "To an European," he writes, "the remedy would be worse than the disease; but this music, which charms the negroes when they are in good health, cannot make them feel, in sickness, a more disagreeable sensation than the most harmonious concert would to one of us."[99] In his reflections on the virtues of music of the "Bedoweens," moreover, Thomas Shaw employs terminology typically reserved for European works: "even in this simplicity of harmony, they observe something of method and ceremony. For in their historical *cantatas* especially, they have their preludes and symphonies." Later he elaborates on the power of this music over other natural forms. "If the account be true, which I have often heard seriously affirmed, that the flowers of mullein and mothwort [*sic*] will drop, upon playing the mismoune, they have something to boast of which our modern music does not pretend to." Here, a "natural" African music becomes the controlling force over other living forms, suggesting a kind of sonic "mother nature." In its difference, however, African music draws comparisons with the performances of European peasantry, reflecting in the texts of Proyart, Lempriere, and others, the continual blurring of distinctions between what is different and same.[100]

The various figurations of Africa's soundscapes might seem on the face of it a fascinating yet obscure body of literature, existing far beyond the bounds of African-America. It is unlikely that Africans consciously embraced European musical constructs of the foreign, let alone carried them across the Atlantic. It is improbable, too, that African people engaged such notions seriously or were even privy to their meanings and implications. Nonetheless, these figurations did come to play in the formation of black music as a consequence of their circulation through the language control centers of an expansionist Europe and its colonial possessions. As part of the conflation of rhetorics constituting European musical concepts of the primitive, barbaric, and savage, the representations of African music laid down the discursive pathways through which a North American "Negro" expression would eventually come into being. As it took shape in metropolitan discourses, "African music" was not, however, the result of a simple act of domination, as if the word of one could be merely imposed onto the sound of another. Rather, African music emerged as the result of a more complicated social contest that amplified the power of blackness in its instability, just as it permanently transformed the understanding of music as such. Theories of the primitive could not exist in isolation but were posited in their relation to (and difference from) the civilized expressions of Europe, and this conversation radically reshaped the understanding of European music's history and character. The engagement of rhetorics of the musically foreign and familiar, the "low" and the "high," reveals, in turn, the importance of elite critical concepts in the study of black expressions. To segregate the dynamic flux of "music" in its various constitutions to the conversations of elites is to ignore the greater impact of music's formation across a broad public sphere. In the relocation of African music's representation to the discourses of the metropole, then, we identify the linchpin for subsequent inventions and reinventions in North America.

What interlinks the radical revision of European music and the invention of the foreign was the enduring question of the nature of nature, figured publicly as a debate over the origins of language. Recognizing humans' special capacity for language, eighteenth-century intellectuals debated the degree to which European speech and music explained the relationship of civilization to its others. The nervousness observed in the travelogues accordingly reflected a wider concern rooted in metropolitan discussions about the very nature of communication as a means of comparing nations and races. As Downing Thomas writes, "The idea of the origin was a way of 'resolving' the difficulty of universality (or generality) and particularity, which became apparent when Europe began to explore and colonize, coming in contact with different practices and beliefs." In an emerging evolutionary racialism, moreover, the matter of the origins of language was bound up with the nature of humanity overall: signifying practices were what distinguished humanity from animality and what provided a ranking system of the world's peoples.[101] Reflecting the impact of the travelogues, the first systematic music historians proposed theories that drew the foreign and the local apart as well as in relation. The English historian Charles Burney, for example, posited that musical creation, while widely varied from place to place, was what joined together the world's cultures. "We hear of no people, however wild and savage in other particulars, who have not music of some kind or other," Burney observed. Employing an organicist metaphor, he also proposed a scheme that distinguished these various cultural expressions: "Music, indeed, like vegetation, flourishes differently in different climates." Another famous music historian suggested that the character of musical communication was what established the limits of savage intelligence. "Man, in the first stage of his development," the German scholar Johann Nikolaus Forkel reasoned, "has not yet developed the capability of being affected by other impressions that require the mind to make comparisons. . . . This explains why we find in all savage and uncivilized nations such great pleasure in the sounds made by noisy instruments such as drums, rattles, and blaring trumpets, as well as very loud and barbaric shouting. Nature has created a direct connection between man's heart and his hearing."[102]

Music came to play such a central role in public discussions because it was thought to identify with the spoken word the essence of humanity. As a matter of course, histories of music's origins, fabricated as they were, traced to a shared primal moment and to a particular expressive capacity within the human voice. In the highly influential theories of Jean-Jacques Rousseau, the towering figure whose "presence prevailed unchallenged [across Europe] throughout the second half of the century," music, in its European form, assumed the same ambiguous position it had sometimes taken in the travelogues, representing simultaneously what distinguished civilization from the savages and the primal utterance (singing) that preceded the spoken word. According to Rousseau, musical singing signified the difference of civilization as it drew its potency from an originary precivilized humanity. Primal singing, derived from the imitation of animals, interplayed with the heightened melodies of sung speech.[103] While such ambiguities have inspired criticisms among modern scholars—most famously by Derrida whose account of Rousseau underpinned his critique of the phonocentrism of modern metaphysics—they nonetheless indicate the crucial positioning of music in the formation of modern European culture. Music is conceived, whether in its unmediated primacy or modern resolution of the primal and civilized, as a perfection toward which humanity, in its incompleteness, aspired. Both a product of civilization and a nature beyond it, music grew from the contradictory interplay of the modern and premodern, the foreign and familiar. Giovanni Battista Martini proposed that song as art derived from the discipline of unlearned, natural singing; Johann Birnbaum spoke of musical art as nature's reflection as well as its corrective; Johann Joseph Fux contended that music "imitates and perfects nature." Poised at the gap between nature and culture, music would become as art the modern form suggesting a completeness according to a supplementary logic forming one through the other. Without civilization there could be no art; without the natural capacities of an originary, primal sound, there could be no civilization.[104]

With respect to the representation of "primitive music," the copious verbiage applied specifically to African sound in the travelogues suggests an expanded attempt to contain that which ultimately exceeded European content, for in that excess critics increasingly located an exterior essence necessary for the perfection of their own national culture. While classification and analysis could translate African and other foreign expressions according to the codes of European musical knowledge (hence, Rousseau's "chanson negre" set to lyrics in Creole), increasing racial intolerance undermined such containing efforts, particularly as it applied to blacks, since the relationships drew uncomfortably close what was thought necessarily far apart.[105] So while the difference of African music depended on the relational circumstance, it could only remain a viable concept as long as African practices assumed their place. But because the descriptions arose from intercultural encounter, they brought with them all the messiness of humanity. We see in this instance the quality of authenticity revised according to the logic of resonance first outlined at the beginning of this chapter. It is a formulation imposed by (in this instance, a modern European) self onto an other, and so is it then "by nature" something constructed out of a relational circumstance. Identifying the difference that moderns, through the processes of civilization, have overcome, authenticity as nature represents the essential quality that modern civility most lacks. The authentic in the form of music would become a particularly powerful signifier of an uncontainability that repeatedly confronted European colonizing strategies, resonating outwardly, increasingly so, with respect to Africans and North American black musics.

The incommensurable and uncontainable nature of music's authentic essence was given textual form in the figure of noise. As a European category imposed on a wide world of sounding practices, noise sought to render familiar an uncontainability, the cross-cultural power and significance of which arose from the very act of its naming. In the texts devoted to Africa in the Pinkerton collection (vols. 15 and 16), "noise" appears repeatedly to mark the sonically transgressive and disruptive. While at times signifying incomprehension, it just as frequently identified a difference that Europeans also recognized as coherent within its local context. Noise, then, assumes a centrality in the discourse of European travel not to identify a resolute and distinct racial otherness as it is commonly understood today (e.g., "bring the noise"). Rather it describes an other that reflects the ambiguity of the colonial relation, affirming Homi Bhabha's insight (after Conrad) that "the experience of colonialism is the problem of living in the midst of the incomprehensible." Because noise was constituted out of a relation, it was for Europeans, like race, theoretically understandable as it remained practically inaccessible. In the form of the sonic projection named "African" and then "black" music, noise became monstrous, reinforcing European assumptions about music's profound cultural significance at the same time epitomizing a diabolical power out of place. This transgressive quality of noise recommends perhaps a literal interpretation of the most horrific depictions in the Pinkerton texts.[106]

The figure of noise also throws light (and sound) on the curious silence of North American colonists. Slave music, we might conjecture, posed an extreme example of noise, a term employed only rarely by New World observers but that cast its shadow over a literature in denial. As a product of continual black/white engagement, the volume of noise was perhaps so great that it quieted the voices of local historical actors, who sought to contain its power by following the Jeffersonian dictum of "silence not merely as a means of self-protection, . . . [but] in a political context of noisy commotion, a studied silence could gain for one a special authority."[107] Acting out themselves the savagery they assigned to others (as Dr. Francis Le Jau described the attitudes among his congregation, "I cannot to this day prevail upon some to make a difference between Slaves, free Indians, and Beasts"), white colonists in North America sought to deny these expressions a musical significance, since such admissions would conflict not only with modern racial thinking but also with the very dangerous undertaking of enslaving a population thought to be less than human.[108] In this respect, the silence among whites was understandable. Indeed, it was entirely appropriate, reflecting circumstances very different from those in Africa where black-white contact was far less systemic and outside the circumstances of European-based society. As a strategy for affirming racial supremacy, white silence served as an antiwriting that asserted Euro-Americans' special authority against the putative noise of Negro inhumanity. By casting the logic of black performance as a kind of transgression, however, white silence inadvertently constituted a New World version of black noise. At this point in the story, finally, we begin to discern an early musical blackness audibly registering its challenges between the lines of text.

Critical Dreamwork: Conjuring Black Music's Essential Relation   Revealing the textual facade of white noise sets the stage for considering "(an)other story" about the origins of black music within the dialogical resonances of the social record. The murmurs of slave sound, once imperceptible beneath the dominant textual order, increase in volume as the weight of their significance becomes more clearly discerned. Reading between the lines, we begin to sense a forgotten realm existing outside the "nonplace" of American historiography, a sounding field resonant with dynamic black humanity.[109] Welling up from normative representation, the brief asides and sporadic references to the sounds of blackness interrupt the typical order of things, breaking the silence to confess a truth of slaves' sounding presence. While forever caught within the figurations of a dominant discourse, while always conforming to a beginning within a resonant double origin, the fragments nonetheless propose a tale that affirms slave music's miraculous significance. If we can now accept the probability of a slave sounding presence in the eighteenth century, we can also gesture to its sonic dimensions, conjuring, as a kind of critical improvisation, its rightful place in the modern history of race. Historical inquiry becomes in this instance a necessarily speculative, negative undertaking, as the enacting of story from the inadvertent admissions and ruptures of denial take form according to the critical practice of dreamwork. By comparing the fragments of text to the potency and resonance of dreams, we begin to get a sense of a musical formation close to the heart of American history.

The "dream of black (musical) form," as Houston A. Baker, Jr., calls it, begins within the mediations of an originary slave resonance, which together create the socioacoustic matrix we name the slaves' place. "Place" identifies not merely a physical, fixed locale but the various zones of social and cultural action taking form as sound-filled, lived experience as well. As understood here, place is a conflation of multiple realms, imagined in their variety according to the diversity of slaves' everyday lives. Because the place of slaves symbolized a culturally shaped humanity, however, it always existed in relational conflict with the master's insistence of Negro debasement. The slaves' place was both public and private, easily witnessed as it endured covertly, secretly, in ways indistinguishable from the formlessness ascribed to it by dominant culture. "Place," then, differs from the Kantian notion of an absolute space that people and things inhabit. It is, rather, the constitution of lives, both personal and social, through the interplay of sensory perception and physical reality. In the sociosonic dimensions that constituted them, the places of slavery drew formidable power, proposing a resonant history that is at once emotive, palpable, heard.

Recent theories of place provide important insight into the rendering of a slave sonic world. In his "Phenomenological Prolegomena" on the nature of place, Edward S. Casey outlines a way of conceiving "placeness," particularly in relation to the body itself. As Casey sees it, place emerges from its

dialectical relation to the body: "The concreteness of a lived body, its density and mass, answers to the thick concreteness of a given place, but the
difference between the two concretions is just as critical because it sets up
a 'coefficient of adversity' that makes ordinary perception itself possible."
In this relation, place emerges from the body, just as the body in its experience gives record of place, representing "the crucial interaction between
body, place, and motion." Thus, Casey continues, we can see place "more
[as] an *event* than a thing . . . places not only *are,* they happen. (And it is because they happen that they lend themselves so well to narration, whether
as history or as story.)"[110]

In his study of the sound of place, moreover, Steven Feld elaborates on
the sensations of the body in the constitution of a perceived sociophysical
realm. Place begins in its negotiation with the sensory array: "As place is
sensed, senses are placed; as places make sense, senses make place."
Proposing what he calls an "acoustemology" of place, Feld seeks to rein-
sert sound and particularly voice into visually dominant phenomenolo-
gies, not as a separate domain within a "visual-auditory great divide" but as
part of a synesthetic interplay. For it is in voice that one finds a neglected
mode of engagement in the constitution of bodily driven experience; voice
is what links the broader sensory state of the body to the outer world. And
as it enters the world, so does voice resonate physically back into the
body, producing a symbiosis of sound and meaning in the construction of
place. "This is why," Feld writes, "hearing and voicing link the felt sensations of sound and balance to those of physical and emotional presence."
The link of voice and emotion, moreover, if not distinct from discourse,
does not subordinate to it. "Emotions may be created in discourse, but this
social creation is contingent on performance, which is always emergent
through embodied voices." Accordingly, bodily sound provides a means of
constituting place that is at once linguistically bound as it is felt and heard;
cast discursively, it also exceeds the full containments of language. If place
grows from the dialectic of self and the social, it finds in this construction a
portion of meaning secure in the resonance of flesh as such.[111]

Read together, Casey and Feld provide a ground of sorts on which to interpret the creation of slave musical practices out of the circumstances of
a lived world. They encourage us to pay attention less to what may have
been retained in favor of what may have been invented and experienced
within a sociodiscursive complex in which Europeans, Africans, and heterodox Euro-African populations engaged and interacted. The previous review of African musical representations together with the teachings of
American social history suggest that what was distinctive about black mu-

sic emerged out of various ideological configurations as a difference constituted, in its plurality, within the relation of master and slave. The character of this "difference," in turn, depended on the precise nature of black/white relations at a given time and circumstance, for in their contests, these relations varied considerably across the eighteenth-century colonial experience. To be sure, black-to-white relations were not static but grew from the dynamics of sociopolitical factors constituting ideological formations: the size of slave populations, the ratio of Africans to African-Americans, the nature of work, the geographical and climatological settings, and so on. The difference of blackness represented a shifting matrix inextricably linked to the dominant conceptions of Europeans as it gave voice to material forms specific to the varieties of local black experience.

To consider the potential range of musical formations and conceptions among eighteenth-century slaves is obviously beyond the scope of this inquiry. Indeed, the notion of place opens up a formidable range of hermeneutical possibility for it acknowledges, at the least, the varieties of lived experience in relation to music making. Beyond the difficulty of locating a body of evidence on which interpretation can be grounded there is the equally daunting challenge of theorizing musical meaning in ways that acknowledge the complexities of slaves' lives and that resist the temptation of assigning to it a singular "black aesthetic." But there is also a need to consider the possibility of locally centered certainties, however constructed they may have been by historical actors and the historians who have more recently studied them. We need to consider the formation of truths within slave cultures if we are to make sense of a similar music-centered truth making that occupies public and private presentations of African-American culture in the twentieth century.[112] For the purpose of making an initial gesture to the matter of musical origins, then, I want to focus here on a particular psychoacoustic place commonly identified in portraits of slave music, namely, the rural settings of the large southern plantations. It is within the pastoral mythologies of slave culture that we can cast an evocation of black musical form sounding its stories from the resonant places of colonial slavery.[113]

Like dreams themselves, the sonic projections of place arose from the slaves' phenomenal, sensing bodies. While places are always constituted in the relation of physical realms to sensory perception, the slaves' place continually referred back to that literal body, for it was the slaves' grasp of their own physicality that profoundly informed their sense of the world. Caught within the lock of a repressive and often brutal regime, slaves constructed place from the last vestige of their material possession, the expressive capacities of their own fleshly selves. Claiming even this was, however, necessarily qualified by the rules of law under slavery. If the creation of place arose from the body's sensory engagement with the physical world, it would be for slaves met with a continual challenge by an ownership denying them a social significance beyond their position within the larger place of the plantation. In this respect, the slaves' place necessarily grew against the dominant perception of Negro placelessness. Accordingly, the body symbolized for slaves the last vestige of possession, as tentative and restricted as it was; it would be the originary site from which place took form against the slaves' status as property. The slaves' place would thus reflect the conflicted nature of slavery, just as the public determinations of black "freedom" arose as a consequence of their enslaved status.

As much as the slaves' place was informed by the social life of slavery, however, it inevitably exceeded that social life. It did so, that is, partially, and to the extent that the felt experience of the slave body constituted an apartness, a semiautonomous realm—what we might think of, evoking the Althusserian determination of the economic, as slave sounding "in the last instance."[114] If bodily felt emotions cannot be reduced entirely to a discursive form, as Feld argues, then the slaves could have conceivably preserved a sense of apartness specific to their own experiences. And yet this "apartness" would have always been understood within the context of slavery and the master-slave relation. Indeed, slave music could not have come about had it not been for the master-slave relation, however perverse and asymmetrical that relation was. Constituted according to the supplementary figures previously conceptualizing African practices, the sound of slaves represented a New World version of difference that at once conformed to the textual order as it exceeded the fixities of a master's place. In this light, we may observe the sonic places of American slaves not as an essence but as a form emerging from an essential relation, the power of which, though constituted in connection with white discursive representations, exceeded the controlling grip of the figurations of placelessness and noise. The origins of the slaves' sounding place depended on the racial motivations of denial that paradoxically assigned to early black music its tremendous power. The essential relation at the heart of black music represented the performative "happening" nature of place, in Casey's formulation, giving re-sonance to this imaginary tale.

If the essential relation was a social contest of two opposing bodies, then the story of black music begins with the consequent of that relation, the objectified slave body. The essential relation of slavery produced in this first instance not creative form but the antiform of physical suffering, through which expressive practices miraculously emerged. In the surreal horror of slavery, we locate an originary contest from which sounding forms of racial difference resonate into the public sphere. According to the social logic of race, slaves were things; in the lived reality of their own sentience, however, they were "things" who endured the constant challenges of subjugation, humiliation, rape, and torture. Slaves could live out their lives in a variety of ways, of course. Some were fortunate enough to have owners with some semblance of decency, enough, at least, to prohibit corporeal punishment. Some too, as previously noted, were even allowed to make a living wage by entering into the market economy. And those less well off could at least cherish the immediacy of their own existence, the sheer significance of their lives remaining unblemished by the suffering they endured. But even the noblest portrait of the slave cannot obscure the enormous psychic damage resulting from enslavement. For a key objective of enslavement was to contain the extent of the slave's humanity. The practices of torture common to the eighteenth-century South sought to preclude an external manifestation of the slave's inner reality, to silence and deny the slave a voice. By shutting down the outward imagining of self, slavery inflicted pain and punishment in an attempt to defuse the creation of that dangerous force we call "culture."[115]

Pain, as Elaine Scarry theorizes, is objectless. It exists solely within the body, having no external object to which it refers. In its extreme, the pained existence of slavery turned the body back into itself to the point where expression was not simply repressed but precluded. If pain has no outlet in the imagination, expression is cut off at its very source, fulfilling the master's plan to deny the slave a sense of self. The miracle of slave music was its manifestation of an inner imagining through physical sound—the last expressive tool of the possessed body. Lacking autonomy, slaves miraculously produced form despite their own formlessness, and they shared and engaged collectively in shaping this form through group performance. The references to an audible slave world that interrupted the narrative of black absence identified not just a sounding practice but the crucial possession of the possessed self, as black music gave outward manifestation to the place of the slave in the world. If the story of black music begins with the slave body as object, it continues in the utterances of those human possessions who created themselves into social existence. The slaves' place takes sonic form through acts of bodily performance.

From this vantage, the power of voice becomes vital to the origins of slave musical expression, arising as an unspecified re-sonance from the relations of blacks and whites, slaves and masters. As the first expression of the body, voice was the primary utterance from which slaves created a sound-filled resonant place. Slaves were "great and loud talkers" who "often sit up after their work is done, over a large fire, even in the heat of summer." They spoke and sang in religious ceremonies, sometimes communing openly with whites. And the stories they told accumulated one upon the other, becoming oral memorials of important social events.[116] Sometimes slaves turned their words into weapons, directly critiquing white mastery. In one extraordinary account from the chronicle of Dr. Francis Le Jau, an unidentified black man ("the best scholar of all the Negroes and Indians") engaged in an act of creative hermeneutics, challenging biblical orthodoxy with an apocalyptic vision of a time when the "Moon wou'd be turned into Blood, and there wou'd be dearth of darkness."[117] More routine representations record a strain of this anxiety, suggesting a growing awareness of the uncontainability of black voicing. Slave sound making had begun to appear omnipresent, as the nighttime "chattering of Negroes in their quarters" re-sounded across America's "virgin landscape." Indeed, the discernible qualities of black performance seemed actually to be unseating the mastery of civic order, transforming through story and song the New World Edenic ideal into what William Byrd called a veritable "New Guinea."[118]

This is not to say that slaves failed to play musical instruments. Evidence shows that instrumental performance continued in North America, as the sheer fact of instrumentalism's ubiquity across cultures encourages us to see slave practices as multiple rather than monolithic. In fact, the broad range of performance expression, from singing to dancing, banjo playing to fiddling, all documented among the fragments of colonial textuality, was most likely (in many instances, at least) part of an overarching expressive capacity, uncontained by the typologies of instrumental versus vocal and, even, dance versus music. But the role of voice in the constitution of the slaves' sense of place suggests it had assumed an importance to which other expressions conformed, not unlike the way critical conceptions of music took shape in European elite culture.[119] As the body's primary sonic extension, voice inhabited the breath of life formed at the limit of existence, poised precariously between the possessed subject and the possession of the master. Voice marked the body's freedom, partial as it was, issuing itself into the audible realm in order to protest and condemn heinous acts of bodily violence and, eventually, to craft miraculous worlds in the slaves' own image.

As a creative force, voice enabled slaves a rare luxury to outline the contours of the physical world and to do so continually, repeatedly, in a variety of social settings, even during acts of labor for the master. The distinctive vocalizations of slaves—"James, . . . his jaw teeth are out, is remarkable fond of singing," "Tom, . . . fond of whistling, which he performs in a peculiar manner with his tongue," "Cajah, . . . his voice sounds as if coming out of a hollow tree"—were the means by which slaves claimed ownership of the world around them.[120] Not only were they in primary control of their voices, they used them to cast the sonic place of the South in their own image, giving sounds and songful names to the broad territory, to the point where black singing and vocal sounding gave audible form and character to the plantation. Such strategies did not exceed the master's understanding. Owners acknowledged the distinctive sound of Virginia slaves' speech as well as the peculiar dialects of Africans in the Lowcountry; as previously noted, ministers such as William Knox struggled with the possibility that such speech practices might need to be learned by whites for the sake of converting blacks. Indeed, ministers feared the performance practices of slave rituals not only because of their "heathenism" but also because of a sonic order that challenged white containments. Nonetheless, they encouraged the use of song in acts of intercultural religious ceremony: the singing of Christian hymns represents the most coherent body of musical evidence prior to the Revolution. Yet the fear of black voicing could also inspire extreme measures, such as the application of a torture device that effectively silenced the slave by securing the victim's tongue and jaw with a metal bit or face clamp (often applied to a black preacher). Less brutal, but with similar intent, were the grand denials of the slaves' sonic significance. The silence of white writers sought to smother the noise of so many slaves singing.[121]

One can certainly imagine from a contemporary perspective the danger of an enemy singing. The familiar image of Fannie Lou Hamer leading Civil Rights protesters in a chorus of song is one of the more powerful sonic examples in recent memory. The rhetorical virtuosity of hip-hop, together with more recent controversies surrounding public prayer, underscore the power in song's uncontainability.[122] But for song to convey such impact it requires a symbolic value that is hardly universal. In the eighteenth-century South, it would have had to acquire a social power of resistance and associations with transcendence not only accessed by slaves but also perceived by white mastery. In recognizing the threat of slaves' singing, whites ascribed a certain rationality to black performative action in the midst of a profusion of denials. These denials grew from assumptions of music's irrational, mystical power, and in situating the cacophony of slave singing within the domain of animal behavior, they would need to hear in it too meanings associated with the natural, the primitive, and the wild so routinely assigned at this point to "savage" expression. As a material difference constituted within the logic of race, black singing gave form to a concentration of transgressive meaning that affirmed difference as its increasing familiarity within the lived relations of blacks and whites contradicted such claims. This contradiction would, in turn, become all the greater as observers transposed to America the noisy challenges of the nature of nature that had been circulating in European culture around this time. While it would oversimplify things to suggest that discourses of elite European culture simply traveled across the Atlantic to inform the musical conceptions of white colonists, it does seem likely that a general sense of music's power had come to inform American understanding, particularly as those conceptions were cast first in the rhetoric of an Anglican ministry and, then, increasingly in the language of authenticity prevalent after the Revolution. The challenge of slave singing, then, while already a threat as a form of musical communication, would double in significance as the transgressive force of black musical difference occupied a version of modern European conceptions of musical others. In this way, it would anticipate the transgressive, spatially displacing power of culture that theorists such as David Harvey have ascribed to a later modernism.[123]

All of this should make one somewhat more cautious about claiming an African essence to be at the center of African-American musical expression. It should also inspire real skepticism about the prevailing view that black music emerged from transpositions of African drumming practices. Judging from the historical record, the incidences of drumming in North America were rare, and surviving material evidence is scant at best; it amounts to a single, West African–style drum housed in the British Museum. While New World practices such as "patting juba" most likely derived from drumming, the absence of drums in North American settings supports a more obvious conclusion: namely, that drumming, while not necessarily uncommon, was not as vital to eighteenth-century slave cultures as we might assume. Many have reasoned that the transposition of drumming to patting came about as a consequence of colonial bans as it reflected the tenacity of an African rhythmic sensibility.[124] Epstein, for one, attributes the end of drumming to the success of Anglican ministers to stamp out "heathenish" practices, even though related efforts to convert slaves to Christianity typically failed at this point. Patting endures, she argues, because the drum bans, which were "so contrary to the natural inclinations of the black population, apparently proved impossible to enforce." Amiri Baraka anticipates this general position, proposing that "it did not occur to [Europeans] that Africans might have looked askance at a music as vapid rhythmically as the West's." Their commitment to drumming, he continues, extends from the use of drums as a surrogate language. Yet he does not explain how a linguistically heterogeneous, North American African population agreed on a particular music-phonetic correlation stemming from an equally heterogeneous system of African tonal languages.[125]

Similarly difficult to explain is the appearance of black drumming in circumstances where it was supposedly a mark of terror. If the banning of drums—the evidence documents only a few, weak laws—reflected deepseated white fears of black rhythm, why did actual drumming practices show up matter-of-factly, sometimes directly after the institution of a prohibition? Recent researches by Edward Widmer and Philip Morgan demonstrate that African-style drumming continued openly in places where bans were recorded, suggesting that it was not nearly as threatening as many have claimed. Particularly striking were the previously noted efforts to recruit black drummers to serve in militias, together with evidence of slaves performing for both sides during the Revolutionary War. Epstein herself notes an advertisement for a South Carolina slave auction appearing directly after the Stono Rebellion, in which drumming is listed as one of a slave's admirable features: "a good Groom, waiting Man, Cook, Drummer, Coachman, and hacks Deer Skins very well."[126] The references to drumming practices in African settings outlined earlier in this chapter support the impression that drums were no more threatening to whites than other forms of black performance. Given their scarcity in North America, it is unlikely that they mattered among colonists to the extent that vocal practices did. Drumming may well have simply died out as a consequence of the processes of acculturation.[127]

At the core of the myth of slave drumming is a belief in the irrepressible, "naturally rhythmic" character of blacks, and it is for this reason above all that we need seriously to reconsider such ways of thinking. Given the near absence of references to drumming in the colonial era, there is no good reason to make claims of drumming's challenging character unless we build a historical theory on a single incident, the Stono Rebellion, and a handful of accompanying accounts: Pinksters, funeral rituals, and so forth. While reports of racial violence in the West Indies and its institution of Black Codes in the mid-eighteenth century may have already informed Caribbean conceptions of black music, they did not draw North American accounts into relation until much later, after the Haitian rebellion.[128] That incident, coupled with the revolutionary challenges of Nat Turner, inspired a new language of rhythmic threat that appears in the literary characterizations of Edgar Allen Poe ("Tale of the Ragged Mountains") and Herman Melville (*Benito Cereno*). Even then, rhythm does not become a dominant signifier of black music until after the Civil War and the European colonization of Africa. As "hot rhythm," American black music assumes the primary racial figure of modernism (see chap. 5).

This is not to say that dynamic percussive performance practices did not exist in eighteenth-century North American slavery. On the contrary, the forms of patting we locate in post-Revolutionary sources were most likely in place well before, together with the highly physical "dance" forms and other percussive actions. To these performances, however, we should avoid casually assigning the designation of "rhythm," or, in the most Africanized settings, "music." For epistemologies of performance are more than a sum of sonic parts; they emerge as thickly textured significations that contour the very stuff of "context." As Klaus Wachsmann and Kenneth Gourlay argued over twenty years ago, simply to name the many versions of acoustical knowing "music" is to impose onto a diversity of experience a peculiarly western European socioartistic construct.[129] Likewise, the discrete European category of rhythm was not likely a part of the slaves' musical epistemology since it, too, is a European discursive formation inconsistent with the broad range of African and African-American performance concepts that would have been intersecting and colliding in North America. More likely, the sounding practices of slaves constituted a heterogeneous assembly of bodily expressions relating to the antagonistic dynamic of the essential relation rather than to a uniform grouping or overarching rhythmic concept. For rhythm specifies not a universal quality but a perception specific to modern, Western musical discourses, a perception that, by the late nineteenth century, had become increasingly associated with notions of blackness, Africa, and race. As Kofi Agawu has demonstrated in an important essay, the social power of rhythm was invented within the discourses of colonialism as a way of defining African difference, and we may see in North America a similar tendency to reduce all of black music to an essential rhythmic difference that underlies contemporary notions of authenticity.[130]

Interrogating performance terminology and conception is important, then, because it honors the slave past by providing it with some freedom from circular containments. It enables, finally, another story to speak. That story is undoubtedly—beyond all conjecture and speculation—one of multiplicity and diversity, rupture and renewal, in which sound ultimately assumes a crucial place in the crafting of the social fabric.[131] Slaves lived their lives, and they did so individually, multiply. As a matter of course, "sound" variously textured and inspired new coherences of those lived experiences, which have now since fallen silent. What finally became "slave music" or "Negro music" in the newly founded United States emerged out of a veritable constellation of practices and conceptions. These diverse formations, representing a spectrum of social configurations, would in turn flow in and out of the multiple meshings of hybrid intra-"African"/ slave concepts and the Euro-centered "musics" that sounded across colonial America.

Beyond the debate of musical origins, we can see why slaves would become so committed to sound as a way of constructing culture, and it is this basic assertion, conceptualized already in the parodies of blackface as it was so responsibly and elegantly presented in the work of modern writers from Du Bois to Baraka, that is affirmed in the present work. Music, and particularly song, as both Du Bois and Baraka have demonstrated, symbolized a body claimed; arising out of the body, it offered a kind of realness amplified by its material relation to the truth of one's own enslavement. Music signified social desire sounding from those for whom freedom was denied, and it is in this irony, once again, that we locate slave music's power and truth in the essential relation. From that unsteady social contest a difference could arise that eventually became acknowledged by white authority. And it is from the atrocity of this same relation, finally, that black music would be constructed as the fullest embodiment of social truth.

Black sounding practices identified a difference that, while constituted within the master-slave relation, gave a material significance to a people under siege. These practices stood in for the slaves' own dispossessed bodies, expressing one of the great miracles of the American experience. Indeed, black music may well represent the ultimate signification of blackness in the way that it sonically resonates a sense of the miraculous. It is the ultimate signification because it speaks at once of blackness and sameness; it is of the local order as it is emblematic of and embodied by a nation's people. As a social phenomenon more so than a natural one, black music realizes a kind of constructed perfection that voices a moral victory in the face of America's enduring racial failure. The great irony of black music would also determine its social power. In its "invisibility," it claims its place at the center of America's history.

3 First Truth, Second Hearing

Audible Encounters in Antebellum Black and White

The Negro is comparison. There is the first truth.—Frantz Fanon

In his sober reflection on the dialectics of modern racial consciousness, Frantz Fanon casts "the Negro's" sorry fate. While acknowledging that blacks have attained a certain recognition within the circumstances of white mastery, Fanon rejects this as a partial and ultimately faulty achievement. For black recognition betrays a crucial flaw: it succeeds "without conflict," without the social contest and ontological giving on the part of whites that, according to Fanon's Hegelian formula, must precede liberating self-consciousness. "Man is human only to the extent to which he tries to impose his existence on another man in order to be recognized by him," Fanon writes. "It is in the degree to which I go beyond my own immediate being that I apprehend the existence of the other as a natural and more than natural reality." Denied by white supremacy the truly conflictive relation that will humanize blackness, the African diasporic subject suffers an incomplete existence within a "vicious circle that throws me back on myself." For Fanon, the circle's closure, its distance from a truly relational social engagement, is what ultimately limits the humanity of African-America.[1]

Within the circumstances of the United States after the Revolution, institutionalized slavery had sought to realize the forms of mastery that Fanon recounts. Observed according to Fanon's formulation, slave existence could only have been incomplete and partial, owing to the repressive regimes that regulated southern black experience. Still subject to the brutalities observed already in the colonial period, slaves in particular would witness an escalation of statist efforts to contain their material rights of existence. Denied a legitimate place in the social world, they lived within a kind of immateriality as possessed subjects legally forbidden autonomous selfhood. Despite new privileges made available through a post-Revolutionary economy (notably, the earning of wages and the buying of freedom), slaves could only rarely attain rights routinely granted to the white population. The comparative, though uncontested, relation that defines the "first truth" also precludes the possibility of real autonomy. As Hortense Spillers observes with some rhetorical flourish, "the 'peculiar institution' elaborated 'home' and 'marketplace' as a useless distinction."[2] What slaves could possess was necessarily limited to the partial claims of ownership they could make of their very bodies.

From this partiality, nevertheless, slaves produced those bodily sounded gestures of the essential relation that would give rise to an exceptional "Negro music." Contrary to Fanon's pessimistic assertions, the sonic projections of African-American slaves produced not an inadequate selfhood but the cultural basis of a black-specific self-awareness. As they were cast within public contexts, slave soundings assumed a discernible social significance as a consequence of their recognition and representation by a white population for whom such performances had previously fallen on deaf ears. From the final decades of the eighteenth century until the time of the Civil War, depictions of slave performances came to occupy a central place in the representation of African-American culture to the point of drowning out all other characterizations. What had once been submitted to a repressive silence consistent with the intention of denying slaves human significance acquired a conspicuous place in public culture, effectively challenging an enduring skepticism about the intellectual and creative capabilities of blacks. "Negro music" now stood between the realms of noise and order, symbolically marking the extremes of the white racial imagination. Operating within a dynamic that mimicked the absurdity of racial ideology itself, "Negro music" assumed qualities of excess ranging from the grotesque to the supernatural, and in its instability it would realize formidable social power. Constituted as a difference existing within as it exceeded the unity of nation, "Negro music" would grow in significance above all in its ability to upend the logic of separating black and white. The many qualities of slave performance would come to represent a miraculous racial magic that drew formidable potency and power as a consequence of a double logic generated in the public sphere.

The audibility of the slave, then, is what challenges the word-specific pessimism characterizing Fanon's text.[3] More than simple acts of "resistance," these black performances proposed a contrary soundscape that proceeded from the decidedly interracial interplay of musical and language-based articulations—all casting about the acousto-discursive realms of post-Revolutionary and antebellum America. The first seventy-odd years of the United States represent a seminal moment in which performative expressions arose in a diversity of slave settings as a fundamental part of the broader emergence of a discernible African-American culture. The presence of the "American Negro" within the national body politic grew out of the acculturative relations of blacks and whites, just as the many forms of black expression reflected the intersecting nature of cross-racial encounter. The naming of "Negro music" spoke to the presence of blacks in American society as it sought to position blackness apart from the exclusive domain of an emerging whiteness. What first arose as a loose interplay of culturally determined performances evolved into separate (though repeatedly interacting) categories of difference that distinguished master from slave. As difference arose from the prior experience of acculturative sharing it produced a never-ending spiral of cultural mimesis in the making of black music.

Within the antebellum racial imagination, "difference" constantly turned back on white authority as it was constructed through it, resulting in an accumulation of mediations that commonly separated the performative experience of slaves from the white world. In constituting what Fanon names the "fact of blackness," the relational character of slavery was precisely what undermined attempts to completely marginalize slaves, just as the logic of race made black music structurally inaccessible to Euro-modernity. As slave performances circulated, they amplified this inaccessibility, giving voice to "another time, another place" simultaneously composed within interracial circumstances as it identified a discernible blackness. Black music consequently took public form only as a second hearing—within the slips and swerves constituting a musical "time lag" of black contramodernity.[4] The authenticity of slave soundings emerges from the logical incongruity of its access by whites, and this authentic quality would increase with each repetition of whites' refusals to engage blackness as something already within themselves.

From this vantage, the formulations of circular resonance proceed into the nineteenth century as a voluble network of interracial cross play that informs the emergence of slave performance. The relational circumstance that Frederick Douglass had witnessed determines the very means by which black music gains public presence. African-America's "first truth" emerges from a second hearing, from the surfacing of blackness within and without of whiteness. The originary nature of the authentic grows from a comparative relation that unseats the stability of both blackness and whiteness as it constitutes an alternative racial sound world. Slaves' sounding places resonate outward, colliding and shifting as they intersect with the discourses of observation that guide, limit, and feed back into slave performative aesthetics. A sound world seeming to arise out of nowhere would miraculously find its way into the center of American cultural identities, into the stories that narrated the idea of an exceptional American nation. Well before Reconstruction's "New Negro," the "face of the race," as Henry Louis Gates, Jr., calls it, had assumed a discernible sonic form named the black voice.[5] The recognition of an expressive blackness was first conceived audibly, however contoured it may have been within and against the conjugations of racial discourses. For "blackness" is recognized through the primacy of a second hearing that translates a once noisy absence into national form.

Getting a Hearing   The initial manifestations of a discernibly public "Negro" utterance appeared in the vocal calls for freedom among northern post-Revolutionary slaves and their white abolitionist sisters and brothers. In fact the rhetorical prominence of blackness had at this moment as important an influence as the "music itself," since it positioned black sounding practices directly within the fabric of public discourse. Speaking from the antislavery sentiments of natural-rights philosophy that had already served to justify the American Revolution, early abolitionists called for the end of a practice of human bondage that mirrored the English tyranny that American colonists had successfully challenged.[6] Slavery, they argued, contradicted the dictates of equality that had underpinned Enlightenment claims of "unalienable rights" and had been written into the Constitution. Northern slaves, having served in respectable numbers in the colonists' fight for freedom, voiced their demands publicly with notable support from Euro-American religious and political organizations.[7] Casting an appeal in the rhetoric of Revolutionary freedom, a group of black petitioners in Massachusetts wrote, "It have Never Bin Considered that Every Principle from which America has Acted in the Cours of their unhappy Dificultes with Great Briton Pleads Stronger than A thousand arguments . . . [that] they may be Restored to the Enjoyments of that which is the Naturel Right of all men." Several others took their appeals directly to the courts, suing for freedom and in some cases, gaining compensation for their past labor.[8] The success of some of these challenges, whether in public forums or in courts of law, inspired further effort as it allowed slaves a hearing. "If we are silent this day, we may be silent for ever," a group of black Philadelphians declared in 1781. Recognized within the auspices of public legal forums, northern blacks eventually won broad emancipatory rulings, whether by formations of state constitutions or judicial decision. By the first years of the nineteenth century, slavery in northern states had been either abolished or legally revised to soon face elimination.[9]

The recognition of a humanized black voice within post-Revolutionary "bodies of law" further destabilized an already unstable discursive field. It aligned incommensurably an ideology of difference, that of race, with an Enlightenment-inspired Revolutionary goal of national identity, which was itself built on a contradictory notion of universalism through exclusion.[10] So, too, did the formation of difference contradict the religious tenets of a Christian rhetoric that claimed for humanity a common, singular whole by excluding as "heathen" those not fulfilling a recognizable religious order. The collision of racism and religious idealism did not pass the notice of critical observers both in Europe and North America. Satirizing racial supremacy, Montesquieu exposed a flawed reasoning: "It is impossible for us to suppose that these beings should be men; because if we supposed them to be men, one would begin to believe that we ourselves were not Christians." Indeed, the paradox of race could produce seemingly insurmountable contradictions that writers directly challenged and more typically subtly critiqued. As Duncan MacLeod puts it, "The Revolutionary struggle with England suggested to many Americans that there was more than a mere inconsistency between the ideals they were propagating and the institution of slavery they succoured: there was a national sin to be purged."[11]

By acknowledging the "black voice" as a sign of African-American humanity and reason, Euro-Americans were forced either to admit blacks into a singular society, contradicting common notions of racial difference, or to live with a second contradiction of egalitarian ideals and divided identities. That the large majority of whites, in keeping with the more virulent expressions of modern racism (and as subjects within a dominant ideological formation) chose the latter course—treating even free blacks as slaves without owners—highlights the sense of anxiety an emerging black public voice would let loose. Recognition would proceed from the fear of encounter. As Etienne Balibar writes, "Racism reveals the nonuniversalistic component of nationalism, which was hidden within it." The subsequent construction of an antebellum "Negro music" would become the consummate symbol of racial difference arising from the unspoken interracialism of the music's constitution. Black music emerges as "a symptom of the contradiction between particularism and universalism which primordially affects nationalism." Its strangely tenuous and paradoxical position within and without of the public sphere fueled the entry of African-Americans into post-Revolutionary society as it served to complicate the false vigor of an Anglo-Saxon supremacy.[12]

The significance of black sounding in the structuring of post-Revolutionary categories poses a challenge to conventional historical explanations of social change. Typically, matters of sound and music are set to the side in order to address more tangible social forces—in traditional histories, wars, royalty, presidents, and famous men; in the newer scholarship, political economy, labor movements, gender relations, family law, and so on. Yet it is precisely within the domain of public rhetoric that audible inventions of nationhood were expressed, debated, and contested, as commentators sought to negotiate between the appeals to unity and the diversity of discourses that Marc Shell names "Babel in America." The Revolutionary character to which these spokespersons gestured was not a stable and secure property built on the rule of law. Rather, it took shape within language itself, revealing what a recent group of literary critics has described as the spoken character of the American Revolutionary ideal. As Christopher Looby argues, the dominant discursive figure of the Revolutionary period was that of the spoken origin of the United States, of a nation founded on a dissonance of words. "[This] revolutionary inception," Looby writes, "was intrinsically undecidable, and . . . that is why it was so aptly figured as a linguistic phenomenon."[13] Challenging the primacy given to print and writing on promoting American Revolutionary ideals, Looby argues that America begins as a consummate orality, as a nation spoken into being.

Taking the example of the Declaration of Independence, Looby shows the announcement of an independent American national entity as being both "constative and performative, at once *referring* to the nation-state (as if it already existed) and *instituting* it (since it did not yet exist)." This paradox, in turn, draws from the instability of language itself, which heightened the mercurial, phantom-like quality of the linguistically bound concept of nation. Spoken into being, the American "nation" verged on the magical, seeming to come out of nowhere as a kind of "mythic present." It is a moment, Looby continues, "in which the state must at once have been already constituted and yet to be, a contradictory fold in time whereby political legitimacy and illegitimacy coincide."[14] The prominence of this calamity of nation-speak was also what crafted the aural materiality of the United States. And the same contradiction between national ideals and heterodox reality inspired still more rhetoric in an exploration of its unstable nature.

I want to consider for a moment the confrontation of these twin formations of African- and Euro-American rhetoric and the potential of their intersection. For while the instability of the rhetoric of nationhood would appear to allow for the entry of black voices into the broader discourses of race, contemporary criticism more typically observes these as realms divided. Looby, for one, acknowledges heterodoxy as he analyzes the fragility of social constructs. "In America," he writes, "racial and ethnic diversity, religious heterogeneity, population dispersal, and geographical unboundedness, practical innovation and exile from historical precedent all contributed to problematize (if not demolish) traditional notions of nationality. Language and languages remained to negotiate the differences and to establish a minimum of social connection."[15] Yet never does he challenge the fixity of racial constructions of whiteness or the role of sound in articulating that challenge; his discussion remains limited to extraracial matters among white authors. For all its admirable Derridian ingenuity, Looby's portrayal of the Revolution follows a remarkably stable racial determination. It misses the opportunity to consider how race exacerbated the discursive instability of nation, as blackness and the parallel miracle of "Negro music" trace to the very center of the anxieties "voicing America."

By accounting for the qualities of blackness among the babble, together with its aural significance beyond a languaged intertextuality, we begin to discern a more nuanced sense of the social contradictions made manifest in performative expression. From this vantage, the emergence of "America" in the contexts of the Revolutionary moment grows from an unsteady resonance of sounds and voices that describe the relational construct of society as a whole. Acknowledging a basic premise of postcolonial criticism, we recognize that "while the imperial metropolis tends to understand itself as determining the periphery, . . . it habitually blinds itself to the ways in which the periphery determines the metropolis—beginning, perhaps, with the latter's obsessive need to present and re-present its peripheries and its others continually to itself."[16] Within the context of the United States, the peripheries of blackness, and black music in particular, no longer remain at the margins but assume a central place in the constitution of post-Revolutionary society. The experiential fact of the slaves' Americanness achieved as a result of an acculturation of European and African traditions collides with the conviction that these two traditions stood apart—that what was cultural in the former was merely instinctual in the latter. The magical quality of the American nation spoken into being consequently encompasses a much broader acousto-discursive network, in which the matters of race and black expressive practices loom as a vague, forbidding presence. The discernibility of black voicings thus reflects the uniqueness of an American "Negro," as black music, a New World expression seeming to come out of nowhere, insistently interrupts the logic of race.

Nowhere was this contradiction more vividly realized than in the interracial musical performances of the South, particularly those of the Chesapeake region. By the 1770s, African-American musicians commonly performed for white dances, as fiddlers and banjo players became increasingly conspicuous on southern plantations. These performances, which date back in North America (specifically, in Virginia) at least to the 1690s, featured accompaniments to European dances such as the cotillion and minuet. At certain moments, however (apparently at the end of evenings), the musicians played music for dances that, according to the British clergyman Andrew Burnaby, were derived or at least informed by slave traditions.[17] Nicholas Cresswell describes one of these events taking place in Virginia in 1775:

Here was about 37 ladies dressed and powdered to the life, some of them very handsome and as much vanity as is necessary. All of them fond of dancing, but I do not think they perform it with the greatest elegance. Betwixt the Country dances they have what I call everlasting jigs. A couple gets up and begins to dance a jig (to some Negro tune) others comes and cuts them out, and these dances always last as long as the Fiddler can play. This is sociable, but I think it looks more like a Bacchanalian dance than one in a polite assembly.[18]

The "Congo minuets" and "Negro jigs" danced by Euro-Americans suggest that some colonists, at least, had become adept at a kind of performance strongly influenced by Negro practices, as the motion and sounds of slaves appeared in translation, according to the actions of whites. Still, the identification of a Negro tune or dance as uniquely "black" might have seemed inappropriate, for the ability of whites to comprehend and engage in these practices shows that they had already been casting about an intercultural body of musical resonance. And so the Englishman Robert Hunter could replace a black fiddler at a dance in Baltimore in 1785, performing not a precolonial African sounding practice but "the savage dance," a primitivist rendering inspired by contemporary racial discourses of naturalism. Similarly, the performance antics of Thomas Jefferson's brother, Randolph (who, according to Isaac, a slave at Monticello, "used to come out among black people, play the fiddle and dance half the night") could happen in the first place only because of the intercultural exchanges that had already occurred. Perhaps most noteworthy is the evidence of performance-based racial crossing among Virginia's youth. Philip Vickers Fithian's observation of black and white children dancing on the estate of the Tidewater planter, Robert Carter, acknowledges the tail end of what was most likely a legacy of performative exchange that whites had only begun to recognize and acknowledge.[19]

The scattered evidence of slaves adopting these practices in the continuation of fiddling and in the dancing and singing of the nineteenth century encourages a view of the Chesapeake performances as a veritable crucible of cultural exchange. Recalling a particularly fascinating moment of interracial engagement, the slave, Old Dick, explained to the English journalist John Davis, "My young master was a mighty one for music and he made me learn to play the Banjer. I could soon tune it sweetly, and of a moonlight night he would set me to play, and the wenches to dance. My young master himself could shake a desperate foot at the fiddle; there was nobody that could face him at a *Congo Minuet;* but Pat Hickory could tire him at a *Virginia Jig.*" Other sources describe blacks "taking off" or copying white manners, and possibly, their performances; still others (notably that of Nicholas Cresswell) observe how Virginia blacks sang songs at the "Negro Ball" in order to "relate the usage they have received from their Masters or Mistresses in a very satirical stile and manner."[20] As "recreation," these interracial engagements tended to perpetuate white authority and black subservience, and probably for that reason they passed by with only limited comment. Yet they also fostered the contradictory expressions of desire and reproach that we encountered earlier. For example, as American and British publishers committed black music to print, distributing versions of "Pompey ran away: Negroe jig" (1782), "Negro Dance," and "Congo—a Jig," a historical account of the British colonies would associate Virginia women's fondness for black-inspired jigs with mental deficiencies and indolence. "They seldom read, or endeavour to improve their minds; however, they are in general good housewives."[21] Symbolically, these works underscored the depth of cross-cultural exchange that underlay the formation of American culture. It is in this context that we might read with a certain attention to music's power Thomas Jefferson's characterization of democratic independence as "the ball of the Revolution." Music becomes a metaphor for a new kind of racial hearing, in which the being of blackness—excised from Jefferson's original version of the Constitution—is finally heard.[22]

The invention of "Negro music," then, may best be understood as a deferral of a potentially transgressive cultural achievement. To evoke Balibar's Lacanian formulation once again, it was a "symptom" growing out of the cross-racial encounters of eighteenth-century slavery. By acknowledging "Negro music," whites would seek to demarcate a distinctive, yet thoroughly hybrid black humanity on racial grounds, and by insisting on the instinctual nature of black performance, they would reinforce this separation. In his famous charge of black inferiority in *Notes on the State of*

Virginia, for example, Jefferson resurrects the trope of natural talent observed already in European depictions of Africans. "In music they are generally more gifted than whites with accurate ears for tune and time, and they have been found capable of imagining a small catch." As a capability aligned with human consciousness, however, natural talent stabilized black inferiority. "Never yet could I find that a black had uttered a thought above the plain level of narration."[23]

Some references to natural ability seemed curiously intended to draw relationships between blacks and whites. Particularly crucial to the recognition of racial encounter were the circumstances surrounding religious worship. Methodist ministers had begun to speak at greater length of slave musicality, sometimes praising blacks' powers of singing and acknowledging a distinctive approach. The Virginia Methodist preacher James Meacham, for example, was overwhelmed when "I awaked in raptures by the sweet Echo of Singing in the Kitchen among the dear Black people." He was so impressed, in fact—"I scarcely heard anything equal to it upon earth"—he proceeded to join them in song.[24] Instances of blacks' more demonstrative expressions became the basis for a conceit in Christian contexts. Bishop Asbury's observation of "tears streaming down" the faces of "Hundreds of Negroes" caught up in the religious fervor would appear slightly revised in Freeborn Garretson's 1777 commentary ("Tears trickled down the faces") and again in Thomas Rankin's 1778 letter to Reverend Wesley ("tears streaming down their faces").[25] Whether these texts reflect three independent observations or repetitions of a common figuration is perhaps less important than the open recognition of highly emotional expressive practices among blacks, whose enthusiasms could inspire a "shout" and sometimes uplift into song. Surely such behavior had gained widespread notice among white Christians, to the point of compelling the Philadelphia-based African-American minister Richard Allen to defend the "bawling," "groaning," "shouting," and "rolling prostrate on the ground" as practices with biblical precedent.[26]

In "Negro music," Euro-Americans had begun to recognize a discernible creativity that, in its separation from a larger and what was increasingly perceived as a less "musical" America, affirmed the racialized tenets of post-Revolutionary white supremacy. The blackness of African-American performance coincided with the escalating desire to group slaves and free blacks into a hardened racial category that would be administered by a new state presence across the South.[27] An unintentional outcome of this was the way racial supremacy also decentered the exclusivity of an emerging whiteness. By excluding "Negro music" from the common tongue of

American interracial resonance, whites constructed an exclusive domain recognizable as it was inaccessible to their own participation and ownership. Indeed, the emergence of "Negro music" reinforced the sense of a miraculous birth seemingly apart from white experience, and it was out of this understanding that the history of an exceptional black music would proceed. Being the product of an unrecognized, "unconsummated" relationship of black and white, "Negro music" was seen as something at once Godlike and illegitimate. The "child" called "Negro music" may have been born of the United States, the product of a population that, according to the Three-fifths Compromise, could legally claim to be part of the American citizenry and therefore partly human.[28] And yet the reality of that "music," while recognized as such and while growing out of the interracial participation of whites, could never be acknowledged as a fruitful interracial offspring. As a result, its value, power, and invention lay completely with African-America. This odd turn of events would give to blacks a remarkable gift, inadvertent as it was, and one they proceeded to employ in casting a viable place in America. Through "Negro music," and singing in particular, slaves and free blacks alike would locate a means of challenging white mastery by crafting expressions that grew in relation to the very domination of white form.

"A Growing Evil": The Formidability of Black Form   The attribution of a particular social danger to the newly identified black vocal forms was famously put forward in Reverend John Fanning Watson's 1819 publication *Methodist Error.* Still keeping with the official evangelical orthodoxy of post-Revolutionary Methodism, Watson directed his charge not at slave participation per se so much as at the irrefutable evidence of African-American musical influence. In the public performances of blacks at Methodist gatherings (and, in particular, at an event staged outside of Philadelphia in 1817), Watson identified "a growing evil" that had corrupted "the practice of singing in our places of public and society worship." According to Watson, black participants had brought to the revivals and open-air camp meetings by then common across the land a performance style and repertory "scarce one of which were in our hymn books" and accompanied by distinctive practices conjuring relations with the ring shout and African dance. What is more, this repertory was not only performed among white congregants but increasingly borrowed and sung by whites themselves. "In the blacks' quarter," Watson observed in an oft-cited comment, "the coloured people get together, and sing for hours together, short scraps of disjointed affirmations, pledges, or prayers,

lengthened out with long repetition *choruses.* . . . The evil is only occasionally condemned, and the example has already visibly affected the religious
manners of some whites." These repetitions were particularly troubling because they seemed to exceed logic, decency, and sense. Describing the refrain of a revival text, Watson observed in an important, though commonly
overlooked footnote:

"Go shouting all yours days," [is sung] in connection with "glory, glory, glory,"
in which ["]go shouting["] is repeated six times in succession. Is there one participle of sense in its connexion with the general matter of the hymn? [A]nd are
they not mere idle expletives, filled to eke out the tunes? They are just exactly
parallel to "*go screaming, jumping* (or any other participle) *all your days! O
splendour, splendour.*" Do those who are delighted with such things, consider
what delights them? Some times too, they are from such impure sources, as I
am actually ashamed to name in this place.[29]

For Watson, repetitious black singing went far beyond the vocal challenges put forward by northern slaves during the time of the Revolution.
The sound of "the coloured people" had not only taken a discernible form;
it now identified a formidable threat to the sanctity of religious expression,
recalling the tropes of terror and "noise" that had dramatized the travelogues. Black singing revealed the ability of an embodied racial sound, figuratively aligned with Satan, "the Prince of Darkness," to cross over and
enter the bodies of unsuspecting white Christians. Immaterial and form-
less, it nonetheless represented a calculable, decidedly physical danger
enacted as a transference from blackness to whiteness, and this corruption carried grave consequences among the higher ranks of the religious.
Watson's rhetoric brims with the kind of racialism that would characterize
the reproving judgments of patrician classes into the mid-nineteenth century, expressing a social-psychic angst that cast cross-racial encounter in
physical and implicitly sexual terms. The same fear of black voice, moreover, would show itself in other places, such as in the occasional writings
of southern planters and the inventors of Sambo, whose uneasy fantasies
of the contented, singing slave contradicted the more ordinary tragedies of
African-American bondage. But because the musically charged religious forums of the revivals represented a seminal and dynamic stage of interracial
encounter, it was in religion that an antebellum concept of "Negro song"
would first emerge and the varieties of its significance play out. In its bodily origin, religious singing revealed the essential relation of black music—
a creative "Negro" form miraculously contradicting the formlessness of

slavery—and its presentation in the public settings of revivalism did more than any other antebellum cultural project to complicate the purity of racial identities. The growing appeal of singing hymns informed by black performance would, as Watson feared, drive patterns of cultural sharing that corrupted the specificity of whiteness as it threatened to overtake the auditory soundscape of American Christianity as a whole.

The passing comments and reminiscences of a colonial ministry have already shown that African-Americans were participating in Christian ceremonies well prior to the nineteenth century. By the 1790s, slaves' participation had become relatively common in churches and particularly at the services of white Protestants, Baptists, and Methodists, whose quotidian religious practices offered a powerful and influential alternative to a stalled Anglican evangelicalism.[30] Slaves were drawn to these gatherings by the rhetorical power of local clergy, together with the circuit riders, itinerant preachers of modest means, who introduced a plainspoken eschatology to a largely rural populace. The appeal of Christian worship had less to do with blacks' natural affinity to enthusiastic expression than with the viable opportunities for cultural emancipation that an early American Christianity seemed to promise. Espousing the antislavery positions of the religious orthodoxy, evangelical preachers frequently welcomed Africans and African-Americans into their congregations, particularly during the early years of the movement. These gestures would enhance public perceptions of a connection between blackness and grassroots revivalism as the visibility of such rituals spread. Already by the turn of the nineteenth century, blacks (particularly in the South, but increasingly across the land) had begun to assume an unmistakable place in the formation of American Christianity, participating in a cross-racial sharing that, David W. Wills contends, came to identify the exceptional character of the American practice of Christian worship.[31]

If revivalism represented a crucible for interracial exchange, it is unclear the extent to which these exchanges were actually acknowledged and endorsed by white participants. Within the circumstances of a post-Revolutionary society in which racial categories had grown increasingly fixed and significant, it would seem unlikely that even the most zealous white Christians wholeheartedly embraced relations with free blacks and slaves. From the beginning, evidence suggests that whites typically took measures to limit "an unaccustomed—and disturbing—intimacy with blacks," segregating the races in religious forums. By the 1820s and 1830s, these divisions would widen significantly as clergy sought to accommodate the members of the laity (particularly, the wealthy white planters) who supported their churches. Some historical observers have claimed, however, that even as the significance of race increased, the congregations of worshipers represented a special class of people, who, in the words of the former slave, Henry Bibb, "despise slavery and see it as degrading to all." In the same vein, Nathan O. Hatch has proposed that class could ultimately trump race, particularly in determining the character of the truly religious. Representing a common stock of agricultural laborers, the white plain folk who made up the early congregations lived within a religious creed that held "divine insight [to be] reserved for the poor and humble rather than the proud and learned." According to this view, the slave sat closer to God than the landed and wealthy did. If we are, finally, to accept the position put forward by Christine Leigh Heyrman, who argues persuasively that the early evangelicals represented not a majority but a cultish minority existing on the fringes of antebellum society, we can more easily imagine the existence of a narrow sector of the white population for a time transcending the more egregious forms of racism.[32]

Beyond the actual inclinations of early white revivalists, what ultimately matters is the plain fact that interracialism took place in various forums of worship and was conspicuously put into play as a form of vocal contact. Judging from the pattern of development in Christian singing (with a racialized black "difference" emerging out of a stylistically familiar musical terrain), it seems likely that a broad base of engagement evolved against the grain of racial segregation, with whites and blacks influencing one another inadvertently and, to some extent, unconsciously. Because the unusual array of behaviorisms present at revivals—seeing visions, hearing voices, dancing to unsung melodies, wailing, shouting, and falling into trance states—had precedents in Europe as well as in Africa, lower-class whites could have engaged in these expressive practices and still considered them "their own." And the common routine of segregating congregations according to race added to the illusion of clear-cut musical-racial delineations. But such fictional delineations could not, in the end, preclude cross influence among those black slaves and white plain folk performing within earshot of one another. Indeed, one of the most powerful aspects of music is its immediacy of comprehension, however inaccurate that comprehension may actually be. One can make sense of logical patterns of sound without prior training or even knowledge of the people from whom it came. In this crucial way, vocal performance exceeded other expressions in its ability to transcend constraints meant to keep the races separate. As a consequence, stylistic exchanges would inevitably take place, with the more disorderly forms of musical conduct marking the categories of difference that ministers such as Watson would assign to black invention.[33]

A critical step in this process was the infusion of racial imagery into the figurative language of everyday religious speech. Such "figures in black," of course, historically marked acts of sin well before race's invention. But the pervasiveness of the racial crisis in American slave society, together with the efforts of whites to contain the extent and degree of interracial engagement, gave to these conceits an aura associated with slavery and slaves. Rather than determining a one-to-one correspondence of words and race, sins of the unholy appeared color coded, suggesting an underlying linkage with the broad base of racial rhetoric circulating in antebellum culture. References to "demons as black as coal" tempting sinners into "chains of bondage, . . . fettered with the cords of unbelief," visions of the church as an oasis within "the wilds of nature" protecting people from "regions of blackness and unspeakable misery" all served to constitute an allusive racial imagery that would be hard to mistake in a society whose oppressed were named "black."[34] Preachers espousing antislavery views were commonly singled out. As Heyrman observes, their enthusiasms and zealous offerings "did not place them in choice company, for the ranks of those believed to do more than dabble in the powers of darkness also included not only a handful of white witches and witch doctors but many more black conjurers and Indian shamans." As these associations were recognized, they produced considerable anxiety among the "many southern [and northern] whites who may have heard echoed their own fears of interracial communion."[35]

As grassroots worship spread, becoming the subject of journals, slave narratives, and public memoirs, revivalism projected a complex racial symbolism that operated within the scripted contours of antebellum public culture.[36] This symbolism commonly aligned with the widening interest in signs of the fantastic that preoccupied religious-minded Americans. Intersecting with a broad circulation of spiritual discourses, the fantastic became an important dimension within the crosshatch of religious orthodoxy, magical beliefs, and occult practices that engaged the antebellum imagination. Volatile and changing in its interplay of evangelicalism and grassroots occultism, this intricate web of discourse—what Jon Butler has named the "antebellum spiritual hothouse"—fostered a revitalization of spiritualist commitments that inevitably informed black religious worship.[37] In this vast ideological formation, race becomes an informing influence, not as a singular causal factor but as an effect arising out of and thus inherent to a similarly dynamic structure. Witnessing a man who "commenced shaking like a leaf in the wind" during a Methodist sermon, for example, members of a South Carolina community unfamiliar with the phenomenon of being stricken down employed a loosely racial language to describe the preacher, who was seemingly practicing "something magical, or wizardly" and relying on "strange powders" that suggested dual associations with the Romish rituals of Anglicanism and vodun. Another group evoked the character of African travel writing when voicing suspicion that revivalists were engaged in "not merely conjuring tricks but a 'devilish necromancy'" associated with a recently re-Africanized slave population. Writing about a black church service in Philadelphia around 1811, finally, Pavel Petrovich Svin'in, a visiting Russian diplomat and artist, employed a mix of metaphors depicting strangeness when recalling the "dim light" and "ejaculations of the possessed" who "howl with wild and piercing voices."[38]

Operating as part of a broader social configuration, revivalist projections of race would be repeatedly sounded and articulated into elaborate, overlapping webs of meaning. They would join with other social symbols as they appeared figuratively within a dynamic, sonic-textural network, all colliding, interacting, and reproducing one another within the broad contexts of revivalist culture. The significance of race derived from the overwhelming primacy given to racial matters within a larger American political economy increasingly dependent on slave labor and making a case for its perpetuation. Despite this primacy, however, race did not determine antebellum culture so much as represent one analytically specifiable dimension of a broader ideological configuration. The intersections of race and music, moreover, identify a particular concentration of sound and text that aligned multiply, expressing both directly and indirectly (denoting and connoting) the powerful image of a contaminating and affecting blackness. These racio-musical constructs existed within an ideology in which blackness was not always recognized directly and was commonly conflated with other forms of difference and excess. Without reducing antebellum black expressive culture to a singular reality or uniform Euro-American order, then, we can still recognize how instances of interracial commingling at grassroots religious meetings profoundly affected the character of African-American performance as it forever complicated the racial complexion of American music as a whole.

Bound as it was to the social texts of antebellum racial ideology, however, historical black music, as direct presence, continues to elude our grasp. We will not, alas, discover in the historical record an unmediated slave world "within the circle," to recall the crucial insight of Frederick

Douglass. While the evidence of shouts and African funeral rites uncovered by Albert Raboteau, Dena Epstein, Eileen Southern, Josephine Wright, and others highlight realms of African distinctiveness, they inevitably come into focus alongside Euro-American performances or, at the least, through the terminology and conceptions of whites. And even if we ourselves turn to the primary sources, we are forced to accept "second hearings": it is Henry Cogswell Knight who recalls the Congo dances on the green in New Orleans in 1819; it is the correspondence of Arthur Middleton to Henry Franklin that documents some characteristics of black churches; it is "H.," an Englishman, who, in his letter to the *Christian Observer,* describes slave holidays and slave preaching in Virginia.[39] Rather than a pure form of African-American expression, black music, as a premodern historical phenomenon, appears at the contact points of the races, and accordingly must be read between the lines of a still dominant repressive textuality. In the analysis of African-American sacred music we return again to the notion of the palimpsest, as discernible traces are "seen and heard" only through the dominant voices of white mastery. The representations of antebellum black religious music call to mind once again what Walter Benjamin called an "echo of the original," a sonic-textual resonance mediated from the beginning and that accumulates new meanings across history.[40]

What we can locate, however, brings us far beyond the illusory truths typically claimed as the story of black music. And it is from this location that we can begin to speculate more deliberately about slave musical epistemologies later in this chapter. If the immediacy of slave music—the characteristics of style, the details of performance, the manner of reception— is forever lost, what is revealed in the representations (and against Fanon's "first truth") is a formidable interruption of the dominant historical themes claiming the clear bifurcation of racial traditions. The simple fact that whites increasingly recognized in black music a racially determined distinctiveness formed out of the essential relation is enough to conclude that slaves created modes of performance that successfully distinguished themselves from others. At the same time, slaves produced this difference by drawing from the general terrain of performance practices interfacing in antebellum culture. In the most basic terms, then, the acknowledged difference of black singing indicated that assimilation was incomplete, largely due to the mechanisms of creative resistance among those denied creative and intellectual capacities. Slaves, it seemed, had miraculously invented a distinctive music that contemporary racial logic had determined they could not have created, just as that musical distinctiveness, though generally familiar to whites (particularly in southern rural regions), could not be fully accessed without stepping over the bounds of race. The incongruity of race is accordingly the place from which public black music emerges. By crafting an art of inaccessibility and interruption, slaves participated in an ideological contest growing out of the give-and-take of performative political action.

In order to comprehend the wider social significance of black religious sound, we need to consider what is perhaps a more radical configuring of musical significance in the construction of race than has been typical of American social history and American music studies. In documenting antebellum religious events, modern social and cultural historians have tended to perpetuate the stability of racial constructs, inadvertently placing limits on the depth of music's transgressive potential. While openly acknowledging black/white intersections (as has been commonplace over the past thirty years), they have also affirmed the stability of antebellum racial categories, missing the real significance of the very subject that would seem to have drawn their attention.[41] Contrary to the more conspicuously material concerns of social history, I want to suggest that the audible engagements in worship did something more than merely reflect the dominance of tangible base forces of religious orthodoxy within an antebellum slave economy. In fact, these engagements helped to constitute the very sensibilities of historical actors taking part in the making and hearing of the religious experience. In one sense, music performed a conservative function, disciplining and asserting difference. Through religious song, revivalists gave audition to racial categories emerging from a common sonic continuum. Yet because music was, as we have seen, part of a broader aural-textual network, it intersected with other dimensions of culture, complicating those same racial categories. While the participation of African-Americans in Christian settings may not have been enough to claim an overarching hybridity crossing class lines, the associations of blackness with other signifiers of difference enabled racial figures to circulate widely through the activity of performance, demonstrating particular effects in their alignment with the similarly disruptive psychic experiences of conversion and transcendence. Signs generated by black singing combined with other meanings, texturing discourses and entering into the social fabric; indeed, their accumulated effect inspired an expression associated with the Methodists Hugh Bourne and Lorenzo Dow: "You sing like a Primitive."[42] Rather than merely contributing to the repression of blacks, the instability of racial discourses accelerated the interruptive capacities of "Negro sound," contributing to greater public recognition of a seemingly miraculous African-American presence.

Putting an ear, so to speak, to the pages of antebellum religious texts, we begin to discern the echoes of a racially heterodox sacred sound. Through an engagement of the sight-soundedness of revivalism, the auditory experience of a sonic spiritualism comes alive, as in the African-American trope of the "talking book."[43] Early reports and memoirs of the revivals brim with a variety of descriptive metaphors that evoke the sacred power of holy utterance, challenging the common assumption of an "unmusical America." As evangelical writings, the texts—typically produced by white clergy and circuit riders—undoubtedly exaggerate the qualities and nature of musical expression as it was routinely experienced. Still, the frequency and the elaborate nature of sonic imagery in these depictions suggest a peculiarly aural commitment that aligns the otherworldly with music's tropic signatures of difference and transcendence. While only rarely making direct reference to black performances, these depictions are nonetheless important in demonstrating a proclivity to sound that would fuel alignments with African-Americans in the settings of religious performance.[44]

If we were to believe the standard documentation of grassroots Methodists and Baptists, soulful sound could be heard nearly everywhere. Converts could be commanded by disembodied voices, to which "every ear was open" as the convicted found salvation through aural guides and celebrated with rapturous exclamation: "It appeared that none could hear, and not acknowledge the mighty power of God."[45] Preachers were admired for their dramatic and rhetorical skills and, especially, for the qualities of their voices. In the memoirs of William Henry Milburn, we find detailed descriptions of his disciplines for vocal training, recounting mnemonic drills for memorizing lyrics and melodies, together with animated discourses on the qualities of the preaching voice. Toward the end of his life, Milburn spoke poignantly about the nature of physical deterioration, considering which loss was greater, his vision or his voice: "I was a preacher for six years before I gained the power and habit of extempore speech. Great as are my losses in the worlds of nature and of art from imperfect vision, I feel now, as I have ever felt, that incomparably my greatest loss is as a speaker."[46] Writing in 1794, moreover, an elderly Devereux Jarratt engages in a good deal of self-admiration of his own auditory and enunciative capacities: "My hearing being as quick, my ear, relish, and perhaps voice as good for music, as ever." Later, he recalls at open-air meetings his youthful "strength of constitution and soundness of lungs, that, without any disagreeable strain of voice, the farthest off could hear as well as the nearest."[47] Congregations, in turn, frequently joined in conversation about religion, sometimes going "from house to house and convers[ing]," engaged in testifying, "daily crying" or a songful exuberance that often exceeded the halls of worship, emanating into the public space. The frequent "concert of prayer" ("attended three times in a week, and sometimes oftener"), copious and animated conversation ("a dish of chat"), and regular, day-to-day gatherings of rural clusters singing hymns to he who "never turns a deaf ear," all contributed to the impression of antebellum religious practices marked by songful, vocalized resonance.[48]

A particularly useful source for studying the sound of Christian worship in the new nation is *Accounts of Religious Revivals in Many Parts of the United States, from 1815–1818,* compiled by the Albany-based minister, Joshua Bradley. Consisting of a series of letters and reports collected from "persons of piety and correct information," the accounts provide useful insight into the auditory dimensions of religious experience in several eastern communities. As a record of revivals and awakenings of the spirit, these descriptions typically document the emotional "exhortations" that accompanied conviction and conversion. On page after page, the reader encounters a highly stylized set of metaphors in which manifestations of God assume various natural forms: "a mighty rushing wind," "marvellous light," "showers of rain." Occasionally the sensation of Godliness seems more abstract and distant, as in "the thunder of Sinai [that] reached [the] ears" of the awakened. In one instance, the rhetoric suggests a sacred contagion that "spread rapidly from house to house."[49] Most compelling, however, were the figurations of the human voice, which together produced a veritable glossary of enunciation describing the physical experience of a blessed sound's inhabitation. Through voice, the believer became intimately connected to God; it was voice that brought forth Godly presence. "Their prayers were heard," reported one minister, "and the spirit of grace descended upon the vilest of the vile." As the power of the word confronted the sinner, the world awakened in sound, as "the mountains and the hills seemed to break forth before them into singing, and all the trees of the fields clapped their hands."[50]

The peculiar references to bodily anatomy and disembodied, unsung voices reflected the importance of sound in evangelical discourse. Throughout Bradley's compendium, we find a recurring rhetorical strategy of employing sonically inflected figures in order to effect a discernible musicality that related more generally to the religious experience. The congregationalists or "hearers," some "with a still small voice," are sometimes portrayed metonymically as "tongue[s that] uttered praise." When one convert witnessed the Lord, "her liberated tongue now broke out in unknown strains." Another, embracing the love of God, finds "his tongue was loosed to speak with the eloquence of an orator," as "the Lord verified his [own] word by perfecting praise from infant lips."[51] A large group of the awakened around Greensborough "begin to speak, as with new tongues *the wonderful works of God.*" Sinners, moreover, could suffer from the nonsound of unspeaking voices, as in the "conscience that could not be quieted," while others responded with a parallel sense of quiet: "The people heard with attention; and by their profound silence, seemed to yield their assent." No wonder a convicted sinner seeking the way of the Lord could only endure sounding places: "No place, but that in which Jesus was preached, in which his saints prayed, sung and exhorted could now be desired by him."[52]

In these passages we sense that the felt, bodily presence of the Christian God derived not from hearing alone but from the exclamation of the hearer. Multisensory spiritual encounters inspired impassioned vocalizing, effecting a version of the prelinguistic, sonorous "grain" so commonly associated with transcendence. Witnessing others prompted the worshiper to "make a noise," as the feeling of resonant sound in one's chest heightened the sensation of group singing, giving way to the kinds of otherworldly encounters associated with bodily possession and being struck. In a typical depiction, an anonymous woman, under the force of conviction, cried continually "until she lost the power of utterance, and then sat . . . for about one hour, speechless, over the pit of destruction." Through the love of God, however, she then regained her voice and "suddenly burst out in raptures of joy and praise." Another woman, upon conversion, "hardly knew how to spend time" in announcing her awakening. Rather than traversing the community, "to go from one to another to tell them individually, [she] wanted some herald with a trumpet to sound it abroad, that they might all at once hear the glorious intelligence." In the same report, the minister described still another convert, who "was so enraptured with his views of the beauties of the Saviour, that he wanted to be on the house top, and have as many as could hear his voice, collected around him, that he might at once publish to them, the excellency of his glorious character."[53]

In his omniscience, the Christian God at times made his presence known merely through a feeling; he "appeared" invisibly and "spoke" without voice. An account from Wilmington, Delaware, for example, reports a vague, spiritual knowingness among those under conviction. As a preacher asked, "Do you feel so much love for Jesus that you could forsake all for him? . . . the Spirit descended, and every cheek appeared bathed in tears, and many cried, What shall we do to be saved." The holy answer appears as a hymn, received by the congregation and sung.[54] A minister from Eaton, New York, moreover, describes a "sinner" who, during a fitful night, discerns a presence. "Before morning, a spirit seemed to reason with him" about his "iniquity." Under conviction, he ultimately encounters his God as song, and seemingly in a dream: "He who turneth *the shadow of death into the morning, and giveth songs in the night,* appeared for his relief."[55] What may have been pedestrian and routine by day underwent transformation by night, as resonant images of the supernatural suffused sacred testimonies. "The fascination with dreams was nearly universal" across the South, and this fascination traced northward as it acquired a discernible tonal power that reinforced God's sonic materiality.[56]

Among the most vivid imagery appeared in the manuscripts of the northern Methodist preacher Reverend Benjamin Abbott, whose coming to the faith was animated by sound-filled dreams. Abbott's memoirs contain a series of night visions and night sounds that he sometimes "interpret[s]" for his readers according to the themes of conviction and sin. Satanic scorpions riddle his spiritually corrupted body with stings as "they roared like thunder"; "regiments of devils" set fire to the condemned, "the screeches of the damned were beyond the expression of man." In an especially powerful account, Abbott recalls a time when "I awoke, and saw, by faith, the Lord Jesus Christ standing by me." As Christ said, "*I died for you,*" Abbott "cried and praised." Moving in and out of dreams throughout the text, Abbott supplies striking illustrations of sound that heighten the sense of God's effect. At one point, a preacher's spoken "word reached my heart in such a powerful manner that it shook every joint in my body." At another, Abbott recalls his first time praying "with a vocal voice," shouting so loud that "I believe I might have been heard half a mile." At still another, while passing through woods, he hears a satanic message "the devil suddenly suggested to my mind, that as I was one of the reprobates and there was no mercy for me, I had better hang myself and know the worst of it."[57]

For Abbott and the others whose perspectives were constituted within the contexts of antebellum evangelicalism, sound represented a medium of direct spiritual contact; it stood equally with sightings and visions as the means by which the awakened "worked the spirit" in relation to God and to others. For believers, there was something truly miraculous about the capacity of voice to enter one's dreams and carry outward, projecting unconscious significance into waking states. Just as distinctions between sound and sight seemed fluid—anticipations of spiritual sightings, for example, could be discerned initially as "voice"—so could the experiences of day and night, together with the conditions of wakefulness and sleep, inform one another. At the more heightened states of emotion and spiritual angst, the convicted seemed to open up, as voice projected the self's acceptance and embrace into the outer world. Versions of subjective openness and dynamism carried over into everyday religious routines. By reciting together and praying together, congregations experienced a social-psychic bonding that was manifested in song: soulful transgression at the contact zones of the spiritual was discernible, felt, heard.

The striking soundfulness of a body's awakening was, then, what made it susceptible to the spirit's intrusion, as one's vocalizing capacities destabilized the completeness of the subject. Singing and other forms of "making noise" in the presence of the Holy Spirit were not simply uplifting but utterly transforming; through the activities of sounding and hearing, worship assumed a kind of sonic significance, an audible materiality that enabled physical-spiritual transgression and allowed the self to become inhabited by Godly presence. The depictions of "conferences" of "hearers" worshiping and testifying, engaging in repetitious recitation, and joining together in cries of Godly recognition indicate a quality of social intercourse that simulated as it exceeded physical contact. Encounters through voice symbolically created a kind of platonic relation, attaining the level of naturalness ascribed to musical iconicity, as it implicitly acknowledged the power of voice shared across the color line. Musical commingling in fact seemed even more real than reality. Hyperreal, it went beyond literal physical relation in its ability to produce a religious ecstasy or "spiritual high."

It was precisely this vulnerability to social contact in vocal acts of worship that threatened the integrity of social categories of race. Communing in sound opened up the faithful to one another in ways that seemed to allow for a kind of symbolic racial crossing in acts of singing and voicing. And if we observe the emphasis on dreams as relating to the long-standing psychoanalytical notion of repression revealed in the unconscious, the alignment of a dynamic subject and racial encounter proposes a kind of racial nightmare actualized in local life. Music and particularly sacred singing played a crucial role in symbolically articulating a return of the racial repressed. What had been cast out and contained as versions of unrecognizable difference or "noise" in the eighteenth century was now infiltrating white domains, entering dreams and welling up into the conscious states of evangelical Christians. The European archetype of music as an expressive practice unbounded by the limits of time, place, and culture became particularly powerful in its antebellum figuration, representing the experience of displacement and transgression associated with both racial encounter and Christian conversion. Vocalizations of difference emerged as part of the very constitution of spiritual meaning, collapsing musical production and discursive signification. They were the stuff of the sacred that came forth as they helped to construct an "awakened" populace.

Understood this way, the connection between spirituality and race was not simply a musical phenomenon but a peculiarly synaesthetic sight-soundedness that revealed music's extradiscursive capacities and, particularly, its alignment with a racialized sacred experience. Still, the spiritual sightings and possessions were played out most vividly in ritual activities as hearing, giving primacy to the aural, which, more than other modes of perception, produced the felt, bodily experience of Godly contact. The recognition of sacred sounds and voices would commonly accompany or even anticipate visions of Jesus and the Holy Ghost, who, while perceived via the eye, entered the body and was given physically informed truth via the ear. The racial is revealed yet again in the constitution of the religious subject through an intermodal transference of meaning. Figures of transcendence commonly associated with the religious experience were not so much reproduced in song as they were iconically engendered in vocal practices historically associated with metaphysics. What is particularly new at this point is the way a "spiritual song" now signifies otherworldly encounters informed discursively by racial figurations.

One of the more compelling depictions of the iconic significance of racio-spiritual transference involving images of race appears as a record of an American Indian's conversion experience, published in the 1807 account of the circuit rider James Gwin.[58] Gwin presents the account in what he claims to be the very words of "an Indian, of the Chickamauga tribe." However fanciful this claim may be, it nonetheless reflects the conspicuous presence of racial-musical associations in the everyday discourses of antebellum Christians. Gwin's informant explains how, at a camp meeting, he was struck down: "I fell to the ground. While there, blackness came over me." He recovers only when things grow brighter: "I tried to get away, but could not until about daylight." Attempting to leave the meeting, he is overwhelmed by the power of the Christ-embodied voices of worshipers: "When they began to sing, something drew me back." Among the congregation once again, he proceeds, "the same weight came upon me, and the darkness. I fell to the ground, and thought I was about to die." What saves him is the vision of lightness and white-inflected sound. "At last a white man came and talked over me, and while he was talking I got lighter and lighter, and everything looked whiter than the sun could make it look. The heavy load and blackness left me. I felt glad in my heart, and jumped up and felt light."

It is more than happenstance that the anonymous Chickamauga's conversion took place at one of the outdoor camp meetings. These grand displays of religious exuberance, both celebrated and admonished in their own time, have in ours narrated the very idea of a "second great awakening." The meetings demonstrated with a particular urgency the exoticism of the religious ritual, a quality heightened by the interracialism common to many events.[59] From this initial phase and continuing across the antebellum era, camp meetings would draw huge crowds in gatherings, first in the West, then in the South and East. For the rural citizen, the campsites seemed like "temporary cities, with all the diverse people, the bustle, the excitement, and even the personal anonymity of street life." This fabricated cosmopolitanism was, in turn, attractive to many black slaves, whose participation was sufficient enough to perpetuate an interracialism of performance. In his study of the seminal meetings in Cane Ridge, Kentucky, in 1801, which drew several thousand worshipers and observers, Paul Conkin explains that the six-day event extended western limits of interracialism in both worship and preaching. The line of influence, Conkin emphasizes, traveled not only from white to black but also from black to white; it is "wrong in seeing all of the influence flowing in one direction," he insists. "In ways impossible to decipher from the evidence, blacks must have had some effect on southern Presbyterianism—at the very least on hymn singing and possibly on the range of physical exercises accepted at times of revival."[60] Speaking of the Kentucky revivals from a contemporary vantage, moreover, the interfaith minister Richard McNemar described great depths of engagements crossing social categories: "Neither was there any distinction, as to age, sex, color, or anything of a temporary nature; old and young, male and female, black and white, had equal privilege to minister the light which they received, in whatever way the Spirit directed." While blacks were increasingly constrained in their worship, sometimes even being physically removed from previously interracial church congregations, the camp meetings still provided greater license than church rituals for exchange and interaction and continued to do so up until the time of the Civil War. (Indeed, their prohibition and removal from services indicated the fact of prior interaction.) If representing a diverse mix of voyeurs and worshipers, opportunists and convicted soldiers of the cross, the meetings, those "happy compounds of illiterateness and fanaticism," also became critical sites of cultural contact and crossing.[61]

The modes of exchange through which such sharing came about were undoubtedly as wide-ranging as the common course of experience. But the primacy of voice both in white spiritualist communities and in slave societies encourages a critical reading of sound's special role as a promoter of relations across the races. At the revivals, nearly every event had its accompanying vocal expression. Contemporary accounts describe a complex dynamic of religious worship involving simultaneous singing, preaching, praying, and conversing. On the journey to the camp meetings, worshipers sang together, lining and chanting hymns that welled up from paths and roadways. At camp, sound typically commenced the day: "A horn is blown about daylight as the signal for getting up; after a while it sounds for family prayers, and soon you may hear strains of song from every tent, celebrating the praise of Him who hath given the slumber and safety of the night."[62] At the larger events, moreover, several preachers might be orating at once all the while groups engaged separately to pray, to sing hymns, and to soothe through sound the emotionally overwrought or "slain." Recollections from the first decades of the nineteenth century describe African-American preachers who had won considerable approval across the South and whose "wild" displays had a "thrilling effect upon the audience."[63] Just as important, however, were the less dramatic incidents of slaves playing an intimate role in white worship, such as Milburn's recollection of an older slave guiding a young master in public oratory.[64] In nearly all of the interracial meetings during the antebellum era, blacks and whites, if not singing together, assembled within the same range of hearing. As a consequence, worshipers carried home their performance practices as an interracial sound complicated existing forms of singing. The strictures of race were continually interrupted through singing's contacts, even as physical relations remained relatively distinct.

The primary texts documenting the emergence of camp-meeting singing repeatedly refer to an invasive sound that resonated across the sites of performance. In many instances, the writers of these texts focused on the more permissive demonstrations of worship, employing a rhetorical style infused with racial imagery. In his account of "American Fanaticism," for example, the English writer John Lambert describes a camp meeting he witnessed around 1808 in a language recalling the extravagant naturalism of African travel writing. "Their camp meetings are generally held in a wood; deep, dark, lonely, and almost impenetrable, far from any human habitation. The native burghers of the forest are frightened from their wild retreat . . . to make way for these midnight worshipers of the most extravagant superstition. . . . During the daytime dramas and 'midnight orgies,' " Lambert continues (mapping what he claims "is by no means an exaggerated picture"), the crowds of worshipers "began their incantations" as "the cauldron is set a-boiling." "They sleep together in tents" (here possibly paraphrasing McNemar), "old and young, men, women, and children indiscriminately; the vigorous male near the unblushing female; black and white, all together." From these bodies emerged sound revealing deep and profound mergings, as references to sonic and bodily contacts drew a metonymic relation describing the extravagances of worship. Making copious reference to the grand displays of vocalization, Lambert reports that "they make all manner of religious gestures [and] discordant noises." At one of these "diabolical meetings," in which about five thousand were assembled, three converts "cried, bellowed, and roared, like persons in the utmost agony begging for their lives. . . . 'Come, O God, come down immediately and save us, or we shall sink.' These exclamations were repeated in the most vociferous manner for a length of time."[65] McNemar, discussing the revivals in Kentucky, similarly acknowledged the sheer volume of interracial sound carrying from body to body and welling up across a broad geographic terrain. He recalls "hundreds" of strangers "moving uniformly into action . . . some uniting their voices in the most melodious songs; others in solemn and affecting accents of prayer: some lamenting, with streaming eyes, their lost situation, or that of a wicked world; others . . . instructing the ignorant and directing the doubtful and urging them, in the day of God's visitation, to make sure work for eternity; . . . the surrounding forest, at the same time, [was] vocal with the cries of the distressed— sometimes to the distance of half a mile or a mile in circumference."[66]

The spontaneous oral nature of camp-meeting performance greatly heightened the possibility of interracial exchange. While the exact character of these performances went largely unrecorded, the subsequent documentation of repertory, coupled with the accumulation of contemporary accounts, give us some general indication of singing practice. Scholars from Louis Benson to Richard Huffman Hulan suggest that singing grew spontaneously from a corpus of preexisting melodic figures taken from hymns, ballads, popular melodies, jigs, and marches.[67] Because the melodies were well known, they could easily bring together large groups of people, supplying the basis for orally generated improvised group singing. To these melodies and melodic fragments singers cobbled together segments of religious lyrics, typically borrowed from well-known hymns. Sung in repetition, the fragments would constitute extended strophes or verses, marked with a closing phrase. At other times, singers would engage in the "ejaculations" and exclamations that Watson admonished or join together in a hymn lined out by a precentor or preacher. With volumes of simple melodies being sung over the course of a camp meeting, it seems likely that, in circumstances where blacks and whites gathered together, interracial exchanges represented not the exception but the rule. Moreover, the ecstatic character of the practices, so vividly depicted by writers such as John Dixon Long, suggest an African basis, although European uses of similar practices, together with verse/chorus form and jig rhythm, forever confuse these debates.[68] As Dena Epstein and Lawrence Levine have both argued (against the white-invention, black-imitation arguments of George Pullen Jackson), the spiritual songs published subsequently in singing-school tune books documented a previously oral performance tradition of seminal interracial singing. Their separation into distinct (though overlapping) black and white repertories reflected the course of race relations and its impact on musical invention rather than the existence of clear and separate traditions from the beginning.[69]

The wealth of indications of interracialism within antebellum revivalism draws us to the conversion ceremonies themselves. At these moments, which appeared repeatedly over the course of a meeting, those lost in sin and faithlessness would be saved through direct godly encounter. In effecting forms of embodied unities, conversion seemed particularly important as a vehicle promoting racial engagement and, above all, in those common circumstances in which the action of spiritual contact came about as a consequence of vocal performance. Singing would establish a sonic medium for interracial intimacy, creating zones of meaning in which metaphors of racial transgression corresponded to the convergence of godly spirit and humanly flesh. While it is impossible to reconstruct the precise ways in which musical and racial meaning converged in the conversion exercise, we may work inductively from the particular circumstances of antebellum musical life to propose a racial quality to religious encounter. Indeed, the sheer fact of musical interracialism taking place within the circumstances of racial apartheid effects a sense of the miraculous complementing spiritual awakening: the miracle of spiritual song arises from the uncanniness of an impossible unity built on a seemingly incommensurable racial difference. Without proposing a one-to-one correspondence of racial transgression and spiritual conversion, we can entertain as part of the tale of black music's emergence one possible reading of the racial variety of religious experience, a reading that gains credibility from the corpus of prior circumstantial evidence of racial-religious intersection cutting across antebellum revivalism.

The conversion ceremony identified the key moment of instability and the apogee of the camp events. It was a form of ontological sacrifice through which a critical encounter with Jesus brought on a transformational shift in one's sense of being and belonging. According to the typical account, the sinner arises from a prior state of conviction, frequently an extended period of suffering in which he or she confronts the moral teachings of Jesus (brought on by visions, sounds, dreams) and, by the time of the ceremony, admits human failing. Conviction could and did destroy individuals who never found their way beyond a condemned state. But the psychic angst also seemed to play a functional role in heightening emotion and making one open to the physical and behavioral excesses commonly associated with conversion. Of all the camp-meeting rituals, these ecstatic states or "physical exercises" were in their representations most closely aligned with race, their trance settings and spiritual articulations recalling the texts of "tribal" cultures—of those unlike "us."[70] While representations do not necessarily communicate the actuality of presentation and experience, the depictions drew from the web of discourses that circulated across antebellum spiritualism and to this extent indicate a possible dimension of the figurative language in which encounters were themselves constituted. In making new and future selves out of the sins of the past, worshipers realized psychic transformations that, in the most profoundly spiritual terms, marked a becoming of something other.[71]

Ecstatic singing and other acts of vocal drama were what commonly brought the sinner into a heightened state where one could access holiness. Encountering godly spirit, victims were said to describe biblically inspired visions of heaven and hell, of Jesus and the Holy Ghost. The sonic drama would soon unfold as "singers and praying persons" surrounded the "slain," providing comfort with healing song as they also accelerated the physical exercises. A spectator at Cane Ridge, Colonel James Paterson, offers this gripping testimony of the sounds accompanying rituals of worship and conversion.

Assembled in the woods, ministers preaching day and night; the camp illuminated with candles, on trees, at waggons, and at the tent; persons falling down, and carried out of the crowd, by those next to them, and taken to some convenient place, where prayer is made for them; some Psalm or Hymn suitable to the occasion, sung. If they speak, what they say is attended to, being very solemn and affecting—many are struck under such exhortations. But if they do not recover soon, praying and singing is kept up, alternatively, and sometimes a minister exhorts over them—for generally a large group of people collect, and stand around, paying attention to prayer and joining in singing. Now suppose 20 of these groups around; a minister engaged in preaching to a large congregation, in the middle, some mourning, some rejoicing, and great solemnity on every countenance, and you will form some imperfect idea of the extraordinary work![72]

Judging from the existing record of camp-meeting singing, participants at these events likely engaged in the spontaneous call-and-response practices that, most scholars assume, lie at the heart of the camp-meeting hymn, for which "rough and irregular couplets or stanzas were concocted out of Scripture phrases and every-day speech, with liberal interspersing of Hallelujahs and refrains."[73] While one could be struck without accompanying song, it was in these vocalized environments that contact with a godly presence often took place, reinforcing the sense, once again, that singing created a sensibility or environment appropriate for spiritual inhabitation, establishing the precondition for an individual to embody sacred immanence. Singing, together with other forms of vocal utterance—prayer, heightened speech, a preacher's emotional rhetoric—amplified the sense of spiritual awakening by destabilizing the solid ground of rational, conventional experience. As the songful utterances of Christians merged with the physical "cries and groans" of the struck, worshipers could be transported in a vibrant responsorial interchange of sonic-sensuous contact. It was at these sound-drenched moments of psychic precariousness that the bodily affecting force of "spiritual" encounter could produce within the frames of interrracial singing a momentary glimpse of racial transcendence.

Blackness, in this way, did not represent for white worshipers an obvious signature determining the conversion experience, according to some elementary mode of signification. Rather, as a critical symbol in an antebellum economy of slavery, it imbued sound with racial inflection, opening up an expansive interpretive range. Within that seemingly endless range, let us consider two basic possibilities. One can imagine how, for instance, the embodiment of racialized song could relate the transcendent qualities of spiritual encounter to miscegenation. The convert realizes a "unity" in which religious transcendence corresponds to a process of racial transgression, whereby disruption of the logic of racial incommensurability heightens the power of conversion overall. Following the tale of the Chickamauga, in contrast, we can locate what would have been perhaps for many whites a more dominant mode of experience, in which conversion identified the path away from the sins of blackness. Even in this instance, however, the acquisition of white purity is racialized through the negative force of blackness whose place is insistent, essential. Singing racially hybrid song becomes a way of passing through the categories of race in order to transcend them in the name of a deracinated (white) godliness. Accordingly, white racial purity derives from the acknowledgment of a relational difference that is deferred and thus denied. In most cases among whites, the experience of performance in interracial religious circumstances probably shimmered between these two extremes, yet rarely could race be entirely eliminated from its comprehension.

The conversion experience of African-American slaves is even more uncertain, and no single gesture could possibly hope to establish a reasonable description of the enormous diversity taking place within that category of people named "Negro." In comprehending the possibilities of song's miraculousness, however, such speculations are nonetheless crucial; finding meaning in a record of absence requires a leap of faith, yet one studied and consistent with both the historical evidence and present strategies of cultural interpretation. We gain a particularly useful critical apparatus from the seminal work of Hortense Spillers, whose reflections on the black worship service establish a contemporary standard for interpreting other aspects of African-American performance. Spillers's attentiveness to the acts of listening and singing serves to propose a strategy for understanding music's role in slave cultures that at once acknowledges the impossibility of historical certainty and the necessity of its consideration. Spillers is insistent that the facts of the black religious past and the slave spiritual world can only be rendered through a mediated textuality. "We are trapped," she writes, "somewhere between the church doors and the library." Still, she contends, these fictions are a necessary part of storytelling: "we *need* the fiction of 'community' in order to speak at all." A reading of the historical documents is accordingly something one "makes up" within and against the inventions of a dominant white culture. For Spillers, the essential fiction is that of a community as a "critical mass" that is at once distinct within the United States and divided from African origins. This is the "*hyphenated* national identity in the first instance both from its new situation and severed from the old one." In the circumstance of conversion, this "hyphenated" identity proceeds not as a stable twoness, but as a kind of simultaneity of cross-racialism effecting a distinctively black sense of dynamic placelessness. Ironically, it is from this precarious state that forms of cultural and spiritual coherence are realized in the services of black Christian worship.[74]

At the helm of devotional singing and the ritual of conversion was the slave preacher, who assumed a special position among the devoted as much for his vocal command as for his insights into the faith. The preacher's skill and holiness carried from his personal relation with the songful life, distilling a special insight or "second sight" constituted out of acts of speaking and singing. The most effective preachers, as several authors have observed, demonstrated a creative oppositionality, engaging in a vocal play that danced across the orthodoxies of white expectation.[75] Crafting their sermons and tales from the mix of local sound and experience, they projected an artistic rendering of the audibility and significance of the slaves' plight and, in this way, provided to those denied a position in the world some gesture toward a viable sense of place. Place in this sense was not a physical realm or restricted territory specified by the master but the terrain of a self responding to the echo of that prior miracle of production: the empirical proof of the slave subject heard in the singing voice. "The sermon," Spillers argues, "as the African-American's prototypical mode of public speaking, locates the primary instrument of moral and political change within the community." It not only "catalyzes" movement but "*embodies* it, is *movement*."[76] Within the responsorial engagements of preacher and laity, black folk could claim through the force of sound a particularity or ground whose value and nature were necessarily interconnected to the conditions of mastery that set the contours of these very acts of self-making. In affirming the dynamic placelessness of the slaves' position, the exhorter gave form to the sound logic of slave exceptionalism growing out of the relation of master and slave, drawing in congregations to the give-and-take of group worship.

"Drawing in" defines the constitution of what Spillers names the sermon's "hermeneutic narrative." In its practice, participation is prescribed: "Everyone is compelled toward the same story." The use of repetition and formulaic structure and phrases—qualities identified by Spillers and others as antebellum in origin—sonically inspire an intimacy among the congregation, as sound constitutes as it reflects a "*fellowship* of belief." During the act of soul-filled worship, these sounds enter the listener's body, as "place" becomes part and parcel of the constitution of self. "The sermon," Spillers writes, "seeks to *inculcate* its words, to make them enter the hearer, and this would account for the rhetorical tenacity of the form." Repetition in this sense was enabling, as singing becomes a key means of cultural production, of actualizing imagined black wholes. The significance of the sermon derives from its interpretive capacity or hermeneutic power to paste over the complexities of so many divided selves and their varieties of experience.[77] By repeating the same story time and again, the sermon constitutes mythical, circular wholes, the veritable "masteries of form" that, employing Houston Baker's Barthesian notion, describe modern virtuosity. While multiple and variable, these "complex wholes" of mastered form establish individually real senses of black difference: sound invents subjectivity and racial identity. The sermon is in effect working within the tradition of the biracial camp-meeting conversion ritual to heal the hyphenated circumstances of an unhealable wounding. Worshipers, in turn, conduct an exercise in self-healing, as song gives form to the unfathomable, through which the convert receives in his or her body a momentary insight into that which exceeds comprehension. Such is the time lag of the songful slave sublime that identifies an antebellum black place emerging out of slavery's essential relation.

One might accordingly think of conversion's state of the fantastic as a kind of translation that draws in associations with racial encounter. Translation in this sense is not meant to convey a literal reproduction of one text as another but a radical ontology through which difference emerges from an irresolvable and tentative social ground and proceeds into history—expressing what Walter Benjamin proposes in appropriately mystical language as translation's sublime "after-life."[78] Figured this way, translation conveys a sense of the immediacy of "first contact" with the indecipherable as it underscores the textually based discourse network from which its romantic conception took shape. It is an uncanny recognition of wholeness in the discovery of the unfathomable even as the individual remains within the inherent partiality of a world of difference. For discovery involves an action that grows from instability. The instability of action, by turns, reveals translation's performative nature, what Homi Bhabha names "the performativity of translation as the staging of cultural difference."[79] In this particular configuration, translation becomes a dynamic instability that draws toward encounter with the unknown, effecting the immaterial place of the sublime. The conversion experience is mimetically related to discourses of the aesthetic sublime within the antebellum "spiritual hothouse." It is a phenomenology at once beautiful and tragic, suggesting a compression of life experiences that brings together opposite extremes of affect. The stagings of the camp meetings locate a double-level encounter with the unknowns of religion and race, as racial and spiritual "passing" join as dominant modes of discovery brought together in sound. The inbetweenness of conversion-as-translation is the sounding place where racial and spiritual instabilities intersect.

Such a characterization, finally, might suggest that the bombastic depictions of camp-meeting conversions were something more than sorry attempts at ethnographic representation. Seen this way, the curious dramas appear to be pointing toward the depths of racial mimesis taking place in the creative production of sound. While some writers noted quieter, more controlled gatherings, so many more described the dramatic exploits and emotional excesses. They seemed to be moved by them as much for their moments of racial exchange as for their sacraments of Christian devotion.

While these sources are unreliable as literal documentary evidence, they serve nonetheless as murky, blemished etchings of a critical moment of racial engagement written under erasure. For it was at these moments that black and white subjectivities were so susceptible to each other's influence, inspiring writers to attempt to capture something of the music's racial effect. From this perspective, we might say that the soundtexts of sacred singing reveal the countenance of race projected on the many details of the camp-meeting rituals. They bring into sight and hearing the convergence of voice and blackness as an overlay, as an informing originary force that generated a constant flood of references to contact and mimesis. In these "forest sanctuaries" of the wild, revivalists and their interpreters imagined a return to a primary humanity, to a basic sentience of being that would transcend race via music's power. Beneath the sky "radiant with golden stars, like glories of Heaven streaming through the apertures of the concave," worshipers complicated through singing and encounter the emerging ideologies of race, acknowledging, if not cherishing, black value. Here, the power of "Negro music" would emerge and for the first time be publicly acknowledged and received.[80]

We can conclude, then, that musical exchanges at the early camp meetings were sufficient in both racial directions to recommend reorienting scholarly inquiry to matters beyond the still dominant "question of origins." Constituted as they were in the inherently dialogical terrain of interracial vocality, spiritual songs could not have been anything but a cross-cultural mixture.[81] Accordingly, if we were to pursue the search for a racially specified origin, we would need to ignore the many vocal intersections and observe history through a monocular lens—to craft inquiry so as to perpetuate the racialist presuppositions that continue to limit African-American musical scholarship. What seems far more important is to explore the reasons why and the processes by which the seminal religious performances evolved from an interracial diversity or "sameness" into forms distinguishing between black and white, even as musical intersections across racial boundaries continued. If the camp meetings at the turn to the nineteenth century represent crucibles of musical and racial intersection, then what becomes essential is identifying the ideologically informed musical signifiers or "soundtexts" that developed according to racial category through the antebellum era. Among slaves, the seminal performance practices became influential within both religious and secular expression in a predominantly oral culture. These markers reflected the continuing cross-racial performative exchanges together with the ideological constraints that established musical notions of difference. The constitution of black singing as a formal difference named "Negro music" creates a metaphysical common sense that denies prior racial contact, as interracial sameness fades under the power of white writers and writing.

The Racial Formation of "Negro" Musical Difference   Out of the originary wellspring of southern Christian expression arose a musical distinctiveness that would be attributed specifically to the African-American slave. Even as blacks and whites lived together, worshiped together, and listened and responded to each other's preaching and performing, an emerging public rhetoric of difference simultaneously sought to specify legacies of musical practice on racial grounds. These stylistic representations of white and black developed from as they reinforced New World racial ideologies stemming as much from the frames of culturally based perception as from patterns manifest in sound. Yet however fabricated they may have been, the musical specifications nonetheless supplied the means of actualizing differing cultural patterns that would repeatedly divide and intersect. The body of textual reference that emerged over the first half of the nineteenth century documents musical significations of blackness that grew increasingly familiar as modes of racial self-identification. By the 1830s, these signifiers would begin to circulate freely; by the 1840s and 1850s, they would proliferate rapidly to the point of specifying a formulaic outline of black practice. Determinations of difference were important in a highly self-conscious way to whites whose perspectives grew as part of the modern ideologies of race informing (as they were constituted by) black music. But they also affected the consciousness of southern African-American slaves in setting constraints that influenced performance and, in turn, senses of belonging and experience. If slaves generated their own modes of music making out of the circumstances of black-to-black encounter in everyday life and labor, so did they continually shape these approaches within and against the parallel performances and receptions of whites. What we might name "slave aesthetics" (and related notions of sublime experience) emerge from this dynamic interstitial relation.

The sounds of blackness welled up from the variety of performance places mapping out antebellum slave cultures. Imagined together, they conjure veritable waves of resonance, the intricacies of which expressed a diversity of sound logics informing African-American life in the South. These musical logics developed from the immateriality of slavery itself. Left with few resources beyond subsistence, slaves held onto and crafted into group artistry productions of value that masters could not so easily claim: the ineffable, ungraspable force of black utterance. In the chronicles of southern slavery, African-American sounding practices trace across the page, animating narratives as they document a power and presence so easily overlooked in more literal readings of the American past. The audibility of black difference supplied African-Americans with this curious immaterial force that, in defining self and crafting identity, carried real-life discernibly material effect.

A portion of the documentary evidence comes from white southerners who interrupted the comfortable silence about slave sounding common to the commentaries of their forebears. While continuing publicly to deny the viability of slave humanity, planters and other occasional writers acknowledged a new black presence of musical form and, in doing so, changed the course of eighteenth-century omission. Expressing a sense of familiarity and attachment consistent with antebellum black-white relations, whites increasingly spoke to the musical inventiveness of African-Americans, whose fiddling, patting, and vocal expressions had found a place in the normal course of daily experience. Typically, the musical indications appeared as passing asides, such as the reference to slave songs in the midst of a planter's record or the description of singing practices in an agricultural journal. When a southern planter employed musical figures to propose slave happiness in refutation of the abolitionist claims of Harriet Beecher Stowe—"the music [of slaves] . . . made the hills and dells of Virginia vocal with its merry notes"—he also acknowledged the power of African-American creativity and its impact across the land.[82] However oblique or inadvertent these references may have been, they provided a sense of the multitude of performative expressions that came to define the southern auditory soundscape. While seeking to deny African-American intellect and to situate slave creative expression within the routines of nature and labor, these commentaries revealed a greater significance in suggesting the sheer omnipresence of a discernible black voice. In this way, the social resonance of black sounding practices that textured public spaces identified a new dimension of music miracle making extending from an eighteenth-century origin.

For the most part, antebellum accounts of African-American performance were written by northern and foreign travelers who visited the southern states as part of their national tours. The chronicles supplied the greatest body of testimony about the remarkable range of slave sounding practices and their conspicuousness in everyday lives. The performances were typically identified as extempore events that signified to whites the spontaneity, liveliness, and unpredictability attributed to the Negro character and that appeared to carry across the broad geography of southern culture. Black sound seemed nearly everywhere, from the cities of Virginia to the plantations of Mississippi, to the intricate waterways of the Sea Islands. Writers supplied new evidence of African-American instrumental approaches. Slaves, we are told, played the banjo but most commonly the fiddle, which represented the instrument of choice in slave quarters and among the whites for whom they performed.[83] Slaves also employed homemade instruments such as the jawbone ("from which they get quite varied sounds"), tin horns, makeshift trumpets, and even one's own body, as in the practice of patting: "Generally, however they have no instruments, but dance to the tunes and words of a leader, keeping time by striking their hands against the thighs, and patting the right foot." Moreover, slaves could be found making music in the unlikeliest places, such as on a stagecoach, where a driver coaxed his horses by playing a fiddle.[84] While references to drums appear, they are rare, limited mainly to performances in New Orleans's Congo Square and to the European-style martial drumming that accompanied parades in Charleston and some northern cities. In many of the references to black instrumental performance, finally, dance appears, so much so as to suggest a kind of symbiosis that complicates easy distinctions between music and accompanying physical demonstrations. What we now call "slave music" may have represented the sonic evidence of a more complex performative gesture that incorporated a variety of bodily action, from singing to stepping to acting out.

It was the slaves' vocal performances that most frequently caught the attention of southern visitors and gained a multitude of renderings. Writers marveled over the ingenuity of vocal expression and the power that it conveyed. Representations covered nearly every possibility of utterance. Slaves whistled, preached, shouted, hummed quietly alone, collectively improvised their own songs, and sang enthusiastically both in quartets and large groups. They sang in leisure and labor, in cotton fields, in tobacco factories, while navigating rowboats along the Carolina rivers and shores, filling the environment with a kind of southern "water music." Some slaves imitated the sounds of musical instruments. In her record of a trip aboard a steamer near New Orleans, Barbara Leigh Smith Bodichon, an English diarist, observed how "they imitate musical instruments very well—so well that for the first time I thought it was an instrument, though I could not conceive of what." Others imitated the sounds and behavior of animals, as the former slave, James Watkins describes in his narrative of 1852. The "peculiarity" of blacks' vocal effects, moreover, encouraged some observers to perpetuate the assumed evolutionary linkages of Negroes and animals—

"monkeys without tails," as one novelist put it. In his recollection of a tour of the South, Frederick Law Olmsted conflated bestial and human sounds of nature, of "two negroes with dogs, barking, yelping, shouting and whistling after 'coons and 'possums.' " In the same essay, he portrayed black voicing as a veritable act of nature. Recalling his first encounter with "The Carolina Yell," Olmsted described a group of yodelers that "raised such a sound as I never heard before; a long, loud, musical shout, rising and falling . . . [their] voice[s] ringing through the woods in the clear, frosty night air, like a bugle call."[85]

As portrayed in the historical record, slave vocal sound seemed to reverberate nearly everywhere, to the point of infiltrating public spaces in which blacks were otherwise absent. Recalling the depictions of camp meetings, the texts documenting slave singing describe a sonic power that had overwhelmed the southern soundscape, and in its omnipresence, assumed a sacred Godlike presence. Such associations with the religious were suggested in two otherwise secular accounts of black singing from the early part of the nineteenth century. Approaching a wharf around 1821, an English traveler recalled the uncanny experience of hearing the disembodied voices of African-American laborers who sang near the water while stowing cotton. Another writer, Francis Hall, an English lieutenant, described a visit to the city of Norfolk in the mid-1810s. While on the street, he paused "when my ears were assailed by the voice of singing, turning around to discover from what corner it came, I saw a group of about thirty negroes [in a coffle] . . . singing a little wild hymn, of sweet mournful melody, flying by a divine instinct of heart, to the consolation of religion, the last refuge of the unhappy, to support them in their distress."[86] Subsequent depictions elaborated on the religious effect of the slave voice, intensifying the sense of an otherworldliness inhabiting southern life. In his recollection of a visit to a Richmond tobacco factory, Samuel Mordecai adopts the language of religion, as if a dreamy spirituality exceeding the common bounds of worship had overtaken everyday secular life. Comparing a factory, that paragon of industry and capitalism, to the church formerly on the same site, Mordecai remarked, judging from "the sounds that proceed from within its walls, might it be mistaken for [a cathedral], . . . for many of the negroes, male and female, employed in the factories, have acquired such skill in psalmody and have generally such fine voices." The sense of a certain religiosity informing the most common labor practices even entered into a passing reference to a slave lining out a hymn as he dug a ditch. If in part intended to mock slave behavior, the commentary only strengthened the sense of an inherent, otherworldly slave musicality reaffirming the bounds of race.[87]

Over the course of the antebellum era, depictions of black singing became more and more grandiose, as an evocatively "spiritual" slave voice assumed a proportion consistent with the figure of the miracle ascribed to eighteenth-century performances. Witnesses in the 1830s wrote passionately, "none wanted voice: they all had it, and to spare." "They possess powerful voices, which can be heard for miles."[88] By the 1850s, writers were extolling the expressive virtues of black singers, as a minister from Maryland reports: "The Negro is as full of music as an egg is full of meat; and music is allied to poetry and eloquence." In a fictional account of an Algerian subject touring the United States, moreover, Mrs. Frances Harriet McDougall depicted slave performance in the familiar language of nature: slave song "is the bird-song, that goes beyond the bloom. . . . It is the human heart-song . . . subliming spirit."[89] These vocal talents also informed the telling of stories by the evening campfire. Lewis W. Paine recalls that the slaves "tell stories, and joke and laugh awhile. At last they get to making all the different noises the human voice is capable of, all at the same time— each one of each party doing his best to win victory." The vocal virtuosity of slaves so impressed southerners and visitors alike that after a while white expressions seemed to grow weary and nearly silent. In his account of experiences traveling the Missouri and Mississippi Rivers, the Swiss artist Rudolph Friedrich Kurz recalled that "whatever singing one hears in the West is usually among the Negroes. The [white] American, who is not of a musical temperament as are the French and Germans, rarely devotes his vocal powers to anything more than psalms." Among the slaves, "there is no silent path for them."[90] This complex figuration of a religious-inspired slave voice would give expression to the idea of the "spirituals" that consumed northern abolitionists by the time of the Civil War.

The disproportionate number of references to the otherworldliness of slave singing speaks to the pervasive aestheticization of politics of which black music became emblematic. In slave song, white observers rarely heard a common, mundane expression consistent with Euro-western experience, even though records from the camp meetings to mid-century depictions of southern life suggest that black singing was both routine and familiar. What they perceived instead were sounds mapping the excesses of human emotion—"loving the extremes," as the seventeenth-century English Chaplain, Lancelot Addison, put it—from the heights of ecstasy to the depths of tragedy and loss.[91] Conceived as a performance of humanity's excesses, black music provided a way of deferring the most challenging and potentially disruptive circumstances of American politics: the ideology of race and its attendant realities in slavery. More than a divertissement or form of light entertainment, slave song, in its various projections, established the discursive ground upon which matters of civilization and nation could most safely be registered and debated. As a sonic projection arising from the non-sense of African-American culture and accessible to all discerning listeners, however, "Negro song" proved a formidable challenge, exacerbating the instability of the white racial self. The formation of black music as difference would become consistent with the groundlessness and insecurity of white nationhood, producing a kind of white double consciousness that would undo the security of the masters themselves.

One important formulation of slave singing as a politics of sound appeared in the antebellum romances that cast "Negro" expression according to the image of slaves' cheerfulness. Acknowledging tropes of natural feeling that trace back to colonial accounts, writers beginning in the 1830s would cast the familiar portrait of Sambo that depended heavily on a sonic dimension. As they were commonly received, these portraits certifying the literally homegrown or "home-born" musical character of the "vernacular slave" helped to justify the practices of slavery.[92] English and northern writers, in turn, played a central role in transmitting the musical formations of slave authenticity, thereby helping to make them conspicuous in broad terms. "Their voices are rich and melodious," a Mrs. Felton pronounced; a second writer, Matilda Houstoun, speculated, "I think that some of the most harmonious sounds I ever heard have proceeded from the lips of young negro girls." Singing happily proved their contentment as music making became the new signature of black accommodation. For one southern planter, the gift of song could be traced to a physical quality that logically precluded comparable skills among whites. "Niggers is allers good singers nat'rally. . . . I reckon they got better lungs than white [folk]."[93] If slaves, as antebellum texts claimed, were "singularly cheerful and good humoured" people—the "happiest creatures in the world"—who "will sit up all night singing if permitted," then slave labor could only assist in their "intense instinct for music and time."[94]

With the rise of blackface minstrelsy, images of the contented slave overwhelmed American public culture, firmly situating the perception of black song as a form of musically generated slave happiness. In donning blackface, white actors had committed a kind of cultural larceny or what Eric Lott calls desire-based "theft": they had not only tarried the honor of slave expression but also, in assuming a rightful access, recast its meaning altogether; by the 1830s, slave song had become something "rich in black fun." In their efforts to counter the enormity of blackface propaganda, moreover, abolitionists, when referring to slave music, routinely proposed a contrary view, insisting that these songs expressed sorrow and pain. The challenge, put forward already in accounts of African travel such as those of Olaudah Equiano, appeared sporadically in antislavery publications, including William Lloyd Garrison's *Liberator* and in the slave narratives. The narrative of Aaron, for example, challenged the Sambo stereotype, explaining "but we are further told that slaves show by their actions that they are happy. They sing, laugh, and make merry. He is a shallow smatterer in human nature, who does not understand this, that mirth is rather often the effort of the mind to throw off trouble than the evidence of happiness."[95]

The theme of sorrow was also featured in the creative acts of fugitive slaves, who performed "authentic" plantation songs in order to convey the trials of bondage. While giving a more accurate depiction than minstrelsy's incessant claims of slave happiness did, these testimonies outlined an opposite emotional extreme that served to reinforce the political suppositions of abolitionist audiences. The common practice of textual borrowing in the accounts themselves prompts a certain skepticism about their originality of form. One lyrical text published in the *National Anti-Slavery Standard* in 1844 was attributed to Henry Bibb, "who was at the Akron Convention, sung it, in connection with several others, with great effect." This same text shows up, unattributed, five years later in the narrative of the former slave and slave driver William Wells Brown. A similar transposition accompanies the reproduction of "eyewitness" accounts of slaves singing and playing fiddles in a coffle, reprinted several times over the course of the antebellum period. In this light, it might be wise to heed Zora Neale Hurston's observation about the dangers of oversimplifying the complexity of slave musical meaning, which she directed toward her Harlem Renaissance colleagues. Speaking specifically of slave songs, she writes: "The idea the whole body of spirituals are 'sorrow songs' is ridiculous. They cover a wide range of subjects from a peeve at gossipers to Death and Judgment." Just the same, the repetition of the conceit of the singing coffle reinforces the sense of an intercultural practice witnessed and even instigated by whites that publicly conveys a singularity of meaning, at least within the frames of literary and political representations of the "slave experience."[96]

The twin projections of excess, mapping extremes of hilarity and horror, were incommensurable with the actualities of slave life. Neither could have possibly captured the complexity of a broad, multiply textured experience, although we can assume that the theme of tragedy came far closer to the truth than the perverse fictions of happiness. As discourses, however, they shared a common role in depicting slave sensibilities according to the outer limits of the antebellum notion of black difference. Conceptualizing realms beyond the ordinariness of the "common" white experience, these racialized portrayals of excess introduced into secular circumstances a version of the religious as aesthetic sublime, conflating unspeakable ecstasy and terror as the twin poles of romantic drama. Over the course, the images became so intertwined and doubled as to confuse the simple binaries of proslavery's happiness and the abolitionist's projections of tragedy. Minstrel performances, for example, had acquired by the 1850s themes of slave suffering that accommodated and surely influenced the mood of sentimentality surrounding midcentury popular song, from Stephen Foster's *Old Folks at Home* (1851) to Henry Clay Work's *Grandfather's Clock* (1875). Dialect and comic stereotypes of the minstrel show, in turn, informed antislavery tracts, which documented lyrics of suffering and occasionally revealed a contempt for black manners consistent with the most offensive white racist. Together the images of excess reinforced the quality of whiteness that Euro-Americans sought to affirm and protect. The peculiarities of "Negro singing" not only stabilized a modern conception of blackness but in its negation what whiteness was not. In its race making, it seemed a miraculous force at the leading edge of blackness's constituting powers.

Drawing in line the disparate figures of racial difference was the trope of the natural musician, a conceit that embodied the exceptional qualities of slave music to the point of defining black character for the next one hundred–odd years. In his happiness, in her pain and sorrow, the slave voiced a certainty of emotion and feeling that precluded the possibility of intellect, something that was assumed to be beyond blacks' capacities. By demonstrating natural musical gifts, blacks rose to a higher power of awareness just as they were effectively removed from the frames of Euro-Western civility. Such thinking among whites was pervasive across the political spectrum. According to Lewis W. Paine, for example, a white southern school teacher who spent six years in prison for aiding the escape of a slave, "if there is a people whom, above all others, the gods themselves have made musical, [blacks] are entitled to the distinction. They hold the mirror up to nature; nay, it is nature's self displayed so fully, and with such graphic power." In their closeness to nature they experienced a kind of pleasure and freedom. "The naturally fine voice and ear for music which seems to have been given to the black race" enabled them "to sing for want of thought." Singing naturally, they seemed to John Pendleton Kennedy the most "happily constructed human beings I have ever seen." And because these qualities were inborn, providing slaves with "better lungs," blacks could not help but possess a musically based gaiety.[97]

The physical superiority of blacks suggested a certain logic of performance that increasingly relegated whites from the nation's public stage.
Given that "the colored people are naturally strongly addicted to music
and dancing," they would, George G. Foster predicted in 1849, ultimately
claim sole possession of the artist's role. "The stage . . . will be eventually
occupied by colored actors and actresses, singers, dancers and instrumental performers, [as] . . . the African race [finds its] power to rise to its
natural level." Around this same time Fredrika Bremer, on witnessing a revival, reasserted the connection between the two Negro natures of religiosity and musicality according to the theme of nationhood, thereby
complicating racial divisions and the security of whiteness. As the sound
of a people naturally disposed to religion, "Negro singing" embodied the
very spirit of America; "their own songs [are] the only original folk-songs
that the New World possess[es]." Such stereotypes were also quite under-
standably embraced by slaves themselves, notably Platt Epps, the fiddler
and writer who would publish under the name, Solomon Northrup. In his
narrative, he suggested that "the African race is a music-loving one,
proverbially; and many there were among my fellow bondsmen whose or-
gans of tune were strikingly developed, and who could thumb the banjo
with dexterity." By the 1840s, figures of musical difference had come to occupy the dominant modes of racial discourse, granting to slaves an exceptional status that logically positioned their voices, if not their selves, at the
center of public conceptions of nation.[98]

The power ascribed to slave music helps to explain the ridicule that frequently accompanied the most sympathetic portraits. Alongside the volumes of praise that accompanied slave song into public culture are those
commentaries suggesting an emphatic retreat from full embrace. Like the
contradictory "Love and Theft" that Lott observes, the texts of the slave
songs record a similar irony. Even within the most vehemently antislavery
texts, one recognizes a disdain for blacks that unmasks racialist sentiments. For with each sign of praise there appears an accompanying expression of contempt, whether overtly voiced or indicated with greater
subtlety. Slaves may have been natural singers, but this prowess owed to
no special claims of intellect, for, as a whole, "they seemed like stupid insensible beings." If Bremer admired the vocal skills of religious blacks, she
could also revel in the pleasures of "bananas, negroes, and negro songs"—
"the greatest refreshments of the mind"—and make passing judgment of a
preacher who "had a countenance which bore a remarkable resemblance
to an ape."[99] "Negro singing" proved a closeness to nature that could lead
the religious-minded white toward ecstasy and wonder. But so did this

depth of feeling seem to preclude the acquisition of reason and intellect. As such, in his noble primitiveness, the "Negro" expressed a doubleness concocted in the white racial imagination. The splendors of transcendence bore witness to the horror of a savage primal end. The slave's song seemed at once to combine moral righteousness and the grotesque, the loveliest sounds with a wicked and diabolical utterance. "It was difficult to believe that tones of such angelic sweetness really issued from such unangelic-looking lips," said a bemused visitor to a northern camp meeting, "But the sweetest birds of song do not boast the brightest plumage."[100] Slave singing drew together dual tropes of nature's sound, the aviary and the ape; beneath the sensuous delights loomed a monstrous, thick-lipped utterance, a resonance that posed a contagion to the innocent and unsuspecting.

The qualifications themselves grew from an anxiety about the place of the black voice in the American cultural landscape. They reflected a discernible uneasiness that had fashioned a prior "noise" into something even more threatening. If slaves possessed a powerful expressive capacity, one might begin to worry that they could also exercise control over the destiny of American expression. While southern whites, in particular, may have consciously paid little heed to the soundings of slaves, they certainly gave them notice and were compelled to consider their value, as a result of the prompting of foreign visitors and the large-scale fantasies of Sambo and blackface. This social empowerment of African-American performance accordingly had a monumental effect on the place of music making on plantations, providing a crucial element in the construction and procuring of racial difference. The process of a superior black sound overwhelming white sonic space was matter-of-factly observed by a southern teacher writing in *Dwight's Journal of Music* in 1853: "The whites first learn them—the negroes catch the air and words from once hearing, after which woods and fields resound with their strains—the whites catch the expression from these sable minstrels—thus Negro Melodies have an effect here not dreamed of at the North."[101] Indeed, the attribution of musical power to blacks identified the very means by which slaves acquired a primary social tool for documenting their significance. Because talent was "in-born," it could not be taken away, beyond the failed attempts to restrict the singing practices overwhelming southern places. For this clearly political reason above all others, slaves claimed the stereotypes of musical practice that assigned a discernible difference to their vocal play. The sonic articulation of a miraculous musical exceptionalism would become perhaps the most enduring feature informing the making and remaking of African-American identities.

The Economy of Play: Selling Difference   As slaves assumed an increasing presence in the routines of antebellum life, they were confronted with new forms of repression that sought to deny the inexorable emergence of a distinctive African-Americanism. Tales of torture and violence that chill the reader of eighteenth-century history take on another level of perversity in antebellum contexts, seeming all the more sordid in the domiciles of the plantation "family."[102] Beyond the literal acts of punishment were efforts to quell the cultural practices through which such distinctiveness could be realized. Efforts to obtain literacy were prohibited by law; preaching by slaves was tightly regulated and frequently quashed. Those attempting to subvert such limits would meet with ruthless measures, such as the iron gag fastened to the face of the more articulate and obstinate leaders, particularly holy men. Representing the most horrendous torture of all was the threat of sale, which stood as a constant reminder of the precarious humanity black bondspeople were forced to endure. Sale of human chattel acted out explicitly the possessed nature of the slave who could be suddenly taken from one's family, one's home, one's self. Living without position or possession, slaves could never forget their material reality as commodities in human form, expressed in the stark terms of the master's threat, "I'll put you in my pocket."[103]

Poised between the status of the commodity and modern notions of individualism, black slaves played out the contradictions of the antebellum political economy, fashioning cultural practices in the image of racial paradox. The force of sale, as Walter Johnson explains in his fascinating analysis of the New Orleans slave market, textured the very flesh of the slave subject with the mark of capitalist exchange. The social actions of slaves repeatedly expressed the tensions between free will and material possession performed over the course of everyday life. While these processes of exchange put blacks at an obvious disadvantage, they also infused into the dynamics of interracial relations an economic dimension that proved oddly enabling in the progress of black cultural construction. Dealing sentient beings, white traders were forced to rely on their chattel to present themselves for purchase, a circumstance that inspired slaves to attempt to influence their own outcomes. As participants in the surreal theater of antebellum capitalism, slaves, serving dual capacities as both sellers and products sold, became astute players in an economic system in which their own expressive capacities—from dancing to preaching to singing to instrumental performance—were among their greatest assets. Even beyond the market and during the course of life's routines, slaves maintained in their relations with whites a performative stance that always left open the possibility of an exchange that somehow centered on their own bodies.

Exchange in fact became closely aligned with the cultural construction of difference, making manifest within a performative economy the distinction between what was free and what was not. Indeed, it produced the very terms of racial authenticity, which could be received by whites only indirectly through access to realms black. The coalescence of processes of exchange and the new visibility of slave musical production would accordingly become a critical factor in crafting the meaning and character of black music as it took shape as a modern phenomenon. Without the economic dimension of black-to-white relations, the modern notion of black music could not possibly have come about in the form we now know it.

For those white agrarians and capitalists finding virtue in the ethos (if not always the actuality) of nose-to-the-grindstone hard work, the difference of blackness was particularly well demonstrated as a form of play acted out in the many varieties of slave performance. If whiteness claimed its character in the labors of capitalists, blackness expressed its opposite, reflected in the putative natural musicality, feeling manner, and childlike demeanor of the docile slave. Play lay at the heart of the entertaining, performative character of authentic "Negroes singing," an image made increasingly popular in the new inventions of blackface that began to circulate across the states from the mid-1840s. In the invention of Sambo, the attribution of playfulness provided an affirmation of the nature of "Negro character," even if the various forms of leisure and entertainment were also commonly a part of white activities.[104] And because this character was limited to the range of earnestness and naïveté, it accordingly helped to rationalize slavery.

As a coalescence of imagined authenticities, "Negro play" fueled white desire for black performance, just as it informed the local constructions of African-American expressive culture that had suddenly gained the attention of the masters. Increasingly, slaves must have realized they had one up on a planter class and to some extent even on the lowly white yeomanry that had increasingly begun to conceive of music making as one of the slave's natural labors. Displaced from the ranks of an emerging performance class, white planters began to see themselves as unmusical. And while many whites continued to sing, whether at work, at worship, or in the parlor, there was a growing perception that blacks were the ones with special musical talents. "The love of music, which characterizes the negro," Olmsted observed in a widely read portrait of the South, "the readiness with which he acquires skill in the art, his power of memorizing and improvising music is most marked and constant. I think, also, that sweet musical voices are more common with the negro than with the white race—certainly than with the white race in America." Even J. K. Paulding, while insisting in a language recalling Jefferson, Hegel, and Hume that "the negro, whether free or a slave, in his own country or elsewhere, [has never] attained distinction in intellectual acquirements, in arts, science, or literature," would finally acknowledge that slave music and dancing were widely praised. The performative skills of slaves, he noted defensively, "would meet with a patronage and excite an admiration, beyond anything which a white man of equal talents could hope to receive."[105]

But play also expressed the dark side of African-American slave behavior; in blacks' putative docility, one could observe a recalcitrance and unpredictability that came to be associated by turns with whites' deep-seated fears of insurrection. According to the logic of play, slaves were not only fun loving but lazy as well. As such, their labor would need to be coerced and extracted, against the natural grain. Of course such perceptions of laziness and light-spirited behavior stood in contradiction with the reality of the tremendous burden of labor that blacks regularly endured. But because they did not perform their tasks willingly, slaves, as a consequence of their social position, were seen as inherently unruly. And because they endured these circumstances against their will, they would always represent as a group the potential of rebellion. In the early nineteenth century, southern whites had witnessed the realization of that potential threat, first with the successful rebellions in Haiti and Saint John's Island, then with the worrisome attempts on the mainland, most notably that lead by Nat Turner in 1831. It would not be too far a leap, accordingly, to observe the performative play of slaves as a signifier of deviousness and danger, even as those attributions intensified white interest in "authentic" expressions and—as this interest was acknowledged by southern blacks—heightened the potency of performance in slave quarters. In a sympathetic portrait, John Dixon Long explains, "If you approach [the slave] from the stand-point of authority, you will never get insight into his real character. He is exceedingly shrewd." According to Alex Mackay, "All his playfulness of disposition is sometimes only a mask used to conceal a burning thirst for vengeance." If whites believed slaves to be full of feeling, they also sensed beneath that well of emotion a seditious potential that could invert relations and leave owners, recalling the words of the eighteenth-century William Byrd, "playing the fool." Play, as wondrous as it was, ran the risk of unseating the stability of slavery as a whole.[106]

In the figurative notion of play, we find the miracle of the essential relation occupying a new social place in the history of African-America. Because racism still tended to deny the possibility of "Negro" creativity, black music arises once again seemingly out of nowhere, suggesting a kind of magic.[107] Slave performance could still be dismissed as something less than a creative practice, but because whites now participated indirectly (and largely voyeuristically) in its creation, such dismissals would be inevitably and repeatedly challenged. For by this time, black song's power derived not simply from the essential relation—as a possession of the possessed—but as a consequence of a particular process of exchange, whereby the volatile play of black racial difference obtains a level of value permitting slaves to earn a recognizable culture. What is particularly fascinating is the way this earning is achieved against the rules of slavery itself. Slaves profit from acts of creative production that signify less than full complacency and commitment to slavery's ideals. The perceived essence of their performative play derives from the putative laziness and insouciance that stood in contradiction to white claims of industry and hard work. It is through these processes that the play of black sounding practices become the centerpiece of culture making in an antebellum racial economy, providing a double-edged accommodation and resistance to the constraints of capitalism. The economy of play perpetuates capitalist logic as its commitment to the authenticity of difference against the reality of white creativity and talent reveals the underlying contradiction of race as such.

In what Olmsted identified as the inimitable "sweet[ness]" of the slave voice, white southerners would finally recognize the "fact of blackness," as Fanon named it, existing within their own cultural and economic circumstances. But this fact seemed less a tangible form than something akin to an algebraic variable; possessed by the slave-as-possession, "Negro sound" derived from an unknown place that gave resonant form to those inaccessible versions of slave authenticity and "freedom." Slave music, in its greater public form (a form that inevitably turned back into the particular circumstances of blacks themselves) depended on the position of the master: as a musical fact, it derived from a relational economy. One can even think of slave music as a kind of surplus value, representing a by-product of labor from which slaves also gained cultural capital through their performances. Importantly, this value was realized most vividly in the process of exchange with whites, through which slaves engaged in acts of what we might call selling difference. Slaves' performances were admittedly coerced, frequently through degradation, whether by tossing coins to prompt dancers or when "whiskey was handed out by the overseers, and the slaves becoming very merry, began to caper and sing more noisily than before." But the slaves also profited from them, not only monetarily but also in accessing a form of cultural power. They became, in fact, critics. Slaves routinely expected payment for services rendered, and if they did not receive it, they could engage in songs ridiculing those who did not show favor. Referring to the social critiques that emerged from the responsorials of nighttime corn shuckings, for example, the Methodist clergyman Thomas C. Thornton observed, "there is nothing that affords a planter so much pleasure, as to hear that the negroes of his farms, give him *abroad* a good name, and nothing mortifies him so much as to hear the reverse." Whites came to depend on the play of black music making in order to reinforce their own social place.[108]

The overall effect was to entrust slaves with a stable role in the rituals and economy of leisure that at once established black identity (as a form of profit) and white loss, a loss that could only be recovered partially through purchase. Increasingly, slaves assumed the role of actors whose expressive practices associated with leisure became a labor-producing value. "In this manner were spent the greater part of the summer evenings," recalled Emily Burke of her time on a Georgia plantation, "and it was usual for the members of the family to assemble on the piazza to witness their pastimes." Observation led to engagement: "and sometimes," Burke continued, "at the request of a favorite slave, I have seen the white children engage in the waltz, or take their places in the quadrille." Over time white southerners grew increasingly dependent on slave musicians, hiring, renting or otherwise inducing blacks to play at their dances, weddings, parades, and other rituals and events. In fact, they grew so dependent on this economy of performance that the failure of a slave to uphold his or her end of the bargain could disrupt community rituals. Francis John Claiborne, for example, tells an apocryphal tale of an African-American fiddler, whose delayed arrival forced the cancellation of a wedding.[109] In competitive circumstances, finally, the racial hierarchy of performance was made plain. In a fascinating portrait, Lewis W. Paine recalls that "all indulge in the dance," only to recognize repeatedly through engagement the effect of constructed difference. "The slaves, as they became excited," Paine writes, "use the most extravagant gestures—the music increases in speed—and the Whites soon find it impossible to sustain their parts, and they retire. This is just what the slaves wish, and they send up a general shout, which is returned by the Whites, acknowledging the victory. Then they all sing out, 'Now show de white man what we can do!' And with heart and soul they dive into the sport, until they fairly exceed themselves. It is really astonishing to witness the rapidity of their motions, their accurate time, and the precision of their music and dance. I have never seen it equaled in my life."[110]

Over time, these performances became deeply ingrained in the crafting of white sensibility. By marking emotional extremes, black performance outlined the range of expression through which southern life was experienced, as slaves became the unofficial actors of life's rhythms. "When you hear them you are half inclined to laugh at their queerness, and yet cannot but be affected at the sincerity and thrilling tones of the singers," admitted an anonymous writer. African-American song, in particular, connoted bedlam and debauchery, conviviality and calm, which together mapped out the discursive range of human emotion. And so purchase continued, whether to acquire a bit of "hilarity" or sentimentality, or even a perverse facsimile of the tragic, what James Hungerford named in reference to slave songs "a state of feeling [that] may be called the luxury of woe . . . to be sad without any personal cause for being so."[111]

Resonating across the southern environment, slave songs gave definition to the sound logic of racial signification. Conceptualized according to white notions of the authentic, the songs accumulated new meanings in acts of cultural translation, just as meaning circled back the other way, as song infused white discourses with discernible sonic shape. The power of slave song, together with other forms of interracial engagement, seemed eventually to give to whiteness an African cast. Novels and journals from the era would sometimes make reference to blacks' predicament in order to describe white experience. Individuals succumbing to desire and infatuation were "enslaved"; embracing minstrel-based behavioral stereotypes they could actually describe themselves from what purported to be the slave's point of view: "We w'ite folks . . . almost burst with laughter." Like the minstrel counterfeits that fetishized black forms, moreover, lyrics in tune books could similarly appropriate black images into a white domain. The tune "Indian Convert," included in William Walker's famous compilation *Southern Harmony* (1835–54), introduces blackface dialect to identify the speaking Native American: "In de dark woods, no Indian nigh, Den me look Heb'n, and send up cry."[112] Northern texts projected a racial kinship of southern masters and slaves engaging in song and laughter, as the factual record referenced a world in which "black and white all take part in the sport" of play, fiddling and playing banjo while camping together and "eating their suppers[,] black and white[,] from the same kettle." The close contact that music produced inevitably drove efforts to keep a safe distance, as sound came to be viewed not simply phenomenally but as active, contagious. Dynamic and unstable, its effect was not easily contained. "Every one appeared to have caught the contagion of the overflowing hilarity," as J. Thornton Randolph put it in his fanciful depiction of a Virginia ball. As a writer summed it up already in the 1820s, in the slave states and across America, "white conversation . . . had darkened in complexion."[113]

The "fact of blackness" at the seat of white recognition was not, in itself, a prerequisite for the emergence of an African-American artistry. Musical expressions would have taken shape quite routinely in any case, just as they did in Africa and as they do within all performative cultures. It is not as if African-Americans needed contact with Europeans and Euro-Americans in order to create music. But to explain the particular formation that black music took requires the kind of socially based analysis proposed in this chapter. Whatever musical gifts may be attributed to antebellum African-America, they evolved as something inextricably linked to the social processes developing from the master-slave relation. Indeed, the power and magic of slave music was constituted as part of this relation, at least as it was realized in southern environs and eventually brought to the stage of American public culture as a whole. For black music, after all, gained its exceptional stature not because of some inherent greatness but because of the emergence of expressions of difference that were recognizable within a familiar racial dialogic. Growing from practices acquired both traditionally (through "retentions") and within New World forums such as the camp meetings, these forms of difference would be developed to a high art, both to perpetuate the growth of insider value systems and, simultaneously and symbiotically, to satisfy the economy of public music making. Neither white containments nor black insiderism was ever absolute. If the construct of black music challenged the stability of white proprietary control over nation and reason, the difference of slave music took shape as a consequence of racial engagement and contact. The slave song's emergence out of the consequences of New World colonialism and white supremacy fulfills once again the projection of cultural encounter as a kind of sublimity: "The experience of colonialism is the problem of living in the 'midst of the incomprehensible.' "[114]

A tentatively recognized "Negro musicality," then, becomes the means by which slaves took hold of American conceptions of self and nation. Concocting surpluses of magical sound through the process of selling difference, slaves profited from their various strategies of play that put into motion a modern social sense of becoming. The dismissive sense of incomprehensibility that informed earlier white interpretations was embraced by slave communities, which garnered from this contempt the difference that precluded white access and grounded expressions of critique. Slaves gained crucial performance power precisely because a once disinterested white class sought so strenuously to specify a racial divide.

By playing the noise of racial difference, slaves found the means of asserting their own human value while issuing a grand critique of the uniformity of white comprehension—a critique that only fueled white desire. Play developed out of the dialectics of racial difference as it worked a prior interracial musical language of sameness into distinctively black forms. The social contradictions these performances advanced would create profound disruptions of white efforts to stabilize racial subjectivity over the course of the antebellum period and into the modern era.

The historical record of slave performance identifies a central manifestation of play that evolved from the flux and flow of slave creativity. In the responsorial practice identified today as call and response, we locate the chief mechanism of dynamic action through which slaves demonstrated and developed a local knowledge of vocal mastery. This sense of play is important because it isolates a particular performance orientation that refers to broad-scale structures of social relation and formations of meaning. Play projects through the primacy of socially derived call-and-response vocalizations a common sense of place; it makes familiar and claims through sound an arena defined by the authority of slave performance. As slaves produced surplus value within the circumstances of a resonant plantation economy, they found the means of structuring a culture during acts ostensibly performed for the master. There is something truly uncanny in this particular manifestation of the essential relation. The dynamic of call and response claimed for blacks a sonic space to the point where the interracial background of responsorial singing would give rise to new perceptions of it as an essential manifestation of blackness. Relational song furnished the language from which life stories would be brought into the world, as art and experience coalesced as a grand play of songful living.

The African-American slave practice of call and response derives from two principal modes of behavior that informed slave cultures: the dynamism of religious performance and the activity of labor. It is the sonic consequence of the preacher/laity relation at the camp meetings proceeding alongside performative engagements in the field. From these key forums, call and response became the crucial marker of black expressive culture, informing diverse practices of improvisation, rhythmic counterpoint, shouting, and testimony, together with repertories of corn songs, rowing songs, and religious spiritual songs. Call and response represented the stuff of the slaves' sonic-social environment. It was so fundamental and inextricably related to the social that it seemed a natural part of it. An artifice of the social, it took form variously as part of the world of life and labor, to the point of texturing daily social motion. Call and response, in Steven

Feld's phrase, assumed the status of "the music of nature" in which nature, as the mix of outdoor performance in the environment of the social, defined "the nature of music." Its inherently relational instability produced a kind of "double singing" that informed the sonic character of the plantation. The polarity of musical exchange constructed the valuative "wholes" of song in which a battery of responsorial procedures would come to characterize slave performance.[115]

Theories of the racial derivation of call and response have occupied a central place in the origins debates, even as the most committed European-roots advocates acknowledged a distinctiveness to African-American contributions. While rejecting the early Afrocentric claims of Henry Krehbiel, John Work, Maud Cuney-Hare, and others, George Pullen Jackson conceded that African-Americans were the most assiduous and inventive in employing call-and-response techniques. Blacks, he wrote in 1943, "went further than their white brothers in song dialogue just as they outdid them and still outdo them in dramatic preaching, dramatic praying, dramatic exhorting, dramatic story-telling and what-not."[116] Early scholars of the sea shanty, moreover, similarly traced responsorial practices to the "Negro influence" of nineteenth-century seafaring towns along the southern coast of the United States and the Caribbean.[117] Among comparative musicologists such as Erich von Hornbostel, finally, call and response was a key indication of African musical practice. While acknowledging that responsorial practices had also existed in European music, Hornbostel believed its widespread use among Africans constituted an informing impulse. Such concessions have prompted many contemporary scholars to assume call and response to be nearly exclusive to the black tradition, representing a centering force that links musical behavior to the imagined collectivity of the African-American past.[118]

While it is inconsistent with the intentions of this project to claim for call and response an exclusive racial origin, we need to acknowledge nonetheless the social forces that encouraged blacks to see it as their own and to innovate musical styles from it. Watson's depiction of the African-American camp meetings suggests already that call and response was widely in practice in religious settings by the 1810s, particularly in the creation of repetition choruses and in orienting preacher/congregation interaction. Significantly, John Garst argues that these practices may owe specifically to the Christian responsorial practices documenting eighteenth- and early-nineteenth-century tune books, from the "dialogues" in the hymnals of George Whitefield to the refrains of "Wonder, Wonder, Wonder" animating Jeremiah Ingalls's *Christian Harmony* (1805). The search for precedents traces back even further as scholars have claimed structural similarities linking call and response to sailors' work songs, group singing among audiences of eighteenth-century French and British opera, sixteenth-century dialogue hymns, the "lining out" practices of Anglican worship, and the responsorial practices of the Catholic Mass.[119] At the least, these precedents complicate easy designations of direct African linkages, theories confused all the more by ethnographic identification of call and response in culture areas most likely uninfluenced by African cultures: in the Middle East, in native North America, in the central Asian village of Makvaneti, Georgia. A transcription of a Chinese rowing song from the late eighteenth century documents antiphonal practices clearly unrelated to those of the African diaspora (fig. 1).[120]

At the time when Jackson was writing, the paucity of references to African practices prior to 1700 seemed to justify the prevailing view that call and response, despite its African-American distinctiveness, had grown from the religious singing traditions of Europe. While now going against the grain of contemporary common sense, such a view cannot be summarily dismissed without evidence. Even if call and response is exceedingly conspicuous in contemporary African-American music and now recognized by

AIR

1. Chinese Boatmen's Song Transcribed from the original notation in John Barrow, *Travels in China* (1806), reprinted in *Time, Place and Music: An Anthology of Ethnomusicological Observation, c. 1550 to 1800,* ed. Frank Harrison (Amsterdam: Frits Knuf, 1973), 209.

authorities such as John Miller Chernoff as "a major characteristic of [contemporary] African musical idioms," we still need to locate some indication of prior use to base claims of African linkages. Historical research since the 1970s shows precisely that: it obtains important precedents that largely discredit theories tracing the origins of call and response entirely to Europe and Euro-America. Epstein's elaboration on the seventeenth-century transcription and analyses of Hans Sloane and the French musician, Baptiste, provide a clear instance of call and response among African slaves in Jamaica. Baptiste's notes (paraphrased or recited by Sloan, who was the actual author) describe dancers and percussionists making "a noise, keeping time with one who makes a sound answering it on the mouth of an empty Gourd or Jar with his Hand." Baptiste's transcription—perhaps the earliest notation of African-derived performance—documents a clear and regular exchange of voices in responsorial fashion (see chap. 4). The contemporaneous notices of Jean-Baptiste Du Tertre, who visited the Antilles around 1640, together with those subsequently documented by Wilham Beckford and Edward Bowdich (in which he notates the call-and-response pattern of "An Accra Fetish Hymn"; see chap. 4) suggest that Baptiste's record was not anomalous. Far more likely, call and response appeared commonly in African and African diasporic musics since at least the seventeenth century.[121]

The widespread use of responsorial practices across Atlantic cultures seriously complicates a simple explanation of the development of call and response in North America. No claim of racial supremacy, no statement of a single cultural origin, black or white, can be defended. Still, the preponderance of responsorial singing in circumstances of labor, documented vividly in seventeenth-century West Indian accounts and in North America, suggests that it was if not a determining influence then at least a frequent practice among slaves. Whites, of course, particularly poor whites, labored too, and the precedents of responsorial work song in Europe give credence to speculations about the formation of Euro-African hybrids within the interracial dimensions of work. But because slaves were the exception of the labor class, subjects who embodied the American "work ethic," they also had a greater variety of experience in engaging in responsorial singing.

Significantly, as slaves developed antiphonal practices, whites appeared to have retreated from these modes of performance as they became increasingly associated with slavery and race. With the help of tune books published widely in the South, white singing masters in the Upland regions introduced rudimentary harmonic practices of eighteenth-century New

England, what Charles Hamm calls "the first system of planned vertical combinations of notes to emerge from oral-tradition Anglo-American music." These texts, together with the singing masters who created them, as David Warren Steel observes, "provided virtually the only [formal] music education available in the Upland South before the Civil War." The application of harmony as a racial signifier of whiteness motivated the landed and wealthy to create distance from call and response even as poorer white southerners continued to sing along these lines well after the Civil War. Advancements in harmony and form promoted by the singing masters betrayed a southern classism interwoven with an emerging white racial supremacy.[122] The formulation of a separate body of "black" notation in the songbooks of northern blackface parody reinforced the perception of separate traditions even while the notations themselves occasionally betrayed some similarity. Together these twin bodies of text helped to craft modes of performance that while growing from the shared experience of responsorial singing increasingly articulated distinctions based on assumptions of racial difference.

Along the interiors of southern rivers and within the dynamic of plantation work rituals slaves practiced a vocal artistry that repeatedly reinforced their claims on double singing. Slaves could be heard singing antiphonally across the landscape. In a typical portrait, "black oarsmen sing songs merrily to the cadence of the oars," inspiring a sense of wonder among the uninitiated. Wonder soon inspired poetic language. "This wild music on the water at night is enchanting; for the broad dome of the skies seems to reverberate the sound," writes Mary Howard Schoolcraft.[123] In fact, call and response was so pervasive that singers could be heard singing alone in responsorial fashion, assuming both dimensions of the dynamic. A source from 1843, for example, describes a slave on a wagon who cracked his whip in response to his "improvisatrized" phrases. The first of two stanzas reads:

Den goin' down to Loudeville,
Long time ago
Where all de wagons chucky fill
Stan' in a row;
Crack! Crack! Crack!

Another notes how a slave, while driving an oxcart, shouted affirmatively to his own verse, "Hilo! Hilo!" A third account describes a soloist bringing into his secular singing connections with sacred worship, lining out a hymn and then singing its melody as he labored.[124]

The pervasiveness of call and response suggested a kind of dialogic swirl of sound into which whites could only occasionally engage or intervene. While instances appear in which white singers joined black performers—notably, at corn-shucking songs and, on one occasion, at the request of a black rower—these pale in comparison with the flood of vivid accounts documenting the development of a dramatic artistry that informed slave experience.[125] The significance of these singing displays eventually forced the acknowledgment of a kind of artistry and intelligence that contributed to the abolitionist challenge of white supremacy. Seemingly rising from the depths of ignorance and unconsciousness, the call and response of the slave showed in the end that he was "one of the smartest men" who possessed verbal ingenuity and an aesthetic sensibility. Describing a corn-shucking ceremony in the 1830s, an anonymous traveler observed, "on the summit of the pile, sat a person, selected for his skill in improvisation, who gave out a line in a sort of rapid chant, at the end of which the whole party joined in chorus. The poet seemed to have no fixed object in view but to sing. He passed from one subject to another without connexion."[126]

Singing "without connexion, . . . the poet" nonetheless demonstrated skill and discernible vocal gifts. To be sure, white listeners had accurately identified a deeply involved and elaborate sense of rhetorical engagement that textured slave life, even while acquiring only a partial sense of its noise-filled mastery. But if whites could glimpse at least a portion of its subtlety and variety, they increasingly suspected they would find a richness and depth otherwise hidden from public meaning. Call and response, the more astute white observers understood, involved a competitive engagement on the part of singers and tellers of tales: "One chick-a-biddy never crows without his challenge answered," Baynard F. Hall recalled in his novel about plantation life, employing the ornithological language common to the period.[127] But rarely could they obtain a real sense of its intricacies even when deeply invested in the culture in which these performances took place. Those travelers from the North and foreign soils who recorded slave practices and who were even less familiar with the complexities of southern cultures were left mainly with mementos in the form of the proliferation of lyrics that documented slavery's generative force of double singing.

Call-and-response practices provided slaves with a mode of communication and critique, an inventive and playful language that by revealing just enough of its critical strategies to whites extended its cultural power. As slaves engaged among themselves in verbal competitions anticipating modern signifyin', they also continued to direct these comments and critiques at whites. The rituals of performative ridicule discussed earlier in this section most typically took the form of responsorial singing, which mediated confrontation through indirection. Depictions of steamboat and corn songs, for example, noted a seemingly common practice among slaves of offering songs to induce whites to share their liquor. Harriet Jacobs's recollection of the performative critique of stingy whites includes a record of antiphonal group singing:

Poor massa, so dey say;
Down in de heel, so dey say;
Got no money, so dey say;
Not one shillin, so dey say;
God A'mighty bress you, so dey say.[128]

Here too we see in the dynamic of call and response whites seeking their place in the responsorial ritual. There is even a sense in these descriptions of white folk as willing accomplices in a form of playful self-humiliation that at once acted out the hierarchy of power as it complicated absolute white authority. Play energized slave culture as long as it did not get out of hand.

The widespread use of call and response among plantation slaves suggests that it had acquired a level of iconicity close to the center of African-American experience. In the dialogic of double singing, slaves heard coalescences of a familiar resonance whose subsequent documentation as a repertory of song texts (and in the 1860s, as notations) brought slave song to an even wider national populace. The public representations ultimately reified responsorial singing into a canon of folk vernacularity. The dynamic of singing became "planting songs," "rowing songs," "corn songs," and "the field harvest." Slaves most likely had their own canons that may or may not have coincided with popularized terminology. Rather than "folk art," however, antebellum slave singing was part and parcel of life's experience: it gave sonic texture to a resonant economy of slavery through which an enslaved populace accessed momentary spaces for making rightful claims to its own humanity. Singing provided the slave, once again, with an audible sense of place.

Seen this way, double singing was something more than a tool for fashioning a uniform, monological identity as if the calamity of experience might be rendered as a singular black experience. Rather, call and response put into action the dynamism of play; free floating, omnidirectional, and spontaneous, it described the precariousness of slave existence as it rendered material a discernible black significance. The sonic texture of responsorial singing disrupted place as it claimed it; in its materiality, call and response spoke of the placelessness and disruption of a possessed people, while simultaneously claiming displacement as home. Groundlessness miraculously gives way to stability and the privilege of hope. If slavery by definition was a denial of self and place, it also signified a dislocation that anticipated a liberative becoming. What pacified in turn inspired the possibility of radical insurgency, gesturing not only forward but also outward (eastward) as it pointed back. In the placelessness that responsorial dynamism evoked, one followed multiple pathways tracing toward forms of liberation: in the excesses of slavery, in the future of postemancipation, in the proposed colonization of slaves, in the prior place of a homeland in Africa. Placelessness, as articulated sonically in call and response, provided the comfort of belonging in situ as well as in spatial and temporal musical projections. Call and response charted the dual ideals of prior and post places that distinguished from a slave present as it acknowledged the already displaced situation of enslavement. This dynamic proposed similarly constructed memories—in an imagined Africa, in the dream of liberation. Call and response's experience thus echoed as a dynamic rich with meaning, finding self in the process of framing pasts and realizing a certain becoming.

4 Magical Writing

The Iconic Wonders of the Slave Spiritual

At the opening of his celebrated collection of black spirituals, the Harlem Renaissance poet and novelist James Weldon Johnson poses a series of searching questions. So deeply touched by the dramatic beauty of America's most celebrated sacred songs, he writes with a bemused sense of wonder as if to say, "how on earth did these musical gems ever come to be?" Johnson, however, isn't looking for simple answers, for he knows full well that the songs' beauty depends on the very fact of their unknown origin. Rather he wants to savor their attendant mysteries, giving pronouncement to the "primitive dignity" of an ancestry cast in "darkness." And as he revels over the slave songs, Johnson eventually succumbs to poetry, reaffirming the sense that what is fundamentally musical exceeds the limits of prose. Brimming with his own charge of noble energy, Johnson directs his questions to the spirituals' anonymous makers, his words verging on song:

O black and unknown bards of long ago
How came your lips to touch the sacred fire?
How in your darkness, did you come to know
The power and beauty of the minstrel's lyre?
Who first from midst his bonds lifted his eyes?
Who first from out the still watch, lone and long,
Feeling the ancient faith of prophets rise
Within his dark-kept soul, burst into song?[1]

Johnson's application of poetry is in part a rhetorical strategy; he wants to create dramatic effect. But he is also seeking to convey the uncanny presence of an artful song produced under the siege of slavery's oppression. "What merely living clod, what captive thing / Could . . . find within its deadened heart to sing, / These songs of sorrow, love and faith, and hope?"

Awestruck, he concludes that their existence is an inexplicable phenomenon, yet one whose mystery depends on the mundane labors of black humanity. It is through "the miracle of its production," through the activity of a vocally inspired populace that the slave song resonates from its forgotten past.[2] For Johnson, the spiritual's basis in the American tragedy of slavery becomes the very source of its magic. Echoing Marxian and Du Boisian sentiments, he claims labor for the master as the basis through which slaves challenge mastery: the songs of blacks establish the ground of a new African-American humanity. Modern-day spirituals assume the form of a supernatural gift arising from the depths of time, from a storyless past that denied blacks the privilege of their own cultural memory. Proposing through sound a story of its own, the spiritual inspires Johnson as the modern mediator and translator to supply the words:

O black slave singers, gone forgot, unfamed,
You—you alone, of all the long, long line
Of those who've sung untaught, unknown, unnamed,
Have stretched out upward, seeking the divine.
. . . .
You sang far better than you knew; the songs
That for your listeners' hungry hearts sufficed
Still live,—but more than this to you belongs:
You sang a race from wood and stone to Christ.

Confronting the utter blankness of the nation's racial memory, Johnson relies on the age-old figure of the miracle in order to comprehend the music's social origin. In "O Black and Unknown Bards," he replaces history with lore: holding their ears to the ground of a mythic racial heritage, slaves excavated the resonances of a timeless African vernacularity, translating them in order to make them their own. At this time, whites still commonly thought that blacks produced song simply by speaking and singing "naturally," free from the burdens of intellect and reason that had complicated European notions of creativity.[3] Johnson supplies the slaves with agency, with a form of action that situates song making in the sphere of public works. Mediating and transforming a prior singing ("African chants"), the slave bards themselves engaged in seminal acts of "writing" on which Johnson's own creation depends. The miracle of the spiritual and the "noble" character he ascribes to it derives not from its spontaneity, but from its magical, composed production as a kind of modern alchemy—a beauty produced out of horror by makers denied ownership of their own labors. "Upon the fundamental throb of African rhythms were reared those reaches of melody that rise above earth and soar into the pure, ethereal blue. And this is the miracle of the creation of the Spirituals."[4]

What finally drives Johnson's celebration of the spiritual is the material fact of its existence as printed, published music. *The Book of American Negro Spirituals* and its companion *Second Book . . .* are above all music collections, compendiums of 122 songs arranged for piano and voice by J. Rosamond Johnson (James Weldon Johnson's brother) and the pianist Lawrence Brown (famed accompanist of Roland Hayes and Paul Robeson). The appeal of the songs derives partly from their appearance in the form of conventional staff notations, which however mediated and constructed, create the illusion of a stable and permanent cultural practice unchanged since its origins in slavery. What seems truly miraculous about the slave spiritual relates precisely to its tenacity, to its human-like perseverance to sustain public prominence against the odds of racism and social inequality. This tenacity, of course, did not express some inner quality in the music itself but depended on the actual efforts of people for whom the songs in various ways represented something worthy of preservation. Cast anew in the public discourses of racial desire around the time of the Civil War, the spiritual would assume purchasable form in the published songbooks and collections that circulated widely in mostly white middle-class households during the second half of the nineteenth century. By the time of Johnson's collection, they had taken the form of arrangements based on earlier transcriptions and harmonizations produced by college instructors and black composers that sought to render plain the "curious turns and twists" and other "peculiarities . . . not susceptible to fixation."[5] While by no means perfect representations, the new arrangements were thought nonetheless to supply the public with a semblance of the spirituals' original character. Indeed, their inadequacy and artificiality as second-level mediations amplified their power: the magic of the spirituals came forward most deliberately as the inadequacy of notation brought into relief that ineffable quality exceeding the bounds of script. Johnson's embrace of the language of miracles exacerbated this condition of artifice, translating the qualities of originality and authenticity for a new black musical modernism and reaffirming the slave song as the cultural centerpiece of African-America as a whole.

The circle of invention now turns full circle, revealing a new coherence in the resonant second nature of racialized slave song.[6] Authenticity becomes constituted within the "origin" of the soundtext, as the purity of folk song derives from the dual forces of representation—verbal description and musical inscription—that create and then seek to isolate black music's excesses. Understood this way, origin is miraculously traceable back to the artifice of slave song's notation, as the ironies of race and the limits of mediation form an alignment: the secrets of blackness at once constructed through and seemingly unfettered by white representation come into focus as that which artistic representation fails to convey. As notations, slave songs bear a resemblance to visual art. "We can never understand a picture unless we grasp what cannot be seen," W. J. T. Mitchell explains. And yet it is the artifice of the picture or of notation itself that becomes obscured, since, as Mitchell continues, "One thing that cannot be seen in the illusionistic picture, or which tends to conceal itself, is precisely its own artificiality."[7] As a version of "picturing the invisible," musical transcription, together with the attendant discourses that help to bring this image into being, give voice to what Johnson calls the "peculiarities" of a previously unspoken slave universe. Notation mystifies as it projects a version of an unheard musical realm and, in so doing, creates the art object. Cast in the polite context of piano and vocal arrangements, the songs materialize for a bourgeois public those special qualities—what the compilers call "their primitive 'swing' "—now ascribed to black singing.[8] The "miracle of . . . production" emerges as a decidedly modern form of magic, a sighting of the nexus of discourses underlying black music as it shifts from the contexts of slavery to freedom.

This chapter charts the making of a new kind of musical miracle that connects the essential relation of antebellum resonances to modern black musical art forms. It seeks to demonstrate further the connections and distinctions between sound and text that have carried through this story. Here we add to the mix the material indication of song as notation, a development that consequently aligns black music with new versions of racial discourses around the mid-nineteenth century. The initial magic of the commodity "slave" creating its own possession to assert a basic freedom takes modern form in the interplay of black music with the magical powers of mechanical reproduction and consumer capitalism. The spiritual's miraculous birth is revealed as a multimediated affair involving sounds, images, and the texts that run through them, all coming together in the form of an ambiguously assertive sheet music that would adorn the pianos of the American parlor. In notation, we locate an emancipatory public force that also constrains the disruptive play of antebellum song. To comprehend the steps in this formation, we begin with the social and ideological circumstances that fueled a new northern interest in the slave music, as the power of black singing once again enters the interstices of society itself.

The Romance of Recovery   The idea of a distinctive black music came into existence at a time when African-Americans themselves were being written into history as a free people. While the various musical formations of difference during the antebellum era had already introduced black musicality into public forums, it was only after witnessing actual slave performances that northerners would ascribe to African-American singing the status of "song" and, with this status, emancipatory significance supporting abolitionism.[9] Such associations appeared in the body of occasional writings, private journals, and popular magazines that together reflected an emerging fascination with folk authenticity and racial difference around the time of the Civil War. Some essays were published anonymously as brief comments and reflections; others featured European visitors such as Fredericka Bremer and Fanny Kemble, who remarked on the unusual displays of expressive talent. However, the main portion of commentary came from white northern intellectuals and reformers who had been committed to the abolitionist cause and worked vigorously to bring slave songs to public knowledge. Perpetuating antebellum figures of excess, they claimed that the slaves possessed an ability to communicate at the height of human emotion, charting realms beyond the access of whites. Typically, these depictions outlined discursive extremes, ranging from saintly freedom to the most debased images of blackface. Hyperbolic references to "wildly excited," "barbaric" songs that were nonetheless "fresh and warm from the heart" appeared across the literature, balancing precariously between paradoxical moods of admiration and contempt.[10]

The rhetoric of extremes recalls earlier accounts of travelers and planters, whose Sambo references fulfilled plantation fantasies of a southern, folkloric sublime. Significantly, however, the double images of freedom and the grotesque now provided some white writers with a means of distinguishing between slave songs and the counterfeit parodies of the minstrel stage. Among northerners in the 1850s and 1860s, the ability to make such distinctions was uncommon and carried special significance among music-minded abolitionists who identified in song the basis of interracial union. If chroniclers of the slave song embraced a minstrel discourse to describe the songs' expressive qualities, so did they revise that language to project a new vision of black music and race relations. Recasting signs of primitive barbarism to fit the ideal of Western freedom, commentators pursued a radical line that ascribed to the make-up of African-American song "elective affinities" of white and black.[11] Ironically, the attribution of special properties of difference to black music logically precluded the music's being acquired by these same observers. By situating a spiritless, if "supe-

rior," Anglo-white culture on a middle ground between expressive extremes, chroniclers of the slave songs affirmed a racial ideology that prevented the very unity they desired.

The double-edged portrayals of the slave songs reflected the legacy of
difference making in the colonial project. More specifically, however, it expressed the contradictions that characterized the aggressive evangelicalism of antebellum reform. Impassioned by a sense of moral righteousness
and New World privilege, northern agents worked with romantic fervor to
erase impediments toward social perfection. Proposals for advancing
women's rights joined with successes in broadening the base of suffrage;
appeals to temperance matched initiatives to grace the land with a lasting,
enlightened peace. These efforts became part of a larger concern with securing the rights of slaves, which ultimately fostered a vigorous abolitionist movement from the 1830s. Describing, in a letter to Thomas Carlyle, the
range of activities taking place around 1840, Ralph Waldo Emerson wrote,
"We are all a little wild here with numberless projects of social reform. Not
a reading man but has a draft of a new community in his waistcoat
pocket."[12] Yet these same pursuits of reform and improvement seemed
also to imply a sense of lack within the reformers themselves. Indeed, we
can read in their initiatives toward a perfectible America the inadequacies
stemming from those very civilizing efforts. While the exaltation of the
slave songs' "perfection" at the moment of armed crisis may have provided
some faith in the possibility of cultural renewal, their collaboration also
mirrored a palpable emptiness infecting reformist circles. For what white
intellectuals gave up in their civilizing ambitions was precisely the transcendent freedom their embrace of slave difference had celebrated. Accordingly, the perceived purity and wholeness of the slave songs—the
very quality of completion associated with slavery's essential relation—
also signified what was missing in whiteness as a consequence of civilization itself. Without reducing reform efforts to a callous solipsism, we can
recognize the white claim to give voice to the slave as an act of ventriloquism, whose motivations were necessarily complicated and ambivalent.
By embracing the ideals of romantic perfectibility associated with folklore
and the spirituals, these reformers described qualities felt to be missing in
themselves, thus revealing a white double consciousness to which they
could only gesture in a series of rather desperate imitative acts.

Stanley Cavell has argued that the rise of romanticism after Kant "is understandable in part as an effort to overcome both skepticism and philosophy's responses to skepticism."[13] Romanticism seeks to heal the "wound
of reflection," as Rousseau called it, by transcending the limits of rational-

ism altogether. Drawing on a vision of the past as a linear recession toward a primal origin—an origin "so secret and fundamental that it can never be quite grasped in itself"—romanticism articulated the basis of the originary trope of authenticity that situated the ancient, the sacred, the primitive, the exotic in an all-encompassing natural world. Intimately tied to this essential matrix was the newly privileged stature of art, which, in its manifestations both high and low, marked through human utterance a point of desire beyond human bounds. Art, and particularly poetry, for Kant provided the means of healing the fracture caused by rationalism, the mode by which an original unity existing in a prior age might be recovered.[14] While Friedrich von Schlegel and Friedrich Wilhelm Joseph von Schelling would subsequently pursue Kant's directive by contemplating authenticity in the recently formulated realm of aesthetics, others, notably a group of nineteenth-century American intellectuals that included Emerson and Walt Whitman, followed the line of Johann Gottfried von Herder.[15] In a series of works beginning in the 1770s, Herder located the height of experiential unity in folk genius.[16] He postulated that a transhistorical folkishness gave rise to a universal spirit, the national particularities of which affirmed a pluralistic, egalitarian conception of race. Uninhibited by the strictures of rational thought, folk forms, from medieval German epics to the ballads of English and Scottish bards, were living vestiges of a free, spiritual truth emanating from the limitless impulses of nature. The age-old vitalism of God speaking through nature assumes a discernibly modern secular form in the emerging concept of an organic national voice. In its universality, the folk voice reflects a spiritually connected complex whole; in its national specificity, however, it reveals peculiarities that acknowledge and legitimize difference. Herder's cultural relativism assigns value to the human quality of art, and particularly vocal art, that would carry important repercussions in the invention of the slave spiritual.[17]

The appeal of Herder tells us something about the broader enthusiasm for folk themes that ran across American culture by the 1820s. It offers, in particular, at least one explanation for the interest in the poet and novelist Sir Walter Scott (1771–1832), whose romantic themes and images of bardic wisdom in *Waverley* (1814) and subsequent "Scotch novels" introduced intellectual conceptions of the authentic to readers across the United States. In his novels and influential poetical works (notably, *Minstrelsy of the Scottish Border* [1825]), Scott cast an authentic world of heroism, noble savagery, and gentlemanly honor that translated easily into New World relations between aristocratic and common classes, masters and slaves, as his portrayals of an invented Highland tradition linked outwardly to Orientalist and Africanist conceptions of otherness.[18] In Scott's Edward Waverley, the young "Man of Feeling" and in his depictions of an earlier medieval age of chivalry in *Ivanhoe* (1820), American readers encountered the basis for the southern patrician affectation central to the creation of plantation decorum.[19] While popular on their own terms, moreover, Scott's inventions had an indirect influence in the adaptations of American authors who identified in the historical romance a basis for a homegrown southern pastoralism. In the works of Thomas Nelson Page and John Pendleton Kennedy, among others, readers encountered versions of Scott's characterizations of rural splendor and noble gallantry, cast within equally fictitious portrayals of plantation culture. Kennedy's *Swallow Barn,* for example, introduces the Scottish author directly into the text: "The picturesque association of falconry with the stories of an age that Walter Scott has rendered so bewitching to the fancy of meditative maidens, had inspired [the plantation belle] Bel with an especial ardor."[20]

Scott's romantic portraits of the Scottish highlands informed yet another creative venture, namely, a series of dramatizations produced nearly simultaneously with each novel. As Anne Dhu Shapiro explains, dramatizations and subsequent stagings of Scott's novels were common during the 1810s and 1820s, when Scott was publishing his "Waverley" texts. Significantly, these performances were accompanied by versions of Scottish song, both original songs brought to America and New World inventions crafted in a Scottish style. The close relation between religious slave songs and Scottish melodies (both widely popular across the South and both sharing in a firmly based pentatonicism) leaves open the possibility that the subsequent record of slave song may have acquired an unacknowledged Scottish gloss. Indeed, the figure of the highland Scot, appropriated by Englanders despite its "wild and barbarous" nature, suggested an important parallel to American figurations of slaves and slave song, both in their discursive formation and in the character of singing.[21]

In the wake of Scott's cosmopolitanism, midcentury northern intellectuals and artists pursued various inquiries into folk expressions, both near and far, from Longfellow's "native ballads," to Melville's South Sea travels, to Whitman's musical poetry, to Thoreau's extensive studies of Hinduism and Native American culture. In the case of Emerson, appeals to the storytelling gifts of "the common" seemed ultimately to celebrate a privileged, self-reliance. Nevertheless, his view that transcendence was not an arcane foreign venture but part of the familiar here and now reinforced the notion that "the highest spiritual cause" existed in the most pedestrian forms of human expression.[22] Indeed, Emerson's statement reflected a wider interest in everyday life among many Northern intellectuals that gave rise to early research in folklore. Of common concern were texts of British Isles ballads that had been a conspicuous part of American musical culture and learning since the colonial era. In the next century, the ballads appeared frequently in published collections and by the 1830s were being taught in public schools. Initial studies conducted by Europeans—along with Scott, Thomas Percy, and Jacob and Wilhelm Grimm—set the background for American inquiries by Harvard-trained amateurs, notably Thomas Wentworth Higginson, Emerson, who praised the ballads' "homespun veracity," and Theodore Parker, who published an essay on ballad literature in 1848.[23] These efforts gave way to formal inquiries into medieval literature and British ballads by the Harvard professors James Russell Lowell and Francis James Child, whose research established the ground of an early, philologically oriented folklore.

It is more than a coincidence that Emerson, Longfellow, Whitman, Thoreau, and Parker were all sympathetic to the abolitionist movement and that Higginson and Lowell were active participants in some of its most radical initiatives.[24] Higginson, a Unitarian minister and one of the secret supporters of John Brown's raid, led a black regiment during the Civil War. Lowell, a distinguished critic and poet, balanced his literary pursuits with work as an editor and contributor to the *National Anti-Slavery Standard* (1845–50). All were party to an evolutionary view of the slaves as inheritors of a primitive spirit descending from a primordial realm. While Whitman is reported to have witnessed slave singing practices firsthand—on occasion, he would "launch forth in his 'vocalism' [of] 'the wild tunes and refrains' he had heard from blacks down South"—most northerners concocted such ideas with little or no familiarity with African-American verbal arts. At best they heard the speeches of former slaves, whose presence at abolitionist rallies was increasingly common. By the early 1840s, slave orators had come to play an important role in the abolitionist initiative, in part because, as John A. Collins observed in a frequently cited letter to William Lloyd Garrison, "The public have itching ears to hear a colored man speak, and particularly *a slave.*"[25] As such, the slave autobiographies that recorded these public "hearings" were more than mere documents; they represented a form of folk authenticity that, for some, signaled the emergence of a national creative voice. "We have never had any doubt that the African race was intended to introduce a new element of civilization," Lowell, a renowned orator and emulator of black dialect, wrote in his discussion of Douglass and other abolitionists. "The Caucasian mind, which seeks always to govern, at whatever cost, can never come to so beautiful or

Christian a height of civilization." Parker, meanwhile, spoke directly to evidence of elements open to the civilizing impulse of the slave autobiographies. In his oration, "The American Scholar" (1849), he declared that "there is one portion of our permanent literature, if literature it may be called, which is wholly indigenous and original. . . . I mean the Lives of Fugitive Slaves. But as these are not the work of the man of superior culture they hardly help to pay the scholar's debt. Yet all the original romance of Americans is in them, not in the white man's novel."[26]

Early chroniclers of slave songs voiced similar notions that subtly challenged the absolutes of black and white. Such references to racial crossing were fairly common, particularly in the context of comparisons between the slave songs and the British ballads. In his famous essay, "Negro Spirituals," Higginson recalls how his early admiration of the ballads gave way to a new love of black song. "The present writer had been a faithful student of the Scottish ballads, and had always envied Sir Walter the delight of tracing them out amid their own heather. . . . It is a strange enjoyment, therefore, to be suddenly brought into the midst of a kindred world of unwritten songs, as simple and indigenous as the Border Minstrelsy, more uniformly plaintive, almost always more quaint, and often as essentially poetic."[27] Writing in *Putnam's Monthly* in 1855, Y. S. Nathanson similarly conflates singing traditions, bringing together "Chevy Chase," "Lord Jamie Douglass," "the 'specimens' of Percy, Ritson, and others, and the most approved poetry of the African school." For Nathanson, folk song seemed to operate in a Herderian mode beyond distinctions of nationality, ethnicity, and race. "Let the words peculiarly Scottish in Hynd Horn . . . or in almost any other ancient ballad, be literally translated into the African dialect, and we have at once a plantation song."[28] Yet it was the accumulation of these markers of difference that assigned to them a powerful otherness and that became so resonant in black singing. By the end of the Civil War, the "discourse of authenticity" that Regina Bendix ascribes to the early study of folklore had focused principally on the slave songs. As "ancient relics," they epitomized a transracial ideal of an original humanity first uttered "from the lips of aged crones."[29]

Crucial to the rising prominence of the slave song was the parallel emergence of classical music in German and American aesthetics. Already by the late eighteenth century, European critics commonly believed that music, the quintessential art of feeling, was the greatest of artistic expressions. Conceived as a naturally intuitive force, it could surpass the limits of rational thought toward which poetry, as writing, merely gestured.[30] Instrumental or "absolute" music, which had been purged of all elements of language, was the most privileged in this scheme, and American elites, in turn, commonly embraced this position wholeheartedly, espousing the greatness of European concert works in cultural journals and in the newly constructed edifice of concert culture in place by the 1840s. Yet like Rousseau and Herder before them, American writers also looked beyond European music for these same qualities, discerning in the most "natural" vocal practices a purity of spirit emanating from an essential humanity.[31] Commentaries on the slave songs frequently involved this romantic language, through which the natural instincts of the plantation singer replaced the intuitive genius of the titanic composer. While supposedly of limited intelligence—"their intellects could only retain the words when assisted by the music"—the slaves nonetheless possessed a knowledge that transcended mere thought. Like the romantic artist, they could sidestep the blocks of reason and, through mysterious acts of improvisation (similarly attributed to Mozart and Beethoven), reach intuitively toward a unified collective unconscious. Moreover, while some aristocrats typically argued that the German concert repertory identified the truest height of the romantic spirit, others believed that the more spontaneous folk forms best expressed nature's power, for "no song of a concert room ever thrilled us like one of these simple African airs."[32] Certain writers, anticipating Dvořák's claim that slave songs were "the most striking and appealing melodies that have yet been found on this side of the water," argued that a union of ballads and slave narratives expressed an emerging national spirit.[33] The paradox of a geographically ambiguous folk music fulfilling the aristocratic yearning for authenticity first associated with German art should have undermined both the hopes for a true music nationalism and a unified measure of aesthetic value. Yet the blurring of discursive spheres only strengthened the notion of a transcultural folkishness, as it confounded racial categories and containment.

Some commentaries suggest that American versions of romanticism had always been informed by images of the vernacular, given how frequently such images appeared in even the most Brahmin appeals to the civilizing of national taste. For John Sullivan Dwight, a Harvard-educated Unitarian minister and transcendentalist who by the 1850s would become the nation's foremost music critic, the masterworks of German classical composers (particularly those of Mozart, Haydn, and Beethoven) were emblematic of the power of music as a "universal language." Despite his commitment to high cultural orthodoxy, however, Dwight also betrayed desires that undermined his views of a pure, European-American musical continuity. For example, in his early criticism published in the *Harbinger,* a transcendentalist journal, he distanced himself from the cult of the master composer, preferring works that emphasized the group over the individual, as if to affirm the Herderian ideal of an anonymous, transhistorical collectivity.[34] Similarly, his distaste for solo efforts, which he felt trivialized creative performance—"it is of *music* rather than of musicians that we intended to speak"—developed from an even more radical collectivist sentiment that anticipated postmodern interrogations of subjectivity. In the end, however, Dwight was a humanist upset with the popularity of virtuoso performers whose superficial exploits obscured the secrets of substantive human expression. Even the weakest execution could be overcome, he stressed, provided that the musicians infuse their performances with qualities of "soul."[35] While Dwight's views generally reflect the influence of Wilhelm Heinrich Wakenroder, F. W. J. Schelling and E. T. A. Hoffmann—critics whom Dwight, fluent in German, may have read—they also suggest the impact of a vernacular discourse associated with black music. In fact, Dwight himself regularly included commentary and debate on the popular phenomenon of blackface in his highly acclaimed magazine, *Dwight's Journal of Music* (1852–81); his coverage of the slave songs begins with the anonymous essay "Songs of the Blacks," published in 1856. While Dwight may have included the material on the slave songs to demonstrate his commitment to the abolitionist movement, their appearance alongside minstrel debates and reviews of elite concert music underscores how deeply the discourses of folk authenticity had affected cultural consciousness, to the point where its traces could be discerned in even the most arcane interpretations of European masterworks.[36]

The reports of "Blind Tom" or "Black Tom" (1849–1908), the "musical wonder" who attracted considerable attention in *Dwight's Journal of Music,* betray the sense of worrisome fascination that accompanied the emergence of black music in northern public culture. While not specifically about the slave songs, this commentary is noteworthy here because it provides but one example of the extent of profound curiosity about the seeming magic of African-American slave performance within polite culture contexts. Tom, who was raised a slave on a Georgia plantation, was born blind and, according to the accounts, "without even ordinary intelligence." As a musician, however, he excelled, particularly in his ability to recall long stretches of music. By the late 1850s, his owner, Perry H. Oliver, who had first employed Tom as an "after-dinner amusement," began profiting from his talents, staging performances at concert halls in southern cities. Tom would play works from memory, reproduce impromptu performances by audience members without prior hearing, and engage in histrionics such as playing the keyboard behind his back or two melodies at once. The demonstrations were marketed as examples of a modern-day miracle: the Negro boy "with a decidedly African type of face—low retreating forehead, flat spreading nose, and projecting upper lip, with every mark of idiocy," who, without an hour's formal training, could perform the masterworks of Europe's finest composers.[37] By 1860, Dwight was reprinting accounts of these spectacles first published in southern newspapers. In 1862, he reproduced a lengthy essay originally appearing in the national magazine *Atlantic Monthly,* which drew considerable reader response. Other essays followed, typically featuring musicians who had witnessed Tom's performances and who debated the accuracy of the most extravagant claims.

Judging from the accounts, what underlay the controversy was an anxiety about the possibility that Tom had, through some kind of devilish mischief, exceeded the talents of the accomplished white concert artist. While the stagings were little more than sideshow acts out of the minstrel theater, they were acknowledged by the nation's upper crust and debated vigorously as if the integrity of white civilization were at stake. And, in a way, it was. For Tom's putative feats went far beyond the musical skills previously granted to blacks, whose facilities were still commonly thought (in the North, at least) to be limited to songs and exercises in imitation. Performing long stretches of musical works with an excellence of command and interpretation, Tom seemed to have demonstrated a kind of intelligence that would have previously been attributed solely to whites. That Tom was said to compose works and to improvise in the style of elite common-practice music was all the more threatening, suggesting a nineteenth-century version of the extraordinary claims surrounding Phillis Wheatley; the playful theatricality of writers who frequently compared Tom to the boy-genius Mozart could have only fueled fears. Here, a blind black boy, who performed "like an ape clawing for food," had somehow acquired skills that challenged the racial sanctity of European music and, by way of association, the very soul of white supremacy.[38]

Perhaps the matter would have mattered less had not so many white observers actually desired to claim for Tom such remarkable gifts. Why else would he have drawn large audiences and gained sustained attention? The more rhapsodic depictions cast his performances as a kind of inversion of Robert Louis Stevenson's Dr. Jekyll and Mr. Hyde, whereby a base "imbecile" attains the stature of the most gracious civilized artist. In the first report on Tom published in *Dwight's Journal of Music,* an anonymous author who had witnessed one of his performances describes how "a feeling of reverence steals over us as we behold this mysterious and sudden

transformation." Another claims Tom's musical memory was "utterly beyond all comprehension" and characterizes his performance as an example of "our music," distinguished from that of the Japanese.[39] The
conflicted desires of these and other writers betray the extent to which
black music had found its way into the sensory fields of a bifurcated American culture, the national identity of which had been destabilized in the
midst of the Civil War. We see here in particular how the power entrusted to
the slave songs had transcended the circumstances of black singing and
entered into a wider domain defining blackness as such. Discourses of musical authenticity became complicated by "Negro" music's growing public
presence, to the point of calling into question the supremacy of whites in
the performance of European art music. While the claims of genius about
Tom are almost certainly exaggerated, elite observers, including Dwight
himself, took the matter seriously, and they did so because even the potential of black creativity was now possible. The new presence of "Negro"
public sound not only unsteadied definitions of national music but also amplified the fractured identity of the nation as a whole. And the stagings of
Tom's performances from southern theaters to the august halls of the
"White House" reflected the confused state of thinking about race together
with music's capacity to articulate and heighten that confusion.[40]

Sacred Songs of the Racial Border   The commentaries observed
thus far are perhaps enough to suggest the paradoxical double meanings
that inform the slave song in their relation to mid-nineteenth-century conceptions of nation and race. Inscribed as an evanescent difference of
formidable power, the songs would subsequently acquire international significance, becoming, by the late nineteenth century, aural signifiers of
blackness for a world populace. In the same representations, we can observe from a specifically domestic vantage the seductive draw of black
difference among an educated northern readership. As part of the abolitionist initiative, the writings were frequently published for the most laudable reasons. They sought to convey the character of the black South and
in some instances to underscore differences between the spirituals and
blackface. Above all, the essays were meant to reinforce for a still skeptical
public the humanity of the African-American slave, offering white autho-
rization of the same positions conveyed by slave orators and writers. Yet
underlying these efforts was another kind of intention that expressed at
times what appeared to be a veritable fantasy of voyeuristic desire. Beneath the admiring portraits of singing blacks one beholds a near fetish of
difference that inspired on the part of the writers themselves profoundly

strange transgressive acts. Working from the rich density of figures and tropes on which pre–Civil War discourses of black music developed, I offer, in this section, a panorama of the wondrous language that brought the spiritual into the folds of public meaning.

In images of "hooting" and "shouting" and scenes of blacks "merry," "caper[ing] and sing[ing]," chroniclers depicted the plantation slaves—"the happiest of the human race"—as masters of play, exercised in barbaric performative action and seemingly continuous bodily motion.[41] "The Negro, whether in Africa or America, is eminently social. His conviviality seems, indeed, exhaustless," writes Daniel Drake to a colleague in Boston. And so they would "shuffle away," dancing a "half 'walk-round' half brea[k]down" to a song from the minstrel stage ("Lucy Long"), creating "such uproarious jollity, such full and perfect enjoyment, I had never seen in humanity, black or white." At moments, however, the slaves would pause to reflect on Christian themes of politeness and civility. Voicing qualities of docility and kindness was a "heavenly sight," although "not always . . . in strains the most reverential and refined." While perhaps "queer," "grotesque," "fantastic," or "strange," the slave songs were nonetheless "original," bespeaking the "natural" musical gifts of the African. "The blacks are a musical race, and the readiness with which many of them improvise words and melody is wonderful," James Robert Gilmore recorded after visiting South Carolina in 1860. As Reverend James Wendell Alexander suggested in 1847, "It is rare to meet with a negro who does not sing."[42] John Pendleton Kennedy would affirm these views in a language evoking ornithological conceits: "Their fondness for music and dancing is a predominant passion. I never met a negro man—unless he is quite old—that he is not whistling; and the women sing from morning till night. . . . Their gayety of heart is constitutional, and perennial, and when they are together they are as voluble and noisy as so many black birds. In short, I think them the most good-natured, careless, light-hearted, and happily constructed human beings I have ever seen."[43]

In all of their "tumming," "glee," and reveries—a "highly pleasurable sensation"—the slaves would ultimately manage a feat believed unattainable by whites since the rise of civilization: they would blend "concord and discord . . . so completely . . . as to produce perfect harmony." Subverting the binaries of Western musical logic, African-American slave culture had begun to achieve humanity's perfection in sound; they created "a *natural* and *rational* expression of devotional feeling" (emphasis mine), "a spirit of rapt abstraction from earth and all earthly things."[44] By the time of the Civil War, the figures of freedom and transcendence would be coupled with direct references to the sacred to produce an exceptional music thought by some whites to be beyond the power of any Euro-Western expression. In images at once Godlike and heathen, the slave songs would come to represent the height of spiritual perfection, merging Christian theology and idealist notions of the sublime with the bestial primitivism of Africa.

Black natural potency was commonly thought to derive from the most literal fact of "Negro" difference: the slaves' lineal connection to Africa. Several midcentury commentaries explored the qualities of this potency as something at once enabling and dangerously unstable. According to the African slaver Captain Canot, the "unmixed Negro" is a "brute" in whom "we behold the animal in all his pristine characteristics—lazy, debauched, incapable as an idiot of self government or forethought, cruel and treacherous as an ape." Yet this "brute," the same author reasons, remains unmistakably happy, particularly when enjoying "sunshine," "cassaxa" (probably "cassava," an edible tropical root), or engaging in "concubinage." Music, in particular, appeared to tame the most debased and licentious proclivities of an inherently performative people. Of the faculties distinguishing man from animal, they are all deficient in the "Negro," excepting "some sensibilities" relating to music. It was sound, he thought, that brought about a contrasting "levity of spirits."[45] As a person of nature the African's "sight is acute, that of taste sufficiently delicate, hearing sharp," all suggesting a "noble character." Trouble was, in his or her present state, the African's performances amounted to a "barbarous music." The contradiction was plain: "They offer therefore a discordant mixture of qualities." Hope lay in the possibility that over time "Negroes" would find their place in humanity by realizing their natural musical abilities and discovering the "melody in their souls." For this quality, according to George G. Foster, not only was a potential for uplift but also identified an exceptional nature relating to the "Negro's" inherent "abstract love for the beautiful." Once something distinguishing Europeans from the rest of the world, beauty now defined black nature: "It is much stronger and universal with the African than any other white race except the modern Italians and ancient Grecians." Given the chance to develop in civilized contexts, the African would realize true greatness, for "the coloured people are naturally strongly addicted to music and dancing—a propensity that one day will be developed into the most astounding results."[46]

As a New World phenomenon, "Negro music," and particularly "Negro song," had begun to acquire the ingredients for the making of an exceptional, rarefied racial signature. While already drawing considerable attention across the South in the 1830s, the slaves' natural musicality would be refigured by midcentury to make whites, in their obsessive commitments to industry and labor, seem like the savages. A fictional portrait from 1852 by the planter Robert Criswell, for example, positions slaves' natural expressivity in contrast to a fallow white technological sophistication, represented in the image of a stalled railroad train. When the locomotive breaks down in a forest, the narrator witnesses a group of two dozen blacks cutting timber and singing "extempore, without regard to rhyme or reason," while others lounged "lazily enough, chattering, laughing and singing, (apparently perfectly happy)." Here, the dynamic free-flowing energy of black expressive play condescends to the disabled technology of European man.[47] As these expressive qualities evolved, they would produce a kind of majesty in sound, for "the voices of this race are generally much richer and more flexible than those of any other, except the Italians; and even they are inferior in that oily suppleness and clinging adaptability so indispensable to the singer." The evolution taking place would ultimately return the African to a precolonial, preslavery state in the image of the Rousseauian noble savage, as Foster describes: "In short, we believe that, after the African race has become purified from the horrible stains and pollutions of centuries of blood, slavery, and oppression, and has found power to rise to its natural level, it will be discovered to correspond to the female sex or the minor key in the grand analogy of the universe."[48]

Perfection, then, was attained not through assimilation into the routines of a male-dominated white culture but, rather, by seeking a higher level, at once marginal (female, minor) and centered within the familiar sphere of Western humanity. This otherness in the common had already begun to produce an aesthetic quality of inimitable drama and beauty. "There is a kind of entrancing power in negro music, which I never felt in any other," Mrs. Francis Harriet McDougall writes through the voice of her protagonist, "It is, as it were, the essence of sweet sound, distilled in the alembic of tearful memories. It affects the nervous system like a species of intoxication."[49] In their new Americanized form, moreover, "Negro" singers exceeded the routines of white vocalists, having achieved the stature of Sir Walter's pride, what John Pendleton Kennedy named (anticipating Johnson) the slave "bard." Performing among "the hanging mosses" of nature's "great Gothic temple," Gilmore reflected, slaves revealed what another writer called an "indescribable humor and pathos"; in church service, he continued, "the negroes, to my ear, [were] making much better music than the whites."[50] An English visitor to Louisiana similarly recalled, "Some of the most harmonious sounds I ever heard have proceeded from the lips of young negro girls." So powerful was black song it could promote healing:

among the slaves, "all is hilarity, fun and frolic. To witness such a scene is a certain cure for ennui, blue-devils, mopes, horrors and dyspepsia." Yet another admirer sought out from a slave her opinion of a white singer. By this point, slaves had not only become expert singers but musical critics with singular cultural authority.[51]

References to the slave songs as spirituals epitomized the new alignment of blackness and the sacred. Prior to the 1860s, slave singing had been consistently identified by the mundane appellation "Negro song," which then gave way to "spiritual" within the contexts of Sea Island commentaries of the Civil War era. While the figure seems to have some basis in slave culture—suggested in one writer's use of a dialect form of "sperichel" to mock slave speech—it acquired stately presence from the imposition of outside ideologies of New England romantic thought.[52] Having moved from a prior absence to a supreme presence, these voicings represented for an increasingly broad group of interpreters an expression that outlined the extremes of sonic significance. Slave song, as spiritual, reflected the grand irony of transcendent freedom through human subjugation. "The Songs of their Captivity . . . are sung with a touching effect," wrote an anonymous observer in the 1850s. In their tunes, one could discern "a decidedly religious character"; indeed, they were "religious . . . without exception."[53] Significantly, only rarely did writers depict the spirituals according to conventional musical images of perceptible beauty. Recalling Foster's theories of African beauty, they proposed that the songs seemed to test the limits of white comprehension, expressing a transcendent musical perfection born out of some uncharted realm—what one writer called, in a fictional account, slave songs' "subliming spirit." Reducing to pure sound the suprarealities of God and nature, the spirituals expressed dialectically that move toward perfection, culminating in a sacred splendor that finally rejoined black folk with an original, natural world. In their exalted naturalness, moreover, the spirituals exceeded the confinements of labor and the legacy of enslavement. Developing from a "native musical capacity" highlighting in-born feats of improvisation, the songs obscured in their perfection, in that "indescribable something," the work that more commonly produces artistic craft.[54] Emerging from beyond the conventions of white understanding, unfettered by "all earthly things," spirituals took form intuitively, seemingly without the necessities of rationality and the effort that embodies more mundane forms of craft. Indeed, as commodities, slave spirituals ironically concealed the labor of blacks' singing efforts, suggesting a purity that distinguished song from the tragedy of enslavement. While cast as musical forms emerging from human bondage, they also suggested a progress beyond it and, in this way, downplayed for many white audiences after the Civil War the memory of slavery's past as such.

Infused with fantastical properties of the mythic other, the slave songs, as a matter of course, inspired a mad gold rush of appropriative desire that continued well into the twentieth century. Already by the time of the Civil War, accounts appearing in diaries and journals had given way to major documents of folkloric study that culminated with the collaborative project *Slave Songs of the United States* (1867). In black sacred song, students of the vernacular now formally identified the means of accessing qualities of emotion that many writers had theorized to be lacking in the Anglo-Saxon personality.[55] Recalling the sentiments of Parker, Lowell, and a host of early slave-song commentators, a new circle of writers vigorously argued that the limits of black intelligence made room for an emotional richness uncharacteristic of whites. While possessing meager intellect, the "Sambo" figure could nonetheless boast traits that, in the romantic imagination, were of far greater importance: qualities of warmth, gentility, and simple happiness that suggested, particularly to the white male mind, a syncretism of blackness and femininity. By this point, the romantic idea of the African slave had grown into a vast compendium of difference, a value-saturated matrix in which images of Christian kindness and womanly perfection intersected, as they provided an enabling strategy for white men to gain hold of an exoticized black masculinity.[56] Perhaps most significantly, many came to believe that these qualities might ultimately be consumed, particularly since blacks' "natural genius" had come forth unwittingly. Relying on gifts of native intuition, slaves in the New World had reclaimed the source of a primordial sound in order to enrich American life as a whole. It was now up to sober-minded whites to acquire these secrets: "All mankind, may be benefited by looking *down* in life, in order to explore the dark corners of nature."[57] A report from 1856 vividly expresses these sentiments:

The only musical population of this country are the negroes of the South. . . . Might not our countrymen all learn a lesson from these simple children of Africa? We are a silent and reserved people. Foreigners think us taciturn and gloomy. So we are, compared with the European nations. . . . Americans, though surrounded with everything to make a people happy, do not show outward signs of uncommon cheerfulness and content. We are an anxious, careworn race. . . .

Let us not be ashamed to learn the art of happiness from the poor bondman at the South. . . . If [the Negroes'] love of music which is inborn in them, could be inbred in us, it would do much to lighten the anxiety and care which brood on every face and weigh on every heart.[58]

Yet just as racial ideology served to define and protect the domain of whiteness, so did it qualify and contain the degree of access to black music. This was not simply a racial matter but a result of the particular ways in which race complicated growing concerns about the expression of national culture. While Europeans could make claims on the folk forms of peasants in the context of a declining feudalism, white Americans' "natural rights" to the slaves, despite their status as "contrabands of war," were certainly more tenuous.[59] Simple gestures to national unity and social completion could not so easily overcome a sturdy assumption about the reality that separated black and white. Just as southern planters acknowledged only a partial purchase of the difference produced by slaves, so could white northerners grasp a mere portion of the racial fullness that rendered whiteness incomplete. As they looked to the slave for answers to the emerging crisis of national identity, whites in the North found certain likenesses that simultaneously conflicted with the ideology of race on which that identity so clearly relied. As a result, the key to reformative fulfillment would once again undermine the successful completion of reform itself. This paradox would lead white writers ironically to blame blacks for the partiality of American society as a whole while continuing to look to black otherness for the cure of a national ill.

Such contradictions help to make more comprehensible the "doubling effect" of the slave-song commentaries at midcentury, which accumulated into a constellation of contrasting figurations tracing back to the travelogues of the early modern period (see chap. 2). If a listener found the songs at once playfully childlike and "depressing," so too could they appear "soul-stirring" and simply "weird." In their sublimely grotesque and primal originality, slave melodies seemed barbaric, uncivilized, wild, mystical; "relic[s] of heathen rites in Congo, or in that mysterious heart of Africa."[60] In turn, however, they could also reflect a Christian kindness and were "infinitely pathetic," qualities attributable to the stereotype of the docile slave. In a fictional recollection of a slave holiday, the Presbyterian minister Bayard R. Hall describes gaiety and frolic falling into disarray: "All society seems resolved into chaos—the darkness only being visible!" After commenting on the "harmonious" sounds of "Negro" girls, moreover, Matilda Charlotte J. F. Houstoun speaks disdainfully of the "little black urchins . . . [who] rolled their great *white* eyes from under their woolly brows," just as Charles Lanman portrays a slave Christmas celebration as a descent into heathenism: "While the more jovial make the night hideous by their animal hilarity, those who are serious accomplish the same end by their moaning and wailings and wild singing." In another instance, however, Lanman could hear "more melody and pure sentiment in this native chant as it echoed over the tranquil waters, than I ever enjoyed in a fashionable concert room."[61]

To be sure, the "songs of the blacks" were certainly a strange mix and match, joining visions of romantic splendor with impressions of a dark and fearful primitive past. Embodying sacred perfection, they assumed the status of spirituals. Yet just as easily they could take the form of "sperichels" that debased all Christian ceremony. Lawrence Levine similarly reflects on how, for many whites, this double image created ambivalences about direct interracial encounters, turning Mrs. Francis Harriet McDougall's recollections of "a species of intoxication" into a tale of horror. Attending a slave service in the 1850s, for example, Frederick Law Olmstead "was at once surprised to find my own muscles all stretched, as if ready for a struggle—my face glowing, and my feet stamping." In another account, the songs of the slaves reduced Mary Boykin Chesnut to an excitability conjuring up images of sexual violence and racial transgression: "I wept bitterly. It was all sound, however, and emotional pathos. . . . It was devotional passion of voice and manner which was so magnetic. . . . It was a little too exciting for me. I would very much have liked to shout, too." In black sacred singing the white observer identified a (feminized) object of desire, together with a (masculinized) difference whose very existence, as "contagion," could infect the sanctity of the white body. Antithetical to the self, blackness became a requirement for self-fulfillment. White society's obsession with the spirituals "render[ed] *delirious* that interior voice that is the voice of the other in us."[62]

From this view, black spirituals were not simply trivial expressions of "primitive purity." In fact, they were vital to the Anglo-Saxon psyche precisely because they constituted the alter ego of the white self, representing the supplement or missing link of American national identity. Over time, that yearning for an unconquerable difference would increase white appropriative desires, for what was perhaps the ultimate expression of romantic transcendence could only recede further with every desperate grasp. As an accumulation of Western otherness stretching from Africa to Valhalla to a Victorian womanly perfection, the spirituals, newly recorded as text, marked the outer limits of a racialized unknown existing beyond its makers' own access. Eventually, the inaccessibility of the spiritual would become in itself a fetish object that generated desperate attempts at recovery and control.

A key discursive element in the containment of blackness appears in the hierarchical relation of light to dark that repeatedly accompanies slave-song depictions. In the resonances of music sung by freed slaves at

night by campfires and along moonlit rivers, the mysteries of a blank musical darkness reverberates with civilization's privileged textual presence,
teetering precariously between visibility and erasure. Laurence Oliphant's
account of "chants . . . [of] pleasant melody" heard at night along the Wac-
camaw in South Carolina links the slave songs to the (dark) mysteries of
nature. Ultimately, however, the materiality that representation enables
gives way, as Negro singing separates from the text to be located in black
absence: "The words," he reports, "are more original than the music." In
another example, the shouts that Higginson heard near a "glimmering fire"
on a "starlit evening: were "chant[ed], often harshly, [in] . . . monotonous
refrain[s]." Yet with the aid of text, he could turn up the light, "writing down
in the darkness . . . with my hand in the safe covert of my pocket," only to
steal away with his newly formed natural object: "Afterwards [I] carried it
to my tent, like some captured bird or insect, and then, after examination,
put it by."[63] A report by "C. W. D.," published in *Dwight's Journal of Music* at
the beginning of the Civil War, further illustrates how the dark mysteries of
African-American musicality depended on the whimsical illumination of
text:

It is one of the most striking incidents of this war to listen to the singing of
the groups of colored people in Fortress Monroe, who gather at their resorts after nightfall. . . . [They recover] simple melod[ies] of nature, fresh and warm
from the heart. . . .
Passing into the yard, I found a large company standing in the open air
round a slow fire. One young man . . . "with a little book in his hand" . . . was
stooping down towards the dim blaze of the fire, to make out the words, as he
lined them for the singers. . . . As the reader progressed one young man threw a
few fresh hoops on the fire, and then . . . the reading became more distinct. . . .
With a word of counsel to the company, and a gentle encouragement, I withdrew.[64]

Here, the enlightenment trope of light opposing the image of a semilit-
erate former slave struggling in the dark affirms the evolutionary path toward rational progress in an emerging Darwinian era. Yet the passage also
implies a more aggressive desire to separate slave voicings from the perceived depravities of the enslaved. Despite the slaves' being reinvented as
authentic wonders of religious simplicity, what figures most dramatically
in this depiction is not the freed slaves—mere vessels of a primordial natural voice—but, rather, echoing a view consistent with the emergence of
absolute music, the sounds themselves. Appropriating the sonic light of

nature from the darkness of Negro bodily insignificance, white Americans possessed the means by which to construct a racially transcendent national selfhood. While the commodification of the freed slaves as contraband helped to overcome the problem of racial difference—mining the use value of the black body's song to enact an exchange for white self-completion—the displacement of the spiritual from its originating environment to the familiar forum of music writing would also contribute to the reform agenda. Through ambitious acts of inscription, whites hoped to extract these anonymous sounds from their real-life slave circumstances, thereby erasing blackness in the name of its preservation. Inscription would reify sound in its taming, anticipating the broad social circumstance that Theodor Adorno later characterized as the "regression of listening."[65]

Visualizing Partials   If white representations had successfully appropriated the slave songs into the sameness of a Euro-American culture of texts, the figure of African-American musical difference would have ended with its own inscription. That difference has informed black music into the present day attests to its generative strengths and effect. As observed over the course of this study, difference was crucial to the sanctity of black music and to the authenticity of the slave song, just as the repeated references to notation's inadequacy, or what I will be calling here "partiality," enhanced the songs' evocative power. Chroniclers, whether describing performances or engaging in transcription, seemed endlessly fascinated with the impossibility of their task, sometimes at the expense of the expressions they were collecting. In an early account, William Smith spoke at the end of his lengthy narrative of the inadequacy of descriptive language: "The beer dance, I have attempted to describe, is a faint representation of what actually occurred. It requires an abler pen to do it justice." More than forty years later, David C. Barrow, Jr., echoed these views, disclaiming in a preface to his transcription of a corn-shucking song that "no full knowledge of the way in which the song is rendered can be conveyed by notes." Gestures to preservation were crucial, of course. "Now that [the slaves'] patience has had its perfect work," Higginson reflected, "history cannot afford to lose this portion of its record."[66] Completion, however, was something else. And so Lucy McKim (Mrs. Wendell Phillips Garrison) worked tirelessly toward the notation, arrangement, and publication of songs while also claiming "there is much more in this new and curious music, of which it is a temptation to write, but I must remember that it can speak for itself better than any one for it." In her famous letter to Dwight, McKim continued, "it is difficult to express the entire character of these negro ballads by mere musical notes and signs. The odd turns made in the throat; and that curious rhythmic effect produced by single voices chiming in at different irregular intervals, seem almost as impossible to place on score, as the singing of birds, or the tones of an Æolian Harp."[67]

The figure of partiality is particularly useful in observing the ingenuity of these midcentury exercises in musical transcription. In acoustics, "partial" refers to the complex of discrete frequencies that resonate simultaneously above a fundamental pitch. Partials are what determine vocal or instrumental timbre or "color"; they give to sound a presence, an identity, even as they themselves remain indiscernible to human listeners. At once, then, partials provide tone with color-bound determination while individually appearing colorless. They are audibly "invisible," absent to common hearing. We can accordingly think of "partial" as a means of speaking musically to the social contradictions of race: the colorlessness of the musical partial provides color just as the comparative nature of race relations—or what I have described here as relational "sameness"—gives rise to the difference of black music. Partiality, then, highlights the close proximity of musical and racial difference in the romantic imagination. This double mystification—of vivid sounds and colors beyond access, seemingly unheard and unseen—helps to explain the enormous power that black music would have in the broader circumstances of American public culture from this time forward.

By recognizing the significance of the partial, we begin to comprehend the true import of the transcriptive act. Partiality in itself carried constituting, even emancipatory potential that drove the repeated desire to inscribe. As slave singing succumbed to the violence of text, songs assumed a graphic similarity. The most reductive recording acts sought merely to bring the spirituals into the familiar notational space of key and time signatures on the staff. Spirituals began to look like a normative music, which in turn encouraged musically literate singers, both black and white, to perform them according to European musical dictates. The performance movement that notation fostered had responded to the visual character of text: formal singing accommodated the discipline of notes on the page. Yet as singing submitted to the effects of writing, so did the original sounds bring about changes in the notations themselves. Seeking to capture the peculiarities of African-American vernacular singing, transcribers altered staff notations to obey a new logic that exceeded the confines of common time and well-tempered scales. The disciplining effects of notation accordingly engendered a kind of counterviolence that related directly to the impossibility of the transcription. Seeking to master, notation succumbed, only to enhance and finally to concretize a modern conception of black difference.

In the emerging "reconstruction" of blackness, partiality implied the possibility of encounters with a sound world existing beyond the transcriptive act. The partiality of text had an enabling effect: it would bring about another mode of listening that revealed the audible "beyond" of the slave era and an African ancestry. In this way, the slave spirituals assumed a place on an intersubjective divide between forgetting and remembering, between a newly constructed "blackness" in song and a musical past refigured through the discipline of writing. As a formation of Western discourse, these sounds-beyond-text were, of course, similarly positioned within racialist frames. Nonetheless, they provided African-Americans with a pathway toward the recovery of memories seemingly vanquished by the convulsions of a profound cultural shift. As partial forms, the transcriptions were akin to memories. They offered static glimpses of what was passed on, glimmers of a former musical collectivity likened to "the singing of birds." While created by the enslaver in the image of the enslaved, these scores exceeded their own powers of containment. As a kind of memorial in text, they referred to a time before the actual textual encounters, much in the same way that memory objectifies a portion of a blurred temporal experience near the edge of forgetting. Just as memory is an "imagetext," "a way of mapping an oral performance, an oration from memory, onto a visual structure," so is slave-song notation a version of the "soundtext." In this instance, the soundtext is literally a sonic picture that refers to the partials of sound notation cannot reveal. From this process of mediation America as a whole would begin to "hear" its collective slave past. And it is from this same intersubjective space that African-Americans would listen back in order to recover a realm of awareness that had been denied to them as slaves.[68]

The efforts to commit slave songs to writing grew out of a prior legacy of documentation reaching back to the early modern era. It is useful, by way of digression, to consider this background for a moment, since it is in the context of "foreign music" that the eventual form of the slave songs would be indicated. While slave songs were commonly understood as expressions growing out of national soil, they were, as we have repeatedly seen, always situated on the exteriors of musical knowledge. As racially inscribed "Negro songs," they stood in between the foreign and the familiar, forever beyond the norms of conventional practice, even as they might be drawn into comparison with the versions of Euro-American religious music to which they were related. Accordingly, a review of the precedents for

transcribing non-European musics can provide some comparative guidance as it helps to magnify the radicalism of the slave-song notations. By
committing the slave songs to print, writers repositioned an already formidable cultural power at the center of an emerging modern conception of
foreignness. Slave songs became a strangely distant sound that simultaneously represented national spirit, a paradoxical configuration that brought
into play what might be called American musicology's "first world music."
The concept of partiality was crucial to this formation, producing repetitions of racial difference that resonated well into the modern era.

Initial efforts by Europeans to transcribe foreign musical performances
arose from the same documentary impulses that historically underlay the
representation of culture. As observed in chapter 2, the primary concern in
these instances was to situate the vague indications of musical order—
what observers would name in the most qualified terms "music"—according to the organizing principles of European text. Notation served as the
handmaiden of an expansionist mission to observe, to understand, to assimilate, and eventually to conquer, with only the most occasional concern
about the terms of its accuracy. In this sense, notation was deemed fully
adequate; any inadequacy or "fault," if one could be assigned, lay in the
performances themselves. Amédée Frézier's (1717) notations of drinking
songs from Chili and Peru, for example, were apparently to be taken as
flawless presentations since the songs themselves were performed "in so
unartificial a Tone, that three Notes would suffice to express the Whole"
(fig. 2). In his two-volume description of the Chinese empire, moreover, the
eighteenth-century French Jesuit, Jean-Baptiste Du Halde (1735) writes of
the degeneration of Chinese music which the accompanying transcriptions by "P. Pereira" serve to demonstrate (fig. 3).[69] In these instances,
transcriptions put on display foreign inferiority while exalting the effi-
ciency of civilized representation to integrate sound and writing. They
served fully and adequately as lenses through which Europeans could observe lesser, purely sonic expressions uncomplicated by civilized thought.
Translating the aural into the more dominant modern European sensory
apparatuses of sight and touch, the notations offered tangible proof of
foreign musics' existence while affirming European descriptive power,
turning mere "hearsay" into the tangible evidence of the "eyewitness" account.[70]

It is from this vantage that we may observe the notations of foreign musics of the early modern period that begin with Jean Léry's *Histoire d'un
voyage faict en la terre du Brésil* (1586–1611).[71] The gallery of notations in
figures 2–14 shows the various efforts by travelers from the sixteenth

through the nineteenth centuries—merchants, civil servants, religious men —to describe non-European expressions. As a group, the transcriptions propose musical similarities: the songs and instrumental performances all look the same in their commitment to the five-line pitch-dominant notations of European music writing. This sameness of look is possible because the sounds have been extracted from, translated out of, the audible—out of the bodies of singers, instrumentalists, and their listeners. When the performances were heard in context, they would have carried some physical effect, since the bodily experience of hearing lies close to the experience of producing sound. Witnessing others perform and sing is but a step away from actually engaging in the act oneself. But once the songs were displaced from the auditory mode, they became comparable, collectible— fair vehicles for analysis subsumed by a dominant textuality. Léry's sixteenth-century songs of the *Caraibes* of Brazil, for example, were hardly the focus of his discussion but, rather, included with the publication of the third edition (1611), without integration or comment in the accompanying text (fig. 4). Similarly, Simon de la Loubère's (1691) transcription of a Siamese court song appears along with an image of an "Intrument de Musique a Timbres" with no explanation of how they relate to his careful descriptions of performance practice (fig. 5). Jean-Jacques Rousseau (1768) reprints portions of Léry's and Pereira's transcriptions, while crediting Marin Mersenne for the former, who had reproduced them in his publication of 1636–37 (fig. 6). The notations of Jean Chardin (1711), Charles Fonton (1751), and Captain J. G. Stedman (1777) have the similar effect of merely putting music on display (figs. 7–9). By giving foreign sound visual form, Europe begins the invention of "world music," while simultaneously distinguishing that music from the exalted strains of its own transcendent musical productions. Transcription performs a colonialist function, rendering non-European performance as a version of the amulet: the notations assume the exoticism of the idol, standing in opposition to the immateriality of European music's spiritual "likeness."[72]

What also seems to drive these reproductions, however, is curiosity

2. South American Song Transcribed from the original notation in Amédée Frézier, *Relation du voyage de la Mer du Sud* (1717), reprinted in *Time, Place and Music: An Anthology of Ethnomusicological Observation, c. 1550 to 1800,* ed. Frank Harrison (Amsterdam: Frits Knuf, 1973), 204.

CHINESE AIRS

3. Chinese Airs Transcribed from the original notation in Jean-Baptiste Du Halde, *Description géographique, historique, chronologique, politique, et physique de l'empire de la Chine et de la Tartarie chinoise* (Paris, 1735), reprinted in *Time, Place and Music: An Anthology of Ethnomusicological Observation, c. 1550 to 1800*, ed. Frank Harrison (Amsterdam: Frits Knuf, 1973), 207.

NOTATIONS MUSICALES CONTENUES
DANS L'EDITION DE 1611

Superposées à cinq paroles de chansons figurant seules dans l'édition de 1580

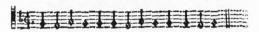

Canidé-ioune, canidé-ioune heura ouch

p. 151 (éd. 1611, p. 174)

*Pira ouaſſou a ouch Kamouroupouy-ouaſ-
ſou a-ouch &*

*Ouara
& Aca
ra-o-
uaſſou,*

p. 165 (éd. 1611, p. 191)

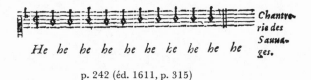

He he he he he he he he he he

*Chantre-
rie des
Sauua-
ges.*

p. 242 (éd. 1611, p. 315)

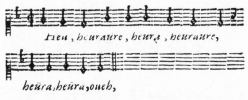

*Heu, heuraure, heura, heuraure,
heüra, heüra, ouch,*

p. 247 (éd. 1611, p. 322)

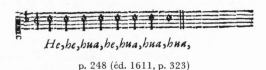

He, he, hua, he, hua, hua, hua,

p. 248 (éd. 1611, p. 323)

4. South American Song (1611) From Jean De Léry, *Histoire d'un voyage fait en la terre du Brésil* (1585/1611), ed. Jean-Claude Morisot (Geneva: Librairie Droz, 1975).

5. Siamese Song (with Drawing of Percussion Instrument) From Simon de la Loubère, *Du royaume de Siam* (Paris and Amsterdam, 1691), reprinted in *Time, Place and Music: An Anthology of Ethnomusicological Observation, c. 1550 to 1800,* ed. Frank Harrison (Amsterdam: Frits Knuf, 1973), illustration sec. D1–2.

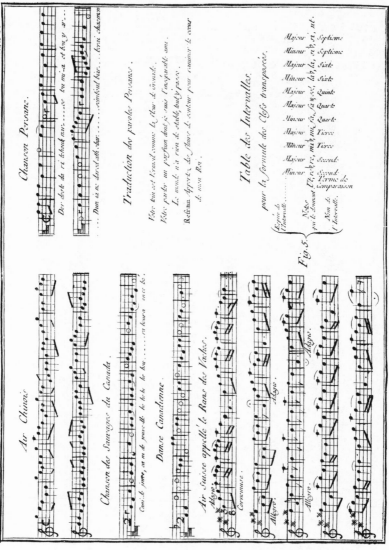

6. Foreign Songs From J. J. Rousseau, *Dictionnaire de Musique* (Paris: Chez la Veuve Duchesne, 1768).

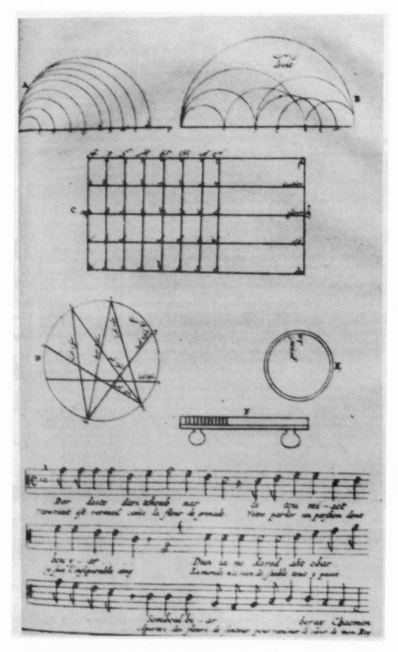

7. Persian Music Diagrams, Instrument, and Song From Jean Chardin, Voyages de monsieur le chevalier Chardin, en Perse, et autres lieux de l'orient, 3 vols. (Amsterdam, 1711), reprinted in *Time, Place and Music: An Anthology of Ethnomusicological Observation, c. 1550 to 1800,* ed. Frank Harrison (Amsterdam: Frits Knuf, 1973), illustration sec. E-1.

8. Turkish Music From Charles Fonton, *Essay sur la musqiue orientale comparée à la musique européene* (1751). Reprinted in *Yüzyilda Turk müzigi: Sark musikisi (Avrupa musikisiyle karsilastirmala bir deneme)* (Çemberilatis, Istanbul: Pan Yayincilik, 1987).

Rather quick

The second slow

Oan bus adiosi - o da so   *adiosso me de - go*   *me lobby fo fighty me man o*
One buss good-by o 'tis so   good-by girl I must go   I love for to fight like a man o

Amimba me dego na boosy o da so   *adiosso me do go.*
Amimba I go to the woods o 'tis so   good-by girl, I must go.

9. Bird Songs and Negro Boat Song From John Gabriel Stedman, *Narrative of a Five Years' Expedition against the Revolted Negroes of Surinam in Guiana* (1777; reprint, Barre, Mass.: Printed for the Imprint Society, 1971), chaps. 10 and 26, respectively.

Koromanti.

Meri Bonbo

mich langa meri wa langa

Upon one of their Festivals when a great many of the Negro Musicians were gathered together, I desired Mr. *Baptiste,* the best Musician there to take the Words they sung and set them to Musick, which follows.

You must clap Hands when the Base is plaid, and cry, *Alla, Alla.*

Angola.

Ho-baognion, Ho-baognion,

Ho—ba Ognion, Ognion.

Papa.

10. Jamaican Music From Sir Hans Sloane, *A Voyage to the Islands of Madera, Barbados, Nieves, S. Christopher and Jamaica . . .* (1707).

HYMNE EN L'HONNEUR DES ANCÊTRES.

Premiere Partie.

Très-lentement.

See hoang fien Tfou , Yu ling yu Tien,

Yuen yen tfing lieou , Yeou kao tay hiuen.

Hiuen fun cheou ming , Tchoui yuen ki fien ,

Ming yn ché tfoung , Y ouan fee ñien.

Seconde Partie.

Toui yué tché tfing , Yen jan jou cheng ,

Ki ki tchao ming , Kan ko tfai ting ;

(*r*) Dans les doubles notes qu'on trouve à la feconde & à la troifieme partie de cet Hymne , le *re* inférieur eft pour la voix , & celui d'en haut pour les inftrumens, d'après ce qu'en a dit le P. Amiot à la page 182. Voyez *Ibid.* note *q.*

Jou

11. Chinese Hymns From Joseph-Marie Amiot, *Mémoire sur la musique des chinois* (1779; reprint, Geneva: Minkoff, 1973), 184–85.

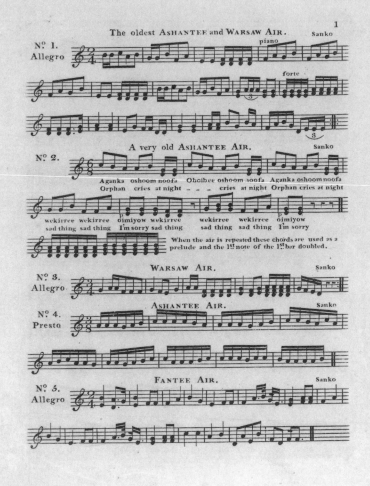

12. Ashantee Airs From T. Edward Bowdich, Esq., *Mission from Cape Coast Castle to Ashantee, with Statistical Account of That Kingdom . . .* (London: John Murray, Albemarle Street, 1819), first example in notational gallery after 364. (Courtesy Widener Library, Harvard University.)

de l'animal, il improvisa à notre louange des paroles qu'il chanta sur un air du pays.

Si, pour comprendre le génie d'un peuple, le
philosophe a besoin d'étudier ses mœurs et sa
religion; si le savant veut, pour l'apprécier, con-
naître ses œuvres d'esprit et de science; si l'indus-
triel doit toucher ces travaux qui exigent de plus
grands efforts de bras que d'imagination, l'artiste,
pour le sentir, demande sa poésie, ses inspirations,
et c'est surtout pour lui que nous allons noter ici
quelques uns de ces airs nationaux, qui lui don-
neront une idée de l'état de la musique chez ce
peuple, et qui l'aideront, sans doute, à voir la
mesure de sa civilisation.

Voici d'abord un air d'Abyssinie :

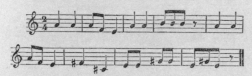

AIR DU ROYAUME DE CHOA.

II.   23

---

13. Abyssinian Airs (as Basis for Improvisation) From [Edmond] Combes
and [Maurice] Tamisier. *Voyage en Abyssinie, dans le pays des Galla, de Choa et D'Ifat
. . . ,* 2 vols. (Paris: Victor Magen, 1839), 2:353–54. (Courtesy Widener Library, Harvard University.)

AIR GALLA.

Ces chants sont peu modulés. Les notes doivent être détachées et fortement accentuées.

Nous allons joindre ici une des dernières productions arabes, pour constater la différence qui existe entre leur musique et celle des Abyssiniens.

Ainsi que les signes l'indiquent, cet air n'a pas de fin, et il se prolonge selon la fantaisie du chanteur.

FIN DU TOME DEUXIÈME.

langages étrangers, rivalisent d'éloquence ; le rameau
du myrobolanier incline la tête pour nous saluer ;
l'odeur que l'on respire sur les joues de la pomme
embaumée, ranime la cendre des morts.

MODE NAOUA.

Mesure douyek.

mah - bou — by là - bas bour

ney - tah Ou dek-ke - thou o'q -

- dah ou chneyt - tah Ta - leb - tou

ouas - lhou qàl ly' *sbey* -

tah[2] Mà - hlà ka - là — mhou hi-t -

[1] Les ornemens de cet air, exé-
cuté comme il l'est ordinairement
par les musiciens ou autres habitans
naturels de l'Égypte, étant un peu
moins baroques que ceux des autres
chansons arabes, nous avons entre-
pris de les noter. Quoiqu'ils ne dé-
figurent pas la mélodie autant que
les autres, cependant toutes les
notes sont tellement chargées de
broderies, que chaque phrase de
musique forme une roulade, et que
le chant simple se trouve comme
enveloppé, au point de devenir
presque insensible. (*M. Villoteau.*)

[2] Ce mot *sbeytah* est pour *esp-*

14. Egyptian Modes and Song From M. Villoteau, *De l'état actuel, de l'art musical en Égypte,* in *Description de l'Egypte,* 36 vols., 2d ed. (Paris: C. L. F. Panckoucke,
1826), 14:155. (Courtesy Eda Kuhn Loeb Music Library, Harvard University.)

and concern with how non-Western performances differ from those of Europe. With Léry's publication, we witness already the commencement of modern Europe's fascination with an outwardly recognized strangeness. While acknowledging musical capacities among South American Indians, Léry seemed above all interested in the way their performances departed from the musical norms of Europe.[73] At this point, however, he is content to describe and observe, which he does with apparent faith in the accuracy of his own descriptive mechanism. Similarly, in his discussion of African music in Jamaica (1707), the British government official Hans Sloane makes clear distinctions between the faculties of European observation and the lesser performances of slaves. "The Negroes are much given to Venery, and although hard wrought, will at nights, or on Feast days Dance and Sing; their Songs are all bawdy, and leading that way." Despite these failings, Sloane provides notations to document them, which were produced by a French musician identified as "Baptiste." While expressing no apparent concern about the notation's accuracy, Sloane's indication that "you must clap Hands when the Base is plaid, and cry, *Alla, Alla*" can be but a vague reference to the intricacies of an undoubtedly dynamic responsorial engagement (see fig. 10).[74]

By the late eighteenth century, the contradictions of notational representation begin to be acknowledged by those documenting foreign music. As scholars devote greater effort to understanding the logic of non-European practices—Joseph-Marie Amiot's *Mémoire sur la musique des chinois* (1779) representing that century's most important example (fig. 11)—they become increasingly aware of the limits of representation, and this realization in turn complicates a once disinterested analytical posture. A primary indication of the blurring of observer and observed is the rising interest in performing foreign music, anticipating what the ethnomusicologist Mantle Hood would name "bi-musicality." According to Ter Ellingson, William Jones, an early student of Indian music and the father of Indo-European language studies, "was apparently first to suggest that Europeans might learn to perform the music they studied abroad" as he demonstrated the value of conducting ethnographic observation rather than simply relying on published representations.

Shortly after this time, we witness a related phenomenon in which transcribers begin to rethink the presumed accuracy of notation itself. Whereas eighteenth-century analysts from Rousseau to Francis Fowke continued to celebrate European notation's precision, early nineteenth-century scholars occasionally questioned its reliability and employed it with circumspection.[75] T. Edward Bowdich (1819) wrote condescendingly of the funeral dirge of the Ashantee as "such a mixture of yells and screeches, that it bids defiance to all notation." Yet he also acknowledged the limits of his inscriptive powers while complementing the character of the airs he prepared as an "annex" of images (fig. 12). "To have attempted any thing like arrangement, beyond what the annexed airs naturally possess," Bowdich writes, "would have altered them, and destroyed the intention of making them known in their original character. I have not even dared to insert a flat or a sharp."[76] In *Voyage en Absyssinie* (1839), moreover, Edmond Combes and Maurice Tamisier offer transcriptions of airs in conventional staff notation while also indicating transcription's limits. Within the context of a perfunctory rendering—they dismiss the musician as someone who merely performs for food—the authors observe that the tunes are played in a staccato and heavily accented way, tacitly acknowledging the fallibility of their own notations (fig. 13).[77] Guillaume-André Villoteau, finally, would take the evolution of musical transcription a step further by introducing new experimental notations in his transcriptions (1826; see fig 14). As a member of the scientific commission accompanying Napoleon to Egypt, he produced a massive volume of regional performances (Arab, Egyptian, Ethiopian, Sudanese, etc.), replete with copious transcription. (The volume, with transcriptions, exceeds five-hundred pages.) In order to correct the "defects" of European musical writing ("Le défaut de signes dans notre musique"), he employed accidental variations indicating microtonal adjustments. At once, Villoteau increased the precision as well as the imprecision of European analytical equipment. He improved it only to magnify its flaws, as the contradictions of representing the foreign now entered into the notations themselves.[78]

In the discovery of the limits of European critical faculties, we see the emergence of the partial. By abstracting sound as writing, transcribers foregrounded notation's own artificiality, prompting the imagination of what lies beyond the notes as such. Ironically, the difference that partiality conceives is recognized only once the songs enter the space of Europe's common logic: what sounds or looks foreign is that which cannot fit into a larger circumstance of comparative familiarity. Like racial difference more generally, foreign music accordingly hovers in a contradictory realm between sameness and otherness, music and noise. At once similar and different, it complicates the stability of inside and outside and, in turn, Europe's certainty of its own place at the center of the world. From this vantage, we can observe the transcription of exotic musics as a disruption of the discursive and textual spaces of European musical supremacy and order. Appearing as a consequence of colonial documentation, transcrip-

tion is increasingly seen as a radical maneuver, whose power and significance would grow as the contests of self and other, of sameness and difference, take on greater consequence in Europe's relation to the world. If, as
W. J. T. Mitchell writes, "part of the power of perspectival illusionism was
that it seemed to reveal not just the outward, visible world but the very nature of the rational soul whose vision is represented," so would the power
of transcription arise from its indications of the unheard.[79] As a matter of
course, transcription moves away from the realistic, becoming a kind of
evocation anticipating modernism. By producing transcription as evocation, scribes concocted a visual form of music's own association with the
beyond. One might even say that the notations were written through with
the sound of music's sociodiscursive formation as a quality of transcendence. It is this welter of representational complexity that establishes the
background for the major initiative of transcribing the spirituals for public
consumption.

The principal "memory text" of slave singing practices is the compendium of 136 musical engravings published as *Slave Songs of the United
States* (figs. 15 and 16).[80] This edition, which brought together for the first
time a large share of the existing transcriptions of southern plantations
songs, represents a watershed moment in the documentation of American
slave music. As a painstakingly prepared tribute to spiritual sound, *Slave
Songs of the United States* appears as part of the stream of nineteenth-
century Christian hymnals and tune books that accompanied the evangelical movements and also bears an important relationship with the volumes
of blackface song published from the 1840s. In its positioning of "Negro civility," moreover, the book betrayed its abolitionist origins in the tradition
of Theodore Dwight Weld's collection of public testimony, *American Slavery as It Is. Slave Songs of the United States* is also a compendium, proposing
an alignment with the emerging body of German masterworks (formalized
later in national collections such as *Denkmäler deutscher Tonkunst*) and
possibly even a tacit challenge to the assumption of European musical superiority.[81] The compendium, to be sure, was very much an artifact of
nineteenth-century reform initiatives that had destabilized racial orthodoxies as a means toward a common good. In fundamental ways, it challenged the post–Civil War white supremacist versions of history that
sought to promote national reconciliation at the expense of blacks. At the
same time, by portraying African-American slaves as models of aristocratic civility, so did it accommodate those very ambitions. More than a
mere document, then, *Slave Songs of the United States* was an ambiguously
radical and at times antidisciplinary text. Most fundamentally, it employed

SLAVE SONGS

OF THE

UNITED STATES.

New York:
A. SIMPSON & CO.,
1867.

15. Title Page of *Slave Songs of the United States* Edited by William Francis Allen, Charles Pickard Ware, and Lucy McKim Garrison (New York: A. Simpson, 1867). (Courtesy Allen Family Papers, Wisconsin Historical Society, University of Wisconsin—Madison.)

CONTENTS.

PAGE.

INTRODUCTION...i—xxxviii
Directions for Singing...xliii

PART I.

South-Eastern Slave States, including South Carolina, Georgia and the Sea Islands ....1—61

  1 Roll, Jordan, roll. *Port Royal Islands, South Carolina.* C. P. W. Variation, L. McK. G.   1
  2 Jehovah, Hallelujah. *Port Royal Islands.* C. P. W..................................... 2
  3 I hear from Heaven to-day. *Port Royal Islands.* C. P. W............................... 2
  4 Blow your trumpet, Gabriel. *Port Royal Islands.* C. P. W. Variation, Mr. Reuben
     Tomlinson. Second version, *Charleston.* Mrs. C. J. Bowen 3
  5 Praise, member. *Port Royal Islands.* C. P. W 4
  6 Wrestle on, Jacob. *Port Royal Islands.* C. P. W..................................... 4
  7 The Lonesome Valley. *Port Royal Islands.* C. P. W................................... 5
  8 I can't stay behind. *Port Royal Islands.* C. P. W................................... 6
  9 Poor Rosy. *Port Royal Islands.* C. P. W. Variation, L. McK. G....................... 7
10 The Trouble of the World. *Port Royal Islands.* C. P. W. Variation, *Savannah.* Mr.
     Arthur L. Ware... 8
11 There's a meeting here to-night. *Port Royal Islands.* C. P. W. Second version,
     Charleston. Mrs. Bowen... 9
12 Hold your light. *Port Royal Islands.* C. P. W...................................... 10
13 Happy Morning. *Port Royal Islands.* C. P. W.. 10
14 No man can hinder me. *Port Royal Islands.* L. McK. G. Second version, C. P. W... 10
15 Lord, remember me. *Port Royal Islands.* C. P. W.................................... 12
16 Not weary yet. *Port Royal Islands.* C. P. W.. 12
17 Religion so sweet. *Port Royal Islands.* C. P. W.................................... 13
18 Hunting for the Lord. *Port Royal Islands.* C. P. W................................. 13
19 Go in the wilderness. *Port Royal Islands.* C. P. W................................. 14
20 Tell my Jesus "Morning." *Port Royal Islands.* C. P. W.............................. 15
21 The Graveyard. *Port Royal Islands.* C. P. W. Variation, W. F. A. 15
22 John, John, of the Holy Order. *Port Royal Islands.* C. P. W........................ 16
23 I saw the beam in my sister's eye. *Port Royal Islands.* C. P. W.................... 17
24 Hunting for a city. *Port Royal Islands.* C. P. W................................... 18
25 Gwine follow. *Port Royal Islands.* C. P. W... 18
26 Lay this body down. *Port Royal Islands.* C. P. W. Variation, Lt.-Col. C. T. Trow-
     bridge].. 19
27 Heaven bell a-ring. *Port Royal Islands.* C. P. W................................... 20
28 Jine 'em. *Port Royal Islands.* C. P. W... 21
29 Rain fall and wet Becca Lawton. *Port Royal Islands.* C. P. W....................... 21

16. First Page of the Table of Contents of *Slave Songs of the United States*
Edited by William Francis Allen, Charles Pickard Ware, and Lucy McKim Garrison (New York: A. Simpson, 1867). (Courtesy Allen Family Papers, Wisconsin Historical Society, University of Wisconsin—Madison.)

mechanically reproduced script in order to make the instabilities of racial logic material, evoking, in acts of veritable alchemy, the sounds of slaves.

The editors of *Slave Songs of the United States* were steeped in the language of aesthetic romance that had previously informed folkoric and ballad studies. Lucy McKim, Charles Pickard Ware, and William Francis Allen were all former abolitionists with family ties to the Unitarian ministry who had left the Northeast in order to participate in wartime educational initiatives on the Carolina Sea Islands.[82] McKim was the first to journey to the Islands, visiting briefly with her father, the abolitionist Reverend James Miller McKim, in June 1862. During the stay, she prepared several transcriptions, which she presented to John Sullivan Dwight in the aforementioned letter to *Dwight's Journal of Music*. Five of the transcriptions were published in *Slave Songs of the United States,* including the lead song, "Roll, Jordan, Roll." Another work, "Poor Rosy," turned up forty years later as one of the unattributed songs concluding W. E. B. Du Bois's *The Souls of Black Folk.*[83] Allen and Ware, moreover, were cousins, born into the aristocratic Ware family of Cambridge. After graduating from Harvard, they traveled to the Sea Islands to teach freed slaves, Ware departing in July 1862 and Allen following in November 1863. By 1864, they had each prepared dozens of transcriptions, many of which were brought together in the slave-song compendium. The volume features thirty-five transcriptions by Allen and the entirety of Ware's collection of fifty-one texts.[84] To these would be added several others prepared by collectors working in a vast geographic area stretching from the Southeast northward to Virginia, Maryland, and Delware, and southwest to Tennessee and Louisiana. Dena Epstein explains that the three editors worked together in planning the volume. Yet it was McKim's prominence in the Garrison family—in 1865, she married Wendell Phillips Garrison, literary editor of the *Nation* and son of William Lloyd Garrison, the abolitionist—that provided a vital institutional forum for the book's production and promotion. Eventually, chief editorial responsibilities were assumed by Allen, who, with the assistance of the magazine's editorial office, prepared the texts, annotations, and a thirty-eight-page introduction. That initial collaboration apparently spawned an ongoing relationship, and Allen would be a common contributor to the magazine over the next thirty years.[85]

Allen's personal interest in the songs reflected a philosophical kinship with the Cambridge circle of folklorists and critics. At the Latin School and then at Harvard (class of 1851), he studied ancient languages and history, a course of learning that would ultimately make him one of the nation's premier classical scholars (fig. 17). According to his colleague Clement

17. Photograph of William Francis Allen, 1830–89
(Courtesy Allen Family Papers, Wisconsin Historical Society,
University of Wisconsin—Madison.)

Lawrence Smith, Allen espoused a social evolutionary perspective that
was deemed radical at the time. For Allen, "No historical fact had any value
'except so far as it helps us to understand human nature, or the working of
historic forces,' which have their root in human nature."[86] By turning to the
ancients for insight into the present, Allen had pursued already in his
youth a line of inquiry that paralleled similar searches for origins in the
scholarly and creative work of Lowell, Child, and Longfellow. Given the exclusivity of Cambridge intellectual culture at midcentury—Allen's Harvard
class totaled sixty-one students—it is likely that he had at least some con-

tact with the critics and collectors of folklore who lived and worked there.[87] Surely he was aware of Longfellow and Child, who were both on the Harvard faculty, as well as Lowell, whose folk-inspired literature was well known. Like Child, moreover, Allen pursued postgraduate studies in Göttingen, the German center of folkloric studies and home of the Grimms. Like Child, too, he joined the Educational Commission of Freedmen (fig. 18); his certificate of admission (not shown here) lists Child as an officer. Also at Harvard at this time was Alexander Wheelock Thayer, whose biography of Beethoven (1856) represented one of the hallmarks of nineteenth-century American musical scholarship. Rounding out the Cambridge circle, finally, were Dwight and Higginson. Both would become directly involved in *Slave Songs of the United States,* Higginson as a contributor, and Dwight, a friend of the Ware family, as one of its publicists.[88]

As a reform text, *Slave Songs of the United States* calls to mind abolitionist depictions of African-Americans as founts of Western propriety and civility. Allen's essay, in particular, bears striking resemblances to the essays of white abolitionists that commonly introduce slave narratives. Like the narratives' introductions, Allen's seeks to lend to slave expressions the honor of white authority and approval. Observed in the context of postwar efforts toward reunion, these comments support progressive claims that blacks owned a rightful place in a reunited America. It is therefore striking how frequently the text's focus shifts from slave music to whites' observations of the music. Like the Civil War commemorations promoting white reconciliation, Allen's introduction obscures the black presence in the name of its celebration. From the outset, Allen speaks in the language of the explorer, recalling how after "discovering the rich vein of music," he and his colleagues became enraptured with the slave singing practices. For visitors from the North, he explains, "there was nothing that seemed better worth their while than to see a 'shout' or hear the 'people' sing their 'sperichels.'" Gathering together every available "specimen" of transcribed song, the editors would pay "tribute to the musical genius of the [Negro] race." In the process of collection, they ultimately bestowed honor on themselves, providing for white history written documentation of "a state of society which has passed away [and] should be preserved while it is still possible." What the editors hoped to preserve, of course, was not simply "civility"—merely an extension of their own whiteness—but the qualities of blackness incommensurable with white experience. With the making of each new specimen, difference would be reaffirmed. For Allen, in particular, the appeal of the slave songs related directly to their "half-barbarous" racial liminality.[89] One could hear in the spirituals a kind of

18. Allen's Certificate of Admission to the Educational Commission for Freedmen (Courtesy Allen Family Papers, Wisconsin Historical Society, University of Wisconsin—Madison.)

sonic closure that overcame the rift between civilization and darkness, coupling forms ancient and modern. Allen observes, "The greater number of the songs which have come into our possession, seem to be the natural and original production of a race of remarkable musical capacity and very teachable, which has long enough associated with the more cultivated race to have become imbued with the mode and spirit of European music—often nevertheless, retaining a distinct tinge of their native Africa."[90] The slave songs had thus sustained a crucial balance: tamed by the formidable powers of reason, they supported the refashioning of an original unity within the context of the civilized world.

Celebrating the slaves' civility while fetishizing their qualities of difference, Allen attempts to negotiate this crucial balance by committing the songs to the "truth" of scientific analysis. The application of analytic and inherently comparative procedures has the striking effect of magnifying notation's inadequacies, bringing the "spiritual effect" of partiality into focus. References to polyphonic textures ("no two appear to be singing the same thing") and intricate techniques of performance ("the 'basers' themselves seem to follow their own whims . . . to produce the effect of a marvellous complication and variety") reveal a logic of slave musicality that ultimately exceeds rational comprehension. Occasional groupings of related variations of a core melody similarly situate slave practices within the frame of studies of European musical style, only to underscore how profoundly they deviate from the norms of classical practice.[91] Similar paradoxes appear when Allen draws comparisons between his research into African-American and Greco-Roman ritual. Slaves wandering through the woods to access the spiritual ("to 'fin' dat ting' ") become familiar as Dionysian "ancient bacchantes"; the oddities of shouting acquire a history along a Western parallel: "it is not unlikely that this remarkable religious ceremony is a relic of some native African dance, as the Romaika is of the classical Pyrrhic."[92] Ultimately, Allen's detached, scholarly posture collapses as praise gives way to a reproachful comment on slave speech practices. Here, Allen's philological analysis of "corruptions" and "phonetic decay" suggests a scholarly version of the minstrel show, in which he mocks the "comic specimens" of Gullah dialect.[93] Minstrel reductions once again maneuver difference into a controllable sphere, just as the songs' articulation in the language of the "sperichel" brings it forward.

Allen and his colleagues' failed attempts to negotiate the incommensurability of sameness and difference appear most strikingly in the 136 transcriptions—revealingly named "songs to be desired and regretted"—that form the centerpiece of *Slave Songs of the United States*.[94] Superficially, the compilation resembles any one of the countless number of song collections common to middle-class homes. Single-voice melodies appear on a standard five-line staff notation, conforming to the disciplines of rhythm and pitch. Lyrics, while written in dialect, assume metric patterns consistent with popular song at the time. For a northern public unfamiliar with the actual singing of the slaves, the spirituals would have seemed patently reasonable. As Allen contends, "There are very few [songs] which are of an intrinsically barbaric character, and where this character does appear, it is chiefly in short passages, intermingled with others of a different character."[95] In these contexts, he works to isolate and contain those expressions of difference. Notation becomes a way of encouraging a particular way of hearing and performing that is consistent with Euro-American song traditions and the edifice of musical knowledge on which they depend. Precision of pitch in the realm of diatonicism, equal temperament, and "four-square" metric simplicity sustain vocal practices specific to the European legacy. Importantly, they encourage a general way of breathing and articulating sound that affects the very nature of bodily posture and feeling. Notation enters the body, shaping and contouring the physicality of vocal expression. Singing the sameness of the spiritual supplies these songs with flesh that is discernibly felt and heard as white.

Yet with each gesture to the songs' sameness, Allen makes another to their difference; undermining his overtly assimilationist intentions, he unleashes a black sense of subversive play. Along margins, between lines, and in superscripts, he employs text to note exceptions to the rule of civilized practice. Indicated editorially, these are the textual variations, the alterations of scale forms, and the alternative versions that appear throughout *Slave Songs of the United States.* "Turn, Sinner, Turn O!" for example, consists of an assembly of tunes, verses, and melodic and lyrical variations that were "constantly interchanged" to produce "the most dramatic of all the shouts" (fig. 19). "The Day of Judgment" includes a minor alteration of the third scale-degree (in modern parlance, a "blue note") to depict what its transcriber, Mrs. C. J. B., calls "a sort of prolonged wail" (fig. 20). Of special interest are the ten titles that Allen claims "may well be purely African in origin." These "Lyra Africana" typically share rhythmic "irregularities" that exceed the capabilities of European notation.[96] In "God Got Plenty o' Room," time signatures shift unpredictably from 2/8 to 3/8 to 2/8 to 2/4 and onward in a "hopeless undertaking to attempt to restore the correct time . . . of negro singing" (fig. 21). "The Trouble of the World" employs frequent eighth-note triplets to render the "rapid, hurried, and irregular [rhythms] to a degree which is very hard to imitate and impossible to represent in notes" (fig. 22). Other "African" texts express more subtle peculiarities, such as the pitch repetitions in "Hunting for the Lord" (fig. 23), the curious lyrics of "Round the Corn, Sally" (fig. 24), the use of French language in the Louisiana-based "Belle Layotte" and "Rémon" (figs. 25 and 26), and the reference to shouting practices in "Shall I Die?" (fig. 27). By this point, the compendium of slave songs seems less a scholarly text than a

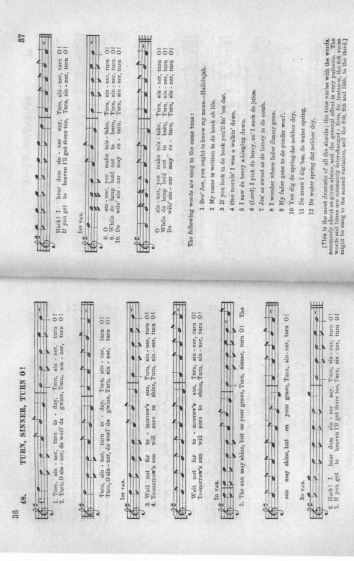

19. "Turn, Sinner, Turn O!" From *Slave Songs of the United States*, ed. William Francis Allen, Charles Pickard Ware, and Lucy McKim Garrison (New York: A. Simpson, 1867). (Courtesy Allen Family Papers, Wisconsin Historical Society, University of Wisconsin—Madison.)

72. THE DAY OF JUDGMENT.

1. And de moon will turn to blood, And de moon will turn to

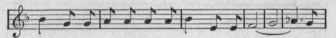

blood, And de moon will turn to blood In dat day—O - yoy,* my

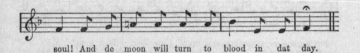

soul! And de moon will turn to blood in dat day.

2 And you'll see de stars a-fallin'.

3 And de world will be on fire.

4 And you'll hear de saints a-singin :

5 And de Lord will say to de sheep.

6 For to go to Him right hand ;

7 But de goats must go to de left.

* " A sort of prolonged wail."—Mrs. C. J. B.

20. "The Day of Judgment" From *Slave Songs of the United States,* ed. William Francis Allen, Charles Pickard Ware, and Lucy McKim Garrison (New York: A. Simpson, 1867). (Courtesy Allen Family Papers, Wisconsin Historical Society, University of Wisconsin—Madison.)

128.   GOD GOT PLENTY O' ROOM.

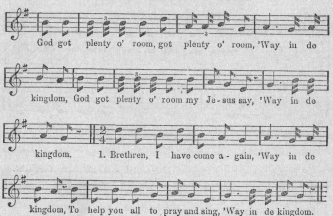

God got plenty o' room, got plenty o' room, 'Way in de kingdom, God got plenty o' room my Je-sus say, 'Way in de kingdom. 1. Brethren, I have come a-gain, 'Way in de kingdom, To help you all to pray and sing, 'Way in de kingdom.

2 So many-a weeks and days have passed
  Since we met together last.

3 Old Satan tremble when he sees
  The weakest saints upon their knees.

4 Prayer makes the darkest cloud withdraw,
  Prayer climbed the ladder Jacob saw.

5 Daniel's wisdom may I know,
  Stephen's faith and spirit sure.

6 John's divine communion feel,
  Joseph's meek and Joshua's zeal.

7 There is a school on earth begun
  Supported by the Holy One.

8 We soon shall lay our school-books by,
  And shout salvation as I fly.

[The above is given exactly as it was sung, some of the measures in 3. some in 3. and some in 2 time. The irregularity probably arises from omission of rests, but it seemed a hopeless undertaking to attempt to restore the correct time. and it was thought best to give it in this shape as at any rate a characteristic specimen of negro singing. The song was obtained of a North Carolina negro, who said it came from Virginia.]

21. "God Got Plenty o' Room" From *Slave Songs of the United States,* ed. William Francis Allen, Charles Pickard Ware, and Lucy McKim Garrison (New York: A. Simpson, 1867). (Courtesy Allen Family Papers, Wisconsin Historical Society, University of Wisconsin—Madison.)

10. THE TROUBLE OF THE WORLD.

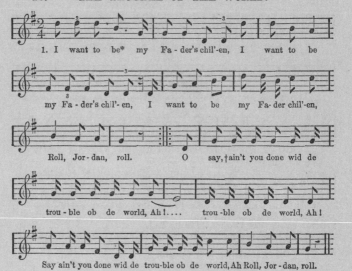

1. I want to be* my Fa-der's chil'-en, I want to be

my Fa-der's chil'-en, I want to be my Fa-der chil'-en,

Roll, Jor-dan, roll. O say,†ain't you done wid de

trou-ble ob de world, Ah!.... trou-ble ob de world, Ah!

Say ain't you done wid de trou-ble ob de world,Ah Roll, Jor-dan, roll.

2 I ask de Lord how long I hold 'em, (*ter*)
Hold 'em to de end.

3 My sins so heavy I can't get along, Ah! &c.

4 I cast my sins in de middle of de sea, Ah! &c.

* O you ought to be.   † My sister, My mudder, etc.

[This is perhaps as good a rendering of this strange song as can be given. The difficulty is in the time, which is rapid, hurried and irregular to a degree which is very hard to imitate and impossible to represent in notes. The following is sung in Savannah, with the same refrain, "Trouble of the world:"]

I wish I was in ju - bi - lee, Ha, ju - bi - lee; I

wish I was in ju - bi - lee, Roll, Jor - dan, roll.

22. "The Trouble of the World" From *Slave Songs of the United States,* ed. William Francis Allen, Charles Pickard Ware, and Lucy McKim Garrison (New York: A. Simpson, 1867). (Courtesy Allen Family Papers, Wisconsin Historical Society, University of Wisconsin—Madison.)

18. HUNTING FOR THE LORD.

Hunt till you find him, Halle - lu - jah, And a - huntin' for de Lord; Till you find him, Halle - lu - jah, And a - huntin' for de Lord.

23. "Hunting for the Lord" From *Slave Songs of the United States,* ed. William Francis Allen, Charles Pickard Ware, and Lucy McKim Garrison (New York: A. Simpson, 1867). (Courtesy Allen Family Papers, Wisconsin Historical Society, University of Wisconsin—Madison.)

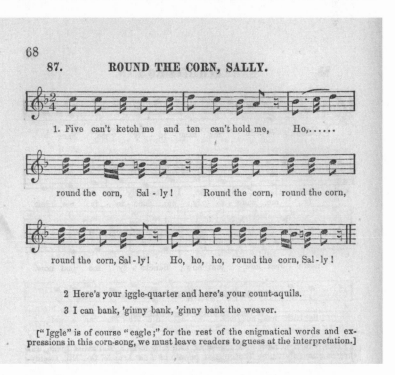

68

87. ROUND THE CORN, SALLY.

1. Five can't ketch me and ten can't hold me, Ho,......

round the corn, Sal - ly ! Round the corn, round the corn,

round the corn, Sal - ly ! Ho, ho, ho, round the corn, Sal - ly !

2 Here's your iggle-quarter and here's your count-aquils.

3 I can bank, 'ginny bank, 'ginny bank the weaver.

["Iggle" is of course "eagle;" for the rest of the enigmatical words and expressions in this corn-song, we must leave readers to guess at the interpretation.]

24. "Round the Corn, Sally" From *Slave Songs of the United States,* ed. William Francis Allen, Charles Pickard Ware, and Lucy McKim Garrison (New York: A. Simpson, 1867). (Courtesy Allen Family Papers, Wisconsin Historical Society, University of Wisconsin—Madison.)

130.   **BELLE LAYOTTE.**

Mo dé-jà rou-lé tout la côte Pan-cor ouar par-eil

belle La-yotte. (*bis*) 1. Mo rou-lé tout la côte,

Mo rou-lé tout la col-o-nie; Mo pan-cor ouar

griffonne la Qua mo gout comme la belle La-yotte.

2 Jean Babet, mon ami,
   Si vous couri par en haut,
   Vous mandé belle Layotte
   Cadeau la li té promi mouin.

3 Domestique la maison
   Yé tout faché avec mouin,
   Paraporte chanson la
   Mo composé pou la belle Layotte.

25. "Belle Layotte" From *Slave Songs of the United States,* ed. William Francis Allen, Charles Pickard Ware, and Lucy McKim Garrison (New York: A. Simpson, 1867). (Courtesy Allen Family Papers, Wisconsin Historical Society, University of Wisconsin—Madison.)

131.   RÉMON.

SOLO.

Mo par - lé Ré - mon, Ré - mon, Li par - lé Si - mon, Si -
- mon, Li par - lé Ti - tine, Ti - tine, Li tom - bé dans chagrin.

CHORUS.

O femme Rom - u - lus, oh! Belle femme Romu - lus, oh!   O
femme Rom - u - lus, oh! Belle femme qui ça vou - lé mo fai.

26. "Rémon" From *Slave Songs of the United States,* ed. William Francis Allen, Charles Pickard Ware, and Lucy McKim Garrison (New York: A. Simpson, 1867). (Courtesy Allen Family Papers, Wisconsin Historical Society, University of Wisconsin—Madison.)

52.   **SHALL I DIE?**

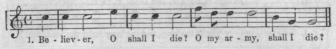

1. Be - liev - er,   O   shall I   die? O my ar - my, shall I   die?

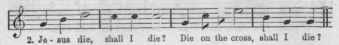

2. Je - sus die, shall I   die? Die on the cross, shall I   die?

3 Die, die, die, shall I die?
Jesus da coming, shall I die?

4 Run for to meet him, shall I die?
Weep like a weeper, shall I die?

5 Mourn like a mourner, shall I die?
Cry like a crier, shall I die?

[This shout was a great favorite on the Capt. John Fripp plantation; its simplicity, wildness and minor character suggest a native African origin. Sometimes the leading singer would simply repeat the words, mournfully : " Die, die,
die,"—sometimes he would interpolate such an inappropriate line as " Jump
along, jump along dere."]

27. "Shall I Die?" From *Slave Songs of the United States,* ed. William Francis Allen,
Charles Pickard Ware, and Lucy McKim Garrison (New York: A. Simpson, 1867). (Courtesy
Allen Family Papers, Wisconsin Historical Society, University of Wisconsin—Madison.)

theosophical offering to a mystical unknown wholly beyond notational containment. "The voices of the colored people have a peculiar quality that nothing can imitate," Allen writes. And as sound resists text, "difference" reveals the peculiarity of transcription itself. The written traces of song call to mind the textual fragments of Robert Carlton Brown's optical poetry: "black riders"—the ink of text—"galloping across a blank page."[97]

The artifice of notation thus constructs the naturalness of song, which in turn heightens awareness of the limits—indeed, the veritable strangeness—of transcription itself. This dialectical interplay never resolves, but it does create an illusory synthesis in the newly conceptualized figuration of difference as an "Africa" existing between the lines. In the bias of pitch-based staff notation deficient in capturing temporal subtlety, an African rhythm would be conceived, giving way to a broad-based language that sought to describe it. In African rhythm, Americans and then the world heard the primitive, the peasant, the agrarian, together with baser forms of danger: the idiot, the savage, the wild man, the beast. For Allen, as for most Americans at the time, black or white, African-inspired rhythm was a mere reference point with vaguely "barbaric" associations, still subordinate to the dominant qualities of spiritually inspired plantation melody. But from this time forward it would become an increasingly significant influence, to the point of informing figurations of race and music by the 1890s and dominating them across the twentieth century. It is important to underscore that this rhythmic quality was not a "true" African feature coming to bear, as if notation had finally revealed a retained musical seed or essence. Rather black musical difference becomes categorized and constructed as that which exceeds notation and is, accordingly, conceptualized as rhythm, the marginal expression of Europe's pitch-centered harmonic system. The publication of *Slave Songs of the United States* thus establishes the basis of a new modern racial discourse informed by rhythm, even while at this point giving central emphasis to melodic features. Rhythm would be increasingly accepted as the cultural ground of a distinctively black musical creation. It is what seems already to fascinate Allen (even as he is only vaguely aware of helping to construct it), as it would a worldwide populace.

A cache of transcriptions found tucked inside Allen's personal copy of *Slave Songs of the United States* dramatically conveys the sense of notation as modernist evocation (fig. 28). Appearing as a handwritten list of melodic sketches, the shout transcriptions seem tentative, partial, and incomplete, lacking the authority of an engraved music text.[98] In fact the simple melodic and rhythmic figures resemble more the preliminary notes of a composer's sketchbook than an accurate portrayal of complex oral singing. Yet what the manuscript loses in authority it gains in the honesty of handwritten script. Paradoxically, the stature of Allen's manuscript increases with the revelation of its inaccuracy. As a historical document of a note taker's futile labor, the transcriptions acquire an aura of transcendent uncontainability that summons the spiritual, inspiring a fictional remembering. If the transcriptions were "but a faint shadow of the original . . . intonations and delicate variations [that] cannot be reproduced on paper," they nonetheless offered the image of an ancient encounter, of the witnessing of living vestiges of primordial sound. The volatility of writing in its sheer violence accomplishes the seemingly impossible task of converting the ancient into the audible, as text moves "the spiritual" toward the modern.[99] According to this double logic, *Slave Songs of the United States* maintains its crucial balance, expressing a difference that undermines notational competence while also fitting comfortably into the domain of nineteenth-century domestic music. This enables Allen to assert without apparent contradiction, "I feel confident . . . that there are no mistakes of importance." In order to reassure his readership, moreover, Allen appears to smooth over discrepancies, converting notational transgressions into the uniformities of printed text (e.g., "Bell Da Ring," which appears in two versions; cf. the third staff, after the first double bar of fig. 28 with fig. 29). The revisions, however inaccurate, remain in their partiality still "correct" since they accommodate white access, just as the prefatory "Directions for Singing," outlining formal inconsistencies (to "help to remove all obscurities with which the reader may be embarrassed"), encourages whites to effect "black song" (fig. 30).[100] That Allen's family, like so many families in the nineteenth century, regularly engaged in domestic singing—to the point that his New England relatives privately published a compendium of Allen family songs (1899)—suggests that *Slave Songs of the United States* may have been a kind of personal testimonial to his prior activism, memory texts through which he and his family could, quite literally, embody black sound (fig. 31). The texts offered a way of hearing voices prior to their being written, evoking Whitmanesque images of singing bodies filtering through the confines of white notations.

Yet whose voicings did Allen and his readers remember when bearing witness to these imaginary sites? If we recall the musical recollections of Frederick Douglass, we observe that he, too, brings to life an audible past after his own psychological transformation through literacy. His reconstruction, however, while different from the actual past, grew out of an immediate, direct encounter. Douglass lived his early life in slavery, whereas

28. Transcription of Melodies from Shouting Ceremonies, Probably Beaufort, South Carolina William Francis Allen, transcriber (Allen Family Papers, Wisconsin Historical Society, University of Wisconsin—Madison).

34

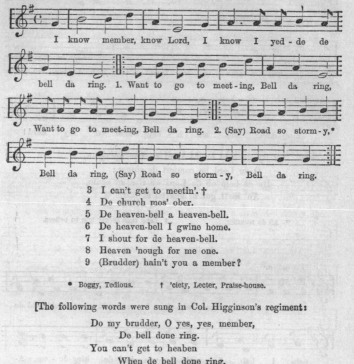

46.   BELL DA RING.

I know member, know Lord, I know I yed - de de

bell da ring. 1. Want to go to meet - ing, Bell da ring,

Want to go to meet-ing, Bell da ring. 2. (Say) Road so storm - y,*

Bell da ring, (Say) Road so storm - y, Bell da ring.

3 I can't get to meetin'. †
4 De church mos' ober.
5 De heaven-bell a heaven-bell.
6 De heaven-bell I gwine home.
7 I shout for de heaven-bell.
8 Heaven 'nough for me one.
9 (Brudder) hain't you a member?

* Boggy, Tedious.   † 'ciety, Lecter, Praise-house.

[The following words were sung in Col. Higginson's regiment:

Do my brudder, O yes, yes, member,
    De bell done ring.
You can't get to heaben
    When de bell done ring.
If you want to get to heaven,
    Fo' de bell, etc
You had better follow Jesus,
    Fo' de bell, etc.
O yes, my Jesus, yes, I member,
    De bell etc.
O come in, Christians,
    Fo' de bell, etc.
For the gates are all shut,
    When de bell, etc.
And you can't get to heaben
    When de bell, etc.

29. "Bell Da Ring" From *Slave Songs of the United States,* ed. William Francis Allen, Charles Pickard Ware, and Lucy McKim Garrison (New York: A. Simpson, 1867). (Courtesy Allen Family Papers, Wisconsin Historical Society, University of Wisconsin—Madison.)

DIRECTIONS FOR SINGING.

In addition to those already given in the Introduction, the following explanations may be of assistance :

Where all the words are printed with the music, there will probably be little difficulty in reading the songs; but where there are other words printed below the music, it will often be a question to which part of the tune these words belong, and how the refrain and the chorus are to be brought in.

It will be noticed that the words of most of the songs arrange themselves into stanzas of four lines each. Of these some are *refrain*, and some are *verse* proper. The most common arrangement gives the second and fourth lines to the refrain, and the first and third to the verse; and in this case the third line may be a repetition of the first, or may have different words. Often, however, the refrain occupies only one line, the verse occupying the other three; while in one or two songs the verse is only one line, while the refrain is three lines in length. The refrain is repeated with each stanza : the words of the verse are changed at the pleasure of the leader, or fugleman, who sings either well-known words, or, if he is gifted that way, invents verses as the song goes on.

In addition to the stanza, some of the songs have a chorus, which usually consists of a fixed set of words, though in some of the songs the chorus is a good deal varied. The refrain of the main stanza often appears in the chorus. The stanza can always be distinguished from the chorus, in those songs which have more than one stanza, by the figure " 1 " placed before the stanza which is printed with the music; the verses below being numbered on " 2," " 3," " 4," &c. In a few cases the first verse below the music is numbered " 3 ;" this occurs when two verses have been printed above in the music, instead of the first verse being repeated. When the chorus has a variety of words, the additional verses are printed below without numbers.

In the following list the first fifty tunes in the collection are classified according

30. First Page of "Directions for Singing" From *Slave Songs of the United States,* ed. William Francis Allen, Charles Pickard Ware, and Lucy McKim Garrison (New York: A. Simpson, 1867). (Courtesy Allen Family Papers, Wisconsin Historical Society, University of Wisconsin—Madison.)

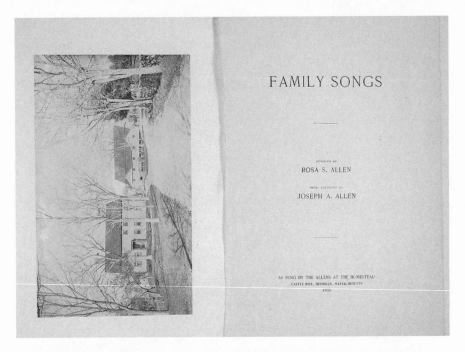

FAMILY SONGS

ROSA S. ALLEN

JOSEPH A. ALLEN

AS SUNG BY THE ALLENS AT THE HOMESTEAD
CASTLE HILL, MEDFIELD, MASSACHUSETTS
1899

31. Frontispiece and Title Page of the Allens' Privately Published Book, *Family Songs* **(1899)** (Courtesy Allen Family Papers, Wisconsin Historical Society, University of Wisconsin—Madison.)

white northerners merely observed it, remaining conspicuously outside the circle. While Allen replicated the kind of cultural translation fostered in the depiction of antebellum song, what he and his colleagues heard between the lines of the slave-song transcriptions could have no direct experiential relation to slavery. At best it expressed an imagined realm cast in the romantic language of race. To distinguish the personal experiences of slaves from the cultivated memories of whites is not to privilege the former as the real truth, the real evidence, so much as to acknowledge the different motivations of subsequent white and black musical projections.[101] Both racial cultures would increasingly rely on the same discourses to articulate how they imagined black music, and both would give special attention to slavery and Africa as an explanatory mode of musical distinctiveness. Thus we see after the Civil War composers and pedagogues embracing the tools of notation to communicate black music's truth, building on the precedents of Allen and his colleagues, together with the facsimile renderings of "Songs of the Contraband" published for polite consumption.[102] Over time, however, African-Americans would more vigorously draw connections between modern expressions and the slave and African pasts, particularly as those associations became privileged in the modern idea of "black experience." By the twentieth century, the figure of Africa increasingly associated with black music would acquire radically diverse meanings, ranging from the signature of an ennobled black spirit (in the image of Johnson's bard) to the playful cannibal of Manhattan primitivism.

The constructions of the past reveal again how black music's meanings evolved as an intersubjective, interracial process, a process at once enormously powerful and invisible. It is this same discursive matrix that enabled African-Americans variously to constitute an exclusive, exceptional music long after the last of the freed slaves had fallen silent, rendering spirituals, according to James Weldon Johnson, as if by magic. It is perhaps fittingly ironic, then, that the trope of black music's immateriality materialized the fiction of continuity for millions of Americans into the twentieth century. If the image of an immaterial black music was variously constructed according to the particulars of time and place, so was it united by the racialist designation "black" that ascribed to African-American musical creativity unique qualities of performance. Difference thus becomes key to figurations of black music, assigning a status of exception that gives to African-Americans a source of racialized power. It is through the idea of difference that a modern black America would finally hear its cultural past, discerning the echoes of an ancestral world saturated with textually invented "Negro sound."

5 Of Bodies and Soul

Feeling the Pulse of Modern Race Music

"What happens to a dream deferred?" Langston Hughes asks at the opening of his poem "Harlem." The dream, of course, is not local, not personal, but of a larger collective kind, as in the hope of African-American equality and freedom. Its ruin takes the form of contrasting, though similarly final, resolutions: "Maybe it just sags / like a heavy load. *Or does it explode?*" (emphasis in the original). A more successful realization is suggested in playful, dynamic movement that dances around stable conceptions of blackness. In the companion poem "Dream Boogie," Hughes proposes such a deferral in terms of musical repetition: "Good morning, daddy! / Ain't you heard / The boogie-woogie rumble / Of a dream deferred?"[1] The rapid eighth-note pulse of a piano bass line gives voice to the possibility of realizing the dream, or even better, of finding one's dream in the very act of seeking it.

For Hughes, black modern living realizes freedom in an energetic musically guided perseverance and play that also acknowledges the inevitability of conflict. One faces choices, and typically they are between places hard and harder. Still, what counts is activity forged out of the sonic drama of the African-American experience. In his poetry, he positions rhythm centrally as a formative power that while originating in the black body and referencing black history and memory gives primacy to contemporary modernist affiliations. As Larry Scanlon argues, "Hughes categorizes this entire process of cultural recovery as rhythmic, but he understands rhythm as a mode of constructing rather than preserving continuity, a mode paradoxically founded on discontinuity."[2] Realizing the "dream deferred" is a process of repeated choice making and encounter that locates the blackness of identity in the crisscrossing experiential action of the boogie-woogie rumble.

The emancipatory potential of free-flowing repetition is similarly at work in Houston Baker's now classic sound-filled portrait of the blues and African-American literature. In the familiar conceit of the crossroads, Baker locates an icon of the fateful contrasts that texture the "black experience": situations none too preferable arise along the many avenues of life-long pursuit and struggle. The legacies of racial oppression make movement necessary, whether in an effort to escape slavery or, after emancipation, to find better opportunities in cities north and south. The crossroads actualizes the topography of the American historical landscape, the surfaces of which regulate the course of black creativity and culture.[3] As Baker suggests, however, these same surfaces also give form to the differences they cannot contain. Figured materially as the railroad junctures through which African-Americans navigated their ways out of the Civil War South, "the crossroads" becomes in its repetition the symbol of the constraints of economy and language that contour experience. Traveling through the crossroads, the black subject ultimately achieves cultural voice in the dynamic and elusive sounding difference of black improvised play. Baker figures this repetition-in-voice musically as "blues": "The 'X' of crossing roadbeds signals the multi-directionality of the juncture and is simply a single instance in a boundless network that redoubles and circles, makes sidings and ladders, forms Y's and branches over the vastness of hundreds of thousands of American miles. Polymorphous and multidirectional, scene of arrivals and departures, place betwixt and between (ever *entre les deux*), the juncture is the way-station of the blues."[4]

And so with the blues, the repetitions of choice making and deferral pulse with a version of the "boogie-woogie rumble," giving rise to the distinctiveness of black expression or what we conventionally call "culture." In its otherness, however, black culture is a difference that grows from the absences uncontained by mainstream common sense. "The blues singer's signatory coda is always *atopic,* placeless: 'If anybody ask you who sang this song / Tell 'em X done been here and gone.' " For Baker, the black voice emerges as an eruption out of the fissures of a dominant economy to reveal its many versions of cultural resistance. African-American creativity builds from its denial, calling to mind the Ellisonian figures of invisibility ushering from Louis Armstrong's horn that began this study, or, in Baker's interpretation, the beauty arising from Robert Johnson's alienation at the axes of America writ large: "Standin' at the crossroad / I tried to flag a ride / Didn't nobody seem to know me /everybody pass me by."[5]

The tropes of repetition and crossing identify a crucial pairing of figurations in the interpretation of black expressive modernism. Together, they form a key relationship that relates the qualities of a musical sensibility forged out of black experience to the sociodiscursive domain of an America dominated by the perverse fantasy of race. At the center of Hughes's dream deferred and what Baker names "a dream of American form" is an underlying sonic dimension of pulsing sound for which the bodily felt dynamism represents something at once prior to and deeply seated within modern social circumstances. This paradox is fundamental to both critical projects as it is to the interpretation of black rhythm more generally. Understood in relation, black music speaks doubly to the artifice and the perceived naturalism of African-American musical sensibilities. What is constituted within the circumstances of the social coalesces as a form claiming a mythic racial origin.

Each in his own way, Hughes and Baker propose a means of celebrating black distinctiveness while acknowledging the social constitution of racial categories of art and culture. They are searching for a way around a radical antiracist skepticism that merely replicates assimilationist programs without succumbing to the likely alternative of a racially determined absolute stability. Recalling a strategy outlined by Hortense J. Spillers earlier in this story, they "want to eat the cake and *have* it."[6] And why not? Those who listen to and care about black music derive enormous pleasure from the power of racially grounded myths and the tales they tell, myths not merely fashioned in our world but that resonate out of the essential relation that gave to America a miraculous musical birth. To simply abrogate the natural laws of rhythm would mean denying the significance of black music as it has come to us and is so treasured today. The challenge, then, is to advance, for this final phase of the story, a music criticism that follows the same paradoxical contours, locating meaning in the "then and now"—at once prior to and deeply seated within modern social circumstances. With particular respect to the idea of black rhythm, the question is this: Can we embrace the claims of vital groove and essence while also challenging the racialism that routinely goes hand in hand with them? Put somewhat differently, can we imagine modes of listening that negotiate between the pleasures of racial fantasy and the critical and political necessities of deferring such dreamy notions?

To do so, I think, requires a forceful positioning of black sound at the crossroads of modern racial understanding. This positioning must necessarily build from the historical ground of language in the formation of modern discourses of rhythm, a formation located not in the recesses of Africa but in the network of texts on Africa and otherness as it intersected with American writing about blacks. Comprehending the modern conception of black rhythm means undertaking a critical genealogy that reaches into the historical depths of American language structures in order to trace the contours of a peculiar musical sensibility bound up with modern notions of race. This chapter traces the early associations of rhythm and race that informed interpretations of black music across the late eighteenth and nineteenth centuries, from early European depictions of Africans to New World representations. After exploring anticipations in philosophical treatises, travelogues, literary texts, and periodical writing, the discussion turns to a specific grouping of discourses emerging during the postbellum era that configured a radically new conception of black music. Constituted as a dynamic and propulsive absence dependent on the rigid commitments of white supremacy, rhythmically oriented black music arose, like prior forms, suddenly and seemingly out of nowhere, to dominate musical understanding from that time forward.

The modern formulation of black rhythm grows from a peculiar set of social alignments that together suggest a new version of the crossroads, cast according to a temporal-spatial axis specific to late-nineteenth-century ideologies of race. In this formulation, what may be conceived as the vertical dimension of the crossroads demonstrates the temporal concept of descent that dominated scientific theory and criticism at the onset of social Darwinism. Most familiarly, perhaps, descent describes familial relations—descendants. As an anthropological term, however, it referred to the search for origins, the act of looking downward into the recesses of history in order to identify the mythical place of human beginnings, an ultimately religious terrain where the "Negro," whether African or African-American, was prominently situated. As an intellectual concept grounded in a series of racial presuppositions, descent served above all to demarcate difference in seemingly benevolent terms. It identified the primordial cure for the ills of a civilized and increasingly mechanized modern society, and in this way, descent advanced in its rhythmic constructs a sense of spirituality and soul akin to midcentury interpretations of the slave songs.[7] Lurking beneath these noble affiliations, however, was the precivilized savagery in which an original blackness was rooted. As an otherness of primal desire, descent's darker side revealed itself in the undulating rhythms of blacks that connected to a savage debased nature.

By the end of the nineteenth century, references to black savagery increasingly appeared in depictions of African-Americans. What had been merely alluded to in prior representations assumed unprecedented circulation and play in connection with a growing fear of transgressive behavior, commonly known as the "Negro problem." The image of the treacherous debased "Negro" grew so influential, in fact, it came to inform the contrasting, spatial side of the axis, what Robert Johnson calls the "east and west" of the crossroads.[8] Whereas descent had identified a primarily intellectual concept, the treachery of what I will call black displacement resonated within the contexts of the American public sphere to express white concerns about the waves of black bodies moving both physically and symbolically from social place to place. Perceptions of black danger exceeded the drawing-board abstractions of descent, becoming the real-life threat for which excessive movements would be increasingly figured in musical terms and above all in the discrete quality of rhythm. An elusive presence that went far beyond the norms of harmonically oriented European musics, the figure of rhythmically generated black displacement provided a compelling metaphor for the massive array of African-Americans transgressing social borders.

In the same way that descent reveals its other, however, displacement epitomized the source of white desire, since it was the threat of contamination by an authentic black potency that also drove fascination. As black music proliferated through the mediations of print, recording, and public performance, the sense of threat would increase, just as its socially widespread appeal supplied emancipatory power to African-Americans. As a white populace contended with the newly rhythmicized projections of bodies and soul, a black America that had evolved out of the same ideological structures would quickly embrace these formations as a modern continuation of the miracle in sound. Constituted within the discourses of descent and displacement, the newly invented rhythmic practices of African-American musicians spoke simultaneously of cultural possibility and actualization, of dreams deferred and life as lived. Sonically evoking forgotten histories, whether in slavery or in the myths of Africa, black rhythm gave voice to distinctively new and modern identities specific to the here and now as it pulsed about the racial fantasies of modern America.[9]

Rhythm's Recognition   References to the bodily affecting power of black rhythm consumed the attention of reporters and readers alike with the rise of the modern as a twentieth-century phenomenon. While rhythm had always been associated with African and African-American musical performances, it had begun to overwhelm other aspects, its propulsive and seductive "hot" qualities—a term linked etymologically to forms of excess—identifying what many believed to be the music's vital essence.[10] Coon songs represent the first modern genre to demarcate the outlines of this new rhythmic sensibility. Referencing prior musical associations with black ferocity within a newly perceived rhythmic energy, the songs emerged as a potent threat engendering fears of a racial menace, depicted in the title of Paul Allen's seminal "New Coon in Town" (1883).[11] In this perverse extension of the minstrel stage, the Sambo figure of the midcentury takes on a more grotesque appearance, assuming a prefigurative version of Richard Wright's Bigger Thomas, a razor-wielding male attacker whose violence was expressed musically as propulsive rhythm. As a musical rendering of the "Negro as Beast," the coon appeared vividly in Charles E. Trevathan's "Bully Song" (1895), which was staged and recorded by May Irwin, generating several popular variants. The lyrics convey both the fear and the excitement that a dynamic Negro population had engendered:

Have you heard about that bully
That just come to town
He's down among the niggers
Laying the bodies down
I'm a looking for that bully and he must be found.

In subsequent verses, Trevathan's narrator proceeds to tell the tale of the ensuing search, discovery, and attack. The fight is described in graphic language animated with images of blood, blades, and razors.[12]

With the emergence of ragtime, interracial public enthusiasm for black rhythm music heightened concerns that a dark terror, figured in terms of metric difference ("ragged rhythms" played by "jerky note groups") was seducing an unsuspecting white populace.[13] What first emerges out of the string bands and medicine shows of the 1880s takes public form (around the time of the World's Columbian Exposition in Chicago in 1893) as an instrumental music fashioned by black musicians that would be subsequently appropriated into Tin Pan Alley.[14] If the white transpositions of black instrumental music into ragtime song and the marches of John Philip Sousa were taken as positive signs of urban progress—"the perfect expression of the American city with its restless, bustling motion"—they also communicated the worst of modernity's consequences, commonly portrayed in a xenophobic rhetoric linking the most palpable social threats: the immigration of foreigners from Asia and southern and eastern Europe; the spread of incurable diseases commonly associated with migrations; the perceived threat of contamination of white women and men by syphilitic African-Americans. Black rhythm becomes all of these: a musical "infection" that had reached the point of "epidemic," fueled by an irrational "craze" to consume practices exceeding the bounds of white propriety. As a form of "syncopation gone mad," this "evil music . . . has crept into the homes and hearts of our American people," plaguing blacks as well as whites. As a 1903 report in the *Negro Music Journal* insisted, ragtime "must be wiped out as other bad and dangerous epidemics have been exterminated."[15]

This "medicomoral discourse" of racial contact should be familiar to students of modern American music, having been ably represented in the seminal work of Neil Leonard and others.[16] The rise of the new genre of syncopated music that inspired the fashionable "animal dance" fad of the 1910s gives way to the public appearances of jass (an early spelling), then jazz, in Chicago, New York, and cities across the Atlantic; by the 1920s, black music's presence had reached a grand scale, to the point of defining an entire era as the Jazz Age. What may be less readily recognized, however, is how the idea of black rhythm music emerges from a specific historical circumstance bound up with the dialectics of modern racial ideology. The musical concept was profoundly and intimately connected to the idea of modernism itself: black rhythm not only reflected society but infiltrated the very texture of American social existence, giving to the social a perceptible musicality expressing "racial" (black) influence. Racialized rhythm becomes the latest in the signatures of difference that served to distance and dislocate African-American otherness, just as these very distancing strategies would reaffirm the vitalism of blackness, prompting difference to be embraced once again.

Circulating unpredictably, wildly, black sounds and their accompanying texts crisscrossed the public sphere, producing dense intersecting layers of racial meaning that solidified rhythm's appearance as a natural, essential form. When J. P. Wickersham, a University of Pennsylvania professor of Romance language and literature decried the scourge of "jazz thinking," he ascribed a sonic quality to a racially determined, irrational condition that was influencing the perception and behavior of urban whites. When Edmund Wilson spoke of "The Jazz Problem" in the *New Republic,* he involved a metonymic relation that conflated an insidious music with an enduring social condition, commonly characterized as "the Negro problem."[17] The "infectious" nature ascribed to black rhythm is particularly revealing, for it focuses attention specifically on fears of material (human) transmission through the immateriality of sound. As a metaphor of contamination, rhythm as infection not only concretized fears of an immigrant menace but identified a mechanism for its transmission as well, as if sound's recognition would bring into the white body the "hot blood" of foreign populations and African-Americans. Entrancing and seductive, hot rhythm emerged as a version of the invisible "airborne menace"—a sonic simulation of Don DeLillo's "White Noise." When cast in the discourse of prohibition, finally, this hot musical menace threatened to intoxicate multiple generations of the American populace. As one writer observed, black music would "get into the blood of some of our young folks, and I might add older folks, too." It would make white America, like the "Negroes dancing in a Harlem cabaret . . . drunk with rhythm."[18]

The modern figure of hotness, which by the 1920s had become the informing epithet for the more rhythmically dynamic versions of jazz, seemed to conflate all qualities of excess, from drunkenness to fever, from violence to sexual promiscuity. Together, they outlined a discursive matrix of extremes that specified the dislocation of white physical and psychological certainty. Correlations between blackness, bodily violation, and aberrant hotness had already appeared by the mid-nineteenth century, when George G. Foster described a trumpeter at Dickens's Place, whose "red-hot knitting needles spirited out . . . [to] pierce through and through your brain without remorse." Shortly after, the British novelist Robert Louis Stevenson equated heat with the monstrous, as "Mr. Utterson began to recover from the hotness of his alarm" about the murderous exploits of Mr. Hyde.[19] By the 1910s and 1920s, fears of racial transmission through sound had assumed a central place among the moralizers and antimodernists, whose opinions helped to inform, if not convince, the public at large. If hot jazz marked the moral decline of civilization, as in the "fall of jazz," it was, as in the popular "rhythm" tunes of George Gershwin, Ellington, and Fields and McHugh, an expression of the pulse of the machine age, giving creative voice in "futuristic rhythm" (1929) to an ethos of speed and "pep" that defined the modern era.[20]

While perhaps rendered in these instances into a form more palatable to middle-class audiences, the songs still reflected the degree to which black expressive forms had inspired racial fantasies that had forever changed the disposition and style of America. It is accordingly important to underscore that the impact of these discourses did not discriminate between black and white. As in ragtime, racial figurations informed perspectives across a populace, including those of Alain Locke, who in his critique of the coon song perpetuated racialist views of natural rhythm, and of W. E. B. Du Bois, who exalted rhythmic power as he ridiculed the baseness of its producers.[21] In his famous essay, "A Negro Explains 'Jazz,'" moreover, James Reese Europe, the African-American leader of syncopated music, claimed that black music's excesses sprang from a racial sensibility. "The Negro loves anything that is peculiar in music, and this 'jazzing' appeals to him strongly. . . . To us it is not discordant, as we play the music as it is written, only that we accent strongly in this manner the notes which originally would be without accent. It is natural for us to do this; it is, indeed, a racial musical characteristic." From the distance of the twenty-first century, the first decades of the 1900s seemed consumed with a rhythmically oriented blackness whose dynamic properties provided a key causal element in the constitution of the modern. Hot rhythm may very well be, in essence, a sonic articulation of what we are, bringing into relief the profound significance of Ralph Ellison's seemingly innocuous comment that "the real secret of the game is to make life swing."[22]

A Smoldering Sense of Rhythmic Anticipation   If the power of black rhythm develops from peculiarly modern determinations of difference, so does it relate to a variety of prior constructions that align sound and race. In his seminal essay "The Invention of African Rhythm," Kofi Agawu argues that the equation of blacks and rhythm amounts to a figure, a topos, and ultimately "a lie" that begins with a musical comment in Ibn Butlan's eleventh-century document on purchasing slaves: "If a black were to fall from the sky to the earth, he would fall in rhythm."[23] Subsequent descriptions of African drumming practices and instrument construction in early modern travelogues show that this perception had carried over to Europe, although we may ultimately choose to qualify Agawu's claims of a consistent perception running across the centuries. In fact, the postbellum conception of rhythm grows rather suddenly out of earlier anticipations, even if rhythm's foreignness seemed always at hand.

By the seventeenth century, Europeans had already taken a casual interest in African percussion instruments, remarking on how they both resembled and departed from Continental analogues. The discussions of Father Denis de Carli, Merolla da Sorrento, and William Bosman cited in chapter 2 demonstrated how percussion instruments served to defend European claims of Africans' foreignness, just as their instruments' similarity to those of modern Greece (Bosman) and appearance in Christian-based rituals (Sorrento) made the foreign seem familiar. During the seventeenth-century slave trade, moreover, African-inspired instruments replicated by West Indian slaves compelled at least a few European observers to commit their thoughts to writing. The comments of Richard Ligon, for example, voiced mixed feelings about the drumming practices of African slaves. While the drum "has but one tone," Ligon was intrigued by the peculiarities of African-style performance: "And yet so strangely they varie their time, as 'tis a pleasure to the most curious eares, and it was to me one of the strangest noyses that ever I heard made of one tone." Ligon's attention was similarly drawn to the process of constructing a marimba, which he details copiously, while claiming "I say this much to let you see that some of these people are capable of learning Arts."[24]

In the next century, travel reports similarly detailed the most distinctive instrumental practices issuing from this "nation of dancers, musicians, and poets," as Olaudah Equiano famously described Africa. As with other observations of African cultures, the references to percussion reflected a spectrum of opinion; a people who seemed to the eighteenth-century Adanson to be "born dancing" could also produce "a horrid noise."[25] Such ambivalence, as already observed in chapter 2, carried over into European theories about the nature of music, some of which focused on qualities of rhythm. If Hegel would dismiss the "temporal vibrations" of Africans as little more than "barbarisms of a uniform rhythm [that produced] sluggishness to the point of gloom and depression," other European philosophers spoke admiringly of foreigners while making particular reference to the bodily effects of pulse. Jean-Jacques Rousseau's neoclassical depictions of vocal stress and strain, for example, revived Platonic notions of physicality that were commonly associated with dark-skinned foreigners. A similar sentiment appears in Johann Gottfried Herder's *Kalligone,* in which he speculates on the bodily consequences of music's rhythmic effect according to the stereotypes of the African and American savage: "Since the tones of music are *temporal* vibrations, they animate the body, the rhythm of their expression expresses itself through its rhythm. . . . Strongly moved, natural man can not abstain from it; he expresses what he hears through appearances of his countenance, through swings of his hand, through posture and flexing."[26]

Some Europeans, at least, had begun to imagine a rhythmically related art emanating from an African diasporic humanity, affirming Ligon's speculations that "if they had the varietie of tune, which gives the greater scope in musicke, as they have of time, they would do wonders in that Art." Suggesting an initial step was Rousseau's recognition of the relativity of European musical greatness. "Why are we so sensitive to impressions that mean nothing to the uncivilized," he writes in his essay *On the Origin of Language.* "Why is our most touching music only a pointless noise to the ear of a West Indian?"[27] But true recognition of a rhythmic basis to African-style performances could only begin after the phenomenon of "Negro music" had been more broadly acknowledged in public culture. In North America, this evolution accompanies white America's dramatic confrontations with the reality of a "Negro" human nature around the time of the Revolution. As we have previously seen, the events in the creation of a "democratic" and "free" United States had long-lasting effect on the conception of blacks across the Atlantic, just as events abroad, and particularly in the West Indies, informed local North American perceptions of black creative expression (chap. 2). We might accordingly imagine the idea of rhythm as an informing concept within a trans-Atlantic conversation, in which the figures of pulse helped increasingly to affirm the racial character of difference. As published accounts appearing in the contexts of colonization and missionary activity carried forward stereotypes of savage Africa, they frequently adopted a dramatic figurative language that introduced rhythm in connection with themes of excess and danger, recalling the moralizing of Christian clerics of centuries prior. Our brief coverage here focuses on British accounts from 1803 to 1853 that were crucial in the shaping of English-language reporting of black music around the Atlantic, giving stress to those depictions of rhythm in anticipation of what comes after.

As a group, nineteenth-century British travel writing extended the practice of referring to an array of musical types as part of an overarching portrayal of African peoples. The commentaries typically appeared alongside or within descriptions of the everyday lives of African populations, such as Joseph Corry's characterization of religious practices and a marriage ceremony along the Windward Coast or James Richardson's recollection of a visit among the Fezzan and Tripoli Arabs. ("It was the usual singing business, with Moorish hammering on tambourines.") In his assembly of the records of Captain Clapperton, moreover, Richard Lander stressed singing practices, documenting lyrics in the context of a discussion of "human sacrifices." Major Alexander Gordon Laing made no distinction between performance types when he described "a horrid din of a variety of barbarous instruments, [which] broke an ear from every direction," even while commenting on the battery of instruments, from flutes to harps, drums to *kora*.[28]

Yet we can also observe in the same documents a tendency to isolate musical practices in ways that are consistent with European perceptions of culture and the arts. Whereas early modern travelogues might cast African performances literally as part of the landscape (recall from chap. 2, e.g., John Windhus's description of music in Morocco as part of an assembly of natural consumables), nineteenth-century British writers were more likely to describe musical practices in ways resembling characterizations of European music. While making frequent reference to instrumental performances, for example, Laing devotes the bulk of his attention in his log of events from June 11, 1823, to songs of the Jelle, the singing skills of women, dancing, and types of percussion instruments.[29] Beecham, for his part, devotes his chapter 6 to "Arts, Trade, Language, National Taste." After elaborating on iron working, tanning, and language practices, he concludes with a commentary on music and musical instruments. Among the Ashantee, Beecham suggests, "a taste for music is also extensively cultivated." He again discusses instrumental types and then explains how natives had assimilated European instrumental practices: "The musical taste of the people is evidenced by the native band at Cape-Coast Castle, which plays admirably, by the ear, several of the most popular English tunes." Especially noteworthy is T. Edward Bowdich's *Mission from Cape Coast Castle to Ashantee,* discussed in chapter 4. Bowdich's chapter 10 is devoted exclusively to music and features nine pages of analysis with accompanying transcriptions.[30]

Ironically, what aggressively motivates the recognition of African music as "music" in the European sense is also what identifies its status as an inferior expressive form. The escalation of references to the musicality of African practices parallels an increase in depictions of Africans as a violent people, whose proclivities toward aggression were said to underlie their fondness for noise and rhythm. At a time of rising intra-African conflicts fueled by the interventions of Europeans, music becomes an emblem of the heightened climate of hostility and danger. Increasingly, this potential danger is referenced in terms of drumming and percussion. While writers might still comment matter-of-factly on various aspects of African rhythmic practices (note, e.g., W. T. Burchell's passing reference to the Kafir people: "Their notion of melody is but very slight, while their timing is perfection itself"), they would more likely by this time associate rhythm directly with the savage capacities of dark-skinned people.[31]

Corry's comments on musical practices, for example, befit the image of Africa as "a country hitherto but little known," filled with mystery and danger. "The European Traveller in that country," he warned his readers, faces a series of hardships. He "has to contend with the combined influence of the native jealousies of its inhabitants, their hereditary barbarism, [and their] obstinate ferocity." Likewise, in place of civilized cultural forms such as religion, Africans were prone to mere "custom . . . added to an avaricious thirst for gain, and the indulgence of sensual gratification." Music in turn seemed to express these qualities of degradation, beginning with the drum, which among African instruments "is the principal" and employed by "the most barbarous musicians that can be conceived." Corry witnessed such barbarisms at the aforementioned wedding in which musicians engaged in "savage yell[s]," gesticulations, and clapping of the hands. In another setting, he observed the same people performing again. This time, "the women fell into loud lamentations, the men beat their drums, and sent forth the most horrid yells." The suggestive dance movements of "the females in particular, . . . [were] highly offensive to delicacy, exhibiting all the gradations of lascivious attitude and indecency."[32]

According to Laing, the "horrid din of a variety of barbarous instruments" was peculiarly functional, accompanying the "extravagant gestures" of the warrior, who "carries with him a cutlass or knife" and moves "to the time of the various sounds produced." The figures of music, death, and violence to which Corry merely gestures become clearly articulated in Laing's account and are frequently figured as qualities of rhythm and noise. "Here the king soon joined me, and the war-drum being beat, the booth was shortly filled with a motley assemblage of armed men." Describing a funeral, Laing observed that "the moment that life fled from the body, a loud yell was uttered from the throats of a hundred people . . . after which, a party of several hundred women, some of them beating small drums, sallied through the town." Threat, finally, could appear more generally by way of association. While traveling through Timannee, Laing is honored by a group of women singers. Soon, however, he realizes that this "honor" could prove dangerous. The song's message said to the men, "to see their wives well dressed, they ought to take some of the money from the white man."[33]

As Laing's descriptions of the behavior of Africans become more grandiose, so do his references to the dangers of African sound. Midway through he provides extensive elaboration on the qualities of musical practices, noting among a diversity of instruments the ponderous drone of drummers who "kept hammering with provoking perseverance, and with the violence of blacksmiths at the anvil." Their playing became so strenuous, so loud, as to produce "a din sufficient almost to crack the tympanum of ordinary ears, and which compelled me to fortify mine with a little cotton." At this point, Laing's skepticism of the intentions of women singers inspires visions of blood. What he names a "diabolical chorus" "bawled till every vein in their throats was distended with blood; it was absolutely terrific; I expected every moment that a blood-vessel would burst. . . . [The singing] brought blood enough into the throat to have almost created suffocation; I was much distressed." Later, he describes the war songs of a female chorus—"Amazons," he calls them—as "savage in the extreme." Such uproarious displays, "marked by repeated discharges of musketry, shouting, blowing of horns, and beating of drums . . . presented a scene of extravagance, which is the delight of an African." If Laing and other commentators sometimes spoke admiringly of individuals and their music, these judgments remained in conflict with an ideological commitment to seeing Africans as a savage people, whose character was cast musically as part of the ensuing colonialist conflict.[34] What had historically signified difference according to European associations of music and otherness now assumed greater qualities of danger anticipating formulations of the latter half of the nineteenth century.[35]

References to the rhythmic capacities of blacks had also begun to enter into the frames of white American perceptions, even if the primary indications of African-American expression continued to specify vocal melody well beyond emancipation. Whether crafted according to the exotic images of travel writing or conceived independently, tales such as the 1803 text depicting Pinkster ceremonies in Albany reflected a public awareness of African-based performance and the role of rhythm making in them. The Pinkster drummer was a synthesis of primitive symbolism, performing while "rolling his eyes and tossing his head with an air of savage wildness; grunting and mumbling out certain inarticulate but hideous sounds and at the same time malling with both hands upon the hollow sounding Guinea drum." This text or one like it may have provided the basis for James Fennimore Cooper's portrait of the Pinkster in *Satanstoe* (1845), which portrays blacks making music "by beating on skins drawn over the ends of hollow logs. . . . This, in particular, was said to be a usage of their African progenitors."[36] Subsequent antebellum reporting on southern musical practices made sporadic reference to percussion instruments employed by slaves, such as the "tom-tom beat" accompanying dancing at New Orleans's Congo Square, the jawbone played in Florida "from which they get quite varied sounds," and the assembly of makeshift devices, including triangles, jawbones, and sheepskin gumbo boxes mentioned by Harriet A. Jacobs.[37] The rhythmic practice of patting, moreover, while referenced only occasionally, seemed particularly fascinating to observers and presumably to those reading about it. The Methodist minister John Dixon Long, for example, explained that slaves generally "have no instruments, but dance to the tunes and words of a leader, keeping time by striking their hands against the thighs and patting the right foot." Lewis Paine's *Six Years in a Georgia Prison* includes a lengthy description of how one "pats juber": "This is done by placing one foot a little in advance of the other, raising the ball of the foot from the ground, and striking it in regular time, while, in connection, the hands are struck slightly together, and then upon the thighs. In this way they make the most curious noise, yet in such perfect order, it furnishes music to dance by."[38]

A report from New Orleans in 1860 is particularly noteworthy in the way that it combines the dominant figure of vocal skill with attention to a seemingly in-born rhythmic sensibility. Commenting on the "peculiar manner" of performance among the "colored people and negroes, bond and free," Colonel James R. Creecy describes in *Scenes in the South* how "groups of fifties and hundreds may be seen in different locations of the square, with banjos, tom-toms, violins, jawbones, triangles, and various other instruments from which harsh or dulcet sounds may be extracted." Subsequently, he shifts from this mode of empirical observation to advance a general theory of race and musical character, in which gifts of song take on an equally peculiar rhythmic dynamism: "All Africans have melody in their souls; and in all their movements, gyrations and attitudenizing exhibitions, the most perfect time is kept, making the beats with the feet, heads, or hands, or all, as correctly as a well-regulated metronome!"[39] Similar variations from the perceptual norm of "Negro song" could even show up in the most visible reports about the spirituals. In his famous study *Army Life in a Black Regiment,* Thomas Wentworth Higginson writes with an obsessive fascination recalling William Francis Allen's detailed commentary on the ring shout: "The dusky figures moved in the rhythmical barbaric dance the negroes call a 'shout,' chanting, often harshly, but always in the most perfect time, some monotonous refrain." With the rise of the publicly performed spirituals or "jubilees," Theodore Seward, the transcriber of the songs performed by the Fisk choir, writes in his preface to the collection, "The first peculiarity that strikes the attention is in the rhythm. This is often complicated, and sometimes strikingly original." A text serving to document the melodic virtues of saintly Negro singing now aligns creativity with a new kind of marker of race.[40]

If midcentury American references to black rhythmic capacities appeared sporadically along the margins of public discourse, they also drew associations that would eventually revise contemporary interpretation. Intermingled with the casual remarks about the utilitarian uses of percussion instruments—such as Fredrika Bremer's comment on the practice of calling slaves to work by sounding a drum—we can identify new social contexts that set the stage for the modern linking of drums with danger.[41] At the center of things was a renewed fear of interracial conflict taking place not in Africa but much closer to home. With the successful revolt of slaves on the island of San Domingo (Haiti) and the bloody massacre of white planters and their families by a group of Virginia slaves lead by Nat Turner, the potential for African-American violence became all the more real, sending tremors through the southern white population with the onset of formalized abolitionist efforts.[42] The images of African threat issuing from

British texts set the parameters for a new figurative language, with the Caribbean serving as a linchpin. A realm with a long history of interracial contest and densely populated by blacks who were visibly perpetuating African-based musical practices, the Caribbean occupied an enduring place in the imagination of rhythm as a signifier of danger. It is at this point that the possibility of a modern conception of black rhythm could begin to take hold in the United States, cast according to the images of violence associated with black bodies in rebellious motion and conceived as part of a viable form of "Negro music" that had recently occupied public perceptions of white Americans. While evidence of a peculiarly rhythmic concept was still relatively rare, the circumstances encouraged a different kind of reading, one that begins to isolate and objectify a particular aspect of African sound and then to claim it as the center of black music's essence.[43]

One of the more compelling anticipations of modern hot rhythm appears in the body of American literary expressions that spoke to the escalating fears of slave rebellion. In "A Tale of the Ragged Mountains" (1844), Edgar Allan Poe depicts the fatal experience of the main character, Augustus Bedloe, who in a morphine-induced dream-made-real is transported through the virgin hills of Charlottesville into the Bazaars of India's Varanasi (formerly Benares). Poe's narrator begins by describing Bedloe as a kind of monstrosity mixing images of civility and savagery. He was a young white man, who also seemed extremely old. Moreover, "his limbs were exceedingly long and emaciated. His forehead was broad and low . . . his teeth were more wildly uneven . . . than I had ever before seen teeth in a human head." "The temperature of Bedloe," the narrator continues, "was, in the highest degree sensitive, excitable, enthusiastic." And those qualities would come to bear as Bedloe encountered the "ragged hills" where, "very suddenly, my attention was arrested by the loud beating of a drum." "A half-naked man" with "hot breath" "rushes past with a shriek." Then a beast appears as images of Africa become intertwined with Orientalist figures: "stately dames close-veiled, elephants, gorgeously caparisoned, idols grotesquely hewn, drums, banners, and gongs, spears, silver and gilded maces." Bedloe eventually succumbs to fever and dies of a failed bloodletting, poisoned by a sangsue "always [to] be distinguished from the medicinal leech by its blackness."[44] In *Benito Cereno* (1854), moreover, Herman Melville employs the clamor of hatchets as a leitmotif to foreshadow a slave mutiny. In the opening pages, Melville introduces the ominous qualities of black noise in the language of the colonial travelogue, as the "Negroes, two and two they sideways clashed their hatchets together, like cymbals with a barbarous din. All six, unlike the generality, had the raw aspect of unsophisticated Africans." According to Edward Widmer, Melville's rhythmic depictions may have subsequently informed related images in Henry Didimus's (Henry Edward Durrell) biography of Louis Moreau Gottschalk, the New Orleans pianist and composer of *Bamboula!* named after a Caribbean drum. The biography "included an enraptured description of Congo Square and its 'saturnalia', with particular praise for the drummer, [who] . . . 'beat with two sticks, to a strange measure incessantly, like mad, for Hours.' "[45]

The coalescence of various temporal references suggests the emergence of a transnational conception of black music increasingly informed by European archetypes of rhythm. Even in this inchoate form, the idea of black rhythm seemed to resonate powerfully in New World circumstances, sonically signifying a social concept that would expand greatly in step with the emergence of African-Americans in public culture. And yet, if the formation of black musical difference specified an increasingly tangible threat, it remained, prior to Emancipation at least, something more or less accommodating to white public listeners. Most mid-nineteenth-century representations of black music making still conformed to the norms of European musical practice, giving stress to the familiar qualities of melody and lyric that together had defined the work-oriented object, "Negro song." While writers such as Thoreau and Emerson made rhythm a central dimension of their thought about life and nature, they did not draw this emphasis directly in connection with African-American music; rhythm identified a marker of the natural, and only later would it be incorporated so extensively into the newly fashioned signature of race.[46] The same held true of references to rhythm in the spiritual. By the time of the Civil War, slave songs had epitomized the best of black music, expressing powers of glory and uplift that represented the ideal of a national voice. While indicating difference, these references to white musical analogues served to accommodate an assimilative process at a time when most African-Americans were still enslaved. When rhythmic features were mentioned, they appeared most typically as oddities cast along the margins of singing practices that could only be comprehended within the frames of plantation or sacred melodies. Even in the more sordid imaginations of blackface, which, as a white musical form, predictably represented the most outward indication of expressive difference, rhythmic features remained far from the center of presentation. While minstrel groups employed nonharmonic instruments (fiddle, banjo, bones, and tambourine) and, judging from published sources, featured syncopated rhythms and rhythmic playing, these elements served mainly as sidelights to a more centrally located melodic emphasis. Compared with the hot fantasies that emerged fifty years later, the rhythmic character of "De Nigger's Banjo Hum" and "De Rattle of De Bones" referred above all to the disciplining of racial difference and the containment of African-American slaves, whose hopes of "Bobolashun" (abolition) were subjected to repeated stage parodies of black on white.[47]

Peering into the Temporal Depths of Human Sound . . .   The slave song as site of wholes and origins becomes increasingly important after the Civil War as a way of aiding the larger social program of reunion. Of all the determinations that might explain the enormous appeal of postwar black performance, none is more significant than the belief in the healing properties of African-American song, a notion first articulated by antebellum observers and subsequently expanded on by the inventors of the public concept of the spiritual. In the jubilees that overwhelmed America in the 1870s and 1880s, advocates and many listeners heard the possibility of civil rebirth and renewal: the "perfection" of black sacred singing would provide the key index for the revitalization of national culture. At Fisk and Hampton Universities, and among the various professional groups that sprang up in the 1880s, African-Americans were seen to be crafting a new kind of music that harkened to an older, more certain truth, secure in the primacy of voice. The soulful spiritual qualities of the jubilees would enact a grand-scale descent: peering into the depths of time, America located a new cultural beginning, crafted out of the imagination of what Nina Silber calls "the romance of reunion."[48]

Musical discussions of the postbellum spirituals and jubilees continued to foreground the dimensions of song, giving emphasis to the qualities of melodism common to midcentury portraits. While evidence remains scarce, reception on the part of white middle-class and elite audiences most likely reinforced these representations, promoting a view of the jubilees and black music in general as a principally vocal-melodic expression that fit comfortably within harmonic settings and conformed to the dictates of common meter. Within the space of thirty years, however, that perception would change dramatically. By the 1920s, when Americans imagined black music, they thought first of rhythmic practices, particularly in instrumental settings. This sea change in comprehension cannot be explained solely in musical terms. The emergence of rhythm takes place symbiotically, relationally, as both a reflection of and the driving force within a greater dynamic of social transformation. Now representing the essential quality of black sound, rhythm introduced a new kind of miracle arising out of the blues of southern invisibility: it would bring about a change in the very nature of black music in America. To observe this construction historically requires us to examine first the new set of discourses defining the temporal axis of modernism's crossroads, named here descent, turning to matters of displacement in the next section.

The search for the origins of black rhythm begins not at the junctures of southern roads and highways but by traveling along another figurative pathway, the root axis of which traces to the intellectual imagination of Europe's cultural elite. Here, the crossroads moves by leaps to the theories of human origin proposed by an interdisciplinary group of British scholars and their European descendants, who speculated variously on the qualities defining human nature. Of particular concern are the theories of those German intellectuals at the forefront of the emerging discipline of musicology, whose racialized views of foreign music and rhythm grew in response to the very cultural forms they helped publicly to conceive. If not a direct influence, the many versions of "Negro sound" put forward by European writers made manifest the existence of a new kind of thinking about the music of people of color, particularly Africans, that had begun to make its way into perceptions of black music in the United States.

The figures of descent that informed social theory of the late nineteenth century were in no small way an extension of Europe's armed encounters with an outer world, a confrontation that would transform European culture in the face of colonization, conquest, and empire building. Napoleon's invasion into the Middle East (which identifies the imperial underpinnings of Villoteau's scholarly achievements) and Britain's forays into China and India, together with the colonization or "scramble for Africa" by European powers in the 1880s, appeared against the background of early modern exploration, conquest, and enslavement, through which foreign peoples took their subordinate positions within a European colonial imagination. Without reducing the intellectual accomplishments of nineteenth-century natural science to a sordid tale of conquest and rapacious greed, we must acknowledge that the conception of the foreign in the theories of descent depended on a literature of encounter based in the imperial past. As a matter of course, the representations of music characteristic of early comparative musicology grew from this same imperial legacy and were consequently informed by the assumptions of cultural and racial difference common to the era. It is, finally, from this same pairing of politics and musical representation that we identify both the background and the consequence of theories of origin that occupied social thinkers from the mid-nineteenth century.

The outward-looking quest for the secret of human origins was in large part an inward-looking exercise that focused primarily on the character of Europe, and in its most egregiously imperialistic demonstrations, it defended claims of white supremacy. But the investigations were also driven by the fact of Europe's difference from a world of foreigners whose presence was palpably felt in the circumstances of their conquest. As Simon Gikandi explains with reference to Britain, "Questions of Englishness cannot be discussed except in relation to different forms of colonial alterity"; difference within oneself grows through comparative encounter, complicating the certainty of cultural distinctiveness.[49] The experience and perception of music played no small role in the shaping of this discursive terrain, as conceptions of difference grew resonant with articulations about black music by the turn of the century.

In his influential essay, "The Origins of Music," which appeared as part of a larger study titled *Illustrations of Universal Progress* (1854), the English scientist Herbert Spencer established the ground for modern speculative thinking about matters of descent.[50] While best known in musicology for postulating music as an extension of heightened speech, Spencer also theorized primitive communication as a triune of integrated dynamic expression: "Rhythm in speech, rhythm in sound, and rhythm in motion, were in the beginning parts of the same thing, and have only in process of time become separate things. Among various primitive tribes we find them still united."[51] Spencer's contemporary, Charles Darwin, in his turn, reversed the formula, proposing that primal sound preceded a more advanced speech practice. As did Spencer, however, Darwin also drew from a legacy of music/speech theory that magnified rhythm's significance. Evoking historical commentaries on the libidinous habits of birds, Darwin theorized that the origins of music could be found in the "musical notes and rhythms" of mating rituals: in "the drumming of the snipe's tail, the tapping of the woodpecker's beat, the harsh trumpet-like cry of a certain waterfowl."[52] While drawing from tropes of the avian, Darwin's ornithological references also betrayed sympathies for prevalent racialist views around the time. His associations of music and sex, for example, perpetuated stereotypes about the heightened sexual desires of primitive peoples, and particularly of foreign women, recalling the tales of "lascivious" dancing and "diabolical singing" by Corry and Laing. While Darwin makes only limited reference to black music in *Descent of Man,* his application of the discourse of foreign travelogues inspired Robert Lach to elaborate on such connections. Writing for Guido Adler's *Handbuch der Musikgeschichte* in 1924, Lach would claim that Darwin had compared these primordial sexual utterances with the speech patterns of "excited Negroes."[53]

Whether or not Darwin makes this association elsewhere, Lach had clearly drawn the matters of origins and race into relation, and in doing so, he expressed the consequences of a generation of theorizing that had established the basis of modern musicology. By the 1880s and 1890s, German scholars were actively pursuing speculations about music's foundations, through which, as Alexander Rehding explains in his essay "The Quest for the Origins of Music in Germany, c. 1900," they hoped to uncover the nature of music as such.[54] In asserting their theories, these writers were doing something more than explaining the entertainment value of art; they were claiming for music a significance in the overall understanding of culture: scientific musical study would provide insight into the nature of "Man." The particular associations of rhythm within the theories of origins consequently provide insight into the conceptions of race and music that were forming at the time. In particular, they supply clues into an emerging ideology linking musical propulsion and blackness across the transnational conversation.

Musicology's exploration of origins may be seen in large part as a solipsistic endeavor consistent with other outward explorations, from colonial encounter to the transcription of the spirituals. For as genuine as the scholars' interests in the foreign may have been, they grew from a primary concern with the place of Europe and European music in an overarching world history. Of particular interest was how a racially conceived "German" identity might have arisen from the musical tones of the folk vernacular. In its local concerns, early musicology's initiatives were consistent with those of contemporary students of human behavior. As did anthropologists, musicologists—and comparatists above all—"took this primitive society as their special subject, but in practice primitive society proved to be their own society (as they understood it) seen in a distorting mirror."[55] If individual researchers pursued different domains (Europe vs. foreign) according to various methodologies, they shared a common interest in the nature and stature of European music within a complex of musical figurations grounded in the primary evidence of foreign exploration and conquest. As Rehding observes, the quest of origins involved a broad consideration of the dimensions of musical practice, from instrumental usages to speculations on speech and song, from the relation of the overtone system to musical evolution. With respect to a developing black music, however, what stood out was the place of rhythm in the understanding of Man's ascent. Within this theoretical circumstance, a primitive originary rhythm becomes a central figuration for determining the superiority of European music. Recalling the role of music more generally in Rousseauian theory, rhythm acts the role of the supplement: what distinguishes the primitive from the civilized also identifies the originary wellspring from which Europe evolved.

Rhythm's primary indication affirmed fantasies of wholes and completion. In his study *Arbeit und Rhythmus* (1896), for example, Karl Bücher proposed that rhythm was inherent to the human organism as it was to the nature of activity from the earliest stages, when art and play were joined as a unity.[56] In this he recalls the eighteenth-century commentary of Johann Nikolaus Forkel: "Rhythm is one of the first means to enlarge and embellish [human] expressions. . . . The most primitive people used it for their monotonous music."[57] Cast within Bücher's modern concern about the rise of labor, rhythm evolves as an economic activity out of an original physical engagement with the natural world. That activity is most productive when generated rhythmically. The sound of rhythm, in turn, inspires work, creating a symbiosis of the audible and the economic. Bücher's study includes a survey of the development of economic principles through rhythmical labor in foreign lands, from "Afrikanische Völker" to "Südslaven" to "Chinesen und andere Ostasiaten." The net effect is to propose a continuity of the rhythmical dimensions of work within a natural history of global economy.

Similarly committed to the rhythmic basis of musical origins was John Frederick Rowbotham, the Scottish rector whose three-volume *History of Music* appeared in 1885. Rowbotham proposed a pattern of musical evolution according to an organological hierarchy: humanity's ascent took place in three stages, "the Drum Stage," "the Pipe Stage," "the Lyre Stage." Drums and rhythm identified an original expression, the primitive essence of which remained intact in the music of contemporary foreign peoples: "The history of savage races is a history of arrested developments . . . all testify[ing] to the high antiquity of the Drum." The drum, as origin, expressed the first instrumental sound: "The savage, who for the first time in our world's history knocked two pieces of wood together . . . had other aims than his own delight—he was trying to re-create a something that had bewildered him. . . . The something he was trying to re-create was Rhythmic Sound—on which roots the whole Art of Music." From that sentiment, Rowbotham proceeds to map out the world dimensions of rhythmic practices and rituals among "savage races," giving primary emphasis to Indians of the Americas. ("The great seat of Drum Worship was South America," he writes.) Africa, while included in this survey, presents an anomaly, since the widespread appearance of lyres contradicts his presumption of the "Negro's" base nature. His appendix "On the Three Stages in Central Africa and especially the Lyre Stage" attempts to explain the lyre's use among "the most degraded savages" as a consequence of cultural diffusion from ancient Egypt. While claiming rhythm as a marker of origins, Rowbotham proposes a discontinuity separating savagery and civilization.[58]

If rhythm supplied the foundations of music, it also identified the crucial quality distinguishing racially superior Europeans from their living descendants in Africa and the Americas. As Rehding explains, a primary trajectory of musicological research sought to determine both the primitive origins and the uniqueness of European expression, which became increasingly associated with the practice of triadic harmony. Scholars such as Guido Adler traced the reliance on intervals of thirds and sixths to a premodern folk sensibility still in practice in the mountain regions of northern Europe. Monophony and rhythm, by contrast, identified respectively the difference of southern and tribal peoples; what may have once represented a primary connection now supplied the critical contrast separating the civilized from savagery and, correspondingly, whiteness from blackness. In this circumstance, difference reveals the sordid dimensions of otherness repressed in civility. If "in the beginning was rhythm" (recalling Hans von Bülow's claim), it now specified qualities not white. As the Austrian musicologist Richard Wallaschek observed in his influential study *Primitive Music* (1893), "the difference between people with or without harmonic music is not a historical but a racial one."[59] Directly contradicting the claims of heightened musical capacities of Negro singers, European scholars now proposed that rhythm determined the difference between the musical and the unmusical in the world's populations. A midcentury account published in *Dwight's Journal of Music* suggests that such thinking had existed for some time. In his lengthy essay translated for publication, F. Rochlitz, identified simply as a "German musician," proposed a view that anticipates late-century evolutionary theory as it recalls the descriptions of noise from earlier eras. "Now savage tribes," Rochlitz writes, "and wholly uncultivated men among us, have properly no tone art and no sense therefor [*sic*], but only a sense of rhythm. What sounds before their ears, is not perceived by them as tones; it only rings and makes a noise; to them it only exists as a condition of the perception of the rhythmical."[60]

Rochlitz's commentary in *Dwight's Journal of Music* shows that such ideas about musical origins had already been circulating in North American public forums. The primary mode of dissemination, however, came not from the writings of the elite but through their transposition into the popular registries of travelogues and mass publications. In these instances, rhythm, as a marker of descent, determines an origin repressed: divided from a civilized culture, the other is revealed as a lurking, encroaching danger. In *The Land of Fetish* (1883), the British writer A. B. Ellis introduces the kind of hyperbolic language extending from early travelogues that had also informed popular literature. His portrait of West Africa is of a world laced with vivid images of war, ritual, and cannibalism: "wattle racks . . . [of] innumerable human skulls . . . sacrificed to the Ju-ju, or fetish." While Ellis's references to music are initially sporadic and diverse (they begin with the now standard overview of common instruments), the most elaborate depictions draw relations between "death drums" and the gruesome violence of human sacrifice: "Screams, the most horrible, the most blood-curdling . . . the most despairing—, it made my blood run cold, [and] was repeated; and then we heard the noise of the beating of drums . . . [as] night closed upon a wild scene of madness and intoxication." Similar references to threat carry over into otherwise innocuous musical discussions. Complaining about the annoyances of Yoruba fifes, Ellis invokes images of African ferocity coupled with the supernatural association of musical power and mysterious physical ailments: instruments "shrieking" against a "diabolical rhythm"; the "torture rapidly grew worse and worse. . . . By 10 A.M. one of our number was down with fever." These gestures to the supernatural recall earlier comments by Richardson and Laing, who described the premonitory power of dreams. Ellis's vivid imagery, however, lies closer to the magical states of Poe or even to the more grotesque parodies of blackface comedy.[61]

The famous adventures of Henry M. Stanley (1872), whose "search for Livingstone" was recounted in regular dispatches to the *New York Herald,* identifies the kind of public vehicle that would popularize the emerging hot fantasies about black music. While showing little interest in the daily lives of American-born blacks, a white readership zealously consumed Stanley's depictions of an exotic world of wild animals, native warriors, and spear-chucking heathens, cast in the language of blackface parody. In Stanley's Africa, the threat of darkness is repeatedly overcome by the superiority of white mastery. It is a world in which Anglo-Saxon masculinity reigns, as if to mourn the passing of the American slave order. Stanley portrays himself in the image of the conqueror-hero, whose command over the jungle and its natives strangely parallels projections of white supremacy in many slave narratives.[62] When he turns to music, Stanley employs figures of rhythmic threat that anticipate late-century depictions yet without engaging the sense of anxious concern that commonly informs those same depictions. In a diary entry from March 12, 1872, for example, he recalls the ritual ceremony marking the end of his visit with Livingstone by juxtaposing tools of violence—axes, spears, guns—with images of "warlike music" and the "appalling energy and thunder of the drums." These are offset by patronizing references to "my braves" and the "chorus-loving children of unyamwezi" that reflect a complicated historical legacy of racial condescension.[63]

The associations between "dark Africa" and a kind of comic-book rhetoric extending from minstrelsy would become increasingly common to turn-of-the-century commentaries of black music. In this new phase, references to bestiality in the blackface songs of "Cannibal Love" (1909), presentations of Dahomey drummers at the World's Columbian Exposition in Chicago, together with the emergence of a new historical literature devoted to Pinkster festivals and the drum bans (in which the absence of drums paradoxically reveals the presence of a slave threat) all contributed to the rise of public displays of black music as a kind of "Negro oddity" or excess.[64] The strenuous commitments to preserving the image of the plantation black as a banjo-playing darky—against the controversial challenges of Joel Chandler Harris—similarly reflected a desire to link the "American Negro" to a lute-playing Old World descendent.[65] Moreover, what had come to blacken the face of a minstrelized African and to Africanize depictions of African-America ultimately cycled back into the heart of darkness, creating an escalating tautology of transnational primitive discourse that intensified fantasies of racial encounter. By the early 1910s, homologies of blackness had commonly informed popular depictions of African and African-American musics. Behind Du Bois's image of the "rhythmic cry of the black slave" lurked the cannibal savage; beneath the surface of Henry Krehbiel's theories of rhythm and engaging depictions of African song was the trope of pathetic slave suffering that traced from Frederick Douglass's autobiographies to Du Bois's own "sorrow songs." As a hybrid discourse of primitivism grew in direct proportion with black music's appeal, Americans became consumed with vivid fantasies of racialized sound that inspired enactments of simian-like "animal dances" and celebrations of a "savage" jazz animated by "jungle rhythms."

Serving, finally, as a kind of textual "missing link" between late-nineteenth- and early-twentieth-century depictions was Edgar Rice Burroughs's best-selling Tarzan series, which commenced with the publication of *Tarzan of the Apes* in 1914. As Marianna Torgovnick and Gail Bederman have both shown, this novel played a crucial role in the formation of the modern primitive idea, as it affirmed newer "tribal" projections of white American manhood specific to a colonialist era.[66] Musical references appearing at a crucial moment in the novel suggest ways in which these masculinist themes could reinforce hot rhythmic desire among a schoolboy readership. In chapter 7, "The Light of Knowledge," Tarzan appears at the center of an ape ritual, the dum dum, through which he is welcomed into the tribe. The dum dum becomes a pathway toward tribal belonging, the journey that enables Tarzan to descend from (white) civilization into the black wholeness of jungle apes. Significantly, what triggers the transference is "the noise of the drums." These black jungle rhythms accompany a "fierce, mad, intoxicating revel" that unites a civilized English boy with his primordial origins and enables his reemergence as "King of the Apes."[67]

...Ascending, Sounds out of Place   On the surface, the tales of Stanley and Burroughs might seem to bring to black rhythm a playfulness and jocularity that finally rendered harmless its "intoxicating" effect. After all, subsequent efforts to assimilate the more dynamic versions of African-American performance into popular entertainment would effectively transform a prior delirium into a merely titillating object of desire, cast in the 1930s as "crazy rhythm" and then as the boozy square hipness of 1950s lounge music. Observed within the context of its initial emergence, however, black rhythm expressed a racial power that our cozier present-day recollections of ragtime and Dixieland fail to capture. Understanding the character of this sonic threat requires us to turn attention to the other dimension of the crossroads, the horizontal axis of social action through which black music acquired a significance relating to the threat of racial transposition and transmission. If the authenticity of an emerging African-American musical modernism carried forward the supplicating conformity of "Negro feeling," it also accrued unprecedented transgressive force that set it apart from all prior manifestations of racial performance. As a sonically inflected scourge, black music would spread laterally, spatially, across the physical landscape, disrupting the tentative security of an African-America in its place. The threat of a potent blackness "on the loose" is what informs the intersecting musico-discursive dimension I am calling here "displacement."

As African-Americans began to move about the territory, traveling south, east, and west, to towns and villages, to southern cities, and then increasingly into the North, they inevitably challenged the rigid norms of behavior that had once constrained them socially and physically. Leaving their homes in search of a job, to acquire an education, or simply to pursue a better life, these black women and men, like their white compatriots, wove their way across the southern environs, where they came face to face with the crossroads that guided life's venture. Throughout the land, large crowds of blacks were participating in what amounted to a grand-scale social interruption: descending into locales where populations had been relatively stable, the conspicuous assemblies of black bodies unsettled the appearance of civil order. Such movements raised the hackles of many white southerners who were desperately seeking to reclaim power after the Civil War. As one observer described, judging "from the sea of black faces round him," an unsuspecting visitor who "jostled his way along the roughly paved sidewalk . . . [might] imagine himself in the realms of the King of Dahomey."[68] The perception of disorder consequently motivated the development of more stringent segregationist guidelines. Over the course of the final decades of the nineteenth century, the separation of black from white would increasingly rule the racial ways of life, first in the South, then in the North, as whites sought to protect the integrity of the color line.

The movements of African-Americans arose in the first place in response to the same social developments that were committed to their containment. What historians commonly name the New South—the era of white supremacy after the collapse of Reconstruction (1877)—was marked by a rapid if unstable growth in industry and labor that developed as part of a desire to revive the economy and restore southern culture. The employment opportunities that increased with the growth in white-controlled industries also attracted a new black labor force eager to avoid the dead-ends of sharecropping and an enduring paternalism, which was worse in rural areas. Increasingly, they sought out jobs in the new industries turning up in places from Birmingham to Charleston, in sawmills, coalmines, turpentine camps, iron fields, and foundries and on railroads.[69] The network of railways that was rapidly developing across the United States was particularly important to postbellum life because it enabled blacks to traverse the land in chase of opportunity. As Arthur Granville Bradley told his readers in *MacMillan's Magazine,* while "some [say] that the negroes are deteriorating, . . . one fact alone can be alleged without much contradiction—that the upper sections of the South are pouring slowly but surely a black tide of emigration towards the states on and about the 'Gulf,' where wages are higher and politics more excited." As a result, travel changed the face of the nation. "The negro exodus now *amounts to a stampede*" an observer in North Carolina commented in 1889, as blacks repeatedly encountered the crossroads of the South's postbellum racial relations.[70]

The broad-scale economic failures that beset the United States in the 1880s and 1890s made their mark on black life and black relations with whites. With economic depressions in and around 1873 and 1893, jobs became exceedingly scarce, and the scarcity drove desperation across the labor force, exacerbating movement as workers searched for jobs. Like the oppressed classes of foreign immigrants arriving in the United States, African-Americans were being blamed for taking away potential work from American-born whites and for the rising tide of crime that went hand in hand with economic crisis. The dramatic migrational shifts of the black population, while obviously motivated by a desire to make a living, only fueled whites' fears, as "one state after another passed laws . . . to check black mobility."[71] By the 1890s, the dramatic efforts to secure blacks in their place would lead to the institution of new racial codes that limited travel by African Americans and social intercourse across the races. The Jim Crow policies enforced over the next seventy-odd years represented a perverse legal solution to fulfill an equally perverse desire to contain the degree of interracial engagement, while the rise in heinous crimes of lynching stood as the most reprehensible method of containment, commonly targeting "strange niggers"—those unknown itinerants with no reputation in a community. Despite these efforts, however, interaction between blacks and whites continued. It is one of the strange ironies of race in America that within an increasingly divided South racial engagements never let up, particularly within the contested domains of travel and labor. If Euro- and African-Americans attended different schools, patronized different stores, slept in different hotels, and worshiped in different churches, so would America as a whole witness a continuation of social engagements that made scenes of "a very black negro and a fair-haired youth drinking out of the same black-bottle" part of the common order.[72]

Black music once again became such a powerful and urgent cultural force because it served to heighten both the specificity of racial difference and the interruption of that difference. While black music arose from a cross-racial interplay—from the engagements of black and white that constituted modern racial form—it would always be actualized through performances by African-Americans. The continuing activities of whites in blackface (and increasingly blacks in blackface) that endured well into the twentieth century might have called attention to the artifice of music's racial categories, but that artificiality would exist in contradiction, both challenging and reinforcing ideological commitments to the authenticity of blackness as such. No matter the sound, the term "Negro music" corresponded directly with the racial identification of the performer; what limited African-Americans to the performance of expressions of questionable artistic value also supplied the naturalism crucial to authenticity. Into the 1890s and 1900s, authentic black music would acquire through its vast public circulation a new kind of potency. As the music accumulated layer upon layer of social meaning, it would come to be identified as a peculiar expressive practice at once aesthetically superior and illegitimate. Curiously, however, as black music's visibility increased, its representations also began to stabilize. The more frequently black music appeared publicly, the more it was described as a rhythm music whose "ragged" edges specified a form associated with a population out of place. In this way, we can say that the interracialism or "sameness" of black musical production would drive the value of authentically black race music, whose power accrues from a nonharmonic descent associated with European theory and its emplotments across the terrain of America's racial figuration. This powerful though contradictory logic sonically enacts a world out of place precisely because it specified racial identity at the same time it built that identity from the relation of black to white.[73]

In black musical production, then, we recognize the emergence of a formidable social expression inextricably related to the creation of American modernism. Its potency derives from its articulation of a radically new conception of racial otherness growing from the spatial dimensions of the crossroads as it intersects temporal affiliations north and south. While Enlightenment conceptions of otherness, according to David Harvey, "perceived 'the other' as necessarily having (and sometimes 'keeping to') a specific *place* in a spatial order that was ethnocentrically conceived to have homogenous and absolute qualities," the new qualities of black music defined the essential nature of blackness by exceeding place in ways that anticipated other fractured dimensions of modernist art and culture.[74] The practices of instrumentally created rhythm would come to play a critical role in articulating this new kind of modernism. And as it defined place by going beyond that which was prescribed by white supremacy, rhythm music appeared uncanny, magical, a force that seemingly "jes grew." Through black music, African-America asserted its own racial presence by reviving the essential relation that would also give voice to America as a whole.

The first public displays of black musical displacement in the postbellum era extended from the spirituals, those emblems of descent that had drawn American listeners directly after the war. With the rise of the jubilee movement in the early 1870s, black choruses introduced the first public performances of music by African-Americans, and the wholesale enthusiasm for these concerts set the stage for black music's prominence as a folk vocal practice from there on. While stemming from midcentury sentimentality about the soulful melodies of slave song, the jubilees also performed critical acts of displacement by challenging the norms of racial order. Making public the formidability of form attributed to spiritual singing, the

jubilees represented the new standard for art. As Paul Gilroy puts it succinctly in a seminal essay on the public circulation of African-American music, "black people singing slave songs as mass entertainment initiated and
established new public standards of authenticity for black cultural expression."[75] Accordingly, our recovery of the origins of black music's hot essence must digress momentarily from rhythmic practices in order to
consider the emergence of the public phenomenon of "Negro singing" that
sets into motion the seditious placelessness of modern artistic expressions.

At the center of things was the well-known concert choir heralding
from Fisk University, an all-black school established in Nashville by white
Methodists and former abolitionists. The widespread popularity of the
Fisk Jubilee Singers from the early 1870s led to a succession of national and
international tours, highlighted by appearances before British and European royalty. As an embodiment of Negro authenticity, the Fisk Jubilee
Singers, together with the countless new groups appearing in its wake,
represented a large-scale challenge to the very efforts to contain racial categories. What many blacks once regarded "as signs of their former dis-
grace[,] . . . prison clothes of the days of [the slaves'] incarceration," had
assumed a new heightened authority rivaling the value of European art.
"We did not realize how precious they would be held by those who had
prayed for us, and with us till we were delivered from slavery, and how
these were the genuine jewels we brought from our bondage."[76] If the appeal of the jubilees remained largely within the white domain and African-
Americans fortunate enough to have found a place in the expanding
working classes, the songs also acquired a substance and a significance
not so easily contained by a Euro-American population fervently committed to maintaining its racial dominance.

The Fisk performances enacted a radical hybrid of songs invented in
the isolation of slavery and of artistic practices based in the common domain of the concert hall. Introducing an extensive repertory of slave
melodies that had been reworked for concert choir, the performances set
the stage for a broad dissemination of a radically new kind of American music. What becomes known as the "Fisk sound" fulfilled a curious contradiction: challenging the conventions of European choral practice, it also
accommodated the norms of white concert music.[77] In their blackness, the
singers had already upset the standards of "good music." But in adopting
the posture, behavior, and performance practices of the concert stage,
they also affirmed the racial sense of place that pleased white audiences.
Even their employment of altered scale forms seemed oddly paradoxical,

identifying a sound beyond conventional understanding as it fulfilled a paternalistic sense of nostalgia, signifying the burdens of the "down-trodden race." A report from Glasgow's *North British Daily Mail,* reprinted in *Dwight's Journal of Music,* conveys these sentiments:

The first thing that strikes us in the singing of the Jubilee Singers is its intense earnestness. The subject of their songs is to them a reality, something they have themselves realized and not a mere sentiment or imagination: they feel the words, and therefore they sing the music. . . . The music is not confined to the usual major and minor forms, as stereotyped in modern music; but it is constructed in such modes as are naturally used by the human voice in speaking, as well as in singing. . . . The character of the music is purely natural as contradistinguished from artistic—hence one great cause of its popular power. . . . The richness and purity of tone, both in melody and harmony, the contrast of light and shade, the varieties of gentleness and grandeur in expression, and the exquisite refinement of the piano, as contrasted with the power of the forte, fill us with delight, and at the same time, make us feel how strange it is that these unpretending singers should come over here to teach us what is the true refinement of music, and make us feel its moral and religions [*sic*] power.[78]

Judging from the Glasgow account, what magnified the sense of paternalism and condescension among white audiences also seemed to be working in reverse: the "strange" character of the Fisk songs taught white listeners about the very concepts of musical refinement they assumed to have invented themselves. And what appeared particularly strange indeed was how "true refinement" apparently derived from the preartistic naturalism explaining "its popular power." Such uneasy admiration expressed once more a general incredulity about the slave songs in relation to contemporary definitions of art. If the "wild harmonies of a band of gentle savages from Tennessee" were gaining widespread admiration, what could be left of the aesthetic achievements of a putatively superior white race?[79] How could "savages" teach whites anything and still remain subservient? Such reasoning not only complicated assumptions of European musical superiority but confidence in the integrity of white civility. The eagerness with which many whites embraced black music seemed to speak of the savage within. As W. E. B. Du Bois observed about the director of the Fisk jubilees himself, he not only taught his singers the songs but so did they teach him, as the jubilees "passed into the soul of George L. White."[80]

The success of the Fisk Jubilees intensified the growing sense of cultural inadequacy that had been inflicting white middle-class Americans since the invention of the idea of "Negro music" as it weakened the effectiveness of black containment strategies. As Houston Baker observes, the pairing of white notation and black song identified a pivotal formulation, effecting "a displacement or deconstruction of western expressive culture by the spirituals."[81] Accordingly, as writers spoke enthusiastically about the jubilees, they also tended to downplay their praise, most commonly by relying on the familiar distancing maneuver of suggesting that the slave songs had grown unconsciously out of a "Negro" folk sensibility. In a concert review published in the *New York Journal,* an anonymous reporter commented, "They are all natural musicians, and doubtless have sung from childhood, like mocking birds because they could not help it."[82] Reporting to the Boston-based *Folio,* another elaborated, "Their performances cannot be judged by any of the ordinary rules of criticism, which makes it a little difficult to describe the secret of their power. . . . The compositions exhibit peculiarities of accent found nowhere else. Many of their old plantation, or camp-meeting hymns, read like the veriest nonsense, yet are rendered in a style which excites a perfect storm, not of amusement, but of genuine, sympathetic admiration."[83] If the jubilees were products of studied practice following the rules of European music, they were also unadulterated wholes of natural purity, akin to the sounds uttered unthinkingly from the mouths of babes.[84]

The widespread appeal of the Fisk Singers and other jubilee choirs set the stage for a grand-scale elaboration on the details of black singing. These texts reflect a last-ditch effort to contain the escalating flow of racial form in a gloss of sentimentality as they revealed the enthusiasm about its entry into the public arena. Across the pages of national magazines, white writers began recalling their first encounters with the slave songs, and the accumulation of these reminiscences gave shape and substance to the postbellum narrative of black song. Represented by southern sentimentalists, they were soon joined by a new generation of northern folklorists who contributed to the making of a modern version of black musical authenticity. To a considerable extent, this new authenticity merely reinforced the racialist concepts of descent common to the paternalism of the Civil War era. Writers continued to insist that "Negroes" were naturally musical, full of spirited play, and lacking in the intellectual equipment necessary to produce art. As they pursued their mission, however, they also gave shape to a newly invented conception of black music that eventually complicated the more secure reminiscences. Reflecting the same structural contradiction that has informed other dimensions of this story, the very efforts to contain blackness in a languid sentimentality would prove empowering to

African-Americans, since it identified in the difference of "Negro" music qualities reflecting an American sensibility.

What is different about this particular historical formation is the unprecedented power black music had now achieved as a result of its dramatic entry into the public sphere and onto the stages of domestic and foreign arenas. The rise of a professional class of African-American music makers gave to the range of black expression the gloss of legitimacy as whites began to recognize and then purchase for personal consumption the inventive practices emerging from black culture. The dialogical process in this give-and-take of cultural production would ultimately inspire the rise of a dramatic refiguring of black music. With the emergence of the modern, African-American music would be increasingly recognized as an expression of black-based creativity, the public legitimacy of which (and to some extent, its artistic value) increased with its purchase. Rather than an unthinking, unconscious emergence, the qualities of black performance assumed a modern form in the image of black cultural production proposed by Hughes and Baker: it signified a generative uniqueness growing from the same racialized notions of natural musicality that reached back to the early modern period.

The copious representations of plantation songs inspired by the success of the jubilees were less an indicator of the reality of postbellum practices than a sentimental monument honoring a rapidly fading era. While the commentaries published in literary magazines and the newly established folklore journals were sometimes based on ethnographic sources, they were inevitably mediated by sensibilities specific to the writers themselves. Writers rarely seemed interested in matters relevant to black music as a contemporary practice—patterns of stylistic evolution, current performance situations, and so forth—although these concerns would inevitably be mentioned in passing.[85] Rather they preferred to look backward through their own imaginations in order to record a precious vestige of slavery, a pure, archaic sound that now seemed to be rapidly slipping away. On visiting Maryland's eastern shore, Fanny D. Bergen was "not a little surprised to find how far back in the history of civilization one turns on entering into the state of mind of the country negro." How far? Apparently, to an uninhibited "arrested development." "His instincts are unchanged by refinement," a *New York Times* writer surmised, making "the negro of the South . . . one of the most interesting studies that can be found."[86] And yet if those same instincts remained, the music itself had begun to sound different, largely as a consequence of blacks' entry into civilization. Writing in *Century Magazine,* Marion Alexander Haskell speculated, "The education of the negro in the South is gradually abolishing a species of folk-song as interesting as it is unique. . . . As the negro becomes educated he relinquishes these half-barbaric, but often beautiful, old words and melodies." Her commitment was to preserve that former primitive quality in all its authenticity. As the Fisk jubilees proposed a racial progress interrupting the certainty of European artistic standards, the recollections of the slave songs would give to America a safer, more secure racial picture. Sentimentalism affirmed the sanctity of the color line.[87]

If the documents of postbellum song were in large part fantasies of white nostalgia consistent with themes of descent, they were nonetheless crucial to the emerging modern narrative of black music. Copiously represented, at times in careful analytical prose, black vocal practices took form in their variety as a folk-based alternative to the innovations of the jubilees. As recorders outlined the various contours of song, they also supplied an accompanying language of black performance that lent to their abstractions the truth of ethnographic context. Situations were presented, from the formal setting of a church to the everyday circumstances of the work yard. In and around these places, witnesses heard a wondrous flow of utterances and turns of phrase that betrayed yet another dimension of the creative activity of black folk. References to "figurated hymns," to ring plays with odd, exotic names such as "Peep Squirrel" and "Jinny put de kettle on," to an assortment of music-dance displays, and to the "peculiar" scale alterations or "songs . . . in the minor key" that had informed characterizations of the jubilees lent a diverting sense of color and animation to black expression.[88] The representations were important in providing a level of realism and humanity to a world still vague in the minds of many curious northerners. In their detail, they helped to establish a new, public vocabulary that revealed something of the intricacies of a black folk creativity that would soon trace across the land.

As if responding to Celia M. Winston's query, "How many people know what a 'darky hymn' is?" writers proceeded to flesh out the dimensions of song specifying aspects of performance, style, history, and local meaning.[89] William Eleazar Barton, for example, supplied extensive commentary on plantation melodies and work songs, including detailed discussions of performance practices, from the use of call and response ("the sledges descend in unison as the long low chant gives the time") to the posture and movements of singers. Portraying a Georgia corn shucking, David C. Barrow, Jr., gave a thorough explanation of the practice of stacking and drying corn (how to "pull the fodder" and prepare "a hand") before turning to the responsorial practices and language of the shucking itself.[90] In his tale of camp-meeting melodies, moreover, Henry Cleveland Wood reasserted the myth of blacks' naturally religious character in his depiction of "the negro at the height of his religious frenzy." "The spell of the fervor," Wood observed, "enwraps [the worshiper] with its intensity, and sways him with its peculiar forces." The continuing fascination with black religious practices drove a flurry of reports by both white southerners and northerners "among the sable singers" that detailed the "lurid" sermons of preachers or "nighthawks," the qualities of the "exhorter," song and hymn texts, instances of shouting (in which "excited feet stamped the dusky floor"), and foot-washing ceremonies where "during the singing the feet of all keep time with the music."[91] Historical depictions of eighteenth-century figures such as Black Harry now paired with descriptions summoned from the accounts of antebellum camp meetings, as in the portrait of a Virginia preacher: "His face was convulsed, and sobs shook his whole frame when he sat down, and a strange, wild hymn was sung, the singers weaving their bodies to and fro to the measure of the music." A few writers, finally, worked directly with former slaves in order to recover the details of musical expression. In *The House of Bondage, or, Charlotte Brooks and Other Slaves,* Octavia Victoria Rogers Albert, herself a former slave, records through a series of interviews the characteristics of sacred singing, hymn lyrics, and the prohibitions on worship. The latter discussion prompts one of the first postbellum recollections of the placement of "a big wash-tub full of water in the middle of the floor to catch the sound of our voices when we sung."[92]

As writers grew increasingly aware of a distinctive body of songs, they more actively speculated on their racial origins. The debate that had originated in North America with Thomas Jefferson's observations of "Negro song" and banjo playing took on a formal, even academic, tone as it centered on the nature of the spirituals. Two kinds of discourses emerge simultaneously, sometimes in the same essay, that reproduce the contradictions surrounding black music's latest manifestation. One kind of discourse downplays the extent of African-American innovation, recalling the criticisms of the slave songs as it depends on the racist assumption of blacks' creative incapacities. According to this position, what seems distinctive about black music was but a corruption of white practices, expressing a pathetic and futile utterance of a declining race. The author of "American Negro Hymns," for example, speaks of a "a writer in the valley of the lower Mississippi" who traced "Negro" hymns to white tune books.[93] The passing of slave songs could also serve to defend claims of an inherent weakness in quality and invention. In "The New Departures in Negro Life," published in the *Atlantic Monthly,* O. W. Blacknall observed how the ribald corn-shucking melodies had become much tamer as black distinctiveness gave way to the dominance and superiority of white civilization. "Doubtless the sense of their decadence adds to their interest," as their passing prompts efforts to document them.[94]

The other kind of discourse elaborated on the innovations of African-American music, noting practices matter-of-factly or sometimes proposing them to be the crucible of a new musical tradition. Writing against the background of Higginson's and Allen's seminal efforts and in the wake of Dvořák's claims about the national significance of the spirituals, observers of "Negro" folk songs proposed them to be a distinctive class of singing that reflected the ingenuity and imagination of African-Americans generally. "The negro of the South is one of the most interesting studies that can be found," O. W. Blacknall, the traveler to Montgomery, Alabama, succinctly put it.[95] Still others recognized this distinctiveness as common fact and sought to embrace it. William E. Barton's extended coverage of "Negro" song and dance, which was published in three installments in *New England Magazine* in 1888 and 1889, describes the efforts of a dancer to learn the "wonderful syncopations" of southern black sound and movement. Brimming with curiosity and excitement, the statement recalls early accounts of shouts as it anticipates the primitivist language of the jazz age:

It is the peculiarity of the negro music that it can nearly all be swayed to and timed with the patting of the foot. No matter how irregular it appears to be, one who ways backward and forward and pats his foot finds the rhythm perfect. A young lady friend of mine was trying to learn some of the melodies from an old auntie, but found that the time as well as the tune baffled her. At length, when the woman had turned to her work, the girl got to swaying and humming gently, patting her foot the while. The old woman turned and, patting the girl on the knee, said: "Dat's right, honey! Dat's de berry way! Now you's a-gittin' it, sho nuff! You'll nebbah larn 'em in de wuld till you sings dem in de sperrit!"[96]

As an accompaniment to these debates, transcription becomes an important tool for those who sought to demonstrate Negro distinctiveness. Yet just as easily it could serve to downplay distinctiveness, ushering black song into the mainstream of notation's conventions and sequestering it safely at a distance from white bodies. For those seeking to claim a viable black innovation, transcription seemed to be a ready tool, one with a secure foundation in the efforts of midcentury slave-song collectors. What better way to specify the character of singing as it departs from the norms of scale and harmony than through the power of inscription, as Allen and his colleagues had already shown? The deviations in normative pitch and time meld to identify the signature of what blackness means, generated out of the peculiar action of swaying bodies and tapping feet.[97] Henry Cleveland Wood's transcriptions of "the old-time melodies" heard near his grandfather's Kentucky home represent "a few fragments" of a "fast disappearing" form prior to "the drilled choir and accomplished organist have fully established their innovations." Mildred Hill's reminiscences about early plantation melodies featured the same monophonic transcription technique employed by Allen, McKim, and Ware, in order to portray the songs' distinctiveness, a practice similarly replicated by Marion Alexander Haskell. In his series of essays for *New England Magazine,* moreover, Barton presented fifty-three transcriptions of songs, together with a discussion of the challenge of transcription itself. Particularly important were the transcriptions performed by Thomas P. Fenner for the Hampton collection, in which he seeks in his fifty versions of songs a middle ground between authentic realism and willfully adorned "improvement."[98]

Yet the intentions of these and others were far from clear. At this point, collectors, despite their sentimentality, seemed less enamored of the putatively magical properties of song claimed by Allen and his contemporaries. More often they seemed more compelled to the practical task of documenting the songs. Such pragmatism could easily become a form of appropriation, whereby the earnest effort to preserve unique qualities secures the melodies in the amber of European harmonic practice. Julia Neeley Finck, for example, supplies a piano arrangement of a melody sung by "the old mammy belonging to my husband's family," making it into a version of the decorum of the domestic place. Arrangements of "Turn Back Pharaoh's Army" and "Go Down, Moses" published in *Dexter Smith's* not only recast melody into decorous harmonic form but turned the songs into commodities that helped to drive magazine sales as well.[99] The renderings were obviously prepared this way in order to make a strange musical world palatable to the skeptics, and they may have been well aware of such distinguished precedents of Lucy McKim and of Charles Carleton Coffin, who in his book, *Four Years of Fighting,* includes a four-part harmonic arrangement of "Roll Jordan," together with a description of its performance. But such transformations also betrayed a lack of comfort with the characteristic racial distinctiveness that the songs displayed. Even Thomas P. Fenner, in his sincere attempt to fastidiously preserve the integrity of black song could not resist the exercise of "bringing out the various parts" in order to "improve" and thus heighten the original racial essence.[100]

Some collectors at the time were clearly dismayed by the civilizing efforts that obscured not only what was characteristically "Negro" about the songs but their origins as well. Barton, who noted the difficulty of transcription ("in writing the notes one has to compromise"), supplemented his sketches with copious discussion of performance practice. Hill, writing under the pseudonym Johann Tonsor, spoke more directly of the failure of the "various attempts . . . at collecting these our only *volkslieder*," identifying that failure principally in the way "the melody is usually sacrificed to the harmony." She proposed, instead, that "the melodies, pure and simple, with no attempt at improving them, should be collected and preserved." According to Alice Mabel Bacon of Hampton Folk-Lore Society, the desire to clothe melodies in harmonized arrangements explained why so many assumed them to be imitations of European practice. "It is my belief that the reason why there is so much doubt to-day in the minds of so many of the best authorities, as to whether the negro spirituals are the product of the negroes, is because they have been subjected to this process of civilizing into regular written forms." Recognizing that even the most scrupulous notation inevitably refashions black singing according to the dictates of European practice, she proposed avoiding it entirely and relying instead on "graphophone" recordings.[101]

As whites debated the nature, origins, and preservation of the black folk melodies, African-Americans pursued a variety of new musical expressions with no clear commitment to any particular avenue of performance. While it is impossible to determine the extent to which public concerns about the characteristics of black music also occupied the attention of black southerners, it is tempting to assume that most were either unfamiliar or unimpressed with such preoccupations. More likely, they continued to make music as a matter of course, constantly fashioning and refashioning it into the texture of their daily lives. The existence of new practices, particularly those stemming from cities, inevitably made their impact. Representations from the 1880s and 1890s suggest a vast range of performance practices through which African-Americans creatively crafted new sonic renderings of place in the new settings they occupied or reoriented familiar approaches to accompany the social changes reaching into even the more remote sites of home. Apart from the extensions of vocal practices already discussed, black southerners seemed increasingly to be playing musical instruments. While instruments had always been conspicuous among African-Americans, they now seemed visible in the pleasures of entertainment, accompanying song and dance and playing a principal role in new genres and settings, such as in the string bands that had become popular by the 1880s. Still often desperately poor under the oppression of a brutal racist regime, black southerners commonly relied on the humblest and most makeshift of instruments, from bones to banjoes to archaic "violins" made of animals' jawbones. Reports also note the coupling of traditional instruments with those new to rural areas: fiddling with the brass instruments introduced in wartime military bands, banjoes accompanying the "French Harp" or harmonica.[102]

In southern cities, black instrumental practices departed markedly from the norms of plantation performance. An 1879 report from Atlanta, for example, referred to one of what were likely several combinations of the old and new. It described "five laborers, each black as the deuce of spades, sitting upon a circle of battered stools and soap boxes, and forming a 'string' band, despite the inconsistency of a cornet." Not far away was another group, this one featuring guitar and banjo, and yet another group of African-American minstrels. An accompanying illustration shows a group playing traditional plantation (minstrel) instruments—banjo, bones, fife, and tambourine—accompanying a concertina player and fiddlers, all "to the amusement of two or three hundred delighted darkies." By 1892, the appeal of fiddling and banjo playing, still prominent after the Civil War, was said to have declined, both in rural settings, where blacks often preferred the accordion, and "among the city negroes [where] the piano is the favorite instrument."[103] What had been, along with the organ, the signature instrument of an aspiring African-American middle-class was now making its way into the saloons and bars of towns and cities. Into the twentieth century, the piano would represent one of the chief components of the new popular genres of ragtime and jazz.

Whether a reflection of changing commitments or a sign of observers' shifting perceptions, southern blacks also seemed to be working more frequently with percussion instruments. What had been extremely rare in antebellum accounts now showed up with some regularity. A report by Hamilton Jay, a Florida correspondent to the *New York Sun,* described how "some dusky warrior" might be seen with a makeshift drum, "made of an empty nail keg with a coon skin stretched over the ends." Similarly, Alcée Fortier described to her readers in the *Journal of American Folk-Lore* a Louisiana drum made out of "a barrel with one end covering with an ox-hide," which a musician "beat with his hands, with his feet, and sometimes, when quite carried away by his enthusiasm, with his head also." Percussion techniques could also be transferred to other instruments. In his portrait of a Georgia corn shucking, David C. Barrow, Jr., portrayed a musician who rattled straws "after the manner of drumsticks [on] that portion of the fiddle-strings between the fiddler's bow and his left hand serving as a drum."[104]

The bulk of references to percussion-playing techniques appeared in the context of performances involving shouting or dancing. The routines of patting and the aggressive physicality of the shout continued to receive vivid melodramatic portrayals recalling the stories of antebellum camp meetings. Now, however, they had begun to suggest a continuity of a discrete category of rhythm as part of a racial legacy. No doubt African-Americans had continued to associate these strenuous exertions with the extremes of religious ecstasy and encounter born out of the slave era. But the essays, together with the well-documented shift in black perceptions by the early twentieth century, suggest that these forms were not static re-creations of slavery but new forms expressing new circumstances. As "the whole body gradually falls into the motion, until it seems as if every muscle moves in perfect time with the music," shouters most likely had begun to understand these practices according to modern conceptions of rhythm. Those standing by, beyond the circle, moreover, may have been resisting the shout precisely because of its associations with the new white fantasies about the rhythmic nature of black music. For white collectors, the evidence of another kind of passing was plain: "Times are changing. Only during Christmas week can be heard the sound of gliding circles on cabin floors."[105] A similar, modern construction grew in association with the cakewalk. If cakewalks actually fulfilled the common representation of a traditional plantation dance, they had also been reinvented in language and approach fulfilling a thoroughly modern perspective. What was new to the public was also seated at the wellsprings of civilization. Cakewalkers, a writer enthused, were "keeping in lively remembrance customs that have become traditional from their remotest ancestors." Having gained a history, a legacy, one linking primal ancestry with "its origin among the French Negroes of the South more than a century ago," the performances assumed a discernibly modern character that would establish the background for the new genre of ragtime and the syncopated "animal dances."[106]

If there was one type of expression that many blacks sought to avoid, it was the singing of spirituals and the more formalized jubilees. While these songs were well represented by a multitude of performances and productions, accordingly sustaining appeal across race and class lines well into the twentieth century, they had, for a time, at least, largely fallen out of favor among many African-Americans. As preachers advocated new forms of gospel singing, the general population grew interested in common secular songs or, at least, in a mix and match of sacred and secular melodies popularized by the vocal quartets. The obvious reason for this departure from the spirituals and jubilees was their association with submissive behavior, propped up by the sentimentalism of folklore itself. If Harriet Tubman had made famous the seditious use of slave songs as a means of secret communication, that practice, while informing the signifyin' aspect of subsequent black expressions, no longer seemed to have much to do with the singing of sacred songs, at least the well-known versions of spirituals and jubilees. Thomas Fenner, who had arranged spirituals for the Hampton singers, spoke to this matter directly. Even as the slave song passes away, "the freedmen have an unfortunate inclination to despise it, as a vestige of slavery."[107] Alice Mabel Bacon of the Hampton Folk-Lore Society once again linked this refusal to the rise in black education, although expressing greater sympathy for its importance than Marion Alexander Haskell had. In an essay on methodological procedures in folklore, she begins, "Any one who has had much to do with the educated negroes of the present day knows that by them the old stories and superstitions and customs of their own race are only too apt to be looked down upon as all bad, and to be forgotten as quickly as possible." Jonathan Baxter Harrison reached a similar conclusion as a result of his own inquiries. "It is very interesting to listen to the singing in the colored schools. . . . One hears everywhere a few rich and powerful voices, and the negro churches in the larger towns have fine choirs." "But the old negro music will soon disappear," Harrison predicted. "All the educated negro ministers discourage or forbid the use of it among their people," most likely in favor of the newly emerging forms of gospel and the cultivated spirituals that Fenner was perpetuating.[108]

Working hand in hand with the resistance to the spirituals were the new opportunities to perform music professionally. By the 1880s, a new class of performer, the professional black musician, had become common to cities and towns across the South, their influence gradually extending into northern regions. Typically young and untried, these musicians entered into the new economy of popular entertainment, performing for black audiences but also commonly for a mixed or white clientele. In many cases, they put up for sale the routines of everyday musical practice, performing the traditions of southern experience. As they appeared increasingly in new settings in distant locales, however, the black musicians who were traversing the South sought to please the tastes of their audiences. Few had the luxury to commit to a single creative impetus. Fewer still had time for the sentimentalism driving white attention, although their music making, now presented for profit, would continually need to accommodate white tastes, particularly among the working classes. Appearing in medicine shows, circuses, and minstrel troupes, performing in brass bands and vaudeville acts and on the concert stage, black musicians featured various approaches and routinely refashioned their offerings. As a matter of course, they also invented new sounds and practices, borrowing widely from the strains of American popular song (verse/chorus form, common meter, functional harmony) and reworking their performances, with little concern that they might breach the norms of authenticity. The adoption of coon songs was itself an infamous example of blacks' adaptability, and unless we discredit this as an act of self-loathing, it would more likely indicate the mercurial shifts of meaning and processes of invention in which African-Americans operated.[109] Southern black music toward the end of the nineteenth century was filled with such anomalies. Indeed, it was unmistakably hybrid. As Edward L. Ayers succinctly describes it, "Seldom staying long in one place, they followed the rail lines across the South, and . . . incorporated new ideas and styles from outside the South into their own distinctly Southern vocabularies."[110]

As black performers entered into more public circumstances controlled by the authority of white taste, they were compelled to work within the parameters defining the nature of race music. In this, they did not simply perform black music but produced those particular expressions that affirmed racial difference within a broad system of relations and according to a structural logic that was unmistakably ideological. While virtually anything performed by African-Americans signified "Negro music," what increasingly drew attention were the more dynamic forms of instrumentally based rhythm music expressing the newness and modernism of a migrant population. African-American musicians would develop this special musical category, generating forms that highlighted rhythmic innovation for the pleasure of audiences across the races. Rhythmic innovation was endemic to music making, determining the common practice of the era, even in the most remote reaches of southern black culture. Witnessing Negro music on successive archeological digs in northern Mississippi (1901–2), the Harvard anthropologist Charles Peabody now noticed how southern blacks worked with rhythmic determination. "These syncopated melodies, sung or whistled, generally in strict tempo, kept up hour after hour a not ineffective rhythm, which we decidedly should have missed had it been absent." Significantly, their performances juxtaposed ragtime tunes learned from passing theatrical troupes (" 'Molly Brown' and 'Goo-goo Eyes' were great favorites") alongside familiar hymns. As Peabody points out, the appearance of urban influence in the most rural of settings "quite inverted the supposed theory of its origin."[111]

The modern versions of black musical difference were not, then, simply imposed onto African-Americans by a white power structure: As extensions of ideological formation, they affected everyone, including black musicians and black audiences. What differed across the races was the nature of the responses to these performances and the conclusions reached about what they signified. As musicians sought to uphold notions of difference embraced by whites, it seems likely that they also did their best to project images and express sentiments benefiting the social position of African-Americans. But because the common sense of a black rhythmic nature had become by the early 1900s so deeply embedded in the matrix of racial ideology, they could only enact creative resistance through the same mechanisms that oppressed them, refiguring details and surfaces as best they could. As professionals, they still lived and worked within a system of accommodation. "The majority of younger negroes must be well paid for their music," Howard W. Odum observed in 1911. "In the smaller towns, such negroes not infrequently organize a small 'orchestra,' and learn to play and sing the new songs. They often render acceptable music, and are engaged by the whites for serenades or for occasions of minor importance. They do not, however, sing the negro folk-songs."[112]

The shift in public perception that reinvented black music as rhythm music occurred over a twenty-year period, during the last two decades of the nineteenth century. At this moment, which represents a veritable watershed in the formation of modern black music, the intellectual concepts of primitivism and African origins aligning with "descent" intersected with the dynamic figurations of displaced Negroes in motion. Modern images of the savage, the original, that constitute Tarzan in the "dum dum" and identify the poisonous scourge of hot jazz grew out of a seminal body of figurations through which rhythm gained both its primal ferocity and its signature of urban-based danger, which together identify fundamental elements of black musical modernism. Not surprisingly, evidence of this shift appears conspicuously in the literature about black folk songs. What had been resolutely melodic in nature acquired a discernible dynamism that would greatly alter the character of song. Singers no longer simply moved but "swayed in rhythmic measure with the music." Performers of hymns were now admired for their temporal sensitivity: "The precision in time of a negro congregation is absolutely marvelous for so untrained a body. Every note is hit with exquisite accuracy." Even Henry Cleveland Wood's admiring depiction of a Negro camp meeting stood in contrast from those of the antebellum era, making precise reference to a discrete rhythmic category. Camp-meeting melodies displayed "rhythmical cadences"; worshipers were "swaying their dusky bodies in rhythmic motion."[113]

Increasingly, the identification of rhythmic character in song spawned associations with Africa. Drawing from the familiar language of colonization and the travelogue, American writers embraced the figures of descent that emphasized rhythmic practices and incorporated them into the new rhythmic appearance of song. On hearing "the songs of the Dahomeyans at the Exposition in Chicago," for example, Charlotte Forten Grimke "was struck with their general resemblance to the shouting and singing of the Sea Island Negroes." It was in this context that she attributed to the shouts a rhythmic aspect that reflected the barbarous nature of black folk "handed down to them from their African ancestors." Similarly, Mildred Hill's sentimental recollections of plantation songs incorporated vivid caricatures of pagans and savages. "I have no doubt that this music, like Voodooism, is a remnant of former idolatry. Doubtless many of these hymns have been sung for centuries before the shrines of fetishes in the dark jungles of Africa." But these were not, she explained, pure African songs but New World inventions that nonetheless expressed "a certain syncopation," which she attributed to their "singing at the top of their voices and swaying their bodies rhythmically to and fro." Hill's depiction of a slave performance employs exotic images to propose a new kind of "Negro," one distinguished from the romantic sentimentality proposed earlier. In this modern rendering, she sees a woman who "sat for a time in a sort of stupor. Everywhere she looked there were gaping throats and fierce eyes glaring at her like those of wild beasts." In order to demonstrate the difference between modern and archaic form, she offers, "in conclusion, . . . two tunes, one of them almost purely African, the other evidently composed in the transition period between the old and new schools."[114]

While discussions of songs secured rhythm in the dominant frames of black music, portrayals of religious rituals involving dancing and drumming drew the most vivid Africanizing treatments. These texts are accordingly key in their anticipation of the modern excitement about twentieth-century black instrumental forms. Whereas the songs would always endure an affiliation with Civil War–era sentimentality, dance-based practices together with their rhythmic accompaniments spoke most directly to modern anxieties of black displacement as they were embellished with images of a distant pagan past. The bulk of these commentaries centered on the voodoo rituals of New Orleans, ceremonies epitomizing the illicit as they would provide a background for interpretations of ragtime, blues, and particularly jazz. References to violence, cannibalism, and carnal desire integrated with an assembly of images of rhythm, drawing the primal figurations of a newly colonized Africa into a New World monstrosity that announced the emergence of the "modern Negro."[115] In his 1887 essay "Voudoo Dance," for example, Charles Dudley Warner stays close to the familiar qualities attributed to black music (song forms, associations with American religious "faith-cure") as he weaves a portrait of strangely foreign and mysterious practice conjuring diabolical images. Prefacing his discussion with a lengthy commentary on the background of voodoosim in Africa and Haiti, Warner draws a portrait of a "wild dance and incantations [that] are accompanied by sacrifice of animals and occasionally of infants, and with cannibalism, and scenes of most indecent license." The actors perform in emphatically rhythmic ways, beginning with "the doctor" who "began in the open space a slow measured dance, a rhythmical shuffle, . . . accelerating his movement as the time of the song quickened and the excitement rose in the room." Soon, "the singing became wilder and more impassioned, a strange minor strain, full of savage pathos and longing, that made it almost impossible for the spectator not to join in the swing of its influence." With all the wildness and passion and heat ("his hands were aflame, his clothes seemed to be on fire") the performance reaches its incendiary height, creating a feeling "so wild and bizarre that one might easily imagine he was in Africa or in hell."[116]

Warner's essay, together with other related portraits of voodoo, shouting, and religious ceremony, appeared against the background of a seminal pair of essays by George Washington Cable, whose grotesque animated accounts of New Orleans rituals set the basis for commentaries appearing after.[117] In a detailed analysis of "Creole Slave Songs" and voodoo ritual, Cable introduces the displays of carnality and violence as an aggregate of excess advanced through rhythmic motion. Like other texts at the time, Cable's characterizes black music as a form of song, offering not only a detailed record of lyrics but transcriptions prepared by the New York critic Henry Krehbiel. Significantly, however, his characterization of black song served not to perpetuate a soulful sentimentalism reminiscent of the spirituals but to advance a secular, more dangerous and finally pagan expression. "Did the slave feel so painfully that the beauties of the natural earth were not for him? . . . His songs were not often contemplative. They voiced not outward nature, but the inner emotions and passions of a nearly naked serpent-worshiper, and these looked not to the surrounding scene for sympathy; the surrounding scene belonged to his master. . . . Sleep was his balm, food his reinforcement, the dance his pleasure, rum his longed-for nepenthe, and death the road back to Africa." This African sang in a rhythmic voice. In the other essay, "The Dance in Place Congo," employs the language of the travelogue to portray the dancing in New Orleans's famous Congo Square as a wild cacophony of ferocity, savagery, flailing bodies, and dynamic sound. At the center was voodoo: "So revolting and so morally hideous, that even in the West Indian French possessions a hundred years ago . . . the orgies of the voudoos were forbidden." As the congregants performed endlessly ("the musicians know no fatigue"), "the rhythm stretches out heathenish and ragged. The quick contagion is caught by a few in the crowd, who take it up with spirited smitings of the bare sole upon the ground, and of open hands upon the thighs." These "swoonings and ravings, nervous trembling beyond control," were the "forbidden fruit" inspired by the drum. It "grew everywhere more and more gross. No wonder the police stopped it in Congo Square."[118]

The challenge of accessing black sound and physicality would shape the character of an emerging racial "sonic fiction" of America on the brink of the modern.[119] Qualities of movement and peculiarities of performance practice assembled as versions of difference defining blackness as such. As images of rhythm circulated, they grew to articulate much of the character of race, betraying a musical quality within texts addressing nonmusical matters. In a perverse parody titled "Chin-Music," for example, the author describes the percussive sound of black pugilists punishing each other's bodies, in which strikes on the body emit the sound of the "natural drum." Introducing images of African ferocity into the category of shiftless urban blacks, he attributes the "rhythmic practice" of chin music to "the rites and ceremonies of wild barbarians on the Gold Coast." A second example of the sonic fiction of blackness appears as a report on the 1885 American Philological Association meeting at Yale. The essay, published in the *Critic,* focused on a paper by J. A. Harrison of Washington and Lee University, which was "the most popular essay of the session." The paper explored the various dialects of "Negro English," explaining that "much of his talk is baby-talk, of an exceedingly attractive sort to those to the manner born. He deals in hyperbole, in rhythm, . . . Negro English is an ear-language . . . built up on what the late Professor Haldemann of Pennsylvania called 'otosis,' an error of ear." This spontaneous, haphazard rhythmic language, Harrison continued, issued from the wilds of the jungle. Dialect, an "ingenious distortion of words," grows as "imitations of sounds, cries and animal utterance," founded on "rhythmic utterance" and "improvisation." "To the negro all nature is alive, replete with intelligence. . . . He is on intimate terms with the wild animals and buds, the flora and fauna of the immense stretches of pine-woods among which for generations his habitation has been pitched." The classic conceits of the early modern travelogue become the basis for explaining the curious grotesque sound world now resonating across a thoroughly modern America.[120]

Over time, the infecting capacities of modern black music would grow more powerful, "louder," as the myths of racial authenticity circulated in a highly mediated public culture. Elaborations on the qualities of hot sound and rhythmic potency accumulated, piling one upon the other and producing a rich network of meaning that packed a punch with every effective rendering of racially pulsating heat. Henry Edward Krehbiel would offer extensive speculations on black music's peculiar properties, proposing a physical basis in African-American bodily form (the vocal cords of blacks were "capable of longer vibrations") and a linkage between kinetic rhythms and the flow of hotness: "The blood of the African black 'has the highest human temperature known—equal to that of the swallow—though it loses that fire in America.' " What could seem "as foreign as the Egyptian," had infiltrated American life, its syncopations coursing through the sound world of white and black. The newness of black rhythm was something magical, akin to the miracle of birth: "It is young, and unhackneyed, and throbbing with life. And it is racial."[121] Such sentiments would circulate ever wider, recasting folklore's representations of the slave songs as fixtures of rhythmic practice (Scarborough, Odum) as they were embraced by African-Americans, from James Reese Europe to Duke Ellington, whose "jungle music" accompanied the frenetic Harlem dancing of voyeuristic white "tourists" uptown.

Black scholars similarly invested in the commonsense opinion of rhythm's naturalism, expressing a dominant ideological formation of race. Maud Cuney-Hare, for example, embraced simple-to-complex evolutionary thinking in her depiction of black music's development, describing a process that begins in primal Africa and ends in twentieth-century artistic practices.[122] With the introduction of African-centered arguments after Herskovits, moreover, the cosmopolitan qualities of swing would be commonly rendered as a foundational essence echoing from the ancestors. The power of rhythm that stood so centrally in the work of Hughes and other Harlem writers would serve as a sturdy basis for defining and redefining difference across the twentieth century. Indeed, it would represent a common sonic identification of an overarching American identity, as blackness infiltrated the core of a modern New World sensibility, resonating outwardly to Europe and across the globe. In jazz, swing, bebop, and rhythm 'n' blues, in the inventions of cool and soul jazz, in the popular forms of soul and funk, and in the later innovations of hip-hop, black America introduced modern versions of racial distinctiveness that many Americans would seek to claim, precisely because these expressions grew from the same circumstances of national culture. Rhythm would supply the basis on which "black essence" was enacted, affirming the mythology of black and white, just as the hybrid character of every rendering of blackness betrayed its grounding in a cross-racial common soil. As a matter of course, America and the rest of the world listened mainly through a coloring lens. With each innovation, we would look on with amazement as miraculous inventions of blackness resonated from its putative African base.

But what if, to return to Hughes and Baker, this "body and soul" of modern American sound were conceived according to a different set of assumptions, such as those outlined in this analysis? What might black music become were we to imagine a "dream of black form" within America, observing racialized sound through a new lens, and thus reworking Zora Neale Hurston's "spy-glass of Anthropology" to adjust for the distortions of an enduring racial fantasy? Put another way—and to turn to the themes discussed at the outset—what might lie beyond the "lies" in the utterances of black voicing?

Epilogue   A Nation's Gift

Already we come not altogether empty-handed:
there is to-day no true American music but the sweet wild
melodies of the Negro slave.—W. E. B. Du Bois

And so we come to the end of the story of black music's various racial contests, of truths and lies, of resonances abounding, of a society's confessions heard in the miraculous creations of those once named invisible and silent. What does this tale of difference making bode for the future? Do we commit to fixed definitions of blackness in an effort to counter the effects of racism and a new rising tide of white supremacy, or do we consider another strategy, one perhaps more consistent with the circuitous patterns of the music's own history in the making? Can we—to return to the matter put forward at the close of chapter 5—perceive the soundtexts of America through a different critical lens, patterning our history with the kind of interpretive flexibility proposed by Langston Hughes, Zora Neale Hurston, Ralph Ellison, and the other heroes of this tale? If so, what appearance might modern black music take if we were to hear it as a cultural expression cast within and against the formations of racial ideology—as a sound form expressive simultaneously of both the difference of blackness and the relation of black to white? The various musical engagements that have appeared throughout *Lying up a Nation* give some indication as to how our story might inform an understanding of music closer to the present. I will conclude with a reflection on race and listening at the onset of the twenty-first century by turning to the seminal study of a master hero as he looked on the twentieth.

A hundred years ago, W. E. B. Du Bois outlined a vision of race relations in the United States that has proven to be remarkably influential across the twentieth century. At the heart of this theory was his notion of the color line, of the division of a united people, a nation, according to a belief in differences of black and white. Du Bois's *The Souls of Black Folk* has continued to seem so modern, so thoroughly up-to-date in large part because this peculiar line of demarcation is still with us, because the deepest structures of race relations have changed so little. Despite the achievements of black protest and the Civil Rights Movement, despite the decidedly American contributions of blacks in the realm of arts and letters, our nation stands firmly committed to its coloring constructs, and it is this commitment above all that explains the effect of race in the deepest layers of social life. As we uphold the notion of color, we perpetuate difference or "twoness," which Du Bois targets as the basis for the precarious state of African-America's racial existence. Commitment to the color line produces a condition he famously names double consciousness, "a double life with double thoughts, double duties, and double social classes." It is from this condition that critics have assembled an analytical strategy for examining a broader black experience. In contemporary black studies, the figure of double consciousness remains the main interpretive starting point for exploring the dimensions of black existence. Despite the diversity of critical literature on African-American culture, it all seems, as Arnold Rampersad suggests, to "come out of . . . *The Souls of Black Folk*—and most precisely from Du Bois's image of the divided souls."[1]

What is less commonly acknowledged in the literature on double consciousness is the subversive logic that Du Bois brings to bear; his theory not only identifies the racial base of American life but a strategy for contending with it. Far from simply acquiescing to the dismal gloom of Jim Crow in slavery's aftermath, Du Bois outlines a form of cultural reasoning that challenges the powerful forces of racism. Significantly, his plan for African-American progress does not depend on a change of heart among whites but calls for a process of self-actualization that begins with recognizing how black experience has informed American life while remaining strangely independent from it. In the paradox of the doubled soul—"gifted with second-sight [that] . . . only lets him see himself through the revelation of the other world"—Du Bois tells a story of tragedy giving way to special insight.[2] Doubleness becomes a mode of black magic, an epistemology affirming flexibility and dynamism to disengage color prejudice while upholding the difference of African-American identity. Rather than merely inverting racial logic (creating a positivity out of negativity), Du Bois celebrates the difference that produces the realness of black experience while simultaneously exposing that realness as an invention of racial ideology that, when brought into the conscious mode, is capable of being transcended. From this posture, African-Americans may continue to claim blackness as a legitimate social experience while its fictiveness offers options out of it.

What enables this dual claim and transcendence of racial identity is the power of black music. As a social scientist with strong aesthetic proclivities, Du Bois affirmed the relation between the aesthetic idea of "Culture" and the anthropological concept of "culture," proposing that in artwork one could discern the mysterious life ways that ethnologists at the time were eagerly attempting to define.[3] In the magical properties of black music, Du Bois heard the most immediate expression of an equally mystified conception of American culture; its sonic forms revealed the unseen depths of the nation, expressing qualities resonant with the shape of things to come. The seemingly boundless signifying capacities of black music accordingly established the material, sonic ground from which one could explore culture's making. In its capaciousness, music expressed the paradoxes of racial existence. References to music in *Souls* do not merely adorn the text but signify the depths of sound in the fashioning of America, a sound revealing black people's equal partnership in the production of culture/Culture. As Houston A. Baker, Jr., puts it, the copious references to musicality and audition suggest that *The Souls of Black Folk* is, after all, a "singing book," the resonant traces of which integrate with social commentary as "cadences of Negro song."[4] The book's chapters brim with sonic references. "Of the Meaning of Progress" speaks of harsh realities "softened by laughter and song," together with fanciful images of a laughing sun, of "jingl[ing] water," of the "patter of little feet" eagerly advancing toward learning. "Of the Golden Fleece" depicts "the hum of the cotton-mills," which gives way to songs of love and laughter and "the clang [of] the day-bell" in "Of the Wings of Atalanta." "Of the Black Belt," in particular, seems almost saturated with vivid tuneful activity, of field hands calling, of cotton gins groaning, of brooks singing, of "five hundred persons" gathered on consecrated space to make spiritual sound. There is a sense that Du Bois seeks to overwhelm the reader with black culture's sonic dimensions as he employs sound more specifically to counter white control on America through language.[5]

But the doubleness of Du Bois's musical America also depends on the language-based modes of representation that attend to the making of modern blackness. In Du Bois's double criticism, the mystified realm of a putatively originary music becomes the basis for advancing his vision of black culture as a social construction. The audible folk soul of *The Souls of Black Folk* is not some primal original domain but a partially texted one that is inevitably accessed through the mediating equipment of representation. If the sorrow songs, those famous inventions of the slaves—"the most beautiful expression born this side the seas"—suggest a pure expression of "the race," they reflect only a partial consciousness until they enter into public culture and are transformed through a texting process that Du Bois takes pains to document.[6] "Art expression in the day of slavery had to be very limited," he observes, "a matter of wild strains of music and still wilder laughter and dancing." What brought forth art and an attendant self-consciousness was the process of inscription, the re-ordering, re-making, and re-membering of song epitomized in the Fisk Jubilee's language of "civilization." This textual process, in turn, supplies a crucial materiality that explains black culture's rightful claims on America. In an important passage, Du Bois identifies the songs that echoed forth from Fisk University's Jubilee Hall as the economically grounded substance of slavery's legacy. This "Chapel of Melody," as he calls it, was literally constituted out of sound and sweaty labor: "To me Jubilee Hall seemed ever made of the songs themselves, and its bricks were red with blood and dust of toil."[7] If Du Bois in his gestures to an exalted folkness seems to be expressing his own longings for a lost innocence, he is also remarkably sensitive to how the peculiarities of social circumstance complicate the romantic ideal of an everlasting, racially determined essence. To be sure, he recognized the power of black song's mystification as a social process in the making of black self-consciousness. But this self-consciousness would be created in the new hybridities of African-American authenticity that were emerging in the late nineteenth century in response to the denials of black creative ability. The material, historical reading of song supplies an important background in the role of black art's expression of a new self-consciousness that challenges the authority of a whitewashed America.

Du Bois is not abiding by our current conventions of authenticity either when he celebrated Jubilee forms over the more firmly planted rural expressions of Tennessee or when he failed to distinguish the privately run Fisk chorus of the 1880s from the original touring ensemble that had been dissolved by the university in 1878 in response to the rash of performances by counterfeit Jubilee troupes. In *The Souls*, as well as in his later writings, he scarcely troubles to justify his membership in Fisk's Mozart Society, his nostalgic recollections of performing the *Hallelujah Chorus*, or his abiding love of Beethoven, Wagner, and the other composers of "real [German] music" that he had discovered at Harvard and Berlin.[8] For Du Bois, progress arises from blacks' rightful claim on all realms of knowledge, a vision depicted powerfully in the pairing of incipits of sorrow songs with quotations from European and Euro-American literature to introduce each chapter of *Souls*. As Shelley Fisher Fishkin and others have observed, "These paired 'quotations,' . . . by their very juxtaposition, reveal the notion of a 'color line' to be a fiction—when it comes to the strivings of the human spirit or the aspirations of the human soul." Racial and cultural purity matter less than the capability of a musical work to articulate real, civilized presence. Evoking the Hegelian master/slave interpretation that he found so compelling, Du Bois identifies true racial freedom in an unresolved dialectical relationship with white America, in a kind of stability in instability. "The genius of *The Souls of Black Folk,*" David Levering Lewis writes, "was that it transcended this dialectic in the most obvious way—by affirming it in permanent tension."[9] Du Bois extends the paradoxes of double consciousness by reconfiguring twoness as black sound, whose properties of "transcendence" in the romantic imagination supply a critique of the presumed whiteness of the American character. Black folks' soul nature becomes a second nature, or what we might call the twoness of oneness—the emancipation of blackness in the reality of doubled difference.

Du Bois is certainly resolute in his commitment to a progressive refashioning of black folk culture. Yet he also recognizes that an unreflective loyalty to the virtues of progress could be as dangerous as a static vernacular origin. Knowledge, reason, and the generative power of writing, he surmises, turned on a "savage irony." As Arnold Rampersad puts it in his study of Du Bois, "For the black man in a racist world, the acquisition of culture is a dangerous and often destructive process."[10] While holding the secrets to power and knowledge, Culture—as the reason behind a history of enslavement—can also turn against its possessor. Accordingly, Du Bois sought to harness reason through the logic of racial difference in order to give voice to a modern version of blackness that ironically recovered a former, "ancient" black self. Extending the logic of Hegel's dictum, Du Bois argues, "Just as lordship shared its essential nature to be the reverse of what it wants to be, so, too, bondage will, when completed, pass into the opposite of what it immediately is: being a consciousness represented within itself, it will enter into itself, and change round into real and true independence."[11] In the aftermath of slavery, black art and culture arise as an articulation of a new independence within and against the forces of white supremacy. The second sight of difference, revealed in the capaciousness of black music, would lend a colored cast to the sound and feel of the nation.

In Du Bois's projection, then, the songs of black folk, refashioned as black art, play an emancipatory role in the making of America. They do so not simply in fashioning a new more modern national vision but by uncoupling white racial logic in order to supply African-Americans with greater claim on American culture as a whole. Key to this critical maneuver is the notion of the gift that blacks bring to America: "Already we come not altogether empty-handed," Du Bois writes in 1897, "there is to-day no true American music but the sweet wild melodies of the Negro slave."[12] The "gift" of the sorrow songs that arose miraculously from the "blood and dust of toil" embody the range of contributions of black people to the making of America, and in their reinvention as jubilees, we identify the emergence of an art form resonant with the depths of national history. As gifts to America, however, the songs of blacks represent something more than an expression of altruism, an offering solely for the benefit of whites. As the work of Marcel Mauss and Natalie Zemon Davis shows, gifts can be double-edged, serving the giver as well as the taker: "Apparently free and gratuitous, [they are] nevertheless constrained and self-interested." Gift giving presumes a gift in return, and "the unreciprocated gift [accordingly] makes the person who has accepted it inferior, particularly when it has been accepted with no thought of returning it."[13]

In the context of American race relations, the gift of black song, so openly embraced by whites during Du Bois's time, seriously undermined the binary logic of race. By taking a gift without thought of reciprocating, whites claimed blackness for themselves, thus committing a selfish act. But this gesture also reveals an inadvertent generosity: it complicates racial purity together with the absolute power of whiteness. For by accepting black song, whites become the receivers rather than the makers, the listeners rather than the producers. Relinquishing creative authority, they participate in a situation that escalates desire and the fetishization of black music. According to Du Bois, such acts of black gift giving were nothing new in the history of race relations, for, after all, the very foundation of the nation, he argued, was built on the backs of slave laborers singing. But Du Bois also saw in this giving a valuable if unintended process of exchange. As a lover of German culture and language as well as a skilled dialectician, he could not have missed the significance of the term "gift" in Teutonic myth and art. Gift, as *das Gift,* or poison, assumes a double meaning, which is built into the very activity of gift giving: "The theme of the fateful gift," Mauss writes, "the present or possession that turns into poison, is fundamental in Germanic folklore. The Rhine Gold is fatal to the man who wins it, the Cup of Hagen, is disastrous to the hero who drinks of it; numerous tales and legends of this kind, Germanic and Celtic, still haunt our imagination."[14] If the sorrow songs voice the passive sorrow of former slaves, they also play a seditious role in undoing white authority, in much the same way that the actual practice of poisoning masters during slavery abruptly concluded the reign of domination.[15]

For the bilingual Du Bois, the gift/*Gift* of black song was a critical poison rich in racially destabilizing power. Its instability infected white America as it emancipated blackness in the modern. African-Americans paradoxically locate completion in a texted assimilation and difference, in an inscribed twoness whose potential for real, conscious presence supplied the supplemental gift/*Gift* to an unblemished white America. The poison in black song, however, meant not the end of America but, rather, its beginning, the cure for its racial sickness. For it is in the engagement of black music as American music, a music whose very composition reflects an inextricable racial crossing, that black people claim America as their own. Songs reflecting the blood and toil of slaves and their contribution to the making of the nation become literal embodiments of a tradition saturated in racial color. The gift of black song thus harkens a new America, revealing doubleness as a condition running across the color line. In the scripted tones of the soulful songs of black folk one hears the sameness of a nation otherwise committed to the logic of race.

Du Bois's intervention into the study of black music reveals how the doubleness of racial identity can work both ways, unsettling both blackness and whiteness toward a greater resuscitation of culture. As we look toward the new century, however, we find ourselves troubled by the same legacies of racial violence, manifested literally in pernicious supremacist acts and more subtly in the representations of blackness that circulate across the public sphere. The soundtexts of black music and the race-complicating hybrids of contemporary expressive culture must work against the tide of modern-day minstrelsies that sustain territories of black and white. We as a nation remain committed to such binary thinking, whether in discussions of classical music, pop, or jazz, or even in the arenas of world beat and electronic dance music, the rhythmic dynamism of which seems underlaid with discourses of dark primal ecstasy. The racial imagination of black music is not only still with us, it exceeds racial and national bounds.

Which is all the more reason for us to wonder about our commitments to stories of racial truths and certainties that equate forms with specific expressive capacities. If we begin to change our modes of hearing in order to listen for the sameness that accumulates in American sound forms, we might discover ways of casting off the masks of racial prescription, of identifying through music a means of seeing the wholes of our national experience. The task at hand, however, is not one of joining and uniting but, rather, in the spirit of *Souls,* of seeking wholes never fulfilled, of engaging the critical force of a seemingly never-ending doubleness. According to this logic, sameness remains perhaps forever linked to difference, to the dynamic, relational tension between blackness and whiteness. For more than two hundred years, black music has evolved as various forms of this dis-closure, registering critiques of the putative unity of America as a means of realizing dynamically changing racial identities. Du Bois teaches us to recognize these dynamic expressions as an outcome of an always-contested racial relation that promotes neither fixity nor assimilation. The stability of instability reverberates loudly from the final pages of *The Souls of Black Folk* as he issues this defiant message to white Americans:

Your Country? How came it yours? Before the Pilgrims landed we were here. Here we have brought our three gifts and mingled them with yours: a gift of story and song—soft, stirring melody in an ill-harmonized and unmelodious land; the gift of sweat and brawn to beat back the wilderness, conquer the soil, and lay the foundations of this vast economic empire two hundred years earlier than your weak hands could have done it; the third a gift of the Spirit. Around us the history of the land has centered for thrice a hundred years. . . . Nor has our gift of the Spirit been merely passive. Actively we have woven ourselves with the very warp and woof of this nation,—we fought their battles, shared their sorrow, mingled our blood with theirs . . . Mercy and Truth, lest the nation be smitten with a curse. Our song, our toil, our cheer, and warning have been given to this nation in blood-brotherhood. Are not these gifts worth giving?[16]

Du Bois asks: "Would America have been America without her Negro people?" In reply, he imagines a second-sighting, one identifying the gift/ *Gift* that blackness brings to America. In its character of twoness, as a black other's double hearing, black music in the modern compromises the singularity of whiteness; from it emerges a new consciousness whose twin appearance transforms the countenance of the nation. The implications of this dis-closure unfold in the song of "The Weary Traveller" (*sic*) that appears at the end of the book (fig. 32). In it we hear the "fresh young voices . . . welling up" over the ancients "from the caverns of brick and mortar below."

30

Hymns of Admonition
Let Us Cheer the Weary Traveler

Let us cheer the wea-ry trav-el-er,—— Cheer the wea-ry trav-el-er;

Let us cheer the wea-ry trav-el-er, A - long the heav-en-ly way.

1 I'll take my gos-pel trum - pet, And I'll be-gin_ to blow,
2 And if you meet with cross - es And tri - als on_ the way,

And if my Sav-iour helps me, I'll blow wher-ev-er I go._
Just keep your trust in Je - sus, And don't for - get_ to pray.

Let us cheer the wea-ry trav-el-er,___ Cheer the wea-ry trav-el-er;

Let us cheer the wea-ry trav-el-er, A - long the heav-en-ly way.

*At Hampton Institute the first two and a half measures are sung as a solo by the "leader"; the whole chorus joins in at the point marked. **

32. "Let Us Cheer the Weary Traveler" From *Religious Folk-Songs of the Negro as Sung at Hampton Institute,* ed. R. Nathaniel Dett (Hampton, Va.: Hampton Institute Press, 1927; reprint, New York: AMS Press, 1972).

"And the traveller," who marks the turn to the twentieth century, "girds himself, and sets his face toward the Morning, and goes his way." So can we, as cultural travelers and storytellers, face our morning afresh with spirits awakened by newly recognized, embodied sound.

Notes

Sources of Opening Quotations

Claude Lévi-Strauss, *The Raw and the Cooked,* vol. 1 of *Mythologiques,* trans. John Weightman and Doreen Weightman (1964; reprint, Chicago: University of Chicago Press, 1983), 12.

James Baldwin, "Everybody's Protest Novel" (1949), *Notes of a Native Son* (1955; reprint, Boston: Beacon Press, 1983), 21.

James M. Phillippo. *Jamaica: Its Past and Present State* (London: J. Snow, 1843), quoted in Sidney W. Mintz and Richard Price, *An Anthropological Approach to the Afro-American Past: A Caribbean Perspective,* ISHI Occasional Papers in Social Change, 2 (Philadelphia: Institute for the Study of Human Issues, 1976), 20.

Martin Heidegger. *Early Greek Thinking,* trans. D. F. Krell and F. A. Capuzzi (1954; reprint, New York: Harper & Row, 1975), quoted in Mark C. Taylor, *Altarity* (Chicago: University of Chicago Press, 1987), 52.

Ralph Ellison, "The Golden Age, Time Past" (1959), in *Shadow and Act* (1964; reprint, New York: Vintage Books, 1972), 199.

Christopher L. Miller. *Theories of Africans: Francophone Literature and Anthropology in Africa* (Chicago: University of Chicago Press, 1990), 81.

Zora Neale Hurston, *Mules and Men,* with a preface by Franz Boas and a new foreword by Arnold Rampersad (1935; reprint, New York: Harper & Row, 1990), 19.

Preface

1. Throughout this study, the term "African-American" appears hyphenated in both its adjectival and noun forms. While perhaps going against the grain of standard practice, this procedure is meant to underscore the book's commitment to the theme of relationality, to the Americanness of African-America. While more and more writers commonly omit the hyphen to assert the authority and autonomy of the black experience, doing so seems also to undermine the place of blackness in America, together with black people's claims of America.

2. LeRoi Jones, "The Changing Same (R & B and New Black Music)," in *Black Music* (New York: William Morrow & Co., 1967), 180–211.

3. Raymond Williams, "Base and Superstructure in Marxist Cultural Theory," in *Problems in Materialism and Culture* (London: Verso, 1980), reprinted in *Rethinking Popular Culture: Contemporary Perspectives in Cultural Studies,* ed. Chandra Mukerji and Michael Schudson (Berkeley and Los Angeles: University of California Press, 1991), 414.

Chapter 1

1. As will be argued, "black music" emerges as a concept in American historical contexts, continually negotiating meaning dialectically against the skepticism of a primarily white dominant culture. This begins with the appearances of "Negro music" at the turn of the nineteenth century and carries forward to the inventions of rhythm music that coalesce around 1900. I employ the term "black music" as part of conventional usage but also to underscore the racial ideological basis from which many of its cultural meanings emerge.

2. Ralph Ellison, *The Invisible Man* (1952; reprint, New York: Vintage, 1972), 8.

3. Experience is one of those dangerous concepts in cultural theory, and I employ it with qualification. In speaking of experience, I mean to imply neither a real presence beyond interpretation nor a singular authentic involvement specified by race. At the same time, I am uneasy with the dismissals of a term that speaks most forcefully to the phenomenally felt realities of historical actors. Perhaps we can maintain the term by abiding by James Clifford's observation with respect to ethnography, namely, that "it is difficult to say very much about experience. Like 'intuition,' it is something that one does or does not have, and its invocation often smacks of mystification. Nevertheless, one should resist the temptation to translate all meaningful experience into interpretation. If the two are reciprocally related, they are not identical" ("On Ethnographic Authority," in *The Predicament of Culture* [Cambridge, Mass.: Harvard University Press, 1988], 35). Or, directly from the perspective of a historian, as Joan Scott famously argues, "It is not individuals who have experience, but subjects who are constituted through experience. Experience, in this definition then becomes not the origin of our explanation, not the authoritative (been seen or felt) evidence that grounds what is known, but rather that which we seek to explain, that about which knowledge is produced." Accordingly, she continues, "*experience* is not a word we can do without. . . . Experience is at once always already an interpretation *and* something that needs to be interpreted" ("The Evidence of Experience," *Critical Inquiry* 17, no. 4 [summer 1991]: 780, 797).

4. In his essay, "What America Would Be Like without Blacks," e.g., Ellison writes:

The problem here is that few Americans know who and what they really are. That is why few of these groups—or at least few of the children of these groups—have been able to resist the movies, television, baseball, jazz, football, drum-majoretting, rock, comic strips, radio commercials, soap operas, book clubs, slang, or any of a thousand other expressions and carriers of our pluralistic and easily available popular culture. And it is here precisely that ethnic resistance is least effective. On this level the melting pot did indeed melt, creating such deceptive metamorphoses and blending of identities, values, and life-styles that most Americans whites are culturally part Negro American without even realizing it.

(*Going to the Territory* [1986; reprint, New York: Vintage, 1995], 108)

5. In this I want to suggest a material aspect to musical expression, as in Louis Althusser's comment, "Of course, the material existence of the ideology in an apparatus and its practices does not have the same modality as the material existence of a paving-stone or a rifle. . . . 'Matter is discussed in many senses,' or rather that it exists in difference modalities" ("Ideology and State Apparatuses [Notes towards an Investigation]," in *Lenin and Philosophy,* trans. Ben Brewster [New York: Monthly Review Press, 1971], 166).

6. Toni Morrison, "Unspeakable Things Unspoken: The Afro-American Presence in American Literature," *Michigan Quarterly Review* (winter 1989): 1–34, reprinted in *Within the Circle: An Anthology of African American Literary Criticism from the Harlem Renaissance to the Present,* ed. Angelyn Mitchell (Durham, N.C.: Duke University Press, 1994), 368–400. For elaboration, see also Morrison, *Playing in the Dark: Whiteness and the Literary Imagination* (New York: Vintage, 1993).

7. Nor am I proposing, for that matter, a deracinated black music without the necessity of a concomitant deracination of "whiteness." This latter concept is so taken for granted and entrenched in the racial imagination that it may seem, at first, not racial at all. For background on essentialism, see Karl Popper, *The Poverty of Historicism,* 3d ed. (New York: Harper & Row, 1961), 26–34.

8. W. E. B. Du Bois, *The Souls of Black Folk,* ed. David W. Blight and Robert Gooding-Williams (Boston: Bedford Books, 1997), 186.

9. Interview with James Baldwin in the documentary film *The Price of the Ticket* (San Francisco: California Newsreel, 1990), directed by Karen Thorsen. An elaboration on this notion in terms of an overarching American modernism appears in Walter Benn Michaels, *Our America: Nativism, Modernism, and Pluralism* (Durham, N.C.: Duke University Press, 1995).

10. In this, I borrow from Stuart Hall, "The Problem of Ideology: Marxism without Guarantees," *Journal of Communication Inquiry* 10, no. 2 (1986): 28–44, reprinted in *Stuart Hall: Critical Dialogues in Cultural Studies,* ed. David Morley and Kuan-Hsing Chen (New York: Routledge, 1996), 31. Moreover, Christopher L. Miller's critique of de Manian deconstruction is relevant here: "But suppose we *had* to care what the difference is . . . suppose we could no longer afford the mandarin detachment from messy differences in the plural; that the matter of difference were simply too urgent to be glorified and homogenized as difference-with-an-A. Such is the question confronting the Western reader of African literature. . . . The challenge is to practice a kind of knowledge that, while remaining conscious of the lessons of rhetorical theory, recognizes European theory as a *local phenomenon* and attempts dialogue with other localized systems of discourse" (*Theories of Africans: Francophone Literature and Anthropology in Africa* [Chicago: University of Chicago Press, 1990], 7–10).

11. I am speaking specifically of my discomfort with the common ground of American music studies that extend versions of "total history": portrayals of the past as a continuous line of events along the even plane of fact. Furthermore, I am employing "structure" here to describe coalescences of events at particular moments without meaning to imply an overarching and continuous historical stream. It is to suggest, as Raymond Williams writes, "structures living in and through human beings" rather than "human beings living in and through structures" ("Structural," in *Keywords: A Vocabulary of Culture and Society,* rev. ed. [1976; New York: Oxford University Press, 1983], 305). For background, see Robert Young, *White Mythologies: Writing History and the West* (New York: Routledge, 1990). The notion of the "relational" is a basic premise of structuralism. See, e.g., Pierre Bourdieu and Loïc Wacquant, *An Invitation to Reflexive Sociology* (Chicago: University of Chicago Press, 1992).

12. Fredric Jameson writes: "Necessity is not . . . a type of content, but rather the inexorable *form* of events; it is therefore a narrative category in the enlarged sense of some properly narrative political unconscious . . . a retextualization of History . . . [as] what Althusser, following Spinoza, calls an 'absent cause.'" Accordingly, we can define "necessity" as "Why what happened . . . had to happen the way it did" without advocating the simple determinism that such a definition implies. Necessity, in this sense, helps to foreground the significance of what we may call "experience" without also insisting on a humanist conception of "the subject in history." It underpins a conception of history in conflictive, experiential terms. As Jameson suggests, "History is what hurts" (*The Political Unconscious: Narrative as a Socially Symbolic Act* [Ithaca, N.Y.: Cornell University Press, 1981], 101–2).

13. In this respect, Kobena Mercer's discussion of soul is relevant, stressing both its constructedness and its phenomenological realism. Working from Iain Chambers's discussion of soul in his book *Urban Rhythms: Pop Music and Popular Culture* ([New York: St. Martin's Press, 1985], 148), Mercer writes:

> Along with the emotional complexity of intimate relationships, sexuality is perhaps *the* central preoccupation of the soul tradition. But as Chambers suggests, the power of soul as a cultural form to express sexuality does not so much lie in the literal meanings of the words but in the passion of the singer's voice and vocal performance. The explicit meanings of the lyrics are, in this sense secondary to the sensual resonance of the individual character of the voice, 'its grain.' While the 'grain' of the voice encodes the contradictions of sexual relationships, their pleasures and pain, the insistence of the rhythm is an open invitation to the body to dance. . . . In its incitement of the listener to dance, to become an active participant in the texture of voice, words and rhythm, soul music is not merely 'about' sexuality, but it is itself a musical means for the eroticization of the body."
>
> ("Monster Metaphors: Notes on Michael Jackson's *Thriller,*" in *Welcome to the Jungle: New Positions in Black Cultural Studies* [New York: Routledge, 1994], 39)

See also Charles Keil's discussion of "soul ideology" in *Urban Blues* (Chicago: University of Chicago Press, 1966).

14. Unique Quartette, *Mama's Black Baby Boy* (1893). This recording has been rereleased on compact disk as part of *The Earliest Negro Vocal Groups,* vol. 2, *1893–1922,* DOCD-5288 (Vienna: Document Records). In his review of LeRoi Jones's (Amiri Baraka) *Blues People,* moreover, Ralph Ellison recalls that, "during the 1870s, Lafcadio Hearn reports that the best singers of Irish songs, in Irish dialect, were Negro dock workers in Cincinnati, and advertisements from slavery days described escaped slaves who spoke in Scottish dialect" ("Blues People," in *Shadow and Act* [1964; reprint, New York: Vintage, 1972], 256). In this light, finally, it is noteworthy that Fanny Kemble observed in her antebellum journal that the "airs" of black Georgian boatmen "have a strong affinity to Scotch melodies in their general character" (Frances Anne Kemble, *Records of Later Life,* 3 vols. [London: Richard Bentley & Son, 1882], cited in *African-American Traditions in Song, Sermon, Tale, and Dance, 1600s–1920,* comp. Eileen Southern and Josephine Wright [New York: Greenwood, 1990], 33).

15. Dena J. Epstein, "African Music in British and French America," *Musical Quarterly* 59, no. 1 (1973): 61.

16. Charles T. Davis and Henry Louis Gates, Jr., *The Slave Narrative* (New York: Oxford University Press, 1985); John Blassingame, ed., *Slave Testimony: Two Centuries of Letters, Speeches, Interviews, and Autobiographies* (Baton Rouge: Louisiana State University Press, 1977). Moreover, is it common for historians to rely on twentieth-century texts of the Works Progress Administration to build theories of antebellum slave culture. For a discussion of the problems with this practice, see Walter Johnson, *Soul by Soul: Life Inside the Antebellum Slave Market* (Cambridge, Mass.: Harvard University Press, 1999), 226, n. 24.

17. As indicated in n. 12 above, the term "absent cause" is Althusser's, and its application here derives from Jameson, who writes:

> What Althusser's own insistence on history as an absent cause makes clear, but what is missing from the formula as it is canonically worded, is that he does not at all draw the fashionable conclusion that because history is a text, the referent does not exist. We would therefore propose the following revised formulation: that history is *not* a text, not a narrative, master or otherwise, but that, as an absent cause, it is inaccessible to us except in textual form, and that our approach to it and to the Real itself necessarily passes through its prior textualization, its narrativization in the political unconscious.
>
> (*The Political Unconscious,* 35)

18. Hortense J. Spillers, "Changing the Letter: The Yokes, the Jokes of Discourse, or, Mrs. Stowe, Mr. Reed," in *Slavery and the Literary Imagination,* ed. Deborah E. McDowell and Arnold Rampersad (Baltimore: Johns Hopkins University Press, 1989), 25–61, as quoted in W. J. T. Mitchell, "Narrative, Memory, and Slavery," in *Picture Theory* (Chicago: University of Chicago Press, 1994), 184.

19. Lawrence Levine, "Slave Songs and Slave Consciousness: An Exploration in Neglected Sources," reprinted in *African-American Religion: Interpretive Essays in History and Culture,* ed. Timothy E. Fulop and Albert J. Raboteau (New York: Routledge, 1997), 59–87. At the opening of the essay, Levine proposes that the sources are unreliable but nevertheless reliable. Sterling Stuckey, *Slave Culture* (New York: Oxford University Press, 1987), 96. Musicological appropriations of Gates's theory of signifying are discussed in the section "Speaking Past" in this chapter. Moreover, continuing the parenthetical discussion of Jameson's view of history as something accessible only indirectly through the narratives that represent it, we may consider this:

> Any rewarding use of the notion of a historical or cultural period tends in spite of itself to give the impression of a facile totalization, a seamless web of phenomena each of which, in its own way 'expresses' some unified inner truth—a world view or a period style or a set of structural categories which marks the whole length and breadth of the 'period' in question. Yet such an impression is fatally reductive. . . . The construction of a historical totality necessarily involves the isolation and the privileging of one of the elements *within* that totality . . . such that the element in question becomes a master code or 'inner essence' capable of explicating the other elements or features of the 'whole' in question.

(Jameson, *The Political Unconscious,* 27–28)
On the "nervous" qualities of historical contexts, see Michael Taussig, *The Nervous System* (London: Routledge, 1992).

20. Winfried Siemerling, "Democratic Blues: Houston Baker and the Representation of Culture," in *Problems of Democracy in the United States: Symposion of the Graduiertenkolleg at the John F. Kennedy-Institut Für Nordamerikastudien, Freie Universität,* ed. Willi Paul Adams et al., Materialien 31 (Berlin: John F. Kennedy-Institut Für Nordamerikastudien, Freie Universität, 1993), 220.

21. Difference has been widely theorized in postmodern and postcolonial theory, typically as a problematic concept we might want to transcend in the name of hybridity. As important as these initiatives have been to my own efforts, I am particularly interested in the way difference is repeatedly reinvented out of the relational circumstances of cultural engagement. It is through the paradoxical expression of difference out of sameness that America first began to recognize the miracle of black singing. Accordingly, difference becomes the necessity from which black music begins. And so will difference as a concept live on as long as we find truth in race. I'm thankful to Susan Stanford Friedman who introduced me to a broad literature on theories of difference in feminism, postcolonial studies, and African-American criticism. One might wisely begin with her book *Mappings: Feminism and the Cultural Geographies of Encounter* (Princeton, N.J.: Princeton University Press, 1994).

22. Ralph Ellison, "The World and the Jug," in *Shadow and Act,* 123.

23. Ellison, "What America Would Be Like without Blacks," 110. This reading of double consciousness, first proposed by Ralph Waldo Emerson writing securely within

the domain of whiteness, is implied in Du Bois's own famous rendering in *Souls of Black Folk.* Sixty years later, Winthrop D. Jordan established the psychoanalytic desire/reproach contradiction that would become so prevalent in "whiteness" studies of the 1990s. See Jordan, *White over Black: American Attitudes toward the Negro, 1550–1812* (Chapel Hill: University of North Carolina Press for Institute of Early American History and Culture, 1968).

24. William Shakespeare, *Merchant of Venice,* 5.1.88–89: "Belmont. The Avenue to Portia's House"; Lorenzo speaking to Jessica. In his studies of seventeenth-century England, moreover, James Stokes has observed references to traveling musicians as "Egiptians," in which figures of the foreign are conflated with those of music and travel (both signifying danger). (Untitled colloquium presentation to the Institute for Research in the Humanities, University of Wisconsin, February 17, 1998.) See references to music and musicians in app. 9 of James Stokes, ed., *Somerset,* vols. 1–2, Records of Early English Drama, ed. Robert J. Alexander (Toronto: University of Toronto Press, 1996). See also Gary Tomlinson, "Ideologies of Aztec Song," *Journal of the American Musicological Society* 48 (1995): 343–79, and *Music and Renaissance Magic: Toward a Historiography of Others* (Chicago: University of Chicago Press, 1993).

25. Jean-Jacques Rousseau, *Essay on the Origin of Languages* (ca. 1760; music sections, ca. 1749); and Johann Gottfried Herder, *Essay on the Origin of Language* (1772), both in *On the Origin of Language: Two Essays,* trans. John H. Moran and Alexander Gode, with an introduction by Alexander Gode (Chicago: University of Chicago Press, 1966).

26. In his essay, "Marx's Immense Theoretical Revolution," Louis Althusser outlines the dimensions of structural causality. "If the whole is posed as *structured,* . . . not only does it become impossible to think the determination of the elements by the structure . . . *it also becomes impossible to think it in the category of the global expressive causality of a universal inner essence immanent in its phenomenon."* Employing the Freudian notion of overdetermination to resist simple causal explanations, moreover, he introduces the previously discussed notion of absent cause in which "the structure is not an essence *outside* the economic phenomena." Continuing, he explains that "effects are not outside the structure, are not a pre-existing object, element or space in which the structure arrives to *imprint or mark:* on the contrary, it implies that the structure is immanent in its effects . . . *the whole existence of the structure consists of its effects"* (in Althusser and Étienne Balibar, *Reading Capital,* trans. Ben Brewster [1970; reprint, New York: Verso, 1997], 187–89: emphasis in original). See also Patrick Brantlinger's succinct overview, "From Althusser to Gramsci," in *Crusoe's Footprints: Cultural Studies in Britain and America* (New York: Routledge, 1990).

27. Retentions literature appeared in the wake of Harlem Renaissance criticism and Melville J. Herskovits's groundbreaking study *Myth of the Negro Past* (1941; reprint, Boston: Beacon Press, 1990). For an excellent background discussion, see the introduction to Roger D. Abrahams and John F. Szwed, eds., *After Africa: Extracts from British Travel Accounts and Journals of the Seventeenth, Eighteenth, and Nineteenth Centuries*

concerning the Slaves, Their Manners, and Customs in the British West Indies (New Haven, Conn.: Yale University Press, 1983). The editors strenuously avoid claims of African origins in favor of patterns of transmission and evolution of African philosophic principles, ideologies, cultural patterns, etc. See also John Szwed and Roger D. Abrahams, "After the Myth: Studying Afro-American Cultural Patterns in the Plantation Literature," *Research in African Literatures* 7, no. 2 (fall 1976): 211–32. On the power of memory in African-American cultures, see Geneviève Fabre and Robert O'Meally, eds., *History and Memory in African-American Culture* (New York: Oxford University Press, 1994).

28. Stuart Hall, "Cultural Identity and Cinematic Representation" (1989), in *Black British Cultural Studies,* ed. Houston A. Baker, Jr., Manthia Diawara, and Ruth Lindeborg (Chicago: University of Chicago Press, 1997), 217. In the same essay, he asks: "Is [research] only a matter of unearthing that which the colonial experience buried and overlaid, brin[g]ing to light the hidden continuities it suppressed? Or is a quite different practice entailed—not the rediscovery but the *production* of identity? Not an identity grounded in the archeology but in the *retelling* of the past?" (211–12; emphasis in original).

29. Kwame Anthony Appiah, *In My Father's House: Africa in the Philosophy of Culture* (New York: Oxford University Press, 1992), 155. Homi Bhabha's related comments may be taken as a response to Afrocentric positions: "The native intellectual who identifies the people with the true national culture will be disappointed. The people are now the very principle of 'dialectical reorganization' and they construct their culture from the national text translated into modern western forms of information technology, language, dress" (*The Location of Culture* [New York: Routledge, 1994], 38).

30. Sandra Adell, *Double Consciousness, Double Bind: Theoretical Issues in Twentieth-Century Black Literature* (Urbana: University of Illinois Press, 1994).

31. In ethnomusicology, such dualisms surface in the still prevalent binarism of "etic" and "emic," which somewhat mangles Kenneth L. Pike's more nuanced original proposal. Pike was very concerned with relations between the observer and observed, which he conceived dialectically. See his *Language in Relation to a Unified Theory of the Structure of Human Behavior* (Glendale, Calif.: Summer Institute of Linguistics, 1954; reprint, The Hague: Mouton, 1967). Moreover, Mary Carruthers challenges "the current opinion that there are radical differences" between oral and literate cultures in *The Book of Memory: A Study of Memory in Medieval Culture* (Cambridge: Cambridge University Press, 1990). See also Steven Feld, "Orality and Consciousness," in *The Oral and the Literate in Music,* ed. Yoshihiko Tokumaru and Osama Yamaguti (Tokyo: Academia Music, 1986), 18–28.

32. "Resonance" may be seen in relation to Walter Benjamin's "echo of the original" as a version of an "afterlife." "Unlike a work of literature, translation does not find itself in the center of the language forest but on the outside facing the wooded ridge; it calls into it without entering, aiming at that spot where the echo is able to give, in its own language, the reverberation of the work in the alien one" ("The Task of the Translator"

[1923], in *Illuminations: Essays and Reflections,* ed. Hannah Arendt; trans. Harry Zohn [New York: Schocken Books, 1968], 76). For elaboration on the concept of resonance, see chap. 2.

33. "The American image of the Negro lives also in the Negro's heart," James Baldwin writes, "and when he has surrendered to this image life has no other possibility" (*Notes of a Native Son* [1955; reprint, Boston: Beacon Press, 1984], 38).

34. I am borrowing this notion of confession from Michel Foucault's "The Repressive Hypothesis," in *The History of Sexuality,* vol. 1, *An Introduction,* trans. Robert Hurley (1976; reprint, New York: Vintage, 1990).

35. "Jes grew" is a term popularized by James Weldon Johnson in *The Book of American Negro Poetry* (New York: Harcourt, Brace, & Co., 1922), 12. See also Kathy J. Ogren, "Controversial Sounds: Jazz Performance as Theme and Language in the Harlem Renaissance," in *The Harlem Renaissance: Revaluations,* ed. Amritjit Singh and Stanley Brodwin (New York: Garland, 1989), 167.

36. Mitchell, *Picture Theory,* 190.

37. Dash's film explores the relationship between a black female film executive who passes for white and an African-American singer who supplies the voiceovers for a white Hollywood actress. Thanks go to Jeff Smith for bringing to my attention the circumstances behind *Carmen Jones.* André Hodeir, *Jazz: Its Evolution and Essence,* trans. David Noakes (1954; reprint, New York: Grove Press, 1956), 92.

38. Jameson, *The Political Unconscious.* See also Eric Lott's application of Jameson's notion of a greater social unconscious to specifically racial formations in "Love and Theft: The Racial Unconscious of Blackface Minstrelsy," *Representations* 39 (summer 1992): 23–50.

39. Carolyn Abbate, *Unsung Voices: Opera and Musical Narrative in the Nineteenth Century* (Princeton, N.J.: Princeton University Press, 1991). Richard Taruskin points to the wider significance of Abbate's book in his review, "She Do the Ring in Different Voices," *Cambridge Opera Journal* 4 (1992): 187–97.

40. Anthony Newcomb, "Sound and Feeling," *Critical Inquiry* 10, no. 4 (June 1984): 623. In her essay on "ventriloquism," Carolyn Abbate locates the rise of the transcendent voice in the period of the turn to the nineteenth century; see *Meaning in the Visual Arts: Views from the Outside,* ed. Irving Lavin (Princeton, N.J.: Institute of Advanced Study, 1995), 305–11. For an informative and relatively recent debate on the power of music in musicology, see Lawrence Kramer, "The Musicology of the Future," *Repercussions* 1 (spring 1992): 5–18; and Gary Tomlinson, "Musical Pasts and Postmodern Musicologies: A Response to Lawrence Kramer," *Current Musicology* 53 (1993): 18–24. Kramer's reply and Tomlinson's counter reply appear in the same issue.

41. Roland Barthes, "The Grain of the Voice"(1972), in *Image Music Text* (New York: Noonday Press, 1977), 179–89.

42. Steven Feld, "Vocal Knowledge" (Columbia University, in preparation). In ethnomusicology, see, e.g., Kofi Agawu, *African Rhythm* (Cambridge: Cambridge University Press, 1995); Jane Sugarman, *Engendering Song: Singing and Subjectivity at Prespa Al-*

banian Weddings (Chicago: University of Chicago Press, 1997); Steven Feld and Aaron A. Fox, "Music and Language," *Annual Review of Anthropology* 23 (1994): 25–53; and Anthony Seeger, *Why Suyá Sing: A Musical Anthropology of an Amazonian People* (Cambridge: Cambridge University Press, 1987).

43. Gary Tomlinson, *Metaphysical Song: An Essay on Opera* (Princeton, N.J.: Princeton University Press, 1999), 4, 24.

44. Ibid., chap. 4.

45. Daniel K. L. Chua, *Absolute Music and the Construction of Meaning* (Cambridge: Cambridge University Press, 1999), 32. The quote by Calvin is on 26–27. See also Tomlinson, *Metaphysical Song,* 59.

46. Mark A. Schneider. *Culture and Enchantment* (Chicago: University of Chicago Press, 1993).

47. A seminal essay in this regard is Jeffrey Kallberg, "The Harmony of the Tea Table: Gender and Ideology in the Piano Nocturne," *Representations* 39 (summer 1992): 102–33. See also Susan McClary, *Feminine Endings: Music, Gender, and Sexuality* (Minneapolis: University of Minnesota Press, 1991); Downing A. Thomas, *Music and the Origins of Language: Theories from the French Enlightenment* (Cambridge: Cambridge University Press, 1995); Lawrence Kramer, *Music as Cultural Practice, 1800–1900* (Berkeley and Los Angeles: University of California Press, 1990); and Charles Dill, *Monstrous Opera: Rameau and the Tragic Tradition* (Princeton, N.J.: Princeton University Press, 1998). Noteworthy, too, among other works are the essays collected in Ian Bent, ed., *Music Theory in the Age of Romanticism* (Cambridge: Cambridge University Press, 1996); and Ruth A. Solie, ed., *Musicology and Difference: Gender and Sexuality in Music Scholarship* (Berkeley and Los Angeles: University of California Press, 1993).

48. Social historians have spearheaded the study of music's role in European working classes. See, e.g., Laura Mason, *Singing the French Revolution: Popular Culture and Politics, 1787–1799* (Ithaca, N.Y.: Cornell University Press, 1996); Robert Isherwood, *Farce and Fantasy: Popular Entertainment in Eighteenth-Century Paris* (New York, 1986); and Anne Fillon, *Les trois bagues aux doigts: Amours villageoises au XVIIIe siècle* (Paris: R. Laffont, 1989).

49. Characterizations of ideology are diverse and often contradictory in contemporary social history and cultural studies. As employed in this study, ideology is a notion consistent with the post-Althusserian attempts to observe the forces constituting social experience within the arrangements of contest, domination, and resistance and giving particular attention to the position of discourse in the articulation, representation, and interpellation of social forces. I am seeking to avoid the concept of false ideology yet without conflating the ideological and the social. This view is indebted to the writings of Fredric Jameson and Louis Althusser, as previously outlined, as well as to the work of Stuart Hall. See, e.g., Hall, "The Problem of Ideology." He employs the term "material force" on p. 27 of that essay.

50. An important contribution to the politicization of European music history is Gary Tomlinson's "Ideologies of Aztec Song," *Journal of the American Musicological So-*

ciety 48 (1995): 343–79. Here, Tomlinson's embrace of ideology suggests a shift away from Foucault, to whom he was previously indebted, and a move toward a Derridian practice aligned with postcolonialism. In this respect, he honors the legacy of Gayatri Spivak's "Can the Subaltern Speak?" (in *Marxism and the Interpretation of Culture,* ed. Cary Nelson and Lawrence Grossberg [London: Macmillan, 1988], reprinted in *Colonial Discourse and Post-Colonial Theory,* ed. Patrick Williams and Laura Chrisman [New York: Columbia University Press, 1994]). And yet, such theoretical forays have their consequences (see the section "Speaking Past," ahead in this chapter).

51. It is perhaps necessary to stress that what new opera studies are concerned with, above all, is the supersensible experience within opera and not with the supersensible as part of a greater examination of musical phenomenology and reception within American culture. In this respect, it is curious that our most sophisticated musical theorists so frequently presume a stability of "Europe" against the challenges of poststructuralism and postcolonial theory. This can be understood according to Jacques Derrida's critique in *Speech and Phenomena and Other Essays on Husserl's Theory of Signs,* trans. David B. Allison (1967; reprint, Evanston, Ill.: Northwestern University Press, 1973): hearing another speak, subjectivity is determined by an other's comprehension. The unsung thus becomes part of the aestheticization of critical practice itself, a mystification that while perhaps evoking the sense of a music beyond writing also perpetuates the privilege of the cultured classes. The "beyond" as a suprasocial place continues the legacy of studying art works apart from society, as something divorced from the social as a consequence of the ascendancy of art. Denying the constitutive nature of art within the social perpetuates metaphysical fantasies as it sides with history's victors, forgetting Benjamin's materialist tenet: "There is no document of civilization which is not at the same time a document of barbarism" ("Theses on the Philosophy of History," in *Illuminations,* 256).

52. John Shepherd and Peter Wicke, *Music and Cultural Theory* (Cambridge: Polity Press, 1997), 13. Shepherd and Wicke's research reflects the legacy of British cultural studies and, more specifically, the informing influence of scholars affiliated with the British journal *Popular Music.* See, e.g., Richard Middleton, *Studying Popular Music* (Buckingham: Open University Press, 1990. Simon Frith's *Performing Rites: On the Value of Popular Music* (Cambridge, Mass.: Harvard University Press, 1996) offers an excellent introduction to the field as part of a proposed return to evaluative criticism. In the anthropology of music, see Judith Becker and Alton L. Becker, "A Musical Icon: Power and Meaning in Javanese Gamelan Music," in *The Sign in Music and Literature,* ed. Wendy Steiner (Austin: University of Texas Press, 1981), 203–15; Sugarman, *Engendering Song;* Seeger, *Why Suyá Sing;* Christopher Waterman, *Jùjú: A Social History and Ethnography of an African Popular Music* (Chicago: University of Chicago Press, 1990); Veit Erlmann, *Music, Modernity and the Global Imagination: South Africa and the West* (New York: Oxford University Press, 1999); and Steven Feld, *Sound and Sentiment: Birds, Weeping, Poetics, and Song in Kaluli Expression* (Philadelphia: University of Pennsylvania Press, 1982).

53. The notion of black music as a countermodernity is first articulated in W. E. B. Du Bois's magisterial *Souls of Black Folk* (1903). More recently, it has been powerfully reinterpreted by Paul Gilroy, *The Black Atlantic: Modernism and Double Consciousness* (Cambridge, Mass.: Harvard University Press, 1993). See the section "Speaking Past" ahead in this chapter for a discussion of Gilroy's highly influential and thoughtful study.

54. Regarding the assertion that we are all a part of the same socially constituted domain, Michel Foucault explains it as discursively inhabiting the "already said": "To this theme is connected another according to which all manifest discourse is secretly based on an 'already-said'; and that this 'already-said' is not merely a phrase that has already been spoken, or a text that has already been written, but a 'never-said', an incorporeal discourse, a voice as silent as a breath, a writing that is merely the hollow of its own mark. It is supposed therefore that everything that is formulated in discourse was already articulated in that semi-silence that precedes it, which continues to run obstinately beneath it, but which it covers and silences" (*Archeology of Knowledge and the Discourse of Language,* trans. A. M. Sheridan Smith [1969; reprint, New York: Pantheon, 1971], 25).

55. In the United States, this premodern sense has been associated equally with the Rousseauian "natural man" and the racialist mythos of Anglo-Saxonism. See Reginald Horsman, *Race and Manifest Destiny* (Cambridge, Mass.: Harvard University Press, 1981).

56. Ralph Ellison, "Remembering Jimmy" (1958), in *Shadow and Act.* In "World and the Jug," published in the same collection, Ellison suggests that Ernest Hemingway came closer to the blues spirit than did Wright. Thanks go to Patrick Burke for redirecting my attention to these articles in his "Black Music and the Abstract Truth" (paper presented during the Black Cultural Studies seminar, University of Wisconsin—Madison, fall 1999).

57. Claude Lévi-Strauss, *The Raw and the Cooked,* vol. 1 of *Mythologiques,* trans. John Weightman and Doreen Weightman (1964; reprint, Chicago: University of Chicago Press, 1969), 16.

58. See Foucault's discussion of primary and secondary relations in *Archeology of Knowledge,* 45. Steven Feld, "Communication, Music, and Speech about Music," *Yearbook for Traditional Music* 16 (1984): 1–18, rev. version in Charles Keil and Steve Feld, *Music Grooves* (Chicago: University of Chicago Press, 1994), 77–95; quote on 91. And, as Feld suggests succinctly in a later essay (expanding on his challenge to simple discursive explanations of music): "Sound, hearing and voice mask a special bodily nexus for sensation and emotion because of their coordination of brain, nervous system, head, ear, chest, muscles, and breathing." As such, "emotions may be created in discourse, but this social creation is contingent on performance, which is always emergent through embodied voices" ("Waterfalls of Sound," in *Senses of Place,* ed. Steven Feld and Keith H. Basso (Santa Fe, N.M.: School of American Research Press, 1996), 97.

59. Johnson, *The Book of American Negro Poetry,* 12.

60. Bhabha, *Location of Culture,* 244–45.

61. James Reese Europe, "A Negro Explains Jazz," *Literary Digest* (April 26, 1919), 28–29, reprinted in Eileen Southern, ed., *Readings in Black American Music,* 2d ed. (New York: W. W. Norton, 1983), 238–241; William Grant Still, "The Structure of Music," *Etude* (March 1950), 17, 61, reprinted in Southern, ed., *Readings,* 314–17.

62. Foucault, *Archeology of Knowledge,* 25.

63. Houston A. Baker, Jr., *Blues, Ideology, and Afro-American Literature* (Chicago: University of Chicago Press, 1984); Max Paddison, *Theodor Adorno's Aesthetics of Music* (Cambridge: Cambridge University Press, 1993), 111.

64. Gilroy writes: "In this setting it is hardly surprising that if it is perceived to be relevant at all, the history of slavery is somehow assigned to blacks. It becomes our special property rather than a part of the ethical and intellectual heritage of the West as a whole" (*Black Atlantic,* 49).

65. "Hear Me Talkin' to Ya" was recorded in Chicago, December 12, 1928, originally released by Okeh Records (Okeh 8649). The tune is by Armstrong. The ensemble included Armstrong (trumpet, vocal), Fred Robinson (trombone), Don Redman (clarinet, alto saxophone), Jimmy Stearns (tenor saxophone), Mancy Carr (banjo), and Zutty Singleton (drums).

66. Ingrid Monson, *Saying Something* (Chicago: University of Chicago Press, 1996). In an important early study of modern black folk practices, Howard W. Odum describes how slide guitarists in the South would mimic singers. With a knife blade, the "instrument can be made to 'sing,' 'talk,' 'cuss,' and supplement in general the voice and the ringing of the fiddle or the tinkling of the guitar." Later, he notes that songs depend on storylines, and the two are interdependent. "Indeed, one may accept the statement that many of their songs are actually derived from story; but there may be as many variations to the song and story as there are negroes who sing it" ("Folk-Song and Folk-Poetry as Found in the Secular Songs of the Southern Negroes," *Journal of American Folk-Lore* 14, no. 93 [July–September 1911]: 261, 264). For a recent exposition on Armstrong's scat performances, see Brent Hayes Edwards, "Louis Armstrong and the Syntax of Scat," *Critical Inquiry* 28 (spring 2002): 618–49.

67. Robert J. C. Young. *Colonial Desire: Hybridity in Theory, Culture, and Race* (New York: Routledge, 1995).

68. For some examples of the copious cultural studies literature focusing on Jackson, see Michelle Wallace, "Michael Jackson, Black Modernisms, and 'the Ecstasy of Communication,' " in *Invisibility Blues* (New York: Verso, 1990), 77–90; Greg Tate, "I'm White! What's Wrong with Michael Jackson," in *Flyboy in the Buttermilk* (New York: Simon & Schuster, 1992), 95–99; Michael Eric Dyson, "Michael Jackson's Postmodern Spirituality," in *Reflecting Black: African-American Cultural Criticism* (Minneapolis: University of Minnesota Press, 1993), 35–63; Kobena Mercer, "Monster Metaphors: Notes on Michael Jackson's *Thriller,*" in *Welcome to the Jungle: New Positions in Black Cultural Studies* (New York: Routledge, 1994), 33–51; and Michael Awkward, " 'A Slave to the Rhythm': Essential(ist) Transmutations; Or, The Curious Case of Michael Jackson," in *Negotiating Difference: Race, Gender and the Politics of Positionality* (Chicago: University

of Chicago Press, 1995), 175–92. Similar ambiguities of racial signature accompany the reception of white stars such as Madonna and historical figures from George Gershwin to Frank Sinatra and Bing Crosby to Elvis Presley.

69. Richard M. Sudhalter, *Lost Chords: White Musicians and Their Contribution to Jazz, 1915–1945* (New York: Oxford University Press, 1999); and Susan Stewart, *Crimes of Writing: Problems in the Containment of Representation* (New York: Oxford University Press, 1991).

70. Nellie Y. McKay, "Naming the Problem That Led to the Question 'Who Shall Teach African American Literature?' Or, Are We Ready to Disband the Wheatley Court?" *PMLA* 113, no. 3 (May 1998): 359–69.

71. Guthrie P. Ramsey, Jr., "Who Hears Here? Black Music, Critical Bias, and the Musicological Skin Trade" (paper presented at the annual meeting of the American Musicological Society, Kansas City, Mo., November 5, 1999). An expanded version of Ramsey's article, covering several additional matters, appears by the same title in *Musical Quarterly* 85, no. 1 (spring 2001): 1–52. For "slow, demanding," see Ramsey, "Cosmopolitan or Provincial? Ideology in Early Black Music Historiography, 1867–1940," *Black Music Research Journal* 16, no. 1 (spring 1996): 11–42.

72. Philip Tagg, " 'Black Music', 'Afro-American Music' and 'European Music'," *Popular Music* 8, no. 3 (1989): 285–98.

73. Gary Tomlinson, "Cultural Dialogics and Jazz: A White Historian Signifies," *Black Music Research Journal* 11, no. 2 (fall 1991): 229–64. The issue, titled "Black Music after Theory," includes essays by Amiri Baraka, Paul Gilroy, Hazel V. Carby, and Houston A. Baker, Jr.; it was guest edited by Bruce Tucker. With reference to theory, Gayatri Spivak writes that this "effectively heliocentric discourse fills the empty place of the agent with the historical sun of theory, the Subject of Europe" ("Can the Subaltern Speak?" in *Marxism and the Interpretation of Culture,* ed. Cary Nelson and Lawrence Grossberg [London: Macmillan, 1988], reprinted in *Colonial Discourse and Post-Colonial Theory,* ed. Patrick Williams and Laura Chrisman [New York: Columbia University Press, 1994], 69). Miller, *Theories of Africans,* 28. Miller, of course, is referring to the legacy of colonialism in Africa, but his comment also serves effectively to describe the legacy of violence imposed on African-Americans in the name of democracy and freedom.

74. This dimension partly explains the objections to theory as they have appeared in black literary studies in the 1980s. For documentation of the debate, see Barbara Christian, "The Race for Theory" (1987) and Michael Awkward, "Appropriative Gestures: Theory and Afro-American Literary Criticism" (1988), both reprinted in *Within the Circle: An Anthology of African-American Literary Criticism,* ed. Angelyn Mitchell (Durham, N.C.: Duke University Press, 1994), 348–59 and 360–67, respectively. Joyce A. Joyce, "The Black Canon: Reconstructing Black American Literary Criticism," *New Literary History* 18, no. 2 (winter 1987): 335–44. Responses by Henry Louis Gates, Jr. (" 'What's Love Got to Do with It'? Critical Theory, Integrity, and the Black Idiom") and Houston A. Baker, Jr. ("In Dubious Battle") are printed in the same issue. Joyce's reply

to both appears directly after as "'Who the Cap Fit': Unconsciousness and Unconscionableness in the Criticism of Houston A. Baker, Jr., and Henry Louis Gates, Jr.," 371–84.

75. For background, see Bernice Johnson Reagon, ed., *We'll Understand It Better By and By: Pioneering African American Gospel Composers,* Wade in the Water series (Washington, D.C.: Smithsonian Institution Press, 1992); Eileen Southern, *Music of Black Americans: A History,* 3d ed. (New York: W. W. Norton, 1997); and Horace Clarence Boyer, *How Sweet the Sound: The Golden Age of Gospel* (Washington, D.C.: Elliott & Clark, 1995).

76. Reagon, ed., *We'll Understand It Better;* Boyer, *How Sweet the Sound;* James H. Cone, *The Spirituals and the Blues: An Interpretation* (New York: Seabury Press, 1972); Jon Michael Spencer, *Theological Music: Introduction to Theomusicology* (New York: Greenwood, 1991); Portia K. Maultsby, "Africanisms in African-American Music," in *Africanisms in American Culture,* ed. Joseph E. Holloway (Bloomington: Indiana University Press, 1990), and "Africanisms Retained in the Spiritual Tradition," in *Report of the Twelfth Congress Berkeley, 1977,* ed. Daniel Heartz and Bonnie Wade (Kassel: Bärenreiter; Philadelphia: American Musicological Society, 1981), 75–82; Melonee V. Burnim, "The Black Gospel Tradition: Symbol of Ethnicity" (Ph.D. diss., Indiana University, 1980); Jacqueline Cogdell Dje Dje, "African American Music to 1900," in *Cambridge History of American Music,* ed. David Nicholls. (Cambridge: Cambridge University Press, 1998), 103–4; Michael S. Harper and Robert B. Stepto, eds., *Chant of Saints: A Gathering of Afro-American Literature, Art, and Scholarship,* foreword by John Hope Franklin (Urbana: University of Illinois Press, 1979).

77. Cornel West, "The Prophetic Tradition in Afro-America," in *Prophetic Fragments* (Grand Rapids, Mich.: William B. Eerdmans; Trenton, N.J.: Africa World Press, 1988), 22–23. West's elaboration on black prophecy shares resemblances to his interpretation of American pragmatism, outlined in *The American Evasion of Philosophy: A Genealogy of Pragmatism* (Madison: University of Wisconsin Press, 1989).

78. Phillip Brian Harper, "Nationalism and Social Division in Black Arts Poetry," in *Identities,* ed. Kwame Anthony Appiah and Henry Louis Gates, Jr. (Chicago: University of Chicago Press, 1995), 233.

79. Henry Louis Gates, Jr., discusses the legacy of such resistance in black studies in *Figures in Black: Words, Signs, and the "Racial" Self* (New York: Oxford University Press, 1987), 27. It is significant that Gates's expression is itself an appropriation of a familiar title by Paul de Man.

80. The term "Afrocentricity" was popularized in the work of Molefi Asante. See, among his many works, *Afrocentricity,* rev. ed. (1980; Trenton, N.J.: Africa World Press, 1988). Marianna Torgovnick's *Gone Primitive* (Chicago: University of Chicago Press, 1990) deftly explains the intellectual and cultural backgrounds of the primitivist movement. In early black-music texts by both black and white authors (e.g., folklorists such as Howard W. Odum and Guy B. Johnson, Newman White, and Dorothy Scarborough, together with journalists such as Henry Krehbiel and Sigmund Spaeth) references to

tribalism were widespread. See, e.g., Maud Cuney Hare, *Negro Musicians and Their Music* (Washington, D.C.: Associated Publishers, 1936). Especially noteworthy are the chapters "Africa," "Africa in Song," and "African Influences in America" and the appendix on African instruments. Furthermore, extensions of tribalist discourses show up in the most "scientific" scholarship in musicology. See, e.g., Erich M. V. Hornbostel, "African Negro Music," *Africa* 1, no. 1 (1928): 30–62; Milton F. Metfessel, *Phonophotography in Folk Music: American Negro Songs in New Notation,* with an introduction by Carl E. Seashore (Chapel Hill: University of North Carolina Press, 1928); and Richard Waterman, " 'Hot' Rhythm in Negro Music," *Journal of the American Musicological Society* 1 (1948): 24–37.

81. On the displacing of African-American examples in the analysis of race, see John F. Szwed, "An Anthropological Dilemma: The Politics of Afro-American Culture," in *Reinventing Anthropology,* ed. Dell Hymes (New York: Pantheon, 1969), 153–81.

82. D. A. Masolo, *African Philosophy in Search of Identity* (Bloomington: Indiana University Press, 1994); and Manthia Diawara, *In Search of Africa* (Cambridge, Mass.: Harvard University Press, 1998).

83. Herskovits outlined his initial position in the seminal treatise of the Harlem Renaissance, *The New Negro*—see, in particular, "The Negro's Americanism," in *The New Negro,* ed. Alain Locke, with a new preface by Robert Hayden (1925; reprint, New York: Atheneum, 1968), 353–60. This argument was subsequently advanced most forcefully by E. Franklin Frazier, who ironically would become Herskovits's principal adversary and critic. For elaboration, see Albert Raboteau, *Slave Religion: The "Invisible Institution" in the Antebellum South* (New York: Oxford University Press, 1978), 43–94.

84. In *Shining Trumpets: A History of Jazz* (New York: A. A. Knopf, 1946), Rudi Blesh proposes a kind of caricature of African influence, one laden with primitivist imagery and written in the wake of Herskovits's texts. Amiri Baraka (LeRoi Jones) acknowledges Herskovits's arguments in chap. 1 of *Blues People.*

85. Roger Abrahams and John Szwed have devoted their professional lives to challenging both visions. See, e.g., "After the Myth."

86. Such resistance ultimately led one prominent African-American historian, Nathan Irvin Huggins, to see the Harlem Renaissance as a failure (*Harlem Renaissance* [New York: Oxford University Press, 1971]). For background, see Kevin Gaines, *Uplifting the Race: Black Leadership, Politics, and Culture in the Twentieth Century* (Chapel Hill: University of North Carolina Press, 1996). For further insight into the notion of blackness in early twentieth-century cultural criticism, see the famous exchange between the African-American writers George S. Schuyler and Langston Hughes published in the *Nation* in 1926 ("The Negro-Art Hokum," "The Negro Artist and the Racial Mountain," respectively) and reprinted in Mitchell, ed., *Within the Circle,* 51–59.

87. See, e.g., LeRoi Jones, *Blues People;* and Gunther Schuller's, *Early Jazz: Its Roots and Development* (New York: Oxford University Press, 1968), the lead chapter of which, "Origins," proposes relationships between New Orleans jazz and Ewe drum ensembles, based on his interpretation of the work of A. M. Jones.

88. Richard Waterman, " 'Hot' Rhythm in Negro Music," and "African Influence on

the Music of the Americas," in *Acculturation in the Americas,* ed. Sol Tax (Chicago: University of Chicago Press, 1952), 207–18; Alan Merriam, "African Music," in *Continuity and Change in African Cultures,* ed. William R. Bascom and Melville J. Herskovits (Chicago: University of Chicago Press, 1959), 49–86; V. Kofi Agawu, "The Invention of 'African Rhythm'," *Journal of the American Musicological Society* 48 (1995): 380–95. An interesting early consideration of these matters appears in William Westcott, "Ideas of Afro-American Acculturation in the U.S.A.: 1900 to the Present," *Journal of the Steward Anthropological Society* 8, no. 2 (spring 1977): 107–36. For background on syncretism, see Carsten Colpe, "Syncretism," in *The Encyclopedia of Religion,* ed. Mircea Eliade (New York: Macmillan, 1987), 14:218–27; Walter Jackson, "Melville Herskovits and the Search for Afro-American Culture," in *Malinowski, Rivers, Benedict, and Others,* ed. George Stocking, History of Anthropology, vol. 4 (Madison: University of Wisconsin Press, 1986), 95–126; E. Franklin Frazier, "Negro Family in Bahia, Brazil," *American Sociological Review* 7 (1942): 465–78; and for a response to Frazier by Herskovits and rejoinder by Frazier, see *American Sociological Review* 8, no. 4 (1943): 394–402, 402–4, respectively.

89. Gates, *Figures in Black,* 27.

90. Michael Awkward, *Negotiating Difference: Race, Gender, and the Politics of Positionality* (Chicago: University of Chicago Press, 1995), 186.

91. Gates, *Figures in Black,* xxx. Baker defends the Black Arts aestheticians even as he departs from them. See his critique of Gates in "Generational Shifts and the Recent Criticism of Afro-American Literature," *Black American Literature Forum,* vol. 15 (spring 1981), reprinted in Mitchell, ed., *Within the Circle,* 282–328.

92. Indeed, Gates was fully aware of the pitfalls of building theory on simplistic racial binaries. In his essay "Preface to Blackness: Text and Pretext," e.g., he observes: "That the base for our literature is an oral one is certainly true; but, as Millman Parry and Albert Lord have amply demonstrated, so is the base of the whole of Western literature, commencing with the Hebrews and the Greeks" (in *Afro-American Literature: The Reconstruction of Instruction,* ed. Dexter Fisher and Robert Stepto [New York, 1978], reprinted in Mitchell, ed., *Within the Circle,* 235–55). The quotation in the text is taken from Mitchell, 250–51.

93. Samuel A. Floyd, Jr., "Ring Shout! Literary Studies, Historical Studies, and Black Music Inquiry," *Black Music Research Journal* 11, no. 2 (fall 1991): 265–88, and *The Power of Black Music: Interpreting Its History from Africa to the United States* (New York: Oxford University Press, 1995); Robert Walser, " 'Out of Notes': Signification, Interpretation, and the Problem of Miles Davis," *Musical Quarterly,* vol. 77, no. 2 (summer 1993), reprinted in *Jazz among the Discourses,* ed. Krin Gabbard (Durham, N.C.: Duke University Press, 1995), 165–88. In *Saying Something,* Ingrid Monson similarly employs Gates's theory while also resisting the temptation of fixing jazz practices into a Procrustean bed of indirection.

94. Diana Fuss, " 'Race' under Erasure? Poststructuralist Afro-American Literary Theory," in *Essentially Speaking* (New York: Routledge, 1989), 73–96.

95. African-American music signified the very essence of a primordial African-

based culture—the "base" of the race/superstructure model that Gates outlines—and accordingly became a crucial element in their definitions of the "black aesthetic." What these critics ultimately affirmed in their evocations was the privileged status of African-American poetry and literature. Despite an obvious respect for the expressive power of black vernacular sound, they turned to music not to delve analytically into the listening experience but in order to facilitate the centering of literary interpretation. Music functioned mainly as a supplement, an exoticized Other that enhanced the sense of mystery and spirit informing the stable ground of text.

96. Paul Gilroy, *The Black Atlantic: Modernity and Double Consciousness* (Cambridge, Mass.: Harvard University Press, 1993). Gilroy's more recent study, *Against Race: Imagining Political Culture beyond the Color Line* (Cambridge, Mass.: Harvard University Press, 2000), would seem to recommend a rethinking of the musical criticism proposed in *The Black Atlantic.* Such a critique can only be inferred, however, since he deals with music in passing.

97. Gilroy, *Black Atlantic,* 187.

98. LeRoi Jones (Amiri Baraka), *Blues People,* 194. Ralph Ellison introduces the figure of the blues impulse to advance a markedly different sentiment in his 1945 essay, "Richard Wright's Blues" (in *Shadow and Act*).

99. Gilroy, *Black Atlantic,* 36, 74, 75, 74, 36, 37, respectively.

100. Lydia Goehr, *The Imaginary Museum of Musical Works: An Essay in the Philosophy of Music* (New York: Oxford University Press, 1992).

101. Scott, "The Evidence of Experience."

102. Frantz Fanon, "The Fact of Blackness," in *Black Skins, White Masks,* trans. Charles Lam Markmann (1952; reprint, New York: Grove Weidenfeld, 1967), 109–40.

103. Gilroy, *Black Atlantic,* 55.

104. Baldwin, *Notes of a Native Son,* 22.

105. Michel Foucault, "Preface to Transgression" (1963), in *Language, Counter-Memory, Practice: Selected Essays and Reviews by Michel Foucault,* ed. Donald F. Bouchard (Ithaca, N.Y.: Cornell University Press, 1977), 35.

106. Walter Benjamin, "Theses of Philosophy of History," in *Illuminations,* 255. "A Dream of American Form" appears as the title of chap. 3 in Baker, *Blues, Ideology, and Afro-American Literature;* Baldwin, "Many Thousands Gone" (1955), in *Notes of a Native Son,* 24. Baldwin writes, in full: "It is only in his music, which Americans are able to admire because a protective sentimentality limits their understanding of it, that the Negro in America has been able to tell his story. It is a story which otherwise has yet to be told and which no American is prepared to hear. As is the inevitable result of things unsaid, we find ourselves until today oppressed with a dangerous and reverberating silence; and the story is told, compulsively, in symbols and hieroglyphics."

107. Gates, *The Signifying Monkey* (New York: Oxford University Press, 1988), 130.

108. Zora Neale Hurston, *Mules and Men,* with a preface by Franz Boas and a new foreword by Arnold Rampersad (1935; reprint, New York: Harper & Row, 1990), 2, 19.

109. Hurston, introduction to *Mules and Men,* 1.

110.Werner Sollors, ed., *Invention of Ethnicity* (New York: Oxford University Press, 1989), xv.

111. Robert E. Hemenway, *Zora Neale Hurston: A Literary Biography,* with a foreword by Alice Walker (Urbana: University of Illinois Press, 1977), 166–67. Thanks go to Ed Pavlic' for guidance on the debates surrounding Hurston's *Mules and Men.* Contemporary historians have acknowledged the constructed nature of folk authenticity. See, e.g., Robin D. G. Kelley, "Notes on Deconstructing 'the Folk,' " *American Historical Review* 97 (December 5, 1992): 1400–1408; Robert Cantwell, *When We Were Good: The Folk Revival* (Cambridge, Mass.: Harvard University Press, 1996); and Benjamin Filene, *Romancing the Folk: Public Memory and American Roots Music* (Chapel Hill: University of North Carolina Press, 2000).

Chapter 2

1. Frederick Douglass, *The Narrative of the Life of Frederick Douglass, an American Slave, Written by Himself,* ed. Benjamin Quarles (1845; reprint, Cambridge, Mass.: Harvard University Press, Belknap Press, 1960), 37. "Tale of woe" is an anticipation of the theme of the "sorrow song" central to W. E. B. Du Bois's *Souls of Black Folk,* ed. David W. Blight and Robert Gooding-Williams (1903; reprint, Boston: Bedford Books, 1997). For an elaboration on Douglass's significance to the formation of spiritual discourses, see my essay "Denoting Difference: The Writing of the Slave Spirituals," *Critical Inquiry* 22 (spring 1996): 506–44. Applications of similar interpretive themes and strategies appear in sections of Jon Cruz's study *Culture on the Margins: The Black Spiritual and the Rise of American Cultural Interpretation* (Princeton, N.J.: Princeton University Press, 1999). For an important consideration of the idea of authenticity and representation, see Henry Louis Gates, Jr., "The Trope of a New Negro and the Reconstruction of the Image of the Black," *Representations* 24 (fall 1988): 129–55.

2. Douglass, *The Narrative,* 65, 52. James Olney develops this reading of the passage in " 'I Was Born': Slave Narratives, Their Status as Autobiography and as Literature," in *The Slave's Narrative,* ed. Charles T. Davis and Henry Louis Gates, Jr. (New York: Oxford University Press, 1985), 148–75.

3. Douglass, *The Narrative,* 37.

4. The terms "un-concealment" and "un-forgetting" are those of Mark C. Taylor, who writes:

> Truth, according to Heidegger, is not *certitudo* or *adequatio;* nor is it *mimesis.* Truth is *aletheia.* A-*letheia* is the un-concealment that arises through un-forgetting. The history of Western metaphysics, I have noted, is inseparably bound up with oblivion. Representational and conceptual thought originate by forgetting their origin. To think what philosophy represses, it is necessary to return to this origin through an act of un-forgetting. A-*letheia,* however, is not simply identical with recollection or remembering. The oblivion that obsesses Heidegger is not an accident that can be avoided. To the contrary, the inevitability of oblivion reflects the necessity of concealment in all

disclosure. To un-forget the origin is to remember *that* one has forgotten and to recognize that such forgetting is inescapable. Since origin remains an inaccessible "abyss," remembering does not issue in the total recollection necessary for transparent self-consciousness. Remembering, therefore, can no more re-member than recollection can re-collect. . . . The truth "known" in the un-forgetting of *a-letheia* is a truth that always carries a shadow in the midst of its lighting.

(*Altarity* [Chicago: University of Chicago Press, 1987], 51)

5. Hortense Spillers, "Changing the Letter: The Yokes, the Jokes of Discourse, or, Mrs. Stowe, Mr. Reed," in *Slavery and the Literary Imagination,* ed. Deborah E. McDowell and Arnold Rampersad (Baltimore: Johns Hopkins University Press, 1989), 29. Comparing colonial and antebellum records, Frank Shuffleton observes, "for the eighteenth century the records are sparser, oral histories are lost, literacy is less common, and the view of African-American culture is consequently more shadowy in its specific features" ("Circumstantial Accounts, Dangerous Art: Recognizing African-American Culture in Travelers' Narratives," *Eighteenth-Century Studies* 27, no. 4 [1994]: 590).

6. Terry Eagleton (*Ideology: An Introduction* [London and New York: Verso, 1991]) observes two central deployments of ideology, one the "epistemological" tradition that "false ideology" inhabits, the other a "sociological" conception relating to the antihumanism that Althusser traces from Marx. See also Louis Althusser, "Ideology and Ideological State Apparatuses (Notes toward an Investigation)," in *Lenin and Philosophy, and Other Essays* (New York: Monthly Review Press, 1972). I am grateful to Christopher Todd and Martin Stempfhuber for many insightful conversations about ideology and contemporary Marxism during our directed study on black studies and cultural theory (Department of Afro-American Studies, University of Wisconsin—Madison, spring 2000).

7. Taylor, *Altarity,* 351.

8. Benjamin, "The Task of the Translator" (1923), in *Illuminations,* ed. Hannah Arendt; trans. Harry Zohn ((New York: Schocken Books, 1969), 76.

9. Ibid.; Homi Bhabha, *The Location of Culture* (New York: Routledge, 1994), 246.

10. Hermann Helmholtz, *On the Sensations of Tone as a Physiological Basis for the Theory of Music,* 2d English ed., adapted from the 4th German ed. (1877) by Alexander J. Ellis, with a new introduction by Henry Margenau (New York: Dover Publications, 1954), quotations on 26.

11. Sterling Stuckey, "Introduction: Slavery and the Circle of Culture," in *Slave Culture* (New York: Oxford University Press, 1987); Robert Farris Thompson, *Flash of the Spirit: African and Afro-American Art and Philosophy* (New York: Random House, 1983); Samuel A. Floyd, Jr., "Ring Shout! Literary Studies, Historical Studies, and Black Music Inquiry," *Black Music Research Journal* 11, no. 2 (fall 1991): 265–88. See also Floyd, *The Power of Black Music: Interpreting Its History from Africa to the United States* (New York: Oxford University Press, 1995).

12. Joseph Campbell, *The Hero with a Thousand Faces* (1949; reprint, Princeton,

N.J.: Princeton University Press, 1973), 41–42; John Warrington, ed., *Aristotle's Metaphysics* (London 1956); Robert G. Olson, *A Short History of Philosophy* (New York: Harcourt Brace & World, 1967), 68–69. In "The Phenomenology of Roundness," moreover, Gaston Bachelard explores the historical connections between the figure of the circle and birds, which dually signify the cosmic perfection of the open horizon. Quoting Michelet, Bachelard writes, "The bird, which is almost completely spherical, is certainly the sublime and divine summit of living concentration. One can neither see, nor even imagine, a high degree of unity" (*The Poetics of Space,* foreword by Etienne Gilson; trans. Maria Jolas (1958; reprint, Boston: Beacon, 1964], 237). For an interesting speculation on celestial motivations for circular motion in ritual, finally (in which participants move in a circle to imitate star motion), see Abraham Seidenberg, "The Ritual Origin of the Circle and Square," *Archive for History of Exact Sciences* 25, no. 4 (1981): 269–327.

13. LeRoi Jones, *Blues People: Negro Music in White America* (New York: William Morrow, 1963).

14. By focusing on music, Baraka disrupted the terrain of historical research, shifting from tangible matters of society to the instabilities of musical practice. Working from this vantage point, he argued that one could read a cultural continuity in sound even while acknowledging the larger disruptions in social development. Despite the losses of material culture, Baraka reasoned, African-Americans maintained a system of coherence through nonmaterial means, projecting a racialized blackness as performative spirit. Baraka developed this line of thinking by working from recent reflections on the nature of blackness so commonly cast within the rhetoric of Marxian social politics (e.g., Richard Wright, Frantz Fanon). Targeted specifically in *Blues People* were those leading figures in music journalism with whom Baraka had once been affiliated, writers who, as a group, tended to interpret black music, and jazz in particular, according to the tenets of a European-based modernism. For his reference to the "blues impulse," see *Blues People,* 194. Ellison first introduces the figure without the essentialisms that Baraka conveys in "Richard Wright's Blues" (1945), reprinted in *Shadow and Act* (1964; New York: Vintage, 1972).

15. Lawrence Levine, *Black Culture and Black Consciousness* (New York: Oxford University Press, 1977); Eileen Southern, *Music of Black Americans,* 3d ed., rev. (New York: W. W. Norton, 1997). Southern proceeded according to the tenets of the musicological positivism in which she was trained. Readers can find more about this legacy and its philological orientation in Joseph Kerman, *Contemplating Music: Challenges to Musicology* (Cambridge, Mass.: Harvard University Press, 1985).

16. Dena J. Epstein, *Sinful Tunes and Spirituals: Black Folk Music to the Civil War* (Urbana: University of Illinois Press, 1977). Melville J. Herskovits proposes such comparisons in chap. 1 of his book *Myth of the Negro Past,* introduction by Sidney W. Mintz (1941; reprint, Boston: Beacon Press, 1990). Epstein's vivid responses to this call have led to the assumption that there is a wealth of sources on early Caribbean musics. While references to Caribbean practices exceed those of the mainland, they are, as a

body of evidence, still fragmentary. For background on the social connections between mainland and Caribbean English colonies, see Michael Mullin, *Africa in America: Slave Acculturation and Resistance in the American South and the British Caribbean, 1736–1831* (Urbana: University of Illinois Press, 1992). Also noteworthy are David C. Littlefield, *Rice and Slaves: Ethnicity and the Slave Trade in Colonial South Carolina* (Baton Rouge: Louisiana State University Press, 1981); and Jack P. Greene, *Pursuits of Happiness: The Social Development of Early Modern British Colonies and the Formation of American Culture* (Chapel Hill: University of North Carolina Press, 1988). Greene's primary concern is with debunking the notion that New England was normative in defining colonial America, which leads him to stress its similarities with other colonies. And yet the distinctiveness of South Carolina and the West Indies (absentee ownership, Draconian slave laws, high black-to-white ratios, single-staple economies, etc.) effectively sets them apart.

17. This is particularly well established in the work of Ira Berlin, notably *Many Thousands Gone: The First Two Centuries of Slavery in North America* (Cambridge, Mass.: Harvard University Press, Belknap Press, 1998), discussed later in this chapter. For a succinct anticipation of the book's argument, see his "Time, Space, and the Evolution of Afro-American Society on British Mainland North America," *American Historical Review* 85, no. 1 (1980): 44–78. See also Winthrop D. Jordan, *White over Black: American Attitudes toward the Negro, 1550–1812* (Chapel Hill: University of North Carolina Press, 1968), who emphasizes South Carolina's ties to the mainland (esp. 141–42); and Littlefield, *Rice and Slaves*. Littlefield writes: "In more ways than one, South Carolina occupied an intermediate position between North America and the tropics" (2).

18. Dena J. Epstein, "African Music in British and French America," *Musical Quarterly* 59, no. 1 (January 1973): 62. In *Sinful Tunes*, Epstein elaborates: "The descriptions of African music from the islands were quite consistent with the more fragmentary accounts surviving from the mainland. Whether the colonies were British or French, on the mainland or in the islands, the culture of the slaves was initially African and, as seen through the eyes of European observers, seemingly homogeneous" (24). Recognizing the limits to European representation she nonetheless subscribed to its conclusions.

19. Sidney W. Mintz and Richard Price, *An Anthropological Approach to the Afro-American Past: A Caribbean Perspective*, ISHI Occasional Papers in Social Change, no. 2 (Philadelphia: Institute for the Study of Human Issues, 1976), 9–10.

20. Epstein argues that the drum bans were "so contrary to the natural inclinations of the black population, apparently proved impossible to enforce" (*Sinful Tunes*, 27). And yet she also acknowledges that there were few recorded instances of drumming in North America. Baraka sees rhythm as the formative essence across the pages of *Blues People*. In his essay on early African music in America, moreover, Richard Cullen Rath sought to defend Epstein's claims in a provocative discussion of notations of Jamaican music recorded by Baptiste, a French musician visiting a plantation. But his assumption that the planters correctly identified the group origins of African slaves, that the musical notations are accurate (typically recorded in common time and 12/8), and that

African practices remained stable are but a few of the variables challenging his argument. See Rath, "African Music in Seventeenth-Century Jamaica: Cultural Transit and Transition," *William and Mary Quarterly,* 3d ser., 50, no. 4 (October 1993): 700–726.

21. Ranajit Guha, "The Small Voice in History," in *Subaltern Studies: Writings on South Asian History and Society,* vol. 9, ed. Shahid Amin and Dipesh Chakrabarty (Delhi: Oxford University Press, 1996), 3. In the case of Eileen Southern, her perspective affirms the racialist-advocacy posture of Black Arts criticism as much as it is indebted to the repertory-oriented conventions of European art-music textbooks. Roger Abrahams, "The Changing Concept of the Negro Hero," in *The Golden Log,* ed. Mody C. Boatright, Wilson M. Hudson, and Allen Maxwell (Dallas: Southern Methodist University Press, 1962), 119–34, and *Deep Down in the Jungle: Negro Narrative Folklore from the Streets of Philadelphia* (Chicago: Aldine Publishing, 1970); and Claudia Mitchell-Kernan, "Signifying as a Form of Verbal Art," in *Mother Wit from the Laughing Barrel: Readings in the Interpretation of Afro-American Folklore,* ed. Alan Dundes (Englewood Cliffs, N.J.: Prentice-Hall, 1973), 310–28.

22. While planters sometimes expressed preferences for slaves from particular African "nations," they routinely sought to disrupt social coherences such as family, ethnicity, and linguistic linkages. In *Many Thousands Gone,* Berlin discusses the enormous dissimilarity of African groups; see 101–3, 107–8, and 114–15.

23. For example, Stanley M. Elkins, *Slavery: A Problem in American Institutional and Intellectual Life* (Chicago: University of Chicago Press, 1968); and Richard Hofstader, *America at 1750: A Social Portrait* (New York, 1973), 90.

24. Jon Butler, *Awash in a Sea of Faith: Christianizing the American People* (Cambridge, Mass.: Harvard University Press, 1990). Quotes and discussions appear respectively on 155, 143–44, 146, and 153. Berlin charts the population growth of slave populations (1680–1810) both numerically and in relation to the total population in *Many Thousands Gone,* 369–71.

25. Butler, *Awash in a Sea of Faith,* 141–42. Berlin, *Many Thousands Gone,* 115–16. Slavery was at its harshest in the eighteenth century, with the rise of slave importations and the institution of severe codes of control and discipline. By one estimation, only one-half of slave births survived ca. 1700. As few as two out of three slaves survived the first year. See Peter J. Parish, *Slavery: History and Historians* (New York: Harper & Row, 1989), 16–17; John B. Boles, *Black Southerners, 1619–1869* (Lexington: University Press of Kentucky, 1984), 30; and Betty Wood, *The Origins of American Slavery: Freedom and Bondage in the English Colonies* (New York: Hill & Wang, 1997), 50–51. By the late eighteenth century, moreover, slave family formations had contributed greatly to the creation of a distinctive African-American culture. Although family formations were encouraged and sometimes based on relations between men and women of neighboring plantations, they were always subject to the real threat of violence and sale. On slave family disruptions, see John W. Blassingame, *Slave Community: Plantation Life in the Antebellum South,* rev. and enlarged (New York: Oxford University Press, 1979), 173–78. The arguments on the relative brutality of slavery forged the debate be-

tween Robert W. Fogel and Stanley L. Engerman (who in *Time on the Cross* argued for a kind of protestant work ethic based on incentives) and Herbert Gutman and Richard Sutch, who detail slavery's brutality. See Paul A. David et al., *Reckoning with Slavery: A Critical Study of the Quantitative History of American Negro Slavery,* with an introduction by Kenneth M. Stampp (New York: Oxford University Press, 1976). According to a consensus of historians, Gutman and Sutch refuted the "work-ethic" argument. Coercion, punishment, or at least the threat of punishment defined the rule not the exception, although as Parish notes in his valuable historiographic review of this debate, the evidence has been widely interpreted (*Slavery: History and Historians,* 33–35).

26. Elaine Scarry, *The Body in Pain: The Making and Unmaking of the World* (New York: Oxford University Press, 1985). Scarry's text figures substantively ahead. Such brutalities were particularly the case in the early part of the eighteenth century in Virginia and across the century in the Lowcountry. Slave importations dropped off considerably in Virginia by the mid-eighteenth century as slave populations reproduced. For additional background on the brutal treatment of Africans and black slaves, see Daniel Mannix, *Black Cargoes: A History of the Atlantic Slave Trade, 1518–1865,* in collaboration with Malcolm Cowley (New York: Viking, 1962); and Leonard Cassuto, *The Inhuman Race: The Racial Grotesque in American Literature and Culture* (New York: Columbia University Press, 1997). Olaudah Equiano's narrative famously accounts such horrors. See *The Interesting Life of Olaudah Equiano, or Gustavus Vassa, the African, Written by Himself,* ed. Werner Sollors (New York: W. W. Norton, 2001), 38–39. The depiction of drowning appears in Philip Morgan, *Slave Counterpoint: Black Culture in the Eighteenth-Century Chesapeake and Lowcountry* (Chapel Hill: University of North Carolina Press, 1998), 590. Benjamin Rush details the slave songs as expressions of misery in *A Vindication of the Address to the Inhabitants of the British Settlements on the Slavery of the Negroes in America . . .* (Philadelphia: Printed by J. Dunlap, 1773), 29–30.

In his account of his travel to the United States in 1791, moreover, Ferdinand-M. Bayard recalled witnessing a "young Negress," blindfolded, her "cherise was hanging from her waist to her feet," beaten by a "white tormentor . . . while, a few steps away, a Negro child, on his knees, his hands clasped, was piercing the air with his cries" (*Travels of a Frenchman in Maryland and Virginia,* trans. and ed. Ben C. McCary [1791; reprint, Williamsburg, Va.: Printed for B. C. McCary, 1948], 14–15). See also M. Le Page du Pratz, *The History of Louisiana or of the Western Parts of Virginia and Carolina,* English trans. (1758; reprint, London: Printed for T. Becket, 1774), 77–79.

A host of references to slave brutalities accompany nineteenth-century depictions of music making: For singing workers on wharves in Savannah, half-starved and beaten, see A. M. Whitman Mead, *Travels in North America: In Three Parts* (New York: Printed by C. S. Van Winkle, 1820), 13–14; for singing in misery and in fear of sale, see Nehemiah Caulkins, "Narrative of Mr. Caulkins," *Liberator* 9, no. 21 (May 24, 1839): 81–82; for tortured Africans aboard a slave ship—"The cries and groans were terrible, notwithstanding there was a whipper on board each vessel, trying to compel the poor creatures to keep silence"—see Moses Grandy, *Narrative of the Life of Moses Grandy, Late a Slave of the United States of America* (Boston: Oliver Johnson, 1844), 28. References to singing as a form of sorrow are related in "Religion in a Cottage," *Liberator* 3, no. 13 (April 31 [April 13], 1833): 60; and [William Ellery] Channing, "Facts Showing the Character of Slavery," *Liberator* 6, no. 25 (June 18, 1836): 99.

27. M. L. E. Moreau de Saint- Méry, *Moreau de St. Méry's American Journey (1793–98),* trans. and ed. Kenneth and Anna M. Roberts; intoduction by Stewart L. Mims (Garden City, N.Y.: Doubleday & Co., 1947), 54. A source from 1786 recommended the use of a "rod of correction" rather than whips, which could create wounds; see *Instructions for the Treatment of Negroes* (1786; reprint, with additions, London: Printed for Shepperson & Reynolds, Oxford-Street, 1797), 109. In 1768, moreover, William Knox reported the brutalizing of slaves to the Society for the Propagation of the Gospel, seeking to impose legal limits on planters' discipline. By the end of the report, however, he was suggesting that slaves were as stupid as animals and could only be compelled through beating. Despite this, he maintained, they "have an ear for musick" (*Three Tracts Respecting the Conversion and Instruction of the Free Indians and Negroe Slaves in the Colonies: Addressed to the Venerable Society for the Propagation of the Gospel in Foreign Parts* [1768] [New Haven, Conn.: Research Publications, (1975)], microfilm, pp. 31–33, 39–41.

Musical references are generally rare in nearly all planters' accounts, as Epstein discusses in *Sinful Tunes and Spirituals.* Those personally inspected include Gideon Johnston, *Carolina Chronicle: The Papers of Commissary Gideon Johnston, 1707–1716,* ed. Frank J. Klingberg (Berkeley and Los Angeles: University of California Press, 1946); Thomas Fairfax, *Journey from Virginia to Salem Massachusetts, 1799,* Fairfax Library Publications no. 1 (London: Printed for private circulation, 1936); Nicholas Cresswell, *The Journal of Nicholas Cresswell, 1774–1777* (New York: Dial Press, 1924); Louis B. Wright, ed., *Letters of Robert Carter, 1720–1727: The Commercial Interests of a Virginia Gentleman* (San Marino Calif.: Huntington Library, 1940); Jack P. Greene, ed., *The Diary of Colonel Landon Carter of Sabine Hall, 1752–1778,* 2 vols. (Charlottesville: University Press of Virginia, 1965); Edward C. Carter II, ed., *The Virginia Journals of Benjamin Henry Latrobe, 1795–1798,* 2 vols. (New Haven, Conn.: Yale University Press, 1977); Alexander S. Salley, Jr., ed., *Narratives of Early Carolina, 1650–1708* (New York: Charles Scribner's Sons, 1911); Thomas Nairne, *A Letter from South Carolina* (London: A. Baldwin, 1710), reprinted in *Selling a New World: Two Colonial South Carolina Promotional Pamphlets,* ed. Jack P. Greene (Columbia: University of South Carolina Press, 1989), 31–73; and J. Hector St. John de Crèvecoeur, *"Letters from an American Farmer"; and, "Sketches of Eighteenth-Century America"* (1781), ed. Albert E. Stone (New York: Penguin, 1981). In Philip Fithian's journal and letters (a tutor to the children of Robert Carter III, a Virginia planter), musical references abound. But these almost entirely have to do with the classical training of Carter's children. See *Journal and Letters of Philip Vickers Fithian, 1773–1774: A Plantation Tutor of the Old Dominion,* ed. Hunter Dickinson Farish (Williamsburg, Va.: Colonial Williamsburg, Inc., 1943).

28. Dipesh Chakrabarty, "Postcoloniality and the Artifice of History: Who Speaks for 'Indian' Pasts?" *Representations* 37 (winter 1992): 1–26. See, in particular, his discussion on 22–23.

29. These studies at their best set aside retentions debates and their commitment

to determining African origins in order to consider more enduring propensities for African cultural expression. They sought to foreground the fragmentary evidence from North America to propose a more nuanced narrative of America, even if at times too vigorously assigning power and influence to seemingly isolated instances of neo-African practices. See Roger D. Abrahams and John F. Szwed's informative historical overview in their introduction to *After Africa,* ed. Roger D. Abrahams and John F. Szwed (New Haven, Conn.: Yale University Press, 1983).

30. Butler, *Awash in a Sea of Faith,* 153. Many scholars have tended to assume that contact with capitalist economies lead inexorably to cultural loss. "The deculturation argument," John Szwed and Roger D. Abrahams write, "was supplied equally to other immigrant groups under the control of capitalist economics. Their loss of culture, it is implied, happens to all traditional peoples when they are forced off the land in search of wages. This divestment provided the *raison d'etre* of sociological study . . . [from] Durkheim through Parsons and Merton even to Frederick Barth" ("After the Myth: Studying Afro-American Cultural Patterns in the Plantation Literature," *Research in African Literatures* ["African Folklore in the New World," ed. Daniel J. Crowley] 7, no. 2 [fall 1976]: 212). In the introduction to their collection *After Africa,* moreover, Szwed and Abrahams provide elaboration, noting that such arguments have been put forward in a variety of ways, from the radical overarching challenges of E. Franklin Frazier and Richard Hofstader, who questioned virtually all forms of continuity, to the more influential positions on the heterogeneity of African peoples in the diaspora outlined by Sidney Mintz and Richard Price.

31. Perhaps an analogy can be made between the erasure of African religious systems and the transformation of polymetric structures that were probably in existence in early modern Africa but had disappeared from North America by the eighteenth century. Reflections along these lines appear in John Miller Chernoff, "The Artistic Challenge of African Music: Thoughts on the Absence of Drum Orchestras in Black American Music," *Black Music Research Journal* 5 (1985): 1–20; and Denis-Constant Martin, "Filiation or Innovation? Some Hypotheses to Overcome the Dilemma of Afro-American Music's Origins," *Black Music Research Journal* 11, no. 1 (1991): 19–38.

32. For an implicit critique of syncretism's unmediated linkage of likenesses, consider Gayatri Spivak's challenge to direct correspondences, particularly those claiming to connect first and third worlds. For elaboration, see Nikos Papastergiadis, *The Turbulence of Migration* (Cambridge: Polity Press, 2000).

33. John Blacking, "The Study of Musical Change" (1977), reprinted in *Music, Culture, and Experience: Selected Papers of John Blacking,* ed. Reginald Brown; foreword by Bruno Nettl (Chicago: University of Chicago Press, 1995), 148–73. See also Veit Erlmann, *African Stars: Studies in Black South African Performance* (Chicago: University of Chicago Press, 1991), 11; and Alan Lomax, "Folk Song Style," *American Anthropologist* 61 (1959): 930.

34. Michel Foucault, *The Archeology of Knowledge,* trans. A. M. Sheridan Smith (New York, 1972), 203.

35. Gayatri Chakravorty Spivak, *The Critique of Post-Colonial Reason: Toward a History of the Vanishing Present* (Cambridge, Mass.: Harvard University Press, 1999), 6. See also Joan Scott, "The Evidence of Experience," *Critical Inquiry* 17, no. 4 (summer 1991): 773–97.

36. Morgan, *Slave Counterpoint*, xvii; Berlin, *Many Thousands Gone*, 13.

37. Morgan, *Slave Counterpoint*, 122–23. The reference to the pot appears on 119.

38. In *Africa in America,* Michael Mullin argues that African ethnicity mattered more in South Carolina than it did in Virginia. When maintained, it reinforced group identity and resistance (15). However, in his discussion of Berlin's and Philip Morgan's studies, Edmund S. Morgan argues the reverse. Citing Philip Morgan, he suggests that the recognition of divisions by linguistic and ethnic group (Igbo, Angolans, etc.) disrupted identity formation ("The Big American Crime," *New York Review of Books* [December 3, 1998], 15). Furthermore, while Philip Morgan tends to qualify the degree of overarching retention, Berlin, for his part, proposes a complex dynamic of culture in both regions. Whereas Philip Morgan depicts Virginia slaves speaking a distinctively black Creole English (aligned with the linguistic practices of white plain folk), Berlin notes that Africans in some areas of the Chesapeake probably spoke Igbo, fueling fears among many whites that Virginia was becoming "New Guinea" (110). In general, both authors build their discussions of retentions from materialist positions, stressing that retentions developed from the sets of socioeconomic relations in the two territories. Morgan finds evidence of retentions in the character of slave architecture (rammed-earth buildings with yards backing one the other) and the pattern of tending yards (clean sweeping to bare ground). They also appear in the idiosyncrasies of slave labor: drugging fish as a means of catching them (both an African and Indian practice), carrying loads atop the head (spreading from the Lowcountry to the Chesapeake), handiwork displayed in blacksmithing and basket making. See, respectively, Morgan, *Slave Counterpoint,* 118, 123, 242, 199, 232–33. For more on retentions, see Mechal Sobel, *The World They Made Together: Black and White Values in Eighteenth-Century Virginia* (Princeton, N.J.: Princeton University Press, 1987).

39. Morgan, *Slave Counterpoint,* 456–57, Berlin, *Many Thousands Gone,* 115, 103–4.

40. Hayden White, *The Content of the Form: Narrative Discourse and Historical Representation* (Baltimore: Johns Hopkins University Press, 1987), 10, 14, 21.

41. Spivak, *The Critique of Post-Colonial Reason,* 6; Hayden White, "The Burden of History," in *Tropics of Discourse: Essays in Cultural Criticism* (Baltimore: Johns Hopkins University Press, 1978). See Joan Scott, "Evidence of Experience."

42. Chakrabarty, "Postcoloniality and the Artifice of History," 22–23; and Steven Tyler, "Post-Modern Ethnography," in *Writing Culture: The Poetics and Politics of Ethnography* (Berkeley and Los Angeles: University of California Press, 1986), 122–40. See also Barbara Maria Stafford, *Body Criticism: Imagining the Unseen in Enlightenment Art and Medicine* (Cambridge, Mass.: MIT Press, 1991). The new historicism identified with Stephen Greenblatt ("I began with the desire to speak with the dead") provides additional background. See his *Shakespearean Negotiations: The Circulation of Social Energy*

in Renaissance England (Berkeley and Los Angeles: University of California Press, 1988), 1. See also Eric Lott, "Love and Theft: The Racial Unconscious of Blackface Minstrelsy," *Representations* 39 (summer 1992): 23–50; and Robert Young, *White Mythologies: Writing History and the West* (New York: Routledge, 1990).

43. John Josselyn, *An Account of Two Voyages to New-England* (London: Giles Widdows, 1674; reprint, Hanover, N.H.: University Press of New England, 1988), 231; and Samuel Sewall, *Diary of Samuel Sewall, 1674–1729,* vol. 2, *1709–1729,* newly edited from the manuscript at the Massachusetts Historical Society by M. Halsey Thomas (New York: Farrar, Straus, and Giroux, 1973), 657, entry dated April 3, 1711.

44. Epstein, *Sinful Tunes,* 119; "An Account of the Negroe Insurrection in South Carolina," in *The Colonial Records of the State of Georgia, Compiled under Authority of the Legislature (1737–40),* comp. Allen D. Candler (Atlanta: Chas. P. Byrd, 1913), vol. 22, pt. 2: 232–36; Alexander Hewatt, *An Historical Account of the Rise and Progress of the Colonies of South Carolina and Georgia,* 2 vols. (London: Printed for Alexander Donaldson, 1779), 2:72. Hewatt argued that most slaves were "great strangers to Christianity and as much under the influence of Pagan darkness, idolatry and superstition, as they were at their first arrival from Africa" (2:72, 100). Rounding out these early references is the 1736 account by Lady Dorothy Oglethorpe (wife of General James Oglethorpe), who describes a slave leading a procession while playing a conch shell. In a letter to her father-in-law, written during the couple's stay on Jeckyl Island, Georgia, Oglethorpe refers to a "trumpeter, a stalwart negro, blowing a conch shell, and producing a dismal and incessant blare." In the same letter she recounts how "about the cavalcade swarmed the negroes, shouting and laughing, rolling their white eyes and . . . singing songs full of melody and pathos." The letter is reproduced in Franklin H. Head, "The Legends of Jekyl Island," *New England Magazine* 8 (May 1893): 397–98.

45. Antoine Bonnefoy, "Journal of Antoine Bonnefoy," trans. J. Franklin Jameson, in *Travels in the American Colonies,* ed. Newton D. Mereness (1741; reprint, New York: Macmillan Company, 1916), 250; Alexander Hamilton, *Gentleman's Progress: The Itinerarium of Dr. Alexander Hamilton,* ed. Carl Bridenbaugh (1744; reprint, Chapel Hill: University of North Carolina Press and the Institute of Early American History and Culture at Williamsburg, 1948), 25. For background on drumming in the colonial era, see Raoul Camus, "Military Music of Colonial Boston," in *Music in Colonial Massachusetts 1630–1820,* vol. 1, *Music in Public Places* (Boston: Colonial Society of Massachusetts and University Press of Virginia, 1980), 75–103.

46. The Somerset County judicial records from 1707–11 can be found in Russell R. Menard, "The Maryland Slave Population, 1658 to 1730: A Demographic Profile of Blacks in Four Counties," *William and Mary Quarterly* 32 (January 1975): 29–54, quoted in Epstein, *Sinful Tunes,* 47. Epstein cites the South Carolina ruling (59) and the New York proceeding (114) and also mentions a 1695 Maryland law prohibiting slaves from assembling, which soon lapsed (59).

47. Morgan Godwyn, *The Negro's and Indians Advocate, Suing for Their Admission into the Church; Or, A Persuasive to the Instructing and Baptizing of the Negro's and Indians in Our Plantations . . .* (London: Printed for the Author by J. D., 1680), 32–33. God-

wyn's principal gripe was with the practice of polygamy and then with the dances and rituals that betrayed "barbarous" behavior. He appeared troubled not with the dances themselves, as Epstein implies (*Sinful Tunes,* 28), but with the association of dancing with idolatry, noting at one point that the Bible records gentiles and Jews who "anciently did esteem and practice Dancing, as part of Divine Worship" (Godwyn, 33). Later, he argues that such barbarisms should be tolerated since even Britains once engaged in similar practices: wearing skins, sharing wives, and fornicating with children. In fact, they exceeded Africans in demonstrating "a greater Barbarity than I have at any time heard amongst the Negro's" (34).

48. *The Carolina Chronicle of Dr. Francis Le Jau, 1706–1717,* ed. Frank J. Klingberg (Berkeley: University of California Press, 1956). The letter is from August 30, 1712 (120–21). On June 13, 1710, Le Jau writes: "The Lord's day is no more profaned by their dancings [*sic*] at least about me" (77). Earlier he describes the slave custom "to have their feasts, dances and merry Meetings upon the Lord's day" (61). Furthermore, Epstein includes additional early eighteenth-century references to the "Heathenish rites" among Africans at funerals in New York in 1712–13, and, in South Carolina in 1712, the dispersing of crowds of slaves and disruption of dancing on Sundays and holidays (*Sinful Tunes,* 38–39, 59, 64). A similar ruling was made in 1723 in Maryland (Epstein, 59).

49. Hugh Jones, *The Present State of Virginia,* ed. Richard Merton (London: John Clarke, 1724; reprint, Chapel Hill: University of North Carolina and the Virginia Historical Society, 1956), 99; Jones notes, in his inventory of personal property, "wheat, 444 barrels of Indian corn, some rye, slaves, and so forth" (42–43). For George Whitefield, see his *A Letter to the Inhabitants of Maryland, Virginia, North and South-Carolina* (n.p., [1740]), 37–39; for Charles Chauncey, see his *Seasonable Thoughts on the State of Religion in New-England: A Treatise in Five Parts* (Boston: Printed by Rogers & Fowle for Samuel Eliot in Cornhill, 1743), pt. 1:226; for Reverend Hutson, see Epstein, *Sinful Tunes,* 104; for Samuel Davies, see *Letters from the Rev. Samuel Davies and Others: Shewing the State of Religion in Virginia* (London: Printed by R. Pardon, 1757), 18, 21–22 (the letter was dated March 2, 1756); on Calinda, see M. Le Page du Pratz, *The History of Louisiana, or of the Western Parts of Virginia and Carolina,* . . . English trans. (1758; London: Printed for T. Becket, 1774), 387. For background on Davies, see Wesley M. Gewehr, *The Great Awakening in Virginia, 1740–1790* (Durham, N.C.: Duke University Press, 1930).

50. Benjamin Fawcett, a Methodist clergyman, quotes Davies's observations in the appendix to his text, *A Compassionate Address to the Christian Negroes in Virginia: With an Appendix Containing Some Account of the Rise and Progress of Christianity among That Poor People* (Salop, England: Printed by F. Eddowes and F. Cotton, 1756), 37; and Knox, *Three Tracts,* 39–41.

51. Lathan N. Windley, comp., *Runaway Slave Advertisements: A Documentary History from the 1730s to 1790,* 4 vols. (Westport, Conn.: Greenwood Press, 1983); and Carter G. Woodson, "Eighteenth-Century Slaves as Advertised by Their Masters," *Journal of Negro History* 1 (1916): 163–216. References to Norfolk's printing houses devoted to slave ads appear in Moreau de Saint-Mery, *Moreau de St. Mery's American Journey,* 52.

52. Windley, comp., *Runaway Slave Advertisements,* vol. 1, *Virginia and North Car-*

olina; Cajah, Tom, Gabriel, and James all appear in ads from Virginia: for Cajah, see Carter Braxton, July 28, 1768 (61); for Tom, John Bannister, July 31, 1779 (204); for Gabriel, John Hudson, January 20, 1776 (334–35); and for James, Fendall Southernland, September 20, 1783 (219).

53. The reference to "new Negroes" appears in Jones, *The Present State of Virginia,* 99.

54. Josselyn, *An Account of Two Voyages to New-England,* 231. In his record of a voyage to Guinea (1554), John Lok shifts from a believable depiction of elephants to a fantastic imaginary world. The elephants, he claims, "have continual war against dragons, which desire their blood because it is very cold." John Hawkins (1564) spoke of Dominica as the "island of the cannibals." See Richard Hakluyt, *Voyages and Discoveries: The Principal Navigations Voyages, Traffiques and Discoveries of the English Nation,* ed. Jack Beeching (New York: Penguin Books, 1972), 68, 107.

55. Janet Schaw, *Journal of a Lady of Quality, Being the Narrative of a Journey from Scotland to the West Indies, North Carolina, and Portugal, in the Years 1774 to 1776,* ed. Evangeline Walker Andrews and Charles McLean Andrews (New Haven, Conn.: Yale University Press, 1921), 168–69. Under its entry for "Music," *The Oxford English Dictionary,* 2d ed. (1989), cites Spenser, *Faerie Queene* 2.6.25 (1590): "She, more sweete then any bird on bough, Would . . . strive to passe . . . Their native musicke by her skilful art." On the meaning of birdsongs in early modern France, see Kate Van Orden, "Sexual Discourse in the Parisian Chanson: A Libidinous Aviary," *Journal of the American Musicological Society* 48 (1995): 1–41.

56. William Bartram, *Travels through North and South Carolina, Georgia, East and West Florida* (Philadelphia: James & Johnson, 1791), 310. Engaged in work song, the slaves sang in what may have possibly been an early recorded version of call and response: "The slaves comparatively of a gigantic stature, fat and muscular, were mounted on the massive timber logs; the regular heavy strokes of their gleaming axes re-echoed in the deep forests" (310).

57. Michel Foucault, *The History of Sexuality,* vol. 1, *An Introduction* (1976; reprint, New York: Vintage, 1990).

58. This "planetary consciousness" is ascribed to the eighteenth century. See Mary Louise Pratt, *Imperial Eyes: Travel Writing and Transculturation* (New York: Routledge, 1992). The African contacts begin first among the Portuguese and Spanish, with the Spanish and then the British principally partaking in slave trading.

59. See Frank Harrison, ed., *Time, Place and Music: An Anthology of Ethnomusicological Observation, c. 1550 to 1800* (Amsterdam: Frits Knuf, 1973), for accounts beginning with Jean de Léry's *Histoire d'un voyage faict en la terre du Brésil,* 3d ed. (La Rachelle, 1585). According to Harrision, neither the first nor the second editions (published in 1578 and 1580, respectively) contains musical notations. The early accounts of Loubère (Paris and Amsterdam, 1691) and Chardin (Amsterdam, 1711) are especially noteworthy for the detail of their musical descriptions and appreciation of European/ foreign differences. These authors also supply transcriptions; see chap. 4.

60. For background on race, see Pratt, *Imperial Eyes;* Ivan Hannaford, *Race: The History of an Idea in the West,* foreword by Bernard Crick (Baltimore and Washington, D.C.: Woodrow Wilson Center Press; distributed by Johns Hopkins University Press, 1996); Michael Adas, *Machines as the Measure of Men: Science, Technology, and Ideologies of Western Dominance* (Ithaca, N.Y.: Cornell University Press, 1989); Jordan, *White over Black;* Anne McClintock, *Imperial Leather: Race, Gender, and Sexuality in the Colonial Context* (New York: Routledge, 1995); David Brion Davis, *The Problem of Slavery in the Age of Revolution, 1770–1823* (1975; reprint, New York: Oxford University Press, 1999); Stephen Jay Gould, *The Mismeasure of Men,* rev. ed. (1981; reprint, New York: W. W. Norton, 1996); and Thomas F. Gossett, *Race: The History of an Idea in America* (1963; reprint, New York: Oxford University Press, 1997). Musical depictions are discussed in John McCall, "The Representation of African Music in Early Documents," in *Africa: The Garland Encyclopedia of World Music,* ed. Ruth M. Stone (New York: Garland Publishing, 1998), 74–99; and in Kofi Agawu's forthcoming *Representing African Music: Post-Colonial Notes, Queries, Questions* (New York: Routledge, 2003), in press.

61. John Pinkerton, *A General Collection of the Best and Most Interesting Voyages and Travels in All Parts of the World: Many of Which Are Now First Translated into English: Digested on a New Plan,* 17 vols. (London: Longman, Hurst, et al., 1807–14). The volumes include English translations of several foreign-language texts. The translator or translators are not identified.

62. Hakluyt, *Voyages and Discoveries.* The entries in this compilation of pre- and early modern English-language travelogues rarely acknowledge musical circumstances. When they do so, they typically focus on the performances of the travelers themselves. For example, Sebastian Cabot (1553) speaks of the allure of drums when seeking to attract the "people" of Cathay (58); John Hawkins (1564), who traveled to the coast of Guinea and the Indies of Nova Hispania exchanged pewter whistles for foodstuffs (107); and John Fox (1577) refers to the use of military music in Alexandria (164). The recorder of Sir Francis Drake's travels (1577) observes how "people of the country showed themselves unto him, leaping and dancing" (174); people in the arctic "in like manner sing and dance, saving only the women, which danced and kept silence" (182). Later, he observes, "The king was a man of tall stature, and seemed to be much delighted with the sound of our music" (184). The report of the voyage of Sir Humphrey Gilbert (1583) to countries north of the cape of Florida notes that the company "continued in sounding trumpets, with drums, and fifes: also winding the cornets" (238–39).

63. "Pinkerton, John (1758–1826)," in *The Dictionary of National Biography,* ed. Sir Leslie Stephen and Sir Sidney Lee (Oxford: Oxford University Press, 1973), 15:1204. David Hume, *A Treatise of Human Nature,* ed. David Fate Norton and Mary J. Norton (1739–40; reprint, Oxford: Oxford University Press, 2000); William Blackstone, *Commentaries on the Laws of England in Four Volumes,* ed. Wayne Morrison (1765–69; reprint, London: Cavendish, 2001); Adam Smith, *An Inquiry into the Nature and Causes of the Wealth of Nations,* ed. Edwin Cannan (1776; reprint, New York: Modern Library, 1994); Edward Gibbon, *The History of the Decline and Fall of the Roman Empire,* ed.

David Wormersley, abridged ed. (1776–80; reprint, London: Penguin, 2000), Edmund Burke, *A Philosophical Enquiry into the Origin of Our Ideas of the Sublime and the Beautiful,* ed. Adam Phillips (1757; reprint, Oxford: Oxford University Press, 1990).

64. Pinkerton was accused of forging ballads and adding them to his collections, an accusation that was widely believed. For background, see Harriet Harvey Wood's introduction to *The Correspondence of Thomas Percy and John Pinkerton,* ed. H. H. Wood, vol. 8 of *The Percy Letters,* ed. Cleanth Brooks and A. F. Falconer (New Haven, Conn.: Yale University Press, 1985), vii–xxxv. See also Dawson Turner, ed., *Literary Correspondence of John Pinkerton* (London: Colburn & Bentley, 1830).

65. Richard Wallaschek, *Primitive Music: An Inquiry into the Origin and Development of Music, Song, Instruments, Dances and Pantomimes of Savage Races* (London: Longmans, Green, 1893). The textual analysis that follows depends heavily on the superb research assistance of Mark Goodale, who combed the Pinkerton collection for much of the material examined here.

66. R. R. F. F. Michael Angelo of Gattina and Denis De Carli, "A Curious and Exact Account of a Voyage to Congo, in the Years 1666 and 1667," in Pinkerton, *General Collection,* 16:148–94; William Bosman, "A New and Accurate Description of the Coast of Guinea, Divided into the Gold, the Slave, and the Ivory Coasts" (1705), in Pinkerton, *General Collection,* 16:337–547. Bosman was chief factor for the Dutch at the Castle of Saint George d'Elmina; Thomas Shaw, "Travels or Observations, Relating to Barbary" (1738). in Pinkerton, *General Collection,* 15:499–680. The excerpt from Mungo Park's chronicle appears in volume 16 of that collection; a nineteenth-century text, it is not discussed here.

67. For useful background, see "British Travel Writers: 1837–1875," in *Dictionary of Literary Biography,* ed. Barbara Brother and Julia Gergits (Detroit: Gale Research, 1996), 166:xi–xxv. The influence of Herodotus was acknowledged in some of the Pinkerton travelogues. See, e.g., Richard Pococke's "Travels to Egypt," 15:163.

68. Recall, e.g., the comments of Morgan Godwyn, who perceived Africans in North America as latter-day versions of primitive Britains (*The Negro's and Indians Advocate,* 32–34).

69. Lancelot Addison, "An Account of West Barbary" (1671), in Pinkerton, *General Collection,* 15:403–41; see, esp., 422, 439. On 439, he writes:

> Their usual instruments are the rabèb and ahlùd; the former resembles our violin, but strung only with one great cord of hair; the other a guitar. In Fez they have lutes, and those who will teach them well. The Alárbs have an instrument called zauphèn, like the bottom of a kettle, on which they tinkle with a stick. The Tituanezes have a less organ, and also use a sort of tabor and pipe when they march in the field. . . . The singing part is performed by negras, not for any peculiar excellency they are happy in, but because singing at public dances is looked upon as slavish.

70. Gattina and Carli, "A Curious and Exact Account," 159–60. Gattina traveled with Carli and died in Congo. The entry consists of letters by Gattina from Africa and text

composed by Carli enroute home. Excerpts examined in this study were written exclusively by Carli. Describing the marimba, Carli writes:

> They take a piece of a stake, which they tie and bend like a bow, and bind to
> it fifteen long, dry, and empty gourds, or calabashes of several sizes, to
> sound several notes, with a hole at top, and a lesser hole four fingers lower,
> and stop it up half-way, covering also that at the top with a little thin bit of
> board, somewhat lifted above the hole. Then they take a cord made of the
> bark of a tree, and fastening it to both ends of the instrument, hang it about
> their neck. To play upon it they use two sticks, the ends whereof are covered with a bit of rag, with which they strike upon those little boards, and so
> make the gourds gather wind, which in some manner resembles the sound
> of an organ, and makes a pretty agreeable harmony, especially when three
> or four of them play together
> (160)

He does not name the instrument, but Father Jerom Merolla da Sorrento's text on Congo from around the same time employs the term "marimba," at least in the English translation. The original text was not consulted. See Merolla da Sorrento, "A Voyage to Congo, and Several Other Countries, Chiefly in Southern Africk" (1682), in Pinkerton, *General Collection,* 16:245.

71. Merolla da Sorrento, "A Voyage to Congo," 245.

72. Ibid., 244–46. On 245, he writes: "Over and above the great drums used in the army, there is another sort of a lesser size, called *Ncamba;* these are made either of the fruit of the tree called Aliconda, or else of hollowed wood with a skin over one end only: they are commonly made use of at unlawful feasts and merry-makings, and are beaten upon with the hands, which nevertheless makes a noise to be heard at a great distance."

73. Ibid., 245, 262.

74. Carli (in Gattina and Carli, "A Curious and Exact Account") continues,

> Then being come into the church, I gave them all holy water. They were
> about two hundred men carrying great logs of wood of a vast weight, for the
> greater penance. I spoke a few words to them of the benefit of penance,
> which if we will not undergo in this world, we shall be forced to endure in
> the next. They were all on their knees, and beat their breasts. I caused the
> candles to be put out, and they disciplined themselves a whole hour with
> leather-thongs and cords made of the bark of trees. After that we said the
> litanies of our Lady of Loretto; and having dismissed them, they returned
> home.
> (169)

75. Ibid., 160; my emphasis.

76. Merolla da Sorrento, 245–46, 282.

77. Pratt, *Imperial Eyes,* 15–37. See also Simon Gikandi, *Maps of Englishness: Writing Identity in the Culture of Colonialism* (New York: Columbia University Press, 1996).

78. Bosman, "A New and Accurate Description of the Coast of Guinea," 16:337–547.

79. Ibid., 530, 394–95.

80. Ibid., 395.

81. White writes: "A given culture is only as strong as its power to convince its least dedicated member that its fictions are truths" ("The Forms of Wildness," in *Tropics of Discourse*, 153).

82. Ibid., 153–54, 174. A parallel discussion of the distancing and isolation of insanity by reason appears famously in Foucault's first major work, *Madness and Civilization: A History of Insanity in the Age of Reason*, trans. Richard Howard (New York: Random House, 1965).

83. Michael Adanson, "A Voyage to Senegal, the Isle of Goree, and the River Gambia" (1759), trans. from the French, in Pinkerton, *General Collection*, 16:598–674.

84. Abbé Proyart, "History of Loango, Kakongo, and Other Kingdoms in Africa," trans. from the French, in Pinkerton, *General Collection*, 16:548–97. The quotation appears in chap. 11, "Of Arts and Trades," 576.

85. Adas, *Machines as the Measure of Men*, 77.

86. Pratt, *Imperial Eyes*, 27. Adas observes, "Though what were held to be scientific techniques for ranking the varieties of humankind were not widely employed or accepted until the nineteenth century, [claims of Negro inferiority] demonstrated what potent weapons allegedly scientific investigations and finds might be in arguing the case for white superiority" (*Machines as the Measure of Men*, 77). For historical conceptions of difference, see Anthony Appiah, "The Uncompleted Argument: Du Bois and the Illusion of Race," *"Race," Writing, and Difference*, ed. Henry Louis Gates, Jr. (Chicago: University of Chicago Press, 1986), 21–37; Jordan, *White over Black;* Frank M. Snowden, Jr., *Blacks in Antiquity: Ethiopians in the Greco-Roman Experience* (Cambridge, Mass.: Harvard University Press, Belknap Press, 1970).

87. John Windhus, "A Journey to Mequinez, the Residence of the Present Emperor of Fez and Morocco . . ." (1725), in Pinkerton, *General Collection*, 15:442–99, quotation on 448. The Pinkerton account is an excerpt of an eight-volume text.

88. C. P. Thunberg, "An Account of the Cape of Good Hope, and Some Parts of the Interior of Southern Africa" (1795), 4 vols., in Pinkerton, *General Collection*, 16:1–147.

89. Ibid., 42, 102, 90. Thunberg's description of what he names a "korà" calls to mind not the modern-day *kora*, a harp-lute, but the musical bow, still common to the region: "It resembles at first a fiddle stick, and was made of a wooden stick, over which was extended a string. At the end of this was fastened the tip of a quill, and upon this they played with their lips, blowing as if it were a wind instrument, so as to produce a jarring sound" (102).

90. Ibid., 143.

91. Hume quoted in Henry Louis Gates, Jr.'s introduction to *"Race," Writing and Difference*, 10; Thunberg, 143.

92. Adas, *Machines as the Measure of Men*, 114–22; Barbara J. Fields, "Ideology and Race in American History," in *Region, Race, and Reconstruction: Essays in Honor of C.*

Vann Woodward, ed. J. Morgan Kousser and James M. McPherson (New York: Oxford University Press, 1982), 155. As Fields writes, "Of course in any society any more complex than the primal horde, there cannot be a single ideology through which everyone apprehends the social world. In any event, what might appear from a distance to be a single ideology cannot hold the same meaning for everyone. If ideology is a vocabulary for interpreting social experience, and thus both shapes and is shaped by that experience, it follows that even the 'same' ideology must convey different meanings to people having different social experiences. To suppose otherwise is to take another false step onto the terrain of racialist ideology" (155).

93. William Lempriere, "A Tour from Gibraltar to Tangier, Sallee, Mogodore, Santa Cruz, Tarudant; and Thence over Mount Atlas, to Morocco," 8 vols., excerpted in Pinkerton, *General Collection,* 15:681–801, quotation on 773. Shaw, "Travels or Observations," 643.

94. Abbé Rochon, "A Voyage to Madagascar and the East Indies" (1792), trans. from the French, in Pinkerton *General Collection,* 16:738–807, quotations on 738. Proyart, "History of Loango," 572. See also Nicholas Hudson, "From 'Nation' to 'Race': The Origin of Racial Classification in Eighteenth-Century Thought," *Eighteenth-Century Studies* 29, no. 3 (1996): 247–64.

95. Jacques Derrida, *Of Grammatology* (Baltimore: Johns Hopkins University Press, 1976).

96. Richard Pococke, "Travels in Egypt" (1743), in Pinkerton *General Collection,* 15:163–402, discussion on 325; Mr. Browne, "A Journey to Dar-Fūr, a Kingdom in the Interior of Africa" (1799), in Pinkerton *General Collection,* 15:108–62, quotation on 153; Windhus, "A Journey to Mequinez," 452; McClintock, *Imperial Leather,* 2–24.

97. Adanson, "A Voyage to Senegal," 612–13.

98. Ibid.; Rochon, "A Voyage to Madagascar," 738; Proyart, "History of Loango, " 576.

99. Proyart, "History of Loango," 572.

100. Ibid.; Shaw, "Travels or Observations," 643. Earlier in the discussion, Shaw mentions the power of song and dance in curing spider bites. The notation of an Apulian "Tarantula" appears as part of a discussion of Saharan cures (635).

101. Downing A. Thomas, *Music and the Origins of Language: Theories from the French Enlightenment,* Perspectives in Music History and Criticism (Cambridge: Cambridge University Press, 1995), 38, 40.

102. Charles Burney, *A General History of Music* (1776); and Johann Nikolaus Forkel, *General History of Music* (1788), both excerpted in Enrico Fubini, ed., *Music and Culture in Eighteenth-Century Europe: A Source Book,* trans. and ed. Bonnie J. Blackburn (Chicago: University of Chicago Press, 1994), 181, 219.

103. Fubini, introduction to *Music and Culture,* 11; Thomas, *Music and the Origins of Language,* 53. For Condillac, this represented the "natural cry," and although Rousseau employed the same term, he gave to it a different order of meaning. See Thomas, 64–65, 105.

104. Excerpts of the writings of Martini, Birnbaum, and Fux appear in Fubini, ed., *Music and Culture,* 179, 276, and 134, respectively.

105. The setting of Rousseau's "chanson negre" to lyrics in Creole is cited in Christopher Kelly, "Rousseau and the Case against (for) the Arts," in *The Legacy of Rousseau,* ed. Clifford Orwin and Nathan Tarcov (Chicago: University of Chicago Press, 1997), 33.

106. Bhabha, *The Location of Culture,* 213. I outline an early consideration of noise in "Black Noise, White Mastery" (paper prepared for the "Unnatural Acts" conference, University of California, Riverside, April 1997, and published under the same title in the conference proceedings *Decomposition: Post-Disciplinary Performance,* ed. Sue-Ellen Case, Philip Brett, and Susan Leigh Foster [Bloomington: Indiana University Press, 2000], 29–49). In developing this concept of noise, I have benefited greatly from discussions with Charles Dill, whose more acutely French poststructuralist rendering appears in his paper "Ideological Noises: Opera Criticism in Early Eighteenth-Century France" (paper presented at the annual meeting of the American Musicological Society, Atlanta, November 15, 2001).

107. Quoted in Christopher Looby, *Voicing America: Language, Literary Form, and the Origins of the United States* (Chicago: University of Chicago Press, 1996), 87.

108. "Le Jau to the Secretary, II, February 18, 1709," from St. James Parish, Near Goose Creek, South Carolina to the Society for the Propagation of the Gospel, in *The Carolina Chronicle,* 52. While members of the clergy demonstrated, on the whole, greater compassion and respect for Africans, they also routinely compared them— when mentioning them at all—with possessions. Gideon Johnston, who served as an Anglican minister in South Carolina from 1708 to 1716, received an indication of the rector's salary at the parish of Phillips, at Charles Town, "a year paid in money halfe yearly Perquisites and presents 100£ a Negro man and Woman, 3 Cowes, a very good House" (*Carolina Chronicle*104).

109. Bhabha, *Location of Culture,* 246.

110. Edward S. Casey, "How to Get from Space to Place in a Fairly Short Stretch of Time: Phenomenological Prolegomena," in *Senses of Place,* ed. Steven Feld and Keith H. Basso (Santa Fe, N.M.: School of American Research Press, 1996), 22, 23, 26, 27. Casey attributes a "coefficient of adversity" to Sartre.

111. Steven Feld, "Waterfalls of Song: An Acoustemology of Place Resounding in Bosavi, Papua New Guinea," in *Senses of Place,* ed. Feld and Basso, 91, 96–97.

112. As Hortense J. Spillers puts it,

> I am predictably selfish in my own desires—I want to eat the cake and *have* it. I *want* a *discursive* "slavery," in part, in order to "explain" what appears to be very rich and recurrent manifestations of neo-slavement in the very symptoms of discursive production and sociopolitical arrangement that govern our current fictions in the United States. At the same time, I suspect that I occasionally resent the spread-eagle tyranny of discursivity across the terrain of what we used to call, with impunity, "experience." But I further suspect that this crucial dilemma is rather common among Afro-American

scholars, who are pledged to the critical work of the *inventory* and its relationship to a community's survival.

("Changing the Letter," 33)

113. As previously noted, the majority of slaves lived in small groups across the colonies, with five or fewer working for a single master. Such masters frequently relocated in search of better land and opportunity, further complicating the stability of "black culture." Plantations, in contrast, while representing fewer slaves, suggest a more stable ground from which eighteenth-century musical cultures would have emerged. On the types of slave groups, see James Oakes, *The Ruling Race: A History of American Slaveholders* (New York: Alfred A. Knopf, 1982).

114. Louis Althusser, "Contradiction and Overdetermination: Notes for an Investigation," in *For Marx,* trans. Ben Brewster (1969; reprint, New York: Verso Classics, 1997), 112.

115. An example of the kind of senseless brutality to which slaves were subjected appears in the *Journals and Letters of Philip Vickers Fithian, 1773–1774,* 51. In his entry from December 1773, Fithian, who was a tutor on the plantation of Robert Carter, recounts the disciplining tactics employed by one overseer.

> He said that whipping of any kind does them no good, for they will laugh at your greatest Severity; But he told us he had invented two things, and by several experiments had proved their success—For Sulleness, Obstinacy, or Idleness, says he, Take a Negro, strip him, tie him fast to a post; take then a sharp Curry-Comb, and curry him severely til he is well scrap'd; & call a Boy with some dry Hay, and make the Boy rub him down for several Minutes, then salt him, & unlose him. He will attend to his Business, (said the inhuman Infidel) afterwards!—But savage Cruelty does not exceed His next diabolical Invention—To get a Secret from a Negro, says he, take the following Method—Lay upon your Floor a large thick plank, having a peg about eighteen Inches long, of hard wood, & very Sharp, on the upper end, fixed fast in the plank—then strip the Negro, tie the Cord to a staple in the Ceiling, so as that his foot may just rest on the sharpened Peg, then turn him briskly round, and you would laugh (said our informer) at the Dexterity of the Negro, while he was releiving [*sic*] his Feet on the sharpen'd Peg!

116. Morgan, *Slave Counterpoint,* 122; Berlin, *Many Thousands Gone,* 139–40; Sobel, *The World They Made Together,* 35, 178–79.

117. Le Jau, *Carolina Chronicle,* 74, 70.

118. Morgan, *Slave Counterpoint,* 122. Sobel includes a drawn map attributed to Byrd that first sees Virginia as Eden, then in 1737, as a "New Guinea" overrun by African slaves and idle poor whites (*The World They Made Together,* 88–91).

119. "In former times," Rousseau writes, "all laws human and divine, exhortations to virtue, the knowledge of what concerned the Gods and heroes, the lives and actions of illustrious men were written in verse and sung publicly by Choirs to the sound of instruments" (quoted in Kelly, "Rousseau and the Case against (and for) the Arts," 29).

120. See n. 52 above, this chap.

121. See Cassuto, *The Inhuman Race,* 78, for an image of a head-instrument torturing device that prevented slaves from speaking, eating, or lying down. In *Roll, Jordan, Roll: The World the Slaves Made* (New York: Pantheon, 1972), Eugene Genovese discusses antebellum suspicion of slave preaching without reference to torture (257–60). The 1856 description of a metal device for gagging an African-American preacher (to prevent him from inciting fellow slaves) is a particularly graphic account of efforts to silence the black voice ("An Inside View of Slavery," *National Anti-Slavery Standard* 16 [January 20, 1856], 4).

122. Fannie Lou Hamer appears in the Public Broadcasting Service film *Freedom on My Mind* (prod. and dir. Connie Field and Marilyn Mulford, 110 min., Clarity Educational Productions, Berkeley, Calif., 1994, videocassette). David Firestone, "South's Football Fans Still Sand Up and Pray," *New York Times,* August 27, 2000, national ed., sec. 1, 1. The 1963 British film *Zulu* (directed by Cy Endfield, 139 min., Diamond Films Ltd., videocassette) offers a dramatic, if romanticized depiction of the effect of song. In the final scene of battle between the Zulu and British forces, the two sides first wage war in a contest of national songs, which heightens tension as a prelude to fighting.

123. David Harvey, *The Condition of Postmodernity* (Oxford: Basil Blackwell, 1989), 252–53.

124. As Morgan observes, "No instance of Lowcountry slaves' using rattles, clappers, or rasps have been found, but two fugitives were tambourine players." He notes that the expression "patting juba" was applied to bodily percussion only later and its link to drumming was given credibility by Sidney Mintz. See Morgan, *Slave Counterpoint,* 583–84. On the absence of drums in North America, see also Chernoff, "The Artistic Challenge of African Music."

125. Epstein, *Sinful Tunes,* 104–5, 27, respectively. Elsewhere she contradicts herself, arguing, "the mainland colonies, with the exception of Louisiana, found it possible strictly to enforce the regulations, judging from the relative absence of drums and drumming in accounts from the mainland" (60). For Baraka, see *Blues People,* 25–26. As John F. Carrington explains in his discussion of African talking drums, moreover, "another obstacle in the relaying of drum messages over great distances is the fact of the tribal nature of most drum languages. Since the drum language is based on the tribal tongue, it is usually understood only by members of the tribe. There is no 'international' drum language in Africa any more than there is a common spoken language" (*Talking Drums of Africa* [London: Carey Kingsgate Press, 1949], 30).

126. Quoted in Epstein, *Sinful Tunes,* 119, 119n; see also 57, 120n. On black military drummers, see Camus, "Military Music of Colonial Boston," which includes references to black drummers. Epstein sees these instances as irrelevant to the matter of retention since they represent "an acculturated kind of drumming" (*Sinful Tunes,* 60).

127. In an antebellum commentary on a 1740 South Carolina statute prohibiting loud instruments, the writer called the law unnecessary: "Who can keep his slaves from blowing loud horns or using other loud instruments?" See John Belton O'Neall, comp., *The Negro Law of South Carolina* (Columbia, S.C.: John G. Bowman, 1848; Chicago: Library Resources, 1970), microfiche, 26.

128. For a valuable overview of research on pinksters, see Sterling Stuckey's essay "The Skies of Consciousness: African Dance at Pinkster in New York, 1750–1840," in his *Going through the Storm: The Influence of African American Art in History* (New York: Oxford University Press, 1994), 53–80. The essay is best read alongside another important publication, which Stuckey critiques: Shane White, "Pinkster in Albany, 1803: A Contemporary Description," *New York History* 70, no. 2 (1989): 191–99. A famous recollection of pinkster is Dr. James Eights, "Pinkster Festivities in Albany Sixty Years Ago," in Joel Munsell, *Collections on the History of Albany: From Its Discover to the Present Time* (Albany, N.Y.: J. Munsell, 1865–71), 2:323–27, reprinted in *Readings in Black American Music,* ed. Eileen Southern, 2d ed. (New York: W. W. Norton, 1983), 41–47.

129. Kenneth Gourlay, "Towards a Humanizing Ethnomusicology," *Ethnomusicology* 26, no. 3 (September 1982): 415; Klaus P. Wachsmann, "Music," *Journal of the Folklore Institute* (Indiana University) 6 (1969): 164–91. "Music" as we know it emerges as a local European concept that becomes a marker of an increasingly racialized conception of civility in the early modern era. This signature of value would be specified to its written, composed manifestations that gain special primacy as "works" with the emergence of romantic aesthetics. See Lydia Goehr, *The Imaginary Museum of Musical Works: An Essay in the Philosophy of Music* (New York: Oxford University Press, 1992). As Steven Feld demonstrates, its transposition onto disparate musical cultural settings creates problems. Discussing the Kaluli of Papua New Guinea, e.g., he writes, "For Kaluli there is no 'music,' only sounds, arranged in categories shared to greater or lesser degrees by natural, animal, and human agents" ("Sound Structure as Social Structure," *Ethnomusicology* 28, no. 3 [September 1984]: 389). For a related argument focusing on the Tiv of Nigeria, see Charles Keil, *Tiv Song: The Sociology of Art in a Classless Society* (Chicago: University of Chicago Press, 1979), 27.

130. Kofi Agawu, "The Invention of 'African Rhythm'," *Journal of the American Musicological Society* 48 (1995): 380–95. If we are to seek an alignment of African and African-American music, we would more sensibly turn to singing, judging from Agawu's subsequent work. For it is song, among the modern-day Ewe of Ghana, that interfaces with the order of the day and provides the medium for the flow of "African rhythm." See Agawu, *African Rhythm: A Northern Ewe Perspective* (Cambridge: Cambridge University Press, 1995).

131. In this respect, I want to affirm Baraka's argument for the privileged role of music in crafting African-American social history.

Chapter 3

1. Frantz Fanon, "The Negro and Recognition," in *Black Skin, White Masks,* trans. Charles Lam Markmann (1952; reprint, New York: Grove Weidenfeld, 1967), 216–17. Fanon's focus is on the Martiniquean experience, but it is routinely transposed across the African diaspora generally and to North American examples particularly.

2. Hortense Spillers, "Changing the Letter: The Yokes, the Jokes of Discourse, or, Mrs. Stowe, Mr. Reed," in *Slavery and the Literary Imagination,* ed. Deborah E. McDowell and Arnold Rampersad (Baltimore: Johns Hopkins University Press, 1989), 28.

3. It is, however, an admittedly "porous" text, as Henry Louis Gates, Jr., suggests, and one inspiring a variety of interpretations. See his "Critical Fanonism," *Critical Inquiry* 17, no. 3 (1991): 458.

4. Homi Bhabha, *Location of Culture* (New York: Routledge, 1994), 238, 244–45.

5. Henry Louis Gates, Jr., "The Trope of a New Negro and the Reconstruction of the Image of the Black," *Representations* 24 (fall 1988): 129–55.

6. Leon F. Litwack, *North of Slavery: The Negro in the Free States, 1790–1860* (Chicago: University of Chicago Press, 1961), 6.

7. Litwack writes that "between 1775 and 1781, Negro soldiers participated in virtually every major military action" (ibid., 12). Furthermore, the place of natural rights in the formation of American Revolutionary thought reflects its close relation to French Enlightenment philosophy. As Duncan J. MacLeod writes, "No study of American slavery and anti-slavery in the eighteenth century would be complete which did not take account of this international backcloth" (*Slavery, Race, and the American Revolution* [Cambridge: Cambridge University Press, 1974], 4).

8. Sidney Kaplan, *The Black Presence in the Era of the American Revolution, 1770–1800* (New York: New York Geographic Society; Washington, D.C.: Smithsonian Institution Press, 1973), 22, 27. The text includes facsimiles of petitions. For an outline of rulings and the dates of abolition, state by state, see Litwack, *North of Slavery,* 3. See also Benjamin Quarles, *The Negro in the American Revolution* (Chapel Hill: University of North Carolina Press for the Institute of Early American History and Culture at Williamsburg, 1961), 38–40.

9. The quotation from the black Philadelphians appears in Ira Berlin, *Many Thousands Gone: The First Two Centuries of Slavery in North America* (Cambridge, Mass.: Harvard University Press, Belknap Press, 1998), 232. See also Joyce Appleby, *Inheriting the Revolution: The First Generation of Americans* (Cambridge, Mass.: Harvard University Press, Belknap Press, 2000); Ira Berlin and Ronald Hoffman, eds., *Slavery and Freedom in the Age of the American Revolution* (Charlottesville: University Press of Virginia and the U.S. Capitol Historical Society, 1983). Those efforts on the part of blacks seeking emancipation would be doubled during a post-Revolutionary period that chronicled a litany of exchanges relating to an emerging "Negro problem." Massive importations of Africans during the final years of the slave trade, influxes of Caribbean blacks brought by white masters after the Haitian Revolution, together with the rapid growth of indigenous black populations increased the sociopolitical presence and the sounds of blackness across the United States (even if their numbers in percentage terms actually declined). Race as a concept grew increasingly visible and audible as the social control of blacks shifted from southern households to the state and as slaves and free blacks alike became more common to the urban place throughout the Atlantic seaboard, where they worked in shops and factories. What we see developing are distinctive African-American cultures that in their racialization within a national concept become more unified and related. Moreover, the conspicuous economic and social presence of blackness within white urban domains helps to explain the clear articulation of an-

tagonistic supremacist responses, whether in the less confrontational proposals of African colonization or the vituperative rhetoric of a hostile polygenetic racism that claimed whites and blacks as separate species. As efforts to drive the cause of blacks in claiming a place in the larger body politic increased with the rise of African-American free economy and the abolitionist movement in the 1820s and 1830s, racial antagonisms swelled, focusing attention more squarely on America's contradictory foundation of race and nation.

10. Alan Hyde, *Bodies of Law* (Princeton, N.J.: Princeton University Press, 1997); David Brion Davis outlines the basic contradiction of slavery and modern concepts of the individual in *The Problem of Slavery in Western Culture* (Ithaca, N.Y.: Cornell University Press, 1966) and *The Problem of Slavery in the Age of Revolution, 1770–1823* (1975; reprint, New York: Oxford University Press, 1999). For an insightful analysis of the particular conflict between revolutionary ideals and slavery within the bounds of race, see MacLeod, *Slavery, Race, and the American Revolution.*

11. Montesqieu appears in David Brion Davis, *The Problem of Slavery in the Age of Revolution,* 302. MacLeod, *Slavery, Race and the American Revolution,* 5. The literary challenges to Revolutionary-era racism has inspired a subfield of critical analysis. Particularly noteworthy is Cathy N. Davidson's discussion of the picaresque, together with her more general efforts to complicate a uniform depiction of American literature in *Revolution and the Word: The Rise of the Novel in America* (New York: Oxford University Press, 1986). See also Jay Fliegelman, *Declaring Independence: Jefferson, Natural Language, and the Culture of Performance* (Stanford, Calif.: Stanford University Press, 1993); Emory Elliott, *Revolutionary Writers: Literature and Authority in the New Republic, 1725–1810* (New York: Oxford University Press, 1982); and David Simpson, *The Politics of American English, 1776–1850* (New York: Oxford University Press, 1986).

12. Etienne Balibar, "Racism as Universalism," in *Masses, Classes, Ideas: Studies on Politics and Philosophy before and after Marx* (New York: Routledge, 1994), 194–95. I am appreciative to Nikhil Singh for introducing me to this essay and for his thoughtful elaboration on its significance.

13. Marc Shell, "Babel in America; Or, The Politics of Language Diversity in the United States," *Critical Inquiry* 20 (autumn 1993): 103–27; Christopher Looby, *Voicing America: Language, Literary Form, and the Origins of the United States* (Chicago: University of Chicago Press, 1996), 22.

14. Looby, *Voicing America,* 23. In his characterization of a "mythic present," Looby is quoting Lynn Hunt.

15. Ibid., 14. When Looby does explore heterodoxy, he focuses exclusively on the Irish. In discussing Washington Irving's *Salmagundi* (1809), he offers no reflection on the choice of this Orientalist gesture beyond its comparative effect, despite Irving's racial references, including a band of blacks with tambourine, drums, fife, and trumpets.

16. Mary Louise Pratt, *Imperial Eyes: Travel Writing and Transculturation* (New York: Routledge, 1992), 6.

17. The banjo was an African prototype, as Dena J. Epstein has persuasively demonstrated, whereas the fiddle derived from British folk practices ("The Folk Banjo: A Documentary History," *Ethnomusicology* 19 [September 1975]: 347–71). For the 1690 reference, see Epstein, *Sinful Tunes and Spirituals: Black Folk Music to the Civil War* (Urbana: University of Illinois Press, 1977), 80. In this instance, a court record recounts a father seeking legal recourse against his daughter's friends, with whom she danced and partied until 11 a.m. into the next Sunday morning. Andrew Burnaby writes in a frequently cited comment, "Towards the close of an evening, when the company are pretty well tired with country dances, it is usual to dance jigs; a practice originally borrowed, I am informed, from the negroes." Less well known is his comment in a footnote, "The author has since had an opportunity of observing something similar in Italy. The trescone of the Tuscans is very like the jigs of the Virginians" (*Burnaby's Travels through North America: Reprinted from the Third Edition of 1798,* introduction and notes by Rufus Rockwell Wilson (1775; reprint, New York: A. Wessels Co., 1904), 57.

18. *The Journal of Nicholas Cresswell* (New York: Lincoln MacVeagh, Dial Press, 1924), 52–53. The entry is from Saturday, January 7, 1775. Cresswell also describes whites dancing "Negro jigs" in Nanemjoy, Maryland, and again farther south, near the Georgia/Florida border, with "plenty of toddy." See Epstein, *Sinful Tunes,* 121, 115. Burnaby observed of the Virginia white women: "They are immoderately fond of dancing, and indeed it is almost the only amusement they partake of." Continuing, he observes, "These dances are without method or regularity: a gentleman and lady stand up, and dance about" (*Burnaby's Travels,* 57). An extraction of this same description of the jig appears as [Paul Wein], *A Concise Historical Account of All the British Colonies in North America, Comprehending Their Rise, Progress, and Modern State* (London: Printed for J. Bew in Pater-Noster Row, 1775), 182–83; and as James Franklin, *A Modern View of the Thirteen United States of America* (London: Printed for David Walker, Bookseller, 1784), 74–75.

19. It is unclear if the "Congo minuet" and "jig" bore a relation to the "Congo-Dances" of Louisiana and Mississippi described in the 1820s. See Epstein, *Sinful Tunes,* 132–33. The "savage dance" is noted in Epstein, 115. For Randolph Jefferson, see Epstein, 122. In his letters and journals for the month of January 1774, moreover, Fithian writes, "Negroes collected themselves into the School-Room, & began to play the *Fiddle,* & dance—I was in Mr Randolphs Room;—I went among them, *Ben,* & *Harry* were of the company—*Harry* was dancing with his Coat off—I dispersed them however immediately" (*Journal and Letters of Philip Vickers Fithian, 1773–1774: A Plantation Tutor of the Old Dominion,* ed. Hunter Dickinson Farish,new ed. (Williamsburg, Va.: Colonial Williamsburg, Inc., 1957), 62. On the engagement of black and white children, see Mechal Sobel, *The World They Made Together: Black and White Values in Eighteenth-Century Virginia* (Princeton, N.J.: Princeton University Press, 1987), 138–39.

20. John Davis, *Travels of Four Years and a Half in the United States of America during 1798, 1799, 1800, 1801, and 1802* (London: T. Ostell et al., 1803; reprint, New York: Henry Holt & Co., 1909), 414. On taking off, see Epstein, *Sinful Tunes,* 82; on the "Negro ball," see Cresswell, *The Journal,* 19. Cresswell's journal entry is dated May 29, 1774.

21. [Wein], *A Concise Historical Account,* 183.The notation of "Pompey" appears in Epstein, *Sinful Tunes,* 122. Epstein speculates that the Negro jig and Irish/English jigs bore little resemblance since observers, all familiar with both traditions, never drew such a connection. But the choice of the term "jig" itself suggests a resemblance already, and the lack of comparison may just as easily indicate that differences were few. See Epstein, 122, 124.

22. Looby, *Voicing America,* 270.

23. Thomas Jefferson, *Notes on the State of Virginia,* ed. William Peden (1787; reprint, Chapel Hill: University of North Carolina Press and the Institute of Early American History and Culture at Williamsburg, Virginia, 1955), 140.

24. James Meacham, "A Journal and Travels of James Meacham. Part 1, May 19 to August 31, 1789." *Historical Papers,* ser. 9 (Durham, N.C.: Trinity College Historical Society and the North Carolina Conference Historical Society, 1912), 88.

25. For Asbury, see Epstein, *Sinful Tunes,* 106; Freeborn Garretson, *The Experience and Travels of Mr. Freeborn Garretson, Minister of the Methodist-Episcopal Church in North-America* (Philadelphia: Printed by Parry Hall, 1791), 72; Rankin's letter appears in the appendix of Devereux Jarratt, *A Brief Narrative of the Revival of Religion in Virginia: In a Letter to a Friend,* 3d ed. (London: J. Paramore, 1786), 32.

26. Garretson, *Experiences and Travels,* 69; Richard Allen, *Spiritual Song,* originally published as a broadside (Philadelphia: Richard Allen, c1800), reprinted in *Early Negro Writing, 1760–1837,* ed. Dorothy Porter (Boston: Beacon Press, 1971), 559–61.

27. Charlotte Haller discusses the hardening of racial categories as a consequence of the transition from colonial-era household governance to post-Revolutionary state controls in her dissertation "Taking Liberties: Households, Race, and Black Freedom in Revolutionary North Carolina" (Ph.D. diss., University of Wisconsin—Madison, 2000).

28. The Three-fifths Compromise, which was written into the Constitution, acknowledged 60 percent of the Negro population as contributing to the overall population of the United States. See John Hope Franklin, *From Slavery to Freedom,* 5th ed. (New York: Alfred A. Knopf, 1980), 94–95.

29. John Fanning Watson, *Methodist Error; Or, Friendly, Christian Advice, to Those Methodists, Who Indulge in Extravagant Emotions and Bodily Exercises* (Trenton, N.J.: D. and E. Fenton; Cincinnati: Looker, Reynolds & Co., 1819), 28–31. In his description of the shout, Watson writes: "With every word so sung, they have a sinking of one or the other leg of the body alternately, producing an audible sound of the feet at every step, and as manifest as the steps of actual negro dancing in Virginia &c." While the ring shout is commonly ascribed to Africa, it is noteworthy that the term itself may have been drawn from Christian rhetoric, as in Samuel Davies's "and how will they cause heaven to ring with shouts of joy and triumph!" (quoted in Sobel, *The World They Made Together,* 187). Watson was also a local historian and reported earlier on the "field frolics" and holidays of slaves, including the New York "Pinxter." See, e.g., his appendix ("Manners and Customs") to *Annals of Philadelphia, Being a Collection of Memoirs, Anecdotes, and Incidents* . . . (Philadelphia: E. L. Corey & A. Hart, 1830), 37, and *Annals*

and Occurrences of New York City and State, in the Olden Time: Being a Collection of Memoirs, Anecdotes, and Incidents . . . (Philadelphia: Henry F. Anners, 1846), 204.

30. Introduced to Christianity in some numbers during the awakenings of the 1730s and 1740s, blacks began to join in Christian worship particularly once more accommodating forms of religious populism spread across western and southern regions around the time of the Revolution. By the early nineteenth century, these engagements had grown more conspicuous. Already among Methodists in eighteenth-century Virginia, "blacks and whites were together in virtually every new congregation" (Sobel, "The Awakening to the Spirit in Virginia," in *The World They Made Together,* 178–203, 207, quotation on 189). See also Albert J. Raboteau, *Slave Religion: The "Invisible Institution" and the Antebellum South* (New York: Oxford University Press, 1978); and Alan Gallay, "Planters and Slaves in the Great Awakening," in *Masters and Slaves in the House of the Lord: Race and Religion in the American South, 1740–1870,* ed. John B. Boles (Lexington: University Press of Kentucky, 1988), 19–36. The latter source focuses on South Carolina.

31. David W. Wills, "The Central Themes of American Religious History: Pluralism, Puritanism, and the Encounter of Black and White," in *African-American Religion: Interpretive Essays in History and Culture,* ed. Timothy E. Fulop and Albert J. Raboteau (New York: Routledge, 1997), 7–20.

32. On prohibitions of intimacy with blacks, see Christine Leigh Heyrman, *Southern Cross: The Beginning of the Bible Belt* (New York: Alfred A. Knopf, 1997), 46. Henry Bibb, *Narrative of the Life and Adventures of Henry Bibb, an American Slave, Written by Himself,* introduction by Lucius C. Matlack (New York: Published by the Author; 5 Spruce Street, 1849), 24–25. Nathan O. Hatch, *The Democratization of Christianity* (New Haven, Conn.: Yale University Press, 1989), 35. Randy J. Sparks argues similarly with regard to revivalism in Mississippi that "many evangelicals, especially ministers, showed a great deal of sympathy for the slaves and often opposed the institution" ("Religion in Amite County, Mississippi, 1800–1861," in *Masters and Slaves in the House of the Lord,* ed. Boles, 63). Moreover, Sobel shows that, in the eighteenth century, supernatural beliefs in charms and magical herbs extended across class lines, even influencing the practices of Anglican ministers, who "often ministered to the ill with all the old panoply of folk remedies" and engaged in what a contemporary observer called "idolatry, sorcery, charming, witchcrafts, [and] conjuring" (*The World They Made Together,* 16). For discussions of the arrangement of services (where segregated seating was typically enforced after 1800), see Hatch, *The Democratization of Christianity;* John B. Boles, *The Great Revival: Beginnings of the Bible Belt* (Lexington: University Press of Kentucky, 1972).

33. For background on the practices of blacks and their relation to whites, see Raboteau, *Slave Religion,* 61–62; Heyrman, *Southern Cross.*

34. For "demons," see Heyrman, *Southern Cross,* 46; for "chains" and "fettered," see Benjamin Abbott, *The Experience and Gospel Labours of the Rev. Benjamin Abbott: To Which Is Annexed, a Narrative of His Life and Death,* ed. John Ffirth (New York: B. Waugh

& T. Mason, 1832), 18–19; for "wilds" and "regions," see Joshua Bradley, A.M., ed., *Accounts of Religious Revivals in Many Parts of the United States from 1815 to 1818* (1819; reprint, Wheaton, Ill.: Richard Owen Roberts Publishers, 1988), 45.

35. Heyrman, *Southern Cross,* 64–65, 46. Later, she writes, "White clergymen touted black spirituality as a marvel for the same reason that they celebrated the virtuosity of white women and children: the conviction that their natural capacities were so limited that supernatural intervention alone could account for such piety and eloquence" (219). Associations of blackness and preachers were enduring, informing, e.g., a characterization of a white preacher in the image of a licentious, Frankenstein monster: "He looked like an ill-constructed machine, set in action by a movement so violent, as to threaten its own destruction" (Mrs. [Frances M.] Trollope, *Domestic Manners of the Americans* [New York: Dodd, Mead, and Co., 1832], 1:236).

36. For discussions of revivals among the slave narratives, see Bibb, *Narrative of the Life and Adventures;* James Watkins, *Struggles for Freedom; Or, The Life of James Watkins, Formerly a Slave in Maryland, U.S . . . ,* 19ᵗʰ ed. (1852; reprint, Manchester: Printed for James Watkins, 1860); and Harriet A. Jacobs, *Incidents in the Life of a Slave Girl, Written by Herself,* ed. L[ydia] Maria Child; reprint ed. Jean Fagan Yellin (1861; reprint, Cambridge, Mass.: Harvard University Press, 1987). For a white-authored narrative on slavery that contains a dialogue with the slave Peter, see Charles Edwards Lester, ed., *Chains and Freedom; Or, The Life and Adventures of Peter Wheeler, a Colored Man Yet Living: Three Volumes in One* (New York: E. S. Arnold & Co., 1839). For revivalism in letters and published memoirs, see, among others, Francis Lieber, ed., *Letters to a Gentleman in Germany, Written after a Trip from Philadelphia to Niagara* (Philadelphia: Carey, Lea & Blanchard, 1834; reprint, New York: Johnson Reprint, 1971), 303–29; Frederika Bremer, *Homes of the New World: Impressions of America,* trans. Mary Howitt, 2 vols. (New York: Harper & Brothers, 1853; reprint, New York: Negro Universities Press, 1968), 1:306–17, 1:392–94, 1:490–93, 2:157–60, 2:234–38; Emily P. Burke, *Reminiscences of Georgia* (Oberlin, Ohio: James M. Fitch, 1850), 92–94, 121–23, 148–50, 229–45; John R. Dix, *Transatlantic Tracings; Or, Sketches of Persons and Scenes in America* (London: W. Tweedie, Strand, 1853), 103–7, 233–36, 280–89, 296–99; Lorenzo Dow, *History of Cosmopolite; Or, The Four Volumes of Lorenzo's Journal Concentrated in One, Containing His Experience and Travels from Childhood to Near His Fiftieth Year,* 4th ed. (1814; reprint, Washington: Joshua Martin, 1848), 124–27, 131, 286, esp. 588–91. For journals, see "The Camp Meeting," *Liberator* 12 (October 28, 1842): 172; Reverend W. L. Ellsworth, "Reminiscences of a Camp-Meeting," *Ladies' Repository* 8 (November 1848): 341–48.

37. Mechal Sobel proposes, for the eighteenth century, a similarly widespread black/white cultural exchange that included religious syncretisms. Without directly discounting this, Butler would seem to disagree, given his claims of an African holocaust. See Mechal Sobel, *The World They Made Together;* Jon Butler, *Awash in a Sea of Faith: Christianizing the American People* (Cambridge, Mass.: Harvard University Press, 1990).

38. Heyrman, *Southern Cross,* 64–65. The cultural origins of evangelical ritual are

difficult to trace since both European and African religions similarly employed physical demonstration and bodily inhabitation. As Albert Raboteau, Mechal Sobel, and others have shown, the vigorous, exercised rituals of west African belief systems bear likenesses to the ecstatic rural practices of British and continental peasants, making it difficult, if not impossible, to draw conclusions about a chief dominant influence in North America. The reference by the Russian diplomat appears in Pavel Petrovich Svin'in, *Picturesque United States of America, 1811, 1812, 1813, Being a Memoir on Paul Svin'in, Russian Diplomatic Officer . . .*, ed. and trans. Avrahm Yarmolinsky (New York: W. E. Rudge, 1930), 20.

39. Arthur Singleton, Esq. [Henry Cogswell Knight], *Letters From the South and West* (Boston: Richardson & Lord, 1824), 127; Priscella Wakefield [Bell], *Excursions in North America: Described in Letters from a Gentleman and His Young Companion, to Their Friends in England* (London: Darton & Harvey, 1806), 9; H., "Letter to the Editor: Remarks during Journey through North America, 1820–1821," *Christian Observer* (New York) 22 (1822): 342–43, 556, 628.

40. "Seen and heard" refers to Frederick Douglass, *The Narrative of the Life of Frederick Douglass, an American Slave, Written by Himself,* ed. Benjamin Quarles (1845; reprint, Cambridge, Mass.: Harvard University Press, Belknap Press, 1960), 37 (see chap. 2). Walter Benjamin, "The Task of the Translator" (1923), in *Illuminations: Essays and Reflections,* ed. Hannah Arendt; trans. Harry Zohn (New York: Schocken Books, 1968), 76.

41. Nathan O. Hatch, e.g., elaborates on the role of black music in the development of revivalism but fails to acknowledge its full significance, limiting his discussions of black religion to two discrete chapter sections. As a result, he reinforces the impression that African-American worship was disconnected from the white public sphere (*Democratization of American Christianity,* 102–13, 154–58). Dickson D. Bruce, Jr., Paul Conkin, and John Boles similarly acknowledge racial crossing, and Boles presents, in an impressive edited collection, a variety of portraits of shared experience. Yet the sense of "race" infiltrating white bodies, so palpable in Watson's text, never comes into focus, above all because of the lack of attention given to the power of musical practices to incite transgression and to engender meaning. See Bruce, *And They All Sang Hallelujah: Plain-Folk Camp-Meeting Religion, 1800–1845* (Knoxville: University of Tennessee Press, 1974); Conkin, *Cane Ridge: America's Pentecost* (Madison: University of Wisconsin Press, 1990); Boles, ed., *Masters and Slaves in the House of the Lord.* Conkin writes, "In ways impossible to decipher from the evidence, blacks must have had some effect on southern Presbyterianism—at the very least on hymn singing and possibly on the range of physical exercises accepted at times of revival. . . . [A]t least from 1750 on southern Presbyterianism was biracial. In fact blacks almost always composed the largest non-Irish component of southern Presbyterian congregations" (39). Lawrence Levine does recognize these engagements in his seminal research from the 1970s, which was brought together as *Black Culture and Black Consciousness* (New York: Oxford University Press, 1977). Levine, however, was principally concerned with demonstrating the distinctiveness of "the slave world" as opposed to white ones.

42. Louis F. Benson, *The English Hymn: Its Development and Use in Worship* (1915; reprint, Richmond, Va.: John Knox Press, 1962), 276.

43. Henry Louis Gates, Jr., "The Trope of the Talking Book," in *The Signifying Monkey* (New York: Oxford University Press, 1988), 127–69. See also Rusticus [John Holt Rice], "The Pious African," *Literary and Evangelical Magazine* 10 (1827): 22–25.

44. Direct references to Negro performance appear in texts by William Henry Milburn, "The Negro," in *Ten Years of Preacher Life: Chapters from an Autobiography* (New York: Derby & Jackson, 1859), 337–52; Bradley, ed., *Accounts of Religious Revivals*, 260; and Abbott, *Experience and Gospel Labours*, 182–89. Abbott refers to "the devil's musicians, the fiddlers" on 49.

45. Bradley, ed., *Accounts of Religious Revivals*, 237, 128.

46. Milburn, *Ten Years of Preacher Life*, 121. On the training of his voice, Milburn writes: "There was work enough of all sorts to be done. The voice to be drilled to an easy obedience, and the development of all its tones. Large portions of the Bible and hymn-book must be committed to memory, for all my reading in public had to be done by rote" (93). He then describes how as a preacher one needed sometimes to be a chorister, and "I therefore armed myself with three tunes—a long, short, and common metre; and when there threatened to be a 'flash in the pan,' from the musical inability of my audience, I would fire away with one of these" (94). (Such warfare imagery was common to preachers' rhetoric.) Later, he recounts how he practiced and memorized hymns while on horseback. "This operation, repeated for hours together, week after week, will be likely to cultivate a man's powers of recollection, and furnish him with an ample store of sacred and lyrical language; when the mind wearied of this, new occupation was found in exploding the radical sounds of speech, or, 'barking' as college-boys call it. This was followed up by practising the articulation of the most difficult words in the language" (95).

47. Jarratt, *The Life of Reverend Devereux Jarratt: Rector of Bath Parish, Dinwiddie County, Virginia* (1806; reprint, New York: Arno Press, 1969), 7, 96.

48. Bradley, ed., *Accounts of Religious Revivals;* the phrases quoted in the text can be found as follows: "house to house," 219; testifying, 139; "daily crying," 149; "concert of prayer," 139; "three times," 42; "dish of chat" and "deaf ear," 216.

49. Ibid.; see, for phrases in the text, the following: "exhortations," 28; "rushing wind," 39, 151; "marvellous light," 39, 116; "showers of rain," 157; "thunder," 92; "house to house," 54.

50. Ibid., 58, 154.

51. Ibid.; for quoted words and phrases, see: "hearers," 84; "small voice," 175; "tongue," 30; "her liberated tongue," 178; "his tongue," 127; "the Lord," 154.

52. Ibid.: "begin to speak," 161; "conscience," 119; "the people," 90; "no place," 90. Of special note is an extended report from the town of Fair-Haven, which is so suffused with sonic imagery that its reading seems nearly audible. Here, the reporting minister describes the behavior of a convicted party who "spoke at considerable length," bringing the minds of listeners "wrought up to an high pitch." "Saying the Lord's prayer" with others, he and they are struck, prompting sinners to redeem themselves "by the repe-

tition of those sacred words." Later, when "he began to see clearly" his sinning ways, "he talked constantly, and often mentioned his abused privileges. . . . They went to conference that evening, and he took an early opportunity to address the assembly. He then talked as he never did before." At the point of his awakening, he suddenly witnesses "a flood of divine light . . . so sudden and unexpected, that he could not forbear crying out, though alone, *glory to God!*" (100–103, 110–16). A final example records the experience of another "sinner" who encounters an embodiment of Jesus, with whom he engages in conversation and spends the night. "When he awoke, the man was gone on his way, but what he had said remained fixed in his soul. *Ask and you shall receive a kingdom* rung in his ears." The report ends with a hymn (92–93), the intended effect perhaps being to make the pages themselves seem to rise up and sing:

> Your harps, ye trembling saints,
> Down from the willows take;
> Loud to the praise of Christ our Lord,
> Bid every string awake.

53. Ibid., 177, 52.

54. The hymn reads, "The people might truly say, on that occasion, Let all with thankful hearts confess / Thy welcome messengers of peace; / Thy power in their report be found / And let thy feet behind them sound" (ibid., 25–26).

55. Ibid., 207. Another example, this from Troy, New York, records the "effusions of the divine Spirit . . . spreading with the greatest rapidity . . . . as showers upon the grass." Here, too, spirit is not seen but implied, felt. Intangible, it takes discernible form in the audible reactions of youthful exuberance: "It was affecting to hear those little creatures speak of the vanity and folly of their lives—talk of the wonders of redeeming love—and singing *Hosanna to the Son of David.*" In the service of God, they, like the unseen spirit, lose material significance, their disembodied voices becoming "the favoured instruments in the hands of God," as "their exhortations and prayers" inspire "awakening" and "converting" (ibid., 170–73).

56. Heyrman, *Southern Cross,* 61. See also Jon Butler, *Awash in a Sea of Faith.* Also noteworthy yet published only after the drafting of this chapter is Mechal Sobel, *Teach Me Dreams: The Search for the Self in the Revolutionary Era* (Princeton, N.J.: Princeton University Press, 2001).

57. Abbott, *Experience and Gospel Labours,* 18, 7, 8, 18, 11, 14, and 12, respectively.

58. The text appears as app. 2-D in Charles A. Johnson, *The Frontier Camp Meeting: Religion's Harvest Time* (Dallas: Southern Methodist University Press, 1955), 260–61. In a few instances, writers made direct associations between race, religious demonry, and music. Many of these texts focus on the practice of fiddling and dancing at balls, which, as we have seen already, represented key sites of performative miscegenation. Joshua Bradley's reports (*Accounts of Religious Revivals*) include, e.g., references to "satanic balls" threatening "the danger of hell fire" (86) and "drunkards and lewd wretches . . . pounding [to] . . . the sound of the violin" (59). In *Experience and Gospel Labours,* Abbott speaks of "devil's musicians, the fiddlers" who instructed the drunken and wicked

(49). A southern Methodist, moreover, faced the evils of a tainted music as a result of a dream, after which he "ran out to a fence corner, and with one fierce blow broke the instrument to shivers" (Heyrman, *Southern Cross,* 62). Pavel Petrovich Svin'in's memoir, finally, contains a watercolor of a diabolical black fiddler performing for white dancers as a couple engages in sexual foreplay (*Picturesque United States of America,* pt. 2, sketch 12). Given the widespread presence of fiddles in antebellum America, it seems likely that they were commonly associated with Negroes regardless of who was performing them, in much the same way that the saxophone denotes black urban cosmopolitanism in twentieth-century contexts.

59. For a critical discussion of the meaning and accuracy of the concept of " great awakening," see Butler, *Awash in a Sea of Faith;* Conkin, *Cane Ridge,* 30–34. Butler dismisses the term while Conkin questions the notion of two historically discrete eruptions. Beyond a few noteworthy precedents in the 1790s—and against the background of evangelical events in New England and Great Britain during the 1740s—awakenings appeared rather suddenly around 1800. The 1801 meeting at Cane Ridge, Kentucky, which commonly identifies the commencement of the movement, drew upwards of five to ten thousand participants; one contemporary estimate listed the attendance at more than twenty thousand. Conkin speculates that about ten thousand could have been there at any one time; twenty thousand may represent the total attendance over the course of six days (*Cane Ridge,* 39, 87–88). For a list of camp meetings from 1800 to 1805, see Richard Huffman Hulan, "Camp-Meeting Spiritual Folksongs: Legacy of the Great Revival in the West" (Ph.D. diss., University of Texas at Austin, 1978), 73–80.

60. As Conkin puts it, "As far as one can tell, whites [at Cane Ridge] often treated blacks in a condescending way but not as less than spiritual equals" (*Cane Ridge,* 174–75). On interracialism, see Conkin, 67, 78. Discussions of racial relations at camp meetings appear sporadically in the primary literature. William Henry Foote, e.g., describes a meeting in North Carolina from 1802 in which blacks and whites participated openly (*Sketches of North Carolina, Historical and Biographical, Illustrative of the Principles of a Portion of Her Early Settlers* [New York: Robert Carter, 1846], 402–3). In *Across the Atlantic* (London: George Earle, 1851), by contrast, the English traveler John Delaware Lewis discusses how worshipers were racially segregated (197). Lieber's *Letters to a Gentleman in Germany,* finally, includes an account of blacks attending a meeting in Philadelphia who are similarly segregated from the main proceedings. "Their boisterous violence is greater in proportion to their greater ignorance," Lieber writes (327).

61. Richard McNemar, *The Kentucky Revival* (1807; reprint, New York: Edward O. Jenkins, 1846), 31. McNemar was a Methodist who converted to Presbyterianism, and then to Shakerism. See Hatch, *The Democratization of Christianity,* 13. On white plainfolk and black relations, see Morgan, *Slave Counterpoint,* 300–317. Conkin notes that at subsequent meetings in Carolina, blacks made up one-half of the crowd (*Cane Ridge,* 174). For "happy compounds," see Singleton [Knight], *Letters from the South and West,* 96–97.

62. Milburn, *Ten Years of Preacher Life,* 62. See also Bruce, *And They All Sang Hal-*

lelujah; Ellen Jane Lorenz, *Glory Hallelujah: The Story of the Camp Meeting Spiritual* (Nashville: Abingdon, 1980).

63. The quotation appears in Ellsworth, "Reminiscences of a Camp-Meeting," 341. For primary sources on black preaching, see, e.g., Fredrika Bremer, *America of the Fifties: Letters of Fredrika Bremer,* selected and ed. Adolph B. Benson (New York: American-Scandinavian Foundation, 1924), 114–23, 130–35, 149–51, 190–91, 261–81; Achille Murat, *America and the Americans,* trans. H. J. S. Bradfield (Buffalo: George H. Derby & Co., 1851), 85, 99 (the text includes a description of a camp meeting); and Frederick Law Olmsted, *A Journey in the Seaboard Slave States, with Remarks on Their Economy* (New York: Mason Brothers, 1859), 107, 408, 450–51.

64. Milburn, *Ten Years of Preacher Life,* 345–46. Attempting to coax his master to preach, a slave named Jake suggested that oratory was divine inspiration: "Don't be afeard; open you mout and de Lord'll fill it. 'Out of de mout of babes and suckling he's ordained praise' " (Milburn, 345).

65. John Lambert, *Travels through Canada, and the United States of North America, in the Years 1806, 1807, and 1808* (London: Cradock & W. Joy, 1814), 2:271–75. See also Mrs. Trollope, "Camp-Meeting," in *Domestic Manners of the Americans,* 1:232–45. Other references appear sporadically throughout the text.

66. McNemar, *The Kentucky Revival,* 31–32.

67. Benson, *The English Hymn;* Hulan, "Camp-Meeting Spiritual Folksongs."

68. John Dixon Long, *Pictures of Slavery in Church and State, including Personal Reminiscences, Biographical Sketches, Anecdotes, Etc., Etc.* (Philadelphia: The Author, 1857), 157–60, 383–84. Attributions of "emotionalism," in particular, fail to betray a distinctive African way of singing and worshiping. The earliest texts suggest that whites and blacks shared in these enthusiasms, as George Pullen Jackson and others have insisted. The revivalist events in southwest Scotland and Ulster in the seventeenth and eighteenth centuries, e.g., together with those in the American colonies from the 1720s, were said to be particularly demonstrative and boisterous. See Conkin, *Cane Ridge,* 3–4, 29–34. Despite its clear favoritism for white singing, John Lambert's reference to "the thundering anathemas of the [white] preacher" supports the contention of interracialism, tracing influence from white to black. "This catches their [the blacks'] attention, and in imitation of their more enlightened *white brethren,* they often fall down in *divine ecstasies,* crying, shouting, bawling and beating their breats [*sic*], until they are ready to faint" (Lambert, *Travels through Canada , and the United States,* 2:175). As Eugene Genovese sums it up, "if emotionalism alone had distinguished black religion . . . no great difference existed between the religion of slaves and that of the lower-class whites" (*Roll, Jordan, Roll,* 239).

69. Given the severe limitations of sources documenting the relationship between black and white singing, we can reach no firm conclusions about the exact nature of musical exchange or, more important for most previous writers, the dominance of one racial group over another. Even the most thorough examinations by Jackson, Tallmadge, Garst, Epstein, and Southern reach decidedly different conclusions simply be-

cause scholars must ultimately speculate on the viability of practices, the permanence of forms and procedures, and the extent of variation across a broad social and geographical territory. While it is reasonable to reach conclusions about performance traditions once they come into conspicuous use, it is entirely unreasonable to draw from a smattering of sources and notational documents anything more than the most tentative assumptions about the purported hierarchy of black/white innovation. In this respect, Garst's research exacerbates the confusion by giving undue privilege to the importance of tune melody in determining the direction of innovation and heritage. As George Herzog had already observed in a seminal discussion of the folkloric researches, "the fact that a spiritual melody, on paper and expressed in terms of analytical features, *looks* very European but does not *sound* so European when listened to, must be significant. There are features involved here with which our music writing and terminology are not accustomed to deal" ("Book Reviews: *Folk Culture on St. Helena Island, South Carolina,* by Guy B. Johnson and *White Spirituals in the Southern Uplands* by George Pullen Jackson," *Journal of American Folklore* 48 [1935]: 396). See William H. Tallmadge, "The Black in Jackson's White Spirituals," *Black Perspective in Music* 9 (1981): 139–60; John F. Garst, "Mutual Reinforcement and the Origins of Spirituals," *American Music* 4, no. 4 (winter 1986): 290–406; George Pullen Jackson, *White Spirituals in the Southern Uplands* (Chapel Hill: University of North Carolina Press, 1933), and *White and Negro Spirituals* (Locust Valley N.Y.: J. J. Augustin, 1943).

70. Conkin discusses the possible interracial basis of the "exercises" in *Cane Ridge,* 100–107. An early essay relevant to the associations between tribalism, sexual inhibition, and worship is Theodore Schroeder, "Revivals, Sex and Holy Ghost," *Journal of Abnormal and Social Psychology* 14, nos. 1–2 (April–June 1919): 34–47. Thanks go to Paul Boyer for introducing me to this article.

71. For background on the complexities of possession, see Raboteau, *Slave Religion.* See also Raboteau, *A Fire in the Bones* (Boston: Beacon, 1995).

72. Colonel Paterson to Reverend John King, September 25, 1801, in *Increase to Piety; Or, The Revival of Religion in the United States of America . . . ,* comp. William Wallis Woodward (Newburyport, Mass.: Angier March, 1802), 39–40, cited in Conkin, *Cane Ridge,* 93.

73. Benson, *The English Hymn,* 292. Benson continues, "Such ejaculatory hymns were frequently started by an excited auditor during the preaching, and taken up by the throng, until the meeting dissolved into a 'singing ecstasy.' Sometimes they were given forth by a preacher, who had a sense of rhythm, under the excitement of his preaching and the agitation of his audience. Hymns were also composed more deliberately out of meeting, and taught to the people or lined out from the pulpit" (292). See also Jackson, *White and Negro Spirituals,* 83 and the apps. titled "A Collection of Wandering Rhyme Pairs" and "A List of Favorite Revival Spiritual Choruses." See also Jackson, "Spiritual Songs Born in Camp-Meetings," in *White Spirituals in the Southern Uplands.*

74. Hortense J. Spillers, "Moving on Down the Line: Variations on the 'African-

American Sermon,'" in *The Bounds of Race: Perspectives on Hegemony and Resistance,*
ed. Dominick LaCapra (Ithaca, N.Y.: Cornell University Press, 1991), 45, 48.

75. Although there is evidence of women preachers, the large majority of references are to men. "Second sight" appears in Levine, *Black Culture and Black Consciousness,* 61.

76. Spillers, "Moving on Down the Line," 44.

77. Ibid., 56–57. Spillers elaborates: "We can either read 'community' as homogeneous memory and experience, laying claim to a collective voice and rendering an apparently unified and uniform Narrative, or we might think of it as a content whose time and meaning are 'discovered,' but a meaning, in any case, that has not already been decided" (48).

78. Benjamin, "The Task of the Translator," 73.

79. Bhabha, *The Location of Culture,* 226.

80. Dix, *Transatlantic Tracings,* 185, 189. A detailed description of a separate black meeting appears as chap. 15 (280–302).

81. The lion's share of modern religious folk song scholarship has been dedicated to the philologically based study of the music's evolution from its first appearance in the tune books. In this respect, it upholds as its ideal a general theory of stylistic progression. Accompanying such respectable scholarly aims, however, has been a parallel desire to specify racially the sources of invention, and this desire has consumed American musical research since the publication of the first compendium of slave songs, *Slave Songs of the United States* (ed. William Francis Allen, Charles Pickard Ware, and Lucy McKim Garrison [New York: A. Simpson, 1867]). While recent integrationist accounts by Lawrence Levine and Dena Epstein would seem to have put an end to such concerns, the debate lives on, largely in its transpositions to popular genres, notably the recent controversy about the contributions of whites to jazz. Despite the turn to other genres, however, this "Question of Origin," as Levine names it, repeatedly turns back to the spiritual song, which, for better or worse, represents the foundation of African-American folk musical practice. What would be later named the "spirituals" identifies in the popular imagination the center of a musical tradition that all Americans seek to claim, however constructed this center may actually be. From this vantage, the theories of white origin that oriented folk musical scholarship since the 1910s may be read as part of an enduring, if rather desperate, effort to preserve the racial purity of a national heritage that had been so obviously corrupted by the insurgencies of African-American music. Spiritual folk songs symbolized the very creation of black music as a concept and became the key cultural defense of a "Negro" expression in the writings of James Trotter, W. E. B. Du Bois, Alain Locke, Nathaniel Dett, and other African-American intellectuals. If antebellum spiritual song could be proved white in origin, it would go a long way toward protecting the mythos of an Anglo-Saxon racial supremacy in America. For background, see D. K. Wilgus, "The Negro-White Spiritual," in *Anglo-American Folksong Scholarship since 1898* (New Brunswick, N.J.: Rutgers University Press, 1959), 344–64, reprinted in *Mother Wit from the Laughing Barrel: Readings in*

the Interpretation of Afro-American Folklore, ed. Alan Dundes (Englewood Cliffs, N.J.: Prentice-Hall, 1973). See also William Westcott, "African-American," in *Ethnomusicology: Historical and Regional Studies,* Helen Myers, ed. (New York: W. W. Norton, 1993), 46–62; and Levine, *Black Culture and Black Consciousness,* chap. 1. The seminal work of Francis James Child and Thomas Wentworth Higginson never seriously considered the possibility of a black cultural influence on white culture, at least according to the cursory review of the Child and Higginson collections at Harvard that was conducted by three members of my seminar on the slave spirituals taught there in 1997. Thanks to Judah Cohen, Charles Starrett, and Blair McLaughlin for their efforts.

82. For example, A Northern Man [David Brown], *The Planter; Or, Thirteen Years in the South* (Philadelphia: H. Hooker, 1853), 84–85; William B. Smith, "The Persimmon Tree and the Beer Dance," *Farmer's Register* 6 (April 1838): 58–61; W. L. G. Smith, *Life at the South; Or, "Uncle Tom's Cabin As It Is": Being Narratives, Scenes, and Incidents in the Real "Life of the Lowly"* (Buffalo: Geo H. Derby & Co., 1852), 163.

83. Joel Chandler Harris's claim that antebellum blacks most typically employed fiddles and fifes rather than banjos became the source of a minor controversy in postbellum discussions of black culture. See Harris, "Plantation Music and the Banjo," *Critic* 3 (December 15, 1883): 505–6, and subsequent responses, as listed in the index of Eileen Southern and Josephine Wright, comps., *African-American Traditions in Song, Sermon, Tale, and Dance, 1600s–1920* (New York: Greenwood, 1990). Robert B. Winans discusses the distribution of instruments among slaves based on an accounting of Works Progress Administration documents. While the reliability of these documents is open to question, his findings coincide with Harris's claim ("Black Instrumental Music Traditions in the Ex-Slave Narratives," *Black Music Research Journal* 10, no. 1 [1990]: 43–53).

84. For "varied sounds," see Francis de La Porte Comte de Castelnau, "Comte de Castelnau in Middle Florida, 1837–38," trans. Arthur R. Seymour, *Florida Historical Quarterly* 26 (July 1947–April 1948): 316; for tin horns and trumpets, see Burke, *Reminiscences of Georgia,* 226; J. Alexander Patten, "Scenes in the Old Dominion. Number Two—a Tobacco Market," *New York Mercury* 21 (November 5, 1859): 8, reprinted in the chapter "Scenes from Lynchburg," in *Travels in the Old South, Selected from Periodicals of the Times,* ed. Eugene L. Schwaab in collaboration with Jacqueline Bull (Lexington: University Press of Kentucky, 1973), 2:537–38, 541. The quotation on patting appears in Long, *Pictures of Slavery in Church and State,* 18. In his story "The Old Plantation," James Hungerford describes how the patter beats time "with his hands alternately against each other and against his body" (in *The Old Plantation, and What I Gathered There in an Autumn Month* (New York: Harper & Brothers, 1859), 195. The reference to the stagecoach and fiddler appears in Mrs. [Anne Jackson] Mathews, *Memoirs of Charles Mathews, Comedian* (London: Richard Bentley, 1839), 3:384–85.

85. For whistling, see [Washington Irving], *A History of New York from the Beginning of the World to the End of the Dutch Dynasty . . .* (1809; reprint, New York: G. P. Putnam's Sons, 1880), 103–4; for improvising and creating songs, see [William Ellery] Channing,

"Facts Showing the Character of Slavery," *Liberator* 6, no. 25 (June 18, 1836): 99. Lewis W. Paine speaks of a range of vocal virtuosity in *Six Years in a Georgia Prison: Narrative of Lewis W. Paine* . . . (Boston: Bela Marsh, 1852), 181; Barbara Leigh Smith Bodichon, *An American Diary, 1857–8,* ed. Joseph W. Reed, Jr. (London: Routledge & Kegan Paul, 1972), 119; Watkins, *Struggles for Freedom,* 12. Watkins focuses mainly on actions performed to entertain whites, while alluding to sound making. For "monkeys without tails," see Reverend Baynard R. Hall, *Frank Freeman's Barber Shop: A Tale* (New York: Charles Scribner, 1852), 22; Olmsted, *A Journey in the Seaboard Slave States,* 394. The yodel itself represents an interesting point of debate relating to Africanisms. It shows up, e.g., in African-American contexts as it is also attributed to white country singers such as Jimmie Rodgers, together with the familiar Swiss practices. Charles Keil suggests that the falsetto to which yodeling relates has African roots and is "the very essence of masculine expression" (*Urban Blues* [Chicago: University of Chicago Press, 1966], 27).

86. William Tell Harris, *Remarks Made During a Tour through the United States of America, in the Years 1817, 1818, and 1819* (London: Sherwood, Neely, & Jones, 1821), 69; Lieutenant Francis Hall, *Travels in Canada and the United States in 1816 and 1817* (London: Printed for Longman, Hurst, Rees, Orme & Brown, 1818), 358–59.

87. Samuel Mordecai, *Richmond in By-Gone Days; Being Reminiscences of an Old Citizen* (Richmond, Va.: George M. West, 1856; reprint, New York: Arno Press, 1975), 296; "Miscellaneous Item," *Musical Gazette* (Boston) 1, no. 15 (July 6, 1846): 91. For additional descriptions of a slave lining out hymns to themselves, see James Dunwoody B. De Bow, "Plantation Life—Duties and Responsibilities," *De Bow's Review* 29 (November 1860): 357–68. See Charles Colcock Jones, *Suggestions on the Religious Instruction of the Negroes in the Southern States* . . . (Philadelphia: Presbyterian Board of Publication, 1847), 56.

88. "Visit to a Negro Cabin in Virginia," *Family Magazine* (New York) 3 (December 1835): 242; An American, "Slavery in the United States," *Knickerbocker* 10, no. 4 (October 1837): 324.

89. Long, *Pictures of Slavery in Church and State,* 26; [Mrs. Frances Harriet McDougall], *Shahmah in Pursuit of Freedom; Or, The Branded Hand,* trans. from the original Showiah and ed. by an American Citizen (New York: Thatcher & Hutchinson, 1858), 274.

90. Paine, *Six Years in a Georgia Prison,* 180–81; Rudolph Friedrich Kurz, *Journal of Rudolph Friedrich Kurz: An Account of His Experiences among Fur Traders and American Indians on the Mississippi and the Upper Missouri Rivers during the Years 1846 to 1852,* trans. Myrtis Jarrell, ed. J. N. B. Hewitt, Bureau of Ethnology Bulletin 115 (Washington, D.C.: Government Printing Office, 1937), 12; Mrs. Caroline Lee Hentz, *The Planter's Northern Bride,* introduction by Rhoda Coleman Ellison (Philadelphia: A. Hart, 1854; reprint, Chapel Hill: University of North Carolina Press, 1970), 409.

91. Lancelot Addison, "An Account of West Barbary" (1671), in John Pinkerton, *A General Collection of the Best and Most Interesting Voyages and Travels in All Parts of the World: Many of Which Are Now First Translated into English: Digested on a New Plan,* 17 vols. (London: Longman, Hurst, et al., 1807–14), 15:422.

92. George M. Fredrickson, "Uncle Tom and the Anglo-Saxon: Romantic Racialism in the North," in *The Black Image in the White Mind: The Debate on Afro-American Character and Destiny, 1817–1914* (1971; reprint, Middletown, Conn.: Wesleyan University Press, 1987), 97–129; Joseph Boskin, *Sambo: The Rise and Demise of an American Jester* (New York: Oxford University Press, 1986). For "vernacular slave" as "home-born," see under "vernacular" in *The Compact Edition of the Oxford English Dictionary* (Oxford, Clarendon Press, 1971).

93. For "their voices are rich," see Mrs. Felton, *American Life: A Narrative of Two Years' City and Country Residence in the United States* (1838; reprint, London: Simpkin, Marshall & Co., 1842), 59; for "some of the most harmonious sounds," see Mrs. [Matilda Charolotte J. Fraser] Houstoun, *Hesperos; Or, Travels in the West* (London: John W. Parker, 1850), 2:157; for "they got better lungs," see [Frederick Olmsted], "A Mississippi Home," *National Anti-Slavery Standard* 21, no. 1052 (August 4, 1860): 1.

94. Frances Wright [D'Arusmont], *Views of Society and Manners in America; In a Series of Short Letters from that Country to a Friend in England* (1820; Cambridge, Mass.: reprint, Harvard University Press, Belknap Press, 1963), 44; "Scenes in North Carolina," *Liberator* 7, no. 22 (May 26, 1837): n.p.; Caroline Howard Gilman, "The Country Visit: Chapter X, Singing Hymns," *Rose Bud, or Youth's Gazette* (Charleston, S.C.) 2 (August 9, 1834): 199. For "intense instinct," see George G. Foster, "Philadelphia in Slices, Slice IX: The Colored Population," *New York Tribune* (December 29, 1848), reprinted in *Pennsylvania Magazine of History and Biography* 93, no. 1 (January 1969): 63.

95. Eric Lott, *Love and Theft: Blackface Minstrelsy and the American Working Class* (New York: Oxford University Press, 1993). On blackface, class, and the formation of the concept of "whiteness," see David R. Roediger's seminal study *Wages of Whiteness: Race and the Making of the American Working Class* (New York: Verso, 1991). Aaron, *The Light and Truth of Slavery, Aaron's History* (1827; Springfield, Mass.: n. p., 1845), 12.

96. Henry Bibb, "The Plantation Song," *National Anti-Slavery Standard* 5, no. 10 (August 8, 1844): 40; [William Wells Brown], *Narrative of William W. Brown, an American Slave* (London: Charles Gilpin, 1849), 51. References to music making in the slave coffles are extensive. See Southern and Wright, comps., *African-American Traditions in Song, Sermon, Tale, and Dance,* source numbers 76, 79, 92, 102, 139, 229, 374, and 434 (all describing fiddling); numbers 410, 417, 443, and 483 (singing). Walter Johnson conjectures that while slaves were made to sing happily in coffles, the real meanings of their songs were more likely consistent with acts of resistance. While Johnson risks reducing the nebulous experience of music to a particular meaning, his assertion seems generally sound (*Soul by Soul: Life Inside the Antebellum Slave Market* [Cambridge, Mass.: Harvard University Press, 1999], 67–70). Zora Neale Hurston, "Spirituals and Neo-Spirituals," in *The Sanctified Church,* foreword by Toni Cade Bambara (New York: Marlowe & Co., 1997), 79.

97. Paine, *Six Years in a Georgia Prison,* 184; Mordecai, *Richmond in By-Gone Days,* 296; J[ohn] P[endleton] Kennedy, *Swallow Barn; Or, A Southern Sojourn in the Old Dominion,* rev. ed. (1832; reprint, New York: George P. Putnam, 1851), 454–55.

98. Foster, "Philadelphia in Slices, Slice IX," 64; Bremer, *America of the Fifties,* 132;

Solomon Northrup, *Twelve Years a Slave: Narrative of Solomon Northrup, Citizen of New-York, Kidnapped in Washington City in 1841, and Rescued in 1853* (1853; New York and Auburn: Miller, Orton and Mulligan, 1855), 216. Northrup goes on to claim that he was the best among the group.

99. Lott, *Love and Theft;* Whitman Mead, *Travels in North America: In Three Parts* (New York: Printed by C. S. Van Winkle, 1820), 31; Bremer, *America in the Fifties,* 147, 190.

100. Dix, *Transatlantic Tracings,* 287.

101. "Letter from a Teacher at the South," *Dwight's Journal of Music* 2, no. 21 (February 26, 1853): 164.

102. Antislavery texts such as Douglass's recorded these incidents and the devices of torture, sometimes graphically. A notable control of the voice of preachers was the iron gag, used against those who refused to refrain from nightly recitations. See the section "Rethinking the Circle" in chap. 2 for a discussion of eighteenth-century treatment of slaves.

103. E. S. Abdy, *Journal of a Residence and Tour in the United States of North America from April 1833, to October 1834* (London: John Murray, 1835), 3:103. In this context, it is noteworthy to recall the references to black vocal power appearing since the seventeenth century. In antebellum writing, Frederick Olmsted refers to the interruption of religious services in North Carolina, during which the black preachers were publicly whipped for their words (*Journey in the Seaboard Slave States,* 408). Arthur Singleton's [Knight's] comments summarize the situation: "Although, south and west, men boast of being most democratic, yet what is more contradictory to their principles, than their tyranny over three fifths of their population? I saw one slave corded up to a tree, with his hands above his head, for wagging an evil tongue at a white man, and stripped, and knouted with a raw-hide thong, until his back was carbonadoed into ridges, and crimson. If two slaves are found quarrelling, it is customary to tie their left wrists together, and order them to lash each other, until one asks of the other pardon" (*Letters from the South and West,* 101).

104. Paine, e.g., in describing the wrestling, jumping, and foot-race competitions, notes that "black and white all take part in the sport, and he who comes off victorious has an extra sip of the 'white eye' " (*Six Years in a Georgia Prison,* 179).

105. Olmsted, *A Journey in the Seaboard Slave States,* 552; J. K. Paulding, *Slavery in the United States* (New York: Harper & Brothers, 1836), 68. Paulding dismissed slave skills of dancing and music as "one, . . . the favourite accomplishment of weak and frivolous minds, the other, the divinity of worn-out nations" (68).

106. Long, *Pictures of Slavery in Church and State,* 196; Alex Mackay, *The Western World; Or, Travels in the United States in 1846–1847; Exhibiting Them in Their Latest Development, Social, Political, and Industrial* (London: Richard Bentley, 1849), 2:133. Etymologically, "play" draws many associations with distrust and indirection. For example, it refers to treating another lightheartedly, revealing a wicked sentiment. If "playing along" suggests obeisance, "make a play for" expresses self-centered purposeful acquisition, typically in the act of sexual or financial competition. (For the

eighteenth-century Virginia planter William Byrd, "to play the fool" meant to have sexual relations with a slave.) Play also implies an instability or unpredictability frequently associated with deviousness. The play in a chain that undermines mechanical function is a cognate of the play in acting (a kind of dishonesty, pretending) as it is of the flitting and darting of unpredictable "playful" movement and of the punning gesture: "play on words." That play also commonly refers to musical performance—to play an instrument or phonograph recording, "to produce sound"—reflects, finally, the close historical relation between music and the unscrupulous, the magical, the unknown.

107. As employed here, "play" evolves from the professed "double meanings" associated with famous slave songs such as "Steal Away," and "the repeated singing of 'O Canaan, Sweet Canaan,' " which, as Frederick Douglass famously explained, had "something more than a hope of reaching heaven. We meant to reach the *north*—and north was our Canaan." By the 1920s, doubleness had been figured more abstractly as a performative strategy with similar political purpose, informing the work of Harlem Renaissance critics such as Joel Rogers, Alain Locke, Langston Hughes, and Zora Neale Hurston. "This indirect mode of expression, it is well known, is one of the characteristic earmarks," the composer Nathaniel Dett observed, "by which the art of the East is distinguished from that of the West. . . . It is characteristic of Negro music, often hiding, mask-like, its fundamental mood and not a little of its real meaning" (*Religious Folk-Songs of the Negro, as Sung at Hampton Institute,* ed. Nathaniel Dett [Hampton, Va.: Hampton Institute Press, 1927; reprint, New York: AMS Press, 1972], xiii–xiv). Since then, writers have cast the word "play" according to the rhetoric of Africanist interpretation, situating the concept within Old World traditions of punning and mockery. Roger Abrahams's research on "playing the dozens" set the framework for post–World War II scholastic interpretations of the qualities of indirection attributed to African-American expressive culture. Henry Louis Gates's widely acclaimed theory of signifying, which postulates an intercontinental legacy of rhetorical mockery and gamesmanship, reflects the tenacity of such notions of instability informing projections of black performative sensibility. On Douglass, see John Lovell, Jr., *Black Song: The Forge and the Flame* (New York: MacMillan, 1972), 494. For a mapping of the history of this usage, see Dett, ed., *Religious Folk-Songs,* xiii–xiv; Roger D. Abrahams, *Singing the Master: The Emergence of African American Culture in the Plantation South,* 1st ed. (New York: Pantheon Books, 1992), 187–88n. See also Charles W. Joyner, *Down by the Riverside: A South Carolina Slave Community* (Urbana: University of Illinois Press, 1984); and Levine's discussion of African insults in chap. 1 of *Black Culture and Black Consciousness.* An important collection dealing with modern phenomena of vocal indirection is Thomas Kochman, ed., *Rappin' and Stylin' Out: Communication in Urban Black America* (Urbana: University of Illinois Press, 1972).

108. On the tossing out of coins, see Edmund Kirke [James Robert Gilmore], *Among the Pines; Or, South in Secession-Time* (New York: J. R. Gilmore & Charles T. Evans, 1862), 146; on handing out of whiskey, see Robert Criswell, *"Uncle Tom's Cabin" Contrasted with Buckingham Hall, the Planter's Home, Or, A Fair View of Both Sides of the Slavery*

Question (New York: D. Fanshaw, 1852; reprint, New York: AMS Press, 1973), 66–67. Harriet A. Jacobs also notes the slave practice of critiquing whites in her book *Incidents in the Life of a Slave Girl,* 119; on the planter's good name, see Thomas C. Thornton, *An Inquiry into the History of Slavery . . .* (Washington, D.C.: William M. Morrison, 1841), 119.

109. Burke, *Reminiscences of Georgia,* 121–22. J. F. H. Claiborne's essay describes a black fiddler who is trapped in a house by wolves and whose playing incites them. While clearly a tall tale, the story nonetheless reinforces the sense of black music's power and presence in white society ("A Trip through the Piney Woods," *Free Trader and Daily Gazette* [December 29, 1841], reprinted in *Publications of the Mississippi Historical Society* 9 [1906]: 535–38).

110. Paine, *Six Years in a Georgia Prison,* 179–80.

111. "Miscellaneous Item," 91; James Hungerford, *The Old Plantation, and What I Gathered There,* 185. Hungerford was a Maryland lawyer, civil engineer, and editor of the *Southern Home Journal.*

112. On being "enslaved" by infatuation and desire, see Criswell, *"Uncle Tom's Cabin" Contrasted with Buckingham Hall,* 122; the quote beginning "We wi'ite folk" can be found in Kirke, *Among the Pines,* 146. See "Indian Convert (or Nashville)," *The Southern Harmony* (1835), comp. William Walker; ed. Glenn C. Wilcox (1854; reprint, Los Angeles: Pro Musicamericana , 1966), 133.

113. On sport, see Paine, *Six Years in a Georgia Prison,* 179; on eating from the same kettle, see Olmsted, *A Journey in the Seaboard Slave States,* 357. J. Thornton Randolph [Charles Jacobs Peterson], *The Cabin and Parlour; Or, Slaves and Masters* (Philadelphia: T. B. Peterson, 1852), 10. On complexion, see Singleton [Knight], *Letters from the South and West,* 101. That same power, of course, compelled others to keep a safe distance. Riding a train in the north, William Henry Milburn observed how white passengers were "avoiding contact with [a black man] as if his presence brought loathsome contagion" (*Ten Years of Preacher Life,* 351).

114. Bhabha, *Location of Culture,* 213.

115. Steven Feld writes about the Kaluli: "The music of nature is heard as the nature of music" ("A Poetics of Place: Ecological and Aesthetic Co-evolution in a Papua New Guinea Rainforest Community," in *Redefining Nature,* ed. Roy Ellen and Katsuyoshi Fukui [London: Berg, 1996], 62). While doubleness often affirms a sense of duality between master positions and subversive others, I am employing it here not only literally—to refer to the musical form from which singing derives from call and response—but figuratively, to stress the mimetic correspondence between slaves and whites. Mimesis grows from the relation of black to white, not as a racial purity or simple "blackness" projected in response of one to the other.

116. Such acknowledgment, however, was qualified, suggesting that call and response as a form of "drama in song" appealed to "children and [the] child-like." Jackson continued, "It is quite understandable that the negroes, where they were unspoiled, uncitified, adopted songs with this dramatic turn." Claiming that John Work's theory of call and response as "unquestionably African in origin" was erroneous, he matter-

of-factly insists without elaboration that Phillips Barry had "completely disproved its African provenience" (*White and Negro Spirituals, Their Life Span and Kinship* [New York: J. J. Augustin, 1943; reprint, New York: Da Capo, 1975], 262–63, 263n).

117. For those acknowledging African-American influence, see Frank T. Bullen and W. F. Arnold, *Songs of Sea Labour* (London: Orpheus Music Publishing Co., 1914), vii–xi; William Main Doerflinger, *Shantymen and Shantyboys: Songs of the Sailor and Lumbermen* (New York: MacMillan, 1951), xii; Stan Hugill, comp., *Shanties from the Seven Seas* (London: Routledge and New York: E. P. Dutton, 1961), xiv, 10–11; and Maud Karpeles, *An Introduction to English Folk Song* (London: Oxford University Press, 1973), 63. Iolo A. Williams discusses the dissenting views of Cecil Sharp and Cicely Fox-Smith in *English Folk-Song and Dance* (London: Longmans, Green, & Co., 1935), 131. For a reference to call and response among sailors in Palestine in 1493, see Hugill, comp., *Shanties from the Seven Seas*, 3. A. L. Lloyd cites a passage in *Daphnis and Chloe* that refers to call-and-response techniques employed by sailors (*Folk Song in England* [London: Lawrence & Wishart, 1967], 287–88). Robert Stevenson notes a call-and-response practice among early sixteenth-century Mayan Indians in "Written Sources for Indian Music until 1882," *Ethnomusicology* 17, no. 1 (1973): 1.

118. Erich von Hornbostel, "African Negro Music," *Africa* 1 (1928): 30–62.

119. Garst, "Mutual Reinforcements and the Origins of Spirituals." Edward Lee discusses a medieval dance that involved a leader and chorus (*Music of the People: A Study of Popular Music in Great Britain* [London: Barrie & Jenkins, 1970], 12–16). That "verse" took only as long as three dance steps and the brevity of some of the texts supplied suggests something along the lines of African-American call-and-response patterns.

120. Examples of call and response on ethnographic recordings beyond Africa include, from Makvaneti, Georgia, "Elessa (work-song)," track 1 of *Chants des Bords de la Mer Noire: Songs from the Shores of the Black Sea,* Le Chant du Monde LDX 274980, 1994; from eastern Georgia, "Farm Work Song," side A, band 4 of *Collection universelle de musique populaire enregistrée,* disk 2, *Asie & Esquimaux,* Notes by Constantin Brailoiu, Recorded by Ernst Emshimer, VDE-Gallo 30-426, ca. 1984; "Duet of Children" (Yemenite Jews), on *Lullabies and Children's Songs,* Unesco Collection 8102, 1972/1996. I thank Patrick Burke for supplying multiple phonographic examples and a detailed summary of the scholarly debate on call and response and Bruno Nettl and Philip V. Bohlman for broader historiographic background. The transcription was taken from an excerpted reproduction of John Barrow's *Travels in China* (1806), reprinted in *Time, Place and Music: An Anthology of Ethnomusicological Observation, c. 1550 to 1800,* ed. Frank Harrison (Amsterdam: Frits Knuf, 1973), 192–94. Barrow was a member of Lord Georg Macartney's embassy, representing the King of England in 1793–94 (Harrison, ed., 167).

121. John Miller Chernoff, *African Rhythm and African Sensibility* (Chicago: University of Chicago Press, 1979), 55. Discussions of Sloan and Baptiste appear subsequently in Roger D. Abrahams and John F. Szwed, ed., *After Africa: Extracts from British Travel Accounts and Journals of the Seventeenth, Eighteenth, and Nineteenth Centuries concerning*

the Slaves, Their Manners, and Customs in the British West Indies (New Haven, Conn.: Yale University Press, 1983); and in Richard Cullen Rath, "African Music in Seventeenth-Century Jamaica: Cultural Transit and Transition," *William and Mary Quarterly,* 3d ser., 50, no. 4 (October 1993): 700–726. For Du Tertre and Beckford, see Epstein, *Sinful Tunes,* 71. A gallery of musical examples appears after 363 in the chapter "Music" in T. Edward Bowdich, *Mission from Cape Coast Castle to Ashantee* (London: J. Murray, 1819).

122. Charles Hamm, *Music in the New World* (New York: W. W. Norton, 1983), 273; David Warren Steel, "Lazarus J. Jones and *The Southern Minstrel* (1849)," *American Music* 6, no. 2 (summer 1988): 125. Steel's essay includes a list of tune books published by southerners, 1816–60. Of these practices, Garst suggests, "one must assume that responsorial singing [in particular] was eliminated by arrangers who considered it inappropriate for singing schools" ("Mutual Reinforcement and the Origins of Spirituals," 391).

123. Mrs. Henry R. [Mary Howard] Schoolcraft, *The Black Gauntlet: A Tale of Plantation Life in South Carolina* (Philadelphia: J. B. Lippincott & Co., 1860), 165.

124. [Samuel Allen], "Sketches of the West," *American Agriculturalist* 2 (1843), 3 (1844), reprinted in the chapter "Sketches of Kentucky," in *Travels in the Old South,* ed. Schwaab, 291; Long, *Pictures of Slavery in Church and State,* 198. The reference to lining out appears in "Miscellaneous Item," 91.

125. For whites engaging in call and response at a corn shucking, see M. A. Malsby, "A Prayer-Meeting at a Corn Shucking," *Southern Christian Advocate* 23 (January 19, 1860): 9. The reference to the rower, while appearing in a novel, most likely derives from actual experience. See Hungerford, *The Old Plantation,* 190. Similar engagements of white singers among slaves are described in Criswell, *"Uncle Tom's Cabin" Contrasted with Buckingham Hall,* 122; and in Hentz, *The Planter's Northern Bride,* 199.

126. Charles Lanman, *Haw-Ho-Noo; Or, Records of a Tourist* (Philadelphia: Lippincott, Grambo & Co., 1850), 142–43; "Visit to a Negro Cabin in Virginia," 244. The latter text includes an excerpt of lyrics.

127. Reverend Baynard R. Hall, *Frank Freeman's Barber Shop: A Tale* (New York: Charles Scribner, 1852), 19.

128. For references to inducing the sharing of alcohol, see Charles Lanman, *Adventures in the Wilds of the United States and British American Provinces* (Philadelphia: John W. Moore, 1856), 2:149; Criswell, *"Uncle Tom's Cabin" Contrasted with Buckingham Hall,* 66–67, 114. For the critique, see Jacobs, *Incidents in the Life of a Slave Girl,* 118–119.

Chapter 4

1. James Weldon Johnson, ed.; musical arrangements by J. Rosamond Johnson; additional numbers by Lawrence Brown, *The Book of American Negro Spirituals* (New York: Viking, 1925). J. R. Johnson produced thirty arrangements, Brown five. A second volume, also from Viking, *The Second Book of Negro Spirituals,* appeared in 1926. Arrangers of individual titles are not specified. An unabridged republication of the original editions appeared as a single volume in 1969 by Viking and again, by Da Capo, as

*The Books of American Negro Spirituals: Including "The Book of American Negro Spiritu-
als" and "The Second Book of Negro Spirituals"* (n.d.). All citations are to the Da Capo
edition; the poem appears on 11–12. Only after completing this chapter did I discover
Brent Edwards's magisterial essay, "The Seemingly Eclipsed Window of Form: James
Weldon Johnson's Prefaces," in *The Jazz Cadence of American Culture,* ed. Robert G.
O'Meally (New York: Columbia University Press, 1998), 580–601.

2. Johnson and Johnson, *The Books of American Negro Spirituals,* 12.

3. As Henry Edward Krehbiel put it succinctly, "[Negro] folk songs are not made;
they grew" ("Folk Music in America," *Music Review* [Chicago] [September 2, 1893]:
603–8). Thanks to Wayne Marshall for bringing this source to my attention.

4. Johnson and Johnson, *The Books of American Negro Spirituals,* 13, 21.

5. Ibid., 30.

6. That Johnson would propose the ring shout as the primal place of this authenticity, otherwise discredited for its "uncivilized" character, suggests an additional layer of
dialectical invention: the shout's supplementarity—simultaneously essential in its
"primitive dignity" and yet outside of civility as such—provides the order of a new
hermeneutic circle or "ring," a second nature as the American musical sublime. Completion, whether in the creation of a black civility within the circumstances of America
or in the efforts of whites to access black nature would prove continually elusive as a
consequence of the ideologies of difference. Racial access remained necessarily partial
as the processes of mimetic interaction were ongoing and continuous.

7. W J. T. Mitchell, *Iconology: Image, Text, Ideology* (Chicago: University of Chicago
Press, 1986), 39. Earlier, Mitchell elaborates on the seen and unseen of the image in relation to consciousness: "The world may not depend upon consciousness, but images
in (not to mention *of*) the world clearly do. And this is not just because it takes human
hands to make a picture. . . . It is because an image cannot be seen *as such* without a
paradoxical trick of consciousness, an ability to see something as 'there' and 'not
there' at the same time" (17).

8. Ibid., 39; Johnson and Johnson, *The Books of American Negro Spirituals,* 30. Johnson writes: "In the arrangements, Mr. Rosamond Johnson and Mr. Brown have been
true not only to the best traditions of the melodies but also to form. No changes have
been made in the form of songs. The only development has been in harmonizations,
and these harmonizations have been kept true in character. And so an old-time Negro
singer could sing any of the songs through without encountering any innovations that
would interrupt him or throw him off. They have not been cut up or 'opera-ated' upon.
The arrangers have endeavored above all else to retain their primitive 'swing' " (50).

9. As we have seen, African-American music making appeared in the North from the
seventeenth century, but the word "music" was applied to such practices only tentatively, even as the notion of black musicality endured. A nineteenth-century version of
this paradox appears in an early review of *Slave Songs of the United States,* ed. William
Francis Allen, Charles Pickard Ware, and Lucy McKim Garrison (New York: A. Simpson,
1867), a text to be discussed later in this chapter. Writing in *Lippincott's,* an anonymous

reviewer commented: "It has been a common idea for many years, accepted without examination or proof, that the negro was essentially musical in nature. . . . [Yet] while the negro possesses a capacity for acquiring a certain degree of musical knowledge which he gets from his organ of imitativeness, he has in his *native* state (to which only we must look in examining the question) no idea whatever of music, so far as melody or harmony is an essential ingredient of such a quality" ("Literature of the Day," review of *Slave Songs of the United States,* ed. Allen, Ware, and Garrison, *Lippincott's Magazine* 1 [March 1868]: 341–43).

10. References regarding song are from Mary Boykin Chesnut, quoted in Dena J. Epstein, *Sinful Tunes and Spirituals: Black Folk Music to the Civil War* (Urbana: University of Illinois Press, 1977), 225. C. W. D., "Contraband Singing," *Dwight's Journal of Music* (September 7, 1861), 182. See also Mary Boykin Chesnut, *Mary Chesnut's Civil War,* ed. C. Vann Woodward (New Haven, Conn.: Yale University Press, 1981), 214; all subsequent quotations from Chesnut's diary can be found on 214. See also William B. Smith, "The Persimmon Tree and the Beer Dance," *Farmer's Register* 6 (April 1838): 58–61, reprinted in *The Negro and His Folklore in Nineteenth-Century Periodicals,* ed. Bruce Jackson (Austin: University of Texas Press, 1967), 3–9. Y. S. Nathanson conflates the slave songs and minstrelsy to form a "golden age of negro literature," of "Zip Coon" and "Long-Tailed Blue" ("Negro Minstrelsy, Ancient and Modern," *Putnam's Monthly* 5 [January 1855]: 72–79, reprinted in *The Negro and His Folklore,* ed. Jackson, 38).

11. Reverend James Miller McKim calls attention to the sorrowfulness of the songs in "Negro Songs," *Dwight's Journal of Music* (August 9, 1862), 148–49, reprinted in *The Negro and His Folklore,* ed. Jackson, 57–60. While McKim had visited the South, his interpretation may have developed directly from a reading of Frederick Douglass, *The Narrative of the Life of Frederick Douglass, an American Slave, Written by Himself,* ed. Benjamin Quarles (1845; reprint, Cambridge, Mass.: Harvard Univerity Press, Belknap Press, 1960).

12. See John L. Thomas, "Romantic Reform in America, 1815–1865," *American Quarterly* 17 (winter 1965): 656–81; Richard J. Carwardine, *Evangelicals and Politics in Antebellum America* (New Haven, Conn.: Yale University Press, 1993); and William E. Gienapp, "Abolitionism and the Nature of Antebellum Reform," in *Courage and Conscience: Black and White Abolitionists in Boston,* ed. Donald M. Jacobs (Bloomington: Indiana University Press, 1993), 21–46. Emerson's quotation appears in Jay B. Hubbell, *The South in American Literature* (Durham, N.C.: Duke University Press, 1954), 187.

13. Stanley Cavell, "Emerson, Coleridge, Kant," in *Post-Analytical Philosophy,* ed. John Rajchman and Cornel West (New York: Columbia University Press, 1985), 84. See also James T. Kloppenberg, "Beyond Kant: Religion and Science in Nineteenth-Century Thought," in *Uncertain Victory: Social Democracy and Progressivism in European and American Thought, 1870–1920* (New York: Oxford University Press, 1986), 15–26.

14. Michel Foucault, *The Archeology of Knowledge,* trans. A. M. Sheridan Smith (New York: Pantheon Books, 1972), 25. My perspectives on the construction of authenticity in early folkloristics have benefited greatly from conversations with Regina Bendix and

a reading of her comparative study of German and American conceptions of the folk, *In Search for Authenticity: The Formation of Folklore Studies* (Madison: University of Wisconsin Press, 1997). Mark C. Taylor, "Introduction: System . . . Structure . . . Difference . . . Other" and "Critique of Judgment" (excerpting Kant's treatment of the sublime from *Critique of Judgment*), in *Deconstruction in Context: Literature and Philosophy* (Chicago: University of Chicago Press, 1986), 1–34 and 35–66, respectively.

15. Definitions of "aesthetics" begin to appear in publications from the late eighteenth century. See Peter le Huray and James Day, introduction to *Music and Aesthetics in the Eighteenth and Nineteenth Centuries,* ed. le Huray and Day (Cambridge: Cambridge University Press, 1981), 1. For Schlegel, poetry was a deeply human energy and the defining expression of culture. It best expressed intuition, a faculty deemed higher than intellect. Schelling, moreover, argued that man could recover through art an original, natural unity. See Friedrich von Schelling, *Ideen zu einer Philosophie der Natur* (Leipzig, 1797), reprinted as *Ideas for a Philosophy of Nature as an Introduction to the Study of This Science,* trans. Errol E. Harris and Peter Heath (Cambridge: Cambridge University Press, 1988); William K. Wimsatt and Cleanth Brooks, *Literary Criticism: A Short History* (1957; reprint, Chicago: University of Chicago Press, 1978), cited in Henry Louis Gates, Jr., *Figures in Black: Words, Signs, and the "Racial" Self* (New York: Oxford University Press, 1987), 277n. 1; and Kloppenberg, "Beyond Kant," 18.

16. Among the first of these works was Herder's 1777 "call to arms," "Von Ähnlichkeit der mittleren englischen und deutschen Dichtkunst" (William A. Wilson, "Herder, Folklore and Romantic Nationalism," in *Folk Groups and Folklore Genres: A Reader,* ed. Elliott Oring [Logan: Utah State University Press, 1989], 30). See also Ira Berlin's overview of Herder in his posthumously published *The Roots of Romanticism* (Princeton, N.J.: Princeton University Press, 1999), 57–67, and Bendix, *In Search of Authenticity.*

17. Saree Makdisi argues that the imperial dimension of folk interest explains the character of romanticism overall. "For romantic discoveries of cultural otherness were dialectically articulated in opposition to the emerging world of modernization even as the latter was being defined; they enabled that definition to begin with. This is what separates romantic 'other worlds' from earlier constructions of cultural otherness" (*Romantic Imperialism: Universal Empire and the Culture of Modernity,* Cambridge Studies in Romanticism. [Cambridge: Cambridge University Press, 1998], 16). See also Gene Bluestein, *The Voice of the Folk* (Amherst: University of Massachusetts Press, 1972).

18. Scott's depiction of the "wild and barbarous" highlander, Evan Dhu Maccombich, becomes a litmus of images of folkish authenticity as it draws alignments with various cultural others from Africa to America to the orient with whom white Americans could easily recognize. See Makdisi, *Romantic Imperialism,* 76. *Minstrelsy of the Scottish Border,* vols. 1–3, and *The Lay of the Last Minstrel: Ballads, Songs,* vol. 5 of *The Poetical Works of Sir Walter Scott, Baronet,* 10 vols. (Edinburgh: A. Constable & Co., 1825). On images of otherness in Scott, see Makdisi, *Romantic Imperialism,* 81–85.

19. Francis R. Hart, *Scott's Novels: The Plotting of Historic Survival* (Charlottesville:

University Press of Virginia, 1966), 19; Rollin G. Osterweis, *Romanticism and Nationalism in the Old South* (Gloucester, Mass.: Peter Smith, 1964), 45.

20. Quoted in Osterweis, *Romanticism and Nationalism,* 62. Osterweis provides a useful synopsis of Scott's novels, their New World appeal, and their influence on American writers (41–53). For additional background on Scott, see Hart, *Scott's Novels;* Alexander Welsh, *The Hero of the Waverley Novels: With New Essays on Scott* (1963; reprint, Princeton, N.J.: Princeton University Press, 1992); Robin Mayhead, *Walter Scott* (Cambridge: Cambridge University Press, 1973); Ina Ferris, *The Achievement of Literary Authority: Gender, History, and the Waverley Novels* (Ithaca, N.Y.: Cornell University Press, 1991); Laura Doyle, "Romanticism and the Race Aesthetic: Scott and Wordsworth," in *Bordering on the Body: The Racial Matrix of Modern Fiction and Culture* (New York: Oxford University Press, 1994), 35–53; Jay B. Hubbell, *The South in American Literature, 1607–1900* (Durham, N.C.: Duke University Press, 1954); William E. Dodd, *The Cotton Kingdom: A Chronicle of the South* (New Haven, Conn.: Yale University Press, 1919); Clement Eaton, *The Mind of the Old South* (Baton Rouge: Louisiana State University Press, 1964); and Jean Fagan Yellin, *The Intricate Knot: Black Figures in American Literature, 1776–1863* (New York: New York University Press, 1972).

21. Anne Dhu Shapiro, "Sounds of Scotland," *American Music* 8, no. 1 (spring 1990): 71–83. Shapiro notes that "Auld Lang Syne" was a popular song for closing public gatherings, possibly as a result of its use as a scene closer and farewell in Scott's *Rob Roy MacGregor* (Edinburgh: Printed by J. Ballantyne for A. Constable, 1818). By the mid-1840s, the tune was commonly sung at antislavery rallies to the words "I am an abolitionist" (74–75). By midcentury, fashion had shifted to Irish songs, which came to inform minstrelsy and songsters. It is in this light that we might recall the first recording of black song, sung in the style of an Irish shanty, "Mama's Black Baby Boy." And it is in this same light that we might also position Ralph Ellison's reflections on the Irish character of early black singing. See chap. 1, n. 14.

22. Ralph Waldo Emerson, "The American Scholar," in *Nature: Addresses and Lectures,* vol. 1 of *The Complete Works of Ralph Waldo Emerson,* ed. Edward Waldo Emerson (1903; reprint, New York: AMS Press, 1968), 111, where he outlines his vision of "the common" ("I embrace the common, I explore and sit at the feet of the familiar, the low"). See chap. 3 of Bendix, *In Search of Authenticity;* and Paul F. Boller, Jr., *American Transcendentalism, 1830–1860: An Intellectual Inquiry* (New York: G. P. Putnam's Sons, 1974), 60. According to F. O. Matthiessen, Melville "jumped ship at the Marquesa Islands" in 1842 "and lived a month among the cannibals in the Taipi Valley before escaping to Tahiti" (*American Renaissance: Art and Expression in the Age of Emerson and Whitman* [New York: Oxford University Press, 1941], 658).

23. Matthiessen notes that Emerson marveled over "the homespun veracity of [English folk songs'] plain style" (*American Renaissance,* 34). See Thomas Wentworth Higginson, "Negro Spirituals," *Atlantic Monthly* (June 1867), 685–94, reprinted as chap. 9 of Higginson's *Army Life in a Black Regiment* (1870; reprint, New York: W. W. Norton, 1984), 197–222. See also Theodore Parker, "Ballad Literature," review of *The Pictorial*

Book of Ballads, Traditional and Romantic, ed. J. S. Moore et al., *Massachusetts Quarterly Review,* no. 2 (March 1848), 240–55. Charles Seeger notes that most of the songs taught in schools were of European origin; see Richard Crawford, "Musical Learning in Nineteenth-Century America," *American Music* 1 (spring 1983): 11n.

24. Gienapp, "Abolitionism and the Nature of Antebellum Reform," 39.

25. For Whitman, see Matthiessen, *American Renaissance,* 560; for Collins, see *The Life and Writings of Frederick Douglass,* ed. Philip S. Foner, 5 vols. (New York, 1950–75), 1:46.

26. James Russell Lowell, "The Prejudice of Color," *National Anti-Slavery Standard* (February 13, 1845), reprinted in *The Anti-Slavery Papers of James Russell Lowell,* 2 vols. (Boston: Houghton Mifflin, 1902), 1:22. Bendix speculates that Lowell's rhetorical gifts may have gotten him the job at Harvard (*In Search of Authenticity,* chap. 3). In "Negro Spirituals," Higginson discusses Lowell's exaggerated use of dialect in the "Biglow Papers" (188).

27. Higginson, "Negro Spirituals," 197.

28. Nathanson, "Negro Minstrelsy, " 38.

29. Bendix, *In Search of Authenticity.* Higginson, "Negro Spirituals," 187.

30. According to le Huray and Day, by the mid-eighteenth century "philosophers and critics were unanimous that of all the arts music spoke most directly to the feelings"; by the early nineteenth century, music would mark the truest form of the sublime, which, paraphrasing Schopenhauer, they call a reality "more 'real' than the phenomenal world itself" (introduction to *Music and Aesthetics in the Eighteenth and Early-Nineteenth Centuries,* 5, 16). Significantly, it was at this point that organicism replaced linguistics as the dominant metaphor of musical depiction. For background, see Foucault, *The Order of Things: An Archaeology of the Human Sciences* (1966; New York: Vintage Books, 1973), xxiii; Leonard Meyer, "Romanticism—the Ideology of Elite Egalitarians," in *Style and Music: Theory, History and Ideology* (Philadelphia: University of Pennsylvania Press, 1989), 163–217; and Ruth A. Solie, "The Living Work: Organicism and Musical Analysis," *Nineteenth-Century Music* 4 (fall 1980): 147–56.

31. See Katherine K. Preston, "Art Music from 1800 to 1860," *Cambridge History of American Music,* ed. David Nicholls (Cambridge: Cambridge University Press, 1998), 186–213; Stanley M. Vogel, *German Literary Influences on the American Transcendentalists* (New Haven, Conn.: Yale University Press, 1955); Henry A. Pochmann, *German Culture in America: Philosophical and Literary Influences, 1600–1900* (Madison: University of Wisconsin Press, 1957); and Carl Dahlhaus, *The Idea of Absolute Music,* trans. Roger Lustig (Chicago: University of Chicago Press, 1989). See also Berthold Hoeckner, "Music as a Metaphor of Metaphysics: Tropes of Transcendence in Nineteenth-Century Music from Schumann to Mahler" (Ph.D. diss., Cornell University, 1994).

32. Nathanson, "Negro Minstrelsy," 48. While Beethoven was an accomplished improviser, he represented above all the turn toward the composer as master over an obedient performer. In fact, Beethoven's anticipation of the eventual canonization of European art may have intensified interest in the declining "freedom" of oral impro-

vised music preserved as folk forms. For background, see William S. Neuman, "The Beethoven Mystique in Romantic Art, Literature, and Music," *Musical Quarterly* 69 (summer 1983): 354–87; and Ora Frishberg Saloman, "Margaret Fuller on Beethoven in America, 1839–1846," *Journal of Musicology* 10 (winter 1992): 89–105. For the quote about concert room singing, see "Songs of the Blacks," *Dwight's Journal of Music* (November 15, 1856), 51–52. The essay was printed again in 15, no. 23 (September 3, 1859): 179–80; subsequent cites are to the 1856 version.

33. Antonin Dvořák, "Music in America," *Harper's New Monthly Magazine* 90 (February 1895): 428–34. Dvořák's comments bear a striking resemblance to W. E. B. Du Bois's observation that the "rhythmic cry of the slave [is] the most beautiful expression born this side the seas" (*The Souls of Black Folk* [1903; reprint, New York, 1989], 182). On the union of ballads and slave narratives, see "Negro Spirituals"; "Letter from a Teacher at the South," *Dwight's Journal of Music,* vol. 2, no. 21 (February 26, 1853); and Louis C. Elson, *The National Music of America and Its Sources* (Boston: L. C. Page, 1899), esp. chap. 10, "Folk-Songs," which includes a section on plantation music.

34. See John Sullivan Dwight, "Musical Review," *Harbinger* (June 14, 1845), 13, and "Great Concert in New York," *Harbinger* (May 16, 1846), 361. The journal was published by Henry James, Sr., and the Brook Farm Phalanx in West Roxbury, Massachusetts. Dwight's abolitionist sentiments are further demonstrated in his friendships with Higginson and Emerson, together with his role as principal planner of the Jubilee Concert at Music Hall, Boston (January 1863), in recognition of the Emancipation Proclamation. See George Willis Cooke, *John Sullivan Dwight, Brook-Farmer, Editor, and Critic of Music: A Biography* (1898; reprint, Hartford: Transcendental Books, 1973), 55.

35. John Sullivan Dwight, "Music in New York," *Harbinger* (July 5, 1845), 59. "Even through bungling repetitions, if you have any soul, such music will inspire it" (Dwight, "Musical Review: Chamber Concerts of the Harvard Musical Association," *Harbinger* (November 28, 1846), 394. This positioning of substance over empty virtuosity is an age-old trope as it prefigures Charles Ives's dichotomy of substance and manner; see Charles Ives, *Essays before a Sonata and Other Writings,* ed. Howard Boatwright (New York: W. W. Norton, 1962).

36. "Songs of the Blacks," 51–52. In his *Harbinger* essays, Dwight's absolute and transcendentalist theories converge in passionate reflections on music's social effect:

> The spirit of such a union [between men] is already felt, and will demand a language, even before it can get an organization. Speech alone will not content; Tone, through all its infinite shades of Modulation, Melody, and Harmony becomes indispensable to the utterance of the full soul. For it would speak a universal language, which Asia and America alike may comprehend. . . . Music is the key to that Divine Order of human society, which is destined yet to be, when these long ages of painful, violent transition, those preparatory discords, shall be resolved into the full accord of Unity and Love.
> (Dwight, "Musical Review," [June 14, 1845], 13)

In his magazine, *Dwight's Journal of Music,* moreover, Dwight gave extensive coverage to black music. This took the form of reprints of essays from major newspapers and magazines, together with newly published essays. During the first year, the magazine published a series of essays under the title of "Music in Mississippi," which included a derogatory reference to "Negro melodies," registering a challenge from a southern-based writer and commentary on the African-American concert singer Elizabeth Greenfield ("the black swan"). See, in *Dwight's Journal of Music,* "Music in Mississippi," 2, no. 17 (January 29, 1853): 132; "Letter from a Teacher at the South," 2, no. 21 (February 26, 1853): 164; "The Black Swan," 3, no. 1 (April 9, 1853): 2–3. A follow up on Greenfield appears as "From New York," 6, no. 23 (March 10, 1855): 180–81. (The latter essay curiously concludes, "pretty cool.") Comments about blackface appear sporadically in the regular column "Musical Chit-Chat." These and other discussions about minstrelsy were revealing, whether pro or con, demonstrating both the pleasure of blackness and the anxiety that pleasure brought about among white Americans. Frequently, the references to black face appeared in the context of reflections on national music. See, e.g., also in *Dwight's Journal of Music,* "Harmony of Tone," 6, no. 13 (December 13, 1854): 98–99; "American Opera," 6, no. 18 (February 3, 1855): 140–41; "The Black Opera," 13–14 (July 3, 1858): 107–8; "Obituary, Not Eulogistic" [On the "death" of Negro minstrelsy], 13, no. 15 (July 10, 1858): 118.

37. The discussions appear respectively in these issues, all *Dwight's Journal of Music:* F., "More About 'Tom'," 22, no. 10 (December 6, 1862): 284; "The Blind Negro Pianist," 17, no. 3 (April 14, 1860): 21; Brown, "St. Louis, May, 1861," 19, no. 7 (May 18, 1861): 55; "Editorial: 'Blind Tom,' " 22, no. 6 (November 8, 1862): 254; "The Blind Negro Boy Pianist," 16, no. 20 (February 11, 1860): 364.

38. "Like an ape clawing for food" can be found in "Editorial: 'Blind Tom.' "

39. "The Blind Negro Boy Pianist," 364; "Blind Tom and the Japanese," *Dwight's Journal of Music* 17, no. 11 (June 9, 1860): 84.

40. This was, presumably, the southern White House of the Confederacy during wartime, located in Montgomery, Alabama. See "Editorial: Blind Tom," 254. For background on Blind Tom, see Geneva Handy Southall's three-volume work: *Blind Tom: The Post-Civil War Enslavement of a Black Musical Genius* (Minneapolis: Challenge Productions, 1979), *The Continuing Enslavement of Blind Tom* (Minneapolis: Challenge Productions, 1983), and *Blind Tom, the Black Pianist-Composer (1849–1908), Continually Enslaved* (Lanham, Md.: Scarecrow Press, 1999). See also Thomas L. Riis's excellent essay on John Davis's compact disk *Plays Blind Tom:* "The Legacy of a Prodigy Lost in Mystery," *New York Times,* March 5, 2000, Sunday Arts and Leisure, pt. 2, 35.

41. For the images of hooting and shouting and for the depiction of slaves as "the happiest of the human race," see Smith, "Persimmon Tree," 9; for scenes of blacks being merry, see Robert Criswell, *"Uncle Tom's Cabin" Contrasted with Buckingham Hall, the Planter's Home; Or, A Fair View of Both Sides of the Slavery Question* (New York: D. Fanshaw, 1852), 66–67.

42. Daniel Drake, *Dr. Daniel Drake's Letters on Slavery to Dr. John C. Warren, of*

Boston, with an introduction by Emmet Field Horine, M.D. (1851; reprint, New York: Schuman's, 1940), 16. The phrase "shuffle away" appears in Edmund Kirke [James Robert Gilmore], *Among the Pines; Or, South in Secession-Time* (New York: J. R. Gilmore & Charles T. Evans, 1862), 147; "heavenly sight" in W. L. G. Smith, *Life at the South; Or, "Uncle Tom's Cabin" As It Is: Being Narratives, Scenes, and Incidents in the Real "Life of the Lowly"* (Buffalo: Geo. H. Derby & Co., 1852), 185; and "not always . . . in strains the most reverential and refined " in Epstein, *Sinful Tunes,* 220. For the use of the words "queer," "grotesque," "fantastic," and "strange" to describe slave songs, see James R. Creecy, *Scenes in the South, and Other Miscellaneous Pieces* (Washington, D.C.: Thomas McGill, 1860), 21. Kirke [Gilmore], *Among the Pines;* Reverend James Wendell Alexander, quoted in Epstein, *Sinful Tunes,* 222.

43. J[ohn] P[endleton] Kennedy, *Swallow Barn; Or, A Sojourn in the Old Dominion,* rev. ed. (New York: George P. Putnam, 1851), 454–55.

44. "Tumming" comes from Smith, "Persimmon Tree," 7, 5; H. G. Spaulding, "Under the Palmetto," *Continental Monthly* 4 (1863): 188–203, reprinted in *The Negro and His Folklore,* ed. Jackson, 68; Reverend C. F. Sturgis, "Melville Letters," in Holland Nimmons McTyeire, C. F. Sturgis, and A. T. Holmes, *Duties of Masters to Servants: Three Premium Essays* (Charleston, S.C.: Southern Baptist Publication Society, 1851), 100, quoted in Epstein, *Sinful Tunes,* 224.

45. Brantz Mayer, "The African Slave Trade," review of *Captain Canot; Or, Twenty Years of an African Slaver,* by Captain Canot, *De Bow's Review* 18 (January 1855): 18; John Campbell, ed., *Negro-Mania: Being an Examination of the Falsely Assumed Equality of the Various Races of Men* (Philadelphia: Campbell & Powers, 1851), 282–83, 371.

46. On the African's discordant mixture of qualities, see Charles Hamilton Smith, *The Natural History of the Human Species, Its Typical Forms, Permanent Distribution, Filiations, and Migrations* (Edinburgh: W. H. Lizars, 1848), reprinted in *Negro-Mania,* ed. Campbell, 171; Creecy, *Scenes in the South,* 21; George G. Foster, "Philadelphia in Slices, Slice IX: The Colored Population," *New York Tribune,* December 29, 1848, reprinted in *Pennsylvania Magazine of History and Biography* 93, no. 1 (January 1969): 63–64. Foster continues, "At present, however, their acquirements are mostly confined to a little, or a good deal, of sawing upon a fiddle, and an intense passion for the real old fashioned Virginny breakdown" (63).

47. Criswell, *"Uncle Tom's Cabin" Contrasted with Buckingham Palace,* 69. Criswell's account recalls another from South Carolina in which slaves bearing torches light the causeways in order to keep trains on track. See Charles Lanman, *Adventures in the Wilds of the United States and British American Provinces,* 2 vols. (Philadelphia: John W. Moore, 1856), 2:98. In their cunning, they appeared almost magical, their powers conveyed in the language of the travelogue: "They sometimes seemed like evil spirits gathering angrily around the locomotive monster which had dared to penetrate their forest home" (98).

48. Foster, "Philadelphia in Slices," 64. Novelist J. Thornton Randolph [Charles Jacobs Peterson] similarly observes that all slave music ("Southern airs") are in the mi-

nor key (*The Cabin and Parlour; Or, Slaves and Masters* [Philadelphia: T. B. Peterson, 1852], 78).

49. Mrs. Frances Harriet McDougall, *Shahmah in Pursuit of Freedom; Or, The Branded Hand,* trans. from the original Showiah and ed. by an American Citizen (New York: Thatcher & Hutchinson, 1858), 273. The text is a fictional account of Shahmah Shah, a Kabyle (Algerian) visitor to the United States, who writes to a friend during his American tour in 1852.

50. Kennedy, *Swallow Barn,* 103; the phrase "hanging mosses" is from Lanman, *Adventures in the Wilds of the United States,* 2:98; on the "indescribable humor and pathos" of the slaves and their making "much better music than the whites," see Kirke [Gilmore], *Among the Pines,* 22, 44.

51. The comment about harmonious sounds was made by Mrs. [Matilda Charlotte J. Fraser] Houstoun, *Hesperos; or, Travels in the West* (London: John W. Parker, 1850), 2:157; for the healing powers of black song, see Creecy, *Scenes in the South,* 22; for the slave as critic, see Mrs. Caroline Lee Hentz, *The Planter's Northern Bride,* with an introduction by Rhoda Coleman Ellison (1854; reprint, Chapel Hill: University of North Carolina Press, 1970), 200. According to the narrator in W. L. G. Smith's *Life in the South,* to hear the fiddle was a way to "dance off 'the blues' " (290).

52. Epstein notes in passing that published references to the songs as spirituals did not appear until the Civil War (*Sinful Tunes,* 219). While this claim seems by and large accurate, Philip Morgan cites a 1741 reference to a "spiritual" among Moravians in South Carolina (*Slave Counterpoint: Black Culture in the Eighteenth-Century Chesapeake and Lowcountry* [Chapel Hill: University of North Carolina Press, 1998], 591). The term was not uncommon, here referring to psalmody: Supply Belcher, *Deep North Spirituals,* ed. Oliver Daniel (1794; reprint, New York, 1973). Moreover, references to the "sperichil" suggest that the term had been employed by slaves themselves. See, e.g., Marcel [William Francis Allen], "The Negro Dialect," *Nation* 1 (December 14, 1865): 744–45. Nonetheless, the term acquired its associations with authenticity only after it had entered national discourse. Whites may have employed it because it affirmed their romantic conceptions; blacks seem to have maintained it as a vehicle of empowerment. In his notice of the forthcoming publication of *Slave Songs of the United States,* finally, John Sullivan Dwight calls attention to the newness of the term by presenting it in scare quotes: "The basis still remains the 'spirituals,' such as were furnished in the *Atlantic* by Mr. Higginson" ("The Songs of the Freedmen," *Dwight's Journal of Music* 27, no. 9 [July 20, 1867]: 71).

53. "Their songs are all religious," even if the most sorrowful of the sorrow songs— "No more driver call for me / many a thousand die!"—seemed to Reverend James Miller McKim "hilarious" ("Negro Songs," 58, 59). In *Slave Songs of the United States,* ed. Allen, Ware, and Garrison, Allen says that all the songs on the island were religious. He then proceeds to ridicule them in a mock scientific analysis; see the section "Visualizing Partials," ahead. The quote about "The Songs of their Captivity" can be found in "Songs of the Blacks," 53; "a decidedly religious character" is from Epstein, *Sinful*

Tunes, 224; and "religious . . . without exception" is the phrasing of James McKim, "Negro Songs," 58.

54. The phrase "indescribable something" appears in Marcel [Allen], "The Negro Dialect," 745. Allen speculated that the act of improvisation developed from natural gifts, as if the slaves were brimming with inventiveness. For "subliming spirit," see McDougall, *Shahmah in Pursuit of Freedom,* 274; for "indescribable something," see Smith, "Persimmon Tree," 5.

55. George M. Fredrickson's now classic discussion of "romantic racialism" offers insight into this interpretation of the spirituals (*The Black Image in the White Mind: The Debate on Afro-American Character and Destiny, 1817–1914* [1971; reprint, Middletown, Conn.: Wesleyan University Press, 1987]). Eric Lott develops this argument in *Love and Theft: Blackface Minstrelsy and the American Working Class* (New York: Oxford University Press, 1993).

56. Christopher Looby explores the paradox of attributions of hyperbolic masculinity and femininity in depictions of slaves in " 'As Thoroughly Black as the Most Faithful Philanthropist Could Desire': Erotics of Race in Higginson's *Army Life in a Black Regiment,*" in *Race and the Subject of Masculinities,* ed. Harry Stecopoulos and Michael Uebel (Durham, N.C.: Duke University Press, 1997), 71–115. Moreover, Nina Silber offers a compelling analysis of the feminization of the South in *The Romance of Reunion: Northerners and the South, 1865–1900* (Chapel Hill: University of North Carolina Press, 1993), while Kristin Hoganson discusses the belief that slaves could not adhere to European-based gender roles in "Garrisonian Abolitionists and the Rhetoric of Gender, 1850–1860" *American Quarterly* 45, no. 4 (December 1993): 558–95.

57. Like the ballads that so charmed Lowell, the spirituals possessed a similar appeal, seemingly because, as Lowell wrote in 1855, "nobody made them. They seem to have come up like violets and we have only to thank God for them" (quoted in Bendix, *In Search of Authenticity,* 81). Similarly, Theodore F. Seward said of the slave songs: "Their origin is unique. They are never 'composed' after the manner of ordinary music, but spring into life, ready made, from the white heat of religious fervour" ("Preface to the Music," in *The Story of the Jubilee Singers with Their Songs,* ed. J. B. T. Marsh, 7th ed. [London: Hodder & Stoughton, 1877], 121). For the phrase beginning "all mankind . . . ," see Smith, "Persimmon Tree," 9.

58. "Songs of the Blacks," 51–52. According to Dr. John H. Van Evrie, a leading southern racialist, Americans could not have developed their vision of egalitarianism without the presence of an inferior race (Fredrickson, *The Black Image in the White Mind,* 93).

59. See C. W. D., "Contraband Singing"; and Lucy McKim, "Songs of the Port Royal Contrabands," *Dwight's Journal of Music* (November 8, 1862): 254–55.

60. Mary Boykin Chesnut's South Carolina diary (1861), quoted in Epstein, *Sinful Tunes,* 225–26; Nathanson, "Negro Minstrelsy," 37.

61. The phrase "infinitely pathetic" comes from Higginson, "Negro Spirituals," 202; "all society" from Reverend Baynard R. Hall, *Frank Freeman's Barber Shop: A Tale* (New

York: Charles Scribner, 1852), 103; "rolled their great . . ." from Houstoun, *Hesperos,* 2:157; and "while the more jovial . . ." and "more melody . . ." from Lanman, *Adventures in the Wilds of the United States,* 120, 150.

62. McDougall, *Shahmah in Pursuit of Freedom,* 273; Levine, *Black Culture and Black Consciousness,* 28–29; Mary Boykin Chesnut, *A Diary From Dixie,* ed. Ben Ames Williams (Boston: Houghton Mifflin Co., 1949), 149. The passage is from her diary entry of October 13, 1861. Similar sentiments appear in [Elizabeth Kilham], "Sketches in Color: IV," *Putnam's Monthly* 15 (March 1870): 304–11, reprinted in *The Negro and His Folklore,* ed. Jackson, 120–33; and John Mason Brown, "Songs of the Slave," *Lippincott's Magazine* 2 (December 1868): 617–23, reprinted in *The Negro and His Folklore,* ed. Jackson, 109–19. Brown provides a good example of this split image. After acknowledging the sorrows of slave life, he turns aboutface and, in the very next sentence, celebrates its pleasures, "as though life were but one long holiday" (116). "Even the fair sex did not escape the contagion," writes J. K[innard], Jr. ("Who Are Our National Poets?" *Knickerbocker Magazine* 26 [October 1845]: 331–41, reprinted in *The Negro and His Folklore,* ed. Jackson, 25. While Kinnard's essay may be satirical, as Jackson argues, it nonetheless reveals racialist views of the time. "Render[ed] delirious . . ." is from Jacques Derrida, quoted in Gayatri Spivak, "Can the Subaltern Speak," in *Marxism and the Interpretation of Culture,* ed. Cary Nelson and Lawrence Grossberg (Urbana: University of Illinois Press, 1988), reprinted in *Colonial Discourse and Post-Colonial Theory,* ed. Patrick Williams and Laura Chrisman (New York: Columbia University Press, 1994), 89.

63. Oliphant's comments are quoted in Epstein, *Sinful Tunes,* 226; Higginson, "Negro Spirituals," 198.

64. C. W. D., "Contraband Singing," 55–56.

65. Theodor W. Adorno, "On the Fetish Character of Music and the Regression of Listening," in *The Essential Frankfurt School Reader,* ed. Andrew Arato and Eike Gebhardt; introduction by Paul Piccone (New York: Continuum, 1982), 270–99. This would mark a new era of reform in the tradition of regular singing, first articulated in a sermon by Reverend Thomas Symmes (1720) on the need for the regulation of sacred singing practices. For post-1865 reforms of secular music, see Joseph A. Mussulman, *Music in the Cultured Generation: A Social History of Music in America, 1870–1900* (Evanston, Ill.: Northwestern University Press, 1971).

66. Smith, "The Persimmon Tree ," 9. David C. Barrow, Jr., "A Georgia Corn-Shucking," *Century Magazine* 24 (1882): 873–78, reprinted in *The Negro and His Folklore,* ed. Jackson, 171; Higginson, "Negro Spirituals," 222. See below for the discussion of Allen's introduction to *Slave Songs of the United States,* ed. Allen, Ware, and Garrison.

67. McKim, "Songs of the Port Royal Contrabands," 254–55. In the same article, McKim continues, "The airs, however, can be reached. They are too decided not to be easily understood, and their striking originality would catch the ear of any musician. Besides this, they are valuable as an expression of the character and life of the race which is playing such a conspicuous part in our history. The wild, sad strains tell, as the sufferers themselves never could, of crushed hopes, keen sorrow, and a dull daily

misery which covered them as hopelessly as the fog from the rice-swamps." Concerning the "repetition" associated with call and response, moreover, McKim writes, "A complaint may be made against these songs on the score of monotony. It is true there is a great deal of repetition of the music, but that is to accommodate the *leader,* who, if he be a good one, is always an improvisator. For instance, on one occasion, the name of each of our party who was present, was dexterously introduced" (255). Moreover, Dena Epstein notes that McKim prepared piano and vocal arrangements of slave songs; Epstein reproduces two of them, "Poor Rosy, Poor Gal" and "Roll Jordan Roll" in her book *Sinful Tunes,* 263–69. Interestingly, a precedent for such renderings of "foreign song" appears as G. G. Ferrari's arrangement of an African melody (with lyrics by the Dutchess of Devonshire), published in Mungo Park, *Travels in the Interior Districts of Africa* (London: Printed by W. Bulmer for the Author, 1799). A copy of Ferrari's song in new notation can be found in Frank Harrison, *Time, Place and Music: An Anthology of Ethnomusicological Observation, c. 1550–1800* (Amsterdam: Frits Knuf, 1973) 219–221.

68. W. J. T. Mitchell, "Narrative, Memory, and Slavery," in *Picture Theory: Essays on Verbal and Visual Representation* (Chicago: University of Chicago Press, 1994), 192. Here, they inadvertently move toward what Walter Benjamin proposed for the most radical translational acts, which recast Western modalities to accommodate the original ("The Task of the Translator" (1923), in *Illuminations: Essays and Reflections,* ed. Hannah Arendt; trans. Harry Zohn (New York: Schocken Books, 1969), 69–82.

69. Harrison, *Time, Place, and Music,* 157, 162–63.

70. Mitchell, "Name and Convention: Gombrich's Illusions," in *Iconology,* 79.

71. Jean Léry, *Histoire d'un voyage faict en la terre du Brésil* (1611). In *Time, Place, and Music,* Harrison lists the original place and date of publication as La Rochelle, 1578. Music notations first appear in the 3d ed., published in Latin in Geneva in 1586 and in a German translation in Frankfurt in 1593. It is unclear if the transcriptions were made by Léry or someone else. Harrison speculates that he may have made them, noting that "he could sing well, in the judgement [*sic*] of an indigenous South American, for he relates that he was given a gift of an *agoutti,* a little animal of the size of a month-old piglet, after he had sung a metrical psalm" (6). Harrison's transcription is a composite of the notations, noting discrepancies in the 3d ed. and subsequent volumes.

72. Mitchell, *Iconology,* 31–35. Stedman's text is particularly noteworthy in its comparison of Surinam singing to the practice of lining out, "not unlike that of some clerks reading to the congregation, one person pronouncing a sentence extempore, which he next hums or whistles" (chap. 26). In the same chapter he compares Suriname singing to bird song and includes two examples of the latter in chap. 10 (see fig. 9) (John Gabriel Stedman, *Narrative of a Five Years' Expedition against the Revolted Negroes of Surinam in Guiana* [1777; reprint, Barre, Mass.: Printed for the Imprint Society, 1871].) Philip V. Bohlman offers what is perhaps a more sanguine view of transcription in "Representation and Cultural Critique in the History of Ethnomusicology," in *Comparative Musicology and the Anthropology of Music: Essays on the History of Ethnomusicology,* ed. Bruno Nettl and Philip V. Bohlman (Chicago: University of Chicago Press, 1991), 131–51.

73. Léry, *Histoire d'un voyage faict en la terre du Brésil* (1585); musical notation first appears in the 1611 edition. The text also discloses admiration for the Indians' musicality: "After these noises and confused howlings were over, . . . we heard them once again singing and making their voices sound with an agreement so delicious that, becoming somewhat reassured through hearing these sweet and more gracious sounds, there is no need to ask if I wanted to see them closely" (in *Time, Place, and Music,* ed. Harrison, 20).

74. Roger D. Abrahams and John F. Szwed, eds., *After Africa: Extracts from British Travel Accounts and Journals of the Seventeenth, Eighteenth, and Nineteenth Centuries concerning the Slaves, Their Manners, and Customs in the British West Indies* (New Haven, Conn.: Yale University Press, 1983), 281. Sloane, who witnessed the performance in 1688, was a physician to the governor of Jamaica and fellow of the Royal Society, charged with preparing a catalog of New World plant and animal life, published as *A Voyage to the Islands of Madera, Barbados, Nieves, St. Christopher, and Jamaica, with the Natural History of the Same,* 2 vols. (London: Printed by B. M. for the Author, 1707, 1725). Biographical information appears in *After Africa,* ed. Abrahams and Szwed, 425–26. Sloane's musical discussion and the accompanying transcriptions form the basis of a speculative inquiry into the character of early New World African performance. See Richard Cullen Rath, "African Music in Seventeenth-Century Jamaica: Cultural Transit and Transition," *William and Mary Quarterly,* 3d ser., 1, no. 4 (October 1993): 700–726.

75. Mantle Hood, "The Challenge of Bi-Musicality," *Ethnomusicology* 4 (1960): 55–59; Ter Ellingson, "Transcription," in *Ethnomusicology: An Introduction,* ed. Helen Myers (New York: W. W. Norton, 1992), 113, 115. William Jones's *On the Modes of the Hindoos* (1784) is published in Sourindro Mohun Tagore, comp., *Hindu Music from Various Authors,* 3d ed. (1875; reprint, Varansi: Chowkhamba Sanskrit Series Office, 1965), 88–112 (originally published in *Asiatick Researches*).

76. T. Edward Bowdich, *Mission from Cape Coast Castle to Ashantee* (London: J. Murray, 1819), 364–65. It is consequently unclear how his commitment to accuracy squares with the omission of accidentals.

77. [Edmond] Combes and [Maurice] Tamisier, *Voyage en Absyssinie* (Paris: Victor Magen, 1839), 2:352–54. I am grateful to Hatim Belyamani, my research assistant at the Du Bois Institute, Harvard University, in the fall 1997. Belyamani conducted a scrupulous and detailed study of nineteenth-century French travel writing, working largely from the bibliographic lists published in Richard Wallaschek's *Primitive Music: An Inquiry into the Origin and Development of Music, Song, Instruments, Dances and Pantomimes of Savage Races* (London: Longmans, Green, 1893). That the review bore only a single notational example and but few musical references makes the above identification all the more precious.

78. The quote about the defects of European musical transcription can be found in M. Villoteau, *De l'art musical en Égypte,* vol. 14 of *Description de L'Égypte: Ou, Recueil des observations et de recherches qui ont été faites en Égypte pendant l'expédition de l'armée française,* 2d ed. (Paris: C. L. F. Panckoucke, 1826), 41. See also Ellingson, "Transcrip-

tion," 115. Thanks to Virginia Danielson of Harvard University for her help in securing a microfilm copy of Villoteau's complete text. Edward W. Said discusses the expedition's scholarly project in "The Scope of Orientalism," *Orientalism* (New York: Vintage Books, 1979), 73–92. For an account of contemporary transcription projects conducted by the British in Java (1817–20), see Benjamin Brinner, "A Musical Time Capsule from Java," *Journal of the American Musicological Society* 46, no. 2 (summer 1993): 221–60.

79. Mitchell, "What Is an Image?" in *Iconology,* 39.

80. All figures from *Slave Songs of the United States* were reproduced from the personal copy of William Francis Allen, courtesy Allen Family Papers, Wisconsin Historical Society, Madison. In her research, moreover, Dena Epstein came across references to an unpublished collection of slave songs reportedly compiled by Mrs. Caroline Gilman in the early nineteenth century. Thus far, the manuscript has not emerged. See Epstein, *Sinful Tunes,* 322–23. Also noteworthy are the transcriptions of "Round' de Corn, Sally" and "Sold Off to Georgy," supplied by James Hungerford in his novel *The Old Plantation, and What I Gathered There in an Autumn Month* (New York: Harper & Brothers, 1859); and Solomon Northrup's inclusion of the notation of "Roaring River" in his *Twelve Years a Slave: Narrative of Solomon Northrup, Citizen of New-York, Kidnapped in Washington City in 1841, and Rescued in 1853* (1853; New York and Auburn: Miller, Orton and Mulligan, 1855). Reprints of both notations appear in Epstein at, respectively, 169–70 and 151.

81. See Theodore Dwight Weld, *American Slavery as It Is: Testimony of a Thousand Witnesses, as Taken from Southern Papers* (New York: American Anti-Slavery Society, 1839). The challenge helps to explain the previously cited critical review of *Slave Songs of the United States,* published in *Lippincott's Magazine;* see "Literature of the Day," vol. 1 (March 1868): 341–43.

82. An overview of this expedition is supplied in Epstein, *Sinful Tunes,* 252–73.

83. See Du Bois, *The Souls of Black Folk,* 184. Lucy McKim does not indicate how many transcriptions she prepared during her stay. "Roll, Jordan, Roll" was commonly sung among the Sea Islands' freed slaves. This song differs from the familiar one known today by the same title. This version also appears in *Slave Songs of the United States,* ed. Allen, Ware, and Garrison as "Lord, Remember Me."

84. Allen and Ware's grandfather, Henry Ware Sr., was Hollis Professor of Divinity at Harvard from 1805 to 1845. Allen's father, Joseph Allen, was also a Harvard graduate and practicing Unitarian minister. Allen recorded his experiences in a daily diary, transferred to typescript by his daughter and housed at the Wisconsin Historical Society, University of Wisconsin—Madison. It is noteworthy that during the course of the stay, Allen's initial idealism about blacks grew into an impatience resembling, at moments, Southern racist sentiment. Epstein offers detailed biographical coverage of the three editors in *Sinful Tunes,* 303–20. See also Allen's indications in his introduction to *Slave Songs of the United States,* ed. Allen, Ware, and Garrison, iii.

85. Epstein, *Sinful Tunes,* 312–33. For the obituary of Allen, see the *Nation* 49 (December 12, 1889): 479–80. An advertisement for the forthcoming collection appeared in the *Nation,* vol. 4 (May 30, 1867). Dwight provided his own backing with an an-

nouncement. See "The Songs of the Freedmen," *Dwight's Journal of Music* 27, no. 9 (July 20, 1867): 71–72.

86. Clement Lawrence Smith, "Obituary: Professor Allen," *Classical Review* 4 (November 1890): 428. The quotation Smith cites is attributed to Allen; Smith was a Harvard classicist. Allen's evolutionary theories would influence the frontier thesis of his future University of Wisconsin colleague Frederick Jackson Turner. See William Cronon, "The Turner Legacy," *L & S Magazine* 8 (summer 1992): 14–16.

87. See *Quinquennial Catalogue of the Officers and Graduates of Harvard University, 1636–1915* (Cambridge, Mass.: Harvard University Press, 1915). Ronald Story reports that Harvard students from the 1840s increasingly socialized with the Cambridge elite (*The Forging of an Aristocracy: Harvard and the Boston Upper Class, 1800–1870* [Middletown, Conn.: Wesleyan University Press, 1980], 92–94). Similarly, Dwight's biographer observes such occasions as when Dwight performed at the home of Higginson (Samuel Eliot Morison *Three Centuries of Harvard, 1636–1936* [Cambridge, Mass.: Harvard University Press, 1936]). Moreover, Morison reports that by the time of the administration of Jared Sparks (1849–53) Southerners comprised about a third of Harvard's student population (see 281). Their presence may have furthered Allen's desire to visit the Sea Islands.

88. James Russell Lowell joined the Harvard faculty in 1855, assuming Longfellow's chair. Francis James Child (class of 1846) was appointed tutor, 1846–51 (see *Who Was Who in America, 1607–1896* [Chicago: Marquis, 1967]). Allen thanks Higginson in the acknowledgments to *Slave Songs of the United States,* ed. Allen, Ware, and Garrison, xxxvii. Epstein reports that Allen had met Thayer while in Germany. However, Thayer was a Harvard graduate (B.A., 1843; L.L.B., 1848) and was subsequently employed at Harvard Library; see *Who Was Who in America, 1607–1896.* Ware's father, Henry Ware, Jr., was, with Dwight, a charter member of the Harvard Musical Association (see Epstein, *Sinful Tunes,* 310). For records of Harvard students and faculty, see *Quinquennial Catalogue of the Officers and Graduates of Harvard University, 1636–1915.*

89. Allen, introduction to *Slave Songs of the United States,* ed. Allen, Ware, and Garrison, i–iii; "half-barbarous" recalls Herder's reference to *halbwild* (half-wild) native peoples. See Gerald Broce, "Herder and Ethnography," *Journal of the History of the Behavioral Sciences* 22 (April 1986): 160–61.

90. Allen, introduction to *Slave Songs of the United States,* viii.

91. Ibid., v. Referring to Spaulding's notations published in the *Continental Monthly* in 1863, Allen writes in his Sea Islands diary, "There is considerable variety in singing these hymns, especially in the shout-tunes: so that I presume the copies in the *Continental* are as correct as mine" (typescript diary, Allen Family Papers, Wisconsin Historical Society, University of Wisconsin—Madison, 149).

92. Allen, introduction to *Slave Songs of the United States,* xii, xiv. Curiously, in her "Glossary of Harlem Slang," Zora Neale Hurston defines "Dat thing" as "sex of either sex," meaning, presumably, genitals (*Spunk: The Selected Stories of Zora Neale Hurston* [New York: Marlowe & Co., 1985], 92).

93. Allen, introduction to *Slave Songs of the United States,* xxv, ix.

94. Ibid., 115.

95. Ibid., vi–vii.

96. Allen, *Slave Songs of the United States,* 37, 53, xxxvii, and vii, respectively. The titles of the "African" notations appear as numbers 10, 12, 18, 29, 52, 87, 93, 128, 130, and 131; see Allen, introduction to *Slave Songs of the United States,* vii, vi.

97. Allen, *Slave Songs of the United States,* 106, 8, iv. Jerome McGann, *Black Riders: The Visible Language of Modernism* (Princeton, N.J.: Princeton University Press, 1993), 85.

98. Allen's transcriptions of hymns appear on the opposite side of the manuscript.

99. Allen, introduction to *Slave Songs of the United States,* iv–v. See Jacqueline Sers, "On the Subject of Violence," interview with Roland Barthes, in Barthes's *The Grain of the Voice: Interviews, 1962–1980,* trans. Linda Coverdale (Berkeley and Los Angeles: University of Californnia Press, 1985), 306–11.

100. Allen, introduction to *Slave Songs of the United States,* iv, xliv.

101. See Joan W. Scott, "The Evidence of Experience," *Critical Inquiry* 17 (summer 1991): 773–97, reprinted in *Questions of Evidence: Proof, Practice, and Persuasion across the Disciplines,* ed. James Chandler, Arnold I. Davidson, and Harry Harootunian (Chicago: University of Chicago Press, 1994), 363–87.

102. The pages of *Dwight's Journal of Music,* e.g., advertise sheet music of "Contraband" songs composed by B. R. Hanly and other popular-song writers. These are listed alongside the titles of a variety of other musical works similarly for purchase. By this time, already, "slave song" had become a commodity, sold without direct involvement of blacks themselves. See "Special Notices," vol. 19, no. 25 (September 21, 1861): 200, vol. 20, no. 21 (February 22, 1862): 376; vol. 20, no. 23 (March 8, 1862): 392.

Chapter 5

1. Henry Louis Gates, Jr., and Nellie McKay, eds., *Norton Anthology of African-American Literature* (New York: W. W. Norton, 1997).

2. Larry Scanlon, " 'Death Is a Drum': Rhythm, Modernity, and the Negro Poet Laureate," in *Music and the Racial Imagination,* ed. Ronald Radano and Philip V. Bohlman (Chicago: University of Chicago Press, 2000), 517.

3. Houston A. Baker, Jr., writes: "What I want explicitly to claim here is that all Afro-American creativity is conditioned by (and constitutes a component of) a historical discourse which privileges certain economic terms. The creative individual (the *black subject*) must, therefore, whether he self-consciously wills it or not, come to terms with 'commercial deportation' and the 'economics of slavery' " (*Blues, Ideology, and Afro-American Literature* [Chicago: University of Chicago Press, 1984], 39).

4. Ibid., 7. Speaking specifically of movement, Baker comments, "The railway juncture is marked by transience. Its inhabitants are always travelers" (7).

5. The first quotation is from ibid., 5; Baker is quoting Robert Johnson's "Cross Road Blues." The second lyrical excerpt appears in both recorded versions of the same song. They were recorded on November 27, 1936, in San Antonio, Texas, and released on Vocalion. See *Robert Johnson: The Complete Recordings,* Columbia C2K 64916.

6. See Hortense Spillers, "Changing the Letter," *Slavery and the Literary Imagination,* ed. Deborah E. McDowell and Arnold Rampersad (Baltimore: Johns Hopkins University Press, 1989), 33.

7. In *Beyond Ethnicity: Consent and Descent in American Culture* (New York: Oxford University Press, 1986), Werner Sollors employs "descent" in a more conventional, anthropological way, referring to bloodlines and generations. But this usage also shares important relationships with my own. On primordial cure, see Tom Lutz, "Curing the Blues: W. E. B. Du Bois, Fashionable Diseases, and Degraded Music," *Black Music Research Journal* 11, no. 2 (fall 1991): 137–56.

8. In take 1 of "Cross Road Blues," Johnson sings: "And I went to the crossroad, baby / I looked east and west / Lord, I didn't have no sweet woman / ooh-well, babe, in my distress" (*Robert Johnson: The Complete Recordings*).

9. Relevant here is Robert H. Crunden, *Body and Soul: The Making of American Modernism* (New York: Basic Books, 2000).

10. In the eighteenth and nineteenth centuries, hotness was commonly equated with displays of anger, passion, and sexual desire. An angry person voiced "hot words"; those lustful were "red hot" or "in heat." By the 1890s, the term had also identified positive attributes ("hot art"), together with extremes of physical display and self-indulgence: hotness evoked images of violence, suffering, danger, and intoxication. See etymologies of "hot" in *The Compact Edition of the Oxford English Dictionary* (Oxford: Clarendon Press, 1971) and *Dictionary of American Regional English,* ed. Frederic G. Cassidy (Cambridge, Mass.: Harvard University Press, Belknap Press, 1985–), vol. 2. See also Sam Dennison, *Scandalize My Name: Black Imagery in American Popular Music* (New York: Garland, 1982), 409–10.

11. Paul Oliver, *Songsters and Saints: Vocal Traditions on Race Records* (Cambridge: Cambridge University Press, 1984), 47–50. See also James H. Dorman, "Shaping the Popular Image of Post-Reconstruction American Blacks: The 'Coon Song' Phenomenon of the Gilded Age," *American Quarterly* 40, no. 4 (1988): 450–71; Karen Linn, *That Half Barbaric Twang: The Banjo in American Popular Culture* (Urbana: University of Illinois Press, 1991), 50. The appearance of the term, "coon," is discussed in David Roediger, *Wages of Whiteness: Race and the Making of the American Working Class* (New York: Verso, 1991).

12. The lyrics are taken from Irwin's 1907 recording, reissued on the compilation *American Pop from Minstrel to Mojo: On Record, 1893–1946,* West Hill Audio Archives, Toronto, 1998, CD-1017. According to Paul Oliver, Trevathan based his lyrics on a song he had heard sung by African-Americans in Tennessee (*Songsters and Saints,* 48). For a discussion of razor images, see Kevin Gaines, "Assimilated Minstrelsy as Racial Uplift Ideology: James D. Corrothers's Literary Quest for Black Leadership," *American Quarterly* 45 (1993): 341–69. For a discussion of the "Negro as beast," see George Fredrickson, *The Black Image in the White Mind: The Debate on Afro-American Character and Destiny, 1817–1914* (1971; reprint, Middletown, Conn.: Wesleyan University Press, 1987).

13. For "ragged rhythm," see Neil Leonard, "The Reactions to Ragtime," in *Ragtime:*

Its History, Composers and Music, ed. John Edward Hasse (New York: Schirmer Books, 1985), 102–16. "Jerky note" appears in Oliver, *Songsters and Saints,* 49.

14. Edward A. Berlin, "Ragtime," in *The New Grove Dictionary of American Music,* ed. H. W. Hitchcock and Stanley Sadie, 4 vols. (London: Macmillan, 1986), 4:3–6.

15. Leonard, "The Reactions to Ragtime," 103, Lutz, "Curing the Blues"; Alan M. Kraut, *Silent Travelers: Germs, Genes, and the "Immigrant Menace"* (Baltimore: Johns Hopkins University Press, 1994). Associations between black music and infection already had appeared in the 1850s, as in John Sullivan Dwight's observation that Stephen Foster's "Old Folks at Home" "breaks out now and then, like a morbid irritation of the skin" (Leonard "The Reactions to Ragtime," 106). The quotations from the *Negro Music Journal* and "syncopation gone mad" appear in Lutz, "Curing the Blues," 149.

16. Lutz, "Curing the Blues," 149.

17. "Decries 'Jazz Thinking'," *New York Times,* February 15, 1925, 17; Edmund Wilson, "The Jazz Problem," *New Republic* 46 (January 13, 1926): 217–19.

18. Alan M. Kraut, *Silent Travelers;* "Wants Legislation to Stop Jazz as an Intoxicant," *New York Times,* February 12, 1922, 1; Stanley R. Nelson, *All About Jazz* (London: Heath Cranton, 1934), 13.

19. George G. Foster, *New York by Gas-Light* (New York: Dewitt & Davenport, 1850), 72–73. At the same point in the essay, Foster noted a similar heat emanating from another rhythm maker, the "frightful mechanical distortions of the bass-drummer as he sweats and deals his blows on every side, in all violation of the laws of rhythm." Robert Louis Stevenson, *"The Strange Case of Dr. Jekyll and Mr. Hyde"* [1886] *and "Weir of Hermiston,"* ed. Emma Letley, Oxford World's Classics (Oxford: Oxford University Press, 1998), 35.

20. Dorothy Fields and Jimmy McHugh published "Futuristic Rhythm" in 1929. George Gershwin's "rhythm" tunes included "Fascinating Rhythm" (1924) and "I Got Rhythm" (1930). The latter soon became standard in the jazz repertory and the basis for many other tunes. Ellington, with Irving Mills, published among others, "Rockin' in Rhythm" (1930) and "It Don't Mean a Thing (If It Ain't Got That Swing)" (1932).

21. Alain Locke called the coon song "a relic of the worst of the minstrel days; slapstick farce about 'razors, chickens, watermelons, hambones.' . . . The appeal was not in what they said, but in the rhythm and swing in which they said it" ("Ragtime and Negro Musical Comedy, 1895–1925," in *The Negro and His Music* [1936; reprint, New York: Arno Press, 1969], 59). See Locke's subsequent section, "The Negro Tempo."

22. James Reese Europe, "A Negro Explains Jazz," *Literary Digest* 61, no. 4 (April 26, 1919): 28; Ralph Ellison, "What America Would Be Like without Blacks," in *Going to the Territory* (New York: Vintage, 1986), 110.

23. Kofi Agawu, "The Invention of 'African Rhythm'," *Journal of the American Musicological Society* 48, no. 3 (fall 1995): 380.

24. Quoted in Dena J. Epstein, *Sinful Tunes and Spirituals: Black Folk Music to the Civil War* (Urbana: University of Illinois Press, 1977), 26.

25. Olaudah Equiano, *The Interesting Narrative of the Life of Olaudah Equiano; Or,*

Gustavus Vassa, the African, Written by Himself, ed. Werner Sollors (New York: W. W. Norton, 2001), 21; the phrase "born dancing" is taken from Michael Adanson, "A Voyage to Senegal, the Isle of Goree, and the River Gambia" (1759), trans. from the French, in John Pinkerton, *A General Collection of the Best and Most Interesting Voyages and Travels in All Parts of the World: Many of Which Are Now First Translated into English: Digested on a New Plan,* 17 vols. (London: Longman, Hurst, et al., 1807–14), 16:598–674; "horrid noise" is from an anonymous source cited in Epstein, *Sinful Tunes,* 31.

26. Georg Wilhelm Friedrich Hegel and Johann Gottfried Herder, cited in Edward A. Lippman, *Musical Aesthetics: A Historical Reader* (New York: Pendragon Press, 1985), 117, 36, respectively.

27. Richard Ligon is quoted in Epstein, *Sinful Tunes,* 26. Rousseau, *Essay on the Origin of Languages* (music sections, 1749), reprinted in Jean-Jacques Rousseau and Johann Gottfried Herder, *On the Origin of Language,* trans. John H. Moran and Alexander Gode. (Chicago: University of Chicago Press, 1966), 59.

28. Joseph Corry, *Observations upon the Windward Coast of Africa . . .* (London: Printed for G. and W. Nicol, 1807), 10–12; James Richardson, *Narrative of a Mission to Central Africa,* 2 vols. (London: Chapman & Hall, 1853), 2:15; Richard Lander, *Records of Captain Clapperton's Last Expedition to Africa,* 2 vols. (London: Henry Colburn & Richard Bentley, 1830), 2:261–64; Major Alexander Gordon Laing, *Travels in the Timannee, Kooranko, and Soolima Countries in West Africa* (London: John Murray, 1825), 9, 218, 231, 368–69.

29. The music discussion begins 231–37 and continues on 242–54 of Laing, *Travels in the Timannee.* For a discussion of John Windhus ("A Journey to Mequinez, the Residence of the Present Emperor of Fez and Morocco . . ." [1725], in Pinkerton, *General Collection,* 15:442–99), see chap. 2, 84–85.

30. John Beecham, *Ashantee and the Gold Coast,* introduction and notes by G. E. Metcalfe (1841; reprint, London: Dawsons of Pall Mall, 1968), 167, 169. T. Edward Bowdich (*Mission from Cape Coast Castle to Ashantee* [London: John Murray, Albemarle Street, 1819]) continues his musical discussion on 449–52, based on an accompanying transcription appearing on the preceding page (between 448 and 449).

31. W. T. Burchell, *Travels in the Interior of Southern Africa,* 2 vols. (London: Printed for Longman, Hurst, Rees, Orme, and Brown, 1822–24), quoted in Richard Wallaschek, *Primitive Music: An Inquiry into the Origin and Development of the Music, Songs, Instruments, Dances, and Pantomimes of Savage Races* (London: Longman's, 1893), 3. According to Wallaschek, Burchell supplies two examples of dance melodies (2).

32. Corry, *Observations upon the Windward Coast of Africa,* viii, 10–11, 153, 11, 100, 67.

33. Laing, *Travels in the Timannee,* 9, 131, 9–10, 11–12, 84–85, 187.

34. On the subject of speaking admiringly of individuals and their music, Corry, e.g., at one moment portrayed the barbarism of African music as a consequence of a luxuriant fantasy: "The Negroe's existence is almost a gratuitous gift of nature; his wants are supplied without laborious exertion, his desires are gratified without resentment, his

soul remains in peaceful indolence and tranquility, and his life glides on in voluptuous apathy and tranquil calm" (*Observations upon the Windward Coast of Africa*, 66).

35. Laing, *Travels in the Timannee*, 231, 234–35, 243–44, 251.

36. The article appeared in the June 3 issue of the *Albany Centinel*, reprinted in the New York *Daily Advertiser* on June 29, 1803. It is reproduced as part of Shane White's "Pinkster in Albany, 1803: A Contemporary Description," *New York History* 70, no. 2 (April 1989): 191–99. James Fennimore Cooper is quoted in James H. Pickering, "Fennimore Cooper and Pinkster," *New York Folklore Quarterly* 22, no. 1 (March 15, 1966): 16–17.

37. For "tom-tom beat," see Brantz Mayer, "The African Slave Trade," review of *Captain Canot; Or, Twenty Years of an African Slaver*, by Captain Canot, *De Bow's Review* 18 (January 1855): 20. See also reference to "the Congo dance" and drumming ("their music often consists of nothing more than an excavated piece of wood, at one end of which is a piece of parchment") in Isaac Holmes, *An Account of the United States of America, Derived from Actual Observation, during a Residence of Four Years in that Republic . . .* (London: Caxton Press, 1823; reprint, New York, Arno Press, 1974), 332. For the jawbone, see Francis de La Porte Comte de Castelnau, "Comte de Castelnau in Middle Florida, 1837–38," *Florida Historical Quarterly* 26 (July 1947–April 1948): 316; Harriet A. Jacobs, *Incidents in the Life of a Slave Girl, Written by Herself*, ed. L[ydia] Maria Child; reprint ed. Jean Fagan Yellin (1861; reprint, Cambridge, Mass.: Harvard University Press, 1987).

38. Reverend John Dixon Long, *Pictures of Slavery in Church and State, including Personal Reminiscences, Biographical Sketches, Anecdotes, Etc. Etc* (Philadelphia: The Author, 1857), 18; Lewis W. Paine, *Six Years in a Georgia Prison: Narrative of Lewis W. Paine . . .* (Boston: Bela Marsh, 1852), 179–80.

39. Colonel James R. Creecy, *Scenes in the South, and Other Miscellaneous Pieces* (Washington, D.C.: Thomas McGill, 1860), 20–21.

40. Higginson, *Army Life in a Black Regiment* (1870; reprint, New York: W. W. Norton, 1984), 188. J. B. T. Marsh, *The Story of the Jubilee Singers, with their Songs*, 7th ed. (London: Hodder & Stoughton, 1877).

41. Fredrika Bremer, *America of the Fifties: Letters of Fredrika Bremer*, selected and ed. Adolph B. Benson (New York: American-Scandinavian Foundation, 1924), 97.

42. Herbert Aptheker, *Nat Turner's Slave Rebellion, Together with the Full Text of the So-Called "Confessions" of Nat Turner Made in Prison in 1831* (New York: Humanities Press for the American Institute for Marxist Studies, 1966).

43. Prior references to drum bans now resurface as inchoate indications of rhythmic danger, as in Paine's reference to the Georgia statute prohibiting drums and horns Paine (*Six Years in a Georgia Prison*, 140–41).

44. Poe, "A Tale of the Ragged Mountains," in *The Complete Tales and Poems of Edgar Allan Poe*, with an introduction by Hervey Allen (New York: Modern Library, 1938), 679–87.

45. Herman Melville, "Benito Cereno," in *Billy Budd and Other Stories*, with an intro-

duction by Frederick Busch (London: Penguin Classics, 1986), 167; Edward Widmer, "African American Percussion in the Twentieth Century" (paper presented at the annual meeting of the American Studies Association, Boston, October, 1993). Thanks to Ed Widmer for supplying me with a copy of his paper.

46. Matthiessen writes, "In 'The Service' Thoreau seems groping to convey his recognition, which was to grow increasingly acute, that a deep response to rhythm was his primary experience" (*American Renaissance: Art and Expression in the Age of Emerson and Whitman* [New York: Oxford University Press, 1941], 84). On Emerson, see Matthiessen, 53 and 46n.

47. Gumbo Chaff, A.M.A. First Banjo Player to the King of Congo, *The Ethiopian Glee Book* (Boston: Elias Howe, 1848). The titles appear in bk. 3; the reference to abolitionism appears in bk. 1. In *Yesterdays: Popular Song in America* (New York: W. W. Norton & Co., 1979), Charles Hamm discusses the emphasis on melody in minstrel song particularly in the nineteenth century (116–17). Eric Lott, in contrast, argues in his book *Love and Theft* for a more subversive reading of the rhythmic character of minstrelsy, focusing on its early expressions. Lott suggests that white musicians had already recognized black music as rhythmic form, then proceeds with an imaginative analysis that links black rhythm with Adornian notions of repetition. While it is true that minstrels emphasized nonmelodic and percussive instrumentation associated with southern slaves and occasionally involved rhythmic ideas in the songs themselves, it is also true that the main feature of emphasis was melodic form and song form. It seems more appropriate, therefore, to observe blackface as a step in the formation of the modern discourse of black rhythm rather than as its full-blown expression. See Lott, *Love and Theft: Blackface Minstrelsy and the American Working Class* (New York: Oxford University Press, 1993), 171–95. For a discussion of the musical dimensions of blackface minstrelsy, see Hans Nathan, *Dan Emmett and the Rise of Early Negro Minstrelsy* (1962; reprint, Norman: University of Oklahoma Press, 1977).

48. Nina Silber, *The Romance of Reunion: Northerners and the South, 1865–1900* (Chapel Hill: University of North Carolina Press, 1993).

49. Simon Gikandi, *Maps of Englishness: Writing Identity in the Culture of Colonialism* (New York: Columbia University Press, 1996), 50.

50. As George W. Stocking, Jr., puts it, Spencer's work was broad both in point of view and influence, having "largely structured the thinking of the two generations of American social scientists before about 1920" ("The Dark-Skinned Savage: The Image of Primitive Man in Evolutionary Anthropology," in *Race, Culture, and Evolution: Essays in the History of Anthropology,* with a new preface (1968; reprint, Chicago: University of Chicago Press, 1982), 117.

51. Warren Dwight Allen. *Philosophies of Music History* (New York: American Book Co., 1939), 115.

52. Charles Darwin, *The Descent of Man and Selection in Relation to Sex,* rev. ed. (New York: Rand, McNally & Co., 1874), chap. 13.

53. Darwin comments: "We see that the musical faculties, which are not wholly de-

ficient in any race, are capable of prompt and high development, for Hottentots and Negroes have become excellent musicians, although in their native countries they rarely practice anything that we should consider music. Georg August Schweinfurth, however, was pleased with some of the simple melodies which he heard in the interior of Africa" (ibid., 565). Robert Lach's comment appears in Allen, *Philosophies of Music History,* 206–7.

54. Alexander Rehding, "The Quest for the Origins of Music in Germany Circa 1900," *Journal of the American Musicological Society* 53, no. 2 (2000): 345–85.

55. Adam Kuper, *The Invention of Primitive Society: Transformations of an Illusion* (New York: Routledge, 1988), 5. For background on the imperialist strains in the emergence of musicology and ethnomusicology, see my introductory essay, cowritten with Philip V. Bohlman, "Music and Race, Their Past, Their Presence," in *Music and the Racial Imagination,* ed. Radano and Bohlman, 1–53. See also Georgina Born and David Hesmondhalgh, "Introduction: On Difference, Representation, and Appropriation in Music," in *Western Music and Its Others: Difference, Representation, and Appropriation in Music,* ed. Georgina Born and David Hesmondhalgh (Berkeley and Los Angeles: University of California Press, 2000), 1–58.

56. Karl Bücher, *Arbeit und Rhythmus,* 2d rev. and expanded ed. (1896; reprint, Leipzig: B. G. Teubner, 1909). A translated excerpt appears in Bojan Bujic, *Music in European Thought, 1851–1912* (Cambridge: Cambridge University Press, 1988).

57. Johann Nikolaus Forkel, *General History of Music* (1788), excerpted in Enrico Fubini, ed., *Music and Culture in Eighteenth-Century Europe,* trans. and ed. Bonnie J. Blackburn (1986; reprint, Chicago: University of Chicago Press, 1994), 223.

58. John Frederick Rowbotham, *A History of Music,* 3 vols. (London: Trübner & Co., Ludgate Hill, 1885), 1:1, xvi, 2–4, 7, 185–87. Rowbotham's biography appears in Albert E. Wier, comp. and ed., *The MacMillan Encyclopedia of Music and Musicians in One Volume* (New York: MacMillan Co., 1938), 1587. Similar views appeared in the work of Willy Pastor, who theorized the soporific and hypnotic effects of "primitive" rhythms ("Music of Primitive Peoples," in *The Annual Report, Smithsonian Institution* [1912], 679–700, originally published in *Zeitschrift für Ethnologie* 42 [1910]: 654–75); and Richard Wallaschek, who contended that "the origins of music must be sought in a rhythmical impulse in man" (*Primitive Music,* 230). Wallaschek, in particular, drew the relationship of rhythm and origins to a primordial impulse emanating from an unchanging African world. See Warren Dwight Allen, *Philosophies of Music History* (New York: American Book Co., 1939), 197, 225n. Wallaschek begins his book with a discussion of the African propensity for rhythmic playing. The essence of sound, once associated with pure melodic affect, now traced backward to rhythmic impulses revealing a discernibly "colored" origin. The book includes a comprehensive bibliography of European travelogues, which represents the primary basis of Wallaschek's evidence. It is noteworthy, finally, that Wallaschek's views of African musical significance did not carry over to the African-American slave songs. These New World practices, he argued, were merely weak imitations of white singing.

59. Hans von Bülow's comments appear in Allen, *Philosophies of Music History,* 195. Wallaschek *Primitive Music,* 144, quoted in Rehding, "The Quest for the Origins of Music," 359.

60. F. Rochlitz, "Of the Different Effect of Music on the Cultivated and the Uncultivated," *Dwight's Journal of Music* 3, no. 14 (July 9, 1853): 105–6. Possibly, though it is unlikely, the author may have been Johann Friedrich Rochlitz, the Leipzig-based music critic who died in 1842.

61. A. B. Ellis, *The Land of Fetish* (London: Chapman & Hall, 1883), 117, 170–71, 269–70. Richardson, *Narrative of a Mission to Central Africa,* xiv; Laing, *Travels in Timannee,* 298.

62. One striking parallel is the drawing of Henry Stanley aiming a pistol as an African crosses a river with Stanley's supplies. The caption reads: "Look out, you drop that box, I'll shoot you" (*How I Found Livingstone: Travels, Adventures and Discoveries in Central Africa* [1872; reprint, New York: Arno Press, 1970], 643). The image recalls Frederick Douglass's tale of Covey shooting a slave in the water in *Narrative of the Life of Frederick Douglass, an American Slave, Written by Himself,* ed. Benjamin Quarles (1845; reprint, Cambridge, Mass.: Harvard University Press, Belknap Press, 1960).

63. Stanley, *How I Found Livingstone,* 621–22.

64. George Rogers Howell, *Bi-Centennial History of Albany: History of the County of Albany, New York, from 1609 to 1886* (New York: W. Munsell & Co., 1886), 725–26; Alice Morse Earle, "Pinkster Day," *Outlook* 49 (April 28, 1894): 743–44; Joel Munsell, *Collections of the History of Albany, from Its Discovery to the Present Time* . . . (1865–71), reprinted in Eileen Southern, ed., *Readings in Black American Music,* 2d ed. (New York: W. W. Norton, 1983); William Chauncey Fowler, "The Historical Status of the Negro in Connecticut," in *Historical Magazine and Notes and Queries concerning the Antiquities, History and Biography of America,* ed. Henry B. Dawson (Charleston: Year Book of the City of Charleston, 1900), 21–22. It is no coincidence that writers at this point began to reconceptualize the history of African-American music with increasing emphasis on the drum bans to suggest an uncontainability of black essence. Rhythm became certifiably constituted as a threat in scholarly discourse, signifying in sonic form the seeds of inexorable black rebellion. See George W. Cable, "The Dance in Place Congo," *Century Magazine* 31, no. 4 (February 1886): 517–32, where he refers to police banning of the bamboula and the suppression of the calinda in 1843 (525, 527).

65. For the literature surrounding the controversial challenges of Joel Chandler Harris, see chap. 3, n. 83.

66. Marianna Torgovnick, *Gone Primitive* (Chicago: University of Chicago Press, 1990); Gail Bederman, *Manliness and Civilization: A Cultural History of Gender and Race in the United States, 1880–1917* (Chicago: University of Chicago Press, 1995).

67. Tarzan is welcomed into the tribe after having killed the bully who attacked his surrogate mother. He was victorious through the help of his deceased father's knife, which he had found, without knowledge of its origins, in his parents' abandoned house. As such, Tarzan embodies a unity, combining primal strength and civilized cunning—

"The Light of Knowledge" that names the chapter. Only then can he descend into his dark past, finding his way through the originary light of ape drumming. Rhythmicized civilization becomes the ultimate agent of regression, the tool by which the rational-minded, when encountering the black (w)hole, gets hot. Edgar Rice Burroughs, "The Light of Knowledge," in *Tarzan of the Apes* (1914; reprint, New York: Ballantine, 1990), 61, 88.

68. Arthur Granville Bradley, "A Peep at the Southern Negro," *Macmillan's Magazine* 39 (November 1878): 61.

69. Edward L. Ayers, *The Promise of the New South: Life after Reconstruction* (New York: Oxford University Press, 1992), 21–22.

70. Bradley, "A Peep at the Southern Negro," 61; Ayers, *The Promise of the New South,* 22.

71. Ayers, *The Promise of the New South,* 154. See also Nell Painter, *Standing at Armageddon: The United States, 1877–1919* (New York: W. W. Norton, 1997).

72. Ayers, *The Promise of the New South,* 157, 33.

73. On emplotment, see Hayden White, *The Content of the Form: Narrative Discourse and Historical Representation* (Baltimore: Johns Hopkins University Press, 1987), 44, 52, 67.

74. David Harvey, *The Condition of Postmodernity* (Oxford: Basil Blackwell, 1989), 252.

75. Paul Gilroy, "Sounds Authentic: Black Music, Ethnicity, and the Challenge of a *Changing Same,*" *Black Music Research Journal* 11, no. 2 (fall 1991): 121.

76. The quotation appears in an unsigned note from the early 1870s that Toni P. Anderson discovered while conducting research in the Fisk Archives in Nashville. She speculates that it was probably from a speech by one of the Jubilee singers ("The Fisk Singers: Performing Ambassadors for the Survival of an American Treasure, 1871–1878" [Ph.D. diss., Georgia State University, 1997], 85). Thomas P. Fenner makes a similar observation: "It may be that this people which has developed such a wonderful musical sense in its degradation will, in its maturity, produce a comoser who could bring a music of the future out of this music of the past. At present, however, the freedmen have an unfortunate inclination to despise it, as a vestige of slavery" (in Mrs. M. F. Armstrong and Helen W. Ludlow, *Hampton and Its Students,* with fifty cabin and plantation songs, arranged by Thomas P. Fenner [New York: G. P. Putnam's, 1874; reprint, Chicago: Afro-Am Press, 1969], 182). The song portion of this publication was republished several times. See, e.g., Fenner, comp., *Cabin and Plantation Songs, as Sung by the Hampton Students* (New York: G. P. Putnam's Sons, 1886).

77. George L. White, the Fisk choral conductor, was on the faculty of Fisk University. His arrangements were subsequently transcribed by the New York–based church musician Theodore Seward, who prepared them for publication. The first written presentation of the Fisk repertory appeared as a section of the chronicle of their success: J. B. T. Marsh, *The Story of the Jubilee Singers: With Their Songs,* 2d ed. (London: Hodder & Stoughton, 1875). For a brief biography of Seward, see Dena J. Epstein, "Theodore Seward," in *The New Grove Dictionary of American Music,* ed. Hitchcock and Sadie, 4:198.

78. "The Jubilee Singers," *Dwight's Journal of Music* 33, no. 17 (November 29, 1873): 131–32.

79. Quoted in Anderson, "The Fisk Jubilee Singers," 99. The quotation appeared originally in the *Newark Evening Courier* (ca. January 1872). Anderson indicates in a footnote that she found the article in the Jubilee Singers Scrapbooks, Special Collections, Fisk University.

80. W. E. B. Du Bois, *The Souls of Black Folk,* introduction by Saunders Redding (1903; reprint, Greenwich, Conn.: Fawcett Premier, 1961), 182.

81. Daniel C. Littlefield, Houston A. Baker, Jr., Henry Louis Gates, Jr., and Gloria Naylor (panelists), "The Afro-American Writer and the South," in *The Southern Review and Modern Literature, 1935–1985,* ed. Lewis P. Simpson, James Olney, and Jo Gulledge (Baton Rouge: Louisiana State University Press, 1987), 136.

82. "Praise Concert," *New York Journal* (December 6, 1871). Quoted in Anderson, "The Fisk Jubilee Singers," 98.

83. "Fisk Jubilee Singers," *Folio* 8, no. 5 (May 1873): 134. Toni Anderson elaborates on the ambivalences in white reporting:

> Whether or not the company was capable of producing "high art" was an issue often addressed by critics. One noted that the troupe's rendition of "Home, Sweet Home" had never been "more exquisitely rendered," but qualified the comment with this statement: "We do not mean, of course, in a modern 'artistic' sense, but we do say that no rendition we ever heard went deeper into the heart of the audience, or more perfectly conveyed the sentiment of the lines." Another wrote, "While the singing did not of course evince what is called high art and the music was simple, it was melodious, was sung in good taste, and evinced rare musical capacity."
>
> ("The Fisk Jubilee Singers," 98)

84. The reference to black speech as baby talk appears in "Philologists in Session," *Critic* 4 (July 18, 1885): 30.

85. An interesting analysis of the evolution of black religious hymns and style (including detailed discussions of vocal timbres and descriptions of rhythmic approaches) appears in "American Negro Hymns," *Musical World* 63 (July 17, 1886): 461–62.

86. Fanny D. Bergen, "On the Eastern Shore," *Journal of American Folk-Lore* 2, no. 7 (October–December 1889): 296; C. H. F., an occasional correspondent, "Negro Worship and Music: The Notes of a Foot Traveler," *New York Times,* February 25, 1877, 5.

87. See Marion Alexander Haskell, "Negro 'Spirituals,'" *Century Magazine* 58, no. 4 (August 1899): 577. Sentimental portrayals proliferated across the pages of magazines around this time. To give but two examples, writing for the New York–based religious newspaper the *Independent* in 1878, Mary W. Porter of "Franklin, St. Mary's Parish, Louisiana," tells the tale of hearing "some genuine negro songs" in a cloying language so overburdened with nostalgia that what ostensibly serves to document a recent performance becomes a testimony to the enduring myth of folk purity ("Some Genuine Negro Songs," *Independent* 30, no. 1536 [May 9, 1878]: 1). In the case of "Johann Tonsor"

(most likely the pseudonym of the Louisville ethnographer Mildred Hill), the timeless past is the same thing as one's personal memory. Recalling the "tenderly pathetic," "uncouthly melancholy" Negro songs of a Kentucky "boyhood," Hill regresses into Tonsor's fictional "childhood in the South." Song triggers memory, and suddenly, "he is again a child in the cradle, and his faithful old 'mammy,' as she rocks him, bends over him in the firelight and croons" ("Negro Music," *Music* 3 [December 1892]: 119–22). Hill's comments are interspersed with incipits of transcriptions that she presumably prepared. The identity of Johann Tonsor is discussed in Michael Beckerman, "Dvořák as Prime Mover, Sitting Duck and More," *New York Times,* November 17, 2002, Arts and Leisure sec., 30, 40.

It is noteworthy, finally, that this musical sentimentalism predominant in the North tended to racialize white southerners. An essay from 1881 concludes: "There is a wide field for interesting study in the South; both among the poor whites and blacks." A. S. Dobbs, "Our Southern Work," *Zion's Herald* (August 4, 1881): 382. A comment during the time of the Civil War graphically speaks to this northern condescension. According to a "Professor Cairnes of Dublin" (author of the study *Slave Power*), whites of the South include a large class of savages: "In the Southern States no less than five millions [*sic*] of human beings are now said to exist in a condition little removed from savage life. . . .Combining the restlessness and contempt for regular industry peculiar to the savage, with the vices of the *prolétaire* of civilized communities, these people make up a class at once degraded and dangerous. . . . Such are the 'mean whites' or 'white trash.' " Cairnes's observations are subjected to debate by Edmund Kirke [James Robert Gilmore] in his essay "The Poor Whites of the South," *Harper's New Monthly Magazine* 29 (June–November 1864): 115–24; the quotation by Cairnes appears on 115.

88. For "figurated" hymns, see "American Negro Hymns," 461; for "peep squirrel" and "Jinny put de kettle on," see Daniel Webster Davis, "Echoes from a Plantation Party," *Southern Workman* (Hampton, Va.) 28 (February 1899): 57, 59; for "peculiar" scale alterations, see Charlotte Forten Grimke, "Folksongs of the Sea Island Negroes," *Independent* 46 (November 1, 1894): 1401–2.

89. Celia M. Winston, "Genuine Negro Melodies—Weird Hymnology of the Colored People of the South," *New York Times,* August 8, 1887, 6.

90. William Eleazar Barton, "Recent Negro Melodies," *New England Magazine* 19, no. 6 (February 1899): 708. See also Barton's earlier essays in the same magazine, "Old Plantation Hymns," 19, no. 4 (December 1898): 443–56, and "Hymns of the Slave and the Freeman," 19, no. 5 (January 1899): 609–24. For other postbellum references to call and response, see, e.g., David C. Barrow, Jr., "A Georgia Corn-Shucking," *Century* 24 (October 1882): 873–78. Barrow supplies musical notation and details the players in a corn-shucking ritual, notably the "general," or "caller-out," whose improvised lines inform the character of responses among the workers: "Rabbit hi oh," "Oh ho ho ho," "Homer Riley ho" (875). In "The Old Way to Dixie," *Harper's New Monthly Magazine* 86 (January 1893): 165, Julian Ralph, a visitor to the South, describes blacks loading flour barrels:

"Every such refrain serves to time their movements." The anonymous author of "American Negro Hymns" explains how "the precision in time of a negro congregation is absolutely marvelous for so untrained a body. Every note is hit with exquisite accuracy, and in their antiphonal hymns, when the men sing a line and the women respond, the intervals are perfect." See also Lillie E. Barr, "Negro Sayings and Superstitions," *Independent* 35 (September 17, 1883): 1222–23, which characterizes responsorial singing during a funeral on John's Island, S.C., and includes a brief excerpt of congregational dialogue.

91. Henry Cleveland Wood, "Negro Camp-Meeting Melodies," *New England Magazine* 6, no. 1 (March 1892): 60–64, quotation on 60. Wood also discusses nighthawks in the same essay and includes several transcriptions. For "among the sable singers" (detailing a "colored revival"), see E. L. Guial, "Among the Sable Singers," *Western Monthly* 2 (December 1869): 421–26. Among the many quotations of song texts are those published by Emma Backus in several installments in *Journal of American Folk-Lore,* from vol. 10, no. 37 (April–June 1897) to vol. 11, no. 40 (January–March 1898); and Porter, "Some Genuine Negro Songs," 1. Unlike preachers, moreover, exhorters were not confined to the sacred testimony of the Bible. See Frank Dingley, "The Negro Creed and Hymnology," *Musical Record* (Boston) 128 (March 12, 1881): 382. For shouts, see Abigail M. Holmes Christensen, "Spirituals and 'Shouts' of Southern Negroes," *Journal of American Folk-Lore* 7 (April–June 1894): 154–55, who describes the shout as a "magic circle," deriving from African fetish worship; and Grimke, "Folksongs of the Sea Island Negroes," 1401–2. Grimke relates shouts to Dahomeyan performances that she witnessed at the Chicago Exposition (1402). Higginson supplies an update of his earlier comment in "The First Black Regiment," *Outlook* 59 (July 2, 1898): 521–31; see esp. 526, 529. For earlier depictions, see Edmund Kirke [James R. Gilmore], "A Merchant's Story," *Continental Monthly* 3 (February 1863): 206–22; W. L. Coan, "Among the Contrabands," *Southern Workman* (Hampton, Va.) 13 (April 1884): 46; "The Freedmen at Port Royal," *North American Review* 101, no. 208 (July 1865): 1–28, esp. 8, 10; H. G. Spaulding, "Under the Palmetto," *Continental Monthly* 4 (August 1863): 188–203, which includes an extended short discussion on 196–200 featuring several transcriptions. For "dusky floor," see Hamilton Jay, "Music among the Negroes," *Musical Record* (Boston) 263 (December 1883): 8; for foot washing, see "Folk-Lore and Ethnology. Beliefs and Customs Connected with Death and Burial," *Southern Workman* (Hampton, Va.) 26 (January 1897): 18–19.

92. The quote "his face was convulsed" is from Edward Smith King, "The Great South. A Ramble in Virginia from Bristol to the Sea," *Scribner's Monthly* 7 (April 1874): 645–74, quotation on 669. An article published in *Southern Workman* announced a new initiative on the part of the Hampton Folk-lore Society to detail preachers' sermons and prayers. See "Folk-Lore and Ethnology," with sections on "Religious Experience" and "Sermons and Prayers," *Southern Workman* (Hampton, Va.) 24 (April 1895): 59–61. For examples of black singing practices appearing at the time in rural churches in Montgomery, Ala., see C. H. F., "Negro Worship and Music," 5. Revivals are discussed with

great detail in Guial, "Among the Sable Singers" and in many later accounts. Mrs. Octavia V. Rogers Albert, *The House of Bondage; Or, Charlotte Brooks and Other Slaves* (New York: Hunt & Eaton, 1891), 12. See also Vivian Njeri Fisher, "Octavia Victoria Rogers Albert," in *Black Women in America: An Historical Encyclopedia,* ed. Darlene Clark Hine (Brooklyn, N.Y.: Carlson Publishing, Inc., 1993), 16–17.

93. In the same essay, the anonymous author acknowledges, speaking of the same writer, "but he is inclined to attribute a considerable portion of them to the negroes themselves." He then proceeds to speculate on how the tunes may have derived from whites, but were then distorted. See "American Negro Hymns," 461–62.

94. O. W. Blacknall, "The New Departure in Negro Life," *Atlantic Monthly* 52 (November 1883): 680.

95. C. H. F., "Negro Worship and Music," 5.

96. William Eleazar Barton, "Hymns of the Slave and the Freedman," *New England Magazine* 19, no. 5 (January 1899): 609. The essay includes musical and lyrical notations of twenty-seven songs.

97. See Charlotte Forten Grimke's discussion of children singing ("they were delighted to sing for us, and sang in low plaintive tones, with a peculiar swaying motion of the body which made their singing all the more effective"), in "Folksongs of the Sea Island Negroes," 1401.

98. Wood, "Negro Camp-Meeting Melodies"; Tonsor [Hill], "Negro Music"; William Eleazar Barton, "Old Plantation Hymns," *New England Magazine* (December 1898), "Hymns of the Slave and the Freedman," and "Recent Negro Melodies"; Haskell, "Negro 'Spirituals,' "; Armstrong and Ludlow, *Hampton and Its Students.*

99. Julia Neeley Finck, "Mammy's Song: A Negro Melody," *Music* (Chicago) 13 (March 1898): 604–5; the arrangements of "Turn Back Pharaoh's Army" and "Go Down, Moses" appeared in *Dexter Smith's* 2 (July 1873): 20.

100. Charles Carleton Coffin, *Four Years of Fighting: A Volume of Personal Observation with the Army and Navy, from the First Battle of Bull Run to the Fall of Richmond* (Boston: Ticknor & Fields, 1866), 230; See Fenner's "Preface to Music," which begins the "Cabins and Plantation Songs" section of Armstrong and Ludlow, *Hampton and Its Students,* 182.

101. Barton, "Old Plantation Hymns," 448; Tonsor [Hill], "Negro Music," 121; Alice Mabel Bacon, "Work and Methods of the Hampton Folk-Lore Society," *Journal of American Folk-Lore* 11 (January–March 1898): 17–21.

102. For banjoes, see Bradley, "A Peep at the Southern Negro," 67; for uses of the jawbone of a mule, see Alcée Fortier, "Customs and Superstitions in Louisiana," *Journal of American Folk-Lore* 1, no. 2 (July–September 1888): 136–37. Fortier's description suggests percussive uses; the reference to a "violin" may have been a form of ridicule. Toward the end of his essay, "Among the Peaches," William C. Lodge describes a group of partygoers dancing in a ring to two fiddlers and brass band (*Harper's New Monthly Magazine* 41 [September 1870]: 511–18). For the reference to the "French harp," see James Lane Allen's "To the Editors of *The Critic,*" *Critic* 4 (January 5, 1884): 10.

103. Ernest Ingersoll, "The City of Atlanta," *Harper's New Monthly Magazine* 60 (December 1879): 43. An illustration appears on 42. For "among the city negroes," see "Folk-Lore Scrap-Book: Negro Superstition concerning the Violin," *Journal of American Folk-Lore* 5 (October–December 1892): 330.

104. Jay, "Music among the Negroes," 8. Jay's reference to the "dusky warrior" and a construction resembling an African drum makes the veracity of this particular portrayal somewhat suspect. But it does indicate that blacks were performing such instruments at the time and whites were noticing it. Fortier, "Customs and Superstitions," 136. The fiddler's drumming appears in Barrow, "A Georgia Corn-Shucking," 878.

105. Christensen, "Spirituals and 'Shouts' of Southern Negroes," 155.

106. " 'The Cake Walk: A Richmond Christmas Festival," *Frank Leslie's Illustrated Newspaper* (New York) 31, no. 796 (December 31, 1870): 261–62; "Origin of the Cake Walk," *Freeman* (Indianapolis) 9, no. 48 (November 27, 1897): 3. In the first of these two sources, the cakewalk is linked to Africa by way of association. The festivals, the author reports, are "loud and long enough to have come from the six-foot throat of a giraffe" (262). Moreover, discussions of ragtime effectively blurred the distinction between music and dance. Rupert Hughes's "A Eulogy of Ragtime" explores the etymology of the term "rag," showing its usage to describe a dance, a way of dancing, and the new musical genre (*Musical Record* [Boston] 447 [April 1, 1899]: 157–59). Other characterizations of black performance suggest newness in the imposition of white discourses, as in Grimke's aforementioned commentary on the Sea Island songs in comparison to the performances of Dahomey musicians at the Chicago Exposition ("Folksongs of the Sea Island Negroes," 1402).

107. In *Scenes in the Life of Harriet Tubman* (Auburn, [N.Y.]: W. J. Moses, Printer, 1869), Sarah H. Bradford writes:

> Harriet wanted to get away without letting her ["poor old mother"] know, because she knew that she would raise an uproar and prevent her going, or insist upon going with her, and time for this was not yet. But she must give some intimation to those she was going to leave of her intention, and send such a farewell as she might to the friends and relations on the plantation. These communications were generally made by singing. They sang as they walked along the country roads, and the chorus was taken up by others, and the uninitiated knew not the hidden meaning of the words. When dat ar ole chariot comes, / I'm gwine to lebe you; / I'm boun' for de promised land, / I'm gwine to lebe you.
> (16–17)

The quotation beginning "the freedmen" can be found in Armstrong and Ludlow, *Hampton and Its Students,* 182.

108. Bacon, "Work and Methods of the Hampton Folk-Lore Society"; Jonathan Baxter Harrison, "Studies in the South: VIII," *Atlantic Monthly* 50 (October 1882): 479.

109. The phenomenon of blacks in blackface was one such accommodation that had become appealing, undoubtedly in some revisionist way, among African-

Americans. Ingersoll, e.g., describes "a vender of patent medicine" at which "two negroes—genuine negroes, but corked in addition to make themselves blacker!—
dressed in the regulation burlesque style familiar to us in the minstrel shows at the
North, are dancing jigs, reciting conundrums, and banging banjo, bones, and tambourine" ("The City of Atlanta," 43). Still a fine source on the early black performing ensembles and situations is Marshall Stearns and Jean Stearns, *Jazz Dance: The Story of
American Vernacular Dance* (New York: Schirmer, 1964). The authors address interracial performances on 66. See esp., pt. 3, "The Vernacular." For a discussion of black
coon songs, see Howard W. Odum, "Folk-Song and Folk-Poetry as Found in the Secular
Songs of the Southern Negroes," *Journal of American Folk-Lore* 24, no. 93 (July–September 1911): 255–94. Among the recorded examples is Luke Jordan, "Traveling Coon"
(1927), reissued on the compact disk *The Songster Tradition* (Document Records, Vienna, DOCD-5045). Jordan's performance is a distinctly hybrid representation that in-
corporates Euro-American-based musical form. For the reference to hearing banjo
playing from outside a Kentucky saloon, see James Lane Allen, "To the Editors of *The
Critic*," 9; A comment on the appearance of black street musicians traveling in groups
across the nation appears in "Wandering Minstrels on Harlem Lane," *Frank Leslie's Illustrated Newspaper* (New York) 34, no. 862 (April 6, 1872): 60–61.

110. Ayers, *The Promise of the New South,* 373.

111. Charles Peabody, "Notes on Negro Music," *Journal of American Folk-Lore* 16
(1903): 148–52.

112. Odum, "Folk-Song and Folk-Poetry," 258.

113. Jay, "Music among the Negroes," 8; "American Negro Hymns,"; Wood, "Negro-
Camp-Meeting Melodies," 60, 62.

114. Grimke, "Folksongs of the Sea Island Negroes," 1402; Tonsor, "Negro Music."

115. "A Voodoo Festival near New Orleans," *Journal of American Folk-Lore* 10 (January–March 1897): 76; A. B. Ellis, "On Vōdu-Worship," *Popular Science Monthly* 38 (March
1891): 651–56; Christensen, "Spirituals and 'Shouts' of Southern Negroes."

116. Charles Dudley Warner, "A Voodoo Dance," *Harper's Weekly* 31 (June 25, 1887):
454–55.

117. Cable, "The Dance in Place Congo," 517–32, and "Creole Slave Songs," *Century
Magazine* 31, no. 6 (April 1886): 807–28. For background on Cable, see Ayers, *The
Promise of the New South,* 30–32, 345–49.

118. Cable, "Creole Slave Songs," 810, and "The Dance in Place Congo," 525.

119. Kodwo Eshun, *More Brilliant Than the Sun: Adventures in Sonic Fiction* (London:
Quartet Books, 1999).

120. "Chin-Music," *Frank Leslie's Illustrated Newspaper* 32 (August 5, 1871): 347;
"Philologists in Session," *Critic* (1885): 30–31.

121. Henry Edward Krehbiel, *Afro-American Folk-Songs* (1914; reprint, New York:
Frederick Ungar Publishing, 1962), 39. Krehbiel is quoting Lafcadio Hearn. Hughes, "A
Eulogy of Rag-Time," 157, 159.

122. Maud Cuney-Hare, *Negro Musicians and Their Music* (Washington, D.C.: The As-

sociated Publishers, 1936). An appendix devoted to African musical instruments highlights the foundation of a primal rhythmic influence.

Epilogue

The epigraph is taken from Du Bois's essay "Strivings of the Negro People," *Atlantic Monthly* 80 (August 1897): 197.

1. W. E. B. Du Bois, *The Souls of Black Folk,* introduction by Saunders Redding (1903; reprint, Greenwich, Conn., Fawcett Premier, 1961), 149; Arnold Rampersad, "Biography and Afro-American Culture," in *Afro-American Literary Study in the 1990s,* ed. Houston A. Baker, Jr., and Patricia Redmond (Chicago: University of Chicago Press, 1989), 199. Rampersad argues that Du Bois's theory represents the exclusive paradigm for all of modern black literature. He elaborates on this point in *The Art and Imagination of W. E. B. Du Bois* (Cambridge, Mass.: Harvard University Press, 1976), 89.

2. Du Bois, *The Souls of Black Folk* 16.

3. See, e.g., Christopher Herbert's excellent essay, "Superstitions of Culture," which introduces his book *Culture and Anomie: Ethnographic Imagination in the Nineteenth Century* (Chicago: University of Chicago Press, 1991), 1–28. See also Adam Kuper, *Culture: The Anthropologists' Account* (Cambridge, Mass.: Harvard University Press, 1999).

4. Houston A. Baker, Jr., *Modernism and the Harlem Renaissance* (Chicago: University of Chicago Press, 1987), 68; Du Bois, *The Souls of Black Folk,* 60. For a detailed investigation of the musical imagery in *Souls,* see my essay, "Soul Texts and the Blackness of Folk," *Modernism/Modernity* 2, no. 1 (January 1995): 71–95.

5. Du Bois, *The Souls of Black Folk,* 55, 57, 104, 69, 93, 95, 102, 104.

6. The quote is from ibid., 182.

7. "As the Negro rises more and more toward economic freedom," Du Bois continued, "he is going on the one hand to say more clearly what he wants to say and do and realize what the ends and methods of expression may be" (quoted in Bernard Bell, "W. E. B. Du Bois's Struggle to Reconcile Folk and High Art," in *Critical Essays on W. E. B. Du Bois,* ed. William Andrews [Boston: G. K. Hall, 1983], 112–13). Du Bois, *The Souls of Black Folk,* 181.

8. A new private touring group was formed by Frederick J. Loudin, who had been a member of the Fisk singers since 1875. See Eileen Southern, *Music of Black Americans,* 2d rev. ed. (New York: W. W. Norton, 1971), 228. This is the group that Du Bois most likely heard at Fisk in the mid-1880s. It is unclear when the chorus's ties to the school were reestablished. W. E. B. Du Bois, *Dusk of Dawn: An Essay toward an Autobiography of a Race Concept* (1940; reprint, New York: Schocken Books, 1968), 45, and *The Autobiography of W. E. B. Du Bois: A Soliloquy on Viewing My Life from the Last Decade of Its First Century* ([New York]: International Publishers, 1968), 120.

9. Shelley Fisher Fishkin, "The Borderlands of Culture: Writing by W. E. B. Du Bois, James Agee, Tillie Olsen, and Gloria Anzaldúa," in *Literary Journalism in the Twentieth Century,* ed. Norman Sims (New York: Oxford University Press, 1990), 140; David Levering Lewis, *W. E. B. Du Bois, Biography of a Race* (New York: Henry Holt, 1993), 281.

10. Rampersad, *The Art and Imagination of W. E. B. Du Bois,* 75–76.

11. Lewis, *W. E. B. Du Bois,* 140. The reference to the "ancient" suggests Africa, about which Du Bois's is appropriately dialectical. In *Dusk of Dawn,* he speaks directly to his African connection: "Living with my mother's people I absorbed their culture patterns and these were not African so much as Dutch and New England. . . . My African racial feeling was then purely a matter of my own later learning and reaction. . . . But it was none the less real and a large determinant of my life character" (115). This makes sense of the subsequent paradox: "Africa is, of course, my fatherland. Yet neither my father nor my father's father ever saw Africa or knew its meaning or cared overmuch for it. My mother's folk were closer and yet their direct connection, in culture and race, became tenuous; still, my tie to Africa is strong" (116).

12. Du Bois, "Strivings of the Negro People," 197.

13. Marcel Mauss, *The Gift: Form and Functions of Exchange in Archaic Societies,* trans. Ian Cunnison; with an introduction by E. E. Evans-Pritchard (1925; reprint, New York: W. W. Norton & Co., 1967), quoted in Natalie Zemon Davis, *The Gift in Sixteenth-Century France* (Madison: University of Wisconsin Press, 2000), 4–5.

14. Mauss, *The Gift,* 62.

15. Peter Wood, *Black Majority: Negroes in Colonial South Carolina from 1670 through the Stono Rebellion* (New York: Knopf, 1974), quoted in a reprinted excerpt in Merritt Roe Smith and Gregory Clancey, eds., *Major Problems in the History of American Technology* (Boston: Houghton Mifflin, 1998), 78–79.

16. Du Bois, *The Souls of Black Folk,* 189–90. All quotes from here to the end of this text appear in ibid., 189–91.

Index

Note: Italicized page numbers indicate figures.

Aaron (slave), 341n95

Abbate, Carolyn, 15, 16, 295nn39–40

Abbott, Benjamin: cited, 330–31n34, 333n44, 334n57; dreams of, 126; on race, demons, and religion, 334–35n58

Abdy, E. S., 342n103

abolition and abolitionists: antislavery tracts of, 146–48, 342n102; "Auld Lang Syne" and, 350n21; blackface propaganda countered by, 144–45; black music's role in, 161, 168–69, 177–78; blacks' petitions for, 108, 326–27n9; involvement as, 140, 172–73, 209, 352n34; in revivalism, 330n32; slave narrative and song collections linked to, 208–9; white fears fostered by, 244–46

Abrahams, Roger D.: on African retentions, 9; cited, 293–94n27, 302n85, 309n21, 311–12n29, 345–46n121, 359n74; on deculturation argument, 312n30; on oral traditions, 58; on playing the dozens, 343n107

absence: of cause in history, 6–7, 291n17; of documentation on black musics, 5–6; of documentation on slave songs and music, 51–52, 57–61, 93, 100; glossing over, 57–58; of materiality in slavery, 139–40; presence in, 17–18, 44–45, 52–53, 66–67; of records of slavery, 51–52, 57–61, 306n5; shadow texts of, 67–74; in whiteness, 169. *See also* silence

absolute music, 17–18, 23, 40, 41

Abundi instruments, 78–79

Abyssinian songs, *201–2,* 205

accommodation, 144, 270–72

accordion, 268

acoustemology, 95

action and activity: of black bodies, as threat, 234; black music and social, 255; instability of, 137; necessity of, 230–31. *See also* interracial exchanges

Adams, Willi Paul, 292n20

Adanson, Michael: cited, 320n83, 321nn97–98, 364–65n25; on nature and instinct, 83; on Senegalese music, 88, 239

Adas, Michael, 83–84, 317n60, 320–21n92, 320nn85–86

Addison, Lancelot, 77, 143, 318n69, 340n91

Adell, Sandra, 10, 294n30

Adler, Guido, 249, 252

Adorno, Theodor W., 44–45, 186, 357n65, 367n47

advertisements, 70–71, 102, 362n102

aesthetics: Black Arts, 303n91, 303–4n95; definitions of, 349n15, 351n31; slave, 139–40. *See also* art; sublime

affective capacities, 15–16, 22, 298n58. *See also* emotions

Africa: colonization of, 248–49; dangers in, 242–43, 249; insults in, 343n107; modern rhythm music linked to, 272–73; as mysterious, 241–42; traditions of, 64–65, 331–32n38. *See also* African music; African retentions theory; Africans

African-American musicians (postbellum): in black face, 375–76n109; instruments used by, 267–68; rhythm music of, 271–72; rise of professional, 262, 270–71; spirituals and jubilees avoided by, 269–70

African-Americans: creativity of, 362n3; economic concerns of, 256–57, 270–71, 377n7; entry into antebellum society, 109; gift giving of, 282–84; marginalization of, 73; migration of, 255–57; physical superiority of, 147; population increase of, 326–27n9; postbellum discourse on, 233–34; purification of, 180–81; unstable rhetoric of, 110–11; use of term, 287n1. *See also* black/white relations; interracial exchanges; slaves

African music: Ashantee, *200,* 204–5, 241; call and response in, 157–59; Dahomey, 254, 273; disparagement of, 204–5; Egyptian, 87, *203,* 205, 252; emergence of, 90; European music compared with, 88–89; instability of meaning of, 80–81; Kafir, 241; missionaries' views of, 76–80; musical notations of, 190, *197, 200*; as "primitive music," 92–93; recognized as music, 241; rhythm and, 238–39, 250–55, 368n58; Sudanese, 87; travel accounts of, 76–88

African retentions theory: Baraka on, 55;

basis for, 33–34; challenge to, 57–58; Du Bois on, 378n11; emergence of concept, 293–94n27; limits of, 10, 60–62; reconsideration of, 9–10; regional differences in, 65, 313n38; religion and, 59–60

Africans: assumptions about, 61–62; barbarism and savagery linked to, 179, 242–43, 253; consciousness/identity as, 65, 281; Europeans compared with, 88–89; humanity of, 86, 88; musical talents of, 147; travel accounts of, 74–75, 81, 240–44; wildness and excess linked to, 82–88, 90, 240. *See also* African music; Congolese

Afrocentrism and Afrocentricity: limits of, 10, 56–58, 61, 294n29; musicological, 33–34; reductionism of, 39; use of term, 301–2n80

Agawu, V. Kofi: cited, 295–96n42, 303n88, 317n60, 364n23; on racial difference, 35; on rhythm, 103, 238, 325n130

Albert, Octavia Victoria Rogers, 264, 373–74n92

Alexander, James Wendell, 178

Alexander, Robert J., 293n24

Allen, James Lane, 374n102, 375–76n109

Allen, Joseph, 360n84

Allen, Paul, 235

Allen, Richard, 114, 329n26

Allen, Samuel, 346n124

Allen, Warren Dwight, 367n51, 368n58, 369n59

Allen, William Francis (pseud. Marcel): background of, 360n84; cited, 338–39n81, 347–48n9, 355–56n53, 355n52, 356n54, 360n83, 361nn88–93, 362nn94–100; in Educational Commission of Freedmen, 211, *212*; family songbook of, 224, *228*; illustration of, *210*; influences on, 209–11; memory of observations of, 224, 228–29; papers of, 360n80, 361n91; perspective of,

211–14, 223, 265, 266; on ring shout, 244; transcriptions by, 223–24, *225*. See also *Slave Songs of the United States* (collection)

Althusser, Louis: on "absent cause," 291n17; cited, 290n12, 296n49, 323n114; on Marx, 293n26, 306n6; on material aspect of ideology, 289n5; mentioned, 97; on psychoanalysis, 52; on structural causality, 293n26

ambiguities: of blackness/whiteness, 2; of blues, 21; in eighteenth-century travel accounts, 87–88; of music's position, 91

American Indians, 128–29, 154, 251–52

American Philological Association, 275

Amin, Shahid, 309n21

Amiot, Joseph-Marie, *199,* 204

Anderson, Toni P., 370n76, 371n79, 371nn82–83

Andrews, Charles McLean, 316n55

Andrews, Evangeline Walker, 316n55

Andrews, William, 377n7

"animal dances," 269

antebellum period: African-Americans in society of, 109; increased importation of slaves in, 326–27n9; political economy of, 149–52; race as dimension in, 120; racial imagery in, 107–8, 119–20, 126, 128–30; rights in, 108–10, 326n7; spirituality in, 119; torture in, 149. *See also* performance practices; slave songs and music; spirituals

anthropology, 19–20, 33–35

antislavery tracts, 146–48, 342n102

Appiah, Kwame Anthony, 10, 294n29, 301n78, 320n86

Appleby, Joyce, 326–27n9

Aptheker, Herbert, 366n42

Arato, Andrew, 357n65

Arendt, Hannah, 294–95n32, 306n8, 332n40, 358n68

Armstrong, Louis: Ellison on, 1–2; perfor-

mances of, 22, 25–27, 299n65; on story, 46

Armstrong, Mrs. M. F., 370n76, 373n107, 374n98, 374n100

Arnold, W. F., 345n117

art: black culture refashioned as, 282–84; intuitive nature of, 173–74; song as, 91, 260; status of, 170; as view into life, 280–81. *See also* aesthetics

Asante, Molefi, 301–2n80

Asbury (bishop), 114

Ashantee songs, *200,* 204–5, 241

Atlanta (Ga.): performance practices in, 268

"Auld Lang Syne," 350n21

authenticity/realness: concept of, 27; debasement of, 85–86; discourse on, 173, 276–77; economic dimension of, 149–52; embodiment of, 259–60; emergence of, 40–41; fascination with/desire for, 168, 174; folklorists' construction of, 169–70, 348–49n14; instability of, 15, 40; music critics on, 261–62; in naturalism, 257–58; representation in constructing, 43; resistance in, 37; resonance in, 22, 53; self-consciousness combined with, 65, 281; of slave autobiographies, 172–73; of sound/music, 92, 107–8, 144, 166–67; in vernacular, 47–48. *See also* original and originality

Awkward, Michael, 29, 36, 43, 299–300n68, 300–301n74, 303n90

Ayers, Edward L., 271, 370nn69–72, 376n110, 376n117

Bachelard, Gaston, 306–7n12

Backus, Emma, 373n91

Bacon, Alice Mabel, 267, 270, 374n101, 375n108

Baker, Houston A., Jr.: on Black Arts, 303n91; on "black (w)holes," 39; on blues, 24, 37; cited, 294n28, 299n63,

Baker, Houston A., Jr. (*continued*)
300–301n74, 300n73, 304n106, 362n5,
371n81, 377n1, 377n4; on creativity,
362n3; on cultural production, 262; on
dream of black form, 94, 277; on Du
Bois, 280; on experience, 231–32; on
modern virtuosity, 136; on movement,
362n4; on musical notations, 261;
White's tropology and, 38
Bakhtin, Mikhail, 30
Baldwin, James: on black music, 45,
304n106; cited, 287n, 289n9, 295n33,
304n104; on thinking of oneself as
black/white, 4
Balibar, Étienne, 109, 113, 293n26, 327n12
ballads, 172–74, 186–87
bamboula, 369n64
Bamboula! (Gottschalk), 246
banjoes and banjo players: Jefferson on,
264; origin of, 328n17; popularity of,
141, 268; references to, 375–76n109;
testimony of, 112–13
baptism, 69–70
Baptiste (musician), 159, 204, 308–9n20,
345–46n121
Baraka, Amiri (LeRoi Jones): as Black Arts
writer, 39; on body and music, 104; on
"changing same," 3, 40; cited, 287n2,
291n14, 300n73, 302n84, 303n87,
304n98, 307n13, 324n125; on continuity in sound, 307n14; on drumming,
101–2; on music, 55, 325n131; perspective of, 307n14; on rhythm, 58, 308–
9n20
barbarism and savagery: Africans linked
to, 179, 242–43, 253; appeal of, 170–71,
211–13, 365–66n34; blackness linked
to, 233–34; civility juxtaposed to, 245,
249–55; creativity and, 88; dances
linked to, 69, 314–15n47; Euro-Americans linked to, 93; excessive emotions
linked to, 168; highland Scot linked to,
171; limited intelligence in, 91; music

linked to, 86–87, 100–101, 239;
pinkster linked to, 243; rhythm linked
to, 223, 233–34, 240–42, 251–52, 273–
75; slaves linked to, 69–70, 71; southerners linked to, 371–72n87
Barr, Lillie E., 372–73n90
Barrow, David C., Jr.: background of,
345n120; cited, 357n66; on corn shucking, 263, 268, 372–73n90; on language,
186; transcriptions by, 372–73n90
Barry, Phillips, 344–45n116
Barthes, Roland, 3, 16, 19, 136, 295n41,
362n99
Barton, William Eleazar: on black song and
dance, 265; cited, 374n98, 374n101; on
slave songs, 263–64, 372–73n90; tran-
scriptions by, 266, 267, 374n96
Bartram, William, 72, 316n56
Bascom, William R., 303n88
Basso, Keith H., 298n58, 322nn110–11
Bayard, Ferdinand-M., 310–11n26
beauty, 179, 180, 181
Beavers, Herman, 43
Becker, Alton L., 19–20, 297n52
Becker, Judith, 19–20, 297n52
Beckerman, Michael, 371–72n87
Beckford, Wilham, 159, 345–46n121
Bederman, Gail, 254–55, 369n66
Bedouin music, 86, 89
Beecham, John, 241, 365n30
Beeching, Jack, 316n54
Beethoven, Ludwig von, 174, 211, 351–
52n32
Belafonte, Harry, 14
Belcher, Supply, 355n52
Bell, Bernard, 377n7
"Bell Da Ring" (song), 224, *225–26*
"Belle Layotte" (song), 214, *220*
Belyamani, Hatim, 359n77
Bendix, Regina: on authenticity, 173, 348–
49n14; cited, 349n16, 350n22, 351n29,
356n57; on Lowell, 351n26
Benjamin, Walter: cited, 297n51, 304n106,

306n8, 332n40, 338n78; on memory, 40, 45; resonance concept and, 53, 121, 294–95n32; on translational acts, 137, 358n68

Benson, Adolph B., 336n63, 366n41

Benson, Louis F., 131, 333n42, 336n67, 337n73

Bent, Ian, 296n47

Bergen, Fanny D., 262, 371n86

Berlin, Edward A., 364n14

Berlin, Ira: on African ethnicity, 313n38; on African traditions, 64–65; approach of, 65–66; cited, 308n17, 323n116, 326–27n9; on diversity, 63–64, 309n22; on Herder, 349n16; on slave populations, 309nn24–25

bestiality, 254. *See also* barbarism and savagery

Bhabha, Homi: on Afrocentrism, 294n29; cited, 298n60, 306n9, 322n106, 322n109, 326n4, 338n79, 344n114; on experience of colonialism, 92–93; on time lag, 23; on translational acts, 137

Bibb, Henry, 118, 145, 330n32, 331n36, 341n96

bi-musicality concept, 204

birds and birdsong: blacks as, 178, 261; circles linked to, 306–7n12; in origins of music, 249; slave songs as, 72, 142, 148, 316n55; Surinam songs as, *197*, 358n72

Birnbaum, Johann, 91

Black Arts Movement: aesthetics of, 303n91, 303–4n95; as influence, 37; metaphysics of, 35–36; racialist advocacy of, 309n21; writers of, as influence, 32

Blackburn, Bonnie J., 321n102, 368n57

Black Codes (West Indies), 102

black culture: in Caribbean vs. North America, 56–57, 308n18; distinctiveness of, 231–32; instability of, 30–31, 43–44, 323n113; music's role in, 11–12;

refashioned as art, 282–84; slave performance represented as, 106; social construction of, 280–81

black expressive modernism: diversity and exploration in, 267–69, 275–77; emergence of, 262; innovation and borrowings in, 264–65, 271; musical notation's role in, 265–66; music critics on, 261–62; power of, 255–56, 276–77; racial differences in responses to, 272; repetition and crossing in, 231–32; rhythm in, 245–47; spirituals avoided in, 269–70; as superior and illegitimate, 258; white appropriations of, 235–38, 263. *See also* African-American musicians (postbellum); blues; jazz; swing

blackface: adoption of, 375–76n109

blackface minstrelsy: on American Indian, 154; commentaries on, 175, 352–53n36; parodies of, 104; persistence of, 257; playfulness and, 150; racism of, 6; rhetoric of, 72, 144–45, 253–54; rhythm and, 246–47, 367n47; slave song compared with, 168–69, 348n10; spirituals compared with, 177–78; theme of slave suffering in, 146. *See also* Sambo stereotype

Blacking, John, 312n33

black music criticism: challenges of, 232–34; emergence of, 35–36; on rhythm's naturalism, 276–77

black musics: accessibility of, 183; approach to, 11–13; betweenness of, 188–89; blackness as center of, 22–23; centrality of, 42–44, 111, 232, 279–85; concept of, 89–90, 116–17, 262, 288n1; construction of, 18–20, 24–25, 26–27, 109; context of, 120–21, 155; countermodernity claimed by, 20, 24, 298n53; demystification of, 59; as exceptional/rarefied/exclusive, 114–15, 179–81; healing through, 89, 180–81, 247–48,

black musics (*continued*)
321n100; hearing of, in public sphere, 24–25, 31, 108–15, 239–40, 257–58, 262; imaginary links in, 7–8; instability of, 52, 80–81; as interracial, 2–3; magical miracle of, 13, 36, 266; modern transnational conception of, 246–47; naming of, 107, 139; otherness of, 8–9, 101, 180–81; power of, 138, 229, 255–56, 257–58, 262280; "prehistory" of, 74–93; publication of, 113; racial formation of, 139–48; reconstruction of, 4–5, 27, 282–84; as romantic recovery, 168–77; significance of, 3–4, 55–56, 232, 255–56; stabilizing representation of, 258; syncretic view of, 35; texting of, 280–81; truths of, 47–48; vocal sound of, 14–15; white appropriations of instrumental, 235–36; whites on excesses of, 143–44; whites' recognition of, 140–41, 155–56, 168, 239–40, 347–48n9. *See also* dances; difference; instruments; performance practices; resonances; slave songs and music; voices

Blacknall, O. W., 264–65, 374n94

blackness: ambiguities of, 2; barbarism and savagery linked to, 233–34; black music's effecting of, 20; collective we of, 32; construction of, 35–36, 41–42; containment of, 184–86, 188, 261–64, 269–70, 371–71n87; deracination of, 289n7; economic and social presence of, 326–27n9; fact of, 152, 155; feminism aligned with, 182, 184; instability of, 107–8, 111, 284–86; maintaining distinction of, 211–13; musical determinism on, 55–56; music's story held together by, 58; as myth, 3; preachers associated with, 119, 331n35; produced in contrast to whiteness, 8–11, 13, 22–23, 292n21; racial coding of, 119–20, 128–29, 134, 334–35n58;

sacred aligned with, 181–86; "sonic fiction" of, 275; sounds of, 139–40; whites' recognition of, 152–53; white worshipers and, 134–35; writing's role in, 45–46

Black Patti, 7

blacks. *See* African-Americans; slaves

Blackstone, William, 317–18n63

Black Tom (or Blind Tom), 175–77, 353n40

black/white relations: acculturation in, 107; changes in, 96; conflicts and white fears in, 244–46; economic dimension in, 149–53; gift of black songs and, 282–84; natural ability discourse and, 114; social place of antebellum, 151–52. *See also* interracial exchanges

black worship and sacred music: call and response in, 156–57; commentaries on, 183–84, 263–64; development of, 371n85; excess in, 114, 143–46, 168–69, 234; interracial influences on, 131–32; resonances of, 121, 123–24, 135; return of racial repressed in, 127–28; social significance of, 122; soundtexts of, 138. *See also* preachers; spirituals

Blassingame, John W., 291n16, 309–10n25

Blesh, Rudi, 302n84

Blight, David W., 289n8, 305n1

Blind Tom (or Black Tom), 175–77, 353n40

blues: ambiguities in, 21; criticism on, 24–25, 37; crossings in, 231

blues impulse concept, 21, 55–56, 304n98, 307n14

Bluestein, Gene, 349n17

Boas, Franz, 33, 46

boatmen's song (China), 158

Boatright, Mody C., 309n21

boat song (black), *197*

Boatwright, Howard, 352n35

Bodichon, Barbara Leigh Smith, 141, 339–40n85

body: advertisements' focus on, 71; authenticity mapped in, 259–60; as basis

for black music, 276; as commodity,
149–50, 186; notation's shaping of,
214; placeness in relation to, 94–96,
163; religious sound and, 124–32, 333–
34n52; rhythm's origin in, 230–32,
234–35; sound of, 97–104, 106–7;
world linked to, 95. *See also* perfor-
mance practices; voices
Bohlman, Philip V., 345n120, 358n72,
362n2, 368n55
Boles, John B., 309–10n25, 330n30, 330n32,
332n41
Boller, Paul F., Jr., 350n22
Bonaparte, Napoleon, 248
Bonnefroy, Antoine, 68, 314n45
Bontemps, Arna, 48
boogie-woogie rumble, 230–31
Born, Georgina, 368n55
Boskin, Joseph, 341n92
Bosman, William: on African/European dif-
ference, 81–83; cited, 318n66,
320nn78–80; perspective of, 76, 87
Bouchard, Donald F., 304n105
Bourdieu, Pierre, 290n11
Bourne, Hugh, 122
Bowdich, T. Edward: on Ashantee funeral
dirge, 204–5; on call and response,
159; cited, 345–46n121, 359n76,
365n30; transcriptions by, *200,* 241
Boyer, Horace Clarence, 31–32, 301nn75–
76
Boyer, Paul, 337n70
Bradford, Sarah H., 373n107
Bradley, Arthur Granville, 256, 370n68,
370n70, 374n102
Bradley, Joshua: cited, 330–31n34,
333nn44–45, 333nn48–51, 334nn53–
55; on race, demons, and religion,
334–35n58; on religious sound, 123–
25, 333–34n52
Brantlinger, Patrick, 293n26
brass instruments, 268, 374n102
Brazilian songs, 190

Bremer, Fredrika: cited, 331n36, 336n63,
341–42n98, 342n99, 366n41; on drums,
244; on musicality, 147, 168
Brett, Philip, 322n106
Bridenbaugh, Carl, 314n45
Brinner, Benjamin, 359–60n78
Broce, Gerald, 361n89
Brodwin, Stanley, 295n35
Brooks, Cleanth, 318n64, 349n15
Brother, Barbara, 318n67
Brown, David, 339n82
Brown, John, 172
Brown, John Mason, 357n62
Brown, Lawrence, 166, 346–47n1, 347n8
Brown, Reginald, 312n33
Brown, Robert Carlton, 223
Brown, William Wells, 145, 341n96
Browne, (Mr.), 87, 321n96
Bruce, Dickson D., Jr., 332n41, 335–36n62
Bücher, Karl, 251, 368n56
Bujic, Bojan, 368n56
Bull, Jacqueline, 339n84
Bullen, Frank T., 345n117
"Bully Song," 235, 363n12
Bülow, Hans von, 252, 369n59
Burchell, W. T., 241, 365n31
Burke, Edmund, 317–18n63
Burke, Emily P., 153, 331n36, 339n84,
344n109
Burke, Patrick, 298n56, 345n120
Burleigh, Harry T., 7
Burnaby, Andrew, 112, 328nn17–18
Burney, Charles, 90, 321n102
Burnim, Melonee V., 31–32, 301n76
Burroughs, Edgar Rice, 254–55, 369–70n67
Butlan, Ibn, 238
Butler, Jon: on African holocaust, 331n37;
on African religion, 59–60, 61, 62;
cited, 309nn24–25, 312n30, 334n56; on
great awakening, 335n59; on spiritual-
ity, 119
Byrd, William, 59, 99, 151, 342–43n106
Byron, Don, 7

Cable, George Washington, 274–75, 369n64, 376nn117–18

Cabot, Sebastian, 317n62

Cairnes, John Elliott, 371–72n87

cakewalk, 269, 375n106

calinda, 369n64

call and response: communication via, 161–62; in conversion ceremony, 134; in corn shucking, 263, 372–73n90; dynamism of play in, 162–63; examples of, *158,* 160, 316n56; origins of, 156–59, 344–45n116; pervasiveness of, 160–61; recordings of, 345n120

Calvin, John, 17

Campbell, John, 354nn45–46

Campbell, Joseph, 306–7n12

camp meetings. *See* baptism; black worship and sacred music; conversion; evangelicalism and revivals; jubilees; spirituals

Camus, Raoul, 314n45, 324n126

Candler, Allen D., 314n44

Cannan, Edwin, 317–18n63

cannibalism, 254, 273–74

"Cannibal Love" (song), 254

Canot (captain), 179

Cantwell, Robert, 305n111

capitalist economies: African-American concerns in, 256–57, 270–71, 377n7; cultural loss and, 312n30; play's role in, 149–52. *See also* commodity

Carby, Hazel V., 43, 300n73

Carey, Mariah, 7

Caribbean traditions: influences in, 56–57, 102; North American traditions compared with, 56–57, 308n18; sources on, 307–8n16. *See also* Haitian Revolution; Jamaican songs

Carli, Denis de: on African sound in Christian ceremony, 79; cited, 318n66; on Congolese music, 78, 319nn74–75; perspective of, 76; travels of, 318–19n70

Carlyle, Thomas, 169

Carmen Jones (film), 14

Carr, Mancy, 299n65

Carrington, John F., 324n125

Carruthers, Mary, 294n31

Carter, Edward C., II, 311n27

Carter, Landon, 59, 311n27

Carter, Robert, 112, 311n27, 323n115

Carwardine, Richard J., 348n12

Case, Sue-Ellen, 322n106

Casey, Edward S., 94–95, 97, 322n110

Cassuto, Leonard, 310–11n26, 324n121

Caulkins, Nehemiah, 310–11n26

Cavell, Stanley, 169–70, 348n13

Chaff, Gumbo, 367n47

Chakrabarty, Dipesh, 61, 309n21, 311n28, 313–14n42

Chambers, Iain, 290–91n13

Chandler, James, 362n101

Channing, William Ellery, 310–11n26, 339–40n85

Chardin, Jean, 190, *195,* 316n59

Chauncey, Charles, 70, 315n49

Chen, Kuan-Hsing, 289n10

Chernoff, John Miller, 159, 312n31, 324n124, 345–46n121

Chesapeake area: African traditions in, 65; Igbo language in, 313n38; interracial performances in, 111–13

Chestnut, Mary Boykin, 184, 348n10, 356n60, 357n62

Child, Francis James, 172, 210, 211, 338–39n81, 361n88

Child, Lydia Maria, 331n36, 366n37

children: singing of, 374n97; slavery and, 60, 183

Chilean songs, 189, *190*

Chinese songs, 158, 189, *191, 199,* 204

chin music, 275

Chrisman, Laura, 296–97n50, 300n73, 357n62

Christensen, Abigail M. Holmes, 373n91, 375n105, 376n115

Christian, Barbara, 300–301n74

Christian ceremony: African sound in, 79–80; call and response in, 158–59; interracial exchanges in, 115–39, 331n37; penance in, 319n74; populism's impact on, 330n30; slave musicality and, 114; sound of, 124–27. *See also* black worship and sacred music; conversion; evangelicalism and revivals; ritual practices; spirituals

Christianity: colonialism and, 77; commitments based in, 36; dialects and, 100; difference as contradiction in, 108–9; emancipatory research and, 31–33; great awakenings in, 129, 335n59; racial categories in, 117–18; racial imagery in, 119–20, 126, 128–30; rhetoric of, 117, 329–30n29; slave practices criticized in, 69–70; slaves as property and, 322n108; slaves' participation in, 70, 115–19, 130, 330n30; travel accounts from perspective of, 76–80

Chua, Daniel K. L., 17–18, 296n45

circles and circularity: being inside/outside of, 50–51; birds linked to, 306–7n12; disruptions in, 58–59; diverse use of, 54–55; reconsideration of, 55–56, 63; repetitions/intersections in, 53–54

civility: racialized conception of, 325n129; savagery juxtaposed to, 245, 249–55; of slaves, 206–7, 211–13

civilization: African sound removed from, 87; black music as ground for discourse on, 144; jubilee's language of, 281; music as product of, 91; wildness as heart of, 82–88, 90, 240

Civil Rights Movement, 100

Claiborne, J. F. H., 153, 344n109

Clancey, Gregory, 378n15

Clapperton, Hugh, 240

class: attitudes toward white plain/poor folk, 371–72n87; harmony vs. call and response as reflective of, 159–60; race vs., 118; supernatural beliefs and, 330n32

classical music: jubilees' incorporation of, 259–61; as universal language, 173–75. *See also* Euro-American elite music

Clifford, James, 288n3

Coan, W. L., 373n91

Coffin, Charles Carleton, 266, 374n100

Cohen, Judah, 338–39n81

collectivist sentiment, 175

Collins, John A., 172, 351n25

colonialism: Africans as savages in, 242–43; challenges to, 92–93; Christianity and, 77; difference making in, 169; disciplining strategies in, 88–89; eighteenth-century views in, 80–88; figures of descent in, 273; musical notation as, 190, 204, 205–6; musical practices under, 74; quest for origins and, 248–51; rhythm in context of, 103; sense of music's power and, 101; seventeenth-century views in, 76–80; textual trail of, 75–76. *See also* Christianity

color line: doubleness and, 284; Du Bois's concept of, 278–79; as fiction, 281–82

Colpe, Carsten, 302n83

Combes, Edmond, *201–2,* 205, 359n77

commodity: musical notations as, 266; performance practice as, 175–77, 270–71; play and, 150–54; slaves as, 149–50, 186; slave songs as, 166–67, 181–82, 362n102

common, the (concept), 171, 350n22

community, 135, 136–37, 338n77

composer, cult of master, 175

Comte de Castelnau, Francis de La Porte, 339n84, 366n37

conch shell, 314n44

Condillac, Étienne Bonnot de, 321n103

Cone, James H., 31–32, 301n76

Congolese: humanity of, 88; music of, 78, 318–19n70, 319nn74–75

Conkin, Paul: on camp meetings, 129, 335nn60–61; cited, 337n72; on ecstatic practice, 337n70; on emotionalism, 336n68; on "exercises," 337n70; on great awakening, 335n59; on revivalism and music, 332n41

consciousness: folk authenticity and cultural, 175; of identity as African, 65, 281; planetary, 74, 80–81, 84, 316n58; racial, 105, 106, 139–40; seen/unseen image and, 167, 347n7; "super-," 39. *See also* double consciousness; unconscious

"Contraband" songs, 362n102

conversion: of American Indian, 128–29; discipline and, 69, 315n48; necessity of, 70; preacher's role in, 135–36; sound's role in, 132–35; as translation, 137–38

Cooke, George Willis, 352n34

"coon": use of term, 363n11

coon songs: blacks' adoption of, 271, 375–76n109; hot rhythm of, 234–35; Locke on, 237, 364n21

Cooper, James Fenimore, 243, 366n36

corn-shucking ceremony, 161, 263, 268, 372–73n90

Corry, Joseph: on African music, 240, 241–42, 249; cited, 365n28, 365n32; on fantasy of barbarism, 365–66n34

Cowley, Malcolm, 310–11n26

Crawford, Richard, 350–51n23

creative agency: barbarism/savagery and, 88; as built from denial, 231–32; in composition, 72; discourse on, 264–65; diversity of, 39, 99; naming practices and, 8–9; persistence in, 362n3; in play, 151–52, 156; possibility for, 176; presumed limit of, 86–87; recognition of, 71, 114–15, 140–41, 148; recording of, 263–64; in song making, 165–66; voice as enabling, 99–100

Creecy, James R., 244, 353–54n42, 354n46, 355n51, 366n39

Cresswell, Nicholas, 112–13, 311n27, 328n18, 328n20

Crèvecoeur, J. Hector St. John de, 311n27

Criswell, Robert: cited, 343–44n108, 344n112, 346n125, 346n128, 353n41, 354n47; on slaves' expressivity, 180

Cronon, William, 361n86

"Cross Road Blues" (Johnson), 362n5, 363n8

crossroads/crossings: black music in, 257–58; black sound at, 232–34; emigration and, 255–57; in hyphenated identity, 135; modern discourse on, 248–49; repetition paired with, 231–32; in resonances, 107–8; of rhythm in public sphere, 236–37; sacred songs of racial, 177–86; transience and, 362n4

Crowley, Daniel J., 312n30

Crunden, Robert H., 363n9

Cruz, Jon, 305n1

cultural relativism, 33–34, 79, 170

cultures: artwork and, 280–81; capitalist economies' impact on, 312n30; circle of, 54; containment of slaves', 98; European perceptions of, 240–41; interracial exchanges in constructing, 113; music's role in, 90–91, 250–55; play in construction of, 149–52; poetry as defining expression of, 349n15; power of, 320n81; race's effect on national, 183; sound as means of constructing, 104. *See also* art; black culture

Cuney-Hare, Maud, 33, 157, 276, 301–2n80, 376–77n122

Dahlhaus, Carl, 351n31

Dahomey drummers, 254, 273

dances: Africanizing commentary on, 273–75; barbarism and savagery linked to, 68–69, 314–15n47; evil linked to, 334–35n58; idolatry linked to, 69–70, 314–

15n47; interracial influences on, 112–13, 328nn17–19; interracial participation in, 153; learning of, 265; modern construction of, 269; nineteenth-century travel accounts on, 141; in pre- and post-Revolutionary U.S., 103; as threat, 115–16. *See also* "animal dances"; cakewalk; jigs; minuets, Congo; shouts

Dandridge, Dorothy, 14

Daniel, Oliver, 355n52

Danielson, Virginia, 359–60n78

dark/light hierarchy, 184–86, 253–54. *See also* racial hierarchy

D'Arusmont, Frances Wright, 341n94

Darwin, Charles, 249–50, 367–68nn52–53

Dash, Julie, 14, 295n37

"dat thing," 213, 361n92

David, Paul A., 309–10n25

Davidson, Arnold I., 362n101

Davidson, Cathy N., 327n11

Davies, Samuel, 70, 315nn49–50, 329–30n29

Davis, Anthony, 7

Davis, Charles T., 291n16, 305n2

Davis, Daniel Webster, 372n88

Davis, David Brion, 317n60, 327nn10–11

Davis, John, 113, 328n20, 353n40

Davis, Miles, 30, 38

Davis, Natalie Zemon, 283, 378n13

Dawson, Henry B., 369n64

Day, James, 349n15, 351n30

"Day of Judgment, The" (song), 214, *216*

De Bow, James Dunwoody B., 340n87

Declaration of Independence, 110

deconstruction, 7, 289n10

deculturation argument, 312n30

DeLillo, Don, 237

"De Nigger's Banjo Hum" (song), 247

Dennison, Sam, 363n10

"De Rattle of De Bones" (song), 247

Derrida, Jacques, 87, 91, 297n51, 321n95, 357n62

descent: displacement's intersection with, 272–73; new beginning in, 247; reinforcement of, 261–63; in social theory terms, 248–55; use of term, 233–34, 363n7

Dett, Nathaniel, 338–39n81, 343n107

dialects: African and Scottish, 173; as baby talk, 261, 275, 371n84; blackface, 154; disparagement of, 213; Lowell's use of, 351n26; white's recognition of slaves', 70, 100

diaspora: Afrocentric view of, 34; call and response in, 159; Gilroy's theory of, 39–42; rhythm as emanating from, 239–40

Diawara, Manthia, 43, 294n28, 302n82

Didimus, Henry, 246

difference: African sound and, 77, 78–79; assumptions of, 8–10, 43–44; celebration and transcendence of, 232, 279–80, 282; codification of African/European, 80–85, 90, 101; as commodity, 149–63; concept of, 42; evidence of, 24; fetish of, 177–78; imperialism in representing, 248–49; instability of, 12–13; interruption of, 257–58; lies that suffuse theories of, 35; logic of, 21, 23–24, 44; maintenance of, 92–93; master/slave relation in construction of, 95–98, 104; musical, 106–7, 139–48, 155–56, 271–77; performativity of, 137–38; power of, 229; race and sound linked in, 238–47; recognition/denial of, 134–35; reinventions of, 292n21; repeated return of, 87; resonance of, 11–12; in revolutionary and religious context, 108–10; sameness (or in-betweenness) implied by, 21, 137, 284–85; signification of, 21–22; in slave song collection, 213–14, 223–24; slaves' production of, 121–22; whites' fascination with, 168. *See also* black musics; racial categories

Dill, Charles, 296n47, 322n106
Dingley, Frank, 373n91
disciplining strategies: in colonialism, 88–89; conversion and, 69, 315n48; of masters, 323n115
discourse: on authenticity/realness, 173, 276–77; in black music criticism, 232–34; black music in context of, 4–5; on civility, 325n129; on creative agency, 264–65; on crossroads/crossings, 248–49; on harmony, 252; on interracial exchanges, 235–36; listening to resonance in, 44–45; nationhood constructed in, 110–11; power of, 23–24; role in music's making, 42. *See also* language
displacement, of black music: concept of, 28–29, 255; examples of, 258–59; musical notation and, 261; primitivism and African origins' intersection with, 272–73; of songs from performance practices, 190; of sound in writing spirituals, 185–86
Dix, John R., 331n36, 338n80, 342n100
Dje Dje, Jacqueline Cogdell, 31–32, 301n76
Dobbs, A. S., 371–72n87
Dodd, William E., 350n20
Doerflinger, William Main, 345n117
Dorman, James H., 363n11
double consciousness: of black music, 8–9; concept of, 43, 279, 292–93n23; as exclusive paradigm for literature, 377n1; twoness as black sound in, 282; of whites, 144, 169
doubleness: as black magic, 279; in gift giving, 283–84; in meanings of songs, 160–63, 177–78, 343n107; representation and, 280–81; in travel accounts, 87–88; use of term, 344n115
Douglass, Frederick: antislavery text of, 342n102; autobiography of, 49–51, 54, 254; on black dancing and music, 43–44; cited, 305nn2–3, 332n40; as influ-

ence, 54, 305n1, 348n11; Lowell on, 172–73; memory of, 224, 228; on relational circumstances, 107; on slave shooting, 369n62; on slave world, 120–21; on song's meanings, 343n107
Dow, Lorenzo, 122, 331n36
Doyle, Laura, 350n20
Drake, Daniel, 178, 353–54n42
Drake, Francis, 317n62
dreams and dreamwork: concept of, 73–74; deferral of, 230, 232, 277; musical instrument in, 334–35n58; place in, 94–96; religious sound in, 126–28; sonic projection as, 96–97; textual fragments compared with, 93–94
drinking songs, 189, *190*
drums and drummers: Africanizing commentary on, 273–75; banning of, 101–2, 254, 308–9n20, 366n43, 369n64; construction of, 268, 375n104; danger, violence, and hostility linked to, 241–42, 244–47, 253, 273–75; in evolution theory, 251–52; judicial records on, 68–69; missionaries on African, 78–80, 319n72; myth of, 102–3; nineteenth-century references to, 141; talking, 324n125; in Tarzan series, 255; techniques of playing, 268–69; travel accounts on, 238–39, 242–44; at World's Columbian Exposition, 254, 273. *See also* pinksters
Du Bois, W. E. B.: on African connection, 378n11; on black music, 3, 44; on body and music, 104; cited, 289n8, 298n53, 338–39n81, 360n83, 371n80, 377n4–6, 377nn1–2, 378n12, 378n16; on double consciousness, 43, 279, 292–93n23; on economic freedom, 377n7; on gift giving, 282–85; influences on, 305n1; on Jubilee Singers, 260; mentioned, 165; musicality in text of, 280–81; quoted, 377n; on rhythm, 237, 254; on slave songs, 209, 352n33; subversive logic

of, 279–80; on touring group, 377n8; vision of, 278–79, 284–85

Du Cille, Ann, 43

Du Halde, Jean-Baptiste, 189, *191*

Dundes, Alan, 309n21, 338–39n81

Durrell, Henry Edward, 246

Du Tertre, 159, 345–46n121

Dvořák, Antonin, 174, 265, 352n33

Dwight, John Sullivan: activities of, 352n34, 361n87, 361n88; backing for, 360–61n85; on Foster, 364n15; as influence, 211; on music as universal language, 174–75; on music's social effect, 352–53n36; on soul, 352n35; on "spiritual," 355n52

Dwight's Journal of Music: advertisements in, 362n102; black music essays in, 185, 352–53n36, 353nn37–39; on black sound covering white sonic space, 148; on Blind Tom, 175–77; contributors to, 209; on Jubilee Singers, 260; on rhythm as unmusical, 252

Dyson, Michael Eric, 299–300n68

Eagleton, Terry, 306n6

Earle, Alice Morse, 369n64

Eaton, Clement, 350n20

economy of loss concept, 23–24

education: in music, 160, 346n122; music effected by, 262–63, 270

Educational Commission of Freedmen, 211, *212*

Edwards, Brent Hayes, 43, 299n66, 346–47n1

egalitarianism, 108–12, 356n58

Egyptian music, 87, *203*, 205, 252

Eights, James, 325n128

Eliade, Mircea, 302n83

Elkins, Stanley M., 309n23

Ellen, Roy, 344n115

Ellingson, Ter, 204, 359n75, 359–60n78

Ellington, Duke, 237, 364n20

Elliott, Emory, 327n11

Ellis, A. B., 253, 369n61, 376n115

Ellis, Alexander J., 306n10

Ellison, Ralph: on Americans and race, 2, 288–89n4; on Armstrong, 1–2; on black singing, 291n14, 350n21; on blues impulse, 21, 304n98, 307n14; cited, 287n, 288n2, 292–93n23, 292nn22–23, 298n56, 364n22; jazz-based silences of, 17; language of, 44; on making life swing, 238; on "prefabricated" blacks, 8

Ellsworth, W. L., 331n36, 336n63

Elson, Louis C., 352n33

Emancipation Proclamation, 352n34

Emerson, Edward Waldo, 350n22, 367n46

Emerson, Ralph Waldo: abolitionism and, 172; cited, 348n12; on "common," 171, 350n22; on double consciousness, 292–93n23; on folk songs, 350–51n23; friends of, 352n34; influences on, 170; on rhythm, 246; on social reform, 169; on transcendence, 171–72

Emmann, Veit, 19–20

emotions: apartness and, 97; in conversion, 133; documentation of, 336n68; God's presence in, 125–26; music's link to, 351n30; in performance practices, 154; possibilities in, 151; religious sound and, 124–30; in vernacular, 182; voice linked to, 95; whites' perception of excessive, 114, 143–46, 168–69, 234. *See also* affective capacities; evangelicalism and revivals; feelingfulness, concept of; hotness

Engerman, Stanley L., 309–10n25

Enlightenment philosophy, 108–9, 326n7. *See also* dark/light hierarchy; other and otherness

enslaved: use of term, 154

entertainment, 14, 270–71

Epps, Platt (Solomon Northrup), 147, 341–42n98, 360n80

Epstein, Dena J.: on absence of documentation, 5–6; on advertisements, 102; on Africanist expressive tradition, 56–57, 307–8n16; on Allen, Ware, and Garrison, 360–61n85, 360n84, 361n88; on call and response, 159; cited, 291n15, 314–15n47, 314n44, 328n20, 329n25, 345–46n121, 348n10, 353–54n42, 354n44, 356n60, 357n63, 360n82, 364nn24–25, 365n27; on dance, 328nn18–19, 329n21; on instruments, 101, 308–9n20, 324nn125–26, 328n17; on interracial exchanges, 336–37n69; on island music, 308n18; mentioned, 121; on musical notations, 357–58n67; on planters' accounts, 311n27; on rhythm, 58; on Seward, 370n77; on slave assemblies, 314n46, 315n48; on slave religion, 315n48; on slave song collections, 209, 360n80; sources of, 68–69; on spirituals, 132, 338–39n81, 355n52, 355–56n53

Equiano, Olaudah, 145, 239, 310–11n26, 364–65n25

Erlmann, Veit, 297n52, 312n33

Eshun, Kodwo, 376n119

essence of black music: assumptions about, 55, 60–61; challenge to, 51, 101–2; concept of, 3–4, 57; persistence of, 27, 38–39, 41–42; rhythm as basis for, 276–77

essentialism, 4–5, 13, 35–36, 41–42

etic/emic binarism, 294n31

Euro-American elite music: African music compared with, 88–89; archetypes of, 246; black music in context of, 121; challenges to dominance of, 176–77, 205–7, 260–61; concepts of, 103; dominance of, 28–29, 89–90, 309n21; Du Bois's interest in, 281; formal rhetoric of, 81, 90; new musicology on, 18–19; primitive rhythm distinguished from, 250–55; role of, 16, 91; slave song collection within/without, 213; slaves' performance of, 71; as universal language, 174–75; world music distinguished from, 190, 204. See also classical music

Europe, James Reese, 7, 24, 237–38, 299n61, 364n22

Europeans: Africans as viewed by, 80–88; Africans compared with, 88–89; colonial imagination of, 248–51

evangelicalism and revivals: abolitionism in, 330n32; auditory experience of, 123–27, 333–34n52; black music's role in, 122, 332n41; call and response in, 156–57; contradictions in, 169; cultural origins of rituals of, 331–32n38; description of, 129–32; in-betweenness of, 137; interracial exchanges in, 115–39, 331n37; race projected onto, 137–38; racial imagery in, 119–20, 126, 128–30; rhythm in modern, 272. See also black worship and sacred music; conversion; hymns; preachers

evil: color coding of, 119–20, 128–29, 134, 334–35n58; in dreams, 126; racial sound linked to, 116; rhythm linked to, 235–36

exceptionalism: of black musics, 114–15, 179–81; black sound embedded in, 108

exoticism: blackness linked to, 34–35; as other, 303–4n95; in religious ritual, 129. See also difference; "foreign musics"

experience: black music's concentration of, 21–22; centrality of black, 279–80; of colonialism, 92–93; of completion, 22–23; diversity of slave, 63–65; expression of, 15–16; hermeneutics of black, 39; memory of lived vs. observed, 224, 228–29; musical determination of, 40–41; oversimplification of, 10; subjects' emergence through, 42; use of term, 288n3. See also materiality expressive practices: in African traditions, 64–65; call and response in, 156–57; as economic asset, 149–53; emergence of, 98–99; implications for whites, 148; literary theory's perspective on, 36–37; place constructed in, 96–97; play in construction of, 150–53; signifying linked to, 37; as threat, 115–39. *See also* black expressive modernism; musical expression

Fabre, Geneviève, 293–94n27
Fairfax, Thomas, 311n27
Falconer, A. F., 318n64
Family Songs (Allen family), 224, *228*
Fanon, Frantz: on blackness, 107, 152; cited, 304n102, 307n14; focus of, 325n1; on racial consciousness, 105, 106; on rhythm, 43
Farish, Hunter Dickinson, 311n27, 328n19
"Fascinating Rhythm" (Gershwin), 364n20
Fawcett, Benjamin, 315n50
feelingfulness, concept of, 22, 298n58. *See also* emotions
Feld, Steven: on call and response, 157; cited, 294n31, 295–96n42, 297n52, 322nn110–11; on feelingfulness, 22, 97, 298n58; investigations by, 19–20; on Kaluli, 325n129, 344n115; on sound of place, 95; on sound structure, 325n129; on vocal knowledge, 16
Felton,Mrs., 144, 341n93
feminism: blackness aligned with, 182, 184
Fenner, Thomas P., 266, 270, 370n76, 374n100
Ferrari, G. G., 357–58n67
Ferris, Ina, 350n20
Ffirth, John, 330–31n34
fiddles and fiddlers: evil linked to, 334–35n58; noted in ads for runaway slaves, 71; origin of, 328n17; popularity of, 112, 141, 268; references to, 268, 374n102; tales about, 153, 344n109

Fields, Barbara J., 86, 320–21n92
Fields, Dorothy, 237, 364n20
Filene, Benjamin, 305n111
Fillon, Anne, 296n48
Finck, Julia Neeley, 266, 374n99
Firestone, David, 324n122
Fisher, Dexter, 303n92
Fisher, Vivian Njeri, 373–74n92
Fishkin, Shelley Fisher, 43, 281–82, 377n9
Fisk University: choral director of, 260, 370n77; Jubilee Concert of, 352n34; Jubilee Singers of, 244, 259–61; music at, 247, 281; touring group and, 377n8
Fithian, Philip Vickers, 112, 311n27, 323n115, 328n19
Fliegelman, Jay, 327n11
Floyd, Samuel A., Jr., 37–38, 54, 303n93, 306n11
Fogel, Robert W., 309–10n25
folklore: authenticity constructed through, 169–70, 175, 305n111, 348–49n14; imperial dimension of, 349nn17–18; otherness established by, 173; popularity of, 170–72, 209, 210–11; rhythm and, 276–77; sentimentalism in, 261–64, 269–70, 371–71n87; sermons and prayers in, 373–74n92
folk music: commentary about, 272–73; education's effect on, 262–63, 270; harmony in, 252; theories of white origin of, 28, 338–39n81. *See also* "foreign musics"; slave songs and music; spirituals
Foner, Philip S., 351n25
Fonton, Charles, 190, *196*
Foote, William Henry, 335n60
"foreign musics": black music as, 273–75; German approach to, 248, 250; invention of, 190, 204; rhythm as unmusical in, 252; sameness/otherness of, 205–6; transcriptions of, 188–90, *190–203*. *See also* "primitive music"
Forkel, Johann Nikolaus, 91, 251, 321n102, 368n57

Fortier, Alcée, 268, 374n102, 375n104
Foster, George G.: on black physicality,
147; on blacks and beauty, 179, 180,
181; cited, 341n94, 341–42n98, 354–
55n48; on hotness, 237, 364n19; on in-
struments, 354n46
Foster, Stephen, 146, 364n15
Foster, Susan Leigh, 322n106
Foucault, Michel: cited, 295n34, 296–
97n50, 298n58, 299n62, 304n105,
312n34, 316n57, 320n82, 348–49n14,
351n30; on history, 62; mentioned, 30,
45; on social domain, 298n54
Fowke, Francis, 204
Fowler, William Chauncey, 369n64
Fox, Aaron A., 295–96n42
Fox, John, 317n62
Fox-Smith, Cicely, 345n117
Franklin, James, 328n18
Franklin, John Hope, 301n76, 329n28
Frazier, E. Franklin, 302n83, 312n30
Fredrickson, George M., 341n92, 356n55,
356n58, 363n12
freedom: blacks' petitions for, 108, 326–
27n9; economic, 377n7; Hughes on,
230; sacred linked to, 178–79; stability
of instability as basis for, 282, 284–85
Freedom on My Mind (film), 324n122
French harp, 374n102
Freud, Sigmund, 293n26
Frézier, Amédée, 189, *190*
Friedman, Susan Stanford, 292n21
Frith, Simon, 297n52
Fubini, Enrico, 321nn102–3, 322n104
Fukui, Katsuyoshi, 344n115
Fulop, Timothy E., 292n19, 330n31
Fuss, Diana, 38, 303n94
"Futuristic Rhythm" (Fields and McHugh),
364n20
Fux, Johann Joseph, 91

Gabbard, Krin, 303n93
Gaines, Kevin, 302–3n86, 363n12

Gallay, Alan, 330n30
gangsta rap, 28
Garretson, Freeborn, 114, 329n25
Garrison, Lucy McKim: abolitionism of,
209; cited, 338–39n81, 347–48n9, 355–
56n53, 356n59, 361nn88–89; as influence, 266; on transcriptions, 186–87,
357–58n67; transcriptions by, 360n83.
See also *Slave Songs of the United
States* (collection)
Garrison, Wendell Phillips, 209
Garrison, William Lloyd, 145, 172, 209
Garst, John F., 157, 336–37n69, 345n119,
346n122
Gates, Henry Louis, Jr.: on authenticity,
305n1; on Black Arts aesthetics,
303n91, 303–4n95; on black voice, 108;
canon making of, 30; cited, 291n16,
300–301n74, 301nn78–79, 303n89,
304n107, 305n2, 320n86, 320n91,
326n5, 333n43, 349n15, 362n1, 371n81;
on deconstruction, 7; on Fanon, 326n3;
as influence, 303n93; on orality,
303n92; on signifying, 292n19,
343n107; on speaking/writing, 45–46;
on "superconsciousness," 39; theory
and vernacular linked by, 37; White's
tropology and, 38
Gattina, R. R. F. F. Michael Angelo of, 318–
19n70, 318n66
Gebhardt, Eike, 357n65
General Collection of Voyages and Travels
(ed. Pinkerton): on African music, 76–
80; context of, 74–76; noise used in,
92–93
Genovese, Eugene, 324n121, 336n68
Gergits, Julia, 318n67
Gershwin, George, 237, 364n20
Gewehr, Wesley M., 315n49
Giaghi (people), 78
Gibbon, Edward, 317–18n63
Gienapp, William E., 348n12, 351n24
gift giving, 282–85

Gikandi, Simon, 249, 319n77, 367n49

Gilbert, Humphrey, 317n62

Gilliat, Simeon, 7

Gilman, Caroline Howard, 341n94, 360n80

Gilmore, James Robert: on black music, 178; cited, 343–44n108, 344n112, 353–54n42, 355n50, 371–72n87, 373n91; on slave characteristics, 180

Gilroy, Paul: cited, 298n53, 299n64, 300n73, 370n75; on cultural expression, 259; on diaspora, 39–42; on musical criticism, 304nn96–97, 304n99, 304n103; on "special property," 25, 299n64

Gode, Alexander, 293n25

"God Got Plenty o' Room" (song), 214, *217*

"Go Down, Moses" (Faulkner), 266, 374n99

Godwyn, Morgan, 69, 314–15n47, 318n68

Goehr, Lydia, 304n100, 325n129

Goodale, Mark, 318n65

Gooding-Williams, Robert, 289n8, 305n1

"Goo-goo Eyes" (song), 271

Gossett, Thomas F., 317n60

Gottschalk, Louis Moreau, 246

Gould, Stephen Jay, 317n60

Gourlay, Kenneth, 103, 325n129

Gramsci, Antonio, 13

Grandy, Moses, 310–11n26

"great awakening," 129, 335n59

Great Britain: songs of, 172, 350–51n23

Greenblatt, Stephen, 313–14n42

Greene, Jack P., 307–8n16, 311n27

Greenfield, Elizabeth, 352–53n36

Grimke, Charlotte Forten, 273, 372n88, 373n91, 374n97, 375n106, 376n114

Grimm, Jacob, 172

Grimm, Wilhelm, 172

Grossberg, Lawrence, 296–97n50, 300n73, 357n62

Guha, Ranajit, 58, 309n21

Guial, E. L., 373n91, 373–74n92

Gullah dialect, 213

Gulledge, Jo, 371n81

Gunning, Sandra, 43

Gutman, Herbert, 309–10n25

Gwin, James, 128–29

Haitian Revolution, 102, 151, 244, 326–27n9

Hakluyt, Richard, 75, 316n54, 317n62

Hall, Baynard R., 161, 183, 339–40n85, 346n127, 356–57n61

Hall, Francis, 142, 340n86

Hall, Stuart, 10, 19, 289n10, 294n28, 296n49

Haller, Charlotte, 329n27

Hamer, Fannie Lou, 100, 324n122

Hamilton, Alexander, 68, 314n45

Hamm, Charles, 160, 346n122, 367n47

Hampton Folk-lore Society, 266, 373–74n92

Hampton University, 247

Hanly, B. R., 362n102

Hare, Maud Cuney. *See* Cuney-Hare, Maud

Harlem Renaissance, 302nn83–84, 343n107

harmony: of black voices, 180–81, 247–48; introduction of, 159–60; as perfection of sound, 178–79; racial discourse on, 252

Harootunian, Harry, 362n101

Harper, Michael S., 31–32, 301n76

Harper, Phillip Brian, 32, 301n78

Harris, Joel Chandler, 254, 339n83, 369n65

Harris, William Tell, 340n86

Harrison, Frank, 316n59, 345n120, 357–58n67, 358n69, 358n71, 359n73

Harrison, J. A., 275

Harrison, Jonathan Baxter, 270, 375n108

Hart, Francis R., 349–50n19, 350n20

Harvard Musical Association, 361n88

Harvey, David, 258, 324n123, 370n74

Haskell, Marion Alexander, 262–63, 266, 270, 371–72n87, 374n98

Hasse, John Edward, 363–64n13

Hatch, Nathan O., 118, 330n32, 332n41, 335n61

Hawkins, John, 316n54, 317n62

Hayden, Robert, 302n83

Haydn, Franz Joseph, 174
Hayes, Roland, 166
Head, Franklin H., 314n44
"Hear Me Talkin' to Ya" (song), 25–27,
  299n65
Hearn, Lafcadio, 291n14, 376n121
Heartz, Daniel, 301n76
"Heebie Jeebies" (song), 22
Hegel, Georg Wilhelm Friedrich, 105, 239,
  282, 365n26
Heidegger, Martin, 51, 287n, 305–6n4
Helmholtz, Hermann, 53–54, 306n10
Hemenway, Robert E., 48, 305n111
Hemingway, Ernest, 298n56
Henderson, Stephen, 39
Hentz, Caroline Lee, 340n90, 346n125,
  355n51
Herbert, Christopher, 377n3
Herder, Johann Gottfried: on body and mu-
  sic, 239; cited, 293n25, 365nn26–27; on
  folk genius, 170, 349n16; mentioned,
  174, 175; on native peoples, 361n89; on
  outsiders' music, 9
Herodotus, 76, 318n67
Herskovits, Melville J.: Afrocentrism of,
  33–34, 61; cited, 293–94n27, 303n88;
  on comparative studies, 56, 307–8n16;
  on Harlem Renaissance, 302nn83–84;
  as influence, 276
Herzog, George, 336–37n69
Hesmondhalgh, David, 368n55
Hewatt, Alexander, 68, 314n44
Hewitt, J. N. B., 340n90
Heyrman, Christine Leigh: cited, 330nn32–
  33, 330–31n34, 331–32n38, 334n56; on
  preachers, 118, 119, 331n35
Hickory, Pat, 113
Higginbotham, Evelyn Brooks, 43
Higginson, Thomas Wentworth: on ballads, 172, 173; cited, 350–51n23,
  357n63, 357n66, 361n88, 366n40,
  373n91; on culture, 338–39n81; friends
  of, 352n34; on "infinitely pathetic,"

356–57n61; as influence, 211, 265; on
  Lowell, 351nn26–27; performances at
  home of, 361n87; on preservation, 186;
  on shouts, 185, 244
Hill, Mildred (pseud. Johann Tonsor):
  cited, 374n98, 374n101, 376n114; on
  collecting black songs, 267; identity of,
  371–72n87; reminiscences of, 266; on
  savages and music, 273
Hine, Darlene Clark, 373–74n92
history: "absent cause" in, 6–7, 291n17; as
  act of un-concealment, 51; double bind
  in, 10–11; Foucault on, 62; intellectual,
  18–19, 248–50; Jameson on, 290n12;
  oversimplification of, 38–39; people's
  apparent lack of, 85–87; periodization
  in, 292n19; racial categories reproduced in, 122, 332n41; shadow texts of
  missing, 67–74; of social change, 109–
  10; social constructionist perspective
  on, 63–67. *See also* music studies
Hitchcock, H. W., 364n14, 370n77
Hodeir, André, 14, 295n37
Hoeckner, Berthold, 351n31
Hoffman, Ronald, 326–27n9
Hoffmann, E. T. A., 175
Hofstader, Richard, 309n23, 312n30
Hoganson, Kristin, 356n56
Holloway, Joseph E., 301n76
Holmes, A. T., 354n44
Holmes, Isaac, 366n37
"Home, Sweet Home" (song), 371n83
Hood, Mantle, 204, 359n75
Hornbostel, Erich M. V., 157, 301–2n80,
  345n118
Horsman, Reginald, 298n55
hotness, 237, 276, 363n10
hot rhythm: concept of, 103, 234–35; fan-
  tasies about, 253–55; modern discourse
  on, 276–77; precursors to, 245–46; sig-
  nificance of, 238; as threat, 236–37
Hot Seven (ensemble), 25, 299n65
Hottentot music, 85–86

Houstoun, Matilda Charlotte J. Fraser, 144, 183, 341n93, 355n51, 356–57n61

Howell, George Rogers, 369n64

Hubbell, Jay B., 348n12, 350n20

Hudson, Nicholas, 321n94

Hudson, Wilson M., 309n21

Huggins, Nathan Irvin, 302–3n86

Hughes, Langston: cited, 302–3n86, 376n121; on cultural production, 262; on dreams deferred, 230, 232, 277; influences on, 343n107; on rhythm, 276

Hughes, Rupert, 375n106

Hugill, Stan, 345n117

Hulan, Richard Huffman, 131, 335n59

humanity: of Africans, 86, 88; denial of blacks', 140; essence of, 91; purity of spirit in, 174, 180–81; recognition of blacks', 105–6, 108–10; rhythm as inherent to, 250–55; sacred linked to, 178–79; search for origins of, 248–50; of slaves, 98, 177–78; spirituals as grounds of, 165–66; temporal depths of sound of, 247–55

Hume, David, 85–86, 317–18n63, 320n91

Hungerford, James, 154, 339n84, 344n111, 346n125, 360n80

Hunt, Lynn, 327n14

Hunter, Robert, 112

"Hunting for the Lord" (song), 214, *219*

Huray, Peter le, 349n15, 351n30

Hurston, Zora Neale: cited, 287n, 304nn108–9, 341n96; on "dat thing," 361n92; influences on, 343n107; scholarship on, 305n111; on slave song, 145; on vernacular, 46–48, 277

Hutson (reverend), 70, 315n49

Hyde, Alan, 327n10

Hymes, Dell, 302n81

hymns: African-American influence on, 116–17, 129, 332n41; appeal of, 117; at camp meetings, 130–31; ecstatic, 337n73; Holy Spirit as source of, 125–26, 334n54. *See also* black worship and sacred music; call and response; Christian ceremony; shouts; spirituals

identity: challenges to, 27; crisis of national, 183; doubleness of racial, 284; formation of, 65, 313n38; hyphenated national, 135; instability of national, 177; specificity in, 37–38; transcendence of racial, 232, 279–80, 282; transferral of, 57. *See also* consciousness; double consciousness

ideologies: black music's role in U.S., 52; black/white relations in context of, 96; central deployments of, 306n6; characterizations of, 296n49; contradictions in, 86, 108–12, 320–21n92; material aspect of, 289n5; music's constitution in, 18–20; of race, 74, 139–40, 142–43, 168–69, 183, 236–37, 279–80; temporal-spatial axis of, 233–34

"I Got Rhythm" (Gershwin), 364n20

Illusions (film), 14, 295n37

imperialism: in representations, 248–51; romanticism linked to, 349nn17–18. *See also* colonialism

improvisation: admiration for, 357–58n67; in call and response, 161; mysteriousness of, 146–48, 151, 174; references to, 339–40n85; as threat, 176

in-betweenness. *See* sameness (or in-betweenness)

individualism: contradictions in, 149–50. *See also* self

Ingalls, Jerome, 157

Ingersoll, Ernest, 375n103, 375–76n109

instruments: of Abundi, 78–79; of Congolese, 78, 318–19n70; contempt for, 81–82; diversity of, 99, 268; fears of rhythm and, 243–44; of Hottentots, 85–86; increased use of, 267–68; laws against loud, 324n127; of Moors, 77; nineteenth-century accounts of, 141, 240–44; preferences in, 141, 339n83;

instruments (*continued*)
Siamese, 190, *193*; supernatural linked
to, 253; suppression of, 369n64
instruments, specific: accordion, 268;
bamboula, 369n64; brass, 268,
374n102; conch shell, 314n44; French
harp, 374n102; "korà," 85, 320n89; lyre,
251–52; marimba, 78, 239, 318–19n70;
percussion, 238–39, 268; piano, 268;
rabekin, 85; slide guitars, 299n66;
trumpet-grass, 85; trumpets, 68. *See
also* banjoes and banjo players; drums
and drummers; fiddles and fiddlers
intellectual history, 18–19, 248–50
intelligence: denied to blacks, 146–48, 151,
174, 175–77, 182
interracial exchanges: ambivalence about,
184; anxiety about physical and sexual, 116–17; black music as symptom
of, 113–14; black music excluded from,
114–15; in conversion ceremonies,
132–34; in dance, 111–13; implications
of, 9; medicomoral discourse on, 235–
36; racial codes on, 257; in religious forums, 115–39, 331n37; shortage of
documentation of, 336–37n69; song's
role in, 168–69; sound's role in, 129–
30; in sports, 342n104; as threat, 127–
30, 244–46; whites' recognition of,
117–18; writing about, 137–38. *See
also* black/white relations
intuitive nature: of art and music, 173–74;
of spirituals, 181–82, 229
Irish songs, 291n14, 350n21
Irving, Washington, 327n15, 339–40n85
Irwin, Mary, 235, 363n12
Isherwood, Robert, 296n48
"It Don't Mean a Thing (If It Ain't Got That
Swing)" (Ellington with Mills), 364n20
Ives, Charles, 352n35

Jackson, Bruce, 348nn10–11, 354n44,
357n62, 357n66

Jackson, George Pullen: on call and re-
sponse, 157, 158, 344–45n116; cited,
336n68, 337n73; on interracial exchanges, 336–37n69; on spirituals, 132
Jackson, Michael, 28
Jackson, Walter, 302n83
Jacobs, Donald M., 348n12
Jacobs, Harriet A., 162, 243, 331n36, 343–
44n108, 346n128, 366n37
Jamaican songs, 159, *198,* 204, 308–9n20
James, Henry, Sr., 352n34
Jameson, Fredric, 67, 290n12, 291n17,
292n19, 295n38, 296n49
Jarratt, Devereux, 123, 329nn25–26,
333n47
Jay, Hamilton, 268, 373n91, 375n104,
376n113
jazz: criticism on, 29, 34; debate over
whites' contributions to, 28, 338–
39n81; in Ellison's writing, 1–2; Hodeir
on, 14; intertextual approach to, 30; re-
visionist properties of, 37; rhythm of,
236–38; standard songs in, 364n20; as
storytelling, 25. *See also specific musicians*
Jefferson, Randolph, 112, 328n19
Jefferson, Thomas, 93, 112, 113–14, 264,
329n23
jigs, 112–13, 328nn17–19, 329n21
Jim Crow laws, 257
Johnson, Barbara, 47
Johnson, Charles A., 334–35n58
Johnson, Frank, 7
Johnson, Guy B., 301–2n80, 336–37n69
Johnson, J. Rosamond, 166, 346–47n1,
347n2, 347nn4–6, 347n8
Johnson, James Weldon: on black music
origins, 33, 36; cited, 295n35, 298n59,
346–47n1, 347n2, 347nn4–5; on ring
shout, 347n6; on spirituals, 164–66,
229; on transcriptions, 347n8
Johnson, Robert, 234, 362n5, 363n8
Johnson, Walter, 149, 291n16, 341n96

Johnston, Gideon, 311n27, 322n108

Jones, A. M., 303n87

Jones, Charles Colcock, 340n87

Jones, Hugh, 69–70, 71, 315n49, 316n53

Jones, LeRoi. *See* Baraka, Amiri Jones, William, 204, 359n75

Jordan, Luke, 375–76n109

Jordan, Winthrop D., 292–93n23, 308n17, 317n60, 320n86

Josselyn, John, 68, 71–72, 314n43, 316n54

Joyce, Joyce A., 300–301n74

Joyner, Charles W., 343n107

jubilees: African-Americans' avoidance of, 269–70; displacement acts of, 258–59; music as healing in, 247; performances at, 259–60; popularity of, 244; slave songs represented in, 262–63; success of, 260–61

Kafir music, 241

Kakongo people, 89

Kallberg, Jeffrey, 296n47

Kaluli (people), 325n129

Kant, Immanuel, 17, 94, 169, 170

Kaplan, Sidney, 326n8

Karpeles, Maud, 345n117

Keil, Charles, 290–91n13, 298n58, 325n129, 339–40n85

Kelley, Robin D. G., 43, 305n111

Kelly, Christopher, 322n105, 323n119

Kemble, Frances Anne, 168, 291n14

Kennedy, John Pendleton: on black music, 178; cited, 341n97, 354n43, 355n50; pastoralism of, 171; on slave singing, 146, 180

Kerman, Joseph, 307n15

Kierkegaard, Søren, 53

Kilham, Elizabeth, 357n62

King, Edward Smith, 373–74n92

Kinnard, J., Jr., 357n62

Kirke, Edmund, 343–44n108, 344n112, 353–54n42, 355n50, 371–72n87, 373n91

Klingberg, Frank J., 311n27, 315n48

Kloppenberg, James T., 348n13, 349n15

Knight, Henry Cogswell, 121, 332n39, 335n61, 344n113

Knox, William, 70, 100, 311n27, 315n50

Kochman, Thomas, 343n107

korà (instrument), 85, 320n89

Kousser, J. Morgan, 320–21n92

Kramer, Lawrence, 295n40, 296n47

Kraut, Alan M., 364n15, 364n18

Krehbiel, Henry Edward: on black music, 276; on call and response, 157; cited, 301–2n80, 376n121; on song development, 254, 347n3; transcriptions by, 274

Kuper, Adam, 368n55, 377n3

Kurz, Rudolph Friedrich, 143, 340n90

LaCapra, Dominick, 337–38n74

Lach, Robert, 249–50, 367–68n53

Laing, Alexander Gordon: cited, 365n33, 365nn28–29, 366n35, 369n61; on dangers in Africa, 242–43, 249; on dreams, 253; on performance practices, 240–41

Lambert, John, 130–31, 336n65, 336n68

Lander, Richard, 240, 365n28

language: of blacks, as baby talk, 261, 275, 371n84; in fetish of difference, 178; inadequacy of, 186–87; origins of, 90–92; power of, 23–24; purged from music, 173–74; racial, 6, 119–20, 126, 223–24, 325n129; retention of, 313n38; slippage between music and, 20–23. *See also* dialects; discourse

Lanman, Charles: cited, 346n126, 346n128, 354n47, 355n50, 356–57n61; on slave Christmas celebration, 183–84

Latrobe, Benjamin Henry, 311n27

Lavin, Irving, 295n40

laws, 108–10, 257

Lee, Don, 39

Lee, Edward, 345n119

Lee, Sidney, 317–18n63

legal records: as resource, 68–69, 328n17
leisure: black identity and white loss in,
153. *See also* entertainment
Le Jau, Francis, 69, 93, 99, 315n48,
322n108, 323n117
Lempriere, William, 86, 321n93
Leonard, Neil, 363–64n13, 364n15
Le Page du Pratz, M., 310–11n26, 315n49
Léry, Jean de: cited, 316n59; transcriptions
by, 189–90, *192,* 204, 358n71, 359n73
Lester, Charles Edwards, 331n36
Letley, Emma, 364n19
"Let Us Cheer the Weary Traveler" (song),
285–86
Levine, Lawrence: on African insults,
343n107; approach of, 56; cited, 292n19,
307n15, 357n62; on double image, 184;
on genre origins, 338–39n81; on revival-
ism, 66; on rhythm, 58; on second sight,
338n75; on slaves' world, 6–7, 332n41;
on spirituals, 132, 338–39n81
Lévi-Strauss, Claude, 21, 287n, 298n57
Lewis, David Levering, 282, 377n9, 378n11
Lewis, John Delaware, 335n60
Lieber, Francis, 331n36, 335n60
Ligon, Richard, 238–39, 365n27
Lindeborg, Ruth, 294n28
lining out practice, 358n72
Linn, Karen, 363n11
Lippman, Edward A., 365n26
listening: Armstrong on, 25; attentiveness
in, 2–3, 67, 284–86; to Du Bois's text,
280–81; Lévi-Strauss on, 21; negative
side of, 44–45; "regression" of, 186;
second hearing as, 121; subversive,
11–14, 27; whites' responsibility in,
283–84. *See also* resonances
literacy, 50, 149
literary theory: on black works, 28, 36–37;
critique of, 18; problematics of, 38–39;
text's dominance in, 15. *See also* text
literature: on African retentions, 293–94n27;
slave autobiographies as, 173. *See also*
travel accounts; *specific authors*

Littlefield, David C., 307–8n16, 308n17,
371n81
Little Richard, 7
Litwack, Leon, 326n6, 326n7, 326n8
Livingstone, David, 253
Lloyd, A. L., 345n117
Locke, Alain, 33, 237, 302n83, 338–39n81,
343n107, 364n21
Lodge, William C., 374n102
"logic of supplementarity" concept, 87
Lok, John, 316n54
Lomax, Alan, 312n33
Long, Edward, 86
Long, John Dixon: cited, 336n68, 339n84,
340n89, 342–43n106, 346n124, 366n38;
on ecstatic practice, 132; on patting,
243; on slaves' abilities, 151
Longfellow, Henry Wadsworth, 171, 172,
210–11, 361n88
Looby, Christopher: cited, 322n107,
327nn13–14, 329n22; on femininity/
masculinity in representation, 356n56;
on heterodoxy, 110–11, 327n15
Lord, Albert, 303n92
"Lord, Remember Me" (song), 360n83
Lorenzo, Ellen Jane, 335–36n62
Lott, Eric: on blackface minstrelsy, 144, 147,
367n47; cited, 295n38, 313–14n42; as influence, 43; on racial unconscious, 67;
on romantic racialism, 356n55
Loubère, Simon de la, 190, *193,* 316n59
Loudin, Frederick J., 377n8
Louisiana: slave dancing in, 70
Lovell, John, Jr., 343n107
Lowcountry: rhythm instruments in,
324n124; task system in, 64
Lowell, James Russell: on Douglass, 172–
73; folklore interests of, 210, 211; as
Harvard faculty, 361n88; rhetorical
gifts of, 351n26; on spirituals, 356n57
Ludlow, Helen W., 370n76, 373n107,
374n98, 374n100
Lutz, Tom, 363n7, 364nn15–16
lying up a nation, concept of, 47–48

lynchings, 257
lyre, 251–52

Mackay, Alex, 151, 342–43n106
MacLeod, Duncan J., 109, 326n7, 327nn10–11
Makdisi, Saree, 349nn17–18
Malsby, M. A., 346n125
"Mamma's Black Baby Boy" (song), 291n14, 350n21
Man, Paul de, 301n79
Mannix, Daniel, 310–11n26
marimba, 78, 239, 318–19n70
Marsh, J. B. T., 356n57, 366n40, 370n77
Marshall, Wayne, 347n3
Martin, Denis-Constant, 312n31
Martini, Giovanni Battista, 91
Marx, Karl, 165, 293n26, 306n6
Maryland: judicial records in, 68–69; slave traditions in, 328n18
Masolo, D. A., 302n82
Mason, Laura, 296n48
materiality: absence of, in slavery, 139–40; of call and response, 162–63; colonialism and, 77; of music, 15–16, 289n5; role of, 64. *See also* experience
Mathews, Anne Jackson, 339n84
Matthiessen, F. O., 350n22, 350–51n23, 351n25, 367n46
Maultsby, Portia K., 31–32, 301n76
Mauss, Marcel, 283, 378nn13–14
Maxwell, Allen, 309n21
Mayer, Brantz, 354n45, 366n37
Mayhead, Robin, 350n20
McCall, John, 317n60
McCary, Ben C., 310–11n26
McClary, Susan, 296n47
McClintock, Anne, 87, 317n60, 321n96
McDougall, Frances Harriet: on black music, 180; cited, 340n89, 355n49, 356n54, 357n62; mentioned, 184; on slave performance, 143
McDowell, Deborah E., 291n18, 306n5, 325n2, 363n6

McGann, Jerome, 362n97
McHugh, Jimmy, 237, 364n20
McKay, Claude, 33
McKay, Nellie Y., 28, 300n70, 362n1
McKim, James Miller, 209, 348n11, 355–56n53
McKim, Lucy. *See* Garrison, Lucy McKim
McLaughlin, Blair, 338–39n81
McNemar, Richard, 129, 130, 131, 335n61, 336n66
McPherson, James M., 320–21n92
McTyeire, Holland Nimmons, 354n44
Meacham, James, 114, 329n24
Mead, A. M. Whitman, 310–11n26, 342n99
melody: emphasis on, 247–48, 367n47; essence of sound linked to, 368n58; as natural ability, 244; transcription's recasting of, 266–67
melting pot concept, 288–89n4
Melville, Herman, 103, 171, 245–46, 350n22, 366–67n45
memory: Benjamin on, 40, 45; black music in national, 3–4; blankness in, 165–66; of lived vs. observed experience, 224, 228–29; musical notation as reconstruction of, 188; narrative and, 358n68; patterns of music's motion and physicality in, 62; sentimentalism and, 261–64, 269–70, 371–71n87
memory texts: concept of, 45; slave song collection as, 206, *207–8,* 209, 224, 228–29
Menard, Russell, R., 314n46
Mercer, Kobena, 43, 290–91n13, 299–300n68
Mereness, Newton D., 314n45
Merolla da Sorrento, Jerom: on Congo, 318–19n70, 319n75, 319nn71–73; on musical instruments, 78–80, 319n72
Merriam, Alan, 34, 35, 303n88
Mersenne, Marin, 190
Merton, Richard, 315n49
metaphysics, 35–36, 91
Metfessel, Milton F., 301–2n80

Meyer, Leonard, 351n30
Michaels, Walter Benn, 289n9
Michelet, Jules, 306–7n12
Middleton, Albert, 121
Middleton, Richard, 297n52
Milburn, William Henry: on black/white re-
    lations, 344n113; on camp meetings,
    130, 336n64; cited, 333n44, 335–36n62;
    on vocal training, 123, 333n46
militia and military: black musicians in,
    68–69; diversity of black roles in,
    326n7; drums in, 79, 102, 324n126
Miller, Christopher L., 30, 287n, 289n10,
    300n73
Mills, Irving, 364n20
Mills Brothers, 24
Mintz, Sidney W., 57, 308n19, 312n30,
    324n124
minuets, Congo, 112–13, 328nn17–19
miscegenation, 82, 134
Mitchell, Angelyn, 289n6, 300–301n74,
    302–3n86, 303nn91–92
Mitchell, W. J. T.: cited, 291n18, 295n36,
    358n70, 358n72, 360n79; on illusion-
    ism, 206; on memory, 358n68; on seen/
    unseen image, 167, 347n7; on what we
    know/don't know, 13
Mitchell-Kernan, Claudia, 58, 309n21
modernism: black social expression in,
    258–59; Euro-Western, 16–17; perfor-
    mance practices constructed in, 269–
    71; rhythm constructed in, 245–47,
    271–73; vernacular concept in, 46–48.
    See also black expressive modernism
"Molly Brown" (song), 271
Monk, Thelonious, 7
monophony, 252
Monson, Ingrid, 25, 299n66, 303n93
Montesquieu, Baron de la Brède et de, 109,
    327n11
Moore, J. S., 350–51n23
Moorish people, 77, 86, 318n69
Mordecai, Samuel, 142, 340n87, 341n97

Moreau de Saint-Méry, M. L. E., 60, 311n27,
    315n51
Morgan, Edmund S., 313n38
Morgan, Philip: on African ethnicity,
    313n38; on African traditions, 64–65;
    approach of, 65–66; cited, 310–11n26,
    313nn36–39, 323n116, 323n118,
    335n61; on diversity of slave cultures,
    63, 64; on rhythm instruments, 102,
    324n124; on spirituals, 355n52
Morison, Samuel Eliot, 361n87
Morley, David, 289n10
Moroccan music, 84–85, 87–88, 240
Morrison, Toni, 2, 289n6
Morrison, Wayne, 317–18n63
Mos Def, 7
movement. *See* action and activity; cross-
    roads/crossings
Mozart, Wolfgang Amadeus, 174, 176
Muddy Waters, 7
Mukerji, Chandra, 288n3
Mullin, Michael, 56–57, 307–8n16, 313n38
Munsell, Joel, 369n64
Murat, Achille, 336n63
music: barbarism and savagery linked to,
    86–87, 100–101, 239; concept of, 41,
    347–48n9; cultures linked by, 90–91;
    as European concept, 325n129; "first
    world," 189; intuitive nature of, 173–
    74; marginalization of, 66; as metaphor
    for racial hearing, 113; origins of, 28,
    33–34, 36, 249–55, 264–65, 338–
    39n81, 368n58; sidelined in social
    change theory, 110; social effect of,
    352–53n36; terminology of, 103–4; as
    universal language, 174–75. *See also*
    black musics; Euro-American elite mu-
    sic; "foreign musics"; slave songs and
    music
musical expression: acquisition of, 66–67;
    black/white categories of, 29; in con-
    struction of difference, 8–9; discursive
    conceptions of, 18–19; as learned vs.

universal, 61–62; material aspect of, 289n5; oversimplification of, 38–39; patterns of motion and physicality in, 62; possibilities in, 4; race linked to, 9, 25; role of discourse in, 42; sameness/stability of, 41; slippage between language and, 20–23. *See also* black expressive modernism; expressive practices

musical notations: audience for, 162; of black and white musics, 159–60; effects of, 166–67, 214, 261, 265–67; of foreign musics, 188–90, *190–203*; inadequacy/artificiality of, 186–87, 205–6, 213–14, 223–24; Johnson on, 347n8; popularity of, 228–29; precursor to, 188–89; questioning accuracy of, 204–5; reasons for, 190, 204, 266; sameness/difference and, 187–88, 213–14, 223. *See also* partiality

music critics: on black expressive modernism, 261–62; on blues, 24–25, 37; development of, 99; on jazz, 29, 34; on jubilees, 261, 371n83; limited perspectives of, 262–64, 371–71n87; musical interpretations in, 307n14; slaves as, 181. *See also* black music criticism; music studies

music studies: Afrocentrism in, 33–34; black music marginalized in, 31; construction of difference and, 8–10; documentation in, 5–6, 291n16; double bind in, 10–11; emancipatory research in, 31–33; essentialism in, 4–5, 13, 35–36; formalism of, 38; imperialism in, 248–51; political commitment in, 7–8; racial and social in, 24–25; racialism's persistence in, 6–7, 138–39; refiguring approach to, 11–14, 18–20, 27; of sonic power, 16; "speaking past" others in, 27–29; stylistic progression assumed in, 338–39n81; "total history" in, 290n11. *See also* musical notations

Mussulman, Joseph A., 357n65
Myers, Helen, 338–39n81, 359n75
myth: concept of, 3–4; music's constitution in, 19, 21; of slave drumming, 102–3. *See also* premodern sense

Nairn, Thomas, 311n27
naming practices, 8–9, 87, 107, 139
narratives: (an)other kind of, 63, 67; constructed nature of, 65–67; containment of black music's, 13–15, 30–31; history as construction of, 51; listening to eruptions in, 2; memory and, 358n68; necessity as category in, 290n12; political commitments and, 208–9; of slaves, 6, 174, 206, 208–9, 291n16; theory vs., 32–33. *See also* story

Nathan, Hans, 367n47
Nathanson, Y. S., 173, 348n10, 351n28, 351–52n32, 356n60
National Anti-Slavery Standard, 172
National Baptist Convention, 31
nation and nationhood: American concept of, 155–56; blacks' musicality and, 147; construction of, 110–11; crisis in identity of, 183; discourse on, 144; memory of, 3–4; narratives as expression of, 174; stability of instability of, 13; transcendence of, 186
Native Americans, 128–29, 154, 251–52
natural abilities: Darwin on, 367–68n53; Jefferson on, 113–14; melody as, 244; music as, 143, 146–48, 174, 175–80, 212–13, 261–62, 347–48n9; potency as, 179; rhythm as, 102–3, 237–38, 275–77
nature and the natural: authenticity as, 92–93; black religion as, 264; black voicing as act of, 142; eighteenth-century representation of, 82–88; instinct in, 83, 87, 88, 113–14, 262; modern discourse on, 276–77; music as product of, 91, 157, 344n115; music's power

nature and the natural (*continued*)
over, 89; origins of language and,
90–92; purity of spirit in, 174; racial
inferiority linked to, 113–14, 146;
rhythm as, 102–3, 237–38, 246; slave
singing linked to, 147–48; spiritual
truths in, 170; wildness linked to, 82–
88, 90, 240

Negro music. *See* black musics

Negro Music Journal, 236

"Negro problem," 233–34, 236, 326–27n9

Nelson, Cary, 296–97n50, 300n73, 357n62

Nelson, Stanley R., 364n18

Nettl, Bruno, 345n120, 358n72

Neuman, William S., 351–52n32

Newcomb, Anthony, 15–16, 21, 295n40

"New Coon in Town" (song), 235

New Orleans: performance practices in,
243–44; rituals in, 273–75

New York: judicial records in, 69

Nicholls, David, 301n76, 351n31

noise: concept of, 92–93, 131; in Melville's
story, 245–46; transformation
through, 127–28

Northrup, Solomon (Platt Epps), 147, 341–
42n98, 360n80

Norton, David Fate, 317–18n63

Norton, Mary J., 317–18n63

Oakes, James, 323n113

"O Canaan, Sweet Canaan" (song),
343n107

Odum, Howard W., 272, 299n66, 301–2n80,
375–76n109, 376n112

Oglethorpe, Dorothy, 314n44

Ogren, Kathy J., 295n35

"Old Folks at Home" (song), 146, 364n15

Oliphant, Laurence, 185

Oliver, Paul, 363nn11–12, 363–64n13

Oliver, Perry H., 175

Olmstead, Frederick Law: on black worship, 184; cited, 336n63, 339–40n85,
341n93, 342n105, 344n113; on repres-

sion of slaves, 342n103; on slaves and
music, 150–52; on slave sound, 142

Olney, James, 50, 305n2, 371n81

Olson, Robert G., 306–7n12

O'Meally, Robert G., 293–94n27, 346–47n1

O'Neall, John Belton, 324n127

opera, 15, 16–17, 297n51

oral-to-written formula, 45–46

oral tradition: in ads for runaway slaves,
71; of camp-meeting performances,
131–32; Gates on, 303n92; protest in,
58; writing vs., 50

Orden, Kate Van, 316n55

original and originality: celebration of, 31;
concept of, 6; constructed nature of,
51; primitive as, 89; repetition and, 53;
romanticism and, 170; understanding
of, 36–42. *See also* authenticity/real-
ness

origins: of banjo, 328n17; of call and response, 156–59, 344–45n116; displacement's intersection with, 272–73; of
evangelicalism and revivals, 331–
32n38; of fiddles, 328n17; of humanity,
248–50; of language, 90–92; of music,
28, 33–34, 36, 249–55, 264–65, 338–
39n81, 368n58; myths of, 4; play's
meaning and, 343n107; quest for, 74–
93, 157; of rhythm, 230–35, 248; scientific approach to, 35; of sea shanty,
157; of shouts, 329–30n29; of slaves,
308–9n20, 309n22; of spirituals, 164–
66, 338–39n81

Oring, Elliott, 349n16

Orwin, Clifford, 322n105

Osterweis, Rollin G., 349–50n19, 350n20

other and otherness: of black music, 8–9,
101, 180–81; center's construction of
periphery as, 111; of civility/savagery,
250–55; in concept of descent, 233–34;
conversion as becoming, 134; in displacement, 258; folklore's establish-
ment of, 173; of "foreign musics," 205–

6; rhythm as marker of, 236–37; slave songs as, 182

Paddison, Max, 299n63
Page, Thomas Nelson, 171
Paine, Lewis W.: cited, 339–40n85, 340n90, 341n97, 344n110, 344n113, 366n38; on dancing, 153; on drums, 366n43; on musical talent of blacks, 146; on patting, 243; on slave storytelling, 143; on sports activities, 342n104
Painter, Nell, 370n71
palimpsest concept, 121
Papastergiadis, Nikos, 312n32
parading, 68. *See also* dances
Parish, Peter J., 309–10n25
Park, Mungo, 76, 318n66, 357–58n67
Parker, Charlie, 25
Parker, Theodore, 172, 173, 350–51n23
Parry, Millman, 303n92
partiality: concept of, 186–88; implications of, 188–89; in limited critical faculties, 205–6; slaves and, 105–6; spiritual effect of, 213; white access allowed in, 224
Pastor, Willy, 368n57
pastoralism, 171. *See also* romanticism
Paterson, James, 133
Patten, J. Alexander, 339n84
patting, 103, 141, 243, 324n124
Paulding, J. K., 151, 342n105
Pavlic, Ed, 305n111
Peabody, Charles, 271, 376n111
Peden, William, 329n23
Percy, Thomas, 172
Pereira, P., 189, *191*
performance practices: black physicality and, 147; as commodity, 175–77, 270–71; complexity of, 103; diversity of, 42, 139–40, 267–68; documentation on, 5–6, 69–70; emotional extremes in, 154; heathenism linked to, 183–84; interracial, 111–13, 129–30, 161; modern con-

struction of, 269–71; nineteenth-century accounts on, 140–44, 240–44; oral nature of camp-meeting, 131–32; as play, 150–53, 156; recording of, 263–64; rise of, in antebellum period, 106–7; of Scottish texts, 171; sermon as, 135–37; social empowerment of, 148; as threat, 115–16; transcribed songs displaced from, 190. *See also* dances; jubilees; rhythm; shouts
Persian songs, 190, *195*
Peruvian songs, 189, *190*
Peterson, Charles Jacobs (pseud. J. Thornton Randolph), 154–55, 344n113, 354–55n48
Phillippo, James M., 287n
Phillips, Adam, 317–18n63
piano, 268
Pickering, James H., 366n36
Pike, Kenneth L., 294n31
Pinkerton, John: cited, 317n61, 317–18n63, 318n64, 318nn66–67, 318n69, 318–19n70, 320n84, 320nn87–88, 321n96, 321nn93–94, 340n91, 364–65n25, 365n29; focus of, 75. See also *General Collection of Voyages and Travels* (ed. Pinkerton)
pinksters, 102, 243, 254, 325n128, 329–30n29
place: in call and response, 156, 163; of other, 258; preacher's gesture toward, 136–37; sonic projection of, 96–100; sound as out of, 255–77; theories of, 94–96. *See also* displacement, of black music
planters: on happy slaves, 140, 144; mobility of, 323n113; slave music and, 59, 311n27; on slave sounding, 100; slaves repressed by antebellum, 149; as unmusical, 150–51; values of, 171. *See also* slavery
play: dynamism of, 162–63; in economic realm, 152–56; logic of, 151; meanings

play (*continued*)
    of, 342–43n106, 343n107; text as sub-
    versive, 214; white desires fueled by,
    150–51. *See also* call and response
playing the dozens, 343n107
Pochmann, Henry A., 351n31
Pococke, Richard, 87, 318n67, 321n96
Poe, Edgar Allen, 103, 245, 366n44
poetry: applied to spiritual songs, 164–65;
    as defining expression of culture,
    349n15; function of, 170; music vs.,
    173–74; rhythm in, 230
politics: aestheticization of, 143–44; of de-
    spair, 61, 67; narratives and, 208–9; of
    sound, 144; of transfiguration, 41
polygamy, 314–15n47
polymetric structures, 312n31
"Poor Rosy, Poor Gal" (song), 209, 357–
    58n67
Popper, Karl, 289n7
Popular Music (British journal), 29, 297n52
Porter, Dorothy, 329n26
Porter, Mary W., 371–72n87, 373n91
poststructuralism, 30–31, 36–37
Pratt, Mary Louise: cited, 316n58, 317n60,
    319n77, 320n86, 327n16; on colonial-
    ism, 74; on science and nature, 84
preachers: blackness associated with, 119,
    331n35; call and response used by,
    156–57; commentaries on, 264; control
    of, 70, 149, 342n102; exhorters com-
    pared to, 373n91; folklorists' interests
    in, 373–74n92; gospel singing and,
    269–70; voices of slave, 135–37;
    women as, 338n75
premodern sense, 21, 298n55. *See also*
    myth
Preston, Katherine K., 351n31
Price, Richard, 57, 308n19, 312n30
Pride, Charlie, 7
"primitive music": black singing as, 122,
    172; representation of, 92–93. *See also*
    "foreign musics"

primitivism: authenticity of, 89; back-
    ground of, 301–2n80; codification of,
    83–84, 90; displacement's intersection
    with, 272–73; missionaries' attitudes
    and, 77; pinkster linked to, 243; in
    rhetorical tradition, 33, 35; rhythm
    linked to, 223, 249–55, 368n58; roman-
    ticism linked to, 184
prohibition, 237
protest tradition, 58. *See also* social
    change
Proyart, Abbé: on African music, 89; cited,
    320n84, 321n94, 321nn98–100; on na-
    ture and instinct, 83, 87, 88
psychoanalysis: desire/reproach in, 292–
    93n23; interpretive strategies in, 52–
    53; overdetermination in, 293n26;
    repression in, 127–28
public sphere: black expressive mod-
    ernism in, 236–37; black music in, 24–
    25, 31, 108–15, 239–40, 257–58, 262;
    blackness in, 15; body and rhythm
    linked in, 234–38; origins of language
    debated in, 90–92; power of discourse
    in, 23–24; racial imagery in antebel-
    lum, 107–8, 119–20, 126, 128–30; reso-
    nance of racial difference in, 98;
    rhetoric of musical difference in, 139;
    rhythm and race linked in, 252–53;
    slave sound in, 106, 141–44; "speaking
    past" others in, 27–29; spirituals in,
    166, 178–86. *See also* jubilees; musical
    notations; performance practices

Quarles, Benjamin, 305n1, 326n8, 332n40,
    348n11, 369n62
rabekin (instrument), 85
Raboteau, Albert J.: cited, 292n19, 302n83,
    330nn30–33, 337n71; mentioned, 121;
    on rituals, 331–32n38
race: binaries of, 3–4, 28, 284–85; black
    music's role in thinking about, 52;
    changing meaning of, 63; class vs., 118;

double vision of, 8–9, 22–23; fantasies of, 232, 237–38; ideological development of concept, 74, 139–40, 142–43, 168–69, 183, 236–37, 279–80; imagery of, in religious speech, 119–20, 126, 128–30; increased visibility of, 326–27n9; interracial interaction as interruption of, 111–13, 130–31; logic of, 13, 98, 107, 283; musical expression linked to, 9, 25; otherworldiness as affirmation of, 142–44; persistent structures of, 278–79; rhythm linked to, 233–34; social construction of, 11–12, 122; sound linked to, 238–47; spirituality linked to, 128–29; transcendence/affirmation of, 232, 279–80, 282. See also blackness; whiteness

racial categories: in Christianity, 117–18; hardening of, 114–15, 329n27; history's reproduction of, 122, 332n41; instability/artificiality of, 28–29, 257–58; jubilees' challenge to, 258–61; local grounding of, 39; of musical expression, 29; slave sound as influence in, 109–10; social/religious contact as threat to, 127–30; soundtexts and, 138–39; state administration of, 114–15, 329n27

racial hierarchy: jubilees' challenge to, 258–61; in performance, 153; scientific concepts in, 233–34. See also dark/light hierarchy; slavery; white supremacy

racial uplift theme, 32

racism: black music as symptom of, 113; Du Bois's challenge to, 279–80; egalitarianism vs., 108–10. See also white supremacy

ragtime, 235–36, 269, 375n106

Rainey, Ma (Gertrude Pridgett), 14

Rajchman, John, 348n13

Ralph, Julian, 372–73n90

Rampersad, Arnold: on black culture, 282;

cited, 291n18, 306n5, 325n2, 363n6, 378n10; on Du Bois, 279, 377n1

Ramsey, Guthrie P. Jr., 300n71

Ramsey, Guthrie P., Jr., 29

Randolph, J. Thornton. See Peterson, Charles Jacobs

Rankin, Thomas, 114

Rath, Richard Cullen, 308–9n20, 345–46n121, 359n74

Reagon, Bernice Johnson, 31–32, 301n75–76

realism: coherence and narrative as basis for, 65–67; perception vs., of work, 151. See also authenticity/realness

recordings of black music, 5, 267, 291n14, 350n21

Redding, Samuel, 377n1

Redman, Don, 25, 26, 299n65

Redmond, Patricia, 377n1

Reed, Joseph W., Jr., 339–40n85

Rehding, Alexander, 250, 252, 368n54, 369n59

relational position: black music's power in, 12–13; of master and slave, 95–98, 104, 107–8, 136–37; of place and body, 94–95; of Revolutionary society, 111–12; of self/difference, 87; in structuralism, 290n11. See also black/white relations; call and response; interracial exchanges; social circumstances

religion: absence of documentation on, 59–60, 135; criticism of slaves', 69–70, 315n48; custom vs., 241; destruction of, 61; ecstatic practice in, 132, 133, 337n70; fear of pagan, 314n44; missionaries' attitudes toward African, 76–80; musicality linked to, 147; racial imagery in, 119–20, 126, 128–30; slave song discussed in, 142–44; transcendence in, 128–29, 134–35. See also black worship and sacred music; Christian ceremony; Christianity; evangelicalism and revivals; spirituality;

religion (*continued*)
    spirituals; sublime; supernatural beliefs
"Rémon" (song), 214, *221*
Renaissance music, 8–9
repetition: in circles and circularity, 53–54; crossroads/crossings paired with, 231–32; emancipatory potential of, 230–31; in sermons, 136–37; in singing, 116–17
representations: of Africans as wildness and nature, 82–88, 90, 240; colonialism's impact on, 74; dark/light hierarchy in, 184–86; of ecstatic practice, 132, 133, 337n70; imperialism in, 248–51; as language-based, 280–81; limits of, 7–8; of "primitive music," 92–93; reception of, 89–90; resonances as disrupted, 45; risks in, 29–31. *See also* African retentions theory; musical notations; travel accounts; *specific concepts and authors*
resonances: authenticity in, 15; in Benjamin's work, 294–95n32; of black music in public sphere, 24–25; concept of, 11–12, 23, 42–45, 67; in concept of America, 111–12; interracial crossplay in, 107–8; interruptions as, 93–94; repetition in, 53–54; of second hearings, 121; subversive listening to, 11–14, 27; of vocal "grain," 16–18, 21. *See also* circles and circularity; dreams and dreamwork
Revolutionary War, 102, 108–12, 326n7
rhythm: barbarism and savagery linked to, 223, 233–34, 240–42, 251–52, 273–75; black music linked to, 223–24; bodily consequences of, 238–40; body as source of, 230–32, 234–35; British accounts of, 240–44; modern conception of, 245–47, 271–73; musical notation of, 214; as "natural," 102–3, 237–38, 246; origins of, 230–35, 248; power of, 230–31, 255–56; as primitive, originary, 223, 249–55, 368n58; privileging of, 42, 58; race linked to, 233–34; recognition of, 234–38; in rhetorical tradition, 33; shift to focus on, 247–55; as threat/infection/danger, 235–37, 364n15, 366n43, 369n54; violence, savagery, and hostility linked to, 241–42, 244–47, 253, 273–75; Waterman's theory of, 34–35. *See also* drums and drummers; hot rhythm
Rice, John Holt (pseud. Rusticus), 333n43Richardson, James, 240, 253, 365n28, 369n61
rights: in antebellum period, 108–10, 326n7; denied to slaves, 105–6; natural, 108–10, 326n7; slaves', 169; women's, 169
ring shout. *See* shouts
Riss, Thomas L., 353n40
ritual practices: Africanizing commentary on, 273–75; of collective cooking, 64; concept of, 61; in corn-shucking ceremony, 161, 263, 268, 372–73n90; Euro-American views of African, 78–79, 100, 240, 253–54. *See also* black worship and sacred music; Christian ceremony
"Roaring River" (song), 360n80
Robeson, Paul, 166
Robinson, Fred, 299n65
Rochlitz, F. (Johann Friedrich Rochlitz?), 252, 369n60
Rochon, Abbé, 86, 88, 321n94, 321n98
"Rockin' in Rhythm" (Ellington with Mills), 364n20
Rodgers, Jimmie, 339–40n85
Roediger, David R., 341n95, 363n11
Rogers, J. A., 33
Rogers, Joel, 343n107
"Roll, Jordan, Roll" (song), 209, 266, 357–58n67, 360n83
romanticism: blacks as represented in, 144, 146; hyperbole of, 72; imperialism

linked to, 349nn17–18; as influence, 23, 169–70; literary theory and, 38–39; in "recovery" of music, 168–77; in rhetorical tradition, 33; slave song as spiritual in, 181–86; values of, 325n129; vernacular and, 174–75

"Round the Corn, Sally" (song), 214, *219, 360*n80

Rousseau, Jean-Jacques: on arts, 323n119; "chanson negre" of, 322n105; cited, 293n25, 298n55, 321n103, 365n27; mentioned, 174, 250; musical notations and, 190, *194,* 204; on music's ambiguous position, 91; noble savage of, 180; on outsiders' music, 9; on romanticism, 169–70; on vocal stress, 239

Rowbotham, John Frederick, 251–52, 368n57

Rush, Benjamin, 310–11n26

Rusticus *See* Rice, John Holt

sacred: in slaves' world, 6–7; in songs of racial crossings, 177–86; in sound-texts, 137–38. *See also* black worship and sacred music

Sadie, Stanley, 364n14, 370n77

Said, Edward W., 359–60n78

Saint John's Island, 151

Salley, Alexander S., Jr., 311n27

Saloman, Ora Frishberg, 351–52n32

Sambo stereotype: challenges to, 144–45; invention of, 116, 143, 150; traits ascribed to, 182, 235

sameness (or in-betweenness): concept of, 9; of "foreign musics," 205–6; implied in difference, 21, 137, 284–85; in musical notations, 190; partiality and, 187; in slave song collection, 213–14, 223; in story, 26; value of authenticity and, 258

Sartre, Jean-Paul, 322n110

"savage dance," 112

Scanlon, Larry, 230, 362n2

Scarborough, Dorothy, 301–2n80

Scarry, Elaine, 98, 310–11n26

Schaw, Janet, 72, 316n55

Schelling, Friedrich Wilhelm Joseph von, 170, 175, 349n15

Schlegel, Friedrich von, 170, 349n15

Schneider, Mark A., 18, 296n46

Schoolcraft, Mary Howard, 160, 346n123

Schroeder, Theodore, 337n70

Schudson, Michael, 288n3

Schuller, Gunther, 303n87

Schuyler, George S., 302–3n86

Schwaab, Eugene L., 339n84, 346n124

Schweinfurth, Georg August, 367–68n53

scientific methods: concept of descent in, 233–34, 363n7; in representation of Africans as natural, 83–85, 88, 320n85; spirituals and, 355–56n53; in travel accounts on music, 75, 76

Scotland: music of, 171; revivalism in, 336n68

Scott, Joan W., 42, 288n3, 304n101, 313n35, 313n41, 362n101

Scott, Walter: on ballads, 172; friends of, 75; mentioned, 173, 180; popularity of, 170–71; romanticism of, 349n18, 350n21; scholarship on, 349–50n19, 350n20

Sea Islands: songs popular on, 360n83; visitors to, 209

sea shanty, 157

Seashore, Carl E., 301–2n80

Seeger, Anthony, 19–20, 295–96n42, 297n52

Seeger, Charles, 350–51n23

segregation: black music as disruption of, 106; hardening of, 256–57; instinct as reason for, 113–14; religious forums and, 117–19, 335n60

Seidenberg, Abraham, 306–7n12

self: American concept of, 155–56; challenges to, 27; healing of, 137; naming difference linked to, 87; place in constitution of, 136. *See also* identity

self/other binarism, 10. *See also* other and
  otherness; self
Senegalese music, 88
Sers, Jacqueline, 362n99
Sewall, Samuel, 68, 314n43
Seward, Theodore F., 244, 356n57, 370n77
sexuality: European fears of, 82; music
  linked to, 249–50; in soul tradition,
  290–91n13
Shakespeare, William, 9, 293n24
"Shall I Die?" (song), 214, *222*
Shapiro, Anne Dhu, 171, 350n21
Sharp, Cecil, 345n117
Shaw, Thomas, 76, 86, 89, 318n66, 321n93,
  321n100
Shell, Marc, 110, 327n13
Shepherd, John, 20, 297n52
Shorty, Bobby, 7
shouts: circularity of, 54; description of,
  244, 373n91; origin of term, 329–
  30n29; percussion-playing techniques
  and, 269; as primal place, 347n6; repetition in, 116; rhythmic aspect of, 273;
  Stuckey on, 7; as threat, 115–16; transcriptions of, 223–24, *225–26*
Shuffleton, Frank, 306n5
Siamese songs, 190, *193*
Siemerling, Winfried, 7, 292n20
sign and signification: black music's concentration of, 21–22; black singing's
  generation of, 122; canon making and,
  30; in double meanings, 343n107;
  Gates's link of black music to, 37; persistence of, 16; in ranking world's people, 90–91; revisionist perspective of,
  38; slave songs in defining racial, 154–
  55
signifiers: authenticity as, 92; "blues" as,
  55–56; harmony as, 160; rhythm as,
  102–3; songs as, 177–78; sound as,
  139–40
Silber, Nina, 247, 356n56, 367n48
silence: black voices in spaces of, 45, 52–
53; criticism of, 32; in Ellison's writing,
  17; of Euro-Americans on slave music,
  51–52, 57–61, 93, 100; implications of,
  73–74; of slave music in colonialism,
  93. *See also* absence
Simpson, David, 327n11
Simpson, Lewis P., 371n81
Sims, Norman, 377n9
sin: color coding of, 119–20, 128–29, 134,
  334–35n58; sound in recognition of,
  125–26
Singh, Amritjit, 295n35
Singh, Nikhil, 327n12
singing: civilized vs. primal, 91; emergence
  of, at camp meetings, 130–32; repetition in, 116–17; in slave coffles, 144–
  45, 341n96; transcendence through,
  118–19, 126–30, 134. *See also* song;
  voices
Singleton, Arthur, 332n39, 335n61,
  342n103, 344n113
Singleton, Zutty, 299n65
slave bard: use of term, 180
slavery: black music as contradiction of,
  116–17; black music's emergence
  from, 113–14; brutality of, 58–60, 98,
  149, 310–11n26, 311n27, 323n115,
  342n103; Douglass's story of, 49–51;
  harshest period of, 309–10n25; immateriality of, 139–40; implications of
  voice in, 14–15, 106–7; institutionaliza-
  tion of, 105–6; North American vs.
  Caribbean, 56–58; records of, 51–52,
  306n5; romanticism in justifying, 144;
  spirituals based in, 165; torture devices in, 100, 323n115, 324n121,
  342n102; whites' commitment to, 74
slaves: ads for runaway, 70–71; audibility
  of, 14–15, 106–7; barbarism and savagery linked to, 69–70, 71; civility of,
  206–7, 211–13; in coffles, 144–45,
  341n96; cultural authority of, 181; cultures of, 63–65, 96, 98; families of, 309–

10n25; fugitive, 145; gender roles of, 356n56; humanity of, 98, 177–78; as incomplete/partial, 105–6; massive importation of, 326–27n9; northerners' characterizations of, 178–79; origins of, 308–9n20, 309n22; place of, 94–98; as preachers and orators, 135–37, 172–73; as property, 25, 299n64, 322n108; rebellions of, 244–46; rights of, 169; "sacred world" of, 6–7. *See also* body

slave songs and music: absence of documentation on, 51–52, 57–61, 93, 100; Africanist expressive tradition in, 56–57; ballads compared with, 173; blackness identified in, 107–8; as commodity, 166–67, 181–82, 362n102; complexity of, 141; as contrary soundscape, 106–7; creation/improvisation of, 339–40n85; critiques in, 153; Douglass on, 50–51; healing potential of, 247–48; interpretive strategies for, 52–53; as interruption, 121–22; in jubilees, 262–63; meanings of, 154–56, 160–63, 177–78, 343n107; as memory texts, 206, *207–8,* 209, 224, 228–29; miracle of, 98–99, 104; nineteenth-century descriptions of, 141–46; northerners double-edged view of, 168–77; as other, 182; as otherworldly, 142–44; power of, 147–48, 152, 161–62, 177, 180–81, 342n103; recording practices of, 263–64; religious texts on, 70–71; Scottish music linked to, 171; sorrow/misery as theme of, 59, 68, 145–46, 310–11n26, 348n11, 357–58nn67; texting of, 280–81; as transgression, 71–72; valuation of, 152–53; whites' perception of excess in, 114, 143–46, 168–69, 234; whites' recognition of, 71, 106–8, 121–22. *See also* jubilees; slave sound; spirituals

Slave Songs of the United States (collection): advertisement for, 360–61n85; black presence obscured in, 211–13; description of, 206, 209; "Directions for Singing" in, 224, *227;* examples from, *215–22, 226;* folklore interests as context of, 182; influences on, 209–12; as memory text, 206, *207–8,* 209, 224, 228–29; as reform text, 211–13; sameness/difference in, 213–14, 223; songs in, 360n83; table of contents of, *208;* title page of, *207. See also* Allen, William Francis; Garrison, Lucy McKim; Ware, Charles Pickard

slave sound: authenticity of, 144; of body in pain, 97–98; complexity and heterogeneity of, 42, 103–4, 106–7, 145–46; as creative force, 99–100; drum's role in, 101–2; as foundation, 73–74; as influence in racial categories, 109–10; production of, 139–40; resonance of, 98–99; significance of, 93–94; symbolic value of, 100–101; travel accounts on, 140–44; whites' recognition of, 71, 106–8. *See also* slave songs and music

slide guitarists, 299n66

Sloane, Hans, 159, *198,* 204, 359n74

Smith, Adam, 317–18n63

Smith, Charles Hamilton, 354n46

Smith, Clement Lawrence, 209–10, 361n86

Smith, Jeff, 295n37

Smith, Merritt Roe, 378n15

Smith, W. L. G., 339n82, 353–54n42, 355n51

Smith, William B.: cited, 339n82, 348n10, 353n41, 354n44, 356n54, 357n66; on language, 186

Snowden, Frank M., Jr., 320n86

Sobel, Mechal: cited, 313n38, 323n116, 323n118, 328n19, 329–30n29, 334n56; on interracial exchanges, 331n37; on rituals, 331–32n38; on slaves' beliefs, 330n30, 330n32

social, the (concept), 46

social change: African-American mobility and, 255–57; new expressions in response to, 267–68; representation of black music and, 247–55; theories of, 109–10. *See also* action and activity

social circumstances: black/white sharing of, 20, 298n54; of call and response, 156–58; as context for black music development, 120–21, 155; as context for musical expression, 65–66; diversity in, 64; music's constitution in, 18–20, 24–25, 26–27, 109; music's resonance in, 11–13; place in relation to, 95–97; of slave sounding, 99–100; travel accounts on, 76. *See also* experience; ideologies; materiality

social reform, 169, 211–13

Society for the Propagation of the Gospel, 69, 70, 311n27

"Sold Off to Georgy" (song), 360n80

Solie, Ruth A., 296n47, 351n30

Sollors, Werner, 47, 305n110, 310–11n26, 363n7, 364–65n25

song: as art, 91; effect of, 324n122; as junction between African and African-American, 325n130; as notation, 167; racially hybrid type of, 134–35; symbolic value of, 100–101

Songster Tradition, The (CD), 375–76n109

sonic power: beyondness of, 21, 23; containment of, 13–15, 30–31; otherness and, 8–9; presence-in-absence of, 17–18, 44–45; significance of, 15–16

soul: as cultural form, 290–91n13; use of term, 175, 352n35

sound: of blackness, 139–40; circular nature of, 53–54; as contagious, 154–55; continuity in, 307n14; displaced in writing spirituals, 185–86; essence of, 368n58; fears of racial transmission through, 235–37, 364n15; harmony as perfection of, 178–79; magic qualities of, 280–81; as means of constructing

culture, 104; as out of place, 255–77; politics of, 144; race linked to, 238–47; religious, 122–34, 333–34n52; Satan linked to racial, 116; sidelined in social change theory, 110; temporal depths of human, 247–55

soundtexts: authenticity constituted in, 166–67; concept of, 3; of sacred song, 137–38; stories of, 46

Sousa, John Philip, 235

Southall, Geneva Handy, 353n40

South American songs, 189, 190, *190, 192,* 204

South Carolina: African ethnicity in, 313n38; African traditions in, 64–65; colonial status of, 307–8n16, 308n17; laws of, 69, 324n127; rebellion in, 68, 102; religious practice in, 70; slave music and dance in, 68–69

Southern, Eileen: approach of, 56; cited, 291n14, 299n61, 301n75, 325n128, 339n83, 341n96, 369n64, 377n8; on interracial exchanges, 336–37n69; mentioned, 121; musical positivism of, 307n15; on rhythm, 58, 309n21

Spaeth, Sigmund, 301–2n80

Sparks, Jared, 361n87

Sparks, Randy J., 330n32

Spaulding, H. G., 354n44, 361n91, 373n91

Spencer, Herbert, 249, 367n50

Spencer, Jon Michael, 31–32, 301n76

Spenser, Edmund, 316n55

"sperichels," use of term, 184. *See also* spirituals

Spillers, Hortense J.: on black worship, 135, 136; cited, 291n18, 306n5, 325n2, 337–38n74, 338n76, 363n6; on community, 338n77; on scholarship, 6; on slavery, 51, 106, 322–23n112; on social change, 232

Spinoza, Benedict de, 290n12

spirituality: multisensory experience of, 125–26; race linked to, 128–29; revitalization of, 119–20; sound as medium of, 126–30, 134; white preachers on, 331n35

spirituals: access to, 182–83, 184; appeal of, 356n57; avoidance of, 269–70; blackface compared with, 177–78; conversion to modern, 224; as cross-cultural mix, 138–39; healing potential of, 247–48; as innovative or derivative, 264–66; as intuitive, 181–82, 229; maintaining otherness of, 211–13; musical notation of, 187–88; origins of, 164–66, 338–39n81; of racial border, 177–86; research on, 31–33; rhythm and, 246; sameness/difference in, 213–14, 223; slave song influenced by, 142–44; sorrow as theme in or not, 145–46; use of term, 355n52; writing and publishing of, 166–67, 185–86. *See also* black worship and sacred music; call and response; hymns; jubilees; shouts

Spivak, Gayatri Chakravorti: cited, 296–97n50, 300n73, 313n35, 313n41, 357n62; on direct correspondences, 312n32; on discourse, 30; on narrative, 62

Stafford, Barbara Maria, 313–14n42

Stanley, Henry M., 35, 253–54, 369nn62–63

Starrett, Charles, 338–39n81

"Steal Away" (song), 343n107

Stearns, Jean, 375–76n109

Stearns, Jimmy, 299n65

Stearns, Marshall, 375–76n109

Stecopoulos, Harry, 356n56

Stedman, John Gabriel, 190, *197,* 358n72

Steel, David Warren, 160, 346n122

Steiner, Wendy, 297n52

Stempfhuber, Martin, 306n6

Stephen, Leslie, 317–18n63

Stepto, Robert B., 31–32, 301n76, 303n92

stereotypes, 33–34. *See also* racism; Sambo stereotype; white supremacy

Stevenson, Robert, 345n117

Stevenson, Robert Louis, 176, 237, 364n19

Stewart, Jimmy, 39

Stewart, Susan, 28, 300n69

Still, William Grant, 24, 299n61

Stocking, George W., Jr., 302n83, 367n50

Stokes, James, 293n24

Stone, Albert E., 311n27

Stone, Ruth M., 317n60

Stono Rebellion, 68, 102

story: as allegory, 65; approach to, 4, 25–26; generalizations in, 6–7; Hurston's use of, 46–48; interruptions/disruptions as basis for, 93–94; repetition of, 136–37. *See also* narratives

Story, Ronald, 361n87

storytelling: black voices as virtuosos in, 143; jazz as, 25; Spillers on, 135; vocal sound of, 14–15

Stowe, Harriet Beecher, 140

structuralism, 290n11, 293n26

structures: use of term, 4, 290n11

Stuckey, Sterling, 7, 9, 54, 292n19, 306n11, 325n128

Sturgis, C. F., 354n44

subjectivities: experience in forming, 42; interracial influences on, 138; musical expression linked to, 20. *See also* identity; self

sublime: conversion linked to, 137; music as truest form of, 351n30; religion linked to, 146; spirituals as, 181–82. *See also* art; aesthetics

substance/virtuosity trope, 175, 352n35

Sudanese music, 87

Sudhalter, Richard M., 28, 300n69

Sugarman, Jane, 19–20, 295–96n42, 297n52

supernatural beliefs: African instruments and, 253; cross-class beliefs in, 330n32; in evangelical religious forums, 119–20; rhythm linked to, 273–75; spirituals and, 165–66

Surinam music, 190, *197,* 358n72

Sutch, Richard, 309–10n25
Svin'in, Pavel Petrovich, 120, 331–32n38, 334–35n58
swing, 276, 364n20
Symmes, Thomas, 357n65
syncretism, 35
Szwed, John F.: on African retentions, 9; cited, 293–94n27, 302n81, 302n85, 311–12n29, 345–46n121, 359n74; on deculturation argument, 312n30

Tagg, Philip, 29, 300n72
Tagore, Sourindro Mohun, 359n75
talking book trope, 123
Tallmadge, William H., 336–37n69
Tamisier, Maurice, *201–2,* 205, 359n77
Tarcov, Nathan, 322n105
Taruskin, Richard, 295n39
Tarzan series, 254–55, 369–70n67
Tate, Greg, 299–300n68
Taussig, Michael, 292n19
Tax, Sol, 303n88
Taylor, Mark C., 53, 305–6n4, 306n7, 348–49n14
technology, 180, 354n47
temperance movement, 169
text: challenge to primacy of, 39–40, 46; privileging of, 15, 27, 303–4n95; shadows of missing, 67–74. *See also* literature; memory texts; musical notations; sound texts
Thai (Siamese) songs, 190, *193*
Tharp, Sister Rosetta, 7
Thayer, Alexander Wheelock, 211, 361n88
theory: in jazz music studies, 30; resistance to, 32–33, 35–36; vernacular linked to, 36–37. *See also* African retentions theory; literary theory; *specific concepts*
Thomas, Downing A., 90, 296n47, 321n101, 321n103
Thomas, George, 47
Thomas, John L., 348n12

Thomas, M. Halsey, 314n43
Thompson, Robert Farris, 54, 306n11
Thoreau, Henry David, 48, 171, 172, 246, 367n46
Thornton, Thomas C., 153, 343–44n108
Thorsen, Karen, 289n9
Three-fifths Compromise, 115, 329n28
Thunberg, C. P.: cited, 320nn88–91; on Hottentot musical instruments, 85–86; on *korà,* 85, 320n89
time lag concept, 23
Tin Pan Alley, 235
Todd, Christopher, 306n6
Tokumaru, Yoshihiko, 294n31
Tomlinson, Gary: cited, 293n24, 295n40, 296nn43–45, 300n73; on jazz studies, 29–30; on music in Euro-Western modernity, 16–17; on politicization, 296–97n50
Tonsor, Johann. *See* Hill, Mildred
Torgovnick, Marianna, 254–55, 301–2n80, 369n66
transcendence: of difference, 232, 279–80, 282; Emerson on, 171–72; modern conceptions of, 17; of national selfhood, 186; of rationalism, 169–70; in religious experience, 128–29, 134–35; sacred linked to, 178–79; in singing, 118–19, 126–30, 134; of spirituals, 181–82; storytelling linked to, 25
transcriptions. *See* musical notations
translations, 137–38, 358n68
travel accounts: anxieties revealed in, 90–92; bibliography of, 368n58; conventions of, 76; eighteenth-century, 80–88; examples of musical references in, 317n62; musical notations and, 189–90; nineteenth-century, 140–44, 240–44; on percussion instruments, 238–39; "planetary consciousness" in, 74, 80–81, 84, 316n58; on "primitive music," 92–93; research on, 359n77; rhythm and race linked in, 252–53;

seventeenth-century, 76–80. See also *General Collection of Voyages and Travels* (ed. Pinkerton)

traveling musicians, 293n24

Trevathan, Charles E., 235, 363n12

tribalist discourse. *See* primitivism

Trollope, Frances M., 331n35, 336n65

Trotter, James, 338–39n81

"Trouble of the World, The" (song), 214, *218*

trumpet-grass, 85

trumpets and trumpeters, 68

truth, 47–48, 73, 96, 305–6n4

Tubman, Harriet, 373n107, 375n107

Tucker, Bruce, 300n73

tune books, 159–60, 166, 346n122. See also *Slave Songs of the United States* (collection)

Turkish songs, 190, *196*

"Turn, Sinner, Turn O!" (song), 214, *215*

"Turn Back Pharaoh's Army" (song), 266, 374n99

Turner, Dawson, 318n64

Turner, Nat, 102–3, 151, 244

Tuscany (Italy), dance in, 328n17

Tyler, Steven, 67, 313–14n42

Uebel, Michael, 356n56

un-concealment/un-forgetting concept, 51, 53, 305–6n4

unconscious, 67, 73, 174

Unique Quartette, 291n14

United States: black music as gift to, 282–84; centrality of black experience/culture in, 42–44, 111, 232, 279–85; contradictions in egalitarianism in, 108–12, 356n58; economic failures of twentieth-century, 256–57; influences in colonial, 307–8n16; "sonic fiction" of, 275

"unsung" concept, 15, 24–25, 297n51

urban areas: plantations vs., 268; professional musicians in, 262, 270–71

Van Evrie, John H., 356n58

vernacular: Du Bois on, 43; emotions in, 182; modern concept of, 46–48; romanticism and, 174–75; theory linked to, 36–37. *See also* story

Vico, Giambattista, 82–83

Villoteau, Guillaume-André, *203,* 205, 248, 359–60n78

Virginia: black Creole English in, 313n38; fiddling in, 71; interracial Methodist congregations in, 330n30; militia and music in, 68; slave traditions in, 112–13

vocal "grain" concept, 16–18, 21

vocal knowledge concept, 16

Vogel, Stanley M., 351n31

voices: body and world linked by, 95; as creative force, 99–100; fear of, 115–26; muted, 13–14; notation of, 214, 223; power of, 14–16, 20–22, 98–99, 342n103; preachers' training of, 123, 333n46; religious encounters through, 126–32; speaking/writing of, 45–46; travel accounts on, 141–44

voodooism, 273–75

Wachsmann, Klaus P., 103, 325n129

Wacquant, Loïc, 290n11

Wade, Bonnie, 301n76

Wakefield [Bell], Priscella, 332n39

Wakenroder, Wilhelm Heinrich, 175

Walker, William, 154, 344n112

Wallace, Michelle, 299–300n68

Wallaschek, Richard: bibliography by, 359n77; cited, 318n65, 365n31, 369n59; on harmony and race, 252; on origins of music, 368n58; on travel accounts, 75

Walser, Robert, 38, 303n93

Ware, Charles Pickard: abolitionism of, 209; background of, 360n84; cited, 338–39n81, 347–48n9, 355–56n53, 360n83, 361nn88–89; as influence, 266

Ware, Charles Pickard (*continued*)
  See also *Slave Songs of the United
  States* (collection)
Ware, Henry, Jr., 361n88
Ware, Henry, Sr., 360n84
Warner, Charles Dudley, 273–74, 376n116
Warren, John C., 353–54n42
Warrington, John, 306–7n12
war songs, 242
Waterman, Christopher, 19–20, 297n52
Waterman, Richard, 34–35, 301–2n80,
  303n88
Watkins, James, 141, 331n36, 339–40n85
Watson, John Fanning: on African-Ameri-
  can musical influence, 115–17; on call
  and response, 157; cited, 332n41; on
  shout, 116, 131, 329–30n29
Watts, Andre, 7
waves analogy, 53–54
Wein, Paul, 328n18, 329n21
Weld, Theodore Dwight, 206, 360n81
Welsh, Alexander, 350n20
Wesley, John, 114
West, Cornel, 32, 43, 301n77, 348n13
Westcott, William, 303n88, 338–39n81
West Indies: call and response in, 159; in-
  struments in, 238–39
Wheatley, Phillis, 176
Wheeler, Peter, 331n36
"When We Do Meet Again" (song), *222*
whistles and whistling, 141, 317n62, 339–
  40n85
White, Charles, 86
White, George L., 370n77
White, Hayden: cited, 313nn40–41,
  320n82, 370n73; on culture's power,
  320n81; on story/narrative, 46, 65;
  tropology of, 38; on wilderness, 82
White, Newman, 301–2n80
White, Shane, 325n128, 366n36
Whitefield, George, 70, 157, 315n49
white music: African cast to, 154–55; bal-
  lads and, 172; blacks' use of, 12; country

singers and, 339–40n85; harmony introduced in, 159–60. *See also* classical music; Euro-American elite music; hymns
whiteness: absences in, 169; African cast
  to, 154–55; ambiguities of, 2; black music as threat to, 42; decentering exclusive, 114–15; deracination of, 289n7;
  desire/reproach contradiction in,
  292–93n23; feared corruption of, 116–
  17, 234; harmony as signifier of, 160; instability of, 107–8, 111, 284–86; produced in contrast to blackness, 8–11,
  13, 22–23, 292n21; reinforcement of,
  146, 183. *See also* white supremacy
White Noise (DeLillo), 237
white plain/poor folk: call and response
  used by, 160; classist attitude toward,
  371–72n87; interracial exchanges of,
  117, 118–19
whites: appropriative desires of, 184; barbarism and savagery linked to, 93, 371–
  72n87; black freedom and, 108; black
  musicians' accommodation to, 270–72;
  black music recognized by, 140–41,
  155–56, 168, 239–40, 347–48n9; black
  music used by, 115–16, 224, *227*, 228–
  29; blackness recognized by, 152–53;
  blacks as stand-ins for, 14; claims of influence on spirituals, 264–65, 374n93;
  double consciousness of, 144, 169; economic difficulties of, 257; failure of, 86,
  104; fears of, 151, 235–36, 244–46; inade-
  quacy/incompleteness felt by, 180, 260–
  61; interracial influences on dances for,
  112–13, 328nn17–19; musical talent absent among, 143; "purity" of, 134–35;
  ragged rhythm and, 235–36; repressive
  tactics of, 58–60, 73; response to gift of
  black song, 283–84; ridicule of, 161–62;
  "self-referential" impulse of, 29; sense of
  music's power and, 101; silence of, on
  slave music, 51–52, 57–61, 93, 100; slave
  sound recognized by, 71, 106–8, 121–22;

spirituals as alter ego to, 184; unstable rhetoric of, 110–11. *See also* black/white relations; colonialism; Europeans; interracial exchanges; planters; travel accounts

white supremacy: African consciousness as response to, 65, 281; assumptions in, 30–31, 33; black gift giving to, 283–84; black humanity denied by, 105; black music as affirmation of, 114–15; challenges to, 14–15, 23–24, 28, 35–36, 161, 176–77, 206–7, 233, 281; criticism of, 109; defense of, 249; identity formation in context of, 65, 313n38; lying acts of, 73; restoration of, 256; silence in service of, 93. *See also* colonialism

Whitman, Walt, 170, 171, 172, 351n25

Wicke, Peter, 20, 297n52

Wickersham, J. P., 236

Widmer, Edward, 102, 246, 366–67n45

Wier, Albert E., 368n57

Wilcox, Glenn C., 344n112

wildness, 82–88, 90, 240

Wilgus, D. K., 338–39n81

Williams, Ben Ames, 357n62

Williams, Iolo A., 345n117

Williams, Patrick, 296–97n50, 300n73, 357n62

Williams, Raymond, 288n3, 290n11

Wills, David W., 117, 330n31

Wilson, Edmund, 236, 364n17

Wilson, William A., 349n16

Wimsatt, William K., 349n15

Winans, Robert B., 339n83

Windhus, John: cited, 320n87, 321n96, 365n29; on Moroccan music, 84–85, 87–88, 240

Windley, Lathan N., 70–71, 315n51–52

Winston, Celia M., 263, 372n89

women: dance preferences of, 113; as preachers, 338n75; as singers, 242

Wood, Betty, 309–10n25

Wood, Harriet Harvey, 318n64

Wood, Henry Cleveland, 264, 266, 272, 373n91, 374n98, 376n113

Wood, Peter, 378n15

Woodson, Carter G., 70–71, 315n51

Woodward, C. Vann, 348n10

Woodward, William Wallis, 337n72

work: call and response songs for, 156–57, 159–62, 372–73n90; diverse circumstances in, 64; interracial engagements in, 256–57; perception vs. reality of, 151; play juxtaposed to, 150; rhythmical dimensions of, 251

Work, Henry Clay, 146

Work, John, 33, 157, 344–45n116

Works Progress Administration (WPA), 291n16, 339n83

world music. *See* "foreign musics"

World's Columbian Exposition (1893), 235, 254, 273

Wormersley, David, 317–18n63

Wright, Josephine, 121, 291n14, 339n83, 341n96

Wright, Louis B., 311n27

Wright, Richard, 235, 298n56, 307n14

writing: antistory of, 67; "crimes" of, 28; generative power of, 50–51; pornotropic character of colonial, 87–88; privileging of, 86–87; role in blackness, 45–46; silence in, 17; song making as, 165–66; sound displaced in, 185–86. *See also* literature; musical notations; text

Yamaguti, Osama, 294n31

Yarmolinsky, Avrahm, 331–32n38

Yellin, Jean Fagan, 331n36, 350n20, 366n37

yodeling (e.g., Carolina yell), 142, 339–40n85

Yoruba fifes, 253

Young, Lester, 25

Young, Robert, 290n11, 313–14n42

Young, Robert J. C., 299n67

Zulu (film), 324n122